Connections

Editorial Board

Psalms Editor

Sidebar Editor

Project Manager

Project Compiler

Year C, Volume 3

Season after Pentecost

A Lectionary Commentary for Preaching and Worship

Joel B. Green
Thomas G. Long
Luke A. Powery
Cynthia L. Rigby
General Editors

2019 Westminster John Knox Press

First edition
Published by Westminster John Knox Press
Louisville, Kentucky

19 20 21 22 23 24 25 26 27 28—10 9 8 7 6 5 4 3 2 1

Book and cover design by Allison Taylor

The Library of Congress has cataloged an earlier volume as follows:
Names: Long, Thomas G., 1946- editor.
Title: Connections : a lectionary commentary for preaching and worship / Joel B. Green, Thomas G. Long, Luke A. Powery, Cynthia L. Rigby, general editors.
Description: Louisville, Kentucky : Westminster John Knox Press, 2018- | Includes index. |
Identifiers: LCCN 2018006372 (print) | LCCN 2018012579 (ebook) | ISBN 9781611648874 (ebk.) | ISBN 9780664262433 (volume 1 : hbk. : alk. paper)
Subjects: LCSH: Lectionary preaching. | Bible—Meditations. | Common lectionary (1992) | Lectionaries.
Classification: LCC BV4235.L43 (ebook) | LCC BV4235.L43 C66 2018 (print) | DDC 251/.6—dc23
LC record available at https://lccn.loc.gov/2018006372

Connections: Year C, Volume 3
ISBN: 9780664262457 (hardback)
ISBN: 9780664264871 (paperback)
ISBN: 9781611649277 (ebook)

PRINTED IN THE UNITED STATES OF AMERICA

♾ The paper used in this publication meets the minimum requirements of the American National Standard for Information Sciences—Permanence of Paper for Printed Library Materials, ANSI Z39.48-1992.

Westminster John Knox Press advocates the responsible use of our natural resources.
The text paper of this book is made from 30% postconsumer waste.

Most Westminster John Knox Press books are available at special quantity discounts when purchased in bulk by corporations, organizations, and special-interest groups. For more information, please e-mail SpecialSales@wjkbooks.com.

Contents

Proper 29 (Reign of Christ)

Sidebars

Publisher's Note

"The preaching of the Word of God is the Word of God," says the Second Helvetic Confession. While that might sound like an exalted estimation of the homiletical task, it comes with an implicit warning: "A lot is riding on this business of preaching. Get it right!"

Believing that much does indeed depend on the church's proclamation, we offer Connections: A Lectionary Commentary for Preaching and Worship. Connections embodies two complementary convictions about the study of Scripture in preparation for preaching and worship. First, to best understand an individual passage of Scripture, we should put it in conversation with the rest of the Bible. Second, since all truth is God's truth, we should bring as many "lenses" as possible to the study of Scripture, drawn from as many sources as we can find. Our prayer is that this unique combination of approaches will illumine your study and preparation, facilitating the weekly task of bringing the Word of God to the people of God.

We at Westminster John Knox Press want to thank the superb editorial team that came together to make Connections possible. At the heart of that team are our general editors: Joel B. Green, Thomas G. Long, Luke A. Powery, and Cynthia L. Rigby. These four gifted scholars and preachers have poured countless hours into brainstorming, planning, reading, editing, and supporting the project. Their passion for authentic preaching and transformative worship shows up on every page. They pushed the writers and their fellow editors, they pushed us at the press, and most especially they pushed themselves to focus always on what you, the users of this resource, genuinely need. We are grateful to Kimberly Bracken Long for her innovative vision of what commentary on the Psalm readings could accomplish, and for recruiting a talented group of liturgists and preachers to implement that vision. Bo Adams has shown creativity and insight in exploring an array of sources to provide the sidebars that accompany each worship day's commentaries. At the forefront of the work have been the members of our editorial board, who helped us identify writers, assign passages, and most especially carefully edit each commentary. They have cheerfully allowed the project to intrude on their schedules in order to make possible this contribution to the life of the church. Most especially we thank our writers, drawn from a broad diversity of backgrounds, vocations, and perspectives. The distinctive character of our commentaries required much from our writers. Their passion for the preaching ministry of the church proved them worthy of the challenge.

As this volume was in production we received the sad news of Blair Monie's passing. Blair was a good friend of Connections, having served as one of our original editors and having remained a steadfast supporter of the project when his struggle with cancer required him to set aside his editorial responsibilities. The resource before you is more insightful, more helpful, and more faithful to the gospel for his leadership.

A project of this size does not come together without the work of excellent support staff. Above all we are indebted to project manager Joan Murchison. Joan's fingerprints are all over the book you hold in your hands; her gentle, yet unconquerable, persistence always kept it moving forward in good shape and on time. Pamela Jarvis skillfully compiled the volume, arranging the hundreds of separate commentaries and Scriptures into a cohesive whole.

Finally, our sincere thanks to the administration, faculty, and staff of Austin Presbyterian Theological Seminary, our institutional partner in producing Connections. President Theodore J. Wardlaw and Dean David H. Jensen have been steadfast friends of the project, enthusiastically agreeing to our partnership, carefully overseeing their faculty and staff's work on it, graciously hosting our meetings, and enthusiastically using their platform to promote Connections among their students, alumni, and friends.

It is with much joy that we commend Connections to you, our readers. May God use this resource to deepen and enrich your ministry of preaching and worship.

WESTMINSTER JOHN KNOX PRESS

Introducing Connections

Connections is a resource designed to help preachers generate sermons that are theologically deeper, liturgically richer, and culturally more pertinent. Based on the Revised Common Lectionary (RCL), which has wide ecumenical use, the hundreds of essays on the full array of biblical passages in the three-year cycle can be used effectively by preachers who follow the RCL, by those who follow other lectionaries, and by nonlectionary preachers alike.

The essential idea of Connections is that biblical texts display their power most fully when they are allowed to interact with a number of contexts, that is, when many connections are made between a biblical text and realities outside that text. Like the two poles of a battery, when the pole of the biblical text is connected to a different pole (another aspect of Scripture or a dimension of life outside Scripture), creative sparks fly and energy surges from pole to pole.

Two major interpretive essays, called Commentary 1 and Commentary 2, address every scriptural reading in the RCL. Commentary 1 explores preaching connections between a lectionary reading and other texts and themes within Scripture, and Commentary 2 makes preaching connections between the lectionary texts and themes in the larger culture outside of Scripture. These essays have been written by pastors, biblical scholars, theologians, and others, all of whom have a commitment to lively biblical preaching.

The writers of Commentary 1 surveyed five possible connections for their texts: the immediate literary context (the passages right around the text), the larger literary context (for example, the cycle of David stories or the passion narrative), the thematic context (such as other feeding stories, other parables, or other passages on the theme of hope), the lectionary context (the other readings for the day in the RCL), and the canonical context (other places in the whole of the Bible that display harmony, or perhaps tension, with the text at hand).

The writers of Commentary 2 surveyed six possible connections for their texts: the liturgical context (such as Advent or Easter), the ecclesial context (the life and mission of the church), the social and ethical context (justice and social responsibility), the cultural context (such as art, music, and literature), the larger expanse of human knowledge (such as science, history, and psychology), and the personal context (the life and faith of individuals).

In each essay, the writers selected from this array of possible connections, emphasizing those connections they saw as most promising for preaching. It is important to note that, even though Commentary 1 makes connections inside the Bible and Commentary 2 makes connections outside the Bible, this does not represent a division between "what the text *meant* in biblical times versus what the text *means* now." *Every* connection made with the text, whether that connection is made within the Bible or out in the larger culture, is seen as generative for preaching, and each author provokes the imagination of the preacher to see in these connections preaching possibilities for today. Connections is not a substitute for traditional scriptural commentaries, concordances, Bible dictionaries, and other interpretive tools. Rather, Connections begins with solid biblical scholarship then goes on to focus on the act of preaching and on the ultimate goal of allowing the biblical text to come alive in the sermon.

Connections addresses every biblical text in the RCL, and it takes seriously the architecture of the RCL. During the seasons of the Christian year (Advent through Epiphany and Lent through Pentecost), the RCL provides three readings and a psalm for each Sunday and feast day: (1) a first reading, usually from the Old Testament; (2) a psalm, chosen to respond to the first reading; (3) a second reading, usually from one of the New Testament epistles; and (4) a Gospel reading. The first and second readings are chosen as complements to the Gospel reading for the day.

During the time between Pentecost and Advent, however, the RCL includes an additional first reading for every Sunday. There is the usual complementary reading, chosen in relation to the Gospel reading, but there is also a "semicontinuous" reading. These semicontinuous readings move through the books of the Old Testament more or less continuously in narrative sequence, offering the stories of the patriarchs (Year A), the kings of Israel (Year B), and the prophets (Year C). Connections covers both the complementary and the semicontinuous readings.

The architects of the RCL understand the psalms and canticles to be prayers, and they selected the psalms for each Sunday and feast as prayerful responses to the first reading for the day. Thus, the Connections essays on the psalms are different from the other essays, and they have two goals, one homiletical and the other liturgical. First, they comment on ways the psalm might offer insight into preaching the first reading. Second, they describe how the tone and content of the psalm or canticle might inform the day's worship, suggesting ways the psalm or canticle may be read, sung, or prayed.

Preachers will find in Connections many ideas and approaches to sustain lively and provocative preaching for years to come. But beyond the deep reservoir of preaching connections found in these pages, preachers will also find here a habit of mind, a way of thinking about biblical preaching. Being guided by the essays in Connections to see many connections between biblical texts and their various contexts, preachers will be stimulated to make other connections for themselves. Connections is an abundant collection of creative preaching ideas, and it is also a spur to continued creativity.

JOEL B. GREEN
THOMAS G. LONG
LUKE A. POWERY
CYNTHIA L. RIGBY
General Editors

Introducing the Revised Common Lectionary

To derive the greatest benefit from Connections, it will help to understand the structure and purpose of the Revised Common Lectionary (RCL), around which this resource is built. The RCL is a three-year guide to Scripture readings for the Christian Sunday gathering for worship. "Lectionary" simply means a selection of texts for reading and preaching. The RCL is an adaptation of the Roman Lectionary (of 1969, slightly revised in 1981), which itself was a reworking of the medieval Western-church one-year cycle of readings. The RCL resulted from six years of consultations that included representatives from nineteen churches or denominational agencies. Every preacher uses a lectionary—whether it comes from a specific denomination or is the preacher's own choice—but the RCL is unique in that it positions the preacher's homiletical work within a web of specific, ongoing connections.

The RCL has its roots in Jewish lectionary systems and early Christian ways of reading texts to illumine the biblical meaning of a feast day or time in the church calendar. Among our earliest lectionaries are the lists of readings for Holy Week and Easter in fourth-century Jerusalem.

One of the RCL's central connections is intertextuality; multiple texts are listed for each day. This lectionary's way of reading Scripture is based on Scripture's own pattern: texts interpreting texts. In the RCL, every Sunday of the year and each special or festival day is assigned a group of texts, normally three readings and a psalm. For most of the year, the first reading is an Old Testament text, followed by a psalm, a reading from one of the epistles, and a reading from one of the Gospel accounts.

The RCL's three-year cycle centers Year A in Matthew, Year B in Mark, and Year C in Luke. It is less clear how the Gospel according to John fits in, but when preachers learn about the RCL's arrangement of the Gospels, it makes sense. John gets a place of privilege because John's Gospel account, with its high Christology, is assigned for the great feasts. Texts from John's account are also assigned for Lent, Sundays of Easter, and summer Sundays. The second-century bishop Irenaeus's insistence on four Gospels is evident in this lectionary system: John and the Synoptics are in conversation with each other. However, because the RCL pattern contains variations, an extended introduction to the RCL can help the preacher learn the reasons for texts being set next to other texts.

The Gospel reading governs each day's selections. Even though the ancient order of reading texts in the Sunday gathering positions the Gospel reading last, the preacher should know that the RCL receives the Gospel reading as the hermeneutical key.

At certain times in the calendar year, the connections between the texts are less obvious. The RCL offers two tracks for readings in the time after Pentecost (Ordinary Time/standard Sundays): the complementary and the semicontinuous. Complementary texts relate to the church year and its seasons; semicontinuous emphasis is on preaching through a biblical book. Both approaches are historic ways of choosing texts for Sunday. This commentary series includes both the complementary and the semicontinuous readings.

In the complementary track, the Old Testament reading provides an intentional tension, a deeper understanding, or a background reference for another text of the day. The Psalm is the congregation's response to the first reading, following its themes. The Epistle functions as the horizon of the church: we learn about the faith and struggles of early Christian communities. The Gospel tells us where we are in the church's time and is enlivened, as are all the texts, by these intertextual interactions. Because the semicontinuous track prioritizes the narratives of specific books, the intertextual connections are not as apparent. Connections still exist, however. Year A pairs Matthew's account with Old Testament readings from the first five books; Year B pairs Mark's account with stories of anointed kings; Year C pairs Luke's account with the prophetic books.

Historically, lectionaries came into being because they were the church's beloved texts, like the scriptural canon. Choices had to be made regarding readings in the assembly, given the limit of fifty-two Sundays and a handful of festival days. The RCL presupposes that everyone (preachers and congregants) can read these texts—even along with the daily RCL readings that are paired with the Sunday readings.

Another central connection found in the RCL is the connection between texts and church seasons or the church's year. The complementary texts make these connections most clear. The intention of the RCL is that the texts of each Sunday or feast day bring biblical meaning to where we are in time. The texts at Christmas announce the incarnation. Texts in Lent renew us to follow Christ, and texts for the fifty days of Easter proclaim God's power over death and sin and our new life in Christ. The entire church's year is a hermeneutical key for using the RCL.

Let it be clear that the connection to the church year is a connection for present-tense proclamation. We read, not to recall history, but to know how those events are true for us today. Now is the time of the Spirit of the risen Christ; now we beseech God in the face of sin and death; now we live baptized into Jesus' life and ministry. To read texts in time does not mean we remind ourselves of Jesus' biography for half of the year and then the mission of the church for the other half. Rather, we follow each Gospel's narrative order to be brought again to the meaning of Jesus' death and resurrection and his risen presence in our midst. The RCL positions the texts as our lens on our life and the life of the world in our time: who we are in Christ now, for the sake of the world.

The RCL intends to be a way of reading texts to bring us again to faith, for these texts to be how we see our lives and our gospel witness in the world. Through these connections, the preacher can find faithful, relevant ways to preach year after year.

JENNIFER L. LORD
Connections Editorial Board Member

Connections

Trinity Sunday

Proverbs 8:1–4, 22–31
Psalm 8
Romans 5:1–5
John 16:12–15

Proverbs 8:1–4, 22–31

[1]Does not wisdom call,
  and does not understanding raise her voice?
[2]On the heights, beside the way,
  at the crossroads she takes her stand;
[3]beside the gates in front of the town,
  at the entrance of the portals she cries out:
[4]"To you, O people, I call,
  and my cry is to all that live.
. . . .
[22]The LORD created me at the beginning of his work,
  the first of his acts of long ago.
[23]Ages ago I was set up,
  at the first, before the beginning of the earth.
[24]When there were no depths I was brought forth,
  when there were no springs abounding with water.
[25]Before the mountains had been shaped,
  before the hills, I was brought forth—
[26]when he had not yet made earth and fields,
  or the world's first bits of soil.
[27]When he established the heavens, I was there,
  when he drew a circle on the face of the deep,
[28]when he made firm the skies above,
  when he established the fountains of the deep,
[29]when he assigned to the sea its limit,
  so that the waters might not transgress his command,
when he marked out the foundations of the earth,
  [30]then I was beside him, like a master worker;
and I was daily his delight,
  rejoicing before him always,
[31]rejoicing in his inhabited world
  and delighting in the human race."

Commentary 1: Connecting the Reading with Scripture

The book of Proverbs belongs to the genre of biblical Wisdom literature, which derives its name from its focus on "wisdom" and "folly." Wisdom literature is didactic, offering teachings grounded in the observations and experiences of daily life and the natural world: "Go to the ant, you lazybones; consider its ways, and be wise" (Prov. 6:6). However, this appointed portion of Proverbs does not contain the kinds of pithy aphorisms we may have come to expect from the rest of the book. Instead, Proverbs 8:22–31 offers a lengthy poem voiced by Wisdom, which is personified as a woman throughout the first nine chapters. Verses 1–4 introduce Wisdom crying out in the public square to all of humanity, echoing a similar call at Proverbs 1:20–21. The remainder of the verses appointed by the lectionary constitute a self-contained poem devoted to Wisdom's reflections on her primacy among all of God's creation.

Though the poem in verses 22–31 can stand alone as an independent unit, one of our first tasks still should be to investigate the intervening lines that have been omitted (vv. 5–21), as we would for any lectionary text that includes nonconsecutive verses. In them Wisdom testifies to the truth, nobility, and righteousness of her speech. Drawing on a favorite metaphor of the wisdom tradition, Wisdom describes her "paths" as straight and just. These characteristics contrast with the seductive speech and dangerous paths of the "strange woman" (NRSV "loose woman"), who is presented as a contrast to Woman Wisdom throughout Proverbs 1–9. In fact, the contrasting parallel of the strange woman, who is essentially the personification of folly, is the first connection to make with Proverbs 8, which itself is dominated by the voice of Woman Wisdom. Though absent from this particular lection, the shadow of the strange woman looms over any discussion of Woman Wisdom in these chapters.

Proverbs 8 is situated within an extended discourse from father to son that stretches throughout Proverbs 1–9. As the father instructs his son on how to navigate the world in ways that will enable him to flourish, the father builds divergent images of these two metaphorical women. Proverbs 7, focused on the strange woman, is a helpful place to see these contrasts, because it is so starkly different from the poems from Wisdom that follow. Carol Newsom describes Proverbs 7 and 8 as a diptych that sets up these two metaphors in a kind of oppositional parallel.[1] The strange woman of Proverbs 7 lurks in the twilight to target the young man, whom she entices into her house with a perfumed bed and "smooth talk." By contrast, Woman Wisdom proclaims aloud at the city gates for all to hear (8:3–4); her words "are all straight to one who understands and right to those who find knowledge" (8:9). Whereas the strange woman incites licentious desire, Woman Wisdom "is better than jewels, and all that you may desire cannot compare with her" (8:11). The strange woman leads to death (7:27), but Wisdom leads to life (8:35–36).

Following the more general observations of verses 4–21, Proverbs 8:22–31 turns our attention to the cosmic realm, broadening its antithesis with the previous chapter. As Newsom notes, "Chapter 8, with its strong mythic overtones, is written largely in the symbolic register; chapter 7 largely in the realistic."[2] The cosmic is often the answer to the mundane in Wisdom literature. Think of God's answer to Job out of the whirlwind (Job 38–41). As a destitute Job scrapes his sores, God takes him on a rhetorical tour of the beginnings of the universe, pointing out the absence of Job's power and the magnitude of God's own. Proverbs, like Job, invites us to connect everyday virtue with the cosmic order, albeit in a slightly different mode. Whereas God's speech all but shuts down Job's complaint, Wisdom's reflections on her position as the first of creation invite her listeners to engage with her in their everyday lives.

Wisdom literature is built on the notion that "the fear of the LORD is the beginning of wisdom" (Prov. 9:10), but God does not feature as a character in Wisdom literature in the same way God does in biblical narrative or prophecy. Though set in a theological framework, much of the content of the book of Proverbs focuses on practicalities like using accurate scales and disciplining children. That emphasis makes the scope of the poem of Proverbs 8:22–31 all the more striking. The poem is replete with vocabulary that emphasizes Wisdom's "first-ness"; Wisdom was there at the beginning, at the first, before the beginning of the earth, before everything else but God. While God created the earth, Wisdom was God's joyful companion. Where the NRSV uses "master worker" in verse 30, an alternative (and, in my evaluation,

1. Carol A. Newsom, "Woman and the Discourse of Patriarchal Wisdom: A Study of Proverbs 1–9," in *Women in the Hebrew Bible: A Reader*, ed. Alice Bach (New York: Routledge, 1999), 85–98.

2. Newsom, "Woman and the Discourse of Patriarchal Wisdom," 95.

God's High, Plenteous Grace

I beheld the working of all the blessed Trinity, and in the beholding I saw and understood these three properties: the property of fatherhood, the property of motherhood, and the property of the Lordship in one God. In our Father almighty we have our keeping and our bliss as regards our human substance, which is ours by our making without beginning. And in the Second Person, in wit and wisdom, we have our keeping as regards our sensuality, our restoring, and our saving: for he is our Mother, Brother, and Savior. And in our good Lord the Holy Spirit we have our rewarding and our recompense for our living and our labors which will far exceed anything we can desire, owing to his marvelous courtesy and his high plenteous grace.

For our whole life is in three. In the first we have our being, and in the second we have our increasing, and in the third we have our fulfilling. The first is kind, the second is mercy, and the third is grace. In the first, I saw and understood that the high might of the Trinity is our Father; and the deep wisdom of the Trinity is our Mother; and the great love of the Trinity is our Lord: and all this we have and own in our natural kind and in the making of our substance.

Julian of Norwich, *Revelation of Love*, chap. 28, trans. John Skinner (New York: Doubleday, 1997), 129.

better) translation is "child." In other words, the poem imagines the first take-your-daughter-to-work day, when God is busy setting limits for the sea, and Wisdom is trailing along as a happy observer, "rejoicing in his inhabited world and delighting in the human race" (v. 31). To walk in the straight and righteous paths of Wisdom, then, is to connect with this same primal joy.

Metaphors are powerful literary devices. They function in two directions. They first serve to describe something unfamiliar or difficult to understand by means of something well established; for example, "folly" is like a "loose woman." At the same time, metaphors can influence our perceptions of those supposedly well-established, well-known ideas. The gendered nature of the wisdom and folly metaphors makes them particularly fraught for today's readers. On the one hand, to imagine wisdom, one of ancient Israelite culture's highest values, as a female companion to God (v. 30) provides a welcome change from some of the more troubling OT metaphors, such as the prophets' descriptions of Israel as an unfaithful wife who must be sexually shamed. On the other hand, pitting wisdom and folly against each other as opposing archetypes of womanhood can reinforce damaging stereotypes and unrealistic expectations, even today. When considering these texts for proclamation, preachers may wish to hold in tension the generativity of these metaphors with their potentially troubling effects.

In the NT, Proverbs 8:22–31 echoes through the Christ hymn of Colossians (Col. 1:15–20), which describes Jesus as the "firstborn of all creation" and "before all things." Although the Colossians text is not one of the lectionary readings this week, the selection of Proverbs 8 for Trinity Sunday will surely give rise to some reflections on the use of this text in the early church's christological debates. Nevertheless, the idea of the Trinity emerges as a theological and doctrinal category long after the composition of this poem. William Brown usefully reminds us, "Poetry is not well suited for settling heated theological debates. The challenge is to look beyond the poem's battle scars and welcome its wonder with eyes wide open, delighting in its richness, come what may."[3] For the preacher, then, perhaps the wisest way forward is to take Brown's advice and to delight in the beauty of Proverbs' poetry: in its rhythms, its imagery, and its journey through the earliest moments of creation.

CAMERON B. R. HOWARD

3. William P. Brown, *Sacred Sense: Discovering the Wonder of God's Word and World* (Grand Rapids: Eerdmans, 2015), 56. Brown devotes a chapter to Prov. 8:22–31, in which he dwells helpfully on Wisdom's childlike playfulness and the poem's inherent beauty.

Commentary 2: Connecting the Reading with the World

A truly stunning natural phenomenon is the sudden appearance of a *murmuration*. This is a large flock of starlings, thousands of starlings, whirling and swooping in exquisite synchronicity over a marsh or field. Murmurations are exuberant living art; they convey joy and vitality. It is impossible not to feel delight in viewing such a natural wonder.

The personified woman of Wisdom in Proverbs 8 would certainly resonate with the marvel and amazement of a murmuration of starlings. The wise woman depicted in this highly structured text delights in the surprising displays of the created world and revels in them. This remarkable text, often the site of theological arguments about Trinity and Christology and creation, is better understood as a bold artistic portrayal of creation's delights. In our frantic, highly competitive, materialistic, and individualistic culture, this text ought to serve as an invitation to a way of life much closer to the delight and joy of the wise woman. Rather than interrogating the text for Trinitarian and christological subtleties or orthodoxies, the judicious reader remains open to the gifts of this wise woman. The insights and instructions she offers for living in this world are multiple, flexible, and practical.

Some of the extensive scholarship crowding around this famous female image of personified Wisdom is argumentative, denying the quasidivine stature of the wise woman as a threat to orthodox Christian Trinitarianism. Taking the text on its own terms, as a celebration of created life in God's wondrous world, it offers evocative insights for a life of flourishing. Two insights emerge that illuminate the challenges of pastoral ministry in a complex world.

First, this text highlights the irreducibly social aspect of creaturely life. The voice of Wisdom calls out in the public square; all are within the range of her voice (vv. 1–4). She is present and active at creation, not as a disinterested bystander, but as a companion and witness, even as an encourager. After all, Wisdom takes up the place of "rejoicing before him always," a place of affirmation and encouragement to the creating actions of God. All of this highlights the deeply social and communal structures of the created world. No fullness of life is possible for the isolated individual who surveys life from a place of cool detachment. Rather, the multiple ways we are connected reach into the structures of creation itself. There is no room in this text for old and damaging anthropologies of human creatures as rational souls encumbered by bodies. The portrayal of both God and all creatures is one of relational connectedness and communication. Wisdom is with God daily (v. 30). Wisdom communicates with God (v. 30). Wisdom collaborates with God (v. 30). Furthermore, Wisdom rejoices in God (v. 31). Here is a portrayal of God's profound and intimate connection with creation and of creation's profound and lively connection with God, both evoked by the image of Wisdom, who relishes that relationship.

The unmistakable implications of the relationship between Wisdom and God reach out both into communities of faith and into communities of the public square. Here is a vision of human life lived fully only insofar as the whole created world lives fully. There are no winners and losers in this vision. This is not a zero-sum game. A Christian vision that looks out onto the world with the eyes of Wisdom constantly sees opportunities for participating in God's own intentions and plans. God is not a Creator gone missing. God is intimately related to each and every creature. This surely motivates social action in every arena.

Furthermore, these relational interconnections happen in the most ordinary patterns of creaturely life. Biblical scholar Roland Murphy once commented, "God's creative intention for the world is fundamentally connected with the actual workings of the human mind and of human society."[4] Scholars sometimes refer to the "quotidian" interests of the book of Proverbs, the day-to-day details that are included in divine care as well as divine call. Christine Roy Yoder underscores this: "[Proverbs] urges us

4. Roland Murphy, "Wisdom and Creation," *Journal of Biblical Literature* 104, no. 1 (1985): 67.

to examine our convictions about the human place in the world, the power and presence of God, the frame and fibers of moral character, the nature of knowledge, the contours of good and evil, the role of tradition, our assumptions about gender and 'strangers,' and the power and contingencies of speech."[5] The scope of interest is both broad, cosmically broad, and detailed, minutely detailed, in this text.

The wise woman of Proverbs 8 calls out to us in all our places of activity with the message that we are at our creaturely roots deeply social and communal. We live in webs of interrelatedness and connection. We experience our true humanity not in isolation but in communion. A perceptive pastoral leader will be shaped by this text in calling communities of faith away from fearful schisms and competitions and toward forgiveness, trust, and wholeness.

The second implication for pastoral ministry that emerges from this text comes from the clear divine invitation to play. In this text, Wisdom takes up her work with such utter delight that work and play mix and merge into one joyful response to God. In fact, the remarkable image of divine Wisdom playing with the creatures that God has created, including human creatures, suggests both that play is part of the palette of God's encounter with creation and that play is part of the proper human response to God.[6] This invitation is a correction to a common assumption that theology and biblical interpretation are serious tasks best undertaken by serious people. The wise woman chuckles and says, "Let's play."

Congregations in some cultural contexts have been trained by well-intentioned pastors to approach God with deadly solemnity. Other cultural contexts express without reserve the palette of play. A pastor who has caught the delight of the wise woman of Proverbs 8 will lead the congregation into all the colors and tones of creaturely life, into joy and play and delight as well as sorrow and grief and loss. The church can certainly better fulfill its mission to communicate the gospel to a jaded world with winsome cheer and joyful delight rather than judgment and blame.

Imagine a congregation who gradually come to understand God as genuinely relishing the common delight of play and joy and wonder shared by both God and creatures. Imagine a congregation who can, however partially, envision their God as one who gets the joke of a murmuration of starlings or the delight of small daily rituals that shape life and bring joy. Such a congregation will come to know that the delights of wisdom are not cognition or knowledge proven by data. The delights of wisdom are a deep disposition, an attitude, a perception. Pastoral leaders who name and nurture that deep disposition of delight and wonder can then also connect it to faithful action in the world. Wonder and witness are twin energies in the life of faith, both born of Wisdom who rejoices daily at the side of God.

LEANNE VAN DYK

5. Christine Roy Yoder, *Proverbs* (Nashville: Abingdon Press, 2009), xxx.
6. Ellen Davis, *Proverbs, Ecclesiastes, and the Song of Songs* (Louisville, KY: Westminster John Knox Press, 2000), 69.

Psalm 8

[1]O LORD, our Sovereign,
how majestic is your name in all the earth!

You have set your glory above the heavens.
[2]Out of the mouths of babes and infants
you have founded a bulwark because of your foes,
to silence the enemy and the avenger.

[3]When I look at your heavens, the work of your fingers,
the moon and the stars that you have established;
[4]what are human beings that you are mindful of them,
mortals that you care for them?

[5]Yet you have made them a little lower than God,
and crowned them with glory and honor.
[6]You have given them dominion over the works of your hands;
you have put all things under their feet,
[7]all sheep and oxen,
and also the beasts of the field,
[8]the birds of the air, and the fish of the sea,
whatever passes along the paths of the seas.

[9]O LORD, our Sovereign,
how majestic is your name in all the earth!

Connecting the Psalm with Scripture and Worship

Psalm 8 is read in response to the first reading, Proverbs 8:1–4, 22–31, in which God is proclaimed as the creator of the universe by the personified Wisdom. While Romans 5:1–5 points to God's reconciling work with humanity through Jesus Christ, and John 16:12–15 explains the work of the Holy Spirit as the Advocate, Psalm 8 connects to the first reading by praising God for the creation of all the creatures in the world, particularly human beings.

In the reading from Proverbs, Wisdom calls for attention from people (Prov. 8:1–4) and discloses to them her identity as the closest one to God (vv. 22–31). Wisdom, being associated with prudence and possessing knowledge and discretion (v. 12), introduces herself as the precedent of the creation of the universe, and stresses that she was with God when God created the universe. More precisely, God as the creator has been by, with, and in Wisdom; and the voice of Wisdom, crying out repeatedly in the most public places, such as "on the heights, beside the way, at the crossroads . . . beside the gates in front of the town, at the entrance of the portals" (vv. 2–3), is an attribute of the voice of God. In the presence of God, she rejoices and delights in the whole world God created (v. 31).

Later, in the Gospel of John, Wisdom is equated with the Logos and is identified with the Christ (John 1:1–2). Moreover, the christological hymn in Colossians 1:15–20 applies the description of Wisdom in Proverbs 8 to Jesus Christ and confesses that "[t]he Son is . . . the firstborn over all creation. . . . in him all things were created: things in heaven and on earth" (NIV). In this way, the relationship between God and Wisdom in the OT became the foundation of understanding the relationship between God and Jesus Christ in the NT. The Council of Nicaea (325 CE) signified the absolute equality of the first person with the second person of the Trinity. Accordingly, Wisdom, who was identified with the second person of the Trinity in the NT, is coequal with God.

A reflection of Wisdom's joy and delight in God's work of creation can be heard in Psalm 8, which is the first hymn of praise in the book of Psalms. Verse 1 directly addresses God in an exclamation of adoration, and then recounts God's creation of the cosmos (Ps. 8:3) and human and nonhuman creatures (vv. 4–8), based on the creation stories in Genesis 1 and 2. The last verse (v. 9) is a refrain of the first verse to conclude the hymn with the tone of the praise of adoration.

The poem says that the essential reason for us to praise God is that God has created and cares for human beings. A profound theological question about humanity is raised in verse 4 ("What are human beings that you are mindful of them, mortals that you care for them?") and is answered in the following verses: God has "made them a little lower than God, and crowned them with glory and honor" (v. 5) and has granted them "dominion" over other creatures that God has created in the world (vv. 6–8).

Do we praise God for creating us and our fellow human beings? How, then, could we praise God the Creator in our reality, where not every human being is regarded as being "a little lower than God" and crowned with "glory and honor"? Our relationships with others are discriminatory and exclusive when we discount people with disabilities, the elderly, the poor, and the racially, sexually, and religiously marginalized as the wonderful work of God. As a result, we make God the Creator not of every human being but of a select, privileged people. What is our relationship with nonhuman creatures? If we misuse the divine gift of "dominion" as domination over them, how can we sing wholeheartedly the hymn of praise for God's creation? Authentic worship with praise and adoration of God is possible when we remember the way God created the world and confess such sins of humanity.

The liturgy of worshiping God the creator may begin with praise songs ("O Lord, our Sovereign, how majestic is your name in all the earth!") and move through lamentation for God's creatures in prayer to the evocation of worshipers' imagination by proclaiming the renewal of God's creation. By praising the sovereign Lord in God's promise of the new creation, the liturgy may end with doxology and remind us of the sovereignty of God over the universe as well as human responsibility for creation.

Psalm 8, therefore, leads us to worship God the creator with joy and delight in humility. It helps us remember who we are and what we are required to do as God's precious creatures, and it invites us to praise God for the continuous work of creation and recreation of all the world.

EUNJOO MARY KIM

Romans 5:1–5

[1]Therefore, since we are justified by faith, we have peace with God through our Lord Jesus Christ, [2]through whom we have obtained access to this grace in which we stand; and we boast in our hope of sharing the glory of God. [3]And not only that, but we also boast in our sufferings, knowing that suffering produces endurance, [4]and endurance produces character, and character produces hope, [5]and hope does not disappoint us, because God's love has been poured into our hearts through the Holy Spirit that has been given to us.

Commentary 1: Connecting the Reading with Scripture

In his book *Open Secrets* Richard Lischer describes his rural Illinois congregation's shared life of intersecting paths, connections, and graced relationships through an image: a vision of the Trinity in stained glass. The window's image, of course, is rather conceptual: a triangle for God, and smaller triangles within for Father, Son, and Holy Spirit,[1] and between them, the paths of the three-in-one God in relation. Lischer later juxtaposes this image with a bird's-eye view of a community from an airplane. From the sky, one can see the paths that run between homes and farms, where people have walked over the many years—reaching out, connecting, helping, sometimes suffering together. There is for Lischer a deep relationship between Trinity as doctrine and life as lived.

If chapter 5 of Paul's Letter to the Romans were to be described visually, it would probably be as a two-sided tapestry. The Trinity, three centuries before the Council of Constantinople, is far from fully defined. Romans 5 bears only indirect witness to a way of thinking about God as Father, Son, and Holy Spirit. Yet at the same time, what are pictured here in starker relief is the relationships between God, Christ, and Holy Spirit, and the corresponding relationships in the church at Rome, to whom Paul writes, possibly around year 57 or 58 CE. Note the relational emphasis here. We moderns are sometimes tempted to read Paul as the introspective individualist. In reading Romans, however, we know that Paul has in mind the relations between Jews and Gentiles in the mystery of the gospel. These relational tensions and possibilities are what we should best juxtapose with the curious language of God, Jesus Christ, and Holy Spirit; this is less than Constantinople, but as close as first-century Paul gets to anything Trinitarian in Romans 5:1–5. For Trinity Sunday, this Pauline interethnic understanding *in nuce* will just have to do. Yet the tapestry's juxtaposition of community life and emerging doctrinal formulation may prove almost as illuminating as Lischer's stained-glass paths.

Within the pericope itself, we note on close reading that the text begins and ends with a grace sandwich. It starts in verse 1 with "justified by faith" and ends in verse 5 with God's love "poured" and Holy Spirit "given." We cannot understand our pericope apart from God's grace in justification and God's love and Holy Spirit poured out as a lavish gift. We may be in a heavy-duty doctrinal section of the middle of Paul's letter to the Romans, but Paul wishes to remind us that his claims are bounded by divine grace. What may surprise us is the point of view. These five verses are doctrinal, but they are not directed to the lonely individual. Throughout

1. Richard Lischer, *Open Secrets: A Memoir of Faith and Discovery* (New York: Doubleday, 2001), 81.

our pericope the pronouns are "we" and "us" and the possessives are "ours."

While we may not wish to pin too much on word choice here, it does help to underline an ongoing feature of Romans overall. Paul is concerned to understand how the gospel can be universal when the communities to whom it speaks are both Jewish and Gentile. The "we" of these texts thus also serves to remind us later readers of the complexity of "we." We are *not* the same; and yet we are graced. Whatever Paul is saying about justification, reconciliation, Spirit, and love must be read through the Jewish/Gentile fabric of his "we" in the letter to the Romans.

Between talk of gifted justification, love, and Spirit is the hard-won naming of suffering and glory, endurance and hope. Gifts are great; but life in human flesh is lived in deeper paradox and shadows—even in the gospel. Paul is here speaking eschatologically—not in some pie-in-the-sky sense, but in an earthy sense, realizing that a gospel promise always points ahead to a future not yet fully present. For now, as is typical for many apocalyptic thinkers of the time, suffering and hope are comingled in the life of the community's faith. Yet this proleptic language is no interloper in the middle of verses 1–5. Justification itself is *also* an eschatological notion, *as is the Spirit*, whose presence is understood as a down payment, a firstfruit of the new age to come. Our text is about struggle bounded by grace. Here you may want to notice: proto-Trinitarian talk of God, Jesus Christ, and Spirit is uttered in the same breath as speech about reconciliation and *shalom* with suffering/hope along the way.

The tapestry threads connect our text to its wider literary context. Chapter 5 helps stitch together the so-called doctrinal section of Romans. Some argue it is the last part of Paul's long treatment of justification. Others claim it is the beginning of a section that concludes in chapter 8, where life in the Spirit, perhaps even sanctification, is in view. The main thing to note for our purposes is that all these are connected. Doctrine is not abstraction over life; it is rather in deep relation to life as lived, like Lischer's well-worn paths in the field.

That is why it is important to remember that even this doctrinal discourse is situated in a letter from Paul to the Romans. Paul must be mindful of connections here: the church is likely not one that he founded. If Paul's goal is as he professes, to stay in Rome on his way to preaching in Spain, he will need to make his gospel clear *and* help a community understand itself more deeply in communion with both Jews and Gentiles. For Paul, these are never just abstractions; just consider the wealth of personal greetings with which Romans concludes.

Thematically, Romans 5:1–5 is of a piece with what follows. There is a similar word cluster of Spirit/suffering/hope in Romans 8:18–25, along with the use of a rhetorical climax. Those who argue for a centrality of life in the Spirit here have the evidence of our text in their favor. Whatever Paul's language of God, Jesus Christ, Holy Spirit offers us on Trinity Sunday is not just about the internal doxology of the mysterious Godhead. It is also about the mystery of human communities, human realities of suffering, and gifts to humans of hope.

Within the lectionary and the church calendar, our text has even wider valence. On Trinity Sunday, we can take any first-century text only so far. If Romans 5 helps with Trinitarian theology, it does so only *in nuce*. Nonetheless, its value on Trinity Sunday is potentially deep. How does the reality of justification in a divided community relate to experience of Spirit and the grace in which "we stand" as God's diverse people together? The payoff may seem modest. At the same time, Paul's lively letter pushes back against any abstract doctrinal focus to the day and instead asks pointedly about the warp and woof, the living texture of community in which such language makes sense.

Within the wider canon, Romans also reminds us about the importance of Holy Spirit language—especially since Trinity Sunday comes right after Pentecost. The Holy Spirit here and elsewhere in the canon (John, for example) is not just some free agent, but precisely the Spirit of Christ. This relation is important for holding things together that at first blush would seem to be spiraling apart. For in the end, only in this way can it possibly lead our communities down the well-worn path from suffering to hope.

DAVID SCHNASA JACOBSEN

Commentary 2: Connecting the Reading with the World

This text encourages us to join Paul and boast in two things: our hope of sharing the glory of God, and our sufferings. While these might seem at odds, if not contradictory, Paul invites us to recognize our sufferings as somehow lying at the root of a journey that, in stages, produces within us the fruit of hope.

How will such a pair of boasts sound in our day? Will they be laughable to those who hear them? Will they in fact stick in our own throats when we try to utter them? How does hope play out in ordinary conversation and discourse today? In particular, how does Paul's sense of the progressive development of our hoping, from sufferings to endurance to character to hope, compare with what the human sciences and contemporary psychological theory have to say about what hope is and how it works? These questions alert us to several key contexts that affect how we hear this text and live in light of it today.

1. The Cultural-Linguistic Context. It is worth listening to the ways the word *hope* is used in everyday conversation, and discerning the grammatical logic evident in the ways it is used. Perhaps we hear things like this: I hope our team wins this weekend. I hope I get a good grade on the exam Friday. I hope he asks me to the prom. I hope I get the job I applied for. While in some ways akin to the idea of wishing, these uses of the word *hope* are stronger. They carry a personal investment in the desired outcome, beyond merely wishing that something would happen apart from any real possibilities or actions. The hopes in view are generally particular, tangible, and immediate. They also have an element of uncertainty about them—what is hoped for may or may not happen.

Our language habits may at times spread out more generally and in reference to longer-term turns of events. I hope our country can become less politically polarized. I hope for a resolution to the conflictual situation in Israel/Palestine. I hope the turmoil in our family will stop. However, our linguistic logic gives little evidence of an ultimate hope for the world. Hope seems mostly to be pinned to what is imaginable.

We also speak of hopes being dashed—that is, things did not materialize as hoped. We may speak of someone as having lost hope. We may speak of a person or group as hopeful, or perhaps another as despairing of hope. A situation may be described as hopeless.

These and many more colloquial expressions of hope are an important context of interpretation. How does our common language illustrate or illumine what the text says? How does the text raise questions about the logic or assumptions to which our language attests? Out of what alternative logic might the text be speaking?

2. The Context of Psychological Research and Psychotherapy Theory. What do the academic field of psychology and the related field of pastoral theology have to say about hope as an element of human experience? In a sense, Paul offers in Romans 5:3–4 a reading of the way a recipient of the peace, access, grace, and love of God lives on a foundation of "the hope of sharing the glory of God." As he does so, he shows the path by which one's hoping in that hope arises as a movement from sufferings to endurance to character formation to hope. Does today's psychological academy see that as a satisfying rendering of human experience? If so, what can be learned from the academy? If not, what dialogue does that set in motion between the text and contemporary theory regarding hope?

Until about four decades ago, the field of psychology had given hardly any attention to hope. In subsequent years it has become a heavily researched aspect of human existence and experience. Hope Theory, as pioneered and championed by C. R. Snyder and his colleagues, has gained dominance in psychotherapeutic practice as well as in pastoral counseling. In Snyder's major study, he characterizes hope, as exhibited in "high-hope" people, as "the sum of the mental willpower and waypower that you have for your goals."[2] As is true of the wider school of thought within which it is situated,

2. C. R. Snyder, *Psychology of Hope: You Can Get Here from There* (New York: Free Press, 1994), 5.

Positive Psychology, Snyder views hope as a cognitive process that is goal oriented. Put another way, hope is construed as a motivational system oriented to achieving positive goals.

Practical theologian Simon Kwan demonstrates the close connections between psychotherapeutic practice and pastoral counseling theory in their respective embrace of the psychology of hope Snyder and others espouse. While Kwan sees that influence as helpful in many ways, he nonetheless worries that the field of pastoral counseling "has been increasingly forgetful of certain unique features of Christian hope, due to its strong inclination to a positive psychology of hope." To stress the difference, Kwan draws on the work of Jürgen Moltmann, who emphasizes that "hope must take root in the future that God promises."[3]

If we follow Kwan's lead, how might the current psychology and psychotherapy of hope shed light on Paul's vision in Romans 5? Might the psychology of hope contradict it?

It should first be noted that psychology and Paul give attention to different questions. The psychology of hope examines what a high-hope person is like, how such a person functions, and how their positive goals are achieved. Paul examines how Christian hope is formed: sufferings to endurance to character to hope.

Beyond that, their views contrast in important ways. Christian hope is not a virtue enabling personal goal achievement but a process of response to God's gifts and promised intentions. God's goals are at the center, and God's agency is primary. Christian hope is not about a person's goal achievement or success; it is about relying in faith on God's actions.

Another difference is even more dramatic. In Snyder's Hope Theory, the focus on achievement sees hope and hopelessness as polar opposites; hope and despair cannot coexist. Paul's formational focus starts with a welcoming embrace of sufferings—of loss, or failure, or proximate hopes not materializing! Paul recognizes that, in Cornel West's words, "Despair and hope are inseparable,"[4] just as Christ's death and resurrection are held together as the ground of hope for the future.

3. The Sacramental-Liturgical Context. Recognizing that hope lies in the tension of cross and resurrection leads us to consider the ways Paul's treatment of hope engages the church's liturgical life. Liturgical traditions suggest that the Lord's Supper is a feast of remembrance and of communion *and of hope*. The first two have the tendency to predominate in our imagination of the Supper. How might that change if we accented the dimension of hope, its hopeful confidence in the coming fulfillment of God's intentions and promises? How, even in churches for whom the celebration of the Supper is more infrequent, can the whole of our liturgy bear the shape of cross and resurrection, of hope in the midst of hopelessness, in such a way that we boast in our hope and boast in our sufferings? How then might attentiveness to the sufferings lead to endurance, and endurance to character, and character to a hope that does not disappoint?

GEORGE R. HUNSBERGER

3. Simon S. M. Kwan, "Interrogating 'Hope': The Pastoral Theology of Hope and Positive Psychology," *International Journal of Practical Theology* 14, no. 1 (2010): 48. Jürgen Moltmann, *Theology of Hope: On the Ground and the Implications of a Christian Eschatology* (New York: Harper & Row, 1967).

4. Cornel West, *The Cornel West Reader* (New York: Basic Civitas Books, 1999), 554.

John 16:12–15

[12]"I still have many things to say to you, but you cannot bear them now. [13]When the Spirit of truth comes, he will guide you into all the truth; for he will not speak on his own, but will speak whatever he hears, and he will declare to you the things that are to come. [14]He will glorify me, because he will take what is mine and declare it to you. [15]All that the Father has is mine. For this reason I said that he will take what is mine and declare it to you."

Commentary 1: Connecting the Reading with Scripture

Perhaps the best way for contemporary readers to understand John's mysterious Gospel generally is to say that it is about the mystery we call *communion*. Readers know that John bears witness to a deep union between the Father and the Son (e.g., John 14:10–11). Yet as we approach our pericope in particular, 16:12–15, John is also aware that the Son's return to the Father begets something of a relational crisis. Readers already know from John's Gospel that the Son comes from the Father and returns to the Father through the Son's glorification on the cross. This very relational return presupposes the Son's *absence* from the disciples and the later Johannine community. It is, therefore, a profound crisis, a crisis not just of presence, but of communion going forward. On this Trinity Sunday, we contemporary readers may also ask: How can the communion of Father and Son benefit a church left behind in lonely absence?

John's Gospel of communion gestures in 16:12–15 toward mystery with an equally mysterious name: the Spirit of truth. The imminent absence of the Son is real enough to the disciples, but it is not the whole story. When the Son is glorified and returns to the Father, the Spirit is sent in his absence. John 16:12 admits the truth about the difficulty of his coming absence: that Jesus has many things to say that his disciples cannot now bear. The disciples themselves cannot know all that there is to know this side of Jesus' "being lifted up." With the introduction of the Spirit of truth in verse 13, the problem of future guidance is solved—only to cause yet another troubling problem: if the Spirit guides into truth not yet known, how is that truth to be judged in relation to the communion already revealed, the one between Father and Son? The answer in John's Gospel keeps their relational communion in view. The Spirit of truth is no free agent, "will not speak on his own," and instead will "speak whatever he hears." This is how the Spirit of truth "will declare to you the things that are to come." The relational mystery thus deepens. If the Son's function is to glorify the Father, and vice versa, it is now the Spirit's role to glorify the Son and in relation to what belongs to the Son to declare things to come. Since in verse 15 communing Father and Son hold all in common, the Spirit is no simple free agent, but a Spirit presence in absence who now carries forward the very communion that the Father revealed through the Son in John's Gospel.

Putting all this communion talk in historical context may make it easier to see. What do communities in crisis like John's do when leadership departs? They feel orphaned. John's Gospel is actually overdetermined by such crises: the leader toward whom the disciples point, the Son, has indeed been "lifted up" and returned to the Father at the time of Jesus' passion and resurrection. At the time of John's composition, however, the Johannine community finds itself being orphaned from a Jewish tradition, probably in a Diaspora setting like

Ephesus toward the turn of the second century. The disciples and then the Johannine community are experiencing, in the span of a few decades, loss upon loss, now orphaned doubly, experiencing absence, longing for presence, for clarity, for truth. Yet the Son who has returned is the means by which the Spirit of truth comes, not to sanction new truth for new times, but for interpreting truth in ever new contexts, as an expression of communion that continues *despite* the absence, the loss, and being orphaned yet again.

The strange content of 16:12–15 for Trinity Sunday makes deeper sense when we stand back and view it in its more immediate context in John. John's Gospel seeks to work through the problem of Jesus' absence through a lengthy speech in John 13–17, the Farewell Discourse. Over the course of these five chapters, John speaks in announcements, promises, instructions, and warnings, culminating in a prayer in chapter 17. The text as a whole is preparing for departure and laying the groundwork for the "lifting up" to follow in the glory of the Son, his passion and resurrection, his return to the Father, and the sending of Spirit. John 13–17 is Jesus' last great opportunity to speak directly to his community before his coming departure. It is direct address. It is about "I" and "y'all," a "you" in this case spoken not in existential loneliness, but in the plural of communion, connection, and community, too.

Thematically our pericope, nestled in the final half of John's Gospel, does more than revisit the Johannine communion theme foregrounded thus far. The text has implications for the Johannine community (14:20), which in relation to Johannine communion is understood like a branch to a true vine and vinegrower (15:1). John's Gospel also underlines the importance of the Holy Spirit through this whole section. The Holy Spirit as Advocate serves to remind believers of what Jesus has said (14:26). This Advocate testifies on the Son's behalf (15:26). The Advocate is also promised after Jesus' departure (16:7). John's Gospel as a whole also has a sense that the story is more than can be fully written. Just as Jesus in our pericope talks about still having "many things to say to you," John's Gospel envisions a story and action beyond its finite chapters. "Greater works than these" (14:12b) shall those who believe in the Son do, even beyond his own works—thanks to his impending departure to the Father. That "Jesus did many other signs . . . not written in this book" (20:30) helps us see a Gospel not easily contained. "But there are also many other things that Jesus did . . . that the world itself could not contain the books that would be written" (21:25). Such language, again, is not license to speculate but does push back on a view unable to receive the transcending mystery of relationship itself.

On Trinity Sunday, John 16:12–15 can be a rich resource. While it does not offer a fully Trinitarian view, its relational vision lays important groundwork. In this sense, it is both similar to and different from the epistolary text for the day, Romans 5. Neither gives us the fullness of church doctrine, which comes centuries later. They do, however, foreshadow the relationship of life in God and life among God's own. For those ready to dig deep into first-century realities of death and loss and the struggling and sometimes traumatized communities of the time, they offer a wealth of understanding on Trinity Sunday for a fragmented age such as ours. The lectionary and calendar may call forth deeper reflection on the relationship of the social Trinity to our own social life. Historically, the lines from them to us may not always be obvious—they are more like dotted lines; but retracing them helps us to see the ellipses of our own human relations more clearly in an age marked not just by a struggle for unity in diversity, but a deep, troubling fragmentation as well.

John's Gospel invites us to live into God's future attuned to a relational vision of life in God and life among us. This does not explain all there is to say about the mystery of Holy Trinity on this Sunday. It is, however, an invitation to see our relations in a different light—the light of God's fecund life, in which departure and coming, presence and absence, crucifixion and lifting up in glory, are both different and one.

DAVID SCHNASA JACOBSEN

Commentary 2: Connecting the Reading with the World

To engage such a brief excerpt drawn from a longer conversation (John 14–16) is challenging enough on its own grounds. To engage it seeking sufficient clues to define or defend the historic doctrine of the Trinity on Trinity Sunday is even more daunting. How do we explore this text in the context of the liturgical traditions that mark the Sunday after Pentecost as Trinity Sunday?

This day stands alone in the yearly liturgical cycle as a Sunday focused on a doctrine. The annual rhythm of the church year is for the most part formed around the unfolding story of God's self-disclosure and redeeming action in Jesus, the promised Christ. Annually, the story is rehearsed and celebrated. It begins with Advent, anticipating the coming of Christ. Then follows his birth and his unveiling to the world. Christ's baptism by John and his transfiguration in the company of disciples are markers along the way. We join the story in Lent, a journey that lands us in Passion Week, the week of Christ's suffering unto death. Easter and Eastertide celebrate Christ's resurrection life. We mark his ascension into heaven, and finally the sending of the Spirit at Pentecost.

In light of this story, what does it mean to follow now with a Sunday focused on a doctrine, specifically the doctrine of the Trinity? Certainly, with only a few lectionary texts in hand, it would be best to avoid trying to do what would be necessary to explain or defend the doctrine fully. Perhaps we would best see this small reading from John 16 as one that offers a glimpse, a few small clues for grasping the triune nature of God. Maybe, in the process, we might find Trinity Sunday not so much of an oddity as it might appear. Maybe what we find in this text is not an explanation of the Trinity, but a kind of recapitulation of the story the church year has been telling.

Can we hear Jesus in this text drawing together the strands of the story of God's self-disclosure as triune? Can we see him projecting forward the persistence of triune divine action? Certainly. Jesus speaks about the Father as one other than himself, and likewise about the Spirit. Yet it is clear that the Father's things (his will, actions, and purposes, we may presume from the rest of the Gospel) have been given to Jesus, and the Spirit will take those things and will testify to them. The Spirit will declare them to us, even after Jesus is no longer physically present to do so. What is made certain is that the three speak and act in the same vein, toward the same ends. One could say, *singularly*. That much is here.

Of course, that also leaves a lot unsaid. It takes more than an excerpt like this for the fullness of the doctrine to flower into view and settle into the church's consciousness. Perhaps Trinity Sunday can serve, positioned as it is in the church year just after Pentecost Sunday, to reprise the annual rhythm of advent/incarnation, cross/resurrection, and ascension/Pentecost, and fill us with wonder at the magnificence of the triune God's astounding action for the redemption of the world.

What is pronounced in this brief passage is the sense that the triune God is a living God who is an active agent. God is the subject of active verbs! The triune God sends, comes, teaches, acts, speaks, chooses, intends, and promises. That portrait suggests another contemporary context that touches our interpretation and preaching of this text: the larger society's belief structures. Increasingly, while pollsters have tended to reassure us that in American society belief in a supreme being has remained strong and somewhat constant over the years, it can be argued that, even if that is so, the *function* of that belief has shifted over time. God is no longer necessary in order to explain anything, and God does not really *do* anything. All of us in the pews are affected by this, whether we wish to admit it or not. How does the text address us then?

In the sociocultural ethos of modern Western societies, there are particular beliefs about what can be known and how that can become known—an epistemology, in other words. The reigning epistemology of our society, whether professionally espoused or popularly presumed, is another of the contexts in which this text is being heard. What Jesus says about the Spirit who is coming puts that in sharp relief. In the foregoing conversation (John 14–16), the Spirit has been mentioned a number of times. Most often the Spirit is called "another Advocate," or simply "the Advocate." The Advocate is called the Holy Spirit at one point, and is twice called the Spirit of truth. The Holy Spirit, says Jesus, will "testify on my behalf" (15:26), "will teach you everything, and remind you of all that I have said to you" (14:26). In the text before us (16:12–15) Jesus returns to those themes and accentuates them: the Spirit of truth will "speak" whatever he hears, and "declare to you" the things that are the Father's and mine, including "the things that are to come." Most pointedly, Jesus says the Spirit will "guide you into all the truth."

This constitutes an epistemology, albeit in embryo. It contains a sense of what things are important and meaningful to know, and a sense of how they may be known—that is, by the declaring, guiding, teaching action of God the Holy Spirit. This epistemology is one that finds itself at odds with the prevailing one. That one, as is often noted, is an epistemology that frames a dichotomy between facts and values. Scientifically established facts are appropriate to public knowledge and action; values lie in the realm of private belief and opinion. In such a world, Christian belief in one who is acclaimed to be Lord of all things faces a dilemma. Can Christ's lordship be believed to be a fact touching the life of the world, or must it be accepted that such a belief belongs only to the realm of private values?

There is too little space here to do justice to the epistemological issues at stake here. However, a suggestive example may be useful.

In his later years, the missionary theologian Lesslie Newbigin gave a great deal of attention to the epistemological context in Western societies. Spurred by the work of Michael Polanyi, a philosopher of science and of knowing, he sketched a way to see that the supposed gulf between scientific knowing and religious knowing is not so great or sharp as presumed. This laid the groundwork for what he commended to be a "proper confidence" to believe the gospel of God and bear witness to it. What follows is a summary of his line of argument in the first five chapters of *The Gospel in a Pluralist Society.*[1]

Scientific, no less than religious, knowing includes the tacit dimension of what is "trusted" as research is pursued; all "reasoning" depends on and is embodied within a particular rational tradition; such a tradition is maintained within a community; innovation occurs not by "reason" of new facts but by a paradigm shift; such shifts typically result from acts of imagination or intuition; all knowing is subjective—it is an act involving personal commitments; but knowing also has an objective referent—it is offered with universal intent.

GEORGE R. HUNSBERGER

1. Lesslie Newbigin, *The Gospel in a Pluralist Society* (Grand Rapids: Eerdmans, 1989).

Proper 3 (Sunday between May 22 and May 28 Inclusive)

Isaiah 55:10–13
Psalm 92:1–4, 12–15
1 Corinthians 15:51–58
Luke 6:39–49

Isaiah 55:10–13

[10]For as the rain and the snow come down from heaven,
and do not return there until they have watered the earth,
making it bring forth and sprout,
giving seed to the sower and bread to the eater,
[11]so shall my word be that goes out from my mouth;
it shall not return to me empty,
but it shall accomplish that which I purpose,
and succeed in the thing for which I sent it.

[12]For you shall go out in joy,
and be led back in peace;
the mountains and the hills before you
shall burst into song,
and all the trees of the field shall clap their hands.
[13]Instead of the thorn shall come up the cypress;
instead of the brier shall come up the myrtle;
and it shall be to the LORD for a memorial,
for an everlasting sign that shall not be cut off.

Commentary 1: Connecting the Reading with Scripture

A congregation will respond vocally to this OT reading with "Thanks be to God!"—a thanksgiving or, in Greek, a "eucharist." After the OT reading, the Psalm, the NT and Gospel readings, the homily, and the prayer of consecration of the body and blood of Christ: all of these liturgical elements will constitute the assembly further. The initial thanksgiving prepares the congregation for the Great Thanksgiving, the Eucharist.

The original congregational response of thanksgiving can help to guide our hearing and our reception of the Word of God from Isaiah 55:10–13. Christian reception of the Scriptures from before modernity invites us to find our life, the life of the congregation, and the life of the world—all of these—within the text itself. In classical Christian reception of Scripture, the text does not simply represent a message that we can then apply to a new situation. This old/new reception proffers a theological understanding that the divine Word takes precedence over our history and our immediate circumstances as the transcendent, eternal Word of God. If this reception is assumed, an exciting task then opens up for the preacher—to find his or her place, and the place of the congregation within the scriptural figuration, as understood in light of the incarnation of God in the one Lord Jesus Christ.

One way to trace the work that Isaiah 55:10–13 does is to follow its pronouns: "my/I," "it," and "you" (plural). Verse 11 provides the center of the text's movement: the "divine Word" (the main "it" of the passage) speaks forth from the divine mouth (the "I/my") and effects the "you" (plural), that is, those of us who receive the Word.

The passage has an "exit and return," a "from-through-and-to" structure. Like rain, the divine Word goes forth, and then it returns to the heavens after having given life on the earth (v. 10). The "you" responds, as does the earth, in the fulfilled mission of the divine Word (v. 12). The passage ends with a third-person structure (v. 13); the prophet speaks. Through the coming forth, the fulfilled purpose, and the return of the divine Word, God becomes named; the Word and the joyous response of those who receive the Word become an eternal sign—a material reality that communicates beyond itself to a reality that is both in, and yet is infinitely beyond, the sign's materiality. Thanks be to God!

Within the context of Christian worship that prepares for the celebration of the Eucharist, Isaiah 55:10–13 expresses the christological center of the Christian Scriptures. We find a common structure in Isaiah 55:10–13, as we do in the great prologue to the Gospel of John and in the Christ hymn of Philippians 2:5–11. Of course, the original author of this oracle did not have any idea of a Word "that became flesh and dwelt among us" or of one who "emptied himself, taking the form of a slave." Nonetheless, through the interweaving of Isaiah 55:10–13 within the structure of Christian worship, the text works exactly in this way.

It may be helpful to think of the passage as though it were a gene expressed differently as the environment of the organism shifts. Its earlier expression is not annulled; rather, it is taken up into a fuller expression in the setting of the relationships within its new environment. The gene itself does not change; however, the network that expresses the gene does change. What was always there, but implicit and unknown in the gene, suddenly bursts forth in a fresh expression. The gene shifts, not only in its expression, but also in expressions that go far beyond it.

Isaiah 55:10–13 appears as a hinge that opens out into Isaiah 56–66. The text seems to close the section of Isaiah that ends with Isaiah 55, with a later editor adding Isaiah 56–66. If we go back to follow the underlying narrative structure of Isaiah 40–55, we can see a drama unfolding. A prophet proclaims God's return of Judah to its homeland from Babylonian captivity through the Persian monarch Cyrus (Isa. 40–48). Starting in Isaiah 49, the pronouns shift. The prophet becomes progressively distanced from his own people; ultimately, the prophet's voice goes silent. In Isaiah 53, "we" now speak of the prophet's demise: "he was wounded for our transgressions" (Isa. 53:5). In the new life of the prophet (Isa. 53:11a), his disciples now go forth to return to Jerusalem following the defeat by Cyrus of the Babylonians. Isaiah 55:10–13 celebrates a future return to Jerusalem, a restoration through the death and life of the prophet. The passage provides a transitional summary to Isaiah 56–66. Isaiah 56–66 looks to a coming future in a new Jerusalem. Isaiah 55:10–13 serves as a confession of faith at a hinge point in the text.

If we step back further into the book of Isaiah, the transitional importance of this text becomes even more apparent. The book of Isaiah has a narrative structure as a whole; the book moves from God's judgment on Jerusalem, to a promise of restoration, to a vision of a future establishment of Jerusalem as the center of the world. Isaiah 49–55 provides the section where the death and the new postmortem life of the servant lead to the new Jerusalem. The servant's death, and then his life, usher forth the witness of the servants to the world as those servants await the restoration. The living-yet-absent servant opens space for faithfulness for the disciples as they continue to gather in his name.

As we step back into a panoramic view to find our lives in Isaiah 55:10–13 within the book of

Isaiah, we hear a confession of faith in God and God's Word that God has sent into the world. The Word, like rain, gives life amid a world broken in sin and injustice. The Word brings forth shade trees rather than brambles. The divine Word comes into creation to bring the full flourishing of creation. This flourishing itself, however, finds its ultimate end in God. The divine Word returns into the ultimate mystery of the divine mouth from which it came forth.

Isaiah 55:10–13 directly names all of those who gather to respond to its reading. The congregation, the church, stands as an everlasting sign. In its witness to the Word of God, in the time of the "between"—that is, between the death and resurrection of Christ and the culmination of all things in God—the life of the disciples allows God to be named in the world, the invisible God is visibly signed. This witness, the result of the coming of the Word of God, stands forever and ever, a sign that God has not left us to ourselves. God, from whom, through whom, and to whom are all things, refuses to let the divine Word collapse the Divine into a dialectical struggle to move history forward. The Word of God calls the receivers of this Word, in repentance and faith, to live the text's description of the congregation as an "everlasting sign."

The text invites a call for the congregation to participate in the holy food and drink of God's people—as God's Word comes again and again in the elements of the bread and wine—to bring forth flourishing now as a sign of life everlasting.

Thanks be to God!

JOHN W. WRIGHT

Commentary 2: Connecting the Reading with the World

These are the last words of what in the modern era is traditionally called Second Isaiah. Isaiah 40–55 was written to people in exile, people in the midst of enormous social and political dislocation, seemingly without political power or voice. The demand for political action, for economic and social justice animating so much of Isaiah 1–39 and 56–66, is lacking here. Second Isaiah focuses instead on the words and promises of the Lord. In Second Isaiah the Lord is described as acting or beginning to act on behalf of these exiled people. The Lord will undo the exile. However, for the Lord to restore these exiled people to their land, they will have to leave Babylon and risk a hard journey home. The deeds and words of the Lord are intertwined with the deeds of the people and their trust in God. It takes both God and God's people to undo this exile.

In moments of loss and dislocation, people of faith throughout history have often turned to the imagery of Isaiah 40–55. The visions of restoration and return that fill the poetry of Isaiah have provided hope and encouragement to countless people. Often these promises seem absurd or impossible. For instance, Isaiah 55 opens with astonishing advice: "Come, buy wine and milk without money and without price." For all the beauty of these promises, the questions remain of why and how to believe they are true.

In some ways, we trust them simply because they are the words of the Lord. We trust the words of the Lord because we trust the speaker. In a sense we need no further proof or data. Sometimes the naked words of the Lord are enough. Yet this passage offers more. It offers a curious and surprising proof of the power and reliability of God's words. It points to the rain and the snow. "As the rain and the snow come down from heaven, and do not return there until they have watered the earth . . . so shall my word be that goes out from my mouth." There is more here than just an analogy. The rain and snow are gifts of God. Yes, the land out there and perhaps your heart is full of thorns and briers, but the rain will come down, and up shall come cypress and myrtle (55:13).

This passage may belong first to people in exile and migration, people away from home in an alien land, people who are dislocated and excluded. To these people this passage proclaims that God is acting or beginning to act to provide a home for them—not just a roof, but a place where the land flourishes, where there is milk and honey. To these people, this passage issues a challenge. To people without political voice, this passage calls for them to engage the political. For God's land to bless them, they must begin a new migration. Exile and migration become the path to home.

It is also the case that people who are apparently safe at home often feel themselves dislocated and in exile. These dislocations can be political, social, personal, or even spiritual. As many people attest, cultures and governments can enforce exile on people who have never left home. In the shadow of political threats, their home is no longer their home; it becomes contested space. Families exile one another; their homes become places of terror. People lose their way in life; their own hearts betray them. Such disconnections haunt all human life. Migration and exile take many forms. Thus, these words of Isaiah have spoken to many people in many moments

When God's word goes forth and people follow, the land blossoms and people come home. In the imagery of Isaiah 55, this flourishing of land and people is a "memorial" to the Lord, an "everlasting sign." This is who God is. God gives life.

Psalm 65 can serve as a helpful conversation partner to our reading from Isaiah, because it uses a similar affirmation about the flourishing of creation. However, here the exile appears to be not from the land but from God. "When deeds of iniquity overwhelm us, you forgive our transgressions." This forgiveness opens the doors to God's presence. "Happy are those whom you choose and bring near to live in your courts." In fact, the return to God seems to happen specifically in the temple. God calls people to live in God's courts. The psalmist, speaking for all who are called, declares, "We shall be satisfied with the goodness of your house, your holy temple." The return seems to be confined to spaces of the temple, to the people of Israel who can find their way to Jerusalem. There is a hint here of exclusiveness, of chosenness in its sectarian echoes.

The rest of the psalm undoes this exclusiveness; God's blessings are not confined to the courts of the temple. Perhaps we might say, God's courts are everywhere. The psalm begins a beautiful litany about God and the abundance of God's creation: "You are the hope of all the ends of the earth and of the farthest seas. . . . You visit the earth and water it, you greatly enrich it; the river of God is full of water; you provide the people with grain." This imagery of abundance moves into celebration by creation itself. "The hills gird themselves with joy, the meadows clothe themselves with flocks, . . . they shout and sing together for joy." All of creation is God's temple. All of creation enjoys God's abundance and sings praises to God.

When we are lost in "our iniquities," whatever they might be, when we cannot imagine walking into the holy courts of God and feel separated from God and ourselves, the psalm calls us to wander among God's mountains and seas and meadows and hills. What we will see is life—good life, abundant life, everywhere. Think of how full of blessings God must be to create and nourish such life. As God fills the valleys with grain, God will fill you with endless blessings.

This imagery, this theological move, this spiritual advice, is nearly everywhere in Scripture. In the Sermon on the Mount Jesus also points us to the abundance of God's creation (Matt. 6:25–34; cf. Luke 12:22–32). Here the issue is people worrying about their "life," specifically what they might eat and wear. This concern fits with the burdens of exile and migration that animated Isaiah 55. On the open road, with no warm hearth waiting, food and clothing and shelter are life-and-death issues. Many historians suggest that most people in ancient Palestine lived on the edge of starvation. To these people, Jesus says, "Do not worry." He gives two reasons. Worry accomplishes nothing. More importantly, we worry like this when we forget who God is. Jesus makes the same move as Isaiah and the psalmist. Look around you. See who God is. Life is everywhere. The flourishing of life on earth, plants and animals both, is proof that God's word "shall accomplish that which I purpose."

To people who live more or less safely and well fed in their homes, these promises might bring warmth and assurance. We all need such. To people who have chosen, for whatever hard reason, to take on the terrors of migration or to people who are forced into migration by, for instance, the immigration laws of the United States, these promises will speak with greater intensity and will perhaps even give pain. People do starve and people do lose their homes. These promises, as fine as they sound, are only partially and occasionally fulfilled.

LEWIS R. DONELSON

Psalm 92:1–4, 12–15

[1]It is good to give thanks to the LORD,
to sing praises to your name, O Most High;
[2]to declare your steadfast love in the morning,
and your faithfulness by night,
[3]to the music of the lute and the harp,
to the melody of the lyre.
[4]For you, O LORD, have made me glad by your work;
at the works of your hands I sing for joy.

. . . .

[12]The righteous flourish like the palm tree,
and grow like a cedar in Lebanon.
[13]They are planted in the house of the LORD;
they flourish in the courts of our God.
[14]In old age they still produce fruit;
they are always green and full of sap,
[15]showing that the LORD is upright;
he is my rock, and there is no unrighteousness in him.

Connecting the Psalm with Scripture and Worship

Psalm 92 is a song for the Sabbath day. Traditionally, the Jewish community has recited it on Friday evenings.[1] The psalm describes the Sabbath as a day of celebration with thanksgiving and joy in a dialogical mode of communication with God. The psalmist's use of the first-person-singular pronoun "I" in the dialogue signifies the intimate relationship between God and the people of Israel, for whom God has done wondrous deeds. Even though the Revised Common Lectionary chose the first four and the last four verses for reading, it is important to appreciate them in the larger context of the entire song.

The first strophe (vv. 1–4) tells what the psalmist does on the Sabbath: giving thanks and praising God with joyful songs and music, and proclaiming the love and faithfulness of God day and night. The following verses (vv. 5–11) provide the reason why he celebrates the Sabbath, echoing an instruction given by Wisdom literature that God treats justly both the wicked and the righteous. It also declares that God will eventually exalt the righteous and destroy the wicked and the evildoers and fulfill God's righteousness, which is future messianic blessing that denotes the true Sabbath. The last strophe (vv. 12–15) reemphasizes that the righteous flourish like palm trees and the cedars of Lebanon, for God, who is upright, stands for them. The song ends with the praise of God as the rock of the righteous.

The historical context for the psalm—when, where, by whom, and for whom the psalm was composed—is obscure. Considering, however, that Psalm 92 is arranged to be the response to the first reading, Isaiah 55:10–13, the preacher may consider the psalm in light of the historical background of Second Isaiah (Isa. 40–55), which could have originated in the Judeo-Babylonian community under the overwhelming political power of the Babylonian Empire during the exilic period.[2] In fact, the observance

1. Annette M. Boeckler, "The Liturgical Understanding of Psalms in Judaism: Demonstrated with Samples from Psalms 90–106, with a Special Focus on Psalm 92, *Mizmor shir le Yom haShabbat*," *European Judaism* 48, no. 2 (2015): 74.

2. Joseph Blenkinsopp, *Isaiah 40–55: A New Translation with Introduction and Commentary*, Anchor Bible 19A (New York: Doubleday, 2000), 102.

Christ for You and Me

I believe that it has now become clear that it is not enough or in any sense Christian to preach the works, life, and words of Christ as historical facts, as if the knowledge of these would suffice for the conduct of life; yet this is the fashion among those who must today be regarded as our best preachers. Far less is it sufficient or Christian to say nothing at all about Christ and to teach instead the laws of men and the decrees of the fathers. Now there are not a few who preach Christ and read about him that they may move men's affections to sympathy with Christ, to anger against the Jews, and such childish and effeminate nonsense. Rather ought Christ to be preached to the end that faith in him may be established that he may not only be Christ, but be Christ for you and me, and that what is said of him and is denoted in his name may be effectual in us. Such faith is produced and preserved in us by preaching why Christ came, what he brought and bestowed, what benefit it is to us to accept him. This is done when that Christian liberty which he bestows is rightly taught and we are told in what way we Christians are all kings and priests and therefore lords of all and may firmly believe that whatever we have done is pleasing and acceptable in the sight of God, as I have already said.

What man is there whose heart, upon hearing these things, will not rejoice to its depth, and when receiving such comfort will not grow tender so that he will love Christ as he never could by means of any laws or works? Who would have the power to harm or frighten such a heart? If the knowledge of sin or the fear of death should break in upon it, it is ready to hope in the Lord. It does not grow afraid when it hears tidings of evil. It is not disturbed when it sees its enemies. This is so because it believes that the righteousness of Christ is its own and that its sin is not its own, but Christ's, and that all sin is swallowed up by the righteousness of Christ. This, as has been said above, is a necessary consequence on account of faith in Christ. So the heart learns to scoff at death and sin and to say with the Apostle, "O death, where is thy victory? O death, where is thy sting? The sting of death is sin, and the power of sin is the law. But thanks be to God, who gives us the victory through our Lord Jesus Christ" [1 Cor. 15:55–57]. Death is swallowed up not only in the victory of Christ but also by our victory, because through faith his victory has become ours and in that faith we also are conquerors.

Martin Luther (1483–1546), "A Treatise on Christian Liberty," trans. W. A. Lambert, in *Works of Martin Luther: Introduction and Notes* (Philadelphia: A. J. Holman Company, 1916), 326–27.

of the Sabbath, along with dietary rules, circumcision, and praying toward Jerusalem, seems to date to that time and place. In order to maintain their religious and cultural identity in the syncretistic sociocultural environment of Babylon, the community of Jewish deportees observed the Sabbath. More precisely, while the deportees and their descendants were settled in a distinct enclave as an ethnic minority group and were permitted to continue religious and cultural practices, many of them were assimilated to the multicultural and multiethnic society of Babylon. In this political and cultural situation, the observance of the Sabbath was a way of seeking God; it was a way to renew the identity of the Judeo-Babylonian community by remembering what God had done for them and hoping that God would have them return home.

Isaiah 55:10–13, which is the finale of Second Isaiah, proclaims the hopeful message of the future of God's creation and convinces the community that the word of God spoken by the prophet will be accomplished (v. 11). The chapter concludes with the joyful praise of God by all creation for the fulfillment of God's righteousness to the people of God and for the restoration of nature (vv. 12–13). These concluding remarks resonate with the Sabbath song of Psalm 92, which illuminates hope in the future true Sabbath where the righteous will be vindicated and flourish. Both texts are prophetic oracles in declarative styles of speech, and both are words of trust of, and comfort for, the people of God.

Reading Psalm 92 in relation to Isaiah 55:10–13 reinforces the theological meaning of the Sabbath. By singing the song, the worshipers are reminded of what God has done for them in the past and the present; they face the future in confidence, spiritually refreshed and strengthened. This is the true spirit of the Sabbath that Psalm 92 is intended to appreciate.

The true spirit of Sabbath imbued by the psalm challenges contemporary Christians to critically reflect on their observance of the Lord's Day. For Christians, Sunday has been celebrated as the Lord's Day just like the Sabbath in the Jewish community. According to Psalm 92, the Sabbath day is not simply a weekly cycle of abstaining from work; it is the day of renewing the identity of believers by remembering the promise of the fulfillment of God's righteousness. What God has done and will do for all creation is called to mind by singing the song of the Sabbath, and that motivates worshipers to celebrate in the true spirit of Sabbath with joy and thanksgiving.

Living in twenty-first-century secular culture, however, many Christians tend to have less regard for the significance of Sunday worship; as a result, many Christian churches in the United States have experienced a decrease of worship attendance. In this situation, Psalm 92 reminds worship leaders and the congregation that the observance of the Lord's Day with joyful songs and music is an act of prophecy about the world to come. Our worship points to the culmination of the righteousness of God, and the word of God, which is a message of hope for all creation, stands firm until it is fulfilled in the messianic time. So every Sunday worship service is a foretaste of the future true Sabbath. In the liturgical context, Psalm 92:1–4, 12–15 can be recited in tandem with Isaiah 55:10–12, either in the beginning of the service or after reading the Isaiah text to celebrate the fulfillment of God's word for all creation in joy and peace.

EUNJOO MARY KIM

1 Corinthians 15:51–58

[51]Listen, I will tell you a mystery! We will not all die, but we will all be changed, [52]in a moment, in the twinkling of an eye, at the last trumpet. For the trumpet will sound, and the dead will be raised imperishable, and we will be changed. [53]For this perishable body must put on imperishability, and this mortal body must put on immortality. [54]When this perishable body puts on imperishability, and this mortal body puts on immortality, then the saying that is written will be fulfilled:

"Death has been swallowed up in victory."
[55]"Where, O death, is your victory?
Where, O death, is your sting?"

[56]The sting of death is sin, and the power of sin is the law. [57]But thanks be to God, who gives us the victory through our Lord Jesus Christ.

[58]Therefore, my beloved, be steadfast, immovable, always excelling in the work of the Lord, because you know that in the Lord your labor is not in vain.

Commentary 1: Connecting the Reading with Scripture

A familiar passage, often read at Christian funerals, today's epistle inspires hope in the transformative power of the resurrection and its promise for human flourishing even beyond death. In the resurrection, the old life is gone; a new life of joy and peace begins. As death is part of life, it seems appropriate for this passage to occur in the lectionary's Ordinary Time. It provides an extraordinary message of God's wondrous power not only to bring life after death, but also to conquer death.

First Corinthians 15:51–58 concludes Paul's summary of his theological teachings on the resurrection. He reveals that those in Christ who are already dead will be raised into an imperishable state. Those who are still alive will change into an imperishability. At this point in Paul's journey, he still believes that he and members of his generation will be alive to see Christ's return. His confidence of his own presence at the Parousia connects with the confidence he expresses in 1 Thessalonians 4:15–18. All must be changed into the imperishability by bearing the likeness of Christ and his righteousness, as promised in the new covenant sealed in his blood (1 Cor. 11:25). The living and the dead will experience the great transformation at the moment of Christ's return.

Paul's description of imperishability in the likeness in Christ is found in his discussion of the resurrection of the body in the preceding verses (15:42–50). There he asserts how humanity was born in "the image of the man of dust," that being the first Adam; later humanity will "bear the image of the man of heaven," meaning Jesus (v. 49). Humanity belongs to both Adam and Jesus. Belonging to Adam represents an earthly existence, and therefore perishability; belonging to Christ represents a heavenly existence, and therefore imperishability. Essentially, Paul provides further evidence for his earlier point about the resurrection: "For since death came through a human being, the resurrection of the dead has also come through a human being; for as all die in Adam, so all will be made alive in Christ" (vv. 21–22). This explanation connects to Paul's expansion on his theology regarding Adam and Christ in Romans 5:12–21. Transformation into the imperishability of Christ's likeness is paramount for the resurrection.

Verses 54–55 mark the climax of Paul's exhortation: "Death has been swallowed up in victory.

Where, O death, is your victory? Where, O death is your sting?" Paul modifies the prophetic language of the LXX in Isaiah 25:8 and Hosea 13:14 to taunt death. Both OT texts describe God's deliverance of God's people from oppressors. For Paul, there is no greater oppressor than the lethality of sin, which is death. By death, he is referring both to the end of physical life and to the end of one's relationship with God.

Sin is the force that kills humanity's relationship with God. At his resurrection, Jesus overcame death's sting when he conquered sin. In verse 56, Paul asserts that the law is the poison that makes the sting of death lethal. Humanity turned the law (the Torah) into a function of sin, giving it power to create death and stifle life. In the natural order, venom, a substance that is deadly, can also have medicinal power to heal and sustain life. Similarly, the law's purpose was to facilitate life and healing in the covenant community. Instead, humanity often milked its lethal properties.

Paul's commentary on the law as the power of sin connects to his later writing to the Romans. In Romans 7, he confirms that the law is not sin. Rather, it made sin observable by revealing human depravity before God and rebellion against God. It created fear and shame, which humanity uses to hide from God, therefore killing one's relationship with God. Humanity also used the law as a basis for false pride in one's sense of achievement in remaining righteous before God. As Christ's righteousness cleansed away sins, it removed the power of death and established the foundation of everlasting life. Therefore, death has no victory. When Jesus returns at the Parousia, death will suffer the ultimate defeat; all earthly suffering, pain, crying, mourning, injustice, and heartache will end (cf. Rev. 21:4).

The lectionary psalm, Psalm 92, also describes the flourishing of life that comes with God's destruction of the enemy and God's steadfastness. Like the epistolary lesson, the psalm announces God's victory and utter destruction of God's enemies. This is the context of the psalm's exclamation, "the righteous flourish like the palm tree, and grow like a cedar in Lebanon" (Ps. 92:12). The palm tree and cedar are symbols of prosperity and longevity. With deliverance, God creates new and everlasting life. Through God's steadfast love and faithfulness, the righteous experience a transformation in their existence and can anticipate the bounty of God's work (vv. 14–15).

While describing the great changes in human existence at the climactic moment of eschaton, Paul does not expect his readers to wait passively for God's transformation during the resurrection. Instead, he encourages their active participation in their transformation and flourishing by God's grace. He concludes his reflection on the resurrection with an ethical admonishment to excel in the work of God while living on this earth. The imperative of his message is driven by the earnestness of his encouragement: "be steadfast, immovable, always excelling in the work of the Lord" (v. 58). This work likely takes multiple forms. Most obviously, it would include righteous activities and relationships in marriage, table fellowship, Eucharist, and ministries of the gospel (chaps. 7–14). Furthermore, consideration and treatment of fellow believers and nonbelievers of the gospel would be work as well. Many of Paul's admonishments incorporate instructions for relationships among various members within the Corinthian church as well as their neighbors. Most importantly, the work of the Lord includes the maintenance of gospel and theological convictions that Paul taught. He encourages the preservation of faith in the resurrection promise of the eternal life in Christ's resurrection.

Paul's final words in verse 58 encourage transformation into the likeness of Christ that begins with current behavior and interactions in this age. While believing in Christ, one should reflect the transformation that freedom in Christ from the power of sin allows. Simply put, Paul's concluding message reflects the modern maxim "When you know better, you do better."

Transformation and flourishing are themes throughout the day's lectionary. In Isaiah 55:10–13, the prophet speaks to the Israelites who are exiled in Babylon as they anticipate their return to Jerusalem. He describes God's promise to give new life to desolate places and desperate people. Upon their return to the land, the people will find creation flourishing with the bounty harvest. The people will experience joy and peace. God will transform both nature and humanity, and both will join together in rejoicing. Verse 12 declares that "all the trees of the field shall clap their hands," a scriptural reference in the popular hymn "You Shall Go Out with Joy (The Trees of the Field)."[1]

As Christ was with God in the beginning, death never had a chance at victory. Yet, in the finality of seeing a loved one physically for the last time, grief can often obfuscate the fact of death's powerlessness. Paul's teaching on the mystery of the resurrection serves as a reminder to the church of Corinth and today of the great transformation and flourishing God has promised through the resurrection that will tie us all together yesterday, today, and forevermore.

BRIDGETT A. GREEN

Commentary 2: Connecting the Reading with the World

Resurrection, a central tenet of the Christian faith and an integral part of the church's liturgical expression for centuries, appears less frequently in sermons today. Are Gospel accounts of bodily resurrection just too peculiar, far-fetched, or unscientific for contemporary sensibilities? Singing an ancient hymn about the glory of an empty tomb is one thing; linking resurrection specifically to our own lives today is quite another. As such, many preachers relegate resurrection talk to mere metaphor, or Easter Messiahs, or vague assurance at funerals (*"Where, O Death, is your sting?"*). Today's pericope invites us to go deeper. Paul's discourse points to resurrection as God's greatest expression of love and power—as essential as it is inscrutable.

Preaching this text is not for the faint of heart. In approaching its astonishing assertions, preachers might do well to remember that incredulity is actually a connection point between first-century and twenty-first-century congregations. Note that this chapter begins with Paul reprimanding his flock for flatly denying that Christ rose from the dead (v. 12), a denial that Paul believes nullifies the entire mission. Theologian N. T. Wright aptly reminds us: "The idea of resurrection is not something which ancient people could accept easily because they didn't know the laws of nature, whereas we moderns, with post-Enlightenment science, have now discovered that resurrection can't be true. That is simply absurd. From Plato to Homer, from Aeschylus to Pliny, the ancients knew perfectly well that dead people didn't rise."[2]

Curiously, life after death has become a lively topic in our current cultural imagination. A plethora of immortal characters—from vampires (*Twilight* series of books and movies) to zombies (*The Walking Dead* TV franchise) to time travelers (*Outlander*) to superheroes (*Wonder Woman*)—now dominate pop culture. Even more surprisingly, bold new ideas from the fields of relativity, cosmology, biocentrism, and quantum theory offer tantalizing new ways of reframing the mysteries of existence.[3] For example, is it possible that some sort of inchoate link exists between science's first law of thermodynamics—energy cannot be created or destroyed, though it can change forms—and Paul's radical description of physical ("perishable") changing or transforming into spiritual ("imperishable")? Although caution must be exercised when applying modern hypotheses to ancient religious texts, is it not incumbent on preachers to explore a full gamut of conceivable connections in order to fire modern imaginations and open us to God's grand limitlessness?

Looking closer, we see that Paul is fearlessly specific on the material and spiritual properties of transformation: "In a moment, in the twinkling of an eye . . . the dead will be raised imperishable, and we will be changed" (v. 52). Grounding the pericope in its broader context of chapter 15, Paul's work in crafting a sturdy set-up is well drawn. He cites the Genesis creation story in illustrating a larger time line flowing from the first Adam to

1. Steffi Geiser Rubin, "You Shall Go Out with Joy (The Trees of the Field)," in *Glory to God* (Louisville, KY: Westminster John Knox Press, 2013), no. 80.

2. Robert B. Stewart, ed., *The Resurrection of Jesus: John Dominic Crossan and N. T. Wright in Dialogue* (Minneapolis: Fortress Press, 2006), 17.

3. See Kirk Wegter-McNelly, *The Entangled God: Divine Relationality and Quantum Physics* (New York: Routledge, 2011); Paul Davies, *God and the New Physics* (New York: Simon & Schuster, 1984).

the last Adam (v. 45), a fluid process in which the physical form is born first, followed ultimately by the spiritual; which is actually a reverse of humanity's first breath in the garden of Eden. Of particular note is 15:49, which contrasts the image of the earthy with the image of the heavenly. What an astounding promise, that one day our fragile, fallible bodies—too fat, too thin, too dark, too white—will each be opulently draped in the dazzling likeness of the cosmic Christ!

In dissecting Paul's language here, it should be stated that not all congregations today need to pause so significantly at the plausibility questions of *if* or *how* regarding resurrection, although all listeners will certainly benefit from reflecting on the *why*. If Paul's epistles are always a pastoral response to particular Christian struggles, what was the problem of the Corinthian community? Unlike some of the bumbling disciples of the NT, the Corinthian faithful are depicted as remarkably powerful believers. Too much so perhaps, since we are told that they acted as though they were Christian elites, already enriched in all power and wisdom (1:5–7), the latter being especially prized in the protognostic/Hellenistic hotbed of Corinth. Because of the awesome giftedness of the community, the Corinthians seemed not to understand that following Christ required a change in behavior or ethical considerations (6:11).

NT scholar Luke Johnson remarks that the Corinthians seem not to have grasped the full implications of resurrection as fundamentally transformative; thus, a kind of spiritual inertia had crept in. This state has alternately been dubbed by many biblical commentators as an "overrealized eschaton," wherein the gifts of the Spirit proved that the Corinthian Christians had "already become as angels" (13:1). Johnson adds: "When Paul reminds them of the fundamental message of the resurrection, he does more than recall historical facts. He reminds them of the structure of their existence 'by which you are *being saved* if you hold fast' (15:2), making that salvation both progressive and conditional."[4]

In other words, Paul is concerned with the impact of the Corinthians' denial of resurrection on their formation as Christians. The implications of resurrection are so intensely radical that to believe is to be changed utterly, which means resurrection becomes an engine for progressive alignment with God now, not simply at the final trumpet.

This is a critical distinction. Are we modern Christians also afflicted at times by an inertia that comes from thinking that this earthly life is all there is (resurrection as metaphor), or that we are already saved though grace, end of story? Despite the privileging of otherworldly paradise by the more fundamentalist among us, it is possible that many modern Christian communities today suffer from an *under*realized eschatology, focusing primarily on the present without much thought of something more. This is the signal flare of our pericope: an assured future should not cause us to grow lazy like entitled trust-fund teenagers. Paul says, "Therefore, my dear brothers and sisters, stand firm. Let nothing move you. Always give yourselves fully to the work of the Lord" (15:58 NIV). This is the critical teaching that will help us live out a perfectly balanced eschatology—living fully in the present moment without discouragement because we are always moving onward toward a magnificent future.

The fact that our individual bodies are not shucked off and thrown away at the end of time illustrates something profound about God's love of our material world, which provides fodder for a fertile sermon topic on ecojustice and a divine desire for the salvation of our beautiful planet as well. Paul's teaching on transformation is ensconced artfully in our lush lectionary collection for Proper 3: from the cultivation of fruit in Sirach, to trees growing in glory in Isaiah, to Psalm 92's depiction of flourishing plants, and finally, the Gospel reading from Luke, which describes how trees are known by their fruit. What shall we grow from our "soilish" (*choikou*) roots, as we turn like heliotrope flowers toward unimaginable light, a Creator who cares about each one of us, tending always and evermore to our flourishing?

SUZANNE WOOLSTON BOSSERT

4. Luke Timothy Johnson, *The Writings of the New Testament* (Philadelphia: Fortress Press, 1986), 289.

Luke 6:39–49

[39]He also told them a parable: "Can a blind person guide a blind person? Will not both fall into a pit? [40]A disciple is not above the teacher, but everyone who is fully qualified will be like the teacher. [41]Why do you see the speck in your neighbor's eye, but do not notice the log in your own eye? [42]Or how can you say to your neighbor, 'Friend, let me take out the speck in your eye,' when you yourself do not see the log in your own eye? You hypocrite, first take the log out of your own eye, and then you will see clearly to take the speck out of your neighbor's eye.

[43]"No good tree bears bad fruit, nor again does a bad tree bear good fruit; [44]for each tree is known by its own fruit. Figs are not gathered from thorns, nor are grapes picked from a bramble bush. [45]The good person out of the good treasure of the heart produces good, and the evil person out of evil treasure produces evil; for it is out of the abundance of the heart that the mouth speaks.

[46]"Why do you call me 'Lord, Lord,' and do not do what I tell you? [47]I will show you what someone is like who comes to me, hears my words, and acts on them. [48]That one is like a man building a house, who dug deeply and laid the foundation on rock; when a flood arose, the river burst against that house but could not shake it, because it had been well built. [49]But the one who hears and does not act is like a man who built a house on the ground without a foundation. When the river burst against it, immediately it fell, and great was the ruin of that house."

Commentary 1: Connecting the Reading with Scripture

Luke's Gospel is carefully structured. Luke tells the story of Jesus like a drama, scene by scene, themes introduced and explored as the drama unfolds. In the first four chapters Jesus takes on his authority—from the astonishing promises to Zechariah and Mary, through the humble but majestic birth, through the temple wisdom foreshadowing how Jesus will interpret the Law, through his baptism and first great test in the wilderness, through his use of the Isaiah text in the synagogue at Nazareth, where Jesus claims for himself the mantle of a great prophet and points to himself as the fulfillment of prophecy. In all these scenes Luke shows his audience that Jesus has been granted authority from God.

From the last verses of chapter 4 to the middle verses of chapter 6, Jesus shows that authority by healing the sick, casting out demons (thereby frustrating the powers of evil), and arguing with religious authorities (thereby frustrating the inordinate attention to inherited piety).

Now, in the Sermon on the Plain, beginning at 6:17, Luke shows us Jesus' teaching authority. This is the longest speech by Jesus in Luke's Gospel; most Lukan scholars think the sermon probably represents a collection of sayings and parables Jesus delivered at different times to different audiences. Matthew uses much of the same material, but in a different setting, with some of Luke's material omitted and some of his own included (Matt. 5–7).

Whether the Sermon on the Plain is a composite drawn from a number of speeches, it certainly includes a number of distinctive sayings, stories, and injunctions. It would be too much to try to preach on the whole sermon. Indeed, it is probably too much to try to cover all the themes Jesus covers in Luke 6:39–49. However, a quick look at the beginning of this sermon suggests an overall perspective on Luke's understanding of Jesus' claims on us.

The sermon begins with the Beatitudes, the blessings. The blessings are similar to those contained in Matthew's Sermon on the Mount, but in two ways at least they show Luke's different understanding of Jesus.

First, in both Matthew and Luke, Jesus describes life in the kingdom of God, but in Matthew the blessings seem to be more directed toward spiritual virtues: "Blessed are the poor in spirit." "Blessed are those who hunger and thirst for righteousness" (Matt. 5:3, 6). In Luke the blessings are pronounced on those who suffer material, physical deprivation: "Blessed are you who are poor." "Blessed are you who are hungry now" (Luke 6:20–21).

Second, Luke includes not only Jesus' blessings on those who live as citizens of the kingdom; he includes Jesus' woes, pronounced on those who ignore the kingdom's possibilities and obligations: "Woe to you are rich, for you have received your consolation. Woe to you who are full now, for you will be hungry" (6:24–25).

In this way, the beginning of the Sermon on the Plain fits beautifully with its last verses. Luke 6:48–49 contrasts those who hear Jesus' words and obey them with those who hear the words but ignore them. The first are blessed, like someone who builds a house on rock. Nothing can shake them. The second are destined for woe, like someone who builds a house on shaky ground. When the inevitable floods come, when the inevitable troubles befall those who hear Jesus in the first century or in the twenty-first, those who have heard and followed will find their lives hold strong. With this in mind we can see what Jesus means when he calls on his listeners to live fruitful lives, to build on solid rock.

In Luke 6:39–49 there are clearly two different ways of responding to Jesus, the way of life and the way of disaster. If you choose the way of woe, you can pretend to know better than your teacher, even if your teacher is Jesus; if you choose the way of life, you will follow your teacher's example (v. 40). If you are hell-bent on disaster, you can notice everything that is wrong with your neighbor and ignore your own faults; if you accept the life of blessedness, you will concentrate on your own faults and be generous of spirit in relation to your neighbor (vv. 41–42). This is one of those passages in the Gospels where Jesus sounds not just like a prophet but like a sage; this is wisdom language. Such generous modesty not only makes for final blessedness; it makes life a lot better in the meantime.

If you choose blessedness, you will cultivate the life of faith and generosity in order to do good works and bear good fruit. If you had rather not bother, you can turn in on yourself in ways that are crabbed and unproductive, perhaps noticing that where you walk thistles spring up, and where you sow, thorns (vv. 43–45). You will trust and obey, and find that even when life turns most painful and unsure, your life is built on a solid rock; or you can simply turn away from Jesus' kind commands and wait for the flood.

In addition to comparing people to builders, in Luke 6:43–45, Jesus compares people to trees; good trees bear good fruit, evil trees evil fruit. A good fruit tree will not bear thistles, but a thorn bush will not bear apples either. The audience hears this two ways. If you are seeking to be faithful, look to your integrity, your faithfulness, your trust in God. Good fruits will flow from good lives.

However, if you have noticed recently that you seem to sow discord, unhappiness, or thorns wherever you go, it may be time for radical tree surgery. In particular, Jesus notes that our fruits, our life products, are often the words that we speak: "for it is out of the abundance of the heart that the mouth speaks" (v. 45).

Put positively, this is the same connection Isaiah notices in another lection for today. Because God purposes good, the words of God are fruitful and fair (Isa. 55:10–13). Put negatively, Jesus notices in Luke that sometimes human words, directed by more insidious purposes, sow weeds instead of flowers, discord instead of peace.

The vision of a house built on bedrock and the picture of the fruitful tree together remind us of the flourishing trees planted near the house of God in Psalm 92:12–14.

> The righteous flourish like the palm tree,
> and grow like a cedar in Lebanon.
> They are planted in the house of the LORD;
> they flourish in the courts of our God.
> In old age they still produce fruit;
> they are always green and full of sap.

The distinction between those who obey and those who disobey reminds us of the distinction between the righteous and the unrighteous in Psalm 1, where the righteous are "like trees planted by streams of water, which yield their fruit in its season, and their leaves do not wither" (Ps. 1:3).

There is a final insight when we compare the beginning of the Sermon on the Plain with its last verses. In this sermon it is not the "poor in spirit" who are blessed, but the poor; not the hungry after righteousness, but the hungry. Perhaps Luke's audience, probably relatively economically comfortable, needs to be reminded that all that comfort may keep us from the faithfulness that God requires. Almost certainly this passage reminds Luke's audience and us that the fruit that we are to bear should issue in bounty to those most in need.

DAVID L. BARTLETT

Commentary 2: Connecting the Reading with the World

Worship remains the basic spiritual formation discipline for most Christians. The readings of the liturgical year play their part by leading participants in present time to connect to the past revelation of God in Christ, as well as to the fulfillment of that revelation in the future. Jesus taught the way of the future in Luke's Sermon on the Plain, which this text concludes. The three sections of Luke 6:39–49 serve as reality checks to those who believe they are enlightened enough to judge and teach like Jesus or in his stead. These narratives caution against blind self-righteousness, separation of being from doing, and the catastrophe of building on a foundation other than Jesus' words and actions.

Any one of them can stand alone as a sermon. Read together the three provide their hearers with linked wisdom about life together in the present between the advent of Jesus and the coming final culmination of his mission. Their elaboration on the necessity of coming to Christ, hearing his words, and doing them as the only sure foundation for the future is both a warning and a word of hope.

Besides serving as a caution sign, Luke 6:39–49 also speaks to the church on mission in the world. If the church does not heed the liturgical words of Luke 6:39–49, it endangers its gospel witness in the world. A church whose words and actions reveal as its main mission judging who is good and who is evil in order to punish the wrongdoer is blind to Jesus' gospel of mercy. The church cannot lead others on a gospel path to which it is itself blind. Any sincere adherents such a church garners become themselves blind followers of its blind teachers. The blind lead the blind into a pit of exclusion and disdain for those they are called to help.

The antidote is a healthy dose of self-reflection. Remove the log in your own eye before trying to excise the splinter in the other. The church that knows and admits its faults is able to repent of them and humbly seek total dependence on God for its life and witness in the world. This does not deny ecclesial moral discernment, but allows it to be employed in effectively helping others. Jesus' teaching here leads the church to judge its own fruits by its own deeds. This is the only sure foundation for the church. G. K. Chesterton wrote that though the church has often fallen into ruin, it is never past rebuilding, "though it rotted away to its first foundation-stone."[1] A confessing church is an attractive church, within and without: the Roman Catholic Church apologizing for sex scandals or the Southern Baptist Convention for its racism.

Jesus' teachings in the liturgical reading of Luke 6:39–49 are not for the church alone. If Luke's Jesus reads humanity correctly, a society that claims for itself the right to implement justice as retributive punishment is building justice on a foundation that will surely fail that society. Luke 6:41–42 clearly has the underlying purpose of helping others who are at fault, not punishing them in equal measure to their sin. A teacher who tempers judgment with mercy

1. Gilbert Keith Chesterton, *St. Francis of Assisi* (New York: Doran, 1924), 46.

that flows from a compassionate heart leads Luke's just society. The goal is to heal and free wrongdoers.

What would taking this seriously mean for a society that considers justice mainly a quid-pro-quo punishment for breaking laws? What would this mean for a society such as the United States, with the highest prison population and the highest prisoner rate per capita in the world, with ten thousand children incarcerated in adult jails or prisons on any given day, most of them people of color and the poor?[2] Surely a society that inflicts lawful violence on such a large scale to a vulnerable population in order to ensure a balance of suffering is a prime target for a "log in the eye" cartoon, and more.

Jesus' teachings in Luke 6:39–49, while radical then and now, are not without connections to the larger human culture, beyond purely Christian structures. A quick internet search will reveal that Jesus' saying about the blind leading the blind is frequently the subject of artists' paintings, the most famous of which is Pieter Bruegel the Elder's sixteenth-century *The Parable of the Blind*. Such a search also reveals similar sayings in other cultures. Two of the oldest are recorded in the Upanishads (ca. 800–200 BCE) and in the Buddhist Pali Canon written in 29 BCE. Clearly the idea of blind teachers leading blind students into error is a widely understood image used to warn students to choose the right teacher in the first place, which Eugene Peterson in *The Message*, his translation of the Bible, writes is the main point of Luke 6:39–40.

Luke 6:39–49 and the larger arena of human knowledge mutually inform one another. Modern psychologists advise us to look for veracity more in what people do than in what they say. The fruits of action as well as words reveal the truth about the communicator (vv. 45–46).

The postwar histories of the First and Second World Wars support Jesus' insights. Harsh punitive measures on the German nation legislated by the victors after WWI partly fueled the dynamics that led to WWII. Alternately, the Allies' generous rebuilding programs on behalf of devastated societies in Germany and Japan after WWII aided the rise of two of the strongest democracies and economies in the world today. Let your discernments of the faults of others be motivated by desire to help them (v. 42).

Today's poisonous political divisions in the Western world are clearly partly due to what is commonly called the echo chamber. Facebook, the primary news source for many people, including as many as 60 percent of millennials, uses logarithmic filters to personalize the content users see. This greatly reduces cross-cutting, defined as exposure to political perspectives other than those one already supports. Similarly, television viewers tend to watch only the channels that support their political assumptions, whether promulgated by MSNBC or Fox News. Liberals see mostly liberal news; conservatives see mostly conservative news. The result is a kind of blind leading the blind in like-minded, judgmental opposing factions.[3] The good news Jesus brought calls for self-reflection, along with compassionate contact with and assistance to those who differ from us. That gospel needs to become cross-cutting news.

Luke 6:39–49 is part of a larger Sermon on the Plain that lays out a great wave of change that will sweep away all before it, except those things that are founded on Christ and his teachings. This is presented as a global and cosmic event.

Yet Jesus' words are directed mostly to persons, not nations or churches or global societies. Student, choose your teacher well, or be the blind led by the blind (vv. 39–40). You hypocrite (singular), remove the log from your own eye before you try to help your neighbor (v. 42). "The good person out of the good treasure of the heart produces good" (v. 45). I will show each of you how to dig a deep foundation that will not fail. At its core, these verses are a call to each hearer to build a foundation by coming to Christ, hearing his words, and doing them. Personal conversion of the head, heart, and hands is essential to Jesus' campaign. What we do matters in the larger scheme of things.

WM. LOYD ALLEN

2. See the website of the Equal Justice Initiative at http://eji.org/.

3. For research on the social-network echo chamber, see Kartik Hosanagar, "Blame the Echo Chamber on Facebook. But Blame Yourself, Too," *Wired*, November 25, 2016, https://www.wired.com/2016/11/facebook-echo-chamber/.

Proper 4 (Sunday between May 29 and June 4 Inclusive)

1 Kings 18:20–21 (22–29), 30–39 and
1 Kings 8:22–23, 41–43
Psalm 96 and Psalm 96:1–9
Galatians 1:1–12
Luke 7:1–10

1 Kings 18:20–21 (22–29), 30–39

[20]So Ahab sent to all the Israelites, and assembled the prophets at Mount Carmel. [21]Elijah then came near to all the people, and said, "How long will you go limping with two different opinions? If the LORD is God, follow him; but if Baal, then follow him." The people did not answer him a word. [22]Then Elijah said to the people, "I, even I only, am left a prophet of the LORD; but Baal's prophets number four hundred fifty. [23]Let two bulls be given to us; let them choose one bull for themselves, cut it in pieces, and lay it on the wood, but put no fire to it; I will prepare the other bull and lay it on the wood, but put no fire to it. [24]Then you call on the name of your god and I will call on the name of the LORD; the god who answers by fire is indeed God." All the people answered, "Well spoken!" [25]Then Elijah said to the prophets of Baal, "Choose for yourselves one bull and prepare it first, for you are many; then call on the name of your god, but put no fire to it." [26]So they took the bull that was given them, prepared it, and called on the name of Baal from morning until noon, crying, "O Baal, answer us!" But there was no voice, and no answer. They limped about the altar that they had made. [27]At noon Elijah mocked them, saying, "Cry aloud! Surely he is a god; either he is meditating, or he has wandered away, or he is on a journey, or perhaps he is asleep and must be awakened." [28]Then they cried aloud and, as was their custom, they cut themselves with swords and lances until the blood gushed out over them. [29]As midday passed, they raved on until the time of the offering of the oblation, but there was no voice, no answer, and no response.

[30]Then Elijah said to all the people, "Come closer to me"; and all the people came closer to him. First he repaired the altar of the LORD that had been thrown down; [31]Elijah took twelve stones, according to the number of the tribes of the sons of Jacob, to whom the word of the LORD came, saying, "Israel shall be your name"; [32]with the stones he built an altar in the name of the LORD. Then he made a trench around the altar, large enough to contain two measures of seed. [33]Next he put the wood in order, cut the bull in pieces, and laid it on the wood. He said, "Fill four jars with water and pour it on the burnt offering and on the wood." [34]Then he said, "Do it a second time"; and they did it a second time. Again he said, "Do it a third time"; and they did it a third time, [35]so that the water ran all around the altar, and filled the trench also with water.

[36]At the time of the offering of the oblation, the prophet Elijah came near and said, "O LORD, God of Abraham, Isaac, and Israel, let it be known this day that you are God in Israel, that I am your servant, and that I have done all these things at your bidding. [37]Answer me, O LORD, answer me, so that this people may know that you, O LORD, are God, and that you have turned their hearts back." [38]Then the fire of the LORD fell and consumed the burnt offering, the wood, the stones, and the dust, and even licked up the water that was in the trench. [39]When all the people saw it, they fell on their faces and said, "The LORD indeed is God; the LORD indeed is God."

1 Kings 8:22–23, 41–43

[22]Then Solomon stood before the altar of the LORD in the presence of all the assembly of Israel, and spread out his hands to heaven. [23]He said, "O LORD, God of Israel, there is no God like you in heaven above or on earth beneath, keeping covenant and steadfast love for your servants who walk before you with all their heart. . . .

[41]"Likewise when a foreigner, who is not of your people Israel, comes from a distant land because of your name [42]—for they shall hear of your great name, your mighty hand, and your outstretched arm—when a foreigner comes and prays toward this house, [43]then hear in heaven your dwelling place, and do according to all that the foreigner calls to you, so that all the peoples of the earth may know your name and fear you, as do your people Israel, and so that they may know that your name has been invoked on this house that I have built."

Commentary 1: Connecting the Reading with Scripture

1 Kings 8. The Johannine Jesus says, "Destroy this temple, and I will raise it again in three days" (John 2:19 NIV). This saying tradition also arises in the Synoptic Gospels during Jesus' trial. Temple language provided a matrix in which first-century Jews spoke of God's presence and revelation to the Jews—and through them to the world.

The location of this temple, however, remained contested in the first century. Competing temples existed to the one in Jerusalem—a temple in Samaria, a Jewish temple in Leontopolis, Egypt. Covenanters at Khirbet Qumran saw their gathering as the temple. There is overlapping imagery in Paul of the church as the body of Christ and the temple; the Epistle to the Hebrews figuratively works with temple language in depicting Christ. This language all presupposes 1 Kings 8, which takes the institution of the temple in Mediterranean and Mesopotamian societies and restructures its language to form a distinctly Jewish institution.

Temples play many roles. They are fortresses to which defenders can withdraw in battle. Mainly, gods dwell and receive sacrifices in temples—transactions of economic goods, redistribution of meat and drink to worshipers, priests, and the poor. In eating food sacrificed to a god—proteins not often received in daily diets—worshipers give thanks to the god. Honoring the god binds sacrificers together in shared meals.

First Kings 8:20–43 witnesses to how the Scriptures take up common Mediterranean temple practices to form the Jews as devoted to the God of Israel, the Lord alone. The passage divides into two parts: (1) Solomon's declaration of the royal provision of the temple (vv. 20–21) and (2) Solomon's prayer before the place of sacrifice (vv. 22–43).

In verses 20–21 Solomon names the temple as a royal gift. The heir of David grants Israel the temple as a place for the ark—the specific location of the divine presence since Israel built it in the wilderness from the divine design at Sinai. The God worshiped in the temple is the God who created all things, elected Abram, delivered Israel from slavery in Egypt, gave the Law at Sinai, and gifted Israel with the land. The narrative shows the gracious constancy of the scriptural God of Israel. The promise to Abram—repeated and focused through the promise to David (2 Sam. 7), that through him all peoples of the earth will receive blessing—is now mediated through the temple.

Solomon's subsequent prayer speaks *of* God *to* God before Israel, witnessing to God's exclusivity. Its language transforms common understandings of the relationship between temples and gods. Temples not only served to honor gods; they also bought divine favor through sacrifices because of fickle divine manifestations. Solomon's prayer names the Lord as faithful, sustaining promises, notwithstanding Israel's sin.

God's faithfulness has a visible sign. Solomon lives as a witness to the promise made to David. The faithfulness of the divine presence in the temple relates directly to God's incomparable faithfulness (vv. 22–26).

Solomon's prayer illustrates how to speak well of God. The language of prayer refuses to localize God within the temple. Even as God's "dwelling place" is "in heaven" (v. 30) and the temple presents one node of God's presence so that worshipers pray toward it (v. 29), Solomon's prayer simultaneously acknowledges that God per se does not dwell in creation; nothing, even all creation, contains God. God is present for supplication within the heavens and the earth, yet is an outside agent. Solomon does not pray as if God dips in and out of creation. God is incomparably One: "there is no God like you in heaven above or on earth beneath" (v. 23).

Nonetheless, the temple represents a saturated location of the mystery of the divine presence. Solomon's prayer evokes God's favor in the temple in three areas: forgiveness for sins (vv. 30, 33–39), righteous judgment within the temple (vv. 31–32), and special favor for the supplications of the foreigner, the non-Israelite (vv. 41–43). The temple is a place of prayer for all people. The request to hear the prayer of the nonelect is a means of witness, so that non-Israelites might name the divine presence as the God of Israel, worshiped in the temple.

This passage plays an important role in the narrative of what some scholars call the Primary History, Genesis through 2 Kings, representing a high point in the narrative structured by the fall of creation and the response of God's promise to Abram: Israel dwells in the land under a Davidic king with the temple established as a witness to divine faithfulness. The precise compositional history of this narrative remains contested. First Kings 8 represents a key text by some who see a Deuteronomistic History written during the reign of Josiah, then edited in exile.

The narrative continues without interruption through 2 Kings 25. The temple, celebrated in 1 Kings 8 as a special intense location of the presence of God, gets destroyed by the Babylonians and the people taken into exile. Only the Davidic line remains as a witness to ongoing divine faithfulness (2 Kgs. 25:27–30). The narrative pins its truthful witness on the future of this Davidic line, itself closely related to the temple.

This background invites us to see today's Gospel reading with new depth. Within the figurative sense of the OT, the temple in 1 Kings 8 functions as a type for Christ's body, the body of the Davidic heir in whom God makes faithfulness visible. The Roman centurion, the foreigner, prays toward the temple in addressing Jesus. The invisible God becomes manifest in the visible healing of the centurion's servant. The foreigner knows that the God of Israel, the God of all creation, is found in the temple, the body of Christ. Witness and invitation to the Gentiles come through the Davidic heir, Jesus Christ. In him God has not abandoned creation to futility; the apostolic witness to his body makes visible the presence of the invisible God whom creation cannot contain.

1 Kings 18. If 1 Kings 8 affirms that God's presence can be signified in royal authority, 1 Kings 18, the high point of Elijah's conflict with Ahab and Jezebel, is an unequivocal declaration that the two can be antithetical. Political authority, cloaked in idolatry, requires confrontation. The Elijah cycle (1 Kgs. 17–2 Kgs. 2) is essential background for this text, detailing both nuances and limitations in long-term strategies of prophetic engagement (as distinct from one-off standoffs).

This story can be compared with other political/religious confrontation narratives: Moses and Pharaoh (Exod. 1–14), Amos and Amaziah (Amos 7:10–17), Daniel and his colleagues and the Babylonian emperors (Dan. 1–6). The question in such biblical narratives is what constitutes confrontation that is not only dramatic and decisive but appropriate and effective.

Paul, in the salvo commencing his letter to the Galatians, heard in today's lectionary, is similarly confrontive. Clearly, for both Elijah and Paul the stakes are high. The alarm must be sounded to awaken sensibilities and redirect behavior. The life and health of the community is in peril. Both Paul and Elijah are drawing on the covenant renewal tradition of Moses and Joshua (Josh. 24:14–16). The question is whether such "prophetic" speech is required (moral excoriation taking seeming priority over perceptive, descriptive vision). There *are* occasions for individuals, communities, and nations when (to borrow Frost's phrase): "two roads diverge in a yellow wood," the choice of which "makes all the difference." Yet in a time of burgeoning tribalism, binary thinking can itself become idolatrous. Error can be explicitly named without mockery (unlike Elijah—and tweet storms). Unlike Paul (who seems to take it personally) those presumed to be in serious error can be addressed with respect—and given space.

JOHN W. WRIGHT

Commentary 2: Connecting the Reading with the World

Psalm 96 is a beautiful and classic celebration of the God of Israel as the God of all people and of the earth itself. "Say among the nations, 'The Lord is king!'" (v. 10). The earth itself rejoices; the sea and the field and the trees and the forest all "sing for joy." People too must celebrate. "O families of the peoples, ascribe to the Lord glory and strength. . . . bring an offering, and come into his courts. . . . tremble before him, all the earth." All people, every created thing, and even creation itself will worship the Lord. There is but one Lord, "for all the gods of the people are idols" (v. 5). It is the God of Israel who created the world and every living thing. It is this only God who "will judge the world with righteousness, and the peoples with his truth" (v. 13).

There is a beauty and comfort in this vision of the victory and glory of the one true God. In this vision there is also danger and terror.

First Kings 8 tells the story of the inauguration of Solomon's temple. The story opens with all the elders and leaders of the tribes gathering in Zion while the priests bring the ark to the house of God that Solomon has built. Solomon addresses the gathering with a royal speech that weaves together the blessings of this God, the chosenness of this place, and the favor and promises to the house of David. It is a traditional ancient combining of the central temple with the power and authority of the king.

Then Solomon prays. The prayer begins with and is full of images reminiscent of Psalm 96: "There is no God like you in heaven above or on earth beneath. . . . Even heaven and the highest heaven cannot contain you, much less this house that I have built" (1 Kgs. 8:23, 27). It is also filled with the religious politics of the time. The people of Israel must obey. As long as Israel is faithful and prays, God will protect them from their enemies, who seem to be everywhere. In the midst of this celebration of the chosenness of Israel and the naming of the blessings of this God for this place and this particular people comes a fragile undoing of the exclusiveness of this vision.

In 8:41 a foreigner, who is "not of your people Israel," arrives at this exclusive and dangerous temple. The person is the outsider, but this person is also not the enemy. Such foreigners "hear of your great name, your mighty hand," and they pray "toward this house." Solomon in turn prays that God "do according to all that the foreigner calls to you" (v. 43). These sentences open a small door out of the exclusiveness of this narrative. This is a political moment that recognizes that the God of Israel is Lord of all.

However, this opening is narrow and surrenders little. It is only the foreigner who submits to the claims of dominance of this temple who squeezes in this door. So it continues to be. We prefer to welcome only the foreigner, stranger, outsider who adopts our language and admits to our superiority. To enter our place, whether it be politics or theology, you must become us.

In the lectionary the story in Luke 7:1–10 of the Roman centurion with the ill slave is nicely paired with this text in 1 Kings 8. This story also opens a door in the exclusiveness of Luke's account of Jesus the Messiah. Throughout his Gospel, Luke insists that, as Messiah, Jesus is sent first to the house of Israel. Here, in this story, a Roman centurion partakes of the blessings of the Jewish Messiah. This centurion seems to be carefully located on the borders of being in the community and not being in the community. Jewish elders tell Jesus, "He is worthy of having you do this for him, for he loves our people, and it is he who built our synagogue for us." His worthiness depends not on his private virtues or his faithfulness to Rome but on his generosity to the Jewish people. They imply that he is almost one of us. Yet in all of this he remains a Roman centurion. The centurion never confesses Jesus as Lord or Messiah. Instead, he reads Jesus out of his own military experiences. His theology, if he has one, comes from the official hierarchy and patterns of submission in the Roman military. He understands Jesus by thinking of himself. He sees Jesus as a centurion who can obey and command. He seems unchanged by Jesus at the end of the story.

This story complicates how we think of the other and how we might imagine the blessings of "our God" touching the outsider. The door here seems a bit wider.

Then there is 1 Kings 18. Here we see the terror in all our dialogues of hospitality and tolerance. The story narrates the famous conflict between Elijah and 450 prophets of Baal, which is a moment in the larger conflict between Elijah, the one prophet of the Lord, and Ahab and Jezebel, who hold all the political power. The story echoes in a terrible way the passing comment in Psalm 96 that "all the gods of the people are idols." The oneness of God means terror for those who do not know this.

The context of this story matters. This is not a question of private faith. This is about public space, about which God and what rulers will rule. In the public arena, compassion and open doors are rare. In that place it is only power that matters. When "all the people" saw the Lord God's power, "they fell on their faces and said, 'The Lord indeed is God'" (1 Kgs. 18:39). In the next verse Elijah commands the people to "seize the prophets of Baal; do not let one of them escape." They do so and then slaughter 450 prophets of the wrong god. Only then does the Lord God release the rain.

It seems as if nothing has changed. These stories create endless echoes among our puzzlements about Jews, Christians, Muslims, immigrants, borders, hospitality, and so on. We too engage in horrible violence and intense compassion.

These stories create a reading experience wherein we the readers are the insiders negotiating our encounter with the stranger, the other. We are haunted by questions: Whom do we welcome? What rules do we enforce? To what extent must they become like us? What do we tolerate, and what do we not? Furthermore, we are often not the host but the stranger. We are ones thinking about crossing the border, haunted by questions: How do we enter? What do we give up? What do we accept? What change is good, what bad?

There are no stable answers to these questions. They must be addressed and decided each and every time. There is much at stake, both for us and for the other.

We must wonder what our visions of God have to do with this. The notion that my God is your God can bring both blessings and terror. The notion that your God is mine can also do both. We should perhaps remain haunted by the founding theology of these stories. There is but one God of all people and all places. If my God is blessing me and not you, then I need to rethink who God is.

LEWIS R. DONELSON

Psalm 96

[1]O sing to the LORD a new song;
sing to the LORD, all the earth.
[2]Sing to the LORD, bless his name;
tell of his salvation from day to day.
[3]Declare his glory among the nations,
his marvelous works among all the peoples.
[4]For great is the LORD, and greatly to be praised;
he is to be revered above all gods.
[5]For all the gods of the peoples are idols,
but the LORD made the heavens.
[6]Honor and majesty are before him;
strength and beauty are in his sanctuary.

[7]Ascribe to the LORD, O families of the peoples,
ascribe to the LORD glory and strength.
[8]Ascribe to the LORD the glory due his name;
bring an offering, and come into his courts.
[9]Worship the LORD in holy splendor;
tremble before him, all the earth.

[10]Say among the nations, "The LORD is king!
The world is firmly established; it shall never be moved.
He will judge the peoples with equity."
[11]Let the heavens be glad, and let the earth rejoice;
let the sea roar, and all that fills it;
[12]let the field exult, and everything in it.
Then shall all the trees of the forest sing for joy
[13]before the LORD; for he is coming,
for he is coming to judge the earth.
He will judge the world with righteousness,
and the peoples with his truth.

Connecting the Psalm with Scripture and Worship

Psalm 96 is a form of hortatory discourse, in which the psalmist exhorts people to praise God. It comprises three sections: verses 1–6, 7–9, 10–13. Each begins with an imperative mood (v. 1: "O sing to the LORD a new song"; v. 7: "Ascribe to the LORD, O families of the peoples"; v. 10: "Say among the nations, 'The LORD is king!'"), and exposits why they have to praise God (vv. 4–6, 12–13) in indicatives (e.g., "For great is the LORD"). Verse 13 concludes the poem with the words of conviction that God is coming to "judge the world with righteousness, and the peoples with his truth," which signifies the ultimate reason for praising God.

The psalm uses three images of God to explain why we should praise God: the creator of the universe, the king, and the judge. Verses 4–6 proclaim that God is not one of the human-made gods, that is, the idols, but the creator of the heavens, who deserves honor and majesty and reveals strength and beauty. Thus, in verses 7–9, the psalmist calls all the earth to "worship the LORD in holy splendor" (v. 9a). In verse 10, God is announced as the king, who not only establishes the world firmly, but also will judge the people fairly. For this reason, all the universe—including the heavens, the earth, all the creatures in the sea, everything in the fields, and all the trees of the forest—is exhorted to rejoice before the Lord (vv. 11–12). In verses 10–13, the psalmist emphasizes that God is not like a worldly king, but the one who is coming to the world to judge the whole world will do so with righteousness and truth. With the eschatological anticipation for the fulfillment of justice and peace on the earth, the psalmist calls all the creatures in the universe to praise and worship God in joy.

Although it is difficult to trace the historical background of Psalm 96, it seems relevant to recite it as the response to the two first readings, 1 Kings 18:20–39 and 8:22–23, 41–43. First Kings 18:20–39 delineates the event on Mount Carmel, the contest between Elijah and the prophets of Baal to demonstrate the truthfulness of their gods. Through that contest, the Lord, who is the God of Israel, is attested to be the true god who controls nature, while Baal, who is worshiped as the god of rain and fertility by the people, is proved not the true deity, but an idol that humans made with imagination. Since the Israelites lived in the same region as the Canaanites who worshiped Baal, and since they were dependent on rainfall in order for their crops to grow, the Baal cult held great allure. It was this cult, in fact, that represented the strongest challenge to the exclusive worship of YHWH.[1]

When Israelites left the desert and entered the agricultural territory of Canaan, they encountered the Baal cult and eventually embraced Baalism in their life in the promised land of Canaan. However, Deuteronomy and later Deuteronomistic writings, to which 1 Kings belongs, condemn Baal worship as a breach of the covenant between God and Israel. The contest on Mount Carmel—which takes place against the historical backdrop of the reign of Ahab, who institutionalized Baalism in Israel—exemplifies the dominant influence of Baal worship on Israel's religious life. The dramatic event on Mount Carmel witnesses that Baal is an idol who is impotent to respond to human needs and that the Lord, not Baal, is the only true God of the earth, the one who promised seasonal rains and has the power to control water and drought. In this context, Psalm 96 can be recited as the joyful response to God's salvation from natural disaster (v. 2: "Sing to the LORD, bless his name; tell of his salvation from day to day") and the proclamation of the Lord as the God of the universe (vv. 4–5: "For great is the LORD, and greatly to be praised; he is to be revered above all gods. For all the gods of the peoples are idols, but the LORD made the heavens").

First Kings 8:22–23, 41–43 is part of King Solomon's inauguration speech dedicating the newly constructed temple (1 Kgs. 8:12–61). The text explicitly presents Deuteronomist theology by emphasizing that the God of Israel is to be praised because the Lord is superior to other gods and faithfully keeps the promise with the people of Israel (vv. 22–23). Foreigners should worship together in God's temple, which is the house of prayers for all the people on the earth (vv. 41–43). Psalm 96 responds to this ceremonial event at the temple by exhorting the people to sing to the Lord (v. 6: "Honor and majesty are before him; strength and beauty are in his sanctuary") and calling all the earth to worship God in honor and awe (vv. 8–9).

The theological claim of the Deuteronomist in 1 Kings 18:20–39 and 8:22–23, 41–43 leads us to think about the God we believe in. How many of us have worshiped Baal, a domesticated god we have made for ourselves, rather than the God who transcends human effort and imagination? We often seek to design God to serve our purpose, especially when we are in such a desperate situation as the Israelites, who suffered from severe drought. Yet both texts from 1 Kings and Psalm 96 remind us that human-made gods are idols that are indifferent to people and powerless to get involved in their lives, and that the Lord is the only living God, who deserves to be praised by all creation.

1. John Day, "Baal (Deity)," in *Anchor Bible Dictionary*, ed. David Noel Freedman, 6 vols. (New York: Doubleday, 1992), 1:547.

Within and beyond Christianity, the concept of God is as diverse as personal and communal experiences of the sacred. It would be arrogant and exclusive to claim that only our own understanding of God is true and those of others are false. Yet not every understanding of God is equally valuable, according to Deuteronomist theology. We need to discern whether the God we believe in is a domesticated god or the living God, who transcends our imagination, but is profoundly concerned with righteousness and truth for all the creatures in the world. In the liturgical context, therefore, singing Psalm 96 is an affirmation of this faith. It can be sung energetically as an anthem. Dave and Jean Perry's composition of Psalm 96 is one of many music pieces available for the choir to sing the psalm in a joyful mood. The psalm can be sung with a congregation. *The Presbyterian Hymnal*, the *United Methodist Hymnal*, and *Glory to God* include Psalm 96 arranged in a "call and response" pattern for singing with the congregation.

EUNJOO MARY KIM

Galatians 1:1–12

[1]Paul an apostle—sent neither by human commission nor from human authorities, but through Jesus Christ and God the Father, who raised him from the dead— [2]and all the members of God's family who are with me,

To the churches of Galatia:

[3]Grace to you and peace from God our Father and the Lord Jesus Christ, [4]who gave himself for our sins to set us free from the present evil age, according to the will of our God and Father, [5]to whom be the glory forever and ever. Amen.

[6]I am astonished that you are so quickly deserting the one who called you in the grace of Christ and are turning to a different gospel— [7]not that there is another gospel, but there are some who are confusing you and want to pervert the gospel of Christ. [8]But even if we or an angel from heaven should proclaim to you a gospel contrary to what we proclaimed to you, let that one be accursed! [9]As we have said before, so now I repeat, if anyone proclaims to you a gospel contrary to what you received, let that one be accursed!

[10]Am I now seeking human approval, or God's approval? Or am I trying to please people? If I were still pleasing people, I would not be a servant of Christ.

[11]For I want you to know, brothers and sisters, that the gospel that was proclaimed by me is not of human origin; [12]for I did not receive it from a human source, nor was I taught it, but I received it through a revelation of Jesus Christ.

Commentary 1: Connecting the Reading with Scripture

Truth and authority are thematic threads that weave throughout this Galatian lectionary lesson. In the epistle, Paul contends for the hearts and minds of the newly converted in the mission field of Galatia and reclaims the efficacy of his past mission there by teaching them once again the true gospel of Jesus Christ. With today's text, he initiates his christological claim that human salvation comes from being justified by faith. To accomplish this mission, not only does Paul have to reassert the foundation of the gospel truth; he must defend his apostolic authority to preach that truth.

To understand Paul's opening remarks to the Galatians, a brief description of the letter's occasion is in order. During his initial evangelism and mission work in Galatia, Paul preached justification through faith, and not by any works (Gal. 2:16). After listening to the gospel of Jesus Christ and believing in his salvific work, many Galatians received the Spirit, converted, and formed churches. After Paul left the area, other missionaries came to the region, subverting his proclamation of the gospel with an alternative version (1:7). They insisted that the recent converts must obey major aspects of Mosaic law to access salvation and to receive the gifts of the Spirit. These missionaries did not seek to dissuade the group of their faith in Jesus; rather, they argued that Gentile converts must be circumcised (5:2) and observe special holidays (4:10) to signify their inclusion in the covenantal community. Luke depicts the intragroup conflict among the Jerusalem council in Acts 15, where Paul, Barnabas, and others successfully argue against a decree that Gentile believers must follow Mosaic law. Believing the other missionaries, though, many among the Galatians followed the alternative gospel.

Therefore, in the salutation, Paul makes his central christological argument. He proclaims that Jesus Christ is the one "who gave himself for our sins to set us free from the present evil age" (1:4). Jesus' self-sacrifice freed humanity,

The Many-Voiced Instrument of the Universe

He who sprang from David and yet was before him, the Word of God, scorned those lifeless instruments of lyre and harp. By the power of the Holy Spirit He arranged in harmonious order this great world, yes, and the little world of man too, body and soul together; and on this many-voiced instrument of the universe He makes music to God, and sings to the human instrument. "For thou art my harp and my pipe and my temple"—my harp by reason of the music, my pipe by reason of the breath of the Spirit, my temple by reason of the Word—God's purpose being that the music should resound, the Spirit inspire, and the temple receive its Lord. Moreover, King David the harpist, whom we mentioned just above, urged us toward the truth and away from idols. So far was he from singing the praises of daemons that they were put to flight by him with the true music; and when Saul was possessed, David healed him merely by playing the harp. The Lord fashioned man a beautiful, breathing instrument, after His own image; and assuredly He Himself is an all-harmonious instrument of God, melodious and holy, the wisdom that is above this world, the heavenly Word.

Clement of Alexandria, "Exhortation to the Greeks," in *Clement of Alexandria*, trans. G. W. Butterworth, Loeb Classical Library 92 (Cambridge, MA: Harvard University Press, 1919), 13, 15.

not ritualistic acts or observances. Contrary to the conditional gospel preached by the other missionaries, Paul maintains that the grace of Christ is salvation given unconditionally, and the Galatians are heirs through God's promise to Abraham (3:1–9). He is foreshadowing the argument that undergirds the body of this letter and becomes a claim central to his most prominent body of work.

The salvific work of Jesus in his death and resurrection introduced in today's lesson is an unpolished version of the Christology that appears in his later writings. Paul develops this point further in the climax of Romans 4, where he explains that the foundation of humanity's righteousness is in Jesus, "who was handed over to death for our trespasses and was raised for our justification" (4:25). In Romans 8:3, he explains that God has done through justification by faith and in the gift of the Holy Spirit what the law could not do: set humanity free from sin and therefore from the present evil age. Therefore, Paul's testimony in the Galatian salutation (Gal. 1:3–4) of humanity's deliverance from sin in Jesus' self-sacrifice is a reassertion of his core message of unconditional salvation, which is the true gospel of Jesus Christ.

While initiating his counterattack on the alternative gospel of the missionaries, Paul begins to defend his apostolic authority as a source of the gospel. It is possible that the Galatians' trust in Paul's message eroded with the attacks on his apostolic authority. Although the letter is not explicit, the bookends of the lesson suggest that the missionaries were misrepresenting the truth while undermining Paul's credibility. In the first line of the letter (1:1) and the ending of this section (vv. 11–12), Paul makes clear that his apostolic commission comes from God only, through Jesus Christ, and that the gospel he proclaimed had no human origins; rather, he received it as revelation from Christ. These claims about his identity and the source of his proclamation set him apart from other second-generation missionaries who learned and were sent out by other humans.

Although not one of the original apostles, Paul asserts that his authority, and therefore the gospel as he preaches it, is as authentic as that of Jesus' disciples, and superior to the missionaries who learned about Jesus only via hearsay, since his comes directly from Jesus (see Acts 9). Paul presumes that these missionaries are circumcised Jewish believers (Gal. 5:2–3). They were possibly missionaries who, unlike him, learned the gospel from apostles. Paul does not provide any biographical information about the missionaries; instead he focuses the anathema of their preaching, their perversion of the gospel of Christ (1:6–7), and the confusion (1:7; cf. 5:12) they have caused among the Galatians.

Reasserting the truth and purity of God's message and of one's own authority is not a stance unique to Paul. He follows in a long scriptural tradition wherein God's appointed leaders must defend the prophetic message that has been preached, and the power of God behind it. Isaiah had to defend his prophecies against Judah and the Judean kings who did not believe him. Ezekiel had to defend his prophecies among Judeans left in Jerusalem and those exiled in Babylon who remained recalcitrant in their ways and struggled in their relationship with God. Issues of truth validity and source credibility connect Paul to one of the most famous prophets in Israel, Elijah. In the OT lectionary lesson, Elijah enters in a battle royal against the prophets of Baal to show the people of Israel and their king that God is the one true God. Through an awesome display of divine actions, he convinces them that the God of Israel is more powerful than Baal. Elijah reestablishes his authority as God's prophet and demonstrates the truth of God's protection and care for the people.

In Luke 7:1–10, Jesus, rather than having his authority challenged, has it affirmed by a Roman centurion, an unlikely source. In the Roman cult of the emperor, Caesar is superior, and Jupiter is supreme. Even in their pantheism and practices of syncretism of various religions and belief systems, Roman citizens, elites, and especially military leaders would adhere to the same cultural, political, and cultic understanding of Roman divine authority. The centurion's depiction as one whom the Jewish elders say loves the people suggests he is a believer of the God of Israel who practices Jewish piety. He addresses Jesus as Lord and believes deeply in Jesus' power to save his slave from death, a recognition of Jesus' divinity as superior over Rome's deities. The centurion's faith in Jesus' authority and his power to heal are so strong that he declares that Jesus could heal his slave from a distance with only a word. The centurion's acknowledgment of the authority of Jesus as a healer and the truth of his power even amazes Jesus (v. 9).

Like Elijah in Israel, Paul must refute the false understanding of the power of God to save the people from the present evil age. He has to prove that his gospel of Jesus Christ is true and defend his authority as mediator, preacher, and teacher of the gospel. People believe a message true once they have confidence that the communicator is an authoritative source. Jesus does not have this problem. Convincing the people that he is a trusted source, Paul's task is to teach God's revelation of the true gospel of Jesus Christ and that its salvific power is unconditional.

BRIDGETT A. GREEN

Commentary 2: Connecting the Reading with the World

Galatia, like many of the brash new communities formed during the dizzying rise of the Way, was giving its founder fits. Paul's opening formulaic greeting—in which his traditional thanksgiving for the recipient goes missing like a knocked-out front tooth—signals immediately that there is trouble. Shards of strife are scattered throughout the Galatians missive, evidence of a community's struggle to absorb the seismic event of Christ and the paradigm shift it detonated. Massive structural pillars have been displaced: What is salvation now? What is righteousness? Does the cross negate law? Who decides? These questions remain profoundly relevant today, as the church continues to discern norms amid the intersection of traditional teachings and unfettered divine grace. Not unlike Galatia, modern faith communities are stretched taut between conservative and progressive polarities, each producing a yearning for either a greater narrowness or expansiveness in defining what it means to be Christian. Preachers might commence an exploration of this pericope by establishing an identification with Galatia's turmoil, showing that American Protestantism's current unsettled state is hardly novel.

Paul's work amid the crash of conflict in early church history is nothing short of breathtaking. Following the fervor of an electrifying movement, Paul is tasked by God to author and shape the theological contours of a sustainable religion. The degree of difficulty in this endeavor is steep for multiple reasons, not least of which was hodgepodge Galatian demographics. It was one thing to form gospel communities in the earliest days, when Jews preached to Jews, but when Gentiles were added to the mix, all the typical headaches of a start-up were compounded exponentially. Foundational was a question of identity: did the gospel herald a new form of Judaism that required non-Jewish pagans and Gentiles to convert, and therefore observe rites such as table fellowship and circumcision? Friction between tradition and innovation caused great instability among the Galatian churches; in the wobble, leaders other than Paul infiltrated with conflicting teachings that threatened the mission itself. Again the question: Who had the authority to speak for God? Similarly today, different truth claims abound about God's vision and requirements for human flourishing. As our culture grapples with hot-button issues like immigration reform and gay marriage, where is Christian moral authority located? Is an evangelical politician quoting Deuteronomy on Fox News "more right" than a progressive blogger quoting Jesus via Dietrich Bonhoeffer in the *Huffington Post*?

Paul validates authority—at both the start and the conclusion of this pericope—by pointing to the message itself, urging the Galatians to look past the cacophony of charismatic experts vying for their attention, and instead to remember their own experience of the power of the gospel. Any other teaching, even if preached by "angels from heaven," should be completely rejected (Gal. 1:8–9). Paul takes a sledgehammer to the "perversions" that had been patched unto the gospel's original scaffolding, pounding out a rebuke that encompasses four chapters (1:6–4:12). Paul writes, "I am astonished [*thaumazō*, "marvel"] that you are so quickly deserting [*metatithēmi*, "remove"] the one who called you in the grace of Christ" (1:6). In this, Paul links their abandonment of him with their abandoning God almighty. His ire toward those who are "bewitching" the people is palpable. Primary suspects are some of James's people and/or a general circumcising faction from either inside or outside the Galatia churches (2:11–12), who mock Paul as a "people pleaser." Paul is accused of seeking approval by preaching a populist message that relaxes Mosaic law for non-Jewish folks, presumably to attract larger numbers to the ranks (1:10). His rivals, in urging a return to Torah's edicts on righteousness, are challenging Paul's core teaching of *pistis Christou* (faith in Christ) as the benchmark for justification (3:11).[1] Preachers might consider a potential parallel to religious extremists today who insist on a return to ancient behavior codes, moral litmus tests, or specifically defined "right behavior" in qualifying for eternal salvation.

Paul grasps the seriousness of the challenge in Galatia, and unequivocally warns against tampering with the radically different modality of living in Christ. No matter how charismatic the preaching or how earnest the religious desire for holiness, Paul is resolute that any addition to the gospel is actually a subtraction, because it implies that Christ alone is inadequate. Paul's genius is protecting the purity of the freedom that Christ offers, which is monumental in its indivisible simplicity: anything other than complete surrender to grace is a form of idolatry. Elements of this theme appear in other selections of the lectionary for Proper 4, such as Luke's praise of the Gentile centurion's singularity of faith in the salvific power of Jesus. How hard it is to believe that we are not required to earn salvation through works, and how difficult it is to have faith that God loves us more than we feel we deserve!

Additionally, the turmoil within Galatia offers another potential connection point, which is the pain of experiencing intense reform. For vastly different reasons, contemporary congregations are also experiencing distress amid rapid change, as the rise of technology, pluralism, and other significant cultural forces continues to rearrange much of our twenty-first-century religious and political landscape. We live in what is now called a post-Christendom age, and although this erosion has happened over many years, grief over what has been lost has become acute in mainline denominations over the past decade, as congregations fight for survival. Forms and practices cherished for generations seem to resonate less

1. Care is urged speaking of these tensions, lest supersessionism creep in.

with today's culture, so congregations are experimenting with many different expressions, such as pub theology, jazz or rock music, podcasts, gender-inclusive language, virtual meetings, and "bite-sized" a la carte programs instead of Christian education for a postcommitment world, just to name a few. These experiments can bring new life even while also heightening a sense of disorientation within many congregations.

Outside of church walls, even more chaos reigns as technology erases traditional ways, and ugly partisan rancor mixes political and religious bickering to fracture our nation. This age calls to mind the darkly moving poem "The Second Coming" by William Butler Yeats, who remarks, "Things fall apart; the center cannot hold; Mere anarchy is loosed upon the world."

Into this tender place of heartache, preachers are called to offer God's word as a shimmering doorway, leading to both soothing comfort as well as necessary galvanization. How has your congregation struggled amid the changing landscape of Christianity and culture? What losses are people grieving most? As in Galatia, are there instances when nostalgia or anger has led to clinging to rituals or programs that are no longer life-giving? One lens to examine the turmoil of Galatia and today is the work of the late theologian Phyllis Tickle, who famously explored the notion that every five hundred years or so—for example, the Reformation, the Great Schism—Christianity and our world undergo massive restructuring across multiple domains, and that we are living through such an epoch right now.[2]

Indeed, Paul's Epistle to the Galatians offers many valuable and healing connection points to our context today. In this deeply unsettling time of transition in the body of Christ, it is fruitful to wonder together what our very alive God is imaginatively innovating in our midst, as well as what impedes us from recognizing it. Then and now, what might our lives look like if we wholeheartedly trusted the spectacular freedom found in living *pistis Christou*, in Christ alone?

SUZANNE WOOLSTON BOSSERT

2. Phyllis Tickle, *The Great Emergence: How Christianity Is Changing and Why* (Grand Rapids: Baker Publishing Group, 2012), 16.

Luke 7:1–10

[1]After Jesus had finished all his sayings in the hearing of the people, he entered Capernaum. [2]A centurion there had a slave whom he valued highly, and who was ill and close to death. [3]When he heard about Jesus, he sent some Jewish elders to him, asking him to come and heal his slave. [4]When they came to Jesus, they appealed to him earnestly, saying, "He is worthy of having you do this for him, [5]for he loves our people, and it is he who built our synagogue for us." [6]And Jesus went with them, but when he was not far from the house, the centurion sent friends to say to him, "Lord, do not trouble yourself, for I am not worthy to have you come under my roof; [7]therefore I did not presume to come to you. But only speak the word, and let my servant be healed. [8]For I also am a man set under authority, with soldiers under me; and I say to one, 'Go,' and he goes, and to another, 'Come,' and he comes, and to my slave, 'Do this,' and the slave does it." [9]When Jesus heard this he was amazed at him, and turning to the crowd that followed him, he said, "I tell you, not even in Israel have I found such faith." [10]When those who had been sent returned to the house, they found the slave in good health.

Commentary 1: Connecting the Reading with Scripture

Perhaps the most surprising moment in this story comes when the centurion sends friends at once to praise and beseech Jesus. Like good messengers they deliver verbatim the words entrusted to them: "For I also am a man set under authority" (Luke 7:8). The second half of the sentence is more what we would expect: "With soldiers under me; and I say to one, 'Go,' and he goes, and to another, 'Come,' and he comes, and to my slave, 'Do this,' and the slave does it."

It seems clear that the centurion's description of his own power is used to profess his faith in Jesus' powers. As the centurion can say to a soldier "Go" and "Come," so Jesus can command the forces that bring illness or healing, and they obey. It is striking that the centurion starts not by affirming his authority over those below him, but the authority of those above him. His authority is not self-contained; he gives orders because he receives them.

Luke's Gospel has many ways of understanding Jesus and his ministry. One of the most important is his continuing claim that Jesus is a prophet. Prophets do not speak on their own authority; they speak the words God gives them to speak. They do not travel on their own authority; they go where God sends them. They do not heal on their own authority; they manifest the authority of the God who works through them.

This prophetic role also provides a key for understanding Jesus' resistance to Satan in the temptation story of Luke 4. When Satan tries to give Jesus authority over the kingdoms of the world, Jesus responds in words appropriate to his own humility and to his prophetic office: "Worship the Lord your God, and serve only him" (4:8b).

For Luke there is no question that Jesus has authority, but like the prophets, and as the greatest prophet, he derives that authority from God's commission. When Jesus sends word to Herod about his own authority to command and heal, he clearly aligns himself with the prophets whose authority came with their commission: "Go and tell that fox for me, 'Listen, I am casting out demons and performing cures today and tomorrow, and on the third day I finish my work. Yet today, tomorrow, and the next day I must be on my way, because it is impossible for a prophet to be killed outside Jerusalem'" (13:32–33).

Because Luke tells his story in two volumes, his Gospel and the book of Acts, it is perhaps most evident that the story of Jesus is continued in the story of the church. In particular, the role of Jesus as prophet is reshaped to define the ways Peter and Paul also are commissioned, speak inspired truth, and do miracles in the name of the one who sent them.

One way to read the ongoing saga of Luke and Acts is to see the succession of authority—from God to Jesus to the apostles to the elders (in Acts 20) and so on to the believers in generations to come. For Luke, Jesus acts under authority and with authority; in a lesser, derivative but essential, way, so do those of us who are the church.

A second theme that informs this story and ties it to the larger drama of Luke and Acts is that of the outsider who has faith. Here the centurion is an outsider because he is a Gentile, not a Jew—perhaps even more an outsider because he is a servant of the imperial power of Rome.

The large theological question the story asks and answers is whether Gentiles can have a place in the kingdom that Jesus proclaims and the community that he begins. The answer is clearly yes, and it is equally clear that what gives the centurion access to kingdom and community is his faith (v. 9). This faith is evident in at least three ways.

First, the centurion shows faith as humility. He does not demand that Jesus help but beseeches him to help. He does not require that Jesus come to him but sends to Jesus.

Second, the centurion shows faith as trust in Jesus' word: "But only speak the word, and let my servant be healed" (v. 7). Here again we see the ways in which Jesus acts in continuity with the prophets. For the classic prophets of the OT, the words that they spoke not only declared; they accomplished. Isaiah's affirmation could serve as a summary of Hebrew prophecy:

> For as the rain and the snow come down
> from heaven,
> and do not return there until they have
> watered the earth,
> making it bring forth and sprout,
> giving seed to the sower and bread to the
> eater,
> so shall my word be that goes out from my
> mouth;
> it shall not return to me empty,
> but it shall accomplish that which I purpose,
> and succeed in the thing for which I sent it.
> Isa. 55:10–11

Third, the centurion shows faith in Jesus' authority. As we have seen, he knows that Jesus is under authority, and that he holds authority to do the good he purposes. The theme of Jesus' authority recurs time and again in this Gospel: he teaches with authority (4:32); he forgives with authority (5:24); he evades his opponents' questions about authority, and thereby demonstrates his own authoritative ability to outfox them (20:1–8)

While it is true that by faith Gentiles may become part of the kingdom and the community, it is equally true that by faith Gentiles can become part of that community. That is one of the essential claims of Luke and Acts.

In many ways the story of Jesus and the centurion is mirrored by the story of Peter and another centurion, Cornelius, in Acts 10. The question for Peter is whether he will follow the example of his Master and reach out to all who come to the faith. The voice from heaven sounds very much like the voice of Jesus: "What God has made clean, you must not call profane" (Acts 10:15).

Our passage in Luke 7 is part of a larger agenda for the author of Luke–Acts (and, he would say, a larger agenda for God): the word of the gospel should be offered to Jew and Gentile alike.

We also notice that both the centurion of Luke 7 and Cornelius have actively supported their local Jewish communities. Luke recognizes that Gentiles come into the kingdom community in company with those Jews who have been the vanguard of God's people, age after age.

When we set this passage in the context of the lectionary readings for this week, we notice that Elijah the prophet foreshadows Jesus, the later and greater prophet of Luke's Gospel. Both our prophets, Elijah and Jesus, perform sign-acts—astonishing demonstrations of power that show the authority of God. More than that, Elijah's self-designation in 1 Kings could easily have been repeated by Jesus in Luke. Elijah speaks as one under authority and acts as one with authority: "O LORD, God of Abraham, Isaac, and Jacob, let it be known this day that you are God in Israel, that I am your servant, and that I have done all these things at your bidding" (1 Kgs. 18:36).

The first verse of Galatians sets Paul in the line of prophets as well, now authorized not only by God but also by Christ: "Paul an apostle—sent neither by human commission nor from human authorities, but through Jesus Christ and God the Father, who raised him from the dead" (Gal. 1:1).

DAVID L. BARTLETT

Commentary 2: Connecting the Reading with the World

Luke 7:1–10 provides a living example of the power of faith in Jesus to bring about the kind of global community the Sermon on the Plain promised. At its center is a dying slave healed. Rippling out from this core at ever farther distances are numerous other figures, with Jesus at the farthest physical remove from the deathbed. Jesus' word—unspoken—brings about the miracle, but Luke ties this work inextricably to a Roman soldier's faith. In the context of the liturgical year, Luke here connects the teachings and ministry of Jesus with believers' faith to bring healing and hope.

This reading is the setting for a liturgical gem. Roman Catholics for centuries have said a prayer modeled on the words of the centurion in Luke 7:6–7 and its parallel Matthew 8:8 just before taking the Communion elements. An older English translation, "Lord, I am not worthy to receive you, but only say the word and I shall be healed," was replaced in the missal in 2011 by, "Lord, I am not worthy that you should enter under my roof, but only say the word and my soul will be healed," which is the exact wording in Matthew's Gospel with the substitution of "soul" for "servant."

This prayer reflects the awe and humility of the faithful who hope to receive Christ "under the roof" of their physical bodies, the temples of his Spirit. They dare to ask, in Charles Wesley's memorable phrasing,

> Love divine, all loves excelling,
> Joy of heaven to earth come down,
> Fix in us thy humble dwelling.

(Some Catholics wryly note that the mouth has a roof, evoking an earthy image of an intimacy the centurion does not experience in this story.)

Luke 7:1–10 has a word for the missional church. The term "missional church" regularly arises in almost any discussion of the nature of the church these days. A missional church's identity is that of an agent of God's mission or *missio Dei* in the world. (The Latin root of "mission" means "sent.") In missional theology, the church does not have a mission; it is a mission. (Yes, like the Blues Brothers, the mobile church is on a mission for God.)

First, the church, like Jesus, is sent into the world, not created for the world to come to it. Jesus learned of the need; he went (v. 6). Too often the church takes its motto from the *Field of Dreams* movie: "If [we] build it, [they] will come." Today, the church that waits for the world to come to it will join the growing ranks of isolated communities funding unattended programs in empty buildings.

Second, the missional church, like the Jewish elders, the centurion, and his friends, serves as a bridge between God's healing and those in need. These three—centurion, Jews, and friends—are mediators in service to Jesus' healing work. Likewise, the missional church is not an end in itself called to perpetuate its existence, but a servant in and to the world.

Third, the church that serves the marginal in society, as Jesus and the centurion served to heal the lowly but beloved slave, may have a far-reaching impact through small gestures. Justo González in his commentary on this section of Luke notes that Jesus' ministry brought him to the attention of Roman power. The empire eventually surrendered to Christ, but not before it crucified him.[1] The missional church needs courage and faith in every age.

Fourth, the missional church should take note of Jesus and the centurion's understanding of spiritual authority: it comes not from inherent self-worth, but from above. The centurion recognized that Jesus, like himself, was "a man set under authority" (v. 8) whose power came from above. It "amazed" Jesus that the centurion recognized and had faith in this hierarchy of power and authority invested in him (v. 9). The church's authority and power rise not from its own worthiness, but from God in Christ. The church is not the center; it is the sent.

The spiritual power revealed in Jesus and trusted by the centurion transforms community social fabric. Jesus and the centurion express power and authority as humility and submission. Jesus humbly obeys the directives of the centurion. Jesus goes when asked to come (v. 6a). He stops when asked to stop coming (v. 6b). Francis's 1221 *Rule* to his disciples, which instructs them to be obedient subjects to their Muslim enemies during the Crusades, echoes Jesus' obedience to a Roman soldier. The centurion exhibits similar humility. He refuses to risk harming Jesus' reputation by either going to him or asking him to come under his unclean Gentile roof. Such mutual submissions do not signify compromise of one's beliefs. They are one's beliefs in an ethical society. Love's authority need not insist on its own way to be effective. Indeed, it must not do so.

The very structure of this story points to the humble exercise of love's authority. Both Jesus and the centurion yield the floor here to others. Neither takes center stage, as they do in the parallel in Matthew 8. They never meet or speak directly to one another in Luke. Jesus is silent, except for his one-liner in verse 10. Even Jesus' answer to the request, "Speak the word" (v. 7), is unrecorded. Jesus and the centurion achieve their desired goal: the slave lives.

This story points to a new community beyond economic, ethnic, religious, vocational, and geographic boundaries. Rich and poor, Israeli and Roman, Jew and pagan, pacifist preacher and military commander, imperial interloper and colonized citizenry all join together for the sake of the common good. This is an interfaith text. It takes a village to heal a slave.

Spiritual realities provide the larger society with powers the state does not possess. Ironically, the centurion states, "I say . . . to my slave, 'Do this,' and the slave does it" (v. 8), yet he cannot say, "Get well." That is a power above his rank, and the rank of his emperor. It is a power above every earthly power, but one every society does well to acknowledge.

Societies growing ever more distant from each other due to nationalism, racism, and impersonal technology are strengthened by what Pope Francis calls a new Christian humanism.[2] He alludes to a willingness to cooperate with any and all of creation in a way that is not narcissistic or self-referential. Technology has the power to make the earth smaller. It also has the potential to reduce human empathy and create emotional distance. This is one of the themes of the movie *Eye in the Sky*, in which teams of varying nationalities in different parts of the world strive to decide whether and/or when to fire a missile at a target containing innocents and terrorists. Watching these modern centurions' agonizing efforts raises questions of power, authority, compassion, and faith. Luke offers clues to the answers.

For all the centurion's amazing faith, one might personally wish more for him. He was compassionate, bold, unfazed by religious boundaries, and diplomatic; he paved the way for Jewish assistance by his community involvement. Still, he knew Jesus only from a distance, through others. As one blogger put it, "Bette Midler's inspirational hit 'From a Distance' has never inspired me one bit."[3] What might it have meant personally for the centurion to welcome Jesus under his unworthy roof?

WM. LOYD ALLEN

1. Justo L. González, *Luke*, Belief (Louisville, KY: Westminster John Knox Press, 2010), 98.
2. Pope Francis, "Address to the Fifth Convention of the Church in Italy," November 15, 2010.
3. Catholic Sensibility at https://catholicsensibility.wordpress.com/2010/11/20/down-with-domine-non-sum-dignus/.

Proper 5 (Sunday between June 5 and June 11 Inclusive)

1 Kings 17:8–16 (17–24) and 1 Kings 17:17–24
Psalm 146 and Psalm 30
Galatians 1:11–24
Luke 7:11–17

1 Kings 17:8–16 (17–24)

> [8]Then the word of the LORD came to him, saying, [9]"Go now to Zarephath, which belongs to Sidon, and live there; for I have commanded a widow there to feed you." [10]So he set out and went to Zarephath. When he came to the gate of the town, a widow was there gathering sticks; he called to her and said, "Bring me a little water in a vessel, so that I may drink." [11]As she was going to bring it, he called to her and said, "Bring me a morsel of bread in your hand." [12]But she said, "As the LORD your God lives, I have nothing baked, only a handful of meal in a jar, and a little oil in a jug; I am now gathering a couple of sticks, so that I may go home and prepare it for myself and my son, that we may eat it, and die." [13]Elijah said to her, "Do not be afraid; go and do as you have said; but first make me a little cake of it and bring it to me, and afterwards make something for yourself and your son. [14]For thus says the LORD the God of Israel: The jar of meal will not be emptied and the jug of oil will not fail until the day that the LORD sends rain on the earth." [15]She went and did as Elijah said, so that she as well as he and her household ate for many days. [16]The jar of meal was not emptied, neither did the jug of oil fail, according to the word of the LORD that he spoke by Elijah.
>
> [17]After this the son of the woman, the mistress of the house, became ill; his illness was so severe that there was no breath left in him. [18]She then said to Elijah, "What have you against me, O man of God? You have come to me to bring my sin to remembrance, and to cause the death of my son!" [19]But he said to her, "Give me your son." He took him from her bosom, carried him up into the upper chamber where he was lodging, and laid him on his own bed. [20]He cried out to the LORD, "O LORD my God, have you brought calamity even upon the widow with whom I am staying, by killing her son?" [21]Then he stretched himself upon the child three times, and cried out to the LORD, "O LORD my God, let this child's life come into him again." [22]The LORD listened to the voice of Elijah; the life of the child came into him again, and he revived. [23]Elijah took the child, brought him down from the upper chamber into the house, and gave him to his mother; then Elijah said, "See, your son is alive." [24]So the woman said to Elijah, "Now I know that you are a man of God, and that the word of the LORD in your mouth is truth."

Commentary 1: Connecting the Reading with Scripture

The OT reading originates toward the beginning of a series of prophetic stories that scholars have entitled the Elijah-Elisha cycle. The cycle appears after the division of Israel into northern and southern kingdoms. The narrative differs from what precedes and follows it. The series of related stories breaks into the predominantly royal narratives of 1–2 Kings. It refocuses the story on prophets, not just kings, as crucial actors. This difference has led to a long dispute about the relationship of the Elijah-Elisha cycle to the composition of 1 and 2 Kings. No consensus about its time and place of origin exists. Most commentators today recognize that whatever its origin, an editor has interwoven the cycle deeply into the narrative context of the end of 1 Kings and the beginning of 2 Kings.

The cycle begins abruptly; Elijah enters the narrative suddenly without introduction (1 Kgs. 17:1). He declares, against Ahab, a coming drought (17:1–2). Of course, after this threat he must flee from the king. The Lord sustains Elijah from his demise through the care of a raven while hiding in a wadi, or ravine (17:2–6).

First Kings 17:7–24 provides more "stable" protection and provision for Elijah as the drought runs its course. The reading entails two related episodes (vv. 7–16 and vv. 17–24). The first generates profound ironies. The narrative had earlier related Ahab's sin to his marriage to Jezebel, the daughter of the king of Sidon (16:31–33). Yet the Lord instructs Elijah to meet a woman from the region of Sidon for his sustenance (17:9). In contrast to Ahab, the non-Israelite widow herself confesses faithfulness to the God of Israel (v. 12a).

Ironically, the narrative emphasizes that Elijah finds himself without necessary sustenance as a victim of the drought that he himself had declared (vv. 1–2); in sustaining Elijah, the Lord also sustains the widow and her son (vv. 7–17). The drought has already impacted the woman. She does not perceive that she has the means to survive this famine (vv. 12b–17). The drought indiscriminately impacts Elijah, the widow, and her son; the Lord's care indiscriminately sustains the Israelite prophet and the non-Israelite widow and her son.

The sign of God's election and care of Elijah, and of the woman and her son through Elijah, comes in the endless flour jar and oil jug. It is not exactly a well-balanced, varied diet; it provides, however, a minimum of calories to sustain the life within the household. The woman's obedience to the prophetic word manifests itself in the survival of the household during the drought. Sometimes survival itself is a moral accomplishment.

Perhaps the largest irony occurs in the core plot of the second episode; the son, sustained through the drought, dies after an extended illness (v. 17). The woman blames herself for the death through the agency of the prophet (v. 18). Elijah, however, turns the blame toward God (v. 20). Even while blaming God, Elijah nonetheless seeks divine aid in responding to the situation. Elijah covers the son with his body and prays to the Lord for life to return to him. The woman, sustained through the drought, receives the gift of her son's life as a vindication of Elijah's status as a prophet (v. 24b). The resuscitation of the son signifies the truthfulness of the woman's words upon her first greeting of Elijah: "as surely as your God lives" (v. 12a). The God of Israel is the living God, not merely for Israel but for all people.

The episode warrants the legitimacy of Elijah in the stories that follow. Moreover, the story indicates the character of the Lord, the God of Israel. The story of the widow from Zarephath reveals God as a God of life, even amid judgment. The following reigns of the kings of Israel and Judah slowly deteriorate in their sole devotion to the Lord, the God of Israel. As a result, the Assyrians destroy the northern kingdom and its capital, Samaria, in judgment (2 Kgs. 17); the Babylonians destroy Jerusalem later as the Primary History reaches toward its end (2 Kgs. 25). Only the heir of David in exile remains as a slight sign of God's faithfulness to God's promise amid judgment.

The sustaining of life amid judgment, drought, and disease in 1 Kings 17:7–24 prepares for the thin hope at the end of 2 Kings 25: the release of Jehoiachin from prison and the continued possibility of the fulfillment of the promise to Abram, the promise to David through the Davidic line. Amid judgment and tragedy, God still signals that God is the God of life.

The lectionary places 1 Kings 17:7–24 in parallel with Luke 7:11–17. Elijah functions as the type for Jesus. The lectionary readings invite us to see how Jesus fulfills the role of prophet, in conjunction with his roles as priest and king. Significantly, the role of prophet comes to its completion in the giving of life. Yet the life given, in both accounts, is not merely to extend the life of the one resuscitated; God gives life for the sake of the living, for widows, as well as the poor and orphans. In the gift of life in the resuscitation of these sons, God opens life to those whose death would seem immanent. The divine Life sustains life by giving life through the word of the prophet.

In such a way, the texts invite us to see how they typologically work to call the congregation into the life of the Father, through the Son, by the power of the Holy Spirit, one God forever and ever. The raising of these sons in accordance with the word of the prophet finds its ultimate fulfillment in the resurrection of Christ, the one who is "the Resurrection and the Life" (John 11:25). Without the fulfillment of the resuscitation of these two non-Israelite sons in the resurrection of Christ, the resuscitations of these sons collapse back into themselves in the play of immanence. What emerges is a heroic, if ultimately tragic attempt to hold the death of the mothers' sons at arm's length through filial obligation. The acts of Elijah and Jesus merely mask the underlying tragedy of human life that moves only toward death, even if delayed momentarily. In the resurrection of Christ, however, the life of these mothers opens into the life of their sons, which returns life to their mothers. The passages point beyond themselves so that all may take hold of the "life that really is life" (1 Tim. 6:19).

The resuscitation of the widows' sons by Elijah and Jesus foreshadows the resurrection of Christ, whose fulfillment of the Jewish Scriptures enfolds non-Jews as well into the fullness of life. The stories signify that beyond the tragedy of death, in the resurrection of Christ, God has transformed death into a witness to eternal life in God, from whom, through whom, and to whom are all things. God shows that God is faithful to the promise made to Abraham and David through the gospel, the life, death, and resurrection of Christ.

Amid the tragedy of life, sin, judgment, social disparities, the always perilous life of the widow, God shows in these passages that we may speak of God as Life itself, for all people, through the defeat of death in the crucifixion and resurrection of Jesus. Life now is not annulled, but lifted, raised, even resuscitated and perfected in the resurrection of Christ.

JOHN W. WRIGHT

Commentary 2: Connecting the Reading with the World

Although these two Elijah stories do not refer directly to the political and religious conflicts that animate the accounts of Elijah, they assume these conflicts and examine the power of God in the midst of such conflict. Ahab, Jezebel, Obadiah, and the various prophets of Baal and the Lord do not appear in these two passages, but they are implicitly present. It is significant that the setting for these stories is Sidon, the hometown of Jezebel. It is also significant that, given the debate over whether Baal or YHWH is more powerful, it is the power of the Lord that is demonstrated in these stories.

Although the passage does not explicitly say so, Elijah appears to be hiding specifically from Ahab. Elijah has announced to Ahab the withdrawing of rain for three years because of Ahab and Jezebel's allegiance to Baal. The word of the Lord tells Elijah to hide by the Wadi Cherith, where the ravens will feed him. There are times when a person of God or the people of God should seek safety from political danger. The instances of this throughout history are beyond counting. The most influential martyrdom story in early Christianity is probably that of Polycarp. He spends much of the story hiding. Even Jesus withdraws and waits for the proper time. How does one know when it is the proper time to hide? Elijah has it easy. The word of the Lord in 1 Kings 17:3 tells him to hide and in 18:1 tells him to confront Ahab.

The question is not only how to determine when to go forth and when to withdraw, but also what God does in the midst of such moments of hiding. Is hiding a sign of the limits of God's power? Does hiding mean that God cannot protect you and care for you? This seems to be a real question in 1 Kings.

It makes sense that this passage is paired with Psalm 146, since this psalm raises the same issue as 1 Kings 17: "Do not put your trust in princes, in mortals, in whom there is no help." Instead, "Happy are those whose help is the God of Jacob." The psalm then sings of God's power and protection. God "made heaven and earth." God "executes justice for the oppressed" and "gives food to the hungry." In fact, "the LORD will reign forever." These classic affirmations about God have offered comfort to believers in countless moments. Such simple confessions travel almost anywhere. The conviction that God feeds the hungry offers hope whenever and wherever someone is hungry. Furthermore, this simple declaration seems to offer comfort even when people are starving.

In 1 Kings 17 the problem is even more theologically complex, since it is God who is withdrawing the food. God is creating starvation. When the land around Wadi Cherith dries out and there is no food for the ravens to bring him, the word of the Lord comes again. It tells Elijah to leave the land of Israel and to go to Zarephath in Sidon. This place is more the proper land of Baal than of the Lord. It is a curious command that becomes even more curious. The word of the Lord says, "I have commanded a widow there to feed you." A widow should be the last place to seek food in a drought. Elijah demands food from her. She affirms the absurdity of God's command, announcing that she has nothing and that she is about to fix her last meal for herself and her son. Then the miraculous power of God changes the story. The jar of meal and jug of oil will not fail until rain comes again. It happens thus.

What do we do with a story like this? On the one hand, it can be read through the lens of Psalm 146 as a narrative affirmation of God's power to feed the hungry. We may not find situations today with much similarity to this story of the widow, but we can hunt for moments where we see and pray for God's power to feed. Beyond that simple move this story becomes hard to read. The main way God feeds the hungry is through the fertility of the land. Here the one who feeds has ceased to feed by way of the land. Furthermore, this God feeds the widow and her son only so that the widow can feed Elijah. There may be hints of divine compassion for the widow, but this seems somewhat secondary to God's primary desire to feed Elijah. Even that desire to feed Elijah seems secondary to God's desire to drive out the prophets of Baal and return Israel to proper worship of the Lord. The story leans more toward issues of divine power than divine compassion. It is significant that little is said about the depth of suffering in the land occasioned by God's withdrawing rain for three years. Furthermore, God does not return the rain until all the prophets of Baal are slaughtered in Wadi Kishon. The message is clear. Be faithful to the Lord, and the land will be blessed. Turn to other gods, and the land will withdraw its blessings.

It is hard to square this account of God with other images we have of God. For example, we might recall Jesus' insistence that God "makes his sun rise on the evil and on the good, and sends rain on the righteous and on the unrighteous" (Matt. 5:45). Yet this portrait of God in 1 Kings persists throughout the Bible and into our theologies and confessions today. We have before us a classic theological puzzle; it is an issue about which believers have long disagreed.

One comment about the larger narrative of 1 Kings might help. God's desire to turn Israel away from Baal and back to worship of the Lord need not be read as an instance of divine jealousy. It is the Lord, not Baal, who created heaven and earth, who causes the rain to fall and the sun to rise, who blesses people with the fertility of the land. Thus, the call to return to the Lord is a call to return to God's blessings.

This passage is also paired with Mark 12:38–44. There we read about scribes who "devour widows' houses." This concern for the fate of the widow fits with the final story of the widow and her son. The son dies or is dying, depending on how you read it. The widow accuses Elijah of causing the death of her son. The death of a widow's son is a familiar story in Scripture. We might recall the story of Elisha in 2 Kings 4:8–37 or the story of Jesus and the widow of Nain (Luke 7:11–17). All these stories build on the intensity of the tragedy of a widow, already bare and unprotected in the world, who is losing her only child. This story seems to have no purpose other than demonstrating God's compassion.

The large theological and historical narratives, in Scripture and outside of Scripture, have a way of overlooking and even devouring the powerless. Whatever its original purpose, 1 Kings 17:17–24 in its canonical form insists that in the midst of God's often terrifying relationship with the nations, God does not neglect the helpless widow and her son. There are many such voices in Scripture and theology that assert the claim of the innocent is more important and powerful than the heartless march of history.

LEWIS R. DONELSON

Proper 5 (Sunday between June 5 and June 11 Inclusive)

Psalm 146

[1]Praise the LORD!
Praise the LORD, O my soul!
[2]I will praise the LORD as long as I live;
  I will sing praises to my God all my life long.

[3]Do not put your trust in princes,
  in mortals, in whom there is no help.
[4]When their breath departs, they return to the earth;
  on that very day their plans perish.

[5]Happy are those whose help is the God of Jacob,
  whose hope is in the LORD their God,
[6]who made heaven and earth,
  the sea, and all that is in them;
who keeps faith forever;
  [7]who executes justice for the oppressed;
  who gives food to the hungry.

The LORD sets the prisoners free;
  [8]the LORD opens the eyes of the blind.
The LORD lifts up those who are bowed down;
  the LORD loves the righteous.
[9]The LORD watches over the strangers;
  he upholds the orphan and the widow,
  but the way of the wicked he brings to ruin.

[10]The LORD will reign forever,
  your God, O Zion, for all generations.
Praise the LORD!

Psalm 30

[1]I will extol you, O LORD, for you have drawn me up,
  and did not let my foes rejoice over me.
[2]O LORD my God, I cried to you for help,
  and you have healed me.
[3]O LORD, you brought up my soul from Sheol,
  restored me to life from among those gone down to the Pit.

[4]Sing praises to the LORD, O you his faithful ones,
  and give thanks to his holy name.
[5]For his anger is but for a moment;
  his favor is for a lifetime.
Weeping may linger for the night,
  but joy comes with the morning.

[6]As for me, I said in my prosperity,
"I shall never be moved."
[7]By your favor, O LORD,
you had established me as a strong mountain;
you hid your face;
I was dismayed.

[8]To you, O LORD, I cried,
and to the LORD I made supplication:
[9]"What profit is there in my death,
if I go down to the Pit?
Will the dust praise you?
Will it tell of your faithfulness?
[10]Hear, O LORD, and be gracious to me!
O LORD, be my helper!"

[11]You have turned my mourning into dancing;
you have taken off my sackcloth
and clothed me with joy,
[12]so that my soul may praise you and not be silent.
O LORD my God, I will give thanks to you forever.

Connecting the Psalm with Scripture and Worship

I have often wondered about the widow of Zarephath's prayers and her disposition toward God. Is she bitter as she gathers kindling for her last meal, or does she have that special strain of piety reserved for those who are nearing the end of this life? Whether she is disappointed or at peace in this moment, she epitomizes one "whose hope is in the LORD" her God (Ps. 146:5). This hope does not exempt her from the fragility of the human condition, but God proves faithful in times of distress and uncertainty—an idea the appointed psalms make quite clear. Psalms 146 and 30 provide a glimpse of the kind of faith that sustains the soul in the face of an ominous future. Preachers can easily explore this faith when preaching 1 Kings 17:8–24, but the task will require lingering on those points in the narrative where the resolution is uncertain. In the tension and ambiguity, a few compelling spiritual postures emerge, postures of adoration, trust, yearning, and protest.

First, contrary to what one might anticipate, both psalms begin with a posture of adoration (Ps. 146:1; 30:1). Adoration reminds the community of the proper relationship between creatures and the creator. Meditating on God's holiness and power brings awareness of one's smallness and finitude. As Susan J. Dunlap explains, "Finitude refers not only to bodily mortality and fragility but also to limited emotional capacity, limited abilities to understand or predict, limited powers to cure, limited control over what is most precious, limited capacity to adjust to new circumstances, limited power to protect the beloved."[1] In Psalm 146, the human finitude that is so often denied or resisted in contemporary North American culture is openly embraced: "I will praise the LORD *as long as I live*; / I will sing praises to my God *while I have my being*" (146:2 [translations by author]; NRSV "all my life long").

Life is too precious to be entrusted to another "child of earth" who may at any moment breathe a final breath and return to the earth (Ps. 146:2–3). Only God, the giver and sustainer of all life, is worthy of such trust. The widow of

1. Susan J. Dunlap, *Caring Cultures: How Congregations Respond to the Sick* (Waco, TX: Baylor University Press, 2009), 189–90.

Zarephath seems to know this, sensing that the Lord has brought her to the current moment of crisis (whether that crisis relates to hunger or her son's illness), and only God can be trusted with the future, whatever it may hold.

By sharing her last meal, the widow of Zarephath also demonstrates surprising generosity. One might expect a starving woman to hoard rather than share, but she is motivated by more than simple largesse; she seems to be driven by a different epistemology or way of knowing. Despite her duress, or perhaps because of it, she is willing to risk. Her generous act reveals an awareness of the limits of human knowledge and control. Psalm 146 makes a comparable point, noting that human "thoughts perish" (v. 4). Verses 7–8 of Psalm 30 also reveal the thinness of human knowledge and the shock of facing the limits of one's control. The preacher might similarly emphasize the limits of human knowledge and control and urge listeners to trust God. A posture of trust often requires being willing to move beyond what we know and face outcomes we cannot control. The preacher may underscore this idea by choosing a structure for the sermon that will move the listeners out of their typical listening patterns or ways of knowing.

Even if the widow of Zarephath has a degree of resignation as she gathers kindling for her last meal, she is not a wholly passive figure. She has a posture of yearning—yearning for her own life and that of her son. In Psalms 146 and 30, the Lord responds to human yearning with miracle. Tears and pleading seem to have a special power in prompting divine action (Ps. 30:2, 6, 9), but it also seems as though the experience of crisis is itself enough to stimulate God's response (Ps. 146:6–8). God does not stop at addressing the illness or material circumstance, but attends to the full depth of human need, bringing the soul from weeping to joy and from wailing to dancing (Ps. 30:6, 12). Psalms 30 and 146 are both anchored in miracle.

In fact, whether it is providing justice to the oppressed (146:7), food to the hungry (v. 7), release to captives (v. 7), or sight to the blind (v. 8), the LORD provides miracle after miracle. One thing that is striking about 1 Kings 17:8–24 is the multiple miracles: Elijah's discovery of the compassionate widow, her provision of water, her willingness to provide food despite her own destitution, the miraculous abundance experienced by her household after feeding Elijah, and her son's resurrection. Since Psalm 146 similarly attests to miracle after miracle, preachers may find it useful to massage this angle of the text. With spotlights on both the simple and dramatic miracles in the text, listeners may pick up on God's pattern of breaking in outside the horizon of human expectation in ways that are "miraculous," "impossible," and "inexplicable."[2]

God's provision continually expands our sense of what is possible, and this expansion is critical. Without this attention to God's power, the weak may appear to be utterly helpless. The postures of praise illustrated in Psalms 146 and 30 attune us to God's presence and action in the world. Psalm 146 includes explicit references to widows and orphans, prisoners, and the hungry, emphasizing God's concern for their protection. When we are preaching on 1 Kings 17:8–24, the widow of Zarephath's story should not be read in isolation but with attention to all who are widowed, orphaned, sick, and impoverished, and to the systems that perpetuate their suffering. In other words, the ethical imperatives of the story are paramount.

Hunger and poverty threaten the body but also chip away at a person's dignity. These psychological effects often prove much harder to resolve than the material effects. God's vision of human justice attends to physical needs as well as the inner life. This idea is illustrated in both Psalm 146 and Psalm 30: "The LORD lifts up those who are bowed down" (146:8) and "I will exalt you, O LORD, because you have lifted me up and have not let my enemies triumph over me" (30:1). Rooting out shame and restoring depressed spirits are essential dimensions of God's healing work and deserve attention alongside the other miracles in 1 Kings 17:8–24.

Ideally, the liturgy will emphasize the postures of adoration, trust, yearning, and protest that arise in the appointed psalms. Hymn

2. Walter Brueggemann, *The Psalms and the Life of Faith* (Minneapolis: Fortress, 1995), 40.

themes might emphasize God's surprising action, the limits of human power, and the need to trust God with the future. If Communion or Eucharist will be celebrated, it may help if the selected approach underscores the shared nature of the bread and the mutual need of those gathered to receive it. As for the communal prayers, petitions for the care and well-being of widows and orphans should also include pleas for their increased political voice, visibility, and ingenuity. The church has a heritage of learning from those who are weak in the eyes of the world, and the prayers should remind parishioners of this perspective. Ultimately, the songs, rituals, and prayers should make it clear that the church consists of widows, orphans, the sick, and others who, despite their station in life, know themselves to be entirely dependent on God's provision.

DONYELLE MCCRAY

Galatians 1:11–24

[11]For I want you to know, brothers and sisters, that the gospel that was proclaimed by me is not of human origin; [12]for I did not receive it from a human source, nor was I taught it, but I received it through a revelation of Jesus Christ.

[13]You have heard, no doubt, of my earlier life in Judaism. I was violently persecuting the church of God and was trying to destroy it. [14]I advanced in Judaism beyond many among my people of the same age, for I was far more zealous for the traditions of my ancestors. [15]But when God, who had set me apart before I was born and called me through his grace, was pleased [16]to reveal his Son to me, so that I might proclaim him among the Gentiles, I did not confer with any human being, [17]nor did I go up to Jerusalem to those who were already apostles before me, but I went away at once into Arabia, and afterwards I returned to Damascus.

[18]Then after three years I did go up to Jerusalem to visit Cephas and stayed with him fifteen days; [19]but I did not see any other apostle except James the Lord's brother. [20]In what I am writing to you, before God, I do not lie! [21]Then I went into the regions of Syria and Cilicia, [22]and I was still unknown by sight to the churches of Judea that are in Christ; [23]they only heard it said, "The one who formerly was persecuting us is now proclaiming the faith he once tried to destroy." [24]And they glorified God because of me.

Commentary 1: Connecting the Reading with Scripture

Galatians 1:11–24 begins Paul's autobiographical account of his call to ministry and his authority to preach the gospel. To reassert his preaching that salvation comes by faith in Jesus Christ and not by the works of the law, Paul must also reestablish his credibility as a messenger of God's revelation.

This section begins with Paul's reason for recalling his autobiography: to prove that his proclamation of the gospel of faith in Jesus Christ is from divine revelation and not from human beings (vv. 11–12). Paul is not a disciple of the original apostles; rather, he is a colleague in ministry whose apostolic authority is on par with these other pillars of the faith. Like them, Paul received his revelation directly from the source, the resurrected Lord and the Holy Spirit. In Acts 9:16 Jesus declares that he will be the one to show Paul, known at the time as Saul, how he must suffer for sake of the gospel. Almost immediately, he began to proclaim Jesus and quickly became increasingly powerful (see Acts 9:19, 22). Paul's account of his past life as a Pharisee and his call to the ministry of Jesus Christ proves his apostolic authority and credibility, and this illustrates his independence from the core group of apostles.

Paul confesses, with an element of boasting, about his zealous nature to spread the good news. Because of his devotion to the traditions of his ancestors, Paul advanced as a leader in the Pharisaic community, where he quickly surpassed many of his peers. Such swiftness in rising through the ranks suggests that Paul was zealous in observance of the statutes and ordinances as written in the law of Moses and of the traditions handed down among Pharisees. Additionally, Paul was committed to enforcing and even punishing those who did not follow the law. When believers of Jesus were seemingly eroding and perverting the traditions of Judaism, Paul pursued them with such force that he became a legend. His devotion and commitment to observing and protecting his traditions led to his violent pursuit and persecution of the church and his determination to destroy it.

Paul understands a life of pleasing others and seeking approval. His fast promotion in the ranks of Judaism indicates his political savvy and the need to ensure everyone's satisfaction with his words and deeds. However, Paul seemingly does not exercise this same political astuteness among his colleagues in the Jesus movement; in this new life, his focus is pleasing Christ (Gal. 1:10). In Galatia, his authority and credibility are undermined by other missionaries in the movement. Some scholars assert that Paul includes his autobiography as a response to a smear campaign designed to impugn him as a people pleaser, and to discredit the truth he proclaimed. Ironically, he goes from destroying the legacy of Jesus to preserving it. Paul becomes a zealot for the gospel of Jesus.

After recounting his commitment to the traditions of Judaism in his former life, Paul testifies to the authenticity of his message of the gospel of Jesus and of its divine source. He begins with his call story, asserting that God had set him apart before he was born (v. 15). This description echoes the call stories of Isaiah and Jeremiah. He recounts his call story using language similar to that found in the prophets Isaiah and Jeremiah. Both declare unequivocally that God called and consecrated them before they were born (Isa. 49:1; Jer. 1:5). Rhetorically, Paul presents himself as a vessel of God's word in the tradition of the ancient prophets.

Crucial to Paul's story is his reference to God's grace in calling him to preach among the Gentiles. When he retells the story of his former life as a zealous Pharisee, Paul shows the Galatians that it would be easy, if not natural, for him to proclaim the gospel while observing the Torah, but salvation through Christ does not require work; it requires faith. His former life served as a tool to help him advance the gospel of faith in Jesus, but it did not justify him before God. As a son of Abraham, Paul's call story foreshadows his later argument that asserts Abraham was justified by faith even before there *was* a Law (Gal. 3:6). Additionally, all who believe are descendants of Abraham (3:7). Through God's grace, the Gentiles, like Paul and even Abraham, are recipients of God's promises and salvation. Paul proclaims the gospel of faith among the Gentiles because he too received the Holy Spirit through faith, independent from his works of the Law.

Furthermore, Paul's call story furthers his argument that the revelation about which he preaches comes from God. He makes clear that God was pleased to reveal God's Son to him and that the revelation he received did not come from a human source. The gospel of faith is a not one of human creation. It is authentic and pure, untainted by word of mouth and tradition. As the gospel of Jesus supplemented by Torah observances is valid among believing, observant Jews, the gospel of faith in Jesus without observant piety is valid among the Gentiles. Although Paul's message is distinctive and somewhat divergent, it is an authentic revelation of God—as credible as, if not more credible than, the gospel preached by the leaders who received their revelation from the previous generation.

Additionally, Paul's direct revelation of Jesus from God makes his apostolic authority equal with the first generation of disciples, who were taught by Jesus himself. The content of his revelation was uninfluenced by "flesh and blood" (v. 16; NRSV "any human being"). Paul did not consult with any human beings or apostles upon receiving it. Instead, he immediately began his preaching ministry. The writer of Acts corroborates Paul's account. Within days after his encounter with Jesus on the way to Damascus, Paul entered synagogues to start his preaching ministry (Acts 9:20). Because his account does not note any in-person encounter or correspondence from the other apostles, one may assume that there was no objection to the gospel that he was preaching. Years later, Paul finally went to Jerusalem and briefly visited with apostles Cephas (the Greek name for Peter) and James. Even then, Paul does not receive either correction or rejection.

Across the regions, Paul's reputation preceded him. People knew him as the one who was formerly persecuting the churches and is now proclaiming the faith that he once tried to destroy. Because of the power and purpose of his preaching, the people glorified God. The revelation of Jesus transforms the staunchest critics and the most dangerous opponents.

By sharing his story, Paul testifies to the source of the gospel and offers evidence that others have believed in Jesus because of his preaching, so that the Galatians may regain their trust in him and his apostolic authority. The unconditional nature of God's amazing love was hard for people to believe then, and it is still hard for many to believe today. Even though this message may seem incredible, Paul proves that the true gospel of Jesus Christ was given to him through a divine revelation for all to hear, to believe, and to be reconciled unto God. As the epistolary lesson, it encourages current listeners that they may trust and believe Paul's words even now. For this, the people give glory to God.

BRIDGETT A. GREEN

Commentary 2: Connecting the Reading with the World

While the scandalous incarnation of Christ stands as one of history's most unexpected events, a case can be made that the Saul-to-Paul conversion is a solid runner-up. Could a more unlikely person have been chosen by God as principal architect of the Christian religion? Paul was a Pharisee fundamentalist who violently persecuted the new church. Paul's shocking shift to Christian apostleship might be akin to imagining an alt-right politico suddenly assuming leadership of the #blacklivesmatter movement. Why would God choose such a vengeful man to midwife Jesus' manifesto of love? What does it mean to follow such an unpredictable God?

The struggle was real for the Galatians. As our epistle commences, Paul bemoans the fact that alternative voices from both inside and outside the community have fomented unrest by challenging the very mission of the gospel. In his defense, Paul first reminds the Galatians of his unique resume, including the fact that his authority was not conferred by any human being or through the usual channels in Jerusalem, but by direct divine revelation. Paul's call was to proclaim a new way of living before God, which was justification through faith in Christ—over against the ancient edicts of Torah—a shift in orientation that was deemed by some as inadequate in determining righteousness (2:16). Many Jewish Christians in the community felt that incoming Gentiles and pagans should convert to Judaism as an additional requirement, including observing table rites and circumcision. Paul rebukes this demand not by disparaging Judaism but, rather, by unfurling God's new vision of salvation. This is an important distinction, and one worthy sermon direction might be to reflect on the ways in which Christians continue, intentionally and unintentionally, to reduce Judaism's rich covenant understanding to a mere "works" mentality, pitting Mosaic law against NT grace in a zero-sum game that has incited anti-Semitism for centuries. Following in the footsteps of the notorious Saul, we moderns remain consistent in our propensity to challenge Christ's message of unconditional grace with our rigid opinions of what constitutes right action and right belief. Like a funhouse mirror refracting and multiplying the same image a thousand ways, we cannot seem to shake our human tendency and desire to control God.

Accordingly, connecting Galatians 1:11–24 to our modern experience is of urgent importance today. Across the globe, the smoldering forces of religious zealotry stir up persecution and hate in many forms, from savage trolling on social media, to punitive political policy making, to violent jihadist bombings and beheadings. Raucous ideological debates—on topics such as the civil rights of LGBTQ persons, abortion, women's equality, and immigration—just to name a few—flood our airwaves and public squares with angry fumes, all in the name of Christ, just as other Christians have perhaps allowed the pendulum to swing too far in the opposite direction, allowing affirmations of universal and unexamined grace to discount the important process of sanctification. Our religious skirmishes are not unlike what stirred the pot in Galatia: what is required for righteousness? Paul's description of his own dark past encourages all believers to examine the many ways the name of Jesus has been weaponized as we rail against each other's mistakes and failings. As Barbara Brown Taylor once said, "As a general rule, I would say that human beings never behave more badly than when they believe they are protecting God."[1] Unchanged for two thousand years, then, is the fact that the gospel is like a fish bone stuck in the throat; it is God's unconditional love that we cannot swallow. If we have problems accepting our personal failures and flaws, we do not imagine that God can either.

Beyond this major theme of righteousness, another path for finding kinship with the text is afforded by the perspective that the passage of time gives us. How shattering and massive the Jesus revolution was! Who could blame the Galatians for craving a return to old ways and past stability (i.e., the "fleshpots of Egypt")? After initial awe in hearing the liberating gospel message, perhaps the Galatians found the stress of having to live into such groundbreaking change overwhelming, creating a yearning to circle back toward Jewish covenantal norms as ballast on the turbulent seas of change (3:3). It is a little like the disorientation we feel when our computer's operating system gets a major overhaul. We know it is an upgrade, but it takes some time to get used to it. Sometimes using the old, inferior system seems more appealing than adapting to the new.

As we traverse the changing landscape of American Protestantism today, many congregations will recognize the allure of "the good old days," when high-steepled churches on town greens represented a particular archetype of established, traditional Christendom. These days we feel disrupted and dislocated, causing us to question what in the world God is thinking, as the status quo crumbles to the ground. In this regard, a provocative sermon theme might be an exploration of a famous statement of theologian Walter Brueggemann: "The world for which you have been so carefully prepared is being taken away from you, by the grace of God."[2] What is God up to?

Our ability to recognize and embrace God's enthusiasm for invention is critical in these days. Confused by the pace and scope of change, today's congregations need to hear the word of hope being spoken to us by Scripture. Indeed, it is a joyful thing to worship a very "woke" God—that is, a most aware and in-tune God—who is ever creating new opportunities for human flourishing. Our Proper 5 lectionary collection paints multiple pictures of new life arising, from a resuscitation of the dead in Luke, to Elijah's encounter with the meager pantry of a widow in 1 Kings. Are we not sometimes like the widow in this passage, clinging to scarcity and dwindling supplies because we simply cannot imagine the bounty of God's benevolent care?

It might be fruitful to begin and end a sermon on Galatians 1:11–24 by acknowledging the role of surrender as both the struggle and triumph of faith. We have already noted the darker tendency of humans to temper or deny entirely the feeling of being out of control, by clinging to judgments about what might guarantee salvation and divine favor. Another reaction to unknowing might be simply summed up as a positive trust and openheartedness. In 1:12, Paul points to a personal, mystical encounter with the risen Christ beyond the handrails of tradition. Paul's reaction to God's big reveal was to go "at once" to Arabia, an exotic place and period of time in Paul's life that we know very little about—and perhaps that is the point. Divine nudges and directives often catapult recipients (Moses, Jesus, Paul, you, and me) into places of shadowy unknowing, which can manifest as lonely wilderness wandering as well as invigorating new adventures that elicit new passion and zeal. Following our ancestors in the faith, it is important that we too make space to discern the movement of the Spirit in our own hearts and communities. Beyond the safety of surety, beyond traditions and expectations, God the creator scans the horizon of uncharted ocean and points us forward, offering eternity.

SUZANNE WOOLSTON BOSSERT

1. Barbara Brown Taylor, *Leaving Church: A Memoir of Faith* (New York: HarperCollins, 2006), 106.

2. Cited in Barbara Brown Taylor, "Preaching into the Next Millenium," in *Exilic Preaching: Testimony for Christian Exiles in an Increasingly Hostile Culture*, ed. Erskine Clarke (Harrisburg, PA: Trinity Press International, 1998), 93.

Luke 7:11–17

[11]Soon afterwards he went to a town called Nain, and his disciples and a large crowd went with him. [12]As he approached the gate of the town, a man who had died was being carried out. He was his mother's only son, and she was a widow; and with her was a large crowd from the town. [13]When the Lord saw her, he had compassion for her and said to her, "Do not weep." [14]Then he came forward and touched the bier, and the bearers stood still. And he said, "Young man, I say to you, rise!" [15]The dead man sat up and began to speak, and Jesus gave him to his mother. [16]Fear seized all of them; and they glorified God, saying, "A great prophet has risen among us!" and "God has looked favorably on his people!" [17]This word about him spread throughout Judea and all the surrounding country.

Commentary 1: Connecting the Reading with Scripture

Luke himself gives us the clue to understanding the significance of Jesus' miraculous raising of the son of the widow of Nain. As is so often the case when Luke tells a story, he lets the chorus of witnesses declare the significance of what they have seen: "A great prophet has risen among us!" and "God has looked favorably on his people!" (Luke 7:16).

We have seen that Luke uses the stories that follow Jesus' Sermon on the Plain to make the claim that Jesus, who has great teaching authority, also has authority to do the acts of God for the healing of humankind. In Luke 7:1–10 Jesus has shown his ability to heal a slave who is "close to death." In Luke 7:11–17 he shows his ability to raise a child who is not only close to death, but simply and sadly is dead.

Of course, what Luke is trying to show is not Jesus' ability, but God's grace in using Jesus. For Luke, Jesus is the greatest of the prophets, God's own representative on earth. Luke does not make the explicit claim that Jesus is God incarnate (like John) or even God with us (like Matthew). Jesus is God's servant for the healing of the people. One sees this claim throughout Luke's Gospel, but perhaps especially when Jesus begins his ministry in Luke 4:18. Jesus opens the "scroll of the prophet" to claim the prophet's words and the prophet's vocation for himself: "The Spirit of the Lord is upon me, because he has anointed me to bring good news to the poor."

Compare Luke 7 to the story of Lazarus in John's Gospel. Jesus raises another dead man for the sake of those who love him. His proclamation there is close to a declaration of his own divinity: "I am the resurrection and the life" (John 11:25). (The phrase "I am" in John's Gospel draws on Exodus 3 and is itself a claim of divine authority.)

Luke does not claim in this story that Jesus is God, but that he is God's prophet. He does not claim that Jesus *is* resurrection, but that Jesus *works* resurrection.

As the Revised Common Lectionary suggests when it pairs this story with the story of Elijah's raising of a widow's son (1 Kgs. 17:8–24), Jesus stands in the line of the prophets.

The dilemma of the two widows is strikingly similar. Each loses a son, in Luke explicitly and in 1 Kings implicitly an only son. Each deals with almost unimaginable grief, and each faces the prospect of spending her last years without the financial and emotional support of children.

The story of Elijah makes clear what is easy to forget: the words of the prophets are illustrated and even enacted by the prophets' deeds. When the widow shows her gratitude to Elijah at the end of the story, she praises him with words that clearly mark him as a faithful prophet: "Now I know that you are a man of God, and that the word of the LORD in your mouth is truth" (1 Kgs. 17:24).

The epistolary reading for the day (Gal. 1:11–24) is probably more helpfully preached as the subject of its own sermon rather than brought into the conversation with Luke 7. If you want to make a connection between the two texts, you might note that the Galatians text represents Paul's story of his own call to be an apostle. He clearly understands his call as embodying the same kind of divine commission that motivated the prophets of the Hebrew Bible. Most directly these verses recall Jeremiah's call in the first chapter of the book of Jeremiah. While Luke sees Jesus as the greatest of the prophets, Paul sees himself as a prophet, but Jesus as something even more remarkable. Paul is the prophet who is called; Jesus is the Lord who calls him.

Sometimes the best way to interweave texts from the lectionary in a sermon is not by multiple attempts at exegesis but by allusion and rhetorical echo. Theologically Psalm 146 reminds us of the claim made by 1 Kings and Luke: it is the power of God and not the power of the greatest of mortals that finally can heal and redeem and even raise from the dead. Literarily there is a line in Psalm 146 whose language might resonate if you preach on the grief of either of the widows in today's lections:

> Do not put your trust in princes,
> in mortals, in whom there is no help.
> When their breath departs, they return to the earth;
> on that very day their plans perish.
> Ps. 146:3–4

Mortals' breath departs. They return to earth. Their plans perish as do the hopes of those who love them. The only hope in which we can live and die is in the Lord our God (Ps. 146:5).

Luke uses this passage to show that Jesus stands in the company of the prophets, and is in fact the greatest prophet of them all. He also uses this passage as a demonstration of the claims he makes throughout his writings about God's power over death.

The NT is consistent in its claim that God raised Christ from the dead and that in Jesus Christ God also promises life to the faithful. However, as Paul makes clear, the victory of God over death is a mystery (1 Cor. 15:51). The efforts of modern scholars notwithstanding, it should not surprise us that different NT writers have different ways of trying to explain the inexplicable.

Of course, when Jesus raises the son of the widow of Nain, he raises him only for his lifetime and not for eternity, but the language of

Into the Broad Daylight

Nothing is more amusing to the convert, when his conversion has been complete for some time, than to hear the speculations about when or whether he will repent of the conversion; when he will be sick of it, how long he will stand it, at what stage of his external exasperation he will start up and say he can bear it no more. For all this is founded on [an] optical illusion about the outside and the inside. . . . The outsiders stand by and see, or think they see, the convert entering with bowed head a sort of small temple which they are convinced is fitted up inside like a prison, if not a torture-chamber. But all they really know about it is that he has passed through a door. They do not know that he has not gone into the inner darkness, but out into the broad daylight. It is he who is, in the beautiful and beatific sense of the word, an outsider. He does not want to go into a larger room, because he does not know of any larger room to go into. He knows of a large number of much smaller rooms, each of which is labelled as being very large; but he is quite sure he would be cramped in any of them. Each of them professes to be a complete cosmos or scheme of all things. . . . Each of them is supposed to be domed with the sky or painted inside with all the stars. But each of these cosmic systems or machines seems to him much smaller and even much simpler than the broad and balanced universe in which he lives.

G. K. Chesterton, *The Catholic Church and Conversion* (New York: The MacMillan Company, 1926), 105.

our text quite clearly indicates a foreshadowing of Jesus' own resurrection and finally of the gift of resurrection for all believers. Translated rather woodenly, here is what Jesus says to the corpse of the young man: "Young man, I say to you, be raised" (7:14). In chapter 8 he will use the same verb to command Jairus's daughter, whose spirit has also departed: "Child, arise!" (8:54).

Later in Luke's Gospel it becomes clear that what Jesus promises is not just temporary resuscitation but final resurrection. The brigand on the cross asks the martyred prophet who is also the crucified Messiah: "Jesus, remember me when you come into your kingdom." Jesus replies: "Truly I tell you, today you will be with me in Paradise" (23:43).

Remember that those who first heard Luke's Gospel already knew the rest of Jesus' story. They had come not only to hear about a famous prophet but to celebrate the presence of a risen Lord. (Most likely, given the story of the meal at Emmaus, they had come to share bread and wine.) So when they hear the story of the widow's son and the story of Jairus's daughter and the story of the thief, they know that the one who delivers life to the children and promises Paradise to the thief has himself been made victorious over death. Those first listeners, our listeners too, look forward to the last chapter of this Gospel because they know what is coming. The goal of the story is also the ground of the story. The two bedazzling men tell the grieving women the good news, using exactly the same word Jesus used to bring life to the young man and the young woman, the same word that restored hope to Jairus and to the widow of Nain. "He has risen" (24:5).

DAVID L. BARTLETT

Commentary 2: Connecting the Reading with the World

Luke 7:11–17 follows Jesus' Sermon on the Plain (Luke 6:17–49). The event at Nain is the second of two miracles revealing Jesus as the embodiment of the new reality announced in the sermon. The miracle at Nain is a living example of the promise of Luke 6:21, "Blessed are you who weep now, for you will laugh."

A funeral is fitting for Ordinary Time. Death is proverbially certain. Into this ordinary event, though, floods extraordinary joy. Pastor Kimberleigh Buchanan catches this reversal nicely in her June 10, 2007, *Day1.org* sermon comparing the funeral at Nain to a New Orleans jazz burial. The somber, muted procession on the way toward the cemetery ends with a joyful street party! A dead man is raised, reminding us of Easter, which has charged every day with new possibilities.

This is the second of two consecutive case studies drawn from real life in which Luke shows that the Sermon on the Plain is more than empty promises. The first was the healing of the centurion's slave (7:1–10), which presents a politically connected military man whose faith in Jesus initiates the physical healing of his slave. The second presents the social healing of a powerless, vulnerable widow who takes no initiative and expresses no faith, yet receives her dead son back alive from a compassionate Jesus. In the first, Jesus praises human faith. In the second, humans praise God's compassion. Taken together, these miracles tell a larger story about the mysterious complexity of God working at ground level to bring the great reversal pledged in the Sermon on the Plain.

Elements of the liturgical rite of Christian baptism surface in the raising of the widow's son at Nain. Jesus walked up to the open coffin and touched it, accepting ritual uncleanness. He then said, "'Young man, I say to you, rise!' The dead man sat up and began to speak, and Jesus gave him to his mother" (vv. 14–15). Jesus made our baptism possible by touching our mortality, joining himself to our death, that we might be joined to his life. The baptized are those who were dead in sin, heard the word of God, and were raised to new life. They rise, proclaiming that Jesus is Lord—we may wonder what the resuscitated man spoke—and are returned to their rightful place in the arms of mother church to live in right relationship with the human community and all creation. Baptized Christians know existentially that the dead can hear and rise.

The people of God can also see themselves in the disciples and seekers who form the crowd who follow Jesus from Capernaum to Nain. As this lively, hopeful crowd nears the gates of the little town, they meet head-on another sort of crowd, one of sorrow and resignation with death at its center, untimely and devastating. Like two great waves advancing, these two crowds meet; and with a touch and a word from Jesus, the new wave of life turns back the old tide of death. In every age and circumstance, the church as the people of God witnesses by word and deed to the power of life over death in the most difficult of circumstances.

The church can see crucial aspects of its true calling in the motive and focus of this miracle as well. The motive is compassion. Its object is the widow.

The centurion's faith is central to performance of the miracle in Luke 7:1–10. Jesus' compassion is crucial to the miracle at Nain (v. 13). No one at Nain asks Jesus to do anything. No faith is required for healing. None is asked for or mentioned. Jesus acts solely out of the gut-wrenching compassion he feels for the wailing widow (*splanchna*, "entrails," is the root of the Greek word translated "had compassion").

Divine compassion is emphasized regularly in Luke's Gospel. The Samaritan's compassion motivates him to help the roadside victim (10:33 NASB). The prodigal father, "filled with compassion" (15:20), rushes to his wayward son. For the church to be the authentic people of God, divine compassion must be its prime motivation, as it was for Jesus at Nain.

The church is called to direct this compassion properly. The church that sees the rightful object of Jesus' compassion at Nain sees its own mission with more clarity. George Buttrick cautioned his students not to let an illustration swallow up the main point of a sermon, as the whale often swallows up preaching on Jonah. Likewise, the church dare not let its eagerness to proclaim Jesus' power over death distract it from its mission to the living, some of whom may think themselves better off dead. Compassion for the dead man is not what motivates Jesus; a woman left bereft of any survival safety net in a patriarchal culture *is*. Jesus "saw *her*, he had compassion for *her* and said to *her*, 'Do not weep'" (v. 13, italics added). He raised her son so she might have him back (v. 15). Jesus raised the departed to restore the family and community relationships of the one left behind. Might that be why the baptized are raised to new life on earth?

Internet images of this story suggest that much Christian visual art misses this point. The son stands at the center of most representations—not the widow, who is the center of Jesus' framework. Is the church expressing its own fear of death when it makes personal salvation the centerpiece of its proclamation? Does the church share God's perspective if it places the desperate poor on the margins or outside the frame of its worldview? Biological death is normal and universal. Social death is sinful. Jesus delays the former to address the latter. The church is called to confront the forces tearing apart the families and social support systems of the poor and vulnerable.

Divine compassion of the kind shown to the widow at Nain connects Christianity and Islam. It is crucial to the ethics of each religion. Compassion is a central divine attribute of God in the Qur'an. It appears in the second verse of the first chapter in a phrase called the *basmalah*, "In the name of God, Full of Compassion, Ever Compassionate,"[1] and in all the additional 113 chapters, save one. Muslims are encouraged to recite the *basmalah* before they begin an action as a reminder to embody this divine compassion within themselves and their conduct.[2] The 138 Muslim leaders who signed the 2007 letter "A Common Word between Us and You" called the compassionate in both faiths to start religious dialogue around this shared value.

1. *The Qur'an: Books that Changed the World*, trans. Bruce Lawrence (London: Atlantic Books, 2006), 201.
2. Mohamed Imran and Mohamed Taib, "The Central Role of Compassion in Muslim Ethics," *Dialogosphere* (March 6, 2016), http://www.islamicity.org/9990/the-central-role-of-compassion-in-muslim-ethics/.

Luke 7:11–17, alongside Jesus' warnings in Luke 6:37–38 against judging others, can inform the ways adherents of the Qur'an and the Bible divide, as Thomas Berry puts it, into "those who appoint themselves as agents of divine anger, and those who understand themselves as called to be agents of divine mercy."[3] Jesus' prophetic action at Nain ends with him hailed as a prophet, but also foreshadows his resurrection, made necessary by his compassion for outsiders, also foreshadowed in 1 Kings 17:17–24 and Luke 4:26–27.

WM. LOYD ALLEN

3. Thomas Berry, Introduction, *My Mercy Encompasses All*, comp. Reza Shah-Kazemi (Berkeley, CA: Shoemaker & Howard, 2007), x.

Proper 6 (Sunday between June 12 and June 18 Inclusive)

1 Kings 21:1–10 (11–14), 15–21a and
2 Samuel 11:26–12:10, 13–15
Psalm 5:1–8 and Psalm 32
Galatians 2:15–21
Luke 7:36–8:3

1 Kings 21:1–10 (11–14), 15–21a

[1]Later the following events took place: Naboth the Jezreelite had a vineyard in Jezreel, beside the palace of King Ahab of Samaria. [2]And Ahab said to Naboth, "Give me your vineyard, so that I may have it for a vegetable garden, because it is near my house; I will give you a better vineyard for it; or, if it seems good to you, I will give you its value in money." [3]But Naboth said to Ahab, "The LORD forbid that I should give you my ancestral inheritance." [4]Ahab went home resentful and sullen because of what Naboth the Jezreelite had said to him; for he had said, "I will not give you my ancestral inheritance." He lay down on his bed, turned away his face, and would not eat.

[5]His wife Jezebel came to him and said, "Why are you so depressed that you will not eat?" [6]He said to her, "Because I spoke to Naboth the Jezreelite and said to him, 'Give me your vineyard for money; or else, if you prefer, I will give you another vineyard for it'; but he answered, 'I will not give you my vineyard.'" [7]His wife Jezebel said to him, "Do you now govern Israel? Get up, eat some food, and be cheerful; I will give you the vineyard of Naboth the Jezreelite."

[8]So she wrote letters in Ahab's name and sealed them with his seal; she sent the letters to the elders and the nobles who lived with Naboth in his city. [9]She wrote in the letters, "Proclaim a fast, and seat Naboth at the head of the assembly; [10]seat two scoundrels opposite him, and have them bring a charge against him, saying, 'You have cursed God and the king.' Then take him out, and stone him to death." [11]The men of his city, the elders and the nobles who lived in his city, did as Jezebel had sent word to them. Just as it was written in the letters that she had sent to them, [12]they proclaimed a fast and seated Naboth at the head of the assembly. [13]The two scoundrels came in and sat opposite him; and the scoundrels brought a charge against Naboth, in the presence of the people, saying, "Naboth cursed God and the king." So they took him outside the city, and stoned him to death. [14]Then they sent to Jezebel, saying, "Naboth has been stoned; he is dead."

[15]As soon as Jezebel heard that Naboth had been stoned and was dead, Jezebel said to Ahab, "Go, take possession of the vineyard of Naboth the Jezreelite, which he refused to give you for money; for Naboth is not alive, but dead." [16]As soon as Ahab heard that Naboth was dead, Ahab set out to go down to the vineyard of Naboth the Jezreelite, to take possession of it.

[17]Then the word of the LORD came to Elijah the Tishbite, saying: [18]Go down to meet King Ahab of Israel, who rules in Samaria; he is now in the vineyard of Naboth, where he has gone to take possession. [19]You shall say to him, "Thus says the LORD: Have you killed, and also taken possession?" You shall say to him, "Thus says the LORD: In the place where dogs licked up the blood of Naboth, dogs will also lick up your blood."

[20]Ahab said to Elijah, "Have you found me, O my enemy?" He answered, "I have found you. Because you have sold yourself to do what is evil in the sight of the LORD, [21]I will bring disaster on you."

2 Samuel 11:26–12:10, 13–15

[26]When the wife of Uriah heard that her husband was dead, she made lamentation for him. [27]When the mourning was over, David sent and brought her to his house, and she became his wife, and bore him a son.

But the thing that David had done displeased the LORD, [12:1]and the LORD sent Nathan to David. He came to him, and said to him, "There were two men in a certain city, the one rich and the other poor. [2]The rich man had very many flocks and herds; [3]but the poor man had nothing but one little ewe lamb, which he had bought. He brought it up, and it grew up with him and with his children; it used to eat of his meager fare, and drink from his cup, and lie in his bosom, and it was like a daughter to him. [4]Now there came a traveler to the rich man, and he was loath to take one of his own flock or herd to prepare for the wayfarer who had come to him, but he took the poor man's lamb, and prepared that for the guest who had come to him." [5]Then David's anger was greatly kindled against the man. He said to Nathan, "As the LORD lives, the man who has done this deserves to die; [6]he shall restore the lamb fourfold, because he did this thing, and because he had no pity."

[7]Nathan said to David, "You are the man! Thus says the LORD, the God of Israel: I anointed you king over Israel, and I rescued you from the hand of Saul; [8]I gave you your master's house, and your master's wives into your bosom, and gave you the house of Israel and of Judah; and if that had been too little, I would have added as much more. [9]Why have you despised the word of the LORD, to do what is evil in his sight? You have struck down Uriah the Hittite with the sword, and have taken his wife to be your wife, and have killed him with the sword of the Ammonites. [10]Now therefore the sword shall never depart from your house, for you have despised me, and have taken the wife of Uriah the Hittite to be your wife. . . . [13]David said to Nathan, "I have sinned against the LORD." Nathan said to David, "Now the LORD has put away your sin; you shall not die. [14]Nevertheless, because by this deed you have utterly scorned the LORD, the child that is born to you shall die." [15]Then Nathan went to his house.

The LORD struck the child that Uriah's wife bore to David, and it became very ill.

Commentary 1: Connecting the Reading with Scripture

The narratives comprising the Elijah cycle appear in 1 Kings 17–19, 1 Kings 21, and 2 Kings 1–2. They are set within the ninth-century reign of King Ahab. As ruler of the northern kingdom of Israel, Ahab's reputation is captured best in 1 Kings 16:30: "Ahab son of Omri did evil in the sight of the LORD more than all who were before him." The defining act to Ahab's evil reign was his Baal worship—a religious practice he shared with his Phoenician wife Jezebel (1 Kgs. 16:31). In typical Deuteronomistic fashion, the rise of an evil monarch necessitated a divine response through a divinely appointed prophet. For King Ahab's reign, Elijah the Tishbite was the designated prophet to speak on behalf of the God of Israel.

As in previous encounters with Ahab, God prompts Elijah in 1 Kings 21 to speak a word of judgment against the king. Different from Elijah's religious critique in 1 Kings 18:18, his message to King Ahab concerned the abuse of power, specifically, murder and unjust land annexation (1 Kgs. 21:17–19). According to the monarchical record, the victim of imperial-sanctioned violence was Naboth, an established Jezreelite viticulturist.

The report begins in verse 1 with details of names and locations: "Naboth the Jezreelite had a vineyard in Jezreel, beside the palace of King Ahab of Samaria." Here, specifying the people and their locations instead of time frame sets the focal points for the report. The location is a borderland defined by Naboth's family vineyard on one side, and Ahab's royal palace on the other. These two domains represent two contrasting worlds: commoner and royalty, household and city-state, labor and luxury. As with other monarchies in the region (e.g., Egypt and Assyria), the governing vision of King Ahab is imperial expansion: "Give me your vineyard, so that I may have it for a vegetable garden" (v. 2). This impulse to possess is predicated on Ahab's seeing difference as a *thing* to be appropriated rather than a *person* to be appreciated. In other words, for Ahab, the difference is between vineyard and vegetable garden, both inanimate objects void of social context. His impulse to possess is less about Naboth than about the object of his desire, the vineyard. King Ahab fails to see the person living on the land—indeed a depersonalizing move that breeds acts of violence against Naboth and his family.

Before mayhem and murder, however, Ahab attempts to acquire Naboth's land by appealing to his notion of the "good" (*tov*), which for some readers may appear fair and generous. With the royal treasury at his disposal, King Ahab offers Naboth two "good" options, a better vineyard or money. His appeal to money assumes that Naboth follows the same value system, in which the ultimate "good" in life is financial gain. Naboth rejects Ahab's notion of the "good," preferring instead to honor God by staying on his ancestral land: "the LORD forbid that I should give you my ancestral inheritance" (v. 3). Here land is intimately linked to ancestral memory, whereby vineyards embody familial dreams, hopes, and joys. According to the regulations and customs concerning ancestral inheritance, Naboth has a duty to maintain ancestral lands and then pass them on to his own children (Num. 27:1–11; 36:1–12).[1] Hence rather than a commodity, Naboth treats his land as a sacred heritage site of God's blessing and family relationships. This may lead readers to imagine the family memories made over the years on Naboth's vineyard, in which particular spots marked moments of celebration or sorrow.

After Naboth rejects King Ahab's notion of the good, the king returns home depressed. His depression bespeaks a mental condition that renders him unfit for leadership. Such is the result of desires that are solely object-driven, for they find fulfillment only in objects and not in people. Afterwards, his wife Jezebel responds to his predicament by pledging to him, "I will give you the vineyard of Naboth the Jezreelite" (v. 7). Using Ahab's royal seal, she mandates a religious fast for the people of Naboth's city. It is important to note how oppressive power makes use of a religious practice to achieve nefarious ends. In more recent times, modern states have found religious institutions like the church to be ideal instruments for accomplishing particular economic, political, or social agendas. Unknown to Naboth are the "two scoundrels" functioning as imperial agents within an officially gathered religious assembly. Their task is to bring a false charge against Naboth, which to the benefit of the king is ultimately punishable by death. What appears to be a familiar religious gathering is instead a hotbed of collusion and conspiracy, all of which lead to Naboth's unjust execution. With him dead, the monarchy proceeds with its annexation agenda, taking hold of Naboth's vineyard with impunity.

It is here that the prophetic word offers a sharp critique of insidious imperial power. Two actions stand out in God's judgment of King Ahab: He kills Naboth, and then he takes possession of his land (v. 19). Although these acts are on the surface performed legally, they hinge on forgery, setup, and false witness. Rather than investigate the details of Naboth's death, King Ahab stays silent and obligingly takes possession of his land. Hence, in God's eyes the crime ultimately falls on the king, in large part because the injustice occurs within his leadership domain. As the chief steward of divine justice, King Ahab prefers to foster corruption; as the prophet Elijah

1. Patrick T. Cronauer, *The Stories about Naboth the Jezreelite: A Source, Composition, and Redaction Investigation of 1 Kings 21 and Passages in 2 Kings 9* (New York: T&T Clark International, 2005), 117.

proclaims, "You have sold yourself to do what is evil in the sight of the LORD" (v. 20).

Critiquing power structures of injustice is not always as straightforward in the Hebrew Bible. Indeed, 2 Samuel 12 reflects a different rhetorical strategy whereby the prophet Nathan critiques King David. Before addressing King David's evil, Nathan uses a parable about a rich man stealing livestock from a poor man, as a first step to addressing David's own crimes against Uriah the Hittite and his wife Bathsheba. For Elijah and Nathan, speaking to power may occur through different rhetorical strategies. In the end, they both achieve their intended result—to transform the hearts of their respective kings and turn them to God.

In the current world, the abuse of power by rulers, governments, nation-states, and other formal power structures seems to be a never-ending reality. Yet in tandem with corrupt power we also discover a prophetic response that effects genuine social change. Similar to Elijah and Nathan, the prophetic message is not void of details; rather it embodies a critical awareness on how corrupt power is operating on both the macro and micro levels. With the goal of the transformation of oppressive power, the prophetic message is such because the prophet refuses to compromise on knowing and communicating the detailed operations of unjust power structures. Conversely, oppressive regimes often show the same sophistication by using complex bureaucracies and networks of affiliation to achieve their purposes. Hence, to assume the prophetic role, at least in the biblical sense, the preacher is willing to be both social critic and spiritual guide.

GREGORY L. CUÉLLAR

Commentary 2: Connecting the Reading with the World

The narratives of two rulers whose unchecked desires inspire deception and even murder confront us with enduring dynamics of greed, duplicity, consequence, and—surprisingly—mercy. While the texts differ regarding the exchange and the ruler's relationship with his victim, both point us to the temptations of power, the reality of suffering under acquisitive logics, and the necessity of reclaiming the moral center of our personhood and our communal systems.

In 1 Kings 21, Ahab desires the adjacent vineyard of Naboth and makes what seems to Ahab to be a perfectly reasonable offer: another better vineyard elsewhere or its equivalent monetary worth. Naboth balks at giving up his ancestral inheritance, and this rejection sends Ahab into dramatic despair—a despair so theatrical that the reader may question why a convenient vegetable garden is so important. But this is a story more about power than proximate healthy food. In this melodrama his wife, Jezebel, reminds him that no one should deny the desires of one who governs Israel, and so she colludes with leaders in Jezreel to have Naboth stoned for blasphemy. In the end, without so much as a question, Ahab takes possession of Naboth's vineyard, willfully ignorant of just how he got his spoils.

Here we see how acquisitive power functions, as Ahab displays a common market logic. Naboth rejects that approach, instead upholding his and his family's land-anchored identity: he/they/it is not merely an exchangeable commodity. Yet in ways that echo into the present, those who do not conform to dominant economic logics are often cast as irrational, even framed as morally or spiritually problematic. Powerful people, nations, and organizations have a long history of seizing lands from indigenous communities, family farmers, and poor communities through appeals to varied logics (e.g., manifest destiny, colonization, corporate scalability, eminent domain, and gentrification) that pay little attention to the vibrant fabric and faithfulness of those grounded in a different sense of place and community.

YHWH sends the prophet Elijah to uphold Naboth's logic and to pronounce God's judgment on the abuse and death of this peasant. In fact, Elijah marches up to Ahab on the stolen ground and tells him he has sold himself to evil, and the consequences will be felt for generations. While not many of us see ourselves in

By Grace You Have Been Saved!

You probably all know the legend of the rider who crossed the frozen Lake of Constance by night without knowing it. When he reached the opposite shore and was told whence he came, he broke down, horrified. This is the human situation when the sky opens and the earth is bright, when we may hear: *By grace you have been saved!* In such a moment we are like that terrified rider. When we hear this word we involuntarily look back, do we not, asking ourselves: Where have I been? Over an abyss, in mortal danger! What did I do? The most foolish thing I ever attempted! What happened? I was doomed and miraculously escaped and now I am safe! You ask: "Do we really live in such danger?" Yes, we live on the brink of death. But we have been saved. Look at our Savior and at our salvation! Look at Jesus Christ on the cross, accused, sentenced and punished instead of us! Do you know for whose sake he is hanging there? For *our* sake—because of *our* sin—sharing *our* captivity—burdened with *our* suffering! He nails *our* life to the cross. This is how God had to deal with *us*. From this darkness he has saved *us*. He who is not shattered after hearing this news may not yet have grasped the word of God: *By grace you have been saved!*

Karl Barth (1886–1968), "Saved by Grace," in *Deliverance to the Captives* (New York: Harper & Bros.; London: SCM, 1961), 38.

the role of the king, the Scripture compels us to ask about the ways in which we are willing to sell ourselves or lose our moral center in order to possess what we think we deserve. Moreover, we are reminded of how often we allow others to do our moral dirty work so we can have what we desire. Ahab relies on hidden systems that serve his selfish ends and never asks questions that would expose the oppression. How might this relate to our relative power in the political economy? What death-dealing dynamics do we ignore (e.g., sweatshops, environmental degradation, unfair tax codes) in order to obtain what we want, with a relatively clean conscience?

These questions are important, in part, also to challenge many of the common interpretations that focus on the corrupting wiles of Jezebel. The character of Jezebel has a long cultural history as one who entices her king to idolatry, crafts the deception and death of Naboth, and uses her sexuality to try to avoid death. Sermons, movies, literature, and visual art continually warn against the temptations of a "Jezebel." We may wish to pause and ask why there is far more cultural obsession with the Jezebel archetype than with Ahab. Ahab aligns with the princess from Phoenicia for political power, embraces varied religious practices to uphold his power, and allows others to do his dirty work while he enjoys the spoils. The Ahab archetype can represent a willful ignorance of responsibility combined with a fragile masculinity that often encourages or requires a more dependent woman to protect his ego. While we must not underestimate Jezebel's moral agency, and thus not ignore her moral culpability in the narrative, we should ask why we spend more time identifying and reprimanding supposed Jezebels than confronting the moral purity and gendered power dynamics of Ahabs.

In 2 Samuel, once again the arrogant desire for something one should not have diffuses a moral center. David's lust for Uriah's wife, Bathsheba, develops from a self-referential morality that assumes he is powerful enough, his masculinity ample enough, that he will take what he wants with ease and impunity. Uriah's faithfulness does not exempt him from the limitless greed of the seemingly noble one. Although arrogant power certainly leads to David's adultery, we should also notice how his need to avoid the exposure of his sin escalates his behavior. Moral panic often leads to more costly consequences for whole communities surrounding a person. Politicians create draconian social policies as distractions from their own moral failings. Deception in an intimate relationship slowly feeds a cycle of criticizing and demeaning a partner. Preserving the moral facade, at all costs, is the costliest of sins, because it fundamentally assumes that we are beyond the gaze, accountability, and *redemption* of God.

This ultimate break from God is precisely when God sends prophets to poke holes in false morality and reminds us of the greater redemptive path. God's prophetic invitation may come in the form of Elijah's blunt confrontation or the subtler parabolic teaching of Nathan. The juxtaposition asks us to consider, as an ecclesial community and as individuals called to prophetic speech, what kind of word someone needs to hear to dissipate a moral mask. What is our strategy for social change and theological transformation? Who stands before us, in their particular social/historical circumstance? What do they need to hear and how do they need to hear it?

The parable of the poor man's ewe and the parasitic hospitality of the rich man invites David to remember his moral core, to regain a sense of righteous (i.e., right-making) anger. Nathan narrates David into a story that evokes real confession; David could have simply continued his moral panic and killed Nathan. David finally understands that his very existence and meaning depend on understanding himself in relation to YHWH. With this recognition, YHWH shows some mercy in sparing David's life, even if his firstborn with Uriah's wife will not receive the same. The redemptive power of confession does not bring instant perfection or restoration. Rather, God's mercy offers continued life to pursue ongoing reconciliation with God and others.

In the end, we encounter these stories of abetted greed, power, and prophetic confrontation and confession during Ordinary Time in the Christian calendar, where we focus on the challenge and gift of forming faithful communities. Readers in the United States may also notice that these passages occur close to a high holy day in the liturgical calendar of civil religion, July Fourth or Independence Day. The lessons on governance and corrupted piety are especially poignant in a country that has often seen itself as a moral standard-bearer for the world. The Scriptures invite us to think more about our role as Christian disciples: In what ways will we claim YHWH's alternative moral logic and value our communities, land, and sense of integrity? In what ways are we called to speak prophetic truth to death-dealing systems of power? In what ways are we called to confession and recognition of the ways "saving face" actually ruptures relationships more deeply? Finally, in what ways will God remind us today that the peasant, the faithful husband, and even the humbled ruler are not outside God's relentless redemption?

C. MELISSA SNARR

Psalm 5:1–8

[1]Give ear to my words, O LORD;
give heed to my sighing.
[2]Listen to the sound of my cry,
my King and my God,
for to you I pray.
[3]O LORD, in the morning you hear my voice;
in the morning I plead my case to you, and watch.

[4]For you are not a God who delights in wickedness;
evil will not sojourn with you.
[5]The boastful will not stand before your eyes;
you hate all evildoers.
[6]You destroy those who speak lies;
the LORD abhors the bloodthirsty and deceitful.

[7]But I, through the abundance of your steadfast love,
will enter your house,
I will bow down toward your holy temple
in awe of you.
[8]Lead me, O LORD, in your righteousness
because of my enemies;
make your way straight before me.

Psalm 32

[1]Happy are those whose transgression is forgiven,
whose sin is covered.
[2]Happy are those to whom the LORD imputes no iniquity,
and in whose spirit there is no deceit.

[3]While I kept silence, my body wasted away
through my groaning all day long.
[4]For day and night your hand was heavy upon me;
my strength was dried up as by the heat of summer.

[5]Then I acknowledged my sin to you,
and I did not hide my iniquity;
I said, "I will confess my transgressions to the LORD,"
and you forgave the guilt of my sin.

[6]Therefore let all who are faithful
offer prayer to you;
at a time of distress, the rush of mighty waters
shall not reach them.
[7]You are a hiding place for me;
you preserve me from trouble;
you surround me with glad cries of deliverance.

[8]I will instruct you and teach you the way you should go;
I will counsel you with my eye upon you.
[9]Do not be like a horse or a mule, without understanding,
whose temper must be curbed with bit and bridle,
else it will not stay near you.

[10]Many are the torments of the wicked,
but steadfast love surrounds those who trust in the LORD.
[11]Be glad in the LORD and rejoice, O righteous,
and shout for joy, all you upright in heart.

Connecting the Psalm with Scripture and Worship

Justo González laments the fact that those who are weak in this world have few opportunities to address the powerful.[1] The lections this week provide a rare flip of the social script. God gives the slain a voice by using prophets to bring their cases to light. In doing so, God emerges as the omniscient judge who sees through corrupt schemes designed to conceal the murder of the innocent. Dramatic revelations and indictments reveal YHWH as the hope of the righteous and offer assurance that human suffering has a divine witness. Ultimately, this week's readings emphasize God's role as righteous judge and reader of human hearts.

Greed, lust, and abuse of power take center stage in the stories about the murders of Naboth and Uriah. In both narratives, the innocent fall prey to the powerful and press an urgent question that runs through much of the Psalter: what is the destiny of the righteous in light of all the power held by the wicked?[2] Naboth and Uriah figure as almost angelic in their innocence. Their deaths become all the more revolting, even obscene, when one remembers that they were murdered by leaders charged with the responsibility of caring for and protecting their citizenry. The stories are disturbing because the righteous seem so outmatched by the wicked.

Psalm 5 suggests the righteous have an invaluable resource in God's listening ear. God hears the voice of the righteous early in the morning, listening not only to the words but to the urgency behind them (v. 3). "Listen to the sound of my cry, my King and my God, for to you I pray" (v. 2). This petition comes from one who worships YHWH as king. In contrast, the psalmist's enemies, the "bloodthirsty and deceitful," serve the gods of their own appetites and are willing to sacrifice the innocent along the way (v. 6). When preachers explore the stories about Naboth and Uriah, the idolatry that drives the murders should not be ignored. The arrogance and narcissism that corrupt David, Ahab, and Jezebel are as dangerous as their actions. Listeners who cannot imagine murdering another human being will probably be able to identify with covetousness and lust and may be prone to minimizing their damaging effects. Ideally, the sermon will somehow prompt listeners to examine their hearts and create a longing for prayer.

Psalm 5 provides an opportunity to overhear the prayer of someone who, like Naboth and Uriah, feels overwhelmed by the forces of evil in the world and finds prayer to be the only forum where a fair hearing is possible.[3] While the petitions in Psalm 5 may seem unremarkable, they have tremendous influence. The pleas and complaints come before a righteous judge who listens attentively and is moved with compassion. In this tenderness, God metes out a level of justice that exceeds what is possible in the

1. Justo González and Catherine González, *The Liberating Pulpit* (Nashville: Abingdon, 1994; Eugene, OR: Wipf & Stock, 2003), 67.
2. Jerome F. D. Creach, "The Destiny of the Righteous and the Theology of the Psalms," in *Soundings in the Theology of Psalms: Perspectives and Methods in Contemporary Scholarship*, ed. Rolf A. Jacobson (Minneapolis: Fortress, 2011), 49–61.
3. Walter Brueggemann, *Psalms and the Life of Faith,* ed. Patrick D. Miller (Minneapolis: Fortress Press, 1995), 220–21.

natural order. The union between God and the righteous is even strong enough to survive death and prompts a confrontation with any mortal who dares to disrupt that union. When Elijah and Nathan raise their voices, they echo the Lord's accusing question for Cain: "What have you done? Listen; your brother's blood is crying out to me from the ground!" (Gen. 4:10). The prophets know that Naboth and Uriah have agency even in their victimization, and a sermon that acknowledges this dynamic will likely empower listeners and encourage them to pray.

When God gives voice to the slain by bringing their hidden suffering to light, the truth can be devastating. David and Ahab wither when confronted by the God who "dwells in unapproachable light" (1 Tim. 6:16). David's response is alarmingly desperate. Here Psalm 32 offers the preacher a helpful question to consider: How can we have hope if we have sinned in a way that has caused immense, irreparable suffering? The reality may seem too much to bear. Members of the congregation who are prone to feeling guilty may have limited tolerance for divine rebuke and, like the psalmist, experience the weight of the Lord's hand (Ps. 32:4). Affirming God's mercy will be essential. Thankfully, the righteous judge has the miraculous ability to balance justice for Uriah with mercy for David. While there is no bliss in the texts, Psalm 32 urges the preacher to offer a subtle glimpse into the future when rejoicing will be possible again (v. 11). Along this line, Psalm 32 cautions the preacher against an approach that saddles listeners with guilt or inhibits the forward movement that David's epiphany is intended to spark.

When David's episode with Nathan is read in light of Psalm 32, it becomes clear that one aim of the narrative is to complicate our estimation of righteousness. The moniker of "righteous" includes those who faithfully serve the Lord, as well as those who fall short but are humble enough to acknowledge their sin and repent. The lections encourage listeners to have supple hearts and pliant wills. Such a disposition is in sharp contrast to the "horse or mule," one "whose temper must be curbed with bit and bridle, else it will not stay near you" (Ps. 32:9). There is good news in the reminder that God is the hope of the righteous as well as the wicked, merciful enough to lead a person from evil to moral purity.

The appointed psalms have the potential to inform the liturgy in dramatic ways. First, the psalms suggest a role for the voices of the oppressed. Perhaps the simplest approach would involve allowing their voices to shape the communal prayers or using them to ground a litany. It would be even better if the congregation could sense the pathos of a song like "Nobody Knows the Trouble I've Seen" or "I'll Fly Away," provided these songs can be incorporated in the liturgy with integrity. African American spirituals articulate the hopes and fears of the oppressed incredibly well. Including one might allow additional historical and contemporary implications of the lections to emerge.

While Christian liturgy should direct people's attention to God and affirm God's sovereignty, this task also requires dethroning competing gods like violence, money, and possessions that hold many Christians captive. Naming these tendencies in the songs and prayers may sensitize worshipers to the plight of the Uriahs and Naboths throughout the world who bear the cost of Western greed. If Communion or Eucharist is celebrated, worship leaders can draw lines between Naboth and Uriah to Jesus.

The appointed psalms have dimensions that might be read over if recited in unison or responsively. Chanting them may prove more fruitful, but including jazz or instrumental interpretations of the psalms will provide the best means of bringing the urgency and tonal shifts to light. The psalm could be recited with alternating musical interludes in order to sound out the dialogical elements or entrusted entirely to a musician for interpretation. If having the congregation speak in unison is essential, the first lesson holds tremendous promise. Rarely do the lessons provide such theatrical lines as, "You are the man!" or "Give me your vineyard." Let the congregation hold forth.

DONYELLE MCCRAY

Galatians 2:15–21

[15]We ourselves are Jews by birth and not Gentile sinners; [16]yet we know that a person is justified not by the works of the law but through faith in Jesus Christ. And we have come to believe in Christ Jesus, so that we might be justified by faith in Christ, and not by doing the works of the law, because no one will be justified by the works of the law. [17]But if, in our effort to be justified in Christ, we ourselves have been found to be sinners, is Christ then a servant of sin? Certainly not! [18]But if I build up again the very things that I once tore down, then I demonstrate that I am a transgressor. [19]For through the law I died to the law, so that I might live to God. I have been crucified with Christ; [20]and it is no longer I who live, but it is Christ who lives in me. And the life I now live in the flesh I live by faith in the Son of God, who loved me and gave himself for me. [21]I do not nullify the grace of God; for if justification comes through the law, then Christ died for nothing.

Commentary 1: Connecting the Reading with Scripture

In order to appreciate the theological richness of Galatians 2:15–21, this text must be situated in a larger literary and historical context. Galatians 2:1–10 recounts events surrounding the Jerusalem conference, a historic event in early Christianity.

The influx of Gentiles into early Christianity occasioned a dilemma. Should Jewish Christians accept Gentile (male) believers without requiring circumcision? Early Christian leaders convened at the Jerusalem conference in approximately 49 CE to address this question. The Jerusalem meeting mentioned in Galatians 2 corresponds with Luke's depiction of the Jerusalem conference in Acts 15, despite some differing details in the two accounts.

According to Galatians 2:1–10, at the Jerusalem conference, Paul defended his missionary tactic of not requiring Gentile converts to be circumcised. Others spoke of God's work among the Gentiles, too, and their approach persuaded the Jerusalem leaders. They agreed that male Gentile converts did not have to be circumcised. At the meeting's conclusion, Paul and the Jerusalem leaders decided on a division of labor: the Jerusalem leaders evangelizing Jews with a law-observant gospel, and Paul evangelizing Gentiles with a gospel free of circumcision.

Implied in this division of labor was a subtle affirmation of unity. The fundamental unifying element was God. The Jerusalem apostles realized that the God operative in those who evangelized the circumcised was the same God at work in Paul, who evangelized the uncircumcised.

Another unifying element was the gospel. The gospel was deemed elastic enough to permit important cultural distinctions to remain in force between Jews and Gentiles, insofar as those distinctions posed no threat to the fellowship of Jews and Gentiles. The pressures of communal life would soon test the strength of the agreement reached in Jerusalem.

Beginning in Galatians 2:11, Paul narrates an episode that occurs at an unspecified time after the Jerusalem meeting. Peter comes to Antioch, an important early Christian center, where Gentile converts to Christianity were not circumcised. According to Paul, Peter ate regularly with Gentiles while in Antioch. The agreement reached earlier in Jerusalem had focused presumably on whether to circumcise Gentile converts. By eating with Gentiles in Antioch, Peter signaled that Jewish dietary laws, which might prohibit fellowship between Jews and Gentiles, could also be repealed in the service of Christian unity.

Yet when powerful representatives from Jerusalem came to Antioch (2:12), Peter separated himself from the Gentiles. Following Peter's lead, Barnabas and other Jews who had shared table fellowship with Gentiles separated themselves as well from Paul and the rest of the Gentiles. Paul indicted all those who withdrew on the charge of hypocrisy.

In Paul's estimation, Peter's fellowship with Gentile converts at Antioch provided *social* expression to a *theological* reality. For the sake of Christian unity, certain Jewish boundary markers that hindered fellowship between Jews and Gentiles could be rescinded. Before these Jewish "power brokers" arrived at Antioch, Peter shared table fellowship with Gentiles in an attempt to foster unity. He relinquished the ancient stereotypical view of Gentiles as "unclean," which was presupposed in the food laws. However, the representatives from James may not have shared Peter's new perspective, and may have pressured him into a more traditional understanding of his Jewish identity. Consequently, Peter withdrew from table fellowship with the Gentiles at Antioch.

Possibly at the root of Paul's indictment was Peter's unfortunate reclaiming of problematic stereotypes symbolized through his withdrawal from Gentile Christians. For Paul, Christ had nullified old ethnic stereotypes about the inherent "uncleanness" of Gentiles. Moreover, Christ had established a new common denominator by which Jews and Gentiles could be sisters and brothers in the same family. Paul considered Peter's withdrawal an affront to the unifying work of Christ.

In Galatians 2:15–21, Paul's rebuke of Peter continues. Paul espouses the common Jewish belief that no person is justified from the works of the law. As the twentieth-century reassessment of ancient Jewish faith has demonstrated, Jews knew that justification—the state of being in a proper covenant relationship with God—was ultimately a result of God's grace. That is, Jews fulfilled the works of the law mentioned in 2:16 (e.g., circumcision, food laws, and keeping the Sabbath) not to earn God's favor, but as a sign that God had already granted them favor. Divine grace and human works of the law were not mutually exclusive.

As *Jews*, Paul and Peter believed that justification was the consequence of divine grace. As *Jewish Christians*, they believed that God, in Jesus Christ, had offered a new, once-and-for-all demonstration of grace. By investing faith *in* Jesus Christ, believers could access the saving power *of* Jesus Christ. Since people could express faith in Jesus Christ regardless of their social identity, faith was the great social equalizer.

Faith in Jesus Christ provided access to God's grace beyond any narrow social boundaries. By withdrawing from the Gentiles at Antioch, Peter insinuated that Jews were superior to Gentiles. Instead of testifying to a divine grace that removes social boundaries, Peter's action established an ethnic fence around grace.

Prior to his conversion experience with Jesus, Paul too had built an ethnic fence around grace, believing that Gentiles were unclean. Jesus Christ compelled Paul to dismantle that ethnocentric wall, and Paul was unwilling to allow anyone to rebuild it (2:18). Paul's life-changing encounter with Jesus "put to death" ancient stereotypical perspectives about Gentiles, and in its place arose a new life of faith, which was open to the surprising ways of God.

Sadly, perspectives and stereotypes that thwart genuine unity are as much a problem today as in this ancient incident at Antioch. Marginalized groups—whether they are racial "minorities," women, economically vulnerable persons, or lesbian, gay, bisexual, and transgender persons—are embraced often by certain dominant groups, only to be rejected later by those dominant groups in crisis moments. In the frenzy, for instance, of a political campaign, representatives from dominant groups talk of building bridges and coalitions with persons who are outside the power structure. These power brokers shake hands and eat with marginalized groups and make sterling promises about building political and economic coalitions.

When the time has come to make good on these promises, these dominant groups often have withdrawn to a sheltered and inconspicuous political position. Instead of offering moral support to those on the fringes and standing on the side of fairness and genuine unity, these dominant groups have separated themselves from the now "unclean" marginalized groups. Such action has exposed a lack of interest in genuine unity and an unwillingness to risk privilege and power for the sake of deep conviction.

The incident at Antioch reveals that from its earliest days Christianity has struggled to transform into a living reality its exalted claims of unity and community. The faults and failures that litter Christian history, however, should teach us about, and not dissuade us from, the possibilities and challenges of "fleshing out" the meaning of Christian unity. Interpreters of Galatians 2:15–21 also might consider the role of stereotypes in today's Gospel reading, Luke 7:36–8:3. The woman in this Gospel text is said to be a "sinner." The real sin in that ancient text and in our contemporary practices might be the stereotypes and biases that divide the world into sinners and saints.

Faith in Jesus Christ compelled Paul to stand boldly for the conviction that God's family was supposed to be socially diverse. In order to comprehend the inclusive nature of God's grace, some of Paul's perspectives had to be relinquished, even "crucified," so that this inclusive grace might live in Paul's ministry and churches. What attitudes, especially about people who differ from us socially, need to be crucified in order that God's inclusive grace might flow more easily through our ministries and churches?

BRAD R. BRAXTON

Commentary 2: Connecting the Reading with the World

The opposite of love is not hate,
it's indifference.[1]
Elie Wiesel

Debt as sin. Debt as lack. Debt as indifference. Ignorance, insensitivity, inertia, or indifference about sin is a tragedy. Perception of sin or debt is itself a hard and challenging grace. Our attitude toward debt or sin stands out explicitly and implicitly in every one of today's readings—a strange and challenging theme to reflect on just after the joys and graces of Easter and Pentecost. Nevertheless, this is the reality of living in the present world.

Proper 6 in Year C, the season *after* Pentecost, signals a transitional moment in the church's worship. Having experienced the power of Jesus' resurrection, and the pouring out of the Holy Spirit, the church now enters a time to reflect on the mixture of grace and sin worked out in the lived experiences of communities and individuals. However, facing this reality can dismay us. We may think we had moved beyond this, or that this was all over, or wonder whether there is anything new under the sun, after all. An example of individual lived experience that dismays us is the resurgence of a habit we have prayed and worked to change—procrastination, negative thinking, a memory of past actions that trap us in a cycle of self-judgment. On a communal or national level, the resurgence of apathy in the face of racism and exclusion, inertia in the face of the suffering of others, the trap of politically correct thinking that subtly undermines loving relationships: all these experiences can tempt communities to slide into insensitivity or indifference, but the comforting fruits of the Holy Spirit received at Pentecost, such as love, joy, peace, patience, kindness (Gal. 5:22–23), do not preclude the gift of self-understanding that is wisdom. Self-understanding or awareness of indifference or inertia is unsettling, but it alerts individuals and communities to areas that are dying, where the active flow of love has been stopped. Discomfort after a season of celebration may not be such a bad thing.

Galatians 2:17 articulates the theological dimensions of sin coexisting with grace in the life of the church: "But if, in our effort to be justified in Christ, we ourselves have been found to be sinners, is Christ then a servant of sin?" Paul's emphatic response, *mē genoito*—"Let it not be!" or "Certainly not!"—is a response he frequently uses after a question that is absurd

1. Elie Wiesel, interview with Alvin P. Sanoff, "One Must Not Forget," *US News and World Report*, October 27, 1986, 68.

(e.g., Rom. 3:4, 6, 31).[2] Appropriating this theological truth into life is the challenge. The mystery of having to struggle with sin in daily life, even while justified by faith in Christ Jesus, threads itself throughout the lived experience of Christians from the early church, through the Reformation, to our present day. We hear the struggle echoing personally and socially through the centuries in the lives of people such as Augustine of Hippo, who struggled with self-surrender; Francis of Assisi, whose lifestyle countered a rising attachment to wealth in society; or Martin Luther, whose personal struggle with justification by faith led to church reform. Self-surrender, attachment to wealth, the need to reform church communities: do we not perceive the need to address these in our communities today? The tension between sin and justification is healthy. It never allows Christians to take for granted our attitude and response to God's love for us. It is the antidote to presumption.

Where self-understanding does not happen spontaneously, however, newcomers to family, neighborhoods, and churches challenge long-held ideas about grace and salvation. They bring to light areas of indifference and inertia in our thoughts, attitudes, religious practices, and worship. This was true for the Galatians, as it is today in our Christian communities. The tension between sin and justification by faith cropped up as new converts from territories outside of Judea and Galilee became Christians. These Gentile Christians brought different perspectives to this debate. Galatians, in fact, presents *three* points of view on the meaning of justification by faith in Christ Jesus: (1) the view of some Jewish Christians, for whom the law and its practices do not justify a person; (2) the view of the "circumcision group" (2:12), Jewish Christians who believed the law and its practices were the route to justification; and (3) the viewpoint of Gentile Christians, whose pagan background probably did not allow them to understand the subtleties of the argument between the previous two groups. People in the Galatian community chafed and irritated each other (and Paul) as they struggled with this issue. Like the Galatians, our churches today, with their official theological positions, bump up against points of view generated by people's lived experiences. Today's ministers, like Paul, may have to take an official stand, while addressing the pastoral needs and beliefs of a diversity of dissenting groups coexisting under one roof.

Like a burr or a thorn rubbing and chafing skin, the mystery of our personal and communal daily struggle with sin, while justified by faith in Christ Jesus, can make us better Christians. How does this help us? Ignorance, indifference, or insensitivity to the issues of personal or social sin or debt can undermine our perception of *our* need for forgiveness and justification in Christ, while being only too conscious of sin in others. This reading from Galatians is followed by Luke's Gospel, which depicts Simon the Pharisee, who is oblivious to his own sin (Luke 7:45–46) but apparently able to perceive sin in others: "Now when the Pharisee who had invited [Jesus] saw it, he said to himself, 'If this man were a prophet, he would have known who and what kind of woman this is who is touching him—that she is a sinner'" (v. 39). The Pharisee is so focused on putting down Jesus and the woman that he fails to perceive his own need for justification. His insensitivity contrasts with the woman, who weeps and anoints and kisses Jesus' feet. Jesus' assessment of her is that "her sins, which were many, have been forgiven; hence she has shown great love. But the one to whom little is forgiven, loves little" (v. 47). Clearly, in the case of this Pharisee, as in today's Christian communities, the opposite of love is not hate; it is indifference, most especially indifference to the desire for forgiveness, goodness, and acceptance found in "outsiders," sometimes even those we may judge to be "beyond justification." Judgments like this can creep in, stealthily setting up camp in the mind-set of a community, shaping its theology, practice, and outreach, until its members become tragically unaware that one "to whom little is forgiven, loves little."

Debt as sin. Debt as lack. Debt as indifference. Preaching or teaching awareness of sin, lack, or indifference as a "hard or challenging

2. Frank J. Matera, *Galatians*, Sacra Pagina 9 (Collegeville, MN: Liturgical Press, 1995), 95.

grace" to be appropriated for oneself or one's community can be a difficult, but necessary experience for church leaders. Awareness of the mystery of sin and justification applied in our lives is a "boomerang" experience. It hits the individuals receiving this teaching in the community, but it also returns to hit the minister. Nevertheless, the Holy Spirit sustains and encourages. The graces received *during* Pentecost provide the community and the leader with strength that is needed to receive the grace of self-awareness that is wisdom, in the season *after* Pentecost.

RENATA FURST

Luke 7:36–8:3

[36]One of the Pharisees asked Jesus to eat with him, and he went into the Pharisee's house and took his place at the table. [37]And a woman in the city, who was a sinner, having learned that he was eating in the Pharisee's house, brought an alabaster jar of ointment. [38]She stood behind him at his feet, weeping, and began to bathe his feet with her tears and to dry them with her hair. Then she continued kissing his feet and anointing them with the ointment. [39]Now when the Pharisee who had invited him saw it, he said to himself, "If this man were a prophet, he would have known who and what kind of woman this is who is touching him—that she is a sinner." [40]Jesus spoke up and said to him, "Simon, I have something to say to you." "Teacher," he replied, "speak." [41]"A certain creditor had two debtors; one owed five hundred denarii, and the other fifty. [42]When they could not pay, he canceled the debts for both of them. Now which of them will love him more?" [43]Simon answered, "I suppose the one for whom he canceled the greater debt." And Jesus said to him, "You have judged rightly." [44]Then turning toward the woman, he said to Simon, "Do you see this woman? I entered your house; you gave me no water for my feet, but she has bathed my feet with her tears and dried them with her hair. [45]You gave me no kiss, but from the time I came in she has not stopped kissing my feet. [46]You did not anoint my head with oil, but she has anointed my feet with ointment. [47]Therefore, I tell you, her sins, which were many, have been forgiven; hence she has shown great love. But the one to whom little is forgiven, loves little." [48]Then he said to her, "Your sins are forgiven." [49]But those who were at the table with him began to say among themselves, "Who is this who even forgives sins?" [50]And he said to the woman, "Your faith has saved you; go in peace."

[8:1]Soon afterwards he went on through cities and villages, proclaiming and bringing the good news of the kingdom of God. The twelve were with him, [2]as well as some women who had been cured of evil spirits and infirmities: Mary, called Magdalene, from whom seven demons had gone out, [3]and Joanna, the wife of Herod's steward Chuza, and Susanna, and many others, who provided for them out of their resources.

Commentary 1: Connecting the Reading to Scripture

It is no secret that women often were not treated well by either original biblical writers or later biblical interpreters. Still, there are some biblical texts that challenge the patriarchal status quo of the ancient world. Luke 7:36–8:3 has mixed together both a support of patriarchy and a challenge to patriarchy. The lection is best understood as two distinct passages connected in Luke because of their focus on women. We will comment briefly on the second passage (8:1–3) before attending more closely to the first (7:36–50), which will more likely be the section of greater interest for a sermon.

While most Gospel passages tell a specific story or offer a specific teaching, some function more as a summary of Jesus' wider ministry than what can be contained in a single narrative. Luke 8:1–3 is such a summary. The summary is striking in that it mentions women accompanying Jesus and supporting him financially in his itinerant ministry. These three women travel with the Twelve (first named in a similar summary passage in 6:12–16) and others (presumably men). Given that rabbis of Jesus' day attracted male students, Luke's inclusion of women in Jesus' entourage clearly challenges patriarchal boundaries to religious community and leadership of the day. That said, Luke never refers to the women as "disciples." The only other time two of them (Mary Magdalene and Joanna) appear in Luke's narrative is at the resurrection (24:1–11). They are given the honored role of being the first witnesses to the empty tomb; but the author reports only that they told the disciples what they saw, instead of giving them direct speech, and that the disciples consider their witness an "idle tale." So Luke 8:1–3 highlights the role of women in the Christ event in a way that challenges the patriarchy of the day but does not go as far as we might like in giving the women characters agency and portraying women as equal to men.

Similar dynamics play out in the first passage of the lection (7:36–50). On the negative side, male commentators throughout the history of the church have often assumed the sinful woman was a prostitute—as if "woman in the city" was an ancient synonym to the modern idiom of "woman of the night," and because her touching Jesus implies a sensual act. Both assumptions are incorrect. The text in no way justifies the assumption that the woman's sin is sexual. Rather, this interpretation reveals men's predilection for assigning sexuality to women's actions. Moreover, not only has interpretation of the passage traditionally been patriarchal; the text itself illustrates the patriarchy of the ancient world in that the narrator neither names the woman nor allows her to speak in the story. Indeed, the men in the story (the Pharisee and Jesus) talk about her without engaging her in conversation. They interpret her actions without inviting her to comment on them.

That said, there are positive elements to the woman's portrayal in the scene. She is clearly a strong character who is willing and able to cross cultural boundaries to express her gratitude to Jesus (see the similar characterization of the woman with the hemorrhage, 8:42b–48). Jesus lifts her up before the Pharisee and the others at the table in both naming that her sins have been forgiven and in claiming that her actions are a demonstration of her faith (vv. 48, 50). In other words, Luke presents this woman as a positive role model for his readers, female and male alike.

With this perspective in hand, we can turn our attention to discovering the author's theological purpose in sharing this passage. Luke's story of the sinful woman anointing Jesus' feet differs considerably from the versions found in Mark 14:3–9 and Matthew 26:6–13. In those versions, a woman anoints Jesus' head as part of the events in and around Jerusalem leading up to his passion. In response to objections regarding how much the oil or ointment cost, Jesus interprets the anointing as preparation for his death and declares the woman will be remembered for her act. Following this scene, Judas agrees to betray Jesus.

In contrast to these christologically orientated versions emphasizing Jesus as the anointed Messiah, Luke's story of the anointing of Jesus' feet appears early in Jesus' ministry and has nothing to do with his death. It is soteriological—focused on the woman's forgiveness.

The particular soteriological perspective of the passage is a recurring theme in Luke. At the banquet held at Levi's house, Pharisees and their scribes complain that Jesus is eating with sinners. In response Jesus declares, "Those who are well have no need of a physician, but those who are sick; I have come to call not the righteous but sinners to repentance" (5:29–32). Later Pharisees and scribes complain that Jesus welcomes and eats with sinners, and Jesus responds by telling the parables of the Lost Sheep, the Lost Coin, and the Lost Son (15:1–32). In the parable of the Pharisee and the Tax Collector, Jesus contrasts the prayer of the former, giving thanks that he is not like sinners, with the prayer of the latter, seeking mercy for his sins, and claims that the tax collector went home justified because those who exalt themselves will be humbled, and those who humble themselves will be exalted (18:9–15). Finally, in 19:1–10 Luke tells the story of Jesus encountering Zacchaeus, the chief tax collector in Jericho, just before entering Jerusalem. When Jesus stays at Zacchaeus's house, "all who saw it" grumbled, saying, "He has gone to be the guest of one who is a sinner." Upon Zacchaeus's repentance, Jesus says, "Today salvation has come to this house, because he too is a son of Abraham. For the Son of Man came to seek out and to save the lost."

The contrast evident in the above four passages also plays out in the story of the sinful woman anointing Jesus' feet. The Pharisee who invited Jesus to dine with him worries that if Jesus were a prophet, he would know that the woman touching him was a sinner (v. 39). Jesus responds with the parable of the Two Debtors, contrasting the Pharisee's and the woman's response to Jesus' presence and illustrating that one who is forgiven more is more grateful.

Given this recurring contrast in Luke, preachers will need to decide whether to ask their congregation to identify with the woman in need of and receiving great forgiveness, or with the Pharisee who is a righteous person in need of less forgiveness but in need of having more mercy. The two different points of identification invite two significantly different sermons, both appropriate to Luke's soteriological perspective but addressing very different existential needs. In the first option, the preacher declares forgiveness to those seeking it and strives to inspire gratitude. In the second option, the preacher urges hearers to move beyond the need for a just recognition of their moral/ethical lives, and to celebrate the pure grace that others receive. At the end of the parable of the Prodigal Son, Jesus does not say whether the elder son chooses to enter the party for the lost, younger son. This allows hearers to complete the story with their own lives. Similarly, in this passage, the narrator does not tell us how the Pharisee responds to Jesus' correction. The open ending invites us to finish the story with obedience and compassion.

O. WESLEY ALLEN JR.

Commentary 2: Connecting the Reading with the World

Simon, the Pharisee, is an ambiguous figure. At one level, he is Jesus' enemy, not just in the religious sense but also in the economic and social sense. When Jesus sent his disciples out to do mission (Luke 9:1–6; Matt. 10:5–16; Mark 6:7–13), he warned them about enemies, that they would be "as lambs among wolves." Why? John Dominic Crossan suggests an answer: the growing divide between those who owned land in first-century Palestine and those who did not.[1]

In order to feed the large Galilean urban populations of Sepphoris and Tiberias (ca. 25,000 each), wealthy landowners bought up smaller farms for mass agricultural production. The result was a growing itinerant population of working poor and artisans. Small landowners, themselves poor, viewed destitute itinerants with fear and disdain. Perhaps they reminded the householders that, with bad luck, they too could become dependent. An avoidance strategy was to reject the itinerants: out of sight and out of mind. We can imagine Simon as one who would be aligned with those who opposed itinerants.

Jesus, as a carpenter, was an itinerant and was followed by other itinerants, including fishermen and tax collectors. He and Simon were then natural enemies, and the distrust went both ways. Itinerants easily could look on self-protective landowners with contempt; but in the previous chapter, Jesus taught those who followed him to "love your enemies, do good to those who hate you" (6:27). Indeed, Jesus' word of rebuke to Simon in this story should be seen as a form of loving one's enemies. When parents stand firm with an addicted child, an abused spouse confronts the abuser, or a group of citizens opposes an injustice, these are not necessarily acts of condemnation. To the extent that they are intended to free the oppressor as well as the oppressed, they are deep acts of love. Jesus confronts Simon, the enemy, not out of contempt but out of love.

Simon is also the host. We cannot overlook the fact that he has opened his home to Jesus

1. John Dominic Crossan, "Jesus and the Kingdom: Itinerants and Householders in Earliest Christianity," in *Jesus at 2000*, ed. Marcus Borg (Boulder, CO: Westview Press, 1991), 21–53.

and invited him to his table. Fred Craddock once remarked that the true measure of one's faith is not whom you are willing to feed, but whom you are willing to eat with. Ethically, householders, even if they were fearful and suspicious, were expected to open their doors to itinerants, to invite them in, listen to them, and provide food and shelter. Simon has at least taken the first steps in this direction.

However, as Jesus' comments to Simon reveal, Simon's hospitality is only skin deep. By contrast, the woman, called a "sinner," who crashes the dinner party, weeps, bathes Jesus' feet with her tears, kisses them, and wipes them with her hair. Her lavish hospitality, motivated by gratitude and love, serves as a contrast to the actions of Simon, who obeys a code of etiquette but displays no deep love.

Theologian Patrick Kiefert has said that churches often display Simon's form of hospitality. They have signs reading "All Are Welcome" and think of themselves as friendly churches, but the profound hospitality for the stranger is not present. It is easy to welcome friends, but to welcome strangers, those not like us, is far more demanding. "I think the church is often at its most inhospitable in public worship," Kiefert writes, but the Spirit keeps sending strangers to the church, and everything vital about church life hangs on how those strangers are received.[2]

So the story in Luke is fraught with tensions: dinner guests who are really enemies, a hospitable host who is not really hospitable, and a woman known as a sinner who embodies the love and grace of the gospel. When Jesus is present, surprising transformations and experiences of healing are possible. Even a begrudging Simon, in opening his home and table to Jesus, moves into a new kind of space where unexpected things happen. The seventy experienced this wonder as they took the gospel to people's homes. They returned giddy with joy and reported, "Even the demons are subject to us in your name" (10:17 RSV). What happened in those homes? What demons possessed the householders—fear, prejudice, dismissiveness? How did those demons distort their lives? How were those demons banished by relating to these traveling "others"? We may need to examine some of our own experiences of reconciliation and healing to understand this, but Jesus is clear about the result: "I watched Satan fall from heaven like a flash of lightning" (10:18). Amazing, powerful stuff here!

Howard Thurman, the African American sage who inspired Dr. King and the nonviolent civil rights movement, also experienced such powerful impact. He trained students to take part in the sit-ins of the early 1960s, and he reports the experience of a female undergraduate trained to tamp down the "fight or flight" response to violence. At her first demonstration, a white man demanded that she leave the lunch counter. She "quietly asked him to identify himself, since he was in plain clothes. He opened his coat to reveal his badge of authority. Whereupon the young lady said, 'That's not a county badge; you have no jurisdiction here.' Nonplussed, the officer seized her by the wrist, his fingers biting into her flesh; and pushed her up against the wall, holding her there." She reflected:

> It was my very first direct encounter with real violence. All the possibilities of what we were up against had been drilled into us in our training and every conceivable kind of situation had been simulated; but even so, I was not prepared for the stark panic that moved through me. This passed quickly and in its place I felt an intense and angry violence—but something in me held. I looked him in the face until I felt his fear and sensed his own anguish. Then I thought, now quite calmly, how desperate a man must be to behave this way to a defenseless girl. And a strange peace came over me and I knew now that violence could be taken, and that I could take it and triumph over it. I suppose that as long as I live I will be winning and losing this battle with myself.[3]

This encounter, between an "itinerant" and "householder," contained the possibility of healing transformation, not only for the young woman but also the police officer. What did

2. Patrick R. Kiefert, *Welcoming the Stranger: A Public Theology of Worship and Evangelism* (Minneapolis: Augsburg Fortress Press, 1992), x.
3. Howard Thurman, *Disciplines of the Spirit* (Richmond, IN: Friends United Press, 1963), 175.

he experience? Maybe somewhere inside he thought, "I did something today I'm not proud of. Why did I? Why was I shaking and afraid?" If he felt anything of this, it was because a young, black woman had the courage and love to expose violent behavior and distorted thinking.

This is the kind of divine space of surprising grace that opens to us when we open ourselves to an "other." Today, we might hear Jesus address us as we are separated from others in many ways. It can be frightening to approach an "other." We all are vulnerable, and Jesus calls for courage, nonviolence, and a willingness to be transformed. There are many reasons not to step across that threshold; but, according to Jesus, that is where healing, peace, and our God-given potential can be realized.

STEPHEN BOYD

Proper 7 (Sunday between June 19 and June 25 Inclusive)

1 Kings 19:1–4 (5–7), 8–15a and
Isaiah 65:1–9
Psalms 42 and 43 and Psalm 22:19–28
Galatians 3:23–29
Luke 8:26–39

1 Kings 19:1–4 (5–7), 8–15a

[1]Ahab told Jezebel all that Elijah had done, and how he had killed all the prophets with the sword. [2]Then Jezebel sent a messenger to Elijah, saying, "So may the gods do to me, and more also, if I do not make your life like the life of one of them by this time tomorrow." [3]Then he was afraid; he got up and fled for his life, and came to Beer-sheba, which belongs to Judah; he left his servant there.

[4]But he himself went a day's journey into the wilderness, and came and sat down under a solitary broom tree. He asked that he might die: "It is enough; now, O LORD, take away my life, for I am no better than my ancestors." [5]Then he lay down under the broom tree and fell asleep. Suddenly an angel touched him and said to him, "Get up and eat." [6]He looked, and there at his head was a cake baked on hot stones, and a jar of water. He ate and drank, and lay down again. [7]The angel of the LORD came a second time, touched him, and said, "Get up and eat, otherwise the journey will be too much for you." [8]He got up, and ate and drank; then he went in the strength of that food forty days and forty nights to Horeb the mount of God. [9]At that place he came to a cave, and spent the night there.

Then the word of the LORD came to him, saying, "What are you doing here, Elijah?" [10]He answered, "I have been very zealous for the LORD, the God of hosts; for the Israelites have forsaken your covenant, thrown down your altars, and killed your prophets with the sword. I alone am left, and they are seeking my life, to take it away."

[11]He said, "Go out and stand on the mountain before the LORD, for the LORD is about to pass by." Now there was a great wind, so strong that it was splitting mountains and breaking rocks in pieces before the LORD, but the LORD was not in the wind; and after the wind an earthquake, but the LORD was not in the earthquake; [12]and after the earthquake a fire, but the LORD was not in the fire; and after the fire a sound of sheer silence. [13]When Elijah heard it, he wrapped his face in his mantle and went out and stood at the entrance of the cave. Then there came a voice to him that said, "What are you doing here, Elijah?" [14]He answered, "I have been very zealous for the LORD, the God of hosts; for the Israelites have forsaken your covenant, thrown down your altars, and killed your prophets with the sword. I alone am left, and they are seeking my life, to take it away." [15]Then the LORD said to him, "Go, return on your way to the wilderness of Damascus."

Isaiah 65:1–9

[1]I was ready to be sought out by those who did not ask,
to be found by those who did not seek me.
I said, "Here I am, here I am,"
to a nation that did not call on my name.
[2]I held out my hands all day long
to a rebellious people,
who walk in a way that is not good,
following their own devices;
[3]a people who provoke me
to my face continually,
sacrificing in gardens
and offering incense on bricks;
[4]who sit inside tombs,
and spend the night in secret places;
who eat swine's flesh,
with broth of abominable things in their vessels;
[5]who say, "Keep to yourself,
do not come near me, for I am too holy for you."
These are a smoke in my nostrils,
a fire that burns all day long.
[6]See, it is written before me:
I will not keep silent, but I will repay;
I will indeed repay into their laps
[7] their iniquities and their ancestors' iniquities together,
says the LORD;
because they offered incense on the mountains
and reviled me on the hills,
I will measure into their laps
full payment for their actions.
[8]Thus says the LORD:
As the wine is found in the cluster,
and they say, "Do not destroy it,
for there is a blessing in it,"
so I will do for my servants' sake,
and not destroy them all.
[9]I will bring forth descendants from Jacob,
and from Judah inheritors of my mountains;
my chosen shall inherit it,
and my servants shall settle there.

Commentary 1: Connecting the Reading with Scripture

The lectionary reading advances us a quarter of the way into the Elijah cycle, moving past his confrontation with King Ahab in 1 Kings 17 and the 450 prophets of Baal in 1 Kings 18. At this point in the story, the prophet Elijah has lived up to his royal title of "troubler of Israel" (1 Kgs. 18:17). Troubling the power structure, especially the tyrannical kind, marks an essential function of Elijah's prophetic call. As God's agent, Elijah even resorts to warriorlike violence as a way to restore God's primacy in Israelite religious belief. As Ahab reports to Jezebel in 1 Kings 19:1, "he killed all the prophets with the sword." Indeed, at first glance, the Wadi Kishon massacre of hundreds of Baal prophets appears harsh and unreasonable, especially given Elijah's decisive victory at Carmel (1 Kgs. 18:36–39).

Rather than define Elijah's actions through Western linear notions of ancient barbarity, this violence points to an important feature of the prophetic call that has a great deal to do with human conflict. This is not to condone physical violence regardless of its justification. As revealed in Jezebel's message to Elijah, violence simply breeds more violence: "So may the gods do to me, and more also, if I do not make your life like the life of one of them by this time tomorrow" (1 Kgs. 19:2). As unsettling as the Wadi Kishon massacre seems in the Elijah story, it does remind us that the prophetic call seeks to establish a counterposition to what has shown to be an unjust power structure. For contemporary readers, this violence is to be imagined but never realized. Herein lies the wisdom in the story: it shows violence to be cyclical and hence leads us to take up nonviolence as the only viable action. Even the Elijah story speaks to the elusive yet empowering nature of divine instruction to the extent that readers take the lead in discovering a third way. Similar to the case of Elijah, divine instruction can sometimes be in the "sheer silence" instead of the wind, earthquake, and fire.

The reputation of troublemaker was not exclusive to Elijah. The ruling establishment viewed the eighth-century prophet Amos as an insurrectionist: "Then Amaziah, the priest of Bethel, sent to King Jeroboam of Israel, saying, 'Amos has conspired [*qashar*] against you in the very center of the house of Israel; the land is not able to bear all his words'" (Amos 7:10). Judean religious leaders considered the sixth-century prophet Jeremiah as a public enemy, announcing at the temple gate, "This man deserves the sentence of death because he has prophesied against this city" (Jer. 26:11). As these prophets demonstrate, clashing with power is an intrinsic and often unavoidable task of the prophetic call. To locate Hebrew prophecy outside of the realms of conflict and power struggle reduces it to a causeless religious discourse. Yet as the Hebrew prophets teach us, their conflict with power was in large part due to the geopolitical, economic, social, and political dimensions of their words. The exilic prophet Third Isaiah (Isa. 56–66) proclaims a divine message that is rife with social and religious critique: "I held out my hands all day long to a rebellious people, who walk in a way that is not good, following their own devices" (Isa. 65:2). For the Hebrew prophets, physical violence was secondary to the prophetic critique, in large part because they viewed their divine words to be sufficient for effecting social change. This is where a divinely inspired social critique can provide the necessary force to topple and transform oppressive power structures.

In response to Jezebel's death threat, Elijah flees for his life by leaving the northern kingdom of Israel and crossing over to Beer-sheba in the southern kingdom of Judah. Here he parts from his servant and proceeds to migrate alone through the desert. Malnourished, exhausted, and isolated, Elijah recedes into suicidal depression.[1] Under the shadow of a broom tree, Elijah asks God to take his life: "It is enough; now, O Lord, take away my life, for I am no better than my ancestors" (v. 4). Here we encounter the hardships of the Hebrew prophetic call, in which the overwhelming burden of speaking to power (i.e., conflict) often produces social isolation (see Jer. 20; Ezek. 24; Jonah 4). For some, this isolation engenders such an extreme form of mental anguish that the prophet ultimately seeks to end his life. Consider for instance Jonah's pleading words, "And now, O Lord, please take my life from me, for it is better for me to die than to live" (Jonah 4:3). Just as depression sets in, so does the healing care of God, which for Elijah comes in the form of an angel: "Suddenly an angel touched him and said to him, 'Get up and eat'" (1 Kgs. 19:5). Similar to the angel in the Hagar story (Gen. 16, 21), Elijah's angel also serves as a travel guide in the desert, providing him with life-giving care over the next forty days and nights. With his

1. Havilah Dharamraj, *A Prophet Like Moses?: A Narrative-Theological Reading of the Elijah Stories* (Crownhill: Paternoster, 2011), 49.

strength restored, Elijah resumes his prophetic call and receives a renewed mission.

From Isaiah 65:1–9, we are reminded that the prophet's isolation is rooted in a counter-message in which the God of Israel has been rejected and hence isolated from Israelite worship. To a certain extent, the prophet's call involves sharing in God's sense of isolation. As admitted in Third Isaiah's divine message, God's loneliness also means the prophet's loneliness: "I was ready to be sought out by those who did not ask, to be found by those who did not seek me. I said, 'Here I am, here I am,' to a nation that did not call on my name" (v. 1). Like the prophets, God desires real and genuine relationships with all God's creation. In the end, this is what drives the prophetic impulse—calling people into genuine relationships with all creation and with God.

Starting with Genesis, the notion of being alone was not what God deemed as the "good" (*tov*); rather, God's ultimate "good" consists of being in peaceful relationships with others and with God. In many ways, contemporary pastors move in and out of a prophetic role so much that their critiques of power can lead to loneliness and isolation. These desertlike conditions can be exhausting and demoralizing for any spiritually mature church leader. At the same time, pastors can also assume the prophetic role by preaching a message of restoration, which is what Third Isaiah gives us in verse 8: "So I will do for my servants' sake, and not destroy them all." Here Third Isaiah points to the compassionate side of the prophetic message. Just as the critique is essential to the prophetic message, so are the prophet's words of hope. For the prophet, the overwhelming sense of isolation was countered by an additional message of hope and restoration. Striking a balance between social critique and social compassion continue to be the pastor's challenge. An overload on social critique can lead to a pastor's isolation, whereas a surplus of sermons on hope can lead to a socially disengaged faith community. Ultimately, the hope of all creation is that God desires not to be alone but rather longs to be found—both in the social critique and the social compassion.

GREGORY L. CUÉLLAR

Commentary 2: Connecting the Reading with the World

"You are not alone. I care for you. Now get back to it."

This may not be the most poetic summary of God's responses to the laments of a refugee prophet and an exiled people, but the passages before us contain this seemingly straightforward sentiment, even as they invite reflection on rich themes of faithful relationship, divine sustenance, and persistent mission. Both the prophet and the people are alienated, exiled, exhausted, and—in different ways—struggling with what will be their next faith chapter. In the midst of their wrestling, God brings different forms of assured care alongside a missional realism that reminds them of their shared strength and the endurance of God's revolutionary covenant.

Although in dissimilar contexts, Elijah and the Israelites are both enduring a season of struggle that seems to have no final victories or respite. On the one hand in 1 Kings 19, Elijah, the great prophet and thorn in King Ahab and Queen Jezebel's side, has just been a conduit of YHWH's decisive victory over the imperial cult and prophets of Baal by bringing rains to the parched land. However, Elijah's faithfulness does not bring him solace and, in fact, puts him under even greater threat. With a death warrant on his head, he flees into the wilderness. He is exhausted physically, emotionally, and spiritually; he is so overwhelmed that his singular hope is death. Then he sleeps. The lack of YHWH's obvious presence, on the other hand, motivates the exiled Israelites' lament in Isaiah 65. In response to YHWH's seeming absence and the loss of Jerusalem and the temple, they almost passive-aggressively ask God to return and stop delivering them into the "hand of our iniquity."

It is fitting that these passages appear during Ordinary Time, a span of time during which there are no grand liturgical events (e.g., Advent,

Christmas, Easter), when we instead are plunged into stories of communal formation and discipleship. Ordinary Time actually refers to the ordinal numbering of the Sundays after Pentecost, but for our purposes here the more common meaning may help us think about what comes after big events for a community. Whether it be victory or exile, where is God when the community is exhausted and has a desperate need for reassurance? Ecclesially, these passages speak particularly to the struggle of faithfulness when final victory seems exceedingly elusive and time is infused with the brutal reality of unrelenting everyday politics and suffering. These Scriptures invite us to reflect on how we embody God when we are not in power and even lack certainty about how the future will unfold. How do we look for the presence of God when we are in despair about our missional future?

Elijah's refuge is sleep and emphatic declarations before God. One could imagine him struggling with why his status as the great righteous prophet of the one true God does not protect him. He has fought the good fight—and yet a death warrant is his reward. How many contemporary Christian activists and/or leaders share this Sisyphean despair? Perhaps it is more disheartening that after a great victory, a seeming break in the oppressive system, the system endures rather than imploding. Ahab is still in power, and Ahab's typical insecure complaint (or perhaps verbal attack on Jezebel's impotent gods; one wonders what their domestic argument entailed) produces a death warrant rather than a resignation to YHWH's reign. Elijah seems to have nothing else to give to his prophetic call.

God does not dismiss Elijah's pain and exhaustion. In fact, the angel of God tenderly touches Elijah and physically rouses him twice to eat and drink. With this renewal, Elijah continues a journey toward a theophany that echoes Moses' forty days and nights. While the storm, earthquake, and fire harken back to Moses' meeting of God, for Elijah God is not present in those natural forces. Instead, God is found in the sheer silence that follows the tumult. The Stillpoint of the universe, who anchors the centripetal energy of all creation, announces divine presence through an awesome hush. This contrast between Moses and Elijah challenges us to think about how we expect God to appear in our lives. Does our experience of God's self-revelation need to parallel another person's or even an iconic religious leader's? God may choose particular moments and manifestations precisely to remind us of a dimension of God we have forgotten and yet desperately need to sustain our call.

Even after all that, Elijah repeats his lament to God. To this, God says simply: go back. Go back into the fray and pronounce with revolutionary certainty that the oppressive powers will fall. With a voice of missional realism, God asserts that Elijah is ready to return, in a verse not included at all in the Revised Common Lectionary (v. 18), and adds that he was *never actually alone* in this mission; there are *seven thousand* faithful who will be with him. In other words, you may think you are the last righteous one standing—but you have missed an entire faithful remnant already journeying on this mission. We can almost hear varied stages of pastoral care in God's acts: physical sustenance, enveloping centering presence, relational reconnection, and decisive sending forth. At some point, your healing will be found again in your mission, alongside others who are walking your collective journey.

In Isaiah 65, we see another temptation that arises in the face of missional despair: taking a shortcut to proximate power. We hear of God's great anger at those who abandon the path of YHWH to secure their future through idols, arcane rituals, and even a false sense of holiness. As the religiopolitical power structure shifts around them, the Israelites set aside God's formative demands and the real divine center to try to secure their own vision of the future. In our contemporary context, what do we embrace, and perhaps even worship, to secure the power we need in a society beyond our control (e.g., the invisible hand of the market, natural social ordering, rugged individualism)? These shortcuts to ephemeral power eventually turn us away from the outstretched hand of God, even as God promises to walk with us to a new heaven and new earth and a new kind of social, economic, and religious reality. God's rebuke and judgment in Isaiah 65 is searing and clear, but notice: there is still a pronouncement of mercy and salvation. There remain good clusters on the weak vine, and that faithful remnant will inherit and inhabit the land again. God's mission abides and so does God's presence with those who truly seek God's heart.

This conclusion assures us, again, that we are not isolated from God or from a faithful community, even if we cannot yet recognize them. Faithful relationships (with God and others) are part of the divine sustenance that enables us to persist in our missional calling. God assures us that care will present itself. But we must say yes to it, sometimes walking toward it in a literal physical manner. We must also know that divine care and revelation will not look, sound, or feel the same for everyone, but rather will meet us in our particular need. Neither of these passages offers a simple, warm, fuzzy kind of care, for extended licking of wounds sometimes means they never heal. Instead, it is our challenge to embrace the steady care and faith in us that God offers: You are not alone. I care for you. Now get back to it.

C. MELISSA SNARR

Proper 7 (Sunday between June 19 and June 25 Inclusive)

Psalm 42

[1]As a deer longs for flowing streams,
  so my soul longs for you, O God.
[2]My soul thirsts for God,
  for the living God.
When shall I come and behold
  the face of God?
[3]My tears have been my food
  day and night,
while people say to me continually,
  "Where is your God?"

[4]These things I remember,
  as I pour out my soul:
how I went with the throng,
  and led them in procession to the house of God,
with glad shouts and songs of thanksgiving,
  a multitude keeping festival.
[5]Why are you cast down, O my soul,
  and why are you disquieted within me?
Hope in God; for I shall again praise him,
  my help [6]and my God.

My soul is cast down within me;
  therefore I remember you
from the land of Jordan and of Hermon,
  from Mount Mizar.
[7]Deep calls to deep
  at the thunder of your cataracts;
all your waves and your billows
  have gone over me.
[8]By day the LORD commands his steadfast love,
  and at night his song is with me,
  a prayer to the God of my life.

[9]I say to God, my rock,
  "Why have you forgotten me?
Why must I walk about mournfully
  because the enemy oppresses me?"
[10]As with a deadly wound in my body,
  my adversaries taunt me,
while they say to me continually,
  "Where is your God?"

[11]Why are you cast down, O my soul,
  and why are you disquieted within me?
Hope in God; for I shall again praise him,
  my help and my God.

Psalm 43

[1]Vindicate me, O God, and defend my cause
against an ungodly people;
from those who are deceitful and unjust
deliver me!
[2]For you are the God in whom I take refuge;
why have you cast me off?
Why must I walk about mournfully
because of the oppression of the enemy?

[3]O send out your light and your truth;
let them lead me;
let them bring me to your holy hill
and to your dwelling.
[4]Then I will go to the altar of God,
to God my exceeding joy;
and I will praise you with the harp,
O God, my God.

[5]Why are you cast down, O my soul,
and why are you disquieted within me?
Hope in God; for I shall again praise him,
my help and my God.

Psalm 22:19–28

[19]But you, O LORD, do not be far away!
O my help, come quickly to my aid!
[20]Deliver my soul from the sword,
my life from the power of the dog!
[21]Save me from the mouth of the lion!

From the horns of the wild oxen you have rescued me.
[22]I will tell of your name to my brothers and sisters;
in the midst of the congregation I will praise you:
[23]You who fear the LORD, praise him!
All you offspring of Jacob, glorify him;
stand in awe of him, all you offspring of Israel!
[24]For he did not despise or abhor
the affliction of the afflicted;
he did not hide his face from me,
but heard when I cried to him.

[25]From you comes my praise in the great congregation;
my vows I will pay before those who fear him.
[26]The poor shall eat and be satisfied;
those who seek him shall praise the LORD.
May your hearts live forever!

[27]All the ends of the earth shall remember
and turn to the LORD;
and all the families of the nations
shall worship before him.
[28]For dominion belongs to the LORD,
and he rules over the nations.

Connecting the Psalm with Scripture and Worship

When I consider the psalms appointed for this week, the face that comes to mind is that of Dr. Martin Luther King Jr. in the early weeks of 1968. By this time, his optimism about the nation's future had waned, and the twin miseries of anxiety and depression pressed in on him. He could relax only in windowless rooms with close friends by his side, and at speaking engagements his eyes would dart from person to person in search of his assassin.[1] The evil he experienced made it hard to trust God. Much like the Hebrew psalmists, King was locked in a struggle against despair.

Haunting questions echo throughout Psalms 42 and 43: "Why are you cast down, O my soul, and why are you disquieted within me?" (42:5, 11; 43:5). These questions are quickly followed with an imperative: "Hope in God, for I shall again praise him, my help and my God" (42:6, 11; 43:5). The refrain has an anchoring effect, and its centrality in both psalms strongly suggests that the two were originally a single unit. The power of the refrain rests in its dialogical articulation of longing for God. On one level, the psalmist is awash in sorrow and restless under its waves. At the same time, the poet is mysteriously buoyed by God's sustaining power. Hope comes in sudden bursts rather than prolonged cycles, but these bursts are vigorous enough to keep him afloat. By embracing the command to trust God and drawing on the power of human will, the psalmist musters enough strength to face the future. Before too long, the somber questions break in again: "Why are you cast down, O my soul, and why are you disquieted within me?" Through these back-and-forth movements, the psalms chart the spiraling nature of despair and reveal how overwhelming the fight can feel.

It will help to keep this spiral in mind when preaching about Elijah's story in 1 Kings 19:1–15. The passage portrays a man who is overwhelmed by his external situation and internally racked with fear and sadness. Listeners may be curious about Elijah's inner turmoil and will likely identify with his terror. This openness on the part of the listener may provide the preacher with opportunity to discuss the ways faith can serve as a resource for people who are experiencing depression and anxiety. The central refrain in Psalms 42 and 43 cautions the preacher against tidy depictions of the struggle against despair and urge recognition of the range of emotions that accompany the journey. Rather than clean portrayals of emotion, the psalmist seems to speak of blurred sentiments such as sorrow tinged with shame (42:3, 9–10), hope numbed by fear (43:1–2), and twists of helplessness and fatigue (42:7). The psalmist's journey is a slow one and is never completely resolved. Preachers might similarly mind their paces when exploring Elijah's despair, make space for a range of emotions, and resist neat solutions.

Psalms 42 and 43 also highlight the role of perspective. On the surface, the psalms provide a window into the psalmist's agony. The reader overhears him as he remembers joyful days (42:4) and compares them to his present suffering. Yet, if the reader takes his questions and petitions seriously, it becomes clear that the psalm is not just about the psalmist; the psalm is about the God the psalmist is addressing.[2]

1. Richard Lischer, *The Preacher King: Martin Luther King Jr. and the Word That Moved America* (New York: Oxford University Press, 1995), 171.
2. Patrick D. Miller, *The Lord of the Psalms* (Louisville, KY: Westminster John Knox, 2013), xi.

Playing with perspective could also serve as a useful strategy when preaching 1 Kings 19. God's self-revelation at Horeb has more impact when one considers all the preceding action that has taken place in the shadows. While Elijah was too frightened to realize it, God enabled Elijah's escape, gave him the gift of deep rest, sustained him with food and water, and empowered him with the strength to travel from Beer-sheba to Horeb. The still small voice is only one dimension of the quiet work of God.

The human-divine dialogue includes spoken and unspoken dimensions, and both deserve the preacher's attention. At the aural level, God asks a question, "What are you doing here, Elijah?" (1 Kgs. 19:9, 13). Elijah rattles off an answer that emphasizes his terror more than anything else. Beneath his words sits a deeper truth worthy of the preacher's excavation. Psalms 42 and 43 provide a series of ricocheting questions that offer clues on Elijah's inner dialogue in the cave. First, there are the three rounds of questions about sorrow, "Why are you cast down, O my soul?" Interspersed among these questions are taunts from an enemy, "Where is your God?" (42:3, 10), and questions directed at God, "Why must I walk about mournfully because the enemy oppresses me?" (42:9; 43:2). The psalmist's deepest prayer is for an interruption that will usher him out of his spiritual-psychological cavern. The miracle for Elijah is that the internal dialogue is heard and interrupted. The right voice prevails.

Human wickedness contributes to Elijah's despair in 1 Kings 19 and similarly drives the lections from Psalm 22 and Isaiah 65. God is outraged by the evil and arrogance described in Isaiah 65:2–5—rebellion, provocation, idolatry, and condescension. When exploring these themes, the preacher should note that venom directed at God also drips on God's people. "Deliver my soul from the sword, my life from the power of the dog! Save me from the mouth of the lion!" (Ps. 22:20–21). The psalmist makes it clear that the wicked rain hatred on the righteous and also make them vulnerable to poverty and deprivation (22:24, 26). So the mourning that propels God's wrath in Isaiah 65:6–7 coalesces with the psalmist's grief.

God appears as the righteous judge in Isaiah 65:1–9. While divine judgement has inextricable elements of terror, the preacher should remember that the holy judge is an answer to the prayers of the righteous. Divine judgment marks an end to the violence, deprivation, and despair that seem to define the lives of the vulnerable. Thriving becomes possible.

The struggle against despair can be explored further by making space in the liturgy for testimonies from members of the congregation who have had similar battles. These testimonies might take the form of short orations woven into the recitation of the psalms or simply written and included in a worship leaflet. If it is not feasible to focus on members of the congregation, stories of saints who struggled with despair provide another option. Ideally, the service will include ordinary and extraordinary people and allow worshipers to see their faces. A classic example is Florence Owens Thompson, the thirty-two-year-old mother of seven depicted in Dorothea Lange's iconic 1936 photograph "Migrant Mother."[3] She epitomizes the despair of the Great Depression with her wrinkled brow, square jaw, and pensive stare. Lange's photo captures Thompson shortly after she sold the tires on the family car for food. Her eyes glow with worry and grit. The unique combination echoes the sentiment of the psalms.

While outside the liturgical calendar, Proper 7 covers Juneteenth, the holiday that commemorates the June 19, 1865, announcement of the abolition of slavery in the United States. This celebration provides another frame for the themes of despair and evil in the lections and also offers a glimmer of hope.

DONYELLE MCCRAY

3. Dorothea Lange, "Migrant Mother," Nipoma, CA, 1936, https://www.loc.gov/rr/print/list/128_migm.html.

Galatians 3:23–29

[23]Now before faith came, we were imprisoned and guarded under the law until faith would be revealed. [24]Therefore the law was our disciplinarian until Christ came, so that we might be justified by faith. [25]But now that faith has come, we are no longer subject to a disciplinarian, [26]for in Christ Jesus you are all children of God through faith. [27]As many of you as were baptized into Christ have clothed yourselves with Christ. [28]There is no longer Jew or Greek, there is no longer slave or free, there is no longer male and female; for all of you are one in Christ Jesus. [29]And if you belong to Christ, then you are Abraham's offspring, heirs according to the promise.

Commentary 1: Connecting the Reading with Scripture

Many scholars maintain that Galatians 3 is the theological center of the letter. Galatians 3 advances three significant theological themes: (1) the role of the Galatians' religious experience, (2) the role of the Jewish law, and (3) the social boundaries of the Christian community.

Paul begins chapter 3 with the frustrated exclamation, "You foolish Galatians!" From his perspective, the Galatians manifest their foolishness by preparing to engage in behavior (i.e., submitting to circumcision) that nullifies their experiences with the Holy Spirit. Such behavior will negate the principle of "ethnic diversity within Christian unity"—a principle hard won at the Jerusalem conference and tragically forgotten at the Antioch incident in last week's epistle reading.

In Galatians 3:1–5, Paul attempts to dissuade the Galatians from their foolishness. He reminds them of their powerful and formative experiences with the Holy Spirit when they initially received the gospel. Paul's emphasis on the Holy Spirit invites preachers to explore the emotive and mysterious dimensions of Christian discipleship. Too often sermons on Pauline texts approach Paul as if he were a dispassionate theologian. Paul was a theologian and also a pragmatic pastor and community builder whose communities regularly experienced passionate demonstrations of the Spirit's presence (e.g., the mention of miracles in Gal. 3:5).

For Paul, the Spirit is the ultimate source of individual and communal power that enables Christian living, and especially the ministry of preaching. Christian preaching that occurs under the auspices of the Holy Spirit should foster not only profound thinking but also life-transforming feelings and actions—both in the one preaching and in the ones listening.

Through their faithful acceptance of the gospel, the Galatians had received the Holy Spirit. Faithful response to the gospel, and not ethnic particularity, is the common denominator on which Christian unity is built. Paul accentuates the importance of faith by appealing to a classic biblical story of a person whose experience with God was rooted in faith: Abraham.

For Paul, Abraham's story does not legitimate an ethnic practice (circumcision) that creates barriers between Jews and Gentiles. Rather, this story demonstrates that the boundaries of the covenant were wider than many Jews had thought. A life of faith, and not circumcision, brings blessings and makes believers true descendants of Abraham (Gal. 3:7–9).

Paul does not categorically oppose the law. Instead, he resists the Jewish imposition of the law on Gentiles, as if law observance were the only authentic manifestation of faith. To demonstrate the incompatibility of law observance and faith for Gentiles, Paul declares in Galatians 3:12, "The law is not by faith" (NRSV

"The law does not rest on faith"). Paul's words are not an unconditionally negative assessment of the law. For Gentiles, faith and law observance are mutually exclusive. A preoccupation with the law causes Gentiles to misunderstand the universal nature of God's covenant, which persons enter through faith alone.

Paul's indignation is not with the law, but with a distorted perspective on the law. He suggests that people who rely on the works of the law are "those who have understood the scope of God's covenant people as Israel per se."[1] According to Paul's logic, those who rely on faith are blessed, and those who rely on anything other than faith are cursed. Christ redeems both Jews and Gentiles from the curse (3:13). Christ's redemptive work releases Jews from a narrow understanding of the law and rescues Gentiles from the necessity of becoming Jews. Christ thereby fulfills God's intent—a covenant family including both Jews and Gentiles.

Later, Paul appeals again to Abraham as justification for the primacy of faith (3:15–20). God established a covenant with Abraham on the basis of God's grace and Abraham's faith. According to Paul's calculation, this covenant predated the giving of the law on Mount Sinai by 430 years. Thus, faith is chronologically prior to the law and is the precondition upon which the law is founded.

Throughout Galatians 3, Paul seeks to devalue the law. Preachers should keep in mind Paul's rhetorical purpose. Since his Gentile converts are being tempted to submit to law observance, Paul speaks negatively about the law *as it pertains to Gentile Christians*, not as it pertains to Jews or Jewish Christians.

Paul's arguments about the law provide preachers an opportunity to courageously examine, and disavow, cultural chauvinism. Cultural chauvinism occurs when dominant social groups dismiss or devalue the cultural histories and practices of minority groups. For example, as an *African American*, heterosexual, middle-class male, I have had to resist cultural chauvinism as certain power brokers in academic and religious communities subtly, and not so subtly, have tried to impose upon me white cultural presuppositions and practices as normative.

Yet, as an African American, *heterosexual, middle-class male*, I am a member of dominant groups and have benefited from male, economic, and heterosexual privilege. Thus I must resist the imposition of my presuppositions and practices upon minority groups. Furthermore, I must repent for the occasions when my impositions have hindered the "diversity within unity" principle championed by Paul.

In Galatians 3:26–29, Paul further emphasizes the faith that creates a community that is both diverse and unified. Even though Gentile faith does not involve law observance, Gentiles who accept Christ are still God's children (v. 26). As God's children, Gentiles have full participation in the blessings of the covenant community.

Paul employs a confession used in ancient baptismal services (v. 28). The confession focuses on three spheres of potential social strife: racial/ethnic relationships ("there is no longer Jew or Greek"), economic status ("there is no longer slave or free"), and gender relationships ("there is no longer male and female"). In order to understand Galatians 3:28, we must correct the misconception that Christian unity entails the absence of social distinctions. Paul pleads for the eradication of *dominance*, not the erasure of *difference*. When they enter the Christian community through belief in Christ and baptism, believers do not lose the social distinctions that have characterized their lives.

Even "in Christ," there is social difference, but Christ abolishes the dominance of one over the other based on these differences. Jews should not dominate Gentiles; free persons should not dominate slaves; men should not dominate women. Christians should foster harmonious relationships characterized by mutuality and respect for social difference.

An analogy from music may be helpful. Harmony is the cooperative union of different voices. The various vocal parts must maintain their distinctiveness, even as they unite, if harmony is to exist.

Paul's famous declaration in Galatians 3:28 can motivate Christian communities to strive for more equitable relationships across racial/

1. James D. G. Dunn, *Jesus, Paul, and the Law: Studies in Mark and Galatians* (London: SPCK, 1990), 227.

ethnic, economic, and gender lines. Christian unity emerges only when the social distinctions that define us are present and acknowledged, but never used as a means of domination. The quest for unity requires ruggedly honest dialogue and deliberate and consistent fellowship among distinct groups.

There remains much unfinished work concerning racial/ethnic, economic, and gender justice in Christian communities. For instance, persons interested in social liberation must raise a critique about the gender politics in many Christian congregations. Many congregations perpetuate a patriarchal culture that assumes that male leadership is "natural." This gender apartheid relegates women to their "proper place," while denying women access to traditional symbols and systems of power (e.g., the pulpit, pastoral leadership, and the right to baptize and administer Holy Communion). According to Galatians 3:28, faith in Christ compels us to dismantle the social barriers that prevent us from truly being sisters and brothers in Christ.

BRAD R. BRAXTON

Commentary 2: Connecting the Reading with the World

"There is no longer Jew or Greek, there is no longer slave or free, there is no longer male and female; for all of you are one in Christ Jesus" (Gal. 3:28). With this one phrase, Paul brings down barriers and overturns categories within the Galatian community. These divisions may reflect the social categories and identities in the dominant culture or categories viewed from a Jewish perspective, which the Galatians adopted when they turned from "the one who called you in the grace of Christ . . . to a different gospel" (1:6). By turning away from the grace of Christ, the Galatians create divisions based on ethnicity, social status, and gender. These proliferate sometimes unnoticed in communities today.

Preaching can bring these divisions into the light and challenge everyone to "live into" their identity in Christ, as "Abraham's offspring, heirs according to the promise" (3:29). How do divisions like these impact communities today? Social (and religious) categories are important because they define the borders of inclusion and exclusion. Typically, social and religious identities are built through layers of separation, divisions that define who is "one of us" and who is "other." These categories are then used to create barriers. Sometimes the dynamics of inclusion versus exclusion can even creep unseen into the language of a community. For example, statements like "we are the old-timers, they are the newcomers," "we have been here for generations, they are illegals," use categories of old versus new to create a division based on antiquity or legality. Those who have been present for generations are at the center of the community, the newcomers are on the periphery. The division can become a barrier, for example, where only those who have belonged to an institution for a long time can have a voice in its governance. Preaching in this context could challenge people to look at the language they use to talk about "others" in the community.

At the same time, people who are marginalized may try to enter the inner circle by accepting their status as "other" who deviate from the norm. This strategy keeps the peace and preserves the structure of the existing community. Under the influence of false preaching, Paul's Galatian addressees seem to have defined themselves as "deviant others" in relation to the "law-abiding" Jews. The Galatians accept submission to the law, which reclassifies them and tears down their identity in Christ. Later in the letter Paul says, "They make much of you, but for no good purpose; they want to shut you out that you may make much of them" (4:17 RSV). To "shut out" (*ekkleiein*) means to "isolate, alienate, or exclude someone or make them 'other,'" here in relation to those who are justified by the law. Encouraging marginalized people to reject alienation and the status of otherness has been one of the great contributions of liberationist movements in the last century. For example, the civil rights and women's liberation movements rejected the inferior status that enslaved these categories of people and affirmed the value of their identity.

Serve and Hope in God's Mercy

O my delight, Lord of all created things and my God! How long must I wait to see You? What remedy do You provide for one who finds so little on earth that might give some rest apart from You? O long life! O painful life! O life that is not lived! Oh, what lonely solitude; how incurable! Well, when Lord, when? How long? What shall I do, my God, what shall I do? Should I, perhaps, desire not to desire You?

But alas, alas, my Creator, what great pain it causes to complain and speak of what has no remedy until You give one! And the soul so imprisoned wants its freedom, while desiring not to depart one iota from what You want. Desire, my Glory, that its pain increase; or cure it completely. O death, death, I don't know who fears you, since life lies in you! But who will not fear after having wasted a part of life in not loving God?

Oh, my soul! Let the will of God be done; this suits you. Serve and hope in His mercy, for He will cure your grief when penance for your faults will have gained some pardon for them. Don't desire joy but suffering. O true Lord and my King! I'm still not ready for suffering if Your sovereign hand and greatness do not favor me, but with these I shall be able to do all things.

Teresa of Avila, "Painful Longing for God," in *The Collected Works of Teresa of Avila*, trans. Kieran Kavenaugh and Otilio Rodriguez, 2nd ed., vol. 1 (Washington: ICS Publications, 1987), 448–49.

Effective preaching with marginalized people affirms their identity and value in God's eyes, emphasizing that "in Christ Jesus you are all children of God through faith" (3:26).

People who live on the margins, as well as those who live in the center of society, need to see freedom from division as the work and gift of God. Galatians echoes the theme of Christ moving across social and ethnic borders found in today's Gospel reading. God moves across the borders between Greek and Jew when Jesus enters the space of pagan people in Gerasa, bringing healing and freedom (Luke 8:26–39). Similarly, Paul's ministry has brought freedom and a new identity to the Galatians, a community composed mainly of pagan converts (Acts 16:6; 18:18–28). They were tempted to embrace the rituals and traditions of Judaism, thus subjecting themselves to the law. Paul's argument against this affirms that God is present in the law *and* in the resurrection. He affirms the value of the law as a pedagogical aid—a barrier or fence that helped to keep the Jewish people from sin and together as a community (Gal. 3:25). Under new circumstances, in view of the resurrection, this is replaced by faith in Christ Jesus. Theologically and practically, preaching this concept challenges people to change their source of identity. How is this so?

For the Galatians, the fence or confinement of the law is not necessary, because their source of identity is the person of Jesus himself: "As many of you as were baptized into Christ have clothed yourselves with Christ" (3:27). God entered their pagan world, allowing them to become part of God's family. Faith in Jesus brings access to the promises of Abraham, so that all may be considered children, heirs, and inhabitants of God's kingdom. The door to enter this family of faith is listening to the gospel and believing—not circumcision. While listening and believing may seem simple—in fact *too* simple for some—this process is actually difficult for people to embrace: What? How can something so simple, that does not require supreme effort, be valued? Whether addressed in public preaching or the privacy of spiritual direction or counseling, *earning* a Christian identity is an issue that lurks under the surface of daily life in our communities. Why? Preaching the fact that Christian identity is a gift *lived into* goes against the grain of an achievement-oriented society. Even today, after centuries of Christian worship and practice, our communities still need to hear the message that faith in Christ is a *gift*, the source of our identity.

Unlike Galatians, who are new Christians, people in our communities have received their faith from their families; few are converts from paganism. Galatians challenges the self-perception of "cradle Christians." After centuries of belief and practice, there are barriers that do not allow present-day listeners of this text to think that they share one identity, that they are "one in Christ Jesus." Just as the Galatians brought their social structures with them into their Christian communities, so too our own are not immune to the divisions that characterize the dominant culture. Barriers today may be based on other categories—race, economic class, gender, disability, age, immigration status—and all are reflected in access to health care, education, housing, full participation in society, and so forth. A minister can help people identify barriers by encouraging a moment of reflection during worship. A prayer addressing this need would bring up these categories, but also allow people to add their own.

When is a social or faith identity a limitation? Galatians can challenge Christian communities' perception of people from other faith traditions, or even those who do not belong to one. The law was a fence that preserved the identity of a people, but a church can function like one as well. While a fence or border encloses and protects those who live within, it also excludes those outside. Where do our fences lie? Whom do we consider to be "in Christ"? Only the baptized? Do the rights and faith of those "outside" Christ matter? Can they also be heirs in the family of God? A surface reading of this text would respond "No" to the idea that people of other traditions may be heirs in the family of God. This is true only if we decide that there is only *one* doorway into God's kingdom. Galatians 3:8 would argue against this by reconnecting to the past: "And the scripture, foreseeing that God would justify the Gentiles by faith, declared the gospel beforehand to Abraham, saying, 'All the Gentiles shall be blessed in you.'"

RENATA FURST

Luke 8:26–39

[26]Then they arrived at the country of the Gerasenes, which is opposite Galilee. [27]As he stepped out on land, a man of the city who had demons met him. For a long time he had worn no clothes, and he did not live in a house but in the tombs. [28]When he saw Jesus, he fell down before him and shouted at the top of his voice, "What have you to do with me, Jesus, Son of the Most High God? I beg you, do not torment me"— [29]for Jesus had commanded the unclean spirit to come out of the man. (For many times it had seized him; he was kept under guard and bound with chains and shackles, but he would break the bonds and be driven by the demon into the wilds.) [30]Jesus then asked him, "What is your name?" He said, "Legion"; for many demons had entered him. [31]They begged him not to order them to go back into the abyss.

[32]Now there on the hillside a large herd of swine was feeding; and the demons begged Jesus to let them enter these. So he gave them permission. [33]Then the demons came out of the man and entered the swine, and the herd rushed down the steep bank into the lake and was drowned.

[34]When the swineherds saw what had happened, they ran off and told it in the city and in the country. [35]Then people came out to see what had happened, and when they came to Jesus, they found the man from whom the demons had gone sitting at the feet of Jesus, clothed and in his right mind. And they were afraid. [36]Those who had seen it told them how the one who had been possessed by demons had been healed. [37]Then all the people of the surrounding country of the Gerasenes asked Jesus to leave them; for they were seized with great fear. So he got into the boat and returned. [38]The man from whom the demons had gone begged that he might be with him; but Jesus sent him away, saying, [39]"Return to your home, and declare how much God has done for you." So he went away, proclaiming throughout the city how much Jesus had done for him.

Commentary 1: Connecting the Reading to Scripture

This exorcism story is one of the longest individual passages in the Synoptic tradition. The length surely points to the high level of significance accorded to it by the early church, but it also makes for a complex passage to interpret and preach.

A problem for the interpreter is determining the setting of the story. Depending on which Gospel you read and which translation you use, the setting might be Gerasa (a major city of the Decapolis that was some thirty miles from Sea of Galilee) or Gadara (a smaller city six miles from the Sea). In truth neither of these make much sense to the Lukan narrative, given that the author presents Jesus as having just arrived from crossing the "lake" (8:22–25) and having just stepped out of the boat (v. 27) when he encounters the possessed man and immediately getting in the boat when asked to leave (v. 37).

The problem of setting shows the Gospel writers either did not know the geography of the region or were not trying to paint a historical, geographical picture at this point. What is clear is that the image presented is that Jesus has crossed from Galilee across the Sea of Galilee/Lake Gennesaret to the Gentile side in the Transjordan. Jesus' healing the Gentile man and then ordering him to offer his testimony in his home/house foreshadows the Gentile mission that will play a key role in the narrative of Acts.

Another complex element of the lengthy passage that bears notice relates to its form—the flow of traditional elements in the telling of the story. Exorcism stories typically have five elements. First, the demoniac and the healer encounter one another, including some description of the manner of the demoniac's suffering. Second, Jesus often asserts power through speech, typically commanding the demon to be silent. Third, Jesus casts the demon out by verbal command. Fourth, evidence is given that the person is now free of the unclean spirit. Fifth, witnesses respond with awe. Preachers should pay attention to ways Luke follows this form and ways he creates his unique emphases by diverging from the standard form.

First, in verse 27 the possessed man and Jesus *encounter one another*. As part of the encounter, the narrator describes the severity of the man's situation; he has for a long time lived naked in the cemetery instead of in a home/house. (The surroundings of tombs were a place ancient minds would have assumed unclean spirits resided.)

Second, in verses 28–29a, Jesus does not simply command the demon to be silent but *engages it in dialogue*. This conversation is narrated in past tense in order to set up what is yet to follow. In other words, the narrator presents the possessed man (that is, the demon) as begging for mercy while recognizing Jesus as the "Son of the Most High" because Jesus has *already* commanded the unclean spirit to come out. All of this sets up in verse 29b the further description of the severity of the man's suffering to highlight the power of the unclean spirit; even though locked up with chains, the demon would break loose and drive the man wild.

In verse 30, Jesus asks the name of the demon, presumably as a way of gaining power over the demon (in contrast to the way the identity of Jesus led the demon to recognize Jesus' power). The answer given is "Legion," revealing that the man is not possessed by *a* demon, but by *many*. (At this point the narrator begins referring to the demons in the plural.) A Roman legion was a military unit of three to five thousand soldiers. No wonder the possessed man had the strength to break out of his shackles! The enormous power of the demons named here highlights all the more the power of Jesus as the one who defeats the legion.

The third element, *the actual casting out of the demon*, takes place in verses 31–33 and is presented as a sort of negotiation continuing the dialogue from above. Jesus' power is highlighted all the more in verse 31 when the demons are presented as begging to be cast into the herd of swine instead of even attempting to resist him. Specifically, they beg not to be sent to the abyss. The use of "abyss" is a Lukan editorial change from Mark, in which the demons simply request not to be thrown "out of the country" (Mark 5:10). This is the only occurrence of *abyssos* in the Gospels. In Revelation, however, the "bottomless pit" is the location of the locusts that will wreak destruction on the earth (Rev. 9:1–11), the place from which the beast will come (11:7; 17:8), and the place to which the dragon will be condemned for a thousand years (20:1–3). Luke's use of this term indicates two things. First, Luke raises the stakes beyond seeing the scene as just another healing to that of an apocalyptic battle. Second, Jesus not only has the power to cast out demons but also has the power to determine their ultimate fate.

The combination of "Legion" and "abyss" in the same story would not have been missed by ancient hearers and readers. Political and apocalyptic perspectives are inseparable for an oppressed people, in ways often difficult for first-world citizens to understand. Jesus is presented here as one powerful enough to conquer the militaristic regime and cast it into the bottomless pit forever. Jesus does not cast them into abyss but allows them to go into the herd of unclean pigs instead. The result is the same, however. By destroying the herd, the demons destroy themselves. Luke seems to be asserting that the Christ event will ultimately exorcise the oppressive Roman Empire in a manner that leads it to self-destruct. In other words, Jesus' nonviolent resistance to the powers that be shows that in actuality they are powerless. (Note that in the next lection from Luke, Jesus sets his face toward Jerusalem.) This exorcism story invites preachers to do something more than preach a Jesus that heals: to preach a Jesus who leads in directions where our faith and politics intersect.

The way Luke combines the fourth and fifth elements, the evidence of the exorcism and the response of the crowd, is perhaps the best homiletical key to how this intersection could be explored. Instead of expressing amazement, the crowds ask Jesus to leave (vv. 34–37). Like the demons, they recognize Jesus' power and are afraid. They prefer the demons they have normalized to the liberating power that is unknown. In a sense they have experienced Stockholm syndrome, in which hostages identify with the evil and destructive powers that kidnap them. Is this not an all-too-normal state of the human condition? Asking a congregation to identify with the townsfolk and consider the ways they have accepted demonic forces in their midst, over against accepting God's liberating work in the world, offers preachers the opportunity to invite hearers into the liberating work of God's reign.

In contrast to the fear of the crowd, the once-possessed man himself responds by asking Jesus to allow him to "be with him" (v. 38). Whereas Jesus granted the demons to go where they requested (albeit to their own demise), Jesus refuses to allow the man to go with him. Instead, he sends him home to tell of what "God" has done for him (v. 39a). Interestingly, the man in his obedience tells what "Jesus" had done for him (v. 39b). Luke could not be clearer: Jesus' work in overcoming the destructive powers that be is God's salvific work in the world.

O. WESLEY ALLEN JR.

Commentary 2: Connecting the Reading with the World

In today's reading, Jesus meets a man "at the country of the Gerasenes, which is opposite Galilee." The text tells us that this man was driven out of the village, wore no clothes, and was homeless, living in the tombs of the dead. Though he was guarded and bound at times, he broke the chains and would "be driven by the demon into the wilds" (Luke 8:29). Contemporary readers might immediately imagine connections between this man and some of those we encounter on the street—homeless, mumbling, or shouting to themselves (or to whoever will listen). We probably have preconceived notions about persons in these situations. Do we see "an angel unawares" (Heb. 13:2), or do we see a mentally ill person, to whom we want to give wide berth? The preacher's work involves noticing what associations the text brings to the preacher's mind and what preachers think their congregations have in mind.

The Gerasene location would have been familiar to Luke's readers. During the First Jewish War it was the site of a Jewish revolt in which the Roman general Lucius Annius massacred one thousand rebels and destroyed Gerasa and all of the villages around it. Perhaps this is why Luke, following Mark's account of this story, identifies the demons driving the man as "Legion," which is the title for a division of about five thousand Roman soldiers. Perhaps Luke, using this exact name, associated the tortured soul with the effects of imperial Rome's brutal exploitation of its colony.

Before the man addresses him, Jesus commands the unclean spirit to leave the man and enter the abyss. Acceding to their plea not to be consigned there, Jesus sends the unclean spirits into a herd of swine. The herd most likely fed Roman soldiers or others of that Gentile population, since Jews were prohibited from eating pork.

Our attention turns to another troubling aspect of the story. Many of us are cautious regarding the notion of evil spirits and possession. We tend to find other causes for the kind of mental anguish described in this text. The preacher might approach this from two different angles, (1) through contemporary research on moral injury and (2) through what Howard Thurman described as the effects of white racism on African Americans during the Jim Crow era. Both approaches address the dynamic of individuals carrying within themselves the traumatic weight of mass, generational, and systematic oppression.

We are currently learning more about the effects of trauma, particularly trauma experienced in war or other armed conflicts involving lethal force and death. Clinicians have recently described a condition called moral injury.[1] The condition can be caused by participating in, or witnessing, the killing or harming of others, events that are perceived as gross moral violations. Moral injury can manifest behaviorally as anomie (alienation, social instability), withdrawal, self-harming, self-handicapping (sabotaging relationships), and failed or harmed relationships with family and friends. The text portrays a man who exhibits all of the symptoms of moral injury: isolation, anger, self-harm and other-harm, and alienation from family and friends. Is it possible that this man witnessed or committed unconscionable acts of violence during these genocidal Roman campaigns? Might they explain the behaviors described in the text?

Moral injury is not limited to our war veterans, though they especially need our attention and the support of communal gratitude and support. The morally injured include those who have witnessed, experienced, or perpetrated emotional or physical abuse in the home; those who have survived the brutal and often violent trauma of incarceration; and those who have seen or been involved in fraudulent financial schemes—legal and illegal. These experiences and others can have the soul-searing impact of anger, self-imposed social isolation, and attempts at self-harm.

When he first encountered the Gerasene, Jesus commanded the unclean spirits to come out. It is interesting to note that one treatment for moral injury encourages a person to describe, in the context of a compassionate, forgiving presence, the experience of having killed or witnessing the killing of another human being. The man in this story fell down and cried out, asking Jesus not to torment him. From today's trauma studies and therapies we know that it is not easy to give up the mechanisms one has developed for coping with violence and terror.

Can we, can our churches, create gracious spaces where the wounded can come to be heard? Can we be honest about our own lives and the lives of others, while avoiding judgment? Can someone, like the man in our text, find healing through those willing to embody incarnational love? Can they find advocates willing to insist that our local, state, and national legislators provide funding for mental health services for our veterans and survivors of abuse? Can the preacher help broker these conversations and welcome?

Another aspect of this text is strange and perplexing. When the swine herdsmen told the people in the city and surrounding country what had happened, they went out to see for themselves. When they found the man clothed, in his right mind, and sitting at the feet of Jesus, they were afraid and asked Jesus to leave. One would expect instead that they would rejoice, since one of their own, who had been lost to them, was healed and coming home. They did not.

In his *Jesus and the Disinherited*, Thurman compared the contemporaries of Jesus, under Roman rule, to his own contemporaries, under white supremacy. Like the Jews and Samaritans in Jesus' day, the African Americans of Thurman's day faced systemic discrimination, economic exploitation, random state-supported violence, cultural invisibility to whites. Distrust and mistreatment at the hands of other African Americans came to those perceived as trying to survive by currying favor with the majority group. This violent, demeaning treatment elicited a series of coping mechanisms in the psyches and bodies of his people. Thurman called these coping mechanisms "the hounds of hell"; numbered among them is fear.[2]

Why were the villagers in our story fearful when they saw their neighbor in his right mind? Thurman observed that African Americans of his day were so fearful of arbitrary violence that it became for them an enduring state of terror as they recognized that there was no legal protection from this ad hoc violence. The terror produced a psychic tendency to be small—to restrict movement, to reduce professional ambition, and to turn away from participation in the country's common life. The villagers may have feared that their neighbor might call attention

1. https://www.ptsd.va.gov/professional/co-occurring/moral_injury_at_war.asp.
2. Howard Thurman, *Jesus and the Disinherited* (Boston: Beacon Press, 1996), 29. The other "hounds" are deception and hatred.

to his healing, his new lease on life, and his lack of fear. What did his healing mean for them? They might become the focus of Roman attention and targets of violence. At the very least, his healing upset their status quo.

According to Thurman, the awareness that one is a child of God stabilizes the self, leading to courage and power.[3] In our story, it is not entirely clear how Jesus cast out all of the demons that led to the living death for this man. What is clear is that the love of God incarnate in Jesus and those drawn to him and sent out by him had the power to heal the man. He was restored to his family and fellow villagers and took with him the power to bring healing to them. Where does the church need that healing? Where do we need it? How might we offer it?

STEPHEN BOYD

3. Thurman, *Jesus and the Disinherited*, 50.

Proper 8 (Sunday between June 26 and July 2 Inclusive)

2 Kings 2:1–2, 6–14 and 1 Kings 19:15–16, 19–21
Psalm 77:1–2, 11–20 and Psalm 16
Galatians 5:1, 13–25
Luke 9:51–62

2 Kings 2:1–2, 6–14

[1]Now when the LORD was about to take Elijah up to heaven by a whirlwind, Elijah and Elisha were on their way from Gilgal. [2]Elijah said to Elisha, "Stay here; for the LORD has sent me as far as Bethel." But Elisha said, "As the LORD lives, and as you yourself live, I will not leave you." So they went down to Bethel. . . .

[6]Then Elijah said to him, "Stay here; for the LORD has sent me to the Jordan." But he said, "As the LORD lives, and as you yourself live, I will not leave you." So the two of them went on. [7]Fifty men of the company of prophets also went, and stood at some distance from them, as they both were standing by the Jordan. [8]Then Elijah took his mantle and rolled it up, and struck the water; the water was parted to the one side and to the other, until the two of them crossed on dry ground.

[9]When they had crossed, Elijah said to Elisha, "Tell me what I may do for you, before I am taken from you." Elisha said, "Please let me inherit a double share of your spirit." [10]He responded, "You have asked a hard thing; yet, if you see me as I am being taken from you, it will be granted you; if not, it will not." [11]As they continued walking and talking, a chariot of fire and horses of fire separated the two of them, and Elijah ascended in a whirlwind into heaven. [12]Elisha kept watching and crying out, "Father, father! The chariots of Israel and its horsemen!" But when he could no longer see him, he grasped his own clothes and tore them in two pieces.

[13]He picked up the mantle of Elijah that had fallen from him, and went back and stood on the bank of the Jordan. [14]He took the mantle of Elijah that had fallen from him, and struck the water, saying, "Where is the LORD, the God of Elijah?" When he had struck the water, the water was parted to the one side and to the other, and Elisha went over.

1 Kings 19:15–16, 19–21

[15]Then the LORD said to him, "Go, return on your way to the wilderness of Damascus; when you arrive, you shall anoint Hazael as king over Aram. [16]Also you shall anoint Jehu son of Nimshi as king over Israel; and you shall anoint Elisha son of Shaphat of Abel-meholah as prophet in your place. . . .

[19]So he set out from there, and found Elisha son of Shaphat, who was plowing. There were twelve yoke of oxen ahead of him, and he was with the twelfth. Elijah passed by him and threw his mantle over him. [20]He left the oxen, ran after Elijah, and said, "Let me kiss my father and my mother, and then I will follow you." Then Elijah said to him, "Go back again; for what have I done to you?" [21]He returned from following him, took the yoke of oxen, and slaughtered them; using the equipment from the oxen, he boiled their flesh, and gave it to the people, and they ate. Then he set out and followed Elijah, and became his servant.

Commentary 1: Connecting the Reading with Scripture

The narratives comprising the Elisha cycle appear in 1 Kings 19:19–21 and 2 Kings 2–13. These stories are set within the ninth-century reigns of several northern kings, which include Ahaziah, Jehoram, Jehu, and Jehoahaz (2 Kgs. 2–9 and 13). At the fore of the designated lectionary readings is the transition of Elijah's prophetic leadership to his successor, Elisha son of Shaphat. In many ways, the aim of the Elijah-Elisha cycles is to affirm the defining traits of a Hebrew prophet. Key acts that have come to define Elijah's prophetic ministry include speaking to power, performing miracles, risking violent confrontation, discerning the voice of God, and overcoming moments of self-doubt. As we read through the Elisha stories, we discover similar prophetic deeds, which in turn serve to reify the identity and role of a Hebrew prophet. Any-one of these themes is worth taking up in a sermon; however, nefarious forms of elite power are an ever-present reality that preachers who claim to have a prophetic voice simply cannot avoid.

As important as the Elijah and Elisha similarities are for defining the Hebrew prophet, they do differ in their respective calls into prophetic ministry. For Elijah, the only hint at a prophetic call lies with the scant phrase, "The word of the LORD came to him" (1 Kgs. 17). In the Elijah narratives, 1 Kings 19:11–16 seems to present a more colorful and dramatic prophetic call. Yet this story qualifies more as a reaffirmation of Elijah's initial prophetic call, which came about after a period of self-doubt and suicidal thoughts. For Elisha, his initial prophetic call unfolds within two parts. The first occurs in 1 Kings 19:19–21, in which Elijah finds Elisha plowing a field with a large team of oxen. As verse 19 states, "Elijah passed by him and threw his mantle over him." This symbolic act marks a shift in Elisha's call from farmer to prophet in training. The second part of Elisha's calling appears in 2 Kings 2:1–14. Here the scene is marked by arduous travel, a water-parting mantle, a sky-flying chariot of fire, and a disappearing prophet master. For contemporary readers, these themes may have more in common with today's science fiction than the ancient imagination. Rather than subject these occurrences to the modern realm of make-believe and fantasy, we should ask: How can preachers expound on the faith that lies behind the miraculous and the supernatural in this passage?

In contrast to Elijah, Elisha appears not as someone who has risen from the established ranks of the monarchical prophets, but rather as an outsider, whose source of livelihood was agriculture. Taking up the ministry of prophecy as an outsider is not, however, exclusive to the Elisha story. To a certain extent, the absence of a dramatic calling event in the Elijah story is not the typical experience for Israel's archetypal Hebrew prophets. Starting with the initial prophetic call of Moses, we discover a scene that is rife with drama, suspense, and divine mystery (Exod. 3), which can also be found in the prophetic call story of Samuel (1 Sam. 3). Adding to the drama of Moses' prophetic call is the notion that he comes to it as an outsider, like Elisha, from the realm of farming (Exod. 3:1; 1 Kgs. 19:19).

This outsider trait for these prophets is less about the readiness of farmers to transfer easily into the ministry of prophecy than about the nature of God's calling process. Viewed more closely, the farmer seems to be the most unlikely candidate for the ministry of prophecy, given that this role requires speaking critically to people in power. Hence the divine principle that registers in God's prophetic call of the outsider is the notion that God can use anyone for this ministry, even the most unlikely (see Amos 7:11–15).

In the transfer of prophetic leadership from Elijah to Elisha, the spirit (*ruach*) serves as a key ingredient to the well-being and authority of the succeeding prophet. Elijah hints at the prophetic value of the spirit in his response to Elisha's spirit request, stating "You have asked a hard thing" (2 Kgs. 2:9–10). Here Elijah's notion of difficulty conversely reflects Elisha's readiness as the next prophetic leader. In other words, to ask for anything other than Elijah's spirit suggests not only a lack of prophetic discernment, but more importantly the absence of divine authority. In both parts of Elisha's prophetic call, which consist of an anointing (*mashach*,

1 Kgs. 19:16) and the spirit (*ruach*, 2 Kgs. 2:9–10), we are reminded of the corporeal and noncorporeal nature of biblical prophetic ministry. To claim such a calling in the biblical sense requires a physical preparedness (i.e., anointing) and a rootedness in the realm of the spirit. Both body and spirit were divinely given sources of life, as well as realms that the Hebrew prophet was called to change—whether with social critique or miraculous deed.

For persons in Western contexts, seeing the world outside of the rational and in the realm of the spiritual can be, in Elijah's words, "a hard thing." Yet the wisdom we receive from the Hebrew prophets is not only a rational social critique against oppressive power but also an awareness of the spirit realm. For the Hebrew prophets, the social and spiritual are intertwined in such a way that to transform them requires reason and faith, body and soul, mind and spirit. As in the Elisha story, prophetic vision understands that belief in the irrational, like a water-parting mantle, is an essential part of how to see the world. The notion that seeing is believing also holds true in Elisha's story: "when the company of prophets who were at Jericho saw him at a distance, they declared, 'The spirit of Elijah rests on Elisha'" (2 Kgs. 2:15).

Integral to a prophetic voice in today's preaching is a balance between critical reasoning and blind faith. It is critical reasoning that equips the prophetic voice of preachers with a disruptive critique against complex social injustices and oppressive forms of power. Yet an overreliance on critical reasoning can lead to a failure to develop a spiritual vision, which is also essential to understanding how evil works in the world. At the same time, an overly spiritualized approach to social realities can lead to a social shortsightedness that can be spiritually debilitating for many facing racism, anti-immigrant sentiment, and chronic poverty. As reflected in the Elisha story, the physical is not separate from the spiritual; rather, they cooperate to effect change. For Elisha, it was from Elijah's mantle that he received a double share of his master's spirit. Here the spiritual and the physical worked together to transform the physical landscape: "When he had struck the water, the water was parted to the one side and to the other, and Elisha went over" (v. 14). For those grounded in reason alone, this sort of event is physically impossible. Yet for those grounded in faith, an event such as parting the Jordan River is completely possible. However, the basis of this miracle hinges on the notion that Elisha desires not to drown, which for any reasonable person

Imitators of His Endurance

Let us . . . turn to the word that was delivered to us from the beginning, being alert in prayer and persistent in fasting. Through our entreaties let us ask the God who sees all things not to bring us into temptation, just as the Lord said, "For the spirit is willing but the flesh is weak."

Thus we should persevere, unremitting in our hope and in the down payment of our righteousness, which is Christ Jesus, who bore our sins in his own body on the tree, who did not commit sin nor was deceit found in his mouth; but he endured all things on our account, that we might live in him.

Therefore we should be imitators of his endurance, and if we suffer for his name, we should give him the glory. For he set this example for us through what he did, and we have believed it.

Therefore I urge all of you to obey the word of righteousness and to practice all endurance, which you also observed with your own eyes . . . in Paul himself and the other apostles.

You should be convinced that none of them acted in vain, but in faith and righteousness, and that they are in the place they deserved, with the Lord, with whom they also suffered. For they did not love the present age; they loved the one who died for us and who was raised by God for our sakes.

Polycarp (ca. 69–ca. 159), "Letter to the Philippians," 7–9, in *The Apostolic Fathers*, vol. 1, *I Clement. II Clement. Ignatius. Polycarp. Didache*, trans. Bart D. Ehrman, Loeb Classical Library 24 (Cambridge, MA: Harvard University Press, 2003), 343, 345.

is what can happen when wading through deep torrent waters. In the end, the prophet utilizes both reason and faith to effect both physical and spiritual change. This is the ultimate trait of the Hebrew prophet, for without both working hand in hand, the result is not prophetic transformation, but simply politics and religion.

GREGORY L. CUÉLLAR

Commentary 2: Connecting the Reading with the World

In 2 Kings 2, we encounter a biblical testimony that is wild, unparalleled, and at points unfathomable. While there are relevant lessons here about vocational calling and leadership succession, we may want to learn most deeply from this text by respecting its inscrutability. The prophetic calling and eventual retirement of Elijah through heavenly ascension behind a chariot of fire does not map easily onto our realities—and perhaps that is just the point. Elijah is the one who will prepare hearts for the coming Messiah (see Mal. 4:5–6); that task must orient us beyond the typical bounds of imagination, politics, and even death. So, while we can listen for lessons with direct, immediate applicability, this text may be most powerful when it illustrates how God ultimately operates beyond our narrow definitions and limited creativity in ways that consistently unsettle our routine sense of religious, social, and political practice. God's vision and salvific ends will exceed our expectations. We should hope that the awesome majesty of God lures us, in the name of love and redemption, beyond the constraints of what we think might be possible.

Our first introduction to Elisha, in 1 Kings 19:16, comes in a decidedly revolutionary moment for Elijah. In instructing his prophet to go back on mission, God declares that Elijah will anoint two new kings as the rightful rulers of Aram and Israel. Mind you, these areas already have living rulers; so Elijah is basically ritualizing a coup as a promise for what is to come. Elijah's third anointing, of Elisha, will identify Elisha as his prophetic successor, thereby folding him into this exceedingly risky journey. Elijah finds Elisha tilling the earth with his twelve oxen and, according to the pithy narrator, merely throws his mantle over Elisha as the indication that he is to follow the great prophet of YHWH. Somehow Elisha recognizes this call and gives his immediate acceptance, but asks if he can go kiss his parents. In contrast with some calling narratives, Elisha does not immediately abandon his family and community but, rather, takes time, albeit brief, to thank them with a meal. His example reminds us to appreciate deeply the communities that send those called to radical mission. The preacher could bring this word as confirmation and blessing to congregations that continue such missional commitments. While his parents and fellow celebrants do not join Elisha on his mission, he does not shame or excoriate those he leaves behind. Rather, he thanks them, perhaps for the fertile spiritual ground they have cultivated in him.

The sudden nature of Elisha's call and his quick acceptance are surprising. Elisha does not require convincing or a grand negotiation from Elijah, but we do not know in what ways Elisha's faith background has prepared him for this moment. While many of us may lack such a decisive call story, Elisha's response invites us personally and ecclesially to consider when and how we prepare ourselves to say yes to what God most needs in our time. Although likely from a wealthy family, Elisha's deep connection to God and carefully listening to the suffering of his people spurred him to say yes to great risk. The Confessing Church in Nazi Germany and the Underground Railroad network during the years of US slavery did not suddenly appear but were built on decades of intentional formation and continual gradual witness against the perverted political power of their day. How might we practice (e.g., through formative prayer, continual acts of service, conscious ethical defiance) a kind of lived faith that fosters willingness to, one day, perhaps risk our lives to say no to evil? With deep formation, we may be more ready and able to act when we feel the mantle fall on our shoulders—to become a sanctuary church (housing persons about to be deported), or to stand in solidarity with the marginalized (for example, registering as a Muslim in the face of a Muslim ban), or to organize disruptive protests (for example, until everyone is guaranteed health care). Elisha invites us to consider how we could say yes to our deepest calling from God, whatever form that may take.

In 2 Kings 2, we rejoin Elijah and Elisha's story at the end of Elijah's prophetic career. Elijah has gone from having missional despair and a death wish in 1 Kings 19:4, to witnessing the anointing of Jehoram come to full fruition in Ahaziah's death. The great prophet has seen the demise of a series of disastrous kings, has developed his successor, and is ready to retire. In a curious test of loyalty, he tries to make Elisha stay behind at each stage of his final tour through central Israel, but Elisha will not leave his side, even as the cohort of prophets keeps reminding him that Elijah will soon be taken away. Elisha shows a vocational persistence and endurance that is vital for succeeding the great prophet. The preacher could connect this insight to ways that people carry on urgent ministries handed down to them by those who have gone before.

When they finally come to the river Jordan, Elijah again uses the mantle to allow them to cross the parted water. As Walter Brueggemann notes, this transitions them beyond the settled territory of the monarchy back to the wilderness, where prophets continually find their renewal.[1] This liminal space, beyond the power and rules of the earthly monarchy, reconnects them with the uncontained power and alternate vision of YHWH. While there, Elijah asks if there is anything that he can do for Elisha, and Elisha asks for double the share of Elijah's spirit. We do not know what motivates his request, but at some level Elisha knows that being named successor is not enough. He needs the spirit of God.

The echoes of Moses' parting the Red Sea are intentional here, but importantly, Elijah's final moments will surpass even Moses', as Elijah will not die but will ascend to heaven, separated from earth by a chariot and horses of fire. This scene has been the subject of numerous paintings and icons; the wonder of it compels—and yet exceeds—creative imagination. The ascension serves to underscore the importance of Elijah as the special messenger who points his people to the coming Messiah (Mal. 4:5–6). During the Passover Seder meal, Jews enact Elijah's importance, pouring him a cup of wine and opening the door for him at the meal's conclusion. The fifth cup of wine, Elijah's cup, is not consumed and represents a return to the land and the future redemption he promised. Elijah both reminds the community of redemptions that have come before and beckons them into the almost unimaginable messianic redemption that awaits them.

In the end, our passage from 2 Kings concludes with Elisha picking up the mantle that has fallen once again upon him, asking where the Lord is, and striking the water to walk back across the river Jordan. Elisha has experienced a prophetic wilderness that deepened his wonder at God's redemptive power and subsequently returned him to his prophetic mission. He rejoins the seeming mundane to show how God's ultimate, and almost unfathomable, redemption continues to manifest in everyday redemptions. Elisha could not linger in the place of truly awesome wonder, but does receive the spirit in order to return and disrupt the routinized expectations of power, healing, and salvation. Perhaps this is precisely what this passage must remind us to do: open ourselves to the undoing of our limited imagination, ask the Spirit of God to help us embrace redemption, and return to our daily task enacting glimpses of the radical new reign of God.

C. MELISSA SNARR

1. Walter Brueggemann, *1 and 2 Kings* (Macon, GA: Smyth & Helwys Publishing, Inc., 2000), 294–95.

Psalm 77:1–2, 11–20

[1]I cry aloud to God,
aloud to God, that he may hear me.
[2]In the day of my trouble I seek the Lord;
in the night my hand is stretched out without wearying;
my soul refuses to be comforted.
. . . .
[11]I will call to mind the deeds of the LORD;
I will remember your wonders of old.
[12]I will meditate on all your work,
and muse on your mighty deeds.
[13]Your way, O God, is holy.
What god is so great as our God?
[14]You are the God who works wonders;
you have displayed your might among the peoples.
[15]With your strong arm you redeemed your people,
the descendants of Jacob and Joseph.

[16]When the waters saw you, O God,
when the waters saw you, they were afraid;
the very deep trembled.
[17]The clouds poured out water;
the skies thundered;
your arrows flashed on every side.
[18]The crash of your thunder was in the whirlwind;
your lightnings lit up the world;
the earth trembled and shook.
[19]Your way was through the sea,
your path, through the mighty waters;
yet your footprints were unseen.
[20]You led your people like a flock
by the hand of Moses and Aaron.

Psalm 16

[1]Protect me, O God, for in you I take refuge.
[2]I say to the LORD, "You are my Lord;
I have no good apart from you."

[3]As for the holy ones in the land, they are the noble,
in whom is all my delight.

[4]Those who choose another god multiply their sorrows;
their drink offerings of blood I will not pour out
or take their names upon my lips.

[5]The LORD is my chosen portion and my cup;
you hold my lot.
[6]The boundary lines have fallen for me in pleasant places;
I have a goodly heritage.

[7]I bless the LORD who gives me counsel;
in the night also my heart instructs me.
[8]I keep the LORD always before me;
because he is at my right hand, I shall not be moved.

[9]Therefore my heart is glad, and my soul rejoices;
my body also rests secure.
[10]For you do not give me up to Sheol,
or let your faithful one see the Pit.

[11]You show me the path of life.
In your presence there is fullness of joy;
in your right hand are pleasures forevermore.

Connecting the Psalm with Scripture and Worship

Psalm 77. Psalm 77 contains expressions of both lament and trust. The psalmist begins, "I cry aloud to God. . . . in the day of my trouble I seek the Lord. . . . my spirit faints" (vv. 1–3). From the pit of despair, the psalmist asks hard questions: Has God's steadfast love ceased forever? Are God's promises at an end? Has God forgotten to be gracious? (vv. 8–9). After the laments of a troubled soul, Psalm 77 changes in tone: "Your way, O God, is holy. . . . You are the God who works wonders; you have displayed your might" (vv. 13–14). The question becomes rhetorical: "What god is so great as our God?" (v. 13). The dramatic shift from lament to trust occurs after the psalmist calls to mind, remembers, and considers the mighty deeds of the Lord (vv. 11–12). Psalm 77 is one of a special group of storytelling psalms, in which the central subject is the recitation of YHWH's mighty deeds in the history of Israel, reminding people of God's faithfulness. Remembering how God has been faithful—redeeming the descendants of Jacob and Joseph (v. 15) and Moses and Aaron (v. 20), leading the people out of slavery and into the promised land—turns the psalmist's turmoil into trust.

The transformation from lament to trust is evident in 2 Kings 2:1–2, 6–14. As Elijah was taken up to heaven, Elisha called out, "Where is the LORD, the God of Elijah?" (v. 14). Like the psalmist, Elisha searched for answers and for God. Then, remembering what Elijah taught him about the mighty acts of God, Elisha picked up the mantle given to him by Elijah and struck the water. Just then, "the water was parted to the one side and to the other" (v. 14), and Elisha went over and continued his work, testifying to the mighty acts of God.

These texts call the preacher to help the congregation remember the central stories of faith and to embolden worshipers to move from lament to trust. Walter Brueggemann concludes, "Everything depends on having the public, canonical memory available which becomes in this moment of pain a quite powerful, personal hope."[1] In the stories of Elijah and Elisha, Jacob and Joseph, Moses and Aaron, one central message is that we cannot do this alone. We need a community to help us remember the promises of our faith. When we can think only of our pain, others remind us of God's presence. When we cannot sing, others sing for us. When we cannot

1. Walter Brueggemann, *Israel's Praise: Doxology against Idolatry and Ideology* (Philadelphia: Fortress Press, 1988), 140.

pray, others pray for us. When we hunger and thirst, others feed us with the bread of life and the cup of salvation, because Jesus says, "Do this in remembrance of me." When we forget, others remind us what is true: God has been our help in ages past and is our hope for years to come.

As Psalm 77 moves from lament to trust, it can be used throughout the liturgy. The first verses (vv. 1–3) can be used as a prayer of confession, the last verses (vv. 11–20) as a declaration of forgiveness or profession of faith. The theme of the psalm lends itself to hymns such as "Great Is Thy Faithfulness," "Our God, Our Help in Ages Past," and "God of the Ages, Whose Almighty Hand." The worship leader might employ a ritual of remembering, in which people are invited to write on a small piece of paper something they want to remember about God on one side, and on the other side, something or someone they want God to remember. After silent reflection, they can put their papers in an offering basket or hang them on a prayer wall, while the congregation sings, "Healer of Our Every Ill."

Psalm 77 reminds us of the God who was faithful, still is faithful, and will transform our lament to trust and our prayers to praise.

Psalm 16. Psalm 16, a psalm of trust that professes confidence in God, begins with a centering prayer: "Protect me, O God, for in you I take refuge" (v. 1), and ends with a sending prayer: "You show me the path of life" (v. 11). Trust is formed in the Lord who gives counsel and instructs (v. 7) and is always present (v. 8), so that the psalmist remains steadfast and secure (vv. 8, 9). With confidence, the psalmist warns against following another god (v. 4) and espouses the blessings of following the Lord (v. 10): fullness of joy and pleasures forevermore (v. 11). In times of being sheltered and in times of being sent out, God is powerfully present.

The theme of trust found in Psalm 16 is also found in 1 Kings 19:15–16, 19–21. When the nation of Israel has divided and the northern kingdom has fallen, and faithful kings are few, God sends Elijah to anoint Elisha as a prophet. Elijah throws the mantle over Elisha, a symbolic act that delivers a summons to go and a sign that God will be with him. It is a call to trust God, and Elisha answers by following Elijah. Psalm 16 could have been the words of Elisha, trusting God as a familiar refuge, to lead him forth into the unknown.

Trust is what Jesus is looking for when he calls people to follow him. In Luke 9:51–62, when Jesus calls, "Follow me," one says, "Yes, but . . . let me go back to my family." Essentially, Jesus' response is that in following him there are no "buts"; if you have trust, like that of the psalmist, you will be confident that God will protect and provide, shelter and send you out.

Psalm 16 reveals two preaching avenues. The first is to preach that God is our refuge (v. 1), to be still and to appreciate the glory and goodness of God (v. 2). To trust is to believe that God is always at work, trying to bring good out of evil—as evidenced through Elijah and Elisha, and in Jesus, who endured the cross, trusting that life would ultimately triumph over death. The second approach is to preach a call to trust and follow God into the world, on the path of life (v. 11), to a life of discipleship. To trust is to step out in faith, to speak a word of justice, to offer a touch of mercy, to walk humbly, to welcome the stranger, trusting that God will show us the way.

Psalm 16 also offers liturgical uses. It can be read responsively, with the Taizé hymn "Bless the Lord" sung as a refrain after verses 1–3, 5–8, and 9–11. The first two verses of Psalm 16 can be used as a call to worship, and the last verse as a charge. If the preacher focuses on God as a refuge, a good hymn choice is "The God of Abraham Praise." If the focus is on the call to follow Jesus on the path of life, an inspiring hymn would be "Will You Come and Follow Me." If both themes were combined in the sermon, an appropriate sending hymn might be "Just a Closer Walk with Thee." Today's texts also lend themselves to a commissioning ritual—for church officers or Stephen ministers or for youth going on a summer mission trip.

Psalm 16 calls people to trust and follow God who calls us in for refuge and calls us out to reshape the world. The people respond with trust in God, who is always before us, always at work through us for good.

DONNA GIVER-JOHNSTON

Galatians 5:1, 13–25

[1]For freedom Christ has set us free. Stand firm, therefore, and do not submit again to a yoke of slavery. . . .

[13]For you were called to freedom, brothers and sisters; only do not use your freedom as an opportunity for self-indulgence, but through love become slaves to one another. [14]For the whole law is summed up in a single commandment, "You shall love your neighbor as yourself." [15]If, however, you bite and devour one another, take care that you are not consumed by one another.

[16]Live by the Spirit, I say, and do not gratify the desires of the flesh. [17]For what the flesh desires is opposed to the Spirit, and what the Spirit desires is opposed to the flesh; for these are opposed to each other, to prevent you from doing what you want. [18]But if you are led by the Spirit, you are not subject to the law. [19]Now the works of the flesh are obvious: fornication, impurity, licentiousness, [20]idolatry, sorcery, enmities, strife, jealousy, anger, quarrels, dissensions, factions, [21]envy, drunkenness, carousing, and things like these. I am warning you, as I warned you before: those who do such things will not inherit the kingdom of God.

[22]By contrast, the fruit of the Spirit is love, joy, peace, patience, kindness, generosity, faithfulness, [23]gentleness, and self-control. There is no law against such things. [24]And those who belong to Christ Jesus have crucified the flesh with its passions and desires. [25]If we live by the Spirit, let us also be guided by the Spirit.

Commentary 1: Connecting the Reading with Scripture

In this text Paul exhorts the Galatians to remain in the freedom that Christ has established (Gal. 5:1, 13). This freedom enables the Galatians to belong to the Christian community without submitting to certain Jewish rituals. This exhortation extends Paul's plea for the Galatians to choose freedom over slavery in the allegory of Hagar and Sarah (Gal. 4:21–31).

The Galatians' submission to the law is tantamount to slavery. Christ had redeemed Gentiles from the necessity of becoming Jews when joining the covenant family (Gal. 3:13). Undergoing circumcision would undercut Christ's redemptive work on behalf of Gentiles. Thus, in Galatians 5:4 Paul asserts, "You who want to be justified by the law have cut yourselves off from Christ; you have fallen away from grace." Separation from Christ is exile of the worst kind. By removing people from the protective covering of God's grace, this separation leaves people vulnerable to the influences of evil.

Paul's warning about falling away from grace emboldens preachers to examine the negative forces that compromise our individual and communal well-being. Paul believes there are evil forces that seek to undermine God's purposes. He refers to these cosmological forces in Galatians as "elemental spirits" (e.g., 4:3, 9). Whether or not we subscribe to Paul's ancient cosmology, significant contemporary forces such as mean-spirited nationalism and predatory capitalism create, and embed themselves in, social systems. These unjust social systems foster suffering and inequality among individuals and entire communities.

Fearing that the Galatians might misinterpret their freedom as a license for immorality, Paul offers ethical instructions throughout this passage. In the history of scholarship, some interpreters have considered Paul's ethical exhortations as inconsequential "filler" with no integral relationship to his theology. On the contrary, Paul's ethical admonitions "are not secondary but radically integral to his basic theological convictions."[1] In other words, authentic Christian discipleship requires *both* righteous beliefs *and* righteous behaviors.

Concerning the connection between theology and ethics, the Galatians' desire to submit to the law might have been the ironic consequence of Paul's theology. The Galatians' acceptance of the gospel was not without social cost. Joining the Christian community would have involved the Galatians' disassociating themselves from their families and former religious practices. The social destabilization of accepting the gospel might have left the Galatians longing for the solid foundation that religious rituals can provide.[2]

Having accepted Paul's message of freedom, the Galatians found, ironically, that the freedom of the gospel made them anxious and gave them a precarious social identity. They were unsure now about the moral rules for everyday living. Consequently, they turned to the Jewish law for guidance and structure. Thus, it may be that Paul's message of freedom paradoxically drove the Galatians to their bondage.

Therefore, Paul explains his notion of freedom and establishes his own paradox. Christian freedom is not unbridled but is manifested in a slavery to the welfare of one's neighbors (5:13). When communities fail to accentuate the primacy of love, a competitive, destructive impulse is unleashed, which consumes individuals and erodes communal bonds (vv. 14–15).

If the law is not the safeguard against sin and the misuse of freedom, what is? Paul responds, "The Holy Spirit!" Thus, in Galatians 5:16 he writes, "Live by the Spirit, I say, and do not gratify the desires of the flesh." Throughout Galatians, Paul has signaled the importance of the Holy Spirit (3:2–5 and 4:6), and here once again he emphasizes the Spirit. The same Spirit that created and confirmed the Galatians' covenant acceptance by God is also sufficient to guide their ethical affairs.

Having instructed the Galatians about the efficacy of the Spirit as an ethical guide, Paul names vices that are characteristic of life under "the flesh." When Paul speaks of the flesh, he often has in mind human existence dominated by sin, and Paul has a robust understanding of sin.

Paul thinks of Sin as a cosmic power that willfully opposes the ways of God (e.g., Rom. 5–6). Thus, when believers live according to the flesh, they invite Sin to rule over their lives like a despotic monarch. The presence of Sin with a capital *S* is what then leads to sin with a lowercase *s*—those vices that Paul refers to as "the works of the flesh" (Gal. 5:19–21).

Paul then names virtues that are characteristic of a life led by the Spirit. These he calls "the fruit of the Spirit" (vv. 22–23). When believers are deeply planted in the sustaining soil of the Spirit, they will produce an abundant harvest of holy living.

Preachers can emphasize that sanctification is a priority of the Holy Spirit. Sanctification is the ongoing invitation to host God's presence—a presence that radically transforms all our relationships, if we would only submit to it and let it have its way. Sanctification is ultimately not asceticism (denying ourselves to death) or athleticism (working ourselves to death). Sanctification is acceptance—allowing God's Spirit to love us into new life, abundant life, and finally everlasting life.

The vices and virtues discussed in Galatians 5:19–23 involve behaviors that either destroy or edify the community. Generally, the works of the flesh destroy unity and community, while the fruit of the Spirit promotes communal well-being. The Spirit empowers believers to seek what is right not only in their relationships with God but also in their relationships with other people. Truly spiritual people seek the common good of all persons, while being especially attentive to the difficulties and needs of fellow believers (6:2, 10).

Preachers should notice the strong social emphasis of Paul's ethical admonitions. Often in traditional Christian piety, moral transgression and transformation are discussed mainly in terms of individuals, not with respect to communities and social systems. Paul teaches,

1. Victor Paul Furnish, *Theology and Ethics in Paul* (Nashville: Abingdon Press, 1968), 13.
2. John M. G. Barclay, *Obeying the Truth: A Study of Paul's Ethics in Galatians* (Edinburgh: T&T Clark, 1988), 58.

however, that ethics entails social, as well as individual, realities.

Paul refers to the forces that destroy community in the plural: "the works of the flesh." The forces that oppose freedom are not singular; nor do they wage war simply on the individual level. They are collective forces that attack entire cultures and institutions. For example, a lust for profit led many large American financial institutions to engage in predatory lending practices that resulted in a national mortgage crisis in 2007. Those practices "devoured" and "consumed" the wealth of many innocent and vulnerable people (5:15). Even a decade later, many of these people have yet to recover from the devastating effects of this social sin.

Similarly, contemporary Christian understandings of "salvation" or "sanctification" that do not address social realities misrepresent the truth of the incarnation. Christ was embodied in order to liberate embodied people from embodied problems. Spiritual people do not retreat from "the world" in order to avoid moral contamination. Rather, the Holy Spirit motivates believers to engage the world with the hopes of returning it to holiness—or, perhaps better, *wholeness*.

Social wholeness occurs when we pursue holiness in two directions. Vertical holiness compels us to establish a right relationship with God. Horizontal holiness compels us to establish right relationships with God's diverse children, who are our sacred siblings.

A congregation might examine carefully the fruit of the Spirit in Galatians 5:22–23, seeking ways to manifest each fruit concretely in the arena of social justice. A congregation's desire to bear the fruit of "love" or "peace" might compel it to lobby state legislatures for the end of the death penalty, or it might prompt a congregation to pursue interfaith collaboration with a neighboring synagogue or mosque.

BRAD R. BRAXTON

Commentary 2: Connecting the Reading with the World

Paul's argument in Galatians circles back again and again to the exhortation to be free from slavery, which is the yoke of the law. "For freedom Christ has set us free. Stand firm, therefore, and do not submit again to a yoke of slavery" (5:1). What is the attraction of slavery? Why would anyone want to return to it? Perhaps, for the Galatians, as for us, a yoke is a known pattern of behavior, "badges" that set us apart and give us a social identity, or a comfortable standard that neatly divides life into black and white. To live into the tension of freedom, we must embrace discomfort, messiness, and gray areas in relationships, worship, belief, and commitment.

The Galatians are a community "in tension that's learning to fly."[3] They live in a world where the things we take for granted today—custom, ritual, worship, a calendar for community celebration, even written Scripture—the things that "ground" their lives, their communities, are in flux. As a pioneering first-century community, they live in the creative tension of faith in Christ Jesus, with little or no tradition to center or ground their experience as Gentile Christians. The preacher may make a connection for us today, as our center or ground is being shifted: we too know that many of our cherished customs, beliefs, and traditions are questioned by our culture. Even so, as the Pink Floyd song puts it, are we free to live in the unsettling "tension of learning to fly"?

In the chapter that precedes this passage, Paul may be describing the attraction for slavery to the law that holds sway over the Galatians. He uses two analogies to explain the role of the law in the life of a Jewish believer. The law is a "fence" or protective custody, to make sure that the identity of the chosen, Israelite community is preserved in the midst of all the nations (3:23). The law can also be a tutor, a guardian or custodian, a servant whose task is to supervise the education of the children of

3. Jon Carin, Bob Ezrin, Dave Gilmour, and Anthony Moore (Pink Floyd), "Learning to Fly," 1979; http://www.azlyrics.com/lyrics/pinkfloyd/learningtofly.html.

a household (3:24). The role of the tutor ends with the child's transition into adult life. In this analogy, the Jews under the law were legally minors, knowing what the law entailed, yet struggling to live by it. This was a stage that would end with the coming of Christ. As the parent of any child transitioning into adult life knows, taking full responsibility for oneself is difficult. The joys of freedom can sometimes seem to be overwhelmed by the trials of responsibility. So a young person may try to regress to his or her role as a minor. This could explain the Galatians' hankering after the boundaries of the law. It may also explain the often outright rejection of preaching that calls an individual or community to maturity. People prefer the familiar boundaries of being a beloved child to the more challenging status of an adult who stands firm in the freedom for which "Christ has set us free."

In Galatians, Paul gives his readers a clear picture of life lived under the law, contrasted with life in the Spirit. He layers a series of polarities—slavery vs. freedom, law vs. faith in Christ, flesh vs. Spirit—to build a trajectory that will shape the Gentiles in the Galatian communities, depending on the path they decide to take. Concretely, a life lived in slavery, subject to law and to the flesh, results in "fornication, impurity, licentiousness, idolatry, sorcery, enmities, strife, jealousy, anger, quarrels, dissensions, factions, envy, drunkenness, carousing, and things like these" (5:19–21). A decision to live in the Spirit, in freedom, through faith in Christ, produces fruits of "love, joy, peace, patience, kindness, generosity, faithfulness, gentleness, and self-control" (5:22–23). The preacher can help hearers reflect on the question: Which trajectory, with its fruits, do *we* choose? Slavery, law, flesh? Freedom, faith in Christ, life in the Spirit? We, ourselves and the communities we serve, freely choose the path we take and the fruit we live by.

Paul turns the concept of slavery upside down. To be set free is to be called out of comfort and self-indulgence, but it does not imply complete disregard for the guidance of the law. The circumcised must adhere to the many precepts of the law, whereas the one justified by faith fulfills the law, "for the whole law is summed up in a single commandment, 'You shall love your neighbor as yourself'" (5:14). "Summed up" in this verse means "fulfilled, completed, finished." This completion or fulfillment requires sacrifice of self, because love can also be a form of slavery: "For you were called to freedom, brothers and sisters; only do not use your freedom as an opportunity for self-indulgence, but through love become slaves to one another" (5:13). Ironically, this "love slavery" tears down boundaries that create exclusion. The preacher can help us know that this love slavery includes and makes neighbors across the divides of class, race, gender, immigration status. Love slavery even stretches out toward "the point of no turning back," to touch the lives of those who betray, hurt, and try to diminish us, to our enemies. Freedom is slavery of a different order; its boundaries are created by love.

Freedom can feel like danger. The overwhelming, raw fear of change can sometimes drive people and communities to the comfort of familiarity, and political correctness. Today's Gospel shows how people can be trapped by a false sense of responsibility: "To another Jesus said, 'Follow me.' But he said, 'Lord, first let me go and bury my father.' But Jesus said to him, 'Let the dead bury their own dead; but as for you, go and proclaim the kingdom of God'" (Luke 9:59–60). The man wants to bury his father, an act of filial love and righteousness; yet to Jesus this is living in a "dead zone," instead of the life-giving kingdom of God. Preachers can help us see that today familiarity, responsibility, and political correctness could look something like pouring our efforts into a career that is not a calling for us; enabling destructive behavior in the name of parental love; keeping quiet about an injustice that bobs up and down in our consciousness. These can become dead zones in our personal and communal lives. Yet they are all created by the righteous role of the quiet, uncomplaining, law-abiding citizen or member of a congregation who gradually becomes enslaved. Familiar social boundaries that once provided guidance, the law that provided a fence for the Jews, no longer hold us in safety; they become a yoke that shapes and creates in us "the mind of a slave" (Rom. 7:23).

What is freedom really like when we embrace it? "But if you are led by the Spirit, you are not subject to the law" (Gal. 5:18). It is a walk in the Spirit, a vision beyond immediate reality. We open our eyes and look up to the skies. Although our feet are anchored in reality, we raise our eyes and dare to live in "love, joy, peace, patience, kindness, generosity, faithfulness, gentleness, and self-control" (5:22–23). Comfort is not on this list. We, ourselves, our communities, our preaching and living, are determined to try, to stand firm, because "for freedom Christ has set us free" (5:1).

RENATA FURST

Luke 9:51–62

[51]When the days drew near for him to be taken up, he set his face to go to Jerusalem. [52]And he sent messengers ahead of him. On their way they entered a village of the Samaritans to make ready for him; [53]but they did not receive him, because his face was set toward Jerusalem. [54]When his disciples James and John saw it, they said, "Lord, do you want us to command fire to come down from heaven and consume them?" [55]But he turned and rebuked them. [56]Then they went on to another village.

[57]As they were going along the road, someone said to him, "I will follow you wherever you go." [58]And Jesus said to him, "Foxes have holes, and birds of the air have nests; but the Son of Man has nowhere to lay his head." [59]To another he said, "Follow me." But he said, "Lord, first let me go and bury my father." [60]But Jesus said to him, "Let the dead bury their own dead; but as for you, go and proclaim the kingdom of God." [61]Another said "I will follow you, Lord; but let me first say farewell to those at my home." [62]Jesus said to him, "No one who puts a hand to the plow and looks back is fit for the kingdom of God."

Commentary 1: Connecting the Reading to Scripture

Luke 9:51 is one of the most explicitly important structural moments in the Lukan narrative. Since 4:15, Jesus has been an itinerant minister in and around Galilee. Now he sets his face to go to Jerusalem. The next, lengthy section of the Gospel is the travel narrative (9:51–19:27), as Jesus slowly makes his way to Jerusalem, teaching his disciples along the way.

When Jesus turns toward Jerusalem, he is heading not only toward the city but also toward his destiny. The symbolic importance of Jerusalem for Luke is highlighted early by narrative elements unique to this Gospel. After his birth, Jesus is taken to the temple to be presented to the Lord (2:22), and his arrival there is accompanied by prophetic acclamations (2:25–38). Jesus attends Passover in Jerusalem every year as a child (2:41), and when he is twelve, he is found conversing with the teachers in the temple (2:42–50). Finally, in his temptation, the climactic trial occurs in Jerusalem (4:9–12; cf. Matt. 4:8–11).

Indeed, Jerusalem is the geographical center of Luke's two-volume narrative. The whole of the Gospel heads toward Jerusalem, and all of Acts moves out from Jerusalem toward Rome (Acts 1:8). Thus Luke 9:51 is a key line pointing to that geographical center and making explicit that Jesus will meet his ultimate fate at that geographical center. That Jerusalem holds his destiny is seen in the phrasing Luke uses to describe what is to come. First, whereas the NRSV is correct in translating the Greek to say that the days "drew near" for Jesus to be taken up, *symplērousthai* can be more thickly translated as "fulfilled." Throughout Luke, Jesus makes clear that "it is necessary" for him to be rejected, suffer, and die in Jerusalem (9:22; 13:33; 17:25; 18:31; 22:37; 24:7), so "fulfilled" is not too heavy of a translation for 9:51. Since at this early point in the narrative Luke presents Jesus as beginning to think about the cross, so should the preacher. Although we are in Ordinary Time, from this point on preachers should attend to ways Luke foreshadows the crucifixion and bring it up as a recurring element of sermons.

Second, even though we have been discussing the cross, it is striking that the narrator actually describes Jesus' fate in terms of his being "taken up," that is, his ascension. While in Mark and Matthew the resurrected Jesus is presented as returning to Galilee to meet with the disciples, in Luke–Acts Christ appears to the disciples in

Jerusalem until he ascends (Luke 24:50–51; Acts 1:9). Certainly here the ascension is not only a specific event but also a symbol for the whole sequence of Jesus' suffering, death, resurrection, and ascension. Still, the figurative use of ascension as opposed to the crucifixion at this key moment hints at a significant element of Luke's soteriology. For Luke the cross is less the locus of salvation and more the necessary death of a martyr. This martyrdom leads to salvation through the resurrection and gift of the Spirit, which becomes the means of God's ongoing salvific presence in the church after Jesus has departed.

Following the key structural element of 9:51, Luke tells of Jesus' being rejected in Samaria. In Acts 1:8, Jesus instructs the disciples to be his witnesses in Jerusalem, in Judea and Samaria, and to the ends of the earth. This outward-moving geography in Acts (ending in Paul's being in Rome, Acts 28:16–31) is a reversal of the Jerusalem-headed structure in Luke. This hourglass movement of Luke–Acts is a theological construct as well as a geographical one: Jesus goes through Samaria and Judea to Jerusalem so that following his death, resurrection, and ascension, salvation in him might spread out through Judea and Samaria to the whole of the world.

Luke's is the only Gospel that presents Jesus as traveling through Samaria. The traditional way Galilean Jews traveled to Judea was to cross the Jordan River in the east, travel south in the Transjordan, and then cross back into Judea to the west. This was done to avoid traveling through Samaria, due to the deep rivalry between Jews and their "unclean" cousins. Luke, however, shows that Samaritans have a place in the church. He lifts up Samaritans in the parable of the Good Samaritan (10:30–37) and in the healing of the ten lepers (17:11–19). In Acts, Luke portrays Samaritans as receiving the gospel and the Holy Spirit (8:5–25). Luke has a constant concern for the outsider, a concern preachers should relay to their congregations, especially in the face of deep divisions in our culture.

Still, Jesus' first encounter with Samaritans in Luke is one in which he is rejected. Two connections help readers see the literary-theological purpose of this portrayal. The first such connection is that Luke 9:51 seems to echo Isaiah 50:7. There the Suffering Servant says, "I have *set my face* like flint, and I know that I shall not be put to shame" (italics added). The context of the line makes it clear that the Servant is expecting rejection and opposition that will lead to suffering. Thus, when the narrator tells us that Jesus "set his face" toward Jerusalem (9:51), we should not be surprised to hear of opposition in the very next scene. Indeed, from this point on in the narrative, Jesus will face more and more opposition, leading to the cross, but God will not allow him to be shamed.

The second connection is found in Jesus' description of the ministry of the Twelve. In 9:1–12, Jesus sends them out with instructions to "take nothing for your journey." They are to rely completely on the hospitality of those to whom they minister. He instructs them, "Wherever they do not welcome you, as you are leaving that town shake the dust off your feet as a testimony against them" (9:5). When James and John ask whether they should command fire to destroy the village for rejecting Jesus (9:54), they show that they have already forgotten Jesus' instructions. Jesus' action of simply leaving the village may seem a weak ending to the story, but that is exactly the point. Christians are not to lash out, condemn, or despise those who reject the gospel we offer. To do so is counter to the gospel we offer and closes us off to other opportunities of ministry with them.

Indeed, in the very next scene (vv. 57–62) Jesus engages three Samaritans who desire to follow him. Often readers assume that Jesus' three pronouncements making clear how radical a call to follow Jesus is (vv. 58, 60, 62) imply that the inquirers do not accept Jesus' call, but the text actually indicates nothing of the sort. Jesus pushes whatever understanding of discipleship they had to a deeper level, and we are left to wonder how they responded to the call.

This open ending, Luke's invitation to readers, becomes the open ending for us as well. Preachers can ask contemporary hearers to identify with those receiving Jesus' radical invitations: hearers are given the opportunity to bring to completion the story's open-endedness by accepting Christ's call to follow in new and more meaningful ways. As with the three invitees in the text, the witness of the text challenges us to acknowledge the many competing claims for our allegiance—family, nation, work, race, class, possessions, even church—and reprioritize our commitments. We must do this if we are to follow the Christ who radically set his face toward Jerusalem to face his fate. Otherwise, the gospel becomes cheap grace.

O. WESLEY ALLEN JR.

Commentary 2: Connecting the Reading with the World

In this text, we come to a pivotal point in Luke's narrative. Jesus prepared for his public ministry and traveled throughout Galilee and Judea teaching, healing, and recruiting followers. For readers today, who know that torture and death await Jesus in the city of David, Luke records one of the most chilling passages in the Gospels; he notes, ominously, that Jesus "set his face to go to Jerusalem." We read these words twice in this passage; the message is underscored by this repetition (9:51, 53). Jesus has now turned to his inevitable passion and death.

Jesus knew what awaited him. Because his disciples did not know what he would face in Jerusalem, Jesus prepared them both for the journey to Jerusalem and for continuing his ministry after he was gone. In fact the disciples already experienced (and contributed to) ways that the foreshadowed events of Jerusalem were already in play: powers that be rose up to thwart the work of the kingdom. The preacher may wish to explore how well contemporary disciples continue Jesus' ministry, especially in the face of powers that be that counter the work of the kingdom. This passage presents one old ethnic and religious conflict, that between the Samaritans and Jews, a hostility that challenges Jesus' work.

Jesus ministered in the context of many human conflicts, including ministry in an area under colonial rule. Rome ruled the region, enriching its own treasury by exploiting that land's natural resources, agricultural products, and even the people's labor. This arrangement was administered by local, indigenous collaborators: the Herodian dynasty, whose kings kept civil order; the temple elite, who occupied the people by overseeing their cultic responsibilities; and the tax collectors who served the Romans, the rulers, and the priests. Jerusalem was the seat of this tripartite system of control and exploitation of the people. Though he spent most of his ministry in and around the Galilee region, Jesus knew that those who "eat the flesh of my people" and "flay their skin off them" (Mic. 3:3) made their homes in Jerusalem.

This powerful economic and political system, centered in Jerusalem, radiated out into the countryside. It divided the villages by turning the haves against the have-nots. In Galilee, as the population of the newly built Roman city of Tiberias grew, pressure for agricultural products induced wealthy landowners to push smaller farmers off their land and into landless itinerant trades and fishing. Some became destitute. These two groups likely found themselves in tension. The itinerants could regard the landowners and their rejection and social distancing with resentment and contempt.[1]

The preacher could connect this textual background to our current cultural situation: Jesus' public ministry was kingdom work that addressed the needs of the poor and outcast. How do we continue this ministry now? In the current American economic environment, characterized in part by job outsourcing, declining wages, and the need of so many people to work multiple jobs and/or retrain midcareer, workers can end up viewing other workers as competition, even as a threat. What might it look like to embrace and pray for those who seem to threaten our economic security? How are we participating in socioeconomic conflicts that deter or promote the work of the kingdom?

Earlier Luke recounts how Jesus traveled through Galilee and to the regions around

1. John Dominic Crossan, "Jesus and the Kingdom: Itinerants and Householders in Earliest Christianity," in *Jesus at 2000*, ed. Marcus Borg (Boulder, CO: Westview Press, 1991), 21–53, esp. 36–37.

Galilee preaching release and liberty (for example, 4:16–44). He announced the coming of God's kingdom, healed the sick, cast out demons, and recruited those who were willing to share in that work. He "called the twelve together and gave them power and authority over all demons and to cure diseases," and sent them out to do what they had seen him do—preach the kingdom of God and heal (9:1–2). They were instructed to take nothing for their journey; they were to be completely dependent on the small landowners for their food and shelter. He also told them, "Wherever they do not welcome you . . . shake the dust off your feet as a testimony against them" (9:5).

This section of Luke, building toward our passage, provides an image of crossing thresholds, both by the itinerant disciples who knock on doors and by the householders who welcome them inside. What thresholds might we step across that could knit our communities together in transformative, healing ways? Sadly, the 11:00 hour on Sunday continues to be one of the most segregated in our country. Could following Jesus today mean that predominately white, African American, and Latino congregations reach toward each other and create joint worship experiences or book studies, or collaborate to improve public schools, all efforts at providing new spaces for developing transformative relationships? An African American woman who joined and became a leader in a multiracial, multicongregational organization spoke in a downtown, predominately white congregation. She grew up in the city, but before she got involved in the organization, she had never been in a white church. Then, she looked out and named four people in the audience whom she now knows and calls friends. There was much joy in the room that night. Can we cross thresholds and make way for such transformative kingdom work? Do we perpetuate actively or passively the powers that Jesus encountered in Jerusalem?

As might be expected, there was a learning curve, as well as resistance, for Jesus' mostly itinerant disciples. Even now, after the disciples had spent much time with Jesus, they still could not comprehend what it meant to follow him. When the Samaritan village would not receive him, the disciples offered to call down judgment and immolation from heaven (9:54). Even after they received his rebuke for their misguided enthusiasm, they still failed to follow him. He again said "Follow me" (v. 59) but they failed. One disciple said he needed to go bury his father first; another needed to go say good-bye to his family. We too might find other, more pressing matters than engaging those for whom we feel contempt, receiving those whom we fear, or challenging the economic and political systems that diminish us all. Jesus is honest with disciples then and now: Let the dead bury the dead; get on with the work of the kingdom, or stop talking about it. I know it is hard, I have nowhere to lay my head.

There is a kind of disorienting sense of itinerancy when one steps out of the comfort of one's own group, whether that group is a particular socioeconomic group, a racial or ethnic group, a gendered group, a religious group, a national group, to engage what might be perceived as a frightening member of another group. Members of one's own group may reject you; members of the other group may reject you. Jesus insists that the risk is necessary for the work of the kingdom.

Even though he knew what he was to face in Jerusalem, Jesus turned and made his way there. He continues to call his disciples to leave everything and follow him. He knows the powers that aim to deter and defeat him. But he continues to bring good news to the poor, release to the captives, and freedom to the oppressed. With the disciples he bids us, "Follow me." Even in the face of inequity, racism, aggression, and violence, we turn our face toward him and follow, seeking to do the work of the kingdom, his work in the world.

STEPHEN BOYD

Proper 9 (Sunday between July 3 and July 9 Inclusive)

2 Kings 5:1–14 and Isaiah 66:10–14
Psalm 30 and Psalm 66:1–9
Galatians 6:(1–6), 7–16
Luke 10:1–11, 16–20

2 Kings 5:1–14

[1]Naaman, commander of the army of the king of Aram, was a great man and in high favor with his master, because by him the LORD had given victory to Aram. The man, though a mighty warrior, suffered from leprosy. [2]Now the Arameans on one of their raids had taken a young girl captive from the land of Israel, and she served Naaman's wife. [3]She said to her mistress, "If only my lord were with the prophet who is in Samaria! He would cure him of his leprosy." [4]So Naaman went in and told his lord just what the girl from the land of Israel had said. [5]And the king of Aram said, "Go then, and I will send along a letter to the king of Israel."

He went, taking with him ten talents of silver, six thousand shekels of gold, and ten sets of garments. [6]He brought the letter to the king of Israel, which read, "When this letter reaches you, know that I have sent to you my servant Naaman, that you may cure him of his leprosy." [7]When the king of Israel read the letter, he tore his clothes and said, "Am I God, to give death or life, that this man sends word to me to cure a man of his leprosy? Just look and see how he is trying to pick a quarrel with me."

[8]But when Elisha the man of God heard that the king of Israel had torn his clothes, he sent a message to the king, "Why have you torn your clothes? Let him come to me, that he may learn that there is a prophet in Israel." [9]So Naaman came with his horses and chariots, and halted at the entrance of Elisha's house. [10]Elisha sent a messenger to him, saying, "Go, wash in the Jordan seven times, and your flesh shall be restored and you shall be clean." [11]But Naaman became angry and went away, saying, "I thought that for me he would surely come out, and stand and call on the name of the LORD his God, and would wave his hand over the spot, and cure the leprosy! [12]Are not Abana and Pharpar, the rivers of Damascus, better than all the waters of Israel? Could I not wash in them, and be clean?" He turned and went away in a rage. [13]But his servants approached and said to him, "Father, if the prophet had commanded you to do something difficult, would you not have done it? How much more, when all he said to you was, 'Wash, and be clean'?" [14]So he went down and immersed himself seven times in the Jordan, according to the word of the man of God; his flesh was restored like the flesh of a young boy, and he was clean.

Isaiah 66:10–14

[10]Rejoice with Jerusalem, and be glad for her,
all you who love her;
rejoice with her in joy,
all you who mourn over her—

[11]that you may nurse and be satisfied
from her consoling breast;
that you may drink deeply with delight
from her glorious bosom.

[12]For thus says the LORD:
I will extend prosperity to her like a river,
and the wealth of the nations like an overflowing stream;
and you shall nurse and be carried on her arm,
and dandled on her knees.
[13]As a mother comforts her child,
so I will comfort you;
you shall be comforted in Jerusalem.

[14]You shall see, and your heart shall rejoice;
your bodies shall flourish like the grass;
and it shall be known that the hand of the LORD is with his servants,
and his indignation is against his enemies.

Commentary 1: Connecting the Reading with Scripture

2 Kings 5:1–14. This story is about paradoxes of power. Nearly every verse makes some reference to the issue of who has status and authority. Almost every initial impression is turned on its head. The seemingly powerful end up dependent on the seemingly powerless. This text is thus perfect for sermons on the limits of human power, the importance of humility, and the God whose power can be found among the powerless.

The passage begins by introducing Naaman as "*commander* of the *army* of the *king* of *Aram*" (2 Kgs. 5:1, emphasis added). Previously, the Arameans killed Israel's king Ahab (1 Kgs. 22:31–35). Here, the text goes on to call Naaman "a *great* man and in *high* favor with his *master*," adding that God used him to achieve victory (5:1, emphasis added). The end of the first verse adds a tragic twist: "The man, though a *mighty warrior*, suffered from *leprosy*" (emphasis added). Suddenly, the man with so much power has a fatal flaw.

This skin disease was not what today is considered leprosy (Hansen's disease). Rather, it was an ailment that typically involved the skin turning white (Num. 12:10–12; 2 Kgs. 5:27). Those who suffered such a disease were often quarantined and forced to live alone (cf. Lev. 13:46; Num. 12:14–15). So, the powerful commander actually has outsider status.

Next, readers encounter Naaman's wife's servant (5:2). She is a slave and a prisoner of war—one of the most powerless people imaginable. Yet God's power can be found in her words. She knows who can heal Naaman (5:3). After she shares her knowledge, Naaman gets permission from his king to go to the king of Israel (vv. 4–5). The Aramean king sends Naaman with extravagant gifts to entice the Israelites to cooperate: ten talents of silver would weigh about 750 pounds, and 6,000 shekels of gold would weigh another 150 pounds. It is more money than hundreds of people would make in a year.

So, a powerful commander from a more powerful kingdom comes to Israel with royal gifts and a request. The Israelite king reacts with fear: although he is supposed to have the most power in Israel, he acts as if he has none. Fearing a trap, he rips his clothes, a sign of deep distress (2 Sam. 1:11; Esth. 4:1).

The prophet Elisha is not so easily shaken though. He has God's power, and he is utterly unimpressed with Naaman's power. Elisha treats

Naaman like an ordinary person. He demands that Naaman come to him (not the other way around). Elisha then sends a messenger to the door to speak to Naaman (rather than go himself). Elisha tells Naaman to wash in the Jordan River (hardly the mightiest of waters in the Middle East; 5:8–10, cf. 12).

Enraged at this lack of royal treatment, Naaman leaves (vv. 11–12). However, Naaman's servants plead with him to do as Elisha orders. In a role reversal, Naaman does what his servants tell him to do. He humbles himself and follows the word of a foreign prophet who did not even have the courtesy to show his face. Naaman obeys a foreign power. He is made clean. Humbling himself, he becomes healed.

The preacher can make clear that, in this story, human power amounts to exceedingly little: neither the powerful commander nor the kings can do very much. Instead, God's power is found only by paying attention to lowly servants and an unimpressed prophet. Later in the Bible, Isaiah talks of God bringing down lofty rulers (Isa. 2:9–22), while Jesus adds that God raises up servants (Mark 9:33–37).

Humility ranks high among biblical virtues (Jas. 4:10). Repeatedly, God sides with the powerless (1 Sam. 2:3–9; Ps. 113:7–9). The Bible tells story after story of bullies who lose, wimps who win, and God's miracles that make it all possible (Exod. 14–15; Josh. 6; Judg. 7:1–25; 1 Sam. 17; Isa. 36–39). One such story comes in the next two chapters, as the Arameans fail in their attempts to raid Israel and besiege its capital Samaria (2 Kgs. 6:8–7:20). In today's lectionary readings, Psalm 30 models humility: knowing one's limits and acknowledging dependence on God. Meanwhile, Paul denounces thinking too highly of oneself (Gal. 6:3), preferring to boast only in the cross of Christ, not circumcision (Gal. 6:13–14). In Luke, Jesus instructs his disciples to rejoice that their names are in heaven—not in their power over others (Luke 10:19–20).

Isaiah 66:10–14. Although this text is brief, it offers preachers wonderful opportunities. It presents a message of hope when the world feels overwhelming. It dares to imagine God in feminine imagery, which can be healing for many congregants. It vividly shows the power of God's justice to set the world right again.

Like other lectionary texts (Ps. 66:1; Luke 10:17–20), this text speaks of joy. What makes the joy of Isaiah 66:10–14 so spectacular is that it is offered to people who have faced so many disappointments that they were afraid of hoping again. The Babylonians destroyed Jerusalem and sent inhabitants into exile in 587 BCE. Although Jews in exile could return in 538, after the Persians conquered Babylon, many of these returnees faced severe difficulties, like opposition from neighboring peoples (see Ezra and Nehemiah).

Amid challenge after challenge, this text insists that God's people can move from grief to joy. Why? Jerusalem—the fallen and abandoned city—will again spring to life (Isa. 66:11). Like a mother (Isa. 66:7–9), Zion will provide her inhabitants with life-giving milk and life-giving rivers (Isa. 66:11–12a). In particular, the poet envisions God extending a river of *shalom* to Zion. This word "shalom" certainly entails "prosperity," as the NRSV translates it. However, it also means holistic peace. In fact, Horatio Spafford's famous hymn "It Is Well with My Soul" begins with the line "When peace, like a river," which is based on this text. Jerusalem—the humiliated city—will come to experience prosperity, peace, honor, and riches. The second half of verse 12 returns to maternal imagery, speaking of being "carried" on the arm or side and "dandled" on the knees. The Hebrew verb for being "carried" has overtones related to being "forgiven" (a reversal of Isa. 2:9 and affirmation of Isa. 33:24), while the verb for being "dandled" evokes images of delight (Ps. 119:16, 47, 70). God brings joy to those who have suffered immeasurably—a timeless message.

In verse 13, Zion is no longer the mother comforting Jerusalem's inhabitants. God is. While this portrayal of God as a woman may be new to some congregants, it can be healing to many mistreated by men. Elsewhere, Isaiah portrays God with maternal imagery in 42:14; 46:3; 49:15. Feminine imagery for God is also found in Jesus' parable of the Lost Coin (Luke 15:8–10; see also Matt. 23:37; Luke 13:34). With maternal comfort from God, the people can rejoice in their hearts (Isa. 66:14). God is making a barren landscape lush with budding vegetation.

The preacher may highlight that to some readers, it may seem odd that this joyful passage ends with a word of God's indignation against enemies. It can be tempting to leave such a word out of sermons on this text. However, divine judgment plays a key role both in the verses to come and in Isaiah as a whole (e.g., 14:3–23). God's anger tells oppressed people that God cares about their suffering and will treat oppressors with justice. It is thus an essential word for people who have suffered abuse, discrimination, and cruelty at the hands of others. Although the world's justice system is too often broken, God remains pure, holy, just, and fair. The OT and NT agree that one day, God will side with those who have suffered unfairly.

MATTHEW RICHARD SCHLIMM

Commentary 2: Connecting the Reading with the World

2 Kings 5:1–14. The story of the healing of Naaman, a mighty Syrian warrior, presents us with both good and disturbing news. According to the biblical text, Naaman is a successful commander of the king of Aram's army because Israel's God made him victorious. Naaman, however, is not healthy; he has leprosy. Thanks to the gentle, unassuming intervention of Naaman's wife's unnamed maidservant, Naaman receives the help he desperately needs from an Israelite prophet, Elisha, who cures him. Strikingly, the young girl—the maidservant—is a sort of prisoner of war herself who was taken captive and then trafficked by a group of Aramean soldiers during one of their raids. The captive one becomes an instrument of liberation for the one oppressed by a deeply feared and contagious skin disease. She becomes the impetus for restoring a contaminated person to his community, since leprosy resulted in the physical and social isolation of the one stricken.

The story of Naaman speaks to our world's leaders today. Like the kings of Aram and Israel, who cannot cure Naaman's disease, no president, prime minister, queen, or king today can cure or stop hunger, poverty, violence, racism, or discrimination, which are just a few of the many afflictions that people globally experience today, and which are like contemporary versions of the leprosy of our story. These afflictions are also all-consuming and result in isolation, shunning, and despair. Like Naaman, who welcomed Elisha, world leaders need to welcome and receive the wisdom and work of today's twenty-first-century prophets who, like Elisha, are trying to free people from the "diseases" that bind them. The preacher might name persons like Dr. Akinwumi Adesina, president of the African Development Bank, a leading voice for hunger, food security, and the structural transformation of African agriculture, or the US Parkland Floridian students who united and organized people against gun violence in an effort to effect legislation. The preacher could help us see in them the example of Elisha, who shows us that the real power of healing and transformation rests in ordinary people acting prophetically.

Additionally, the plight of the nameless Israelite maidservant brings to light the plight of many women today, especially in war-torn countries in the Middle East like Syria and Yemen. Human trafficking occurred thousands of years ago and still continues in the twenty-first century. In the text she is a person of faith who has enough love in her heart to be concerned about the one in whose household she remains captive. She is not an object, and neither are trafficked women today. She is someone through whom God works. The preacher could connect this part of the story with that social issue. The plight of trafficked women calls the human community to expose those places rampant with this crime, to push for legislation against it, and to create safe houses so that women rescued from trafficking can regain their dignity, receive counseling and vocational training, and be reintegrated into society. Trafficked women, like the maidservant, can be a source of societal healing and transformation. The maidservant's spirit continues in two nameless Nepalese women who, once trafficked victims rescued by the Indian government, opened Skabti Samucha, a shelter for other trafficked women.

Finally, Naaman's story has implications for our personal lives. If we are the ones in need of healing, then we have to surrender to the power of God, whose presence rests within people we may deem as insignificant.

Isaiah 66:10–14. Isaiah's marvelous vision offers us a word of hope. After the Israelites had lost everything—their monarchy, many of their people, their temple, and their holy city Jerusalem—the poet promises new life for the devastated city. The poet envisions Jerusalem as being prosperous and wealthy, capable of nursing her children (v. 11) to whom she gave birth (vv. 7–9), and a cause for gladness and rejoicing. Jerusalem will become a place of welcome, comfort, and consolation for the righteous who are afflicted by their own (vv. 12–13). Furthermore, the poet tells his listeners that Jerusalem's new life will be a sign of God's presence among God's servants, which is not the case for God's enemies, whose experience is divine indignation (v. 14).

In Isaiah 66:10–14 and in earlier chapters of Isaiah (e.g., Isa. 60–62), the poet offers us a mixed metaphor for Jerusalem. Jerusalem is God's Holy City; Jerusalem becomes a metaphor for God's holy people and the nation of Israel as a whole. As the Holy City experiences new life, so will God's people experience new life. Jerusalem also becomes a manifestation of God. The ancient, traumatized Israelites begin to ponder anew who their God is after their devastating experience of loss. The image of God dwelling once again in Jerusalem (Ps. 135:21; Jer. 3:17; Zech. 1:16) now shifts in verse 13 from God as the sovereign one who dwells in Jerusalem and who will be worshiped by kings and nations, to God the compassionate one who, like a mother who comforts a child, will comfort the people in Jerusalem. Both God and Jerusalem become sources of comfort and maternal care.

The preacher can help us hear how this message of a renewed city and people is pertinent for contemporary listeners. Certainly today's Middle East cities—from Aleppo to Mosul—are ones ravished by war, with many of the cities' inhabitants either exiled or killed. Reconstruction of these cities and communities is complicated, perhaps even doubtful. Yet God's renewing Spirit, working through the human condition and its agents, continues to rebuild Jerusalem and its communities, as well as other Middle East cities. In the face of violence and terrorism, persons continue to work for peace and human rights. The witness of the text is that devastation is not the final word and experience: Jerusalem restored is a sign of God's benevolent and creative Spirit being poured out again and again to renew the face of the earth. The preacher can make connections between the restoration of Jerusalem and all the ways God's restoring Spirit is at work rebuilding cities and places of safety, shelter, economy, and well-being.

Jerusalem, as a metaphor for God's holy people, has profound implications for what is meant by the "people of God" today. Like Jerusalem, God's people are called to be a source of comfort and consolation for people today who have suffered and are suffering, particularly those traumatized by warfare and any form of violence and oppression. Today's sanctuary cities that welcome and protect immigrants are like Jerusalem, which offered comfort to its suffering people. Those who welcome immigrants are like Jerusalem—a holy "city"—a people of God. Every liturgical gathering carries these overtones. The gathered people of God are a community of restoration, of new life. The preacher can help us know that we live into that promise in our ecclesial gatherings each week as we aim to be a sign of that new life in the world.

Finally, as God's dwelling place and as a metaphor for God's holy people, Isaiah's image of Jerusalem calls each person to recognize the indwelling presence of God in his or her life, and thus to become people of profound compassion, knowing that God's presence dwells in each person and has the capacity to work in and through each person within the human community to heal and to restore life. Such is the noble work of counselors who work to liberate people from the shackles of addiction, spiritual directors who reach deep into people's lives to help them recover their hearts, and social workers who help victims of abuse reclaim their dignity and find safe havens to live.

CAROL J. DEMPSEY, OP

Proper 9 (Sunday between July 3 and July 9 Inclusive)

Psalm 30

[1]I will extol you, O LORD, for you have drawn me up,
and did not let my foes rejoice over me.
[2]O LORD my God, I cried to you for help,
and you have healed me.
[3]O LORD, you brought up my soul from Sheol,
restored me to life from among those gone down to the Pit.

[4]Sing praises to the LORD, O you his faithful ones,
and give thanks to his holy name.
[5]For his anger is but for a moment;
his favor is for a lifetime.
Weeping may linger for the night,
but joy comes with the morning.

[6]As for me, I said in my prosperity,
"I shall never be moved."
[7]By your favor, O LORD,
you had established me as a strong mountain;
you hid your face;
I was dismayed.

[8]To you, O LORD, I cried,
and to the LORD I made supplication:
[9]"What profit is there in my death,
if I go down to the Pit?
Will the dust praise you?
Will it tell of your faithfulness?
[10]Hear, O LORD, and be gracious to me!
O LORD, be my helper!"

[11]You have turned my mourning into dancing;
you have taken off my sackcloth
and clothed me with joy,
[12]so that my soul may praise you and not be silent.
O LORD my God, I will give thanks to you forever.

Psalm 66:1–9

[1]Make a joyful noise to God, all the earth;
[2]sing the glory of his name;
give to him glorious praise.
[3]Say to God, "How awesome are your deeds!
Because of your great power, your enemies cringe before you.
[4]All the earth worships you;
they sing praises to you,
sing praises to your name."

[5]Come and see what God has done:
he is awesome in his deeds among mortals.
[6]He turned the sea into dry land;
they passed through the river on foot.
There we rejoiced in him,
[7]who rules by his might forever,
whose eyes keep watch on the nations—
let the rebellious not exalt themselves.

[8]Bless our God, O peoples,
let the sound of his praise be heard,
[9]who has kept us among the living,
and has not let our feet slip.

Connecting the Psalm with Scripture and Worship

Psalm 30. The psalmist begins with praise and exaltation (v. 1), for God healed the one who cried out for help (vv. 2–3). After another description of distress (vv. 8–10), the remainder of the psalm contains expressions of individual thanksgiving (v. 12) and communal praise: "Sing praises to the LORD, O you his faithful ones" (v. 4). One can interpret this psalm simplistically: pray long enough and God will make everything all right. However, a more nuanced reading reveals a deeper theological meaning. The psalmist has learned to give thanks in times when God's presence is manifest and in times when the face of God is hidden (v. 7), trusting that "weeping may linger for the night, but joy comes with the morning" (v. 5). The psalmist testifies to the truth that even when trouble comes, people can hope, pray, and praise. Praise is "the language of joy and gladness" that people use to give witness to God's faithfulness in all seasons of life.[1] Even in times of distress, the psalmist finds joy and offers praise to God.

The theme of healing is also found in 2 Kings 5:1–14. Naaman, a mighty warrior and "great man held in high favor" (2 Kgs. 5:1) by the king of Aram, suffered from leprosy. Through a young girl, the king of Aram heard of a prophet in Israel who could heal. Naaman sought the prophet Elisha, who said to him: "Go, wash in the Jordan seven times, and your flesh will be restored" (v. 10). Naaman immersed himself in the water, and he was healed. Although the lectionary reading ends there, it is instructive to read the rest of the story. After his miraculous healing, Naaman asked Elisha how he could repay him. Elisha refused, so Naaman said, "I will no longer offer burnt offering or sacrifice to any god except the LORD" (v. 17), thus vowing to offer praise to the God of Israel alone. Psalm 30 provides words of thanks that those who are healed might offer to God. Even in the midst of suffering, with hope for healing, people respond to God with thanks and praise.

These texts offer rich themes for preaching. The preacher can take this opportunity to name the reality of suffering and dispel the myth that bad things happen only to bad people and witness to the powerful, sometimes mysterious gift of healing. The presence of hope is what allows both the psalmist and Naaman to endure times of weeping and mourning, trusting that joy will come in the morning (v. 5). This little word "but" creates a contrast between what was and what will be; it does not deny the reality of suffering, nor does it minimize the power of hope. Even through the night of weeping, we know that sadness does not have the last word. God does, and it is a word of grace, hope, and joy.

The psalmist gives witness to the truth that throughout history, even when trouble comes,

1. James L. Mays, *Psalms*, Interpretation (Louisville, KY: Westminster John Knox Press, 1994), 141.

Reverence for Life

The idea of Reverence for Life offers itself as the realistic answer to the realistic question of how man and the universe are related to each other. Of the universe, man knows only that everything that exists is, like himself, a manifestation of the will to live. With this universe, he stands in both a passive and an active relationship. On the one hand he is subject to the flow of world events; on the other hand he is able to preserve and build, or to injure and destroy, the life that surrounds him.

The only possible way of giving meaning to his existence is to raise his physical relationship to the world to a spiritual one. If he remains a passive being, through resignation he enters into a spiritual relationship with the world. True resignation consists in this: that man, feeling his subordination to the course of world events, makes his way toward inward freedom from the fate that shapes his external existence. Inward freedom gives him the strength to triumph over the difficulties of everyday life and to become a deeper and more inward person, calm and peaceful. Resignation, therefore, is the spiritual and ethical affirmation of one's own existence. Only he who has gone through the trial of resignation is capable of accepting the world.

By playing an active role, man enters into a spiritual relationship with this world that is quite different: he does not see his existence in isolation. On the contrary, he is united with the lives that surround him; he experiences the destinies of others as his own. He helps as much as he can and realizes that there is no greater happiness than to participate in the development and protection of life.

Once man begins to think about the mystery of his life and the links connecting him with the life that fills the world, he cannot but accept, for his own life and all other life that surrounds him, the principle of Reverence for Life. He will act according to this principle of the ethical affirmation of life in everything he does. His life will become in every respect more difficult than if he lived for himself, but at the same time it will be richer, more beautiful, and happier. It will become, instead of mere living, a genuine experience of life.

Albert Schweitzer, *Out of My Life and Thought: An Autobiography,* trans. Antje Bultmann Lemke (Baltimore: Johns Hopkins University Press, 1998), 233–34.

even when the world seems to be on the verge of chaos, people of faith join their voices in singing psalms and hymns and spiritual songs (Eph. 5:19).[2] So we do. Choose hymns that allow people, wherever they are on the journey of faith, to sing praises to the God of all the seasons of life. "Come Sing to God" (based on Ps. 30) is a good choice for a hymn that follows the sermon. Water is a medium of God's healing in the text and can be utilized in the liturgy. Pour water into the baptismal font—visibly and audibly—to remind people of the promise of God's mercy. Invite people to touch the water and remember the hope and healing we have in God.

In summary, these texts give to both those who are struggling and those who are celebrating, the words to cry out for help, but also the voice to sing God's praise.

Psalm 66:1–9. Psalm 66 is a psalm of thanksgiving in response to God's faithful intervention on behalf of the community. Because of its characteristic antiphonal structure, it is well suited for corporate worship. Psalm 66 is a universal call to worship God ("Make a joyful noise to God, all the earth," v. 1) because of particular things God has done for God's people ("He turned the sea into dry land; they passed through the river on foot," v. 6). By inviting people to "come and see what God has done" (v. 5), then telling the story of how God "has kept us among the living" (v. 9), the psalmist

2. Bernhard W. Anderson, *Out of the Depths: The Psalms Speak for Us Today* (Philadelphia: Westminster Press, 1983), 14.

effectively links the recounting of divine deeds of salvation to the praise of the people. In response to God's faithfulness, the people give glorious praise (v. 2), worship (v. 4), sing praises (v. 4), rejoice (v. 6), and bless God (v. 8).

The connection between Psalm 66 and Isaiah 66:10–14 is evident in the first verse: "Shout with joy" (Ps. 66:1) and "Rejoice" (Isa. 66:10). This part of Isaiah was written after Israel's return from Babylonian captivity to their home in Jerusalem, which had been destroyed but was being rebuilt with God's help. Isaiah uses the imagery of a mother comforting her children (v. 13) to help the people see with the eyes of faith not what is, but what will be, as God promised: Jerusalem as a city of abundance, blessing, and peace. "You shall see; and your heart shall rejoice" (v. 14).

Preaching on this Sunday can be a summons to praise God in response to the particular deeds of salvation seen in history and the world today. As the psalmist points to the exodus and Isaiah to the restoration of Jerusalem, the preacher can cite examples of historic and current events that reveal God's salvific purpose. The Christian preacher can proclaim the fulfillment of God's promise as the universal Word became flesh in the particular person of Jesus. A sermon calling people to a deeper gratitude can change hearts and lives for good.

Psalm 66 lends itself to multiple liturgical uses. In a call to worship, the leader and congregation can alternate, beginning with verse 1, and together proclaim, "Come and see what God has done. Let us worship God!" (v. 5). Then people can sing "Make a Joyful Noise to God!" (based on Psalm 66). For the prayers of the people, the leader might name particular blessings of God, ending with, "Say to God," with the congregation responding, "How awesome are your deeds" (v. 3). If the sermon focuses on the power of telling the stories of God's faithfulness, a hymn of response might be "I Love to Tell the Story." Texts about "seeing" the mighty deeds of YHWH lend themselves to ritual, so that worshipers might experience directly the power and meaning of what God has done in and through God's people throughout history.[3] A meaningful ritual to help people "taste and see the goodness of God" is the sacrament of Holy Communion. As Isaiah portrays God as a mother who nurses her children at her breast, so people are invited to come to the Lord's Table to taste the bread of life and drink the cup of salvation and live anew.

The texts offer provocative imagery to powerfully illustrate God's enduring faithfulness throughout history and in today's world. In response, we are invited to join with the whole earth in worship and praise.

DONNA GIVER-JOHNSTON

3. Anderson, *Out of the Depths*, 135.

Galatians 6:(1–6), 7–16

[1]My friends, if anyone is detected in a transgression, you who have received the Spirit should restore such a one in a spirit of gentleness. Take care that you yourselves are not tempted. [2]Bear one another's burdens, and in this way you will fulfill the law of Christ. [3]For if those who are nothing think they are something, they deceive themselves. [4]All must test their own work; then that work, rather than their neighbor's work, will become a cause for pride. [5]For all must carry their own loads.

[6]Those who are taught the word must share in all good things with their teacher.

[7]Do not be deceived; God is not mocked, for you reap whatever you sow. [8]If you sow to your own flesh, you will reap corruption from the flesh; but if you sow to the Spirit, you will reap eternal life from the Spirit. [9]So let us not grow weary in doing what is right, for we will reap at harvest time, if we do not give up. [10]So then, whenever we have an opportunity, let us work for the good of all, and especially for those of the family of faith.

[11]See what large letters I make when I am writing in my own hand! [12]It is those who want to make a good showing in the flesh that try to compel you to be circumcised—only that they may not be persecuted for the cross of Christ. [13]Even the circumcised do not themselves obey the law, but they want you to be circumcised so that they may boast about your flesh. [14]May I never boast of anything except the cross of our Lord Jesus Christ, by which the world has been crucified to me, and I to the world. [15]For neither circumcision nor uncircumcision is anything; but a new creation is everything! [16]As for those who will follow this rule—peace be upon them, and mercy, and upon the Israel of God.

Commentary 1: Connecting the Reading with Scripture

Paul writes this letter to the churches of Galatia, a region in the central plateau of Asia Minor. While our knowledge of the individual churches in the region is scarce (1:2; 3:1), it is clear that the recipients are Gentiles, perhaps a mixture of Greeks and ancient Celts, tribal people from the northern part of the region. Paul's epistle is written to settle controversies and to provide ethical instruction and pastoral care to new believers who are struggling with their new faith.

Paul writes in the traditional epistolary fashion of the Greco-Roman world, the formulaic literary style of the day. The literary movements follow Greco-Roman literary categories: epistolary prescript (1:1–5), to offer greeting and to set the intention of the letter; exordium (1:6–11), to present a summary of the facts; narration (1:12–2:14), to establish the story line or reason for writing; proposition (2:15–21), to define the nuances of the arguments or the opposing sides; probation (3:1–4:31), to present the central argument of the writer; exhortation (5:1–6:10), to provide clear injunctions for future behavior; epistolary postscript (6:11–18), to provide a summary of the main points. Our section of focus, 6:7–16, belongs clearly to the concluding arguments that Paul makes to underline the points found in the entire letter. The importance of this concluding section is made clear: Paul has chosen not to dictate the material through a scribe (amanuensis) but to write the words personally with his own style of handwriting (6:11).

From this small section, the epistolary postscript, we understand the central points of the entire letter. First, Paul has opponents (6:12).

Outside voices have called the believers to turn to a different gospel (1:6), one that Paul has not been teaching and certainly will not support. These adversaries have been undermining Paul's apostolic authority by saying that Paul's gospel message is a commercial enterprise (1:11) from a false teacher seeking personal gain and prestige (1:10), developed from his own machinations for economic gain (1:12) and not from the Spirit of Christ. Paul spends a lot of words defending his authenticity, because the opponents have worked diligently to undermine his reputation among these believers (1:10–24).

Second, the theology of the opponents is clear (6:13). The opponents—perhaps coming from Jerusalem, representing the Jewish Christian position of the new faith, which was still locked within a framework of laws, religious customs, and ancient traditions—were earnestly trying to "save" this group of young believers from what they thought was abomination: freedom from the law. The message cannot be any clearer in this letter: neither circumcision nor uncircumcision count. A new creation is the most important (6:15).

Third, Paul's ministry stands in opposition to these opponents (6:14). Paul once again makes his position clear: "For in Jesus Christ neither circumcision nor uncircumcision is of any avail, but faith working through love." What a challenge to the hundreds of years of religious tradition! Radical to the core, Paul, even though having shared the religious heritage of legalism before his dramatic conversion, now teaches that the faith works through love, not the cutting of the flesh (5:6). Using highly figurative language, Paul then makes his point: "you were running well, who 'cut into you' from obeying the truth?" (5:7, my trans.). Paul makes a counterargument to that of his opponents by saying that their motives are for their own glory, not for the glory of the cross of Christ (6:13–14). Furthermore, they themselves are unable to abide by every mandate they require of the young believers in Galatia. With similar metaphorical style, Paul wishes that the opponents who have unsettled these young believers would just let the knife slip, meaning that they would mutilate themselves as they perform the religious act of self-circumcision (5:12).

The preacher could connect this ancient, religious form of separation to current forms of religious separation. What ritual or belief, in its own merit not divisive, is used to create hostilities between groups of people who all aspire to belong to the same family of God? What is "circumcision" for your congregation? What is used to sever the fellowship? It could be sexual orientation, women's ordination, racial divides, rituals related to communion or church polity, style of clothing, or doctrine. The list is long. While circumcision was related to hygiene and longevity for male members of the community, the act of cutting the flesh became a symbolic divide between those who did (the faithful) and those who did not (the unfaithful).

Fourth is the single most important aphorism in the letter (6:15). Even though lodged in the postscript at the very end of the letter, this statement becomes the banner for this entire correspondence, and perhaps for Paul's entire ministry: "Neither circumcision nor uncircumcision matters for anything; what really matters is a new creation" (my trans.). What is a new creation? The new creation is a believer whose life is known by the fruits of the spirit: love, joy, peace, patience, kindness, goodness, gentleness, self-control (5:22–24)—rather than mutilated flesh. These fruits cannot be bound up in a law book or a dogmatic presentation. To be a new creation is to live and walk by the Spirit (5:25), not by the law.

The preacher can fill in the blank: "Neither ______ nor ______ is of any avail, but faith working through love." Place in the blank: gay nor straight, black nor white, female nor male, European brown nor Hispanic brown, Baptist nor Catholic, evangelical nor mainline, rural nor urban, liberal nor conservative, and on and on. These attributes, just like circumcision, are not to be used to define the life of faith. Rather, the preacher can help us see that believers who desire to fulfill the entire law of God understand that these attributes do not matter. What matters is how we serve one another through love.

Fifth is the blessing for those who follow the teaching (6:16). Paul's words are earthy, argumentative, forceful, and passionate. For Paul, the believer cannot be bound by the dictates of the past definitions of faith; something new is becoming clear with the cross of Christ. The challenge for the faithful is to speak this truth in ways that convince. This will not be easy.

Preachers do well to notice that Paul's words to the Galatians are poignant, earthy, unadorned, and basic. Gone are the flowery, philosophical arguments that in their best and worst displays can both obfuscate and illuminate truth because of their polyvalence. Galatians, instead, is almost pure binary—it is either this or that. Then nothing. Neither circumcision, seen as an outer sign for some internal conviction, nor uncircumcision, seen as an outer sign for the *lack* of some internal conviction, counts for anything. These external markings that identify who is in and who is out are useless. In fact, Paul's blunt language appears this way: "I wish those who would unsettle you would mutilate themselves" (Gal. 5:12). "Just Let the Circumcision Knife Slip" may not be the most acceptable title for Sunday's sermon, but would be the best summation of Paul's insistence on viewing faith from the inside out rather than the outside in. For all that we do in order to manifest outward signs of faith, be it through pious practices of prayer and devotion or engagement with God's world through acts of social justice, we encounter Paul's insistence on faith that dwells within. The preacher will help us encounter, again, faith that works through love.

LINDA MCKINNISH BRIDGES

Commentary 2: Connecting the Reading with the World

The connections between this remarkable letter, written two millennia ago, and the church, culture, and world in our day are palpable.

> We know that a person is justified not by the works of the law but through faith in Jesus Christ.
>
> 2:16

> There is no longer Jew or Greek, there is no longer slave or free, there is no longer male and female; for all of you are one in Christ Jesus.
>
> 3:28

> For freedom Christ has set us free. Stand firm, therefore, and do not submit again to a yoke of slavery.
>
> 5:1

> Let us not grow weary in doing what is right . . . let us work for the good of all.
>
> 6:9, 10

Great, important, and inspiring ideas emerge from the arguments in this document, no doubt dictated by a scholarly, passionate follower of Jesus Christ. Conflict between Paul, who has been preaching and teaching the gospel of Jesus Christ in Gentile communities, and the leaders of the Jewish Christian community in and around Jerusalem has pushed Paul into deep waters—theologically, socially, and politically. It was Paul who broke through religious and social boundaries by discovering and arguing the broad universality he had encountered in Jesus Christ.

The precipitating event was a visit by representatives of the Jerusalem church to the Pauline community in Galatia. The conflict seems a lot like the timeless encounter between conservative and progressive social thought. The Jerusalem representatives have told the new Galatian Christians that their religion was not yet complete or authentic, and would not be so until they adopted the older traditions of Jerusalem. In the process they apparently questioned Paul's own faith, experience, and authority, even though he was not present. The passionate scholar missionary is offended, insulted, and angry. When personal faith and experience are called into question for whatever reason, it is deeply offensive. In the letter he wrote in response, at times he is virtually white hot in anger; at other times, he is gentle and tenderly pastoral.

His letter has been called the "Magna Carta of Christian Freedom." Paul's argument is that salvation is a gift, not to be earned by good works, but only gratefully received and then lived through a life of generous love.

Speaking directly to the tragic results of the conflict within the Galatian congregation, which had become clearly and openly divided, Paul counsels patience and gentleness, with the goal of restoration and reconciliation. He then moves on to his hopes for the community: "Bear one another's burdens. . . . let us not grow weary in doing what is right. . . . let us work for the good of all" (6:2, 9, 10).

The sad reality of our experience is that we have witnessed the church today become as deeply divided as Paul's beloved Galatian community. We are beginning to understand that our conflicts and divisions are in part a reflection of the profound divide in the world around us. Brexit and the weakened European community, recent political campaigns in America that drove a wedge into the center of our common life, conflicts over the status and role—and even the believability—of women, fear in the face of growing numbers of neighbors of other faiths (or no faith at all), and times of further pulling apart around issues that are vital to our future and indeed to our survival as a democratic republic that is open, welcoming, generous, and compassionate, have found their way into our own beloved churches and communities. Never have Paul's words rung more true or more urgently: "There is no longer Jew or Greek, there is no longer slave or free, there is no longer male and female; for all of you are one in Christ."

As heirs of Paul, the contemporary churches must remember the power of the claim that Christ has broken down all the barriers that continue to divide us in church and—dare we imagine—beyond our local communities in the nation and the world. All are one: Christian, Muslim, Jew, nonbeliever, secular humanist, liberal, conservative, Republican, Democrat. All, because of what God has done in Jesus Christ, are finally, fundamentally, one.

As borders are walled and immigrants kept out, as politicians threaten to deconstruct institutions and policies laboriously established in our history to protect and affirm and liberate, the church, the church of Jesus Christ, must never tire of proclaiming and then living out in its own life the good news that barriers have been overcome and divisions are gone. All, in Christ, are one.

It is not possible to avoid or ignore the unique and radical idea of inclusiveness that runs through this letter as Paul pastorally concludes: "let us not grow weary in doing what is right. . . . let us work for the good of all." In a time and context of religious tribalism, then and now, Paul loves that word "all": "*all* are one . . . work for the good of *all*."

The opposite of "all" seems to be deeply embedded in our humanity and has produced some of history's most deplorable tragedies: Christian crusaders slaughtering Muslims and Jews (and Christians); Muslims slaughtering Christian infidels; Catholics burning Protestants at the stake and Protestants reciprocating. The current persistent insistence in some political as well as religious rhetoric that Islam is fundamentally flawed and necessarily threatening is similarly tragic, often reflective, as it is, of assumptions about a white, Christian America.

There is another, better way: a religion that transcends boundaries, a religion moved and motivated by compassion for the "other" as a beloved child of God deserving of love, care, acceptance, dignity, freedom, security, and full life: black-white, female-male, gay-straight, Muslim-Jew, liberal-conservative, immigrant, Republican, Democrat. Goodness, according to this religion, is having compassion for the other, doing what is helpful, never tiring of doing what is right, and always working for the good of all. Churches are one place in our society where doing good is the essence of the project. It is deep in our tradition with its origins in the Hebrew notion of Tikkun Olam, the healing, repairing, and transforming of the world as the purpose of religion. Preachers can make the connection that all churches should always be seen to be doing good, however small: feeding the hungry, clothing the naked, sheltering the homeless, welcoming the stranger.

There are social and political as well as religious implications here. There are deeply personal implications. From the beginning, up to and including Paul, Scripture is consistent: we will be measured ultimately by how well we have loved, helped, healed, and welcomed.

When the five-hundredth anniversary of the Reformation was observed not long ago, Christians acknowledged that the result of the Reformation was not only reform and renewal but separation, division, and the shattering of unity.

This text calls us to remember both the necessity and the tragedy of the Reformation. We have come such a long way along the difficult journey of restoring our lost unity. Slowly gentleness has replaced suspicion and hostility. Over time, dialogue has replaced silent separation. Christians now agree that we are saved—all of us—by grace through faith, and slowly we are acknowledging that our continued separation as denominations and as Protestants and Roman Catholics is a scandal to the world, which is simply not interested in Christian infighting, and an offense to the Lord, in whom we are one—all of us.

Would it not be remarkable if the holy catholic church revisited this ancient letter and then sat down and talked—listening carefully to one another—instead of proclaiming our version of the truth? In doing that, we would extend that gentle patience Paul encouraged and in the process demonstrate to a fractured world what our Creator wills and intends for all of us.

JOHN M. BUCHANAN

Luke 10:1–11, 16–20

[1]After this the Lord appointed seventy others and sent them on ahead of him in pairs to every town and place where he himself intended to go. [2]He said to them, "The harvest is plentiful, but the laborers are few; therefore ask the Lord of the harvest to send out laborers into his harvest. [3]Go on your way. See, I am sending you out like lambs into the midst of wolves. [4]Carry no purse, no bag, no sandals; and greet no one on the road. [5]Whatever house you enter, first say, 'Peace to this house!' [6]And if anyone is there who shares in peace, your peace will rest on that person; but if not, it will return to you. [7]Remain in the same house, eating and drinking whatever they provide, for the laborer deserves to be paid. Do not move about from house to house. [8]Whenever you enter a town and its people welcome you, eat what is set before you; [9]cure the sick who are there, and say to them, 'The kingdom of God has come near to you.' [10]But whenever you enter a town and they do not welcome you, go out into its streets and say, [11]'Even the dust of your town that clings to our feet, we wipe off in protest against you. Yet know this: the kingdom of God has come near.' . . .

[16]"Whoever listens to you listens to me, and whoever rejects you rejects me, and whoever rejects me rejects the one who sent me."

[17]The seventy returned with joy, saying, "Lord, in your name even the demons submit to us!" [18]He said to them, "I watched Satan fall from heaven like a flash of lightning. [19]See, I have given you authority to tread on snakes and scorpions, and over all the power of the enemy; and nothing will hurt you. [20]Nevertheless, do not rejoice at this, that the spirits submit to you, but rejoice that your names are written in heaven."

Commentary 1: Connecting the Reading with Scripture

Luke's account of the mission of the seventy winds together so many seemingly disparate images and themes that it becomes difficult for readers to be sure where we should focus our attention and what the bigger story is. To make sense, we have to be aware of the underlying narrative threads that Luke is working on in the larger context. One of these is the question of whether and how Jesus' mission involves judgment. In the synagogue of his hometown, Jesus claimed the mantle of the eschatological prophet, citing Isaiah 61:1–2a (Luke 4:18–19), but his citation stops just short of Isaiah's promise of a coming day of vengeance. In Luke 7:18–23, John the Baptizer sends his disciples to ask Jesus if he is really the one coming, or if they should look for someone else. Jesus' reply again highlights the blessings that attend his ministry (7:22–23), but makes no mention of judgment. By the time we reach Luke 10, however, motifs focused on judgment are becoming more common and more prominent (e.g., 7:29–32; 8:4–9). As the Gospel continues, Luke carefully winds motifs of salvation and healing together with announcements of judgment, not least in this passage.

The intertwining of redemption with judgment may be difficult for modern audiences to grasp, but it is common throughout Israel's prophetic traditions. Blessing and judgment both turn on human responses to God's coming; they are two sides of a single coin, linked inextricably. Even Paul, in the reading from Galatians 6 for this Sunday, while not explicitly focused on judgment, nonetheless mingles images of judgment and restoration, of suffering and hope, in the same exhortation. In the prophetic tradition, judgment comes to induce repentance, which may then lead to redemption. Israel itself was as much subject to this judgment as were the nations, and as is the church today. As Luke moves in this passage between images of dawning power and hope, on the one hand, and harsh condemnation, on the other, the audience is reminded that Jesus' mission has deep roots in this prophetic tradition, including its refusal to preserve the supposed insiders from judgment.

Israel often expected that the focus of God's judgment would be directed toward the nations, but the blessings to themselves, only to find themselves repeatedly enduring harsh judgment. Modern Christians also tend to see God's judgment as directed primarily toward others. The biblical paradigm, however, is that judgment always comes on us, whether as individuals or as a nation, when we become complicit with the powers of this world, rather than trusting God. One approach to this passage, then, is to lead congregations to explore why and how judgment comes upon us in both world and church, and how we might nurture hope even in the midst of judgment.

The seventy disciples Jesus sends, equaling the number of nations in Genesis 10, symbolizes mission to all the nations. In this story, Jesus is still focusing his ministry on the people of Israel, but as he already suggested in his rebuke to the people of Nazareth, his calling is also to announce the coming of God's reign to the nations, in both judgment and blessing (4:24–28). Both here and in the earlier mission of the Twelve (9:1–6), the disciples are to travel light. The means of mission is a crucial embodiment of the message itself: the disciples' mode of mission signals their dependence on God's provision—a crucial element of faith that goes all the way back to Israel's wilderness experience and, before that, to Eden. God's agents depend on others to recognize and respond to their need in hospitality. In congregations where success is measured primarily in numbers, wealth, and programming, the model of mission Jesus affirms will be unsettling. Do we want those to whom we go in mission to see our power and privilege, or God's power and blessing? How are God's presence and character evident in the actions and practices that comprise our mission?

Jesus then narrows the focus to hospitality as the decisive expression of God's mission. Jesus first tells the seventy to "greet no one on the road" (10:4), because peace and hospitality do not take root in the transience of the road, but in the households of God's people. The houses that receive the disciples receive the greeting of peace, with the expectation that it will continue to reciprocate (10:5–6). Twice Luke also signals that the offer of hospitality requires the disciples to accept whatever food is set before them (10:7, 8). Why? The missionaries are bringing the blessing of peace, healing the sick (10:9), and announcing the arrival of God's kingdom, so they are "laborers" who "deserve their pay" (10:7). The pay they accept is hospitality, which they must accept on their hosts' terms. Embedded in this practice is the principle that missionaries act not out of self-interest, but to draw attention to God's power, and they accommodate themselves to their hosts, not the other way around. The preacher can help us know that mission is not a one-way enterprise, but a partnership and peacemaking between the missionary and those to whom the missionary comes. The lectionary reading for this Sunday from 2 Kings 5, the story of Naaman and Elisha, also describes a scene in which human agency is stripped to the bare minimum, so that only God and God's power are at stake, resulting in Naaman's conversion. Elisha also refuses Naaman's offer of a tribute.

Finally, twice Luke tells the disciples to announce that "the kingdom of God has come near" (10:9, 11). Remarkably, in both cases this announcement is not the first thing the missionaries say, but the last, because blessing and judgment both turn on the acceptance or rejection of the missionaries themselves, made evident in the presence or absence of hospitality, which manifests the reality of God's presence. In both the Gospel and Acts, table fellowship and hospitality are the definitive locus of God's presence and power (e.g., Luke 24:13–35; Acts 10, esp. 10:23, 48). What kind of hospitality do we offer to the stranger, the outsider, the enemy? Do we go as colonizers or as peacemakers? What of ourselves are we prepared to give up in order to make peace?

What does it mean that the kingdom of God has come near? Modern readers often hear this claim primarily in temporal terms, as if Jesus were saying that it is almost here, but not yet. To "draw near" (*engizō*), however, carries more the spatial sense that something is already present, at hand, or among you (cf. 17:21). The preacher can help us know that Luke's vision here is typical of early Christian eschatological convictions, which were more clearly rooted in the sense that God was already present and at work in the world—both bringing transformation and fomenting powerful resistance—than in a sense that we are still waiting for God to come at the end of history to set things right. The varied responses we see in Luke 10 in the wake of the disciples' mission—from Jesus' pronouncements of judgment on the towns where he has already ministered (10:12–15), to the rejoicing of the seventy over the submission of the demons to them in Jesus' name (10:17), as well as in Jesus' vision of Satan falling from heaven (10:18)—signal that the kingdom of God has indeed come in power. Apparently, God's power is already loose in the world. Proclamation of these texts should lead Christians to grapple with the ways God is already active among us, in judgment as well as redemption, and especially in those practices that make for peace.

STANLEY P. SAUNDERS

Commentary 2: Connecting the Reading with the World

In commissioning seventy disciples, Jesus invites them—and us—into practices of risk. Risk traveling lightly. Risk rejection and welcome. Risk protest and proclaiming the good news of God's kingdom, which is coming near to every circumstance (Luke 10:9). This passage nurtures our capacity for risking, and preachers who engage it with a willingness to practice and explore will find a multitude of ways for the Word to enter the church's life.

Jesus' instructions, "Carry no purse, no bag, no sandals" (v. 4), sound counterintuitive to many in our congregations. Should we not bring along extra, just in case? Minds snared by scarcity may miss that this extensive episode in Luke 10 begins with abundance: Jesus sends these *seventy* disciples (plus two more, according to some translations) out in pairs. No one goes the road alone here. Preachers may take this opportunity to explore how to undo understandings of the Christian journey that emphasize the individual and encourage overpacking.

Similarly, we may miss Jesus' words about receiving hospitality: Whether or not your hosts share the peace you bring, stay, eat, and drink with them (vv. 5–8). This should come as no surprise to preachers familiar with Luke's focus on meals; thousands feasted on multiplied bread just a chapter earlier (9:10–17), and later on in this chapter Jesus will dine with Martha and Mary (10:38–42). However, in our increasingly polarized society, where people self-select into like-minded groups (churches included), Jesus invites contemporary listeners into a risky and creative tension. Preachers can lead a congregation into this tension, imagining receiving hospitality unburdened by extra baggage.

The thirty-five pairs of disciples return to Jesus with joy (v. 17); the risks of the journey have all been worthwhile. Inexplicably, Jesus chooses to tell them at this moment about the authority they possess, that nothing will harm them (v. 19). Without knowing that ahead of time, how did these disciples sustain their trust, with only the clothes on their back, the company of a friend, and Jesus' name on their lips? Here is one way to find out: Go searching for some risk takers. There are probably a good number in the congregation, and even more in the wider community. Learn from them how the church can live in Jesus' abundance.

Preachers with their senses tuned to risk can stumble on the most unlikely examples of discipleship. For example, consider this far-from-joy scenario: a congregation that is closing their doors, reflecting the shifting landscape of religion in North America. Even here there are risk takers who trust that the kingdom of God is close by and that Jesus continues to call them to live out that good news. Preachers can listen through heartbreak for brave questions: How will we eat and drink with the members of other congregations that we may join? More than anyone, these disciples know the authority of bearing Jesus' name in the world (v. 19), ultimately authoring more life than any institution. They know what it means to live knowing that no matter the circumstance, their names are written in heaven (v. 20).

Placing their trust in Jesus, the disciples risk rejection. For that, Jesus has a Plan B: "Go out into its streets and say, 'Even the dust of your town that clings to our feet, we wipe off in protest against you. Yet know this: the kingdom of God has come near'" (vv. 10–11). In congregations that value politeness or diplomacy, such a protest might be Plan Z. In our current political and social context, protest has reemerged as a strategy for change. The good news of the kingdom can and should engage protest, and, if Jesus' words are to be believed, protest can also shape how we proclaim the good news.

Preachers do not need to stage an impromptu protest during the sermon to make this point; they may wonder aloud, "Who is protesting right now, close by or far away? Why and how?" Search locally and globally. When you have found your protesters, ponder what it might be like to care so much about that particular issue to take a public stance. Protesters may hold up a mirror about churches' willingness to demonstrate the gospel in provocative ways. Like protesters of our time and place, the disciples in Luke interrupt the flow of ordinary life to heal and denounce. Local congregations may even draw inspiration from these disciples to confront in public the ways of life that poison and possess.

It is possible that the protesters you find might be protesting *you*—or, someone like you. In that case, preachers can help the congregation slip into this perspective and take a look around. Where has the church rejected visiting disciples? Where have we said, "No, thank you, our town is fine the way it is" (v. 10)? While crying "Woe!" against the congregation seems ill-advised (vv. 12–15), it might be useful for preachers to cry, "Whoa!" to caution people about their inhospitality and instead invite them into a season of discernment about how God is calling them to live out the risky and joyful good news.

Preachers might also find it useful to repurpose the act of wiping the dust from one's feet (v. 11). Beyond protest, these words carry an existential importance for rejected disciples. Notice that none of the returning seventy dwell on their "failed" missions (and from vv. 12–15 one assumes there have been some). Like familiar actions in worship such as the prayer of confession or pouring water into the baptismal font, wiping the dust from one's feet conveys cleansing and reminds disciples that neither fear nor failure can undo their belonging to Jesus' kingdom. Throughout worship, no less in the sermon, preachers can give people permission to dust off accumulated layers of guilt, shame, or rejection.

In his poem "Shake the Dust," spoken-word artist Anis Mojgani makes a similar move. Mojgani uncovers a redemptive quality to shaking the dust off one's feet: it is risking rejection in order to know life's fullness; falling down and still rising; reaching out to "grab the world by its clothespins, and shake it out / again and again."[1] The invitation to "shake the dust" is for all people—"the fat girls . . . the little brothers . . . the former prom queen . . . the schoolyard wimps and the childhood bullies that tormented them."[2] Preachers looking for grace in the text may uncover it in verse 11, imaginatively approaching the verse both from the perspective of the rejected disciples bending down to wipe their feet and from that of the townspeople watching them retreat into the distance, still pondering the words that were too hard to accept at first hearing.

In the final analysis, the risks into which Jesus invites us and the seventy come down to the greatest risk: to live as Jesus lived. Jesus traveled lightly, without a home to call his own (9:58). He ate and drank whatever his hosts

1. Anis Mojgani, "Shake the Dust," in *Songs from Under the River* (Austin, TX: Write Bloody Publishing, 2013), 88.
2. Mojgani, "Shake the Dust," 87.

provided. Sometimes he protested, crying woe and toppling tables. In another memory circulating through the early church, he washed his disciples' feet (John 13:1–17). It is the humbling task of preachers to invite people—starting with ourselves—into that journey, in miniature and sometimes momentous ways. Whatever success or setbacks the congregation encounters along the way, remind them that the kingdom of God has come near, particularly in the grace of Jesus Christ, and will sustain us on every traveling road.

HIERALD E. OSORTO

Proper 10 (Sunday between July 10 and July 16 Inclusive)

Amos 7:7–17 and Deuteronomy 30:9–14
Psalm 82 and Psalm 25:1–10
Colossians 1:1–14
Luke 10:25–37

Amos 7:7–17

[7]This is what he showed me: the Lord was standing beside a wall built with a plumb line, with a plumb line in his hand. [8]And the LORD said to me, "Amos, what do you see?" And I said, "A plumb line." Then the Lord said,

"See, I am setting a plumb line
in the midst of my people Israel;
I will never again pass them by;
[9]the high places of Isaac shall be made desolate,
and the sanctuaries of Israel shall be laid waste,
and I will rise against the house of Jeroboam with the sword."

[10]Then Amaziah, the priest of Bethel, sent to King Jeroboam of Israel, saying, "Amos has conspired against you in the very center of the house of Israel; the land is not able to bear all his words. [11]For thus Amos has said,

'Jeroboam shall die by the sword,
and Israel must go into exile
away from his land.'"

[12]And Amaziah said to Amos, "O seer, go, flee away to the land of Judah, earn your bread there, and prophesy there; [13]but never again prophesy at Bethel, for it is the king's sanctuary, and it is a temple of the kingdom."

[14]Then Amos answered Amaziah, "I am no prophet, nor a prophet's son; but I am a herdsman, and a dresser of sycamore trees, [15]and the LORD took me from following the flock, and the LORD said to me, 'Go, prophesy to my people Israel.'

[16]"Now therefore hear the word of the LORD.
You say, 'Do not prophesy against Israel,
and do not preach against the house of Isaac.'
[17]Therefore thus says the LORD:
'Your wife shall become a prostitute in the city,
and your sons and your daughters shall fall by the sword,
and your land shall be parceled out by line;
you yourself shall die in an unclean land,
and Israel shall surely go into exile away from its land.'"

Deuteronomy 30:9–14

[9]The LORD your God will make you abundantly prosperous in all your undertakings, in the fruit of your body, in the fruit of your livestock, and in the fruit of your

soil. For the LORD will again take delight in prospering you, just as he delighted in prospering your ancestors, [10]when you obey the LORD your God by observing his commandments and decrees that are written in this book of the law, because you turn to the LORD your God with all your heart and with all your soul.

[11]Surely, this commandment that I am commanding you today is not too hard for you, nor is it too far away. [12]It is not in heaven, that you should say, "Who will go up to heaven for us, and get it for us so that we may hear it and observe it?" [13]Neither is it beyond the sea, that you should say, "Who will cross to the other side of the sea for us, and get it for us so that we may hear it and observe it?" [14]No, the word is very near to you; it is in your mouth and in your heart for you to observe.

Commentary 1: Connecting the Reading with Scripture

Amos 7:7–17. The book of Amos overflows with images of destruction and judgment coming upon the nations, especially Israel. As our passage begins, Amos sees God beside a wall with a plumb line (7:7). Both in ancient times and today, construction workers ensure a wall is plumb (straight up and down) by dropping a weight attached to a string a short distance from the top of a wall. If the string measures the same distance from the wall at its bottom as at its top, then the wall is plumb—and gravity will not turn it to rubble. If the wall does not stand true, or if the ground settles and the wall tilts out of plumb, then it needs to be corrected, or gravity will eventually take its toll, causing the building to collapse. The idea is that Israel's buildings—especially its high places and sanctuaries (7:9)—will collapse with God's coming judgment.

Preachers have many options for developing Amos's image sermonically. For example, they can introduce listeners to biblical ideas of justice: if something is evil, it simply cannot stand for very long. It will collapse on itself. In fact, the same Hebrew word (*raah*) means both "evil" and "disaster." People who do evil (*raah*) will end up experiencing terrible things (*raah*). This idea is present, for example, in Deuteronomy 31:29; 1 Kings 2:44; 21:20–21; Jeremiah 2:19; 18:8; and Jonah 3:10.

Alternatively, preachers can emphasize the importance of pointing straight, true, and plumb toward God. When we orient our lives around ourselves or idols, we lack the right posture toward God. We are bent in on ourselves (what theologians, using Latin, call *incurvatus in se*). It is like building our homes on sand rather than solid rock (Matt. 7:24–27). Disobedience leads to ruin. Faithfulness to God, on the other hand, means we are in sync with the world's Creator.

After talking about the plumb line, the passage suddenly shifts, moving from an account of Amos's prophecies to a story about Amos's life. For nearly two hundred years, the kingdom of Israel had been divided in two. Judah was in the south and home to Jerusalem, while Israel was in the north and home to alternate places for worship such as Bethel. Amos likely was from Judah, but he forecasts grave destruction against Israel. Threatened by Amos's words about the destruction of Israel's high places and sanctuaries (7:9), Amaziah (priest of Bethel) accuses Amos of conspiring against the Israelite king Jeroboam II.

The priest orders Amos to return to his homeland and receive pay for prophesying there. Amos, however, explains that he does not see himself as a professional prophet who might charge or receive a fee for his prophesying. He is not even a prophet's son, which likely means that he has not received training under a professional prophet (see the reference to "their father" in 1 Sam. 10:12). Instead, Amos earns a living tending sheep and trimming sycamore trees (Amos 7:14). He has brought God's message against Israel only because of God's commands (v. 15). Such news would no doubt be frightening to Amaziah and Jeroboam II. It is clear that professional prophets often told rulers soothing words that authorities would welcome

(1 Kgs. 22:6–28; Jer. 6:13–15; 28:1–17). The fact that Amos is not in Israel to earn money suggests he is there solely to give an authentic word from God.

This text from Amos can be a way of empowering church members for ministry in the world: preachers can emphasize that often the best people to share God's word are laypeople like Amos. One does not need a seminary degree, an ordination certificate, a clergy collar or robe to bring God's word to people who desperately need it. The body of Christ is not made up of pastors alone (see Rom. 12:4–8; 1 Cor. 12:4–31). God works through all sorts of people—sometimes even those whom we least expect. Bringing God's word to others is not easy: the opposition Amos faces makes this abundantly clear (Amos 7:10–17). Despite difficulties, the church is called to speak God's word to a world needing direction.

Deuteronomy 30:9–14. The Bible insists that obeying God leads to a good and beautiful life. This passage makes that idea concrete, talking about abundant prosperity, children, wealth, and God's taking delight in us (30:9). It reiterates ideas present in Deuteronomy 28:1–14. (In fact, Deut. 28:11 is nearly identical to Deut. 30:9.)

Should this text be equated with the prosperity gospel common among many American televangelists and others today? Given the immense popularity of the health-and-wealth gospel, preachers may want to spend considerable time wrestling with this question in sermons. On the one hand, both Deuteronomy and prosperity theology say that good things come in this lifetime for those who obey God. They also emphasize the good in human beings. On the other hand, much of the health-and-wealth gospel today focuses on having the right mind-set, being optimistic, forgetting about the past, and trusting that God has good things in store for the future. Sometimes, prosperity preaching even encourages indifference toward the poor, who do not seem to be receiving God's blessings. The book of Deuteronomy, meanwhile, stresses remembering our past—including sinful mistakes (Deut. 1–4). It does not assume that everything will automatically turn out okay, especially when people lead wicked lives (28:15–68). It stresses not only having the right things in our minds, but also translating those good thoughts into concrete obedience. It teaches compassion toward the poor (15:7–11).

The text assures people that God's instructions are practical and attainable. God's commandment is not "too hard . . . too far away . . . in heaven . . . or beyond the sea" (30:11–13). Instead, God's word is within reach: already in people's mouths and hearts (30:14). The language is similar to Jeremiah 31:31–33, where God writes the law on people's hearts as a sign of a new covenant. There are also connections with the lectionary's epistle reading, which talks of being "filled with the knowledge of God's will in all spiritual wisdom and understanding" (Col. 1:9). Another way of developing this text into a sermon, therefore, is to talk about how God gives power for faithful and holy lives. The Holy Spirit not only provides comfort (Acts 9:31) but also sanctifies us so that we can serve God with joyful hearts (1 Cor. 6:11; 1 Pet. 1:2).

This text in Deuteronomy may contain the Bible's most optimistic estimation of what God's people can do. Other passages talk of humanity's continual proclivity for evil (e.g., Gen. 6:5; Rom. 3:23). Later, Joshua will speak to the same people as they make a covenant with God—much as Moses does here. However, Joshua warns them that they will utterly fail at what God has commanded (Josh. 24:19). It is useful, therefore, to see Deuteronomy 30:9–14 as one voice in the Bible's conversation about obedience and consequences. There are times when people desperately need to hear this voice—to learn that wonderful things come from obeying God and that it is possible at least to stumble in the right direction. However, there are other times when people need to hear the truths told in other parts of the Bible: Job's righteous suffering, the wicked reaping tragic consequences, and the difficulties of obedience. Wise pastors exegete not only the biblical text but also their congregations, so that they know which word is most appropriate on which occasion (cf. Prov. 25:11). At times, sermons need to give voice to more than one biblical perspective, reflecting the conversations that take place within the Bible.

MATTHEW RICHARD SCHLIMM

Commentary 2: Connecting the Reading with the World

Amos 7:7–17. Amos 7:7–17 consists of a vision (vv. 7–9) and a judgment speech concerning Amaziah, his family, and Israel (vv. 10–17). The vision that Amos sees foreshadows the demise of the northern kingdom of Israel, otherwise known as the house of Jeroboam. Without any hesitation, he makes known what he has seen, even though the vision is a terrible one and will have devastating effects for a people and their homeland (vv. 7–9).

The exchange between Amaziah, the priest of Bethel, and Amos is one that discloses the corruption of religious and political leadership and the courage of one person who acts prophetically to confront, challenge, and deliver a stinging message to counter the hypocrisy of the day. Amaziah sets up Amos in an attempt to silence him, because Amos's word is challenging and uncomfortable. Amaziah, however, is unsuccessful in his plot, and Amos's prophecy is later directed, ironically, against the priest and his family. In both verses 7–9 and verses 10–17, Amos does what he has to do in the spirit of being faithful to his commitment to his God and his commitment to speak the truth, even in times of personal peril.

The preacher can help us see how Amos's poetic prose narrative informs our communal mission in the world today. When Amos shared his divine vision, it provoked a conflict with Amaziah. Speaking truth to power is no easy task, especially when words are often misconstrued, misinterpreted, or even rejected altogether when the message threatens the listeners. Yet speaking truth cannot be sidestepped, and it cannot be something done when the moment is convenient and the climate is right. The mission to speak the truth supersedes all other personal concerns.

As God's people, our mission addresses physical as well as spiritual concerns. For example, we are called today to challenge the easing of environmental regulations that would undoubtedly lead to increased climate change, economically damage poor countries, and perhaps devastate the whole planet. Lands will become desolate and will be laid waste, not because of God's deeds but because of human deeds. In Amos's time, all of the northern kingdom and its people suffered devastation because of the corrupt deeds of those in power. Amos's situation is no different than our situation today, except that we have different and yet similar life-threatening issues that need to be addressed. The mission of the church is to address the pressing issues of the day, just as Pope Francis has done in his encyclical *Laudato Si*. The preacher can help us know again that the mission of the people of God is to advance such concerns by speaking truth to power locally, nationally, and globally, while living in a way that shows a fidelity to the word we teach and preach.

Finally, Amos shows us that when we dare to speak truth to power, especially to corrupt religious and political leaders, we run the risk of losing our lives. Other encounters with powerful leaders could cause us to be ostracized, slandered, unwelcomed in houses of worship, or silenced. Such roadblocks did not stop Amos, who faithfully tried to bring forth the reign of God, which is characterized by justice and ethical praxis. Such was his challenge, and such is ours today. The preacher ought not to shy away from addressing the ways that such truth-telling can have costly repercussions for individuals and congregations.

Deuteronomy 30:9–14. Prosperity and fertility are the gifts that God promises to give to the Israelite people if they obey God by observing God's commandments and decrees written in the book of the law. Such obedience begins with being in right relationship with God, which includes turning to God with one's whole being—heart and soul. Love is the essence of the law (Deut. 10:12–22), and the commandment that God enjoins on the people is the command to love (6:1–9). Hence, the law and the commandment are one and the same: the call to love. This commandment is said to be neither too hard for the people nor far from them. It is already in their mouths and hearts and waits to be observed. Observance of the law guarantees the "good life" with peace and security for all. The decision to follow God's ways and commandments is not just a matter of doing what is supposed to be done and thereby affirming the law. Rather, obeying God's commands involves choosing a way of life characterized by right relationship with God, with one another, and with all life (30:15–20).

This passage from Deuteronomy is a profound source of knowledge and wisdom for the church's mission of evangelization today. Too often believers become too focused on the letter of the law and make it an end in itself, instead of seeing it as a means to an end, with the end being love. How many times have people allowed their misinformed interpretation of God's ways and commands to become a source of division within a community? How many times have people been judged by others for not following the letter of the law? Surely these situations were prevalent in ancient Israel as well as in Jesus' day in NT times. As part of their mission of evangelization, the people of God as church have the task of educating others to the essence of the law, which is love, just as the character Moses offers instruction to the Israelites in this reading from Deuteronomy.

The mission of evangelization also calls the church to educate others in their faith, then teach people how to think critically about faith and its many issues. Believers who are well informed—well educated in the breadth and depth of theology, biblical studies, historical theology, pastoral studies, liturgical studies, and spirituality—will have the knowledge they need to avoid falling into a fundamentalist understanding of God and faith. Fundamentalism often leads to judgment. Thus the work of evangelization involves the church in education and faith formation.

For the ancient Israelite community, ethical praxis and worship went hand in hand. Hence, adherence to God's ways and commandments has profound social and ethical implications for today. Faithfulness to an ethical way of life as prescribed by God's commands is always for the purpose of safeguarding relationships. In every nation across the globe, laws exist; yet our world continues to be fraught with violence, injustice, and broken relationships, in spite of governing bodies' best attempt to lay down laws to safeguard people's rights and lives. Not until societies begin to function on a higher ethic, namely, the law of love, will the world's people live themselves into the divine promise of prosperity and the good life. As long as laws exist without a change of heart among the world's people, the laws will be broken, and the transformative presence of God stifled. This passage from Deuteronomy calls people everywhere to reclaim their hearts, to listen to their hearts, and to follow their hearts. In the heart rests the Spirit and word of the sacred Presence who will reveal to us how we should live our lives.

Finally, this text from Deuteronomy calls for each person to enter deeply into a personal relationship with God so that God can soften and change one's heart. Beverly Lanzetta, in her book *Emerging Heart: Global Spirituality and the Sacred*, makes the point that people have to recover their hearts and rekindle their desire for God.[1] Only when one's heart is completely given over to God can a new ethic begin to take shape, one that is rooted in a divine transformative love instead of a set of legalistic codes.

CAROL J. DEMPSEY, OP

1. Beverly Lanzetta, *Emerging Heart: Global Spirituality and the Sacred* (Minneapolis: Augsburg Fortress Press, 2007).

Psalm 82

[1]God has taken his place in the divine council;
in the midst of the gods he holds judgment:
[2]"How long will you judge unjustly
and show partiality to the wicked?
[3]Give justice to the weak and the orphan;
maintain the right of the lowly and the destitute.
[4]Rescue the weak and the needy;
deliver them from the hand of the wicked."

[5]They have neither knowledge nor understanding,
they walk around in darkness;
all the foundations of the earth are shaken.

[6]I say, "You are gods,
children of the Most High, all of you;
[7]nevertheless, you shall die like mortals,
and fall like any prince."

[8]Rise up, O God, judge the earth;
for all the nations belong to you!

Psalm 25:1–10

[1]To you, O LORD, I lift up my soul.
[2]O my God, in you I trust;
do not let me be put to shame;
do not let my enemies exult over me.
[3]Do not let those who wait for you be put to shame;
let them be ashamed who are wantonly treacherous.

[4]Make me to know your ways, O LORD;
teach me your paths.
[5]Lead me in your truth, and teach me,
for you are the God of my salvation;
for you I wait all day long.

[6]Be mindful of your mercy, O LORD, and of your steadfast love,
for they have been from of old.
[7]Do not remember the sins of my youth or my transgressions;
according to your steadfast love remember me,
for your goodness' sake, O LORD!

[8]Good and upright is the LORD;
therefore he instructs sinners in the way.

[9]He leads the humble in what is right,
and teaches the humble his way.
[10]All the paths of the LORD are steadfast love and faithfulness,
for those who keep his covenant and his decrees.

Connecting the Psalm with Scripture and Worship

Psalm 82. Psalm 82 is an enthronement psalm, likely used as a temple liturgy to celebrate YHWH's kingly triumph over all earthly powers hostile to divine rule. In this courtroom drama, Israel's God puts the other "gods" on trial (v. 1), indicts and charges them (vv. 2–4), summarizes the case (v. 5), and pronounces the guilty sentence (vv. 6–7). In the end, Psalm 82 "affirms again the message that forms the theological heart of the book of Psalms: God rules the world."[1] Despite the powers that threaten to plunge the world into chaos, the psalmist proclaims the sovereignty of God in the eternal realm and professes faith in the presence of God on the earth with a summons: "Rise up, O God, judge the earth; for all the nations belong to you!" (v. 8). With a strong judgment on the gods of the cosmos and a tender word for the needy on the earth, the psalmist proclaims that ultimate power lies in the one true God of justice (v. 3) and of mercy (v. 4).

Like Psalm 82, Amos 7:7–17 reveals a God who is not afraid to pronounce judgment on the wicked and unjust, delivering a divine judgment of harsh punishment on God's own people of Israel, including exile and death (v. 17). The people's disregard for the divine will of justice violates the sacred covenant and will not be tolerated. Both Amos and the psalmist echo the refrain: "Yahweh is the King who was, who is, and who is to come—to judge the earth with righteousness."[2]

In Christian worship, Psalm 82 is read in context of the gospel to proclaim that Jesus is Lord, through whom God's kingdom has been inaugurated on earth, and by whom God's will shall be done. Trusting that God's kingdom has come, but is not yet complete, people are called to new responsibility—to "Rise up" against injustice, evil, and oppression. In the Gospel lesson (Luke 10:25–37), Jesus reminds the lawyer to love God and neighbor (v. 27). To answer the question "Who is my neighbor?" (v. 29), Jesus tells the story of the man who was robbed and left to die; two people passed by, while the third person who stopped to help the man in need was the one who showed mercy. Jesus said, "Go and do likewise" (v. 37).

The biblical texts present an opportunity for the preacher to proclaim the sovereignty of the God of justice and mercy. In today's world, we see injustice and evil all around us—in our cities and neighborhoods and workplaces, in our homes and schools and churches. People cannot help but search for God. The psalmist's words can be a powerful prayer for God to "Rise up" and defeat the powers of evil, as well as a powerful plea for the people of God to "Rise up" and be the hands of Jesus on the earth, helping, healing, and bringing hope.

In the liturgy, the psalmist's words "Rise up, O God" can be used as a refrain throughout the prayers of the people, ending with the Lord's Prayer. Hymns that sound the chorus of the sovereignty of God are appropriate: "Holy, Holy, Holy" or "God of the Ages, Whose Almighty Hand." To reinforce the call to be disciples, consider "Jesu, Jesu, Show Us How to Love," "Come! Live in the Light," or "What Does the Lord Require of You?" The bold worship leader might play Bruce Springsteen's "My City of Ruins," with the refrain "Rise up!"

These Scripture readings illustrate the God who was, is, and forever will be judging and caring for the earth and all the people in it with justice and mercy. In response, the people sing

1. J. Clinton McCann Jr., "The Book of Psalms," in *The New Interpreter's Bible*, ed. Leander E. Keck, 10 vols. (Nashville: Abingdon, 1996), 4:1006.
2. Bernhard W. Anderson, *Out of the Depths: The Psalms Speak for Us Today* (Philadelphia: Westminster Press, 1983), 176.

praise, pray, and participate in the kingdom of God on earth.

Psalm 25:1–10. Psalm 25 is a lament that contains the characteristic elements: summons to YHWH (vv. 1–2a), complaint of enemies (vv. 2–3), petition of teaching and leading in right paths (vv. 4–5), appeal to divine attributes of mercy, steadfast love, and goodness (vv. 6–7), and conviction of pardon for those who keep God's commandments and decrees (vv. 8–10). However, this lament functions as a form of praise based on the psalmist's belief that, in contrast to the capricious gods of the ancient world, YHWH is steadfast in doing good, showing mercy, and remembering the covenantal relationship with the people of Israel. In fact, even the laments and petitions are offered along with a word of praise, for example, "Do not remember my sins . . . for your goodness' sake, O Lord!" (v. 7). Lament and praise can coexist in Psalm 25 because of the trust the psalmist has in God. Trusting in God's merciful nature, the psalmist offers a plea for forgiveness and deliverance, knowing it will be granted; while waiting, the psalmist can exalt God's holy name and offer thanks and praise.

Psalm 25 hearkens back to the days of old, when God was steadfast in love and mercy (v. 6) for the assurance that God will be so again. Deuteronomy 30:9–14 offers such an example of God's steadfast love. Despite the Israelites' repeated attempts to revoke the covenant God made with them, God was faithful in leading them out of slavery and through the trials and temptations of the wilderness. Now on the brink of the promised land, Moses reminds the people of the covenantal relationship with God: God will take care of you and bless you if you will obey God's commandments. This commandment, this God, is not far away, but is very close, in fact is within each person's mouth and heart (v. 14).

With these texts, the preacher may proclaim a powerful word about the faithfulness of God in every time, from generation to generation. God's love and mercy have stood the test of time. Another homiletic possibility is to explore the tension between lament and praise and the fruitfulness and faithfulness that are produced in that in-between place. Psalm 25 offers a model of prayer as we wait for God to abundantly prosper (Deut. 30:9), and a model for living as we trust that we will learn the ways of truth and love (v. 10).

Liturgically, Psalm 25 can be used in part as a prayer of confession, and Deuteronomy can be used as a declaration of forgiveness. The themes of Psalm 25 suggest hymns of God's faithfulness ("Great Is Thy Faithfulness"), mercy ("There's a Wideness in God's Mercy"), and love ("Love Divine, All Loves Excelling"). After the sermon or prayer, consider hymns that invite people to offer themselves in response to God's mercy ("Just As I Am" or "Take My Life"). With the focus on offering, some of the words of the psalm can be used in the prayer of dedication or sending prayer. The psalm's references to the "paths and ways of the Lord" can be visually portrayed in worship for the children's time, as well as after worship in the form of a prayer walk in the community.

In summary, these readings invite the hearer to live in the tension between lament and praise, not as one without hope, but one who trusts that the God who has been faithful for generations will remember the covenant of steadfast love and mercy forever. So we respond with the psalmist, "O my God, in you I trust" (Ps. 25:2).

DONNA GIVER-JOHNSTON

Colossians 1:1–14

[1]Paul, an apostle of Christ Jesus by the will of God, and Timothy our brother,

[2]To the saints and faithful brothers and sisters in Christ in Colossae:

Grace to you and peace from God our Father.

[3]In our prayers for you we always thank God, the Father of our Lord Jesus Christ, [4]for we have heard of your faith in Christ Jesus and of the love that you have for all the saints, [5]because of the hope laid up for you in heaven. You have heard of this hope before in the word of the truth, the gospel [6]that has come to you. Just as it is bearing fruit and growing in the whole world, so it has been bearing fruit among yourselves from the day you heard it and truly comprehended the grace of God. [7]This you learned from Epaphras, our beloved fellow servant. He is a faithful minister of Christ on your behalf, [8]and he has made known to us your love in the Spirit.

[9]For this reason, since the day we heard it, we have not ceased praying for you and asking that you may be filled with the knowledge of God's will in all spiritual wisdom and understanding, [10]so that you may lead lives worthy of the Lord, fully pleasing to him, as you bear fruit in every good work and as you grow in the knowledge of God. [11]May you be made strong with all the strength that comes from his glorious power, and may you be prepared to endure everything with patience, while joyfully [12]giving thanks to the Father, who has enabled you to share in the inheritance of the saints in the light. [13]He has rescued us from the power of darkness and transferred us into the kingdom of his beloved Son, [14]in whom we have redemption, the forgiveness of sins.

Commentary 1: Connecting the Reading with Scripture

This addition to the collection of Paul's writings, the letter of Colossians, with its lofty language and unusual descriptions of Christ, nature, and the cosmic life of faith, clearly enhances our understanding of the development of this community formed early after the death of Christ. Multiple issues, multiple ways to address those issues, multiple letters, and multiple writers all serve to give us a colorful view of the variety of form and thought in the communities of believers that formed after the death of Jesus in the first-century world. The community of believers in Colossae are accustomed to lofty visions, such as one identifying God, who has qualified us to share in the inheritance of the saints in light, and us, who have been delivered from the dominion of darkness (1:12–13).

There are several distinctive attributes of this letter. The language is reminiscent of poetry and philosophical thought. It is less concerned about practical concerns but instead describes faith more in philosophical, abstract language. Indeed, the language of Colossians bears close resemblance to the writings of the ancient Greek philosophical schools where beautiful, abstract language is used to describe the commonplace, rather than reading like a practical manual for living intended to instruct those who are living in the *Way*—those followers of Jesus in the early hours of the development of the church. Clearly absent from this letter are the practical, common injunctions for daily living, so obvious in other letters like the ones to the Thessalonians. This letter to the believers in Colossae almost sings—like a hymn dedicated to a Greek deity, or at least an elegant statement of religious rigor energized by philosophy and Greek thought.

A Closer Neighbor

The Samaritan, "who took pity on the man who had fallen among thieves," is truly a "guardian," and a closer neighbor than the Law and the prophets. He showed that he was the man's neighbor more by deed than by word. According to the passage that says, "Be imitators of me, as I am of Christ," it is possible for us to imitate Christ and to pity those who "have fallen among thieves." We can go to them, bind their wounds, pour in oil and wine, put them on our own beasts, and bear their burdens. The Son of God encourages us to do things like this. He is speaking not so much to the teacher of the Law as to us and to all men when he says, "Go and do likewise." If we do, we shall obtain eternal life in Christ Jesus, to whom is glory and power for ages and ages. Amen.

Origen (ca. 185–ca. 254), "Homily 34," in *Origen Homilies on Luke; Fragments on Luke*, trans. Joseph T. Lienhard, SJ, Fathers of the Church (Washington, DC: Catholic University Press of America, 1996), 141.

"Singing passages" are not unusual in the NT, which includes passages that move into poetry and perhaps were even actual hymns sung during the worship of the first-century believers. The tuned homiletical ear can hear voices of the choir, for example, in Philippians 2:5–11, "Have this mind in you. . . ." Perhaps one can hear the notes and the sounds from the Johannine community as they sing the prologue: "In the beginning was the Word . . ." (John 1:1–14). Sometimes words on a page or screen must, in order to be received and understood, turn into song, into music, into doxology. The preacher can help listeners tune in to this genre with its doxological implications for our lives of faith.

Whether Paul actually wrote this letter is not clear, and maybe authorial authentication is not all that important if understanding the early life of the Christian community is truly our final goal. The practice of communicating significant messages using the name of already-accepted leaders to gain credibility and acceptance was not uncommon in the first-century world. We do know that Colossae was a city of Phrygia on the bank of the River Lychus, in the province of Asia, settled by wealthy indigenous Phrygians and Greeks. This predominantly Greek community also included a strong population of Jewish colonists by the time of this writing, around the first half of the first century (52–55 CE).

The person named Epaphras, mentioned in this letter, most likely brought the community of believers in Colossae together; his reports (1:7) appear to be the obvious connecting links between the author of this letter and the believers in Colossae. Epaphras appears to be closely connected to this community (4:12) as he accounted for the community's well-being and spiritual growth. No major problems are reported, which is in sharp contrast to the reports received in the communities of Thessalonica and Corinth. Rather, Epaphras gives account of the love that is present in the community (1:8).

The key word, *therefore*, introduces the next section of text in 1:9. The writer of Colossae prays that their relationship with God will go even deeper, bringing spiritual wisdom and good fruit (1:9–10). By way of comparison, a quick review of 1 Corinthians (undisputedly Paul's) shows the list of problems the members of the Corinthian community were facing, which clearly becomes the occasion for the writing of the letter. (See 1 Cor. 4–10, paying careful attention to the "now concerning" literary form.) The members of the Corinthian church are ethically challenged, facing immoralities of every type, from incest to poor table etiquette. For the members of the church in Colossae, that does not appear to be the catalyst for the letter. Rather, the letter appears to be generous in praise for the readers, with the use of extravagant language belonging to a wider religious community. The preacher can take a cue from Colossians and look for instances in their local church that are worthy of praise such as the writer of Colossians offered that community. Along with those words of praise the preacher could give directions, guidance, ways that persons in that community might deepen their individual and collective relationship with God, growing in spiritual wisdom and good fruit (1:9–10).

The epistolary introduction (1:1–8) that offered thanksgiving to the deity now opens into language of prayer (vv. 9–14). It is a style of writing that closely resembles Qumran literature, wherein God reveals what has been hidden and makes all mysteries known, moving from darkness into light. Interestingly, the traditional Pauline corpus lacks the literary allusions to Qumran literature, with the exception of Ephesians and Colossians. In this letter the believers share in the "inheritance of the saints in the light" and have been delivered from the "darkness" (vv. 12–13). Yet the preacher can help us here by pointing out that there is no eschatological or apocalyptic language in the epistolary introduction of Colossians. This is language belonging to the here and now.

This author remembers the people of a little mountain church in southern Appalachia who learned about the here and now. It was this congregation's custom on every Easter Sunday morning to gather for the Easter sunrise service in the two-hundred-year-old church cemetery. It was still dark on that early Easter morning. With sleepy but confident voices, the people prayed for Jesus to return and the rapture to appear as they sang about "that resurrection morning when the dead in Christ shall rise . . . we shall rise, and have a new body." Nothing happened. I was a young daughter of the church and was waiting for the graves to burst open wide in that mystical mountain Easter morning. No trumpets. No bursting of graves. No clouds parting for Jesus' return. The preacher preached while we stood remembering the loved ones who were buried beneath our feet. Still nothing happened. Jesus did not descend from on high. The graves did not open. The songs were over, the preacher had finished, and all of the sudden the sun was peeking over the mountain. The final prayer. No, Jesus did not come that morning, but the Light did. That was enough.

That little group of people walked back into their lives knowing that they were surrounded by a great host of witnesses, that God was present, and that in the living of their normal lives, the rapturous presence of Christ could be experiences of grace and holiness. Like those readers of Colossians, they could understand that there was no need for prolonged waiting for the light to emerge; the light is here already (1:12). Preachers today, of every land, could help listeners know how this is true for us, in our contexts, too: the light is here already.

LINDA MCKINNISH BRIDGES

Commentary 2: Connecting the Reading with the World

There are few words more comforting, more strengthening, and more empowering than "I am praying for you." We have said those words to persons facing surgery or in the depths of grief and perhaps we have heard those words as we encountered a particularly daunting challenge. They come from the heart, those words do, and there is something about them that is mysteriously powerful. Likewise, there are few words happier or more personally affirming than "I thank God for you." Those words are church language, the language of Christian love, and they carry and convey life both to those who hear them and to those who speak them.

So begins the letter to the first-century church in the city of Colossae, either written by Paul or dictated by Paul (or possibly written by someone who knew the apostle's thoughts and wished to honor him by writing a letter in his name), which is theologically bold, imaginative, and beautifully poetic. Surely it was read aloud when the Christians in Colossae gathered in a member's home for worship, and it may have become an official part of that church's liturgy.

It addresses issues that had begun to emerge in and around the church in Colossae that have a contemporary ring: thinking theologically in a way that engaged the intellect and imagination of people inside and outside the church, and preparing for an unknown and quite possibly dangerous future. The writer will quickly move to universal, cosmic ideas but first wants the people to know that others have heard about them and are praying for them, and that they are the object of profound gratitude for their faithfulness and clear witness—by their life together—to the truth of the Gospel. "In our prayers for you we always thank God . . . for we have heard of your faith in Christ Jesus and the love that you have for all the saints. . . . Since the day we heard it, we have not ceased praying for you" (Col. 1:3, 4, 9).The Christians in Colossae surely stood taller and viewed the future with more hope and confidence when they heard those words.

The future that church faced was going to be challenging, perhaps even frightening at times. The gospel, along with the churches it spawned, was becoming more visible and viable, and was therefore a formidable threat to other, competing ideologies. Because early Christians were becoming a public and growing enterprise on the way to becoming a public institution, they inevitably would be viewed with suspicion by other religions and philosophies and finally by the empire itself. The issue of power loomed. What would be the power that saved and assured security? What would be the power to which followers of Jesus gave their ultimate allegiance and obedience? Would it be empire and emperor, or Jesus Christ?

The admonition within the prayer, "May you be made strong with all the strength that comes from his glorious power, and may you be prepared to endure everything with patience" (v. 11), indicates that leaders of the early church understood that their future would not be easy.

Authoritarian ideology does not look kindly on a religion that invites alternative ultimate allegiance. Authoritarian regimes understand the ultimate threat posed by a system of thought, a morality, and a way of life that trusts someone other than the state for security and salvation. Dictators know intuitively the threat posed by a religion that designates someone other than the leader or dictator or emperor as Lord, and so it is no coincidence that one of the things an authoritarian ideology and the empire it spawns must do is neutralize the threat of religion. So persecution of one form or another has hovered close to the church throughout its history. Sometimes that persecution would be soft and almost seductive.

The Nazi government in Germany during the 1930s succeeded in neutralizing the church by co-opting it, establishing a state office of religious affairs, and giving church leaders a visible presence at Nazi functions and public rallies. A photograph of two Lutheran bishops standing near Adolf Hitler at a Nazi rally—both giving the Nazi straight-arm salute—offers a chilling reminder of how effective soft persecution can be.

An indirect and recent example comes in the form of the successful efforts of some American politicians to co-opt susceptible Christian leaders and to persuade an entire swath of American Christianity to join the demonization of immigrants and adherents of another religion, thereby marginalizing and disenfranchising racial minorities, while publicly supporting increased investment in defense and reduced funding for programs that help poor, vulnerable, and underserved populations.

Sometimes persecution can be direct, too, and as harsh and lethal as it was later in the Roman Empire. The Third Reich, which co-opted German Christianity into the official German Christian Church, turned on the Confessing Church, forcing it underground, jailing and executing its leaders, including theologian and pastor Dietrich Bonhoeffer. During the cold war, communist governments in the Soviet Union, the Eastern Bloc, and Cuba cruelly persecuted those Christians who refused to avow their allegiance to the state and who instead claimed their ultimate faithfulness to Jesus Christ.

Sometimes persecution could be demonically cruel. Martin Scorcese's motion picture *Silence,* based on a novel by Shusako Endo, recounts the story of two seventeenth-century Portuguese Jesuits who travel to Japan to find their missionary teacher and mentor who was rumored to have renounced his faith and vocation under fierce persecution. They discover that Christian clergy and leaders were given the choice of denying their faith by tramping on an image of Jesus or watching as members of their congregations were horribly tortured and executed.

The letter to the Colossians is a reminder that being strengthened to endure is important for Christians and churches in every time and place. The writer also wants believers to know that faithful discipleship is never a choice between correct theological beliefs or living a faithful, loving life with one's neighbors in the world. Both matter. Theology matters. There were plenty of religious options within the first century's polytheistic culture. Knowing what Christianity believed about God, Jesus Christ, the Spirit, and the human prospect was essential. In our time, as digital technology allows us to communicate with anyone anywhere, engaging with people of other faith traditions is critical. Those encounters are not much enhanced by scrubbing our faith of its own specific intellectual constructs. Interfaith relationships are enhanced when people understand and can articulate what we believe. Preachers can help us know that the best way to relate with those of other faiths is not to dumb down our own, nor to expect then to minimize the particularities of their faith, but to listen and perhaps to learn new truth.

In the next section of the letter, the author expands the theological horizons into eternity with bracing, imaginative assertions. The writer also wants to encourage women and men to bear witness to the truth of the gospel by the way they live their lives in the world—to lead lives pleasing to God, as women and men who have been forgiven, renewed, and transferred to the kingdom of God's beloved Son.

Sometimes our religion and our churches seem more concerned with having our doctrine remain orthodox than that our life and the lives of individual Christians demonstrate the grace and love and kindness of that beloved Son. The early church knew that its witness to the lordship of Jesus Christ depended just as much on the way of life it displayed to the world as the eloquence and correctness of its theology and doctrine.

JOHN M. BUCHANAN

Luke 10:25–37

[25]Just then a lawyer stood up to test Jesus. "Teacher," he said, "what must I do to inherit eternal life?" [26]He said to him, "What is written in the law? What do you read there?" [27]He answered, "You shall love the Lord your God with all your heart, and with all your soul, and with all your strength, and with all your mind; and your neighbor as yourself." [28]And he said to him, "You have given the right answer; do this, and you will live."

[29]But wanting to justify himself, he asked Jesus, "And who is my neighbor?" [30]Jesus replied, "A man was going down from Jerusalem to Jericho, and fell into the hands of robbers, who stripped him, beat him, and went away, leaving him half dead. [31]Now by chance a priest was going down that road; and when he saw him, he passed by on the other side. [32]So likewise a Levite, when he came to the place and saw him, passed by on the other side. [33]But a Samaritan while traveling came near him; and when he saw him, he was moved with pity. [34]He went to him and bandaged his wounds, having poured oil and wine on them. Then he put him on his own animal, brought him to an inn, and took care of him. [35]The next day he took out two denarii, gave them to the innkeeper, and said, 'Take care of him; and when I come back, I will repay you whatever more you spend.' [36]Which of these three, do you think, was a neighbor to the man who fell into the hands of the robbers?" [37]He said, "The one who showed him mercy." Jesus said to him, "Go and do likewise."

Commentary 1: Connecting the Reading with Scripture

Augustine read Jesus' parable about the dying man and three travelers as an allegory of the Christian story of salvation: the devil and his minions rob Adam (humankind), leaving him for dead; the Law and the Prophets, or Judaism generally, fail to help; but Christ (in disguise as the Samaritan) saves us. Augustine went on to allegorize virtually every detail of the parable, often with fanciful, arbitrary associations. Many scholars now challenge the validity of allegorical interpretation, but the basic elements of Augustine's scheme are still with us in popular imagination, and often in pulpits, today, in ways that turn this story into a condemnation of Judaism, purportedly represented in the story by the priest and Levite. The preacher's first task in engaging this story may be to put our Christian triumphalism firmly in check.

Luke sets this story early in the material that describes the journey of Jesus and his disciples toward Jerusalem (Luke 9:51–19:27). The section begins with an account of a Samaritan village that refuses to accept Jesus, because they know that he intends to go up to Jerusalem (9:51–56). Jesus rebukes his disciples when they want to call down fire from heaven to consume the village, a plan that reflects the sorry character of Judean-Samaritan relations, even among Jesus' followers. Samaritans and Jews had a long, deeply intertwined, and often hostile history, focused on such questions as whose temple was God's true dwelling place. The lectionary reading for this day from Amos 7:7–17 also features the ancient conflict between the northern and southern kingdoms. Telling a parable in which a Samaritan is the hero was thus certain to be provocative. In fact, as Jesus and his entourage continue their journey, he supplies a steady stream of provocative teachings about discipleship (e.g., 9:57–62; 10:1–12), much of which touches on a recurrent Lukan theme: the importance of what one does, especially in offering hospitality and making peace. The story of the neighborly Samaritan illustrates risky, limitless hospitality, both by and for the stranger or enemy.

Luke frames the parable with the story of a lawyer who means to "test" Jesus, the same term used in 4:2 to designate the devil's temptation of Jesus. The lawyer's first question (10:25) may strike modern audiences, trained to focus on personal salvation, as a reasonable question that any seeker might ask: to what confessions or doctrines should I give assent? Should I be sprinkled or immersed? Are there other necessary actions I must undertake to secure my salvation? Jesus and most of his audience, however, did not see themselves as individuals seeking personal salvation. Salvation was understood, rather, in corporate terms: it was Israel's life that was at stake. One did not secure eternal life by oneself. "Eternal life" in God's presence is only and always a gift from God, not something humans can demand or achieve. In short, the lawyer's question is based on false premises. Jesus, therefore, simply turns the question back to him: "What is written in the law? What do you read there?"

The lawyer recites the commandments from Deuteronomy 6:5 and Leviticus 19:18, widely seen in ancient Judaism as the hooks on which the whole law hung: one part focused on devotion to God with one's whole being and one part on love of neighbor. They necessarily go together. Throughout this chapter, Luke correlates devotion to God with actions that represent God's love and mercy for humankind. Jesus' reply affirms the lawyer's answer but carries a barb. The lawyer's answer is "right" (Greek *orthos* means "correct" or "straight") but not necessarily complete, for *orthos* is not the same as *dikaios*, "just" or "righteous," which would depend on what the lawyer actually does to fulfill the commandments: "Do this, and you will live." The preacher can help us know that Psalm 82, another reading for this day, affirms that God's justice requires doing righteousness, especially toward the vulnerable, neighbors and enemies alike.

The lawyer, however, does not seek justice, but rather to "justify himself." His question "Who is my neighbor?" seeks again to narrow the quest for eternal relationship with God to a fixed, manageable determination. He is really asking, "Who is *not* my neighbor?" "Where are the limits?" Defining the neighbor inevitably narrows the focus: this one, not that one; Jews, not Samaritans; Judeans, not Galileans; Protestants, not Catholics; Republicans, not Democrats. Again, his enquiry is focused neither on God nor the neighbor, as the commandments require, but on himself. Modern listeners should hear in this story a challenge to our deeply held tendencies to divide the world into ever smaller circles of insiders and outsiders, friends and enemies.

The figures in the parable itself are drawn mostly from central casting: robbers, an unidentified traveler, a priest, a Levite. A typical Jewish audience might have expected the third character coming down the road to be an everyday Israelite. Instead, we meet a Samaritan. No indication is given—or necessary—as to why the priest and Levite pass by. Although many commentators argue that they are seeking to avoid defilement from touching, or even coming in proximity to, a dead or bleeding body, they were obliged under the law to care for those in distress, even the dead, if they were first on the scene. They are, moreover, coming from, not on their way up to, Jerusalem, so defilement would not be an overriding concern. The priest and Levite are not symbols of what is wrong with the law or with Judaism, as many have claimed, but simply a failure to do what needs to be done. They are, rather, highly religious people who fail to act in compassion, or even out of obligation, toward one who is in desperate need. Like the lawyer, they may be people of privilege, interested more in their entitlements than in a stranger in need. Jesus invites us to reconsider our foundational understandings of neighbors, neighborliness, and justice, upon which salvation hangs.

Luke presents the Samaritan, in contrast to the other characters in the story, in generous detail, adding layer upon layer of discomforting force to the Samaritan's portrayal. Like the priest and Levite, he comes near and sees, but he alone is moved with compassion (see 7:13; 15:20). He goes to the wounded man rather than around him. He attends to the wounds, pouring on oil and wine, puts him on his animal, brings him to the inn, cares for him, pays the innkeeper to continue care, and promises to repay the costs.

The details demonstrate complete, relentless, boundless care. All this from a despised Samaritan, the enemy who has nothing to gain from this kind of care for an unknown victim. He demonstrates what it means to act as a neighbor and thus to fulfill the commandments.

This parable easily lends itself, first, to translation into more contemporary terms. The Samaritan could be an immigrant, an Arab, a released felon. Which enemy/neighbor seems most threatening and risky? Second, at the heart of all Christian practice is the dangerous impulse to reach out in compassion and genuine care, without regard for one's self-interest or even one's own salvation. Salvation is found not in building walls, but in joining arms with the enemy and the alien—notions directly contrary to current political tendencies. Are our deeply held and ever-hardening political binaries congruent with our faith? Finally, when we read this story through our modern highly individualized and self-interested notions of salvation, we may end up in the same camp as the lawyer, who seems to have the right answers, but the wrong questions. How does this story challenge narrow, individualistic, formulaic, and self-justifying notions of salvation?

STANLEY P. SAUNDERS

Commentary 2: Connecting the Reading with the World

If you could ask Jesus any question, what would it be? On the road to Jerusalem (Luke 9:51), an expert in the Torah gets his chance: "Teacher, what must I do to inherit eternal life?" (10:25). Jesus takes the question seriously and, in doing so, places his listeners in a story that shocks their sensibilities. The preacher can help the congregation recover the unnerving news about the neighbor in this passage, moving beyond familiar assumptions about the "good" Samaritan and finding the healing touch of Jesus at its heart.

"Just then a lawyer stood up to test Jesus" (v. 25). Luke portrays Torah experts as a negative foil to Jesus (e.g., 7:30; 11:46–47), yet here is one such person in Jesus' company. Contemporary disciples may rush to judge him for testing (or tempting) Jesus, but Jesus himself does not respond defensively. Preachers can start making connections to the nature of the church: "What are some of the concrete differences in politics or piety within the congregation? What connects us?" These questions will be useful later on in reflecting on this passage.

When the Torah expert pushes Jesus to expand on who the "neighbor" is, Jesus tells us a story about a person left half-naked and half-dead by a band of criminals (v. 30). As for other details—ethnicity, occupation, class—Jesus says nothing. In this way, Jesus begins to answer the question: the neighbor is one you do not know. Leviticus 19:34 makes the same move: "The alien [immigrant, *ger*] who resides with you shall be to you as the citizen among you; you shall love the alien [immigrant] as yourself, for you were aliens [immigrants] in the land of Egypt." Preachers can invite their congregation to ponder: "Who are the neighbors we do not know? Why not? How might God call us into new relationships?"

While parishioners need to explore *why* they might not know certain neighbors, they likely already know *how* they do not know. Like the priest and Levite, we know all about passing by on the other side (vv. 31–32). These characters offer a pair of opportunities for personal self-reflection.

First, these figures represent upstanding members of the community. Jesus' listeners expect them to stop, and yet they do not. Similarly, around the nation and close to home, people who have earned our respect betray our trust. Preachers can invite the congregation to link to their own experience: perhaps a politician who suddenly resigned after the scandal broke or a beloved family member who looked away from abuse. How can followers of Jesus respond? (Luke 6:32–36 could provide the start to an answer.)

Second, the priest and the Levite prompt listeners who are aware of their own tendency to avoid the neighbor to cultivate self-compassion, a key strategy in counseling practices such as compassion-focused therapy. Preachers should not confuse this with self-justification; reflecting on one's hardness of heart requires intentional effort and honest prayer. However, in a culture that easily converts guilt ("I have done something bad") into shame ("I am bad"), self-compassion helps Christians identify habits or assumptions that keep them from living into the mandate of neighbor love and affirm God's love for them that redeems and restores. Though they have not responded to the gracious gift of God's Torah, the priest and Levite still belong to the covenant people. Likewise, preachers can remind the congregation that in Christ we are grafted into the same covenant, in which nothing can separate us from God's love (Rom. 11:17; 8:37–39).

After the priest and Levite passed by, Jesus' listeners likely expect the next character to be an ordinary Judean; instead, he shocks them with a Samaritan (v. 33). The history between these two peoples connected to Moses and ancient Israel and is written in blood (e.g., the Judean Hasmoneans destroyed the Samaritan temple on Mount Gerizim in the second century BCE). Just a chapter before this parable, Samaritan villagers refused to welcome Jesus' messengers because he was traveling to Jerusalem, inflaming the disciples to potential violence (9:52–55). Yet it is a Samaritan here whose gut wrenches with pity (or compassion, cf. 7:13; 15:20) at the state of the unknown victim and moves to help.

Connecting the Samaritan to the congregation's contemporary equivalent may be the most important connection preachers can make. Who do members of the community tend to disparage—wrongly, yes, but even rightly? Jesus does not introduce the Samaritan in order to dissolve his listeners' preconceptions but in order to play off them. If the temptation arises to place on Jesus' lips some equivalent to, "See, not *all* Samaritans are bad," then the preacher may want to substitute "white supremacists," "homophobes," or "abusers" in place of "Samaritans" and judge whether that statement holds water. The issue at hand is not whether God loves or redeems white supremacists, homophobes, abusers, or Samaritans; nor should preachers reduce their personhood to the violence they commit. Yet Jesus seems to be making a point in the parable (wherein he never calls the Samaritan "good") that he makes in the succeeding chapter: "If you then, who are evil, know how to give good gifts to your children, how much more will the heavenly Father give the Holy Spirit to those who ask him!" (11:13). In other words, if the "bad" Samaritan can show compassion, then surely someone who knows the Torah's commandments to love can do likewise!

Of course, we disparage some communities without merit; we project onto particular others our fears, insecurities, and qualities we like the least about ourselves. Research into implicit bias can help preachers unpack for their congregations the unconscious attitudes into which we have been socialized. It may be helpful to ask for testimony, connecting with trusted individuals to discuss their memories of direct and indirect messages about other people they received growing up, messages based on characteristics of race, ethnicity, gender, or social class. These illustrations in a sermon (granted permission, of course) demonstrate vulnerability and establish trust in the congregation. Recalling the strategy of self-compassion, preachers should affirm how God's grace precedes and empowers us in braving conversations about healing harmful stereotypes. This work prepares congregations to follow Jesus in his vision of cultural transformation (4:16–21), undoing the structural effects of bias.

Making these connections around the Samaritan prepares preachers to do more than encourage people to identify their neighbor as the person they dislike the most or the person with whom they have the least in common. Notice how Jesus turns the Torah expert's question around (v. 36), provoking us to imagine receiving care and hospitality from that person! Recalling the questions raised earlier regarding the Torah expert, preachers can point out how this vulnerability begins even in the congregation: How will we allow ourselves to receive care from the person in the pews who disagrees with us most? That answer for many will center on Jesus and the good news of the kingdom he proclaims.

It is curious, considering all of this, that patristic interpreters often read Jesus, the great physician (Luke 5:31), in the character of the Samaritan. John Chrysostom likened the oil and wine with which the Samaritan dressed the injured one's wounds to the sacraments: the oil for anointing the newly baptized; the cup of costly salvation. Preachers may lift up these elements as ways in which we receive Jesus' healing touch today, even as they promise that Jesus will come to us—wounded, biased, ashamed ones—in unlikely ways as well, transforming us into willing neighbors in God's kingdom.

HIERALD E. OSORTO

Proper 11 (Sunday between July 17 and July 23 Inclusive)

Amos 8:1–12 and Genesis 18:1–10a
Psalm 52 and Psalm 15
Colossians 1:15–28
Luke 10:38–42

Amos 8:1–12

[1]This is what the Lord GOD showed me—a basket of summer fruit. [2]He said, "Amos, what do you see?" And I said, "A basket of summer fruit." Then the LORD said to me,

"The end has come upon my people Israel;
I will never again pass them by.
[3]The songs of the temple shall become wailings in that day,"
says the Lord GOD;
"the dead bodies shall be many,
cast out in every place. Be silent!"

[4]Hear this, you that trample on the needy,
and bring to ruin the poor of the land,
[5]saying, "When will the new moon be over
so that we may sell grain;
and the sabbath,
so that we may offer wheat for sale?
We will make the ephah small and the shekel great,
and practice deceit with false balances,
[6]buying the poor for silver
and the needy for a pair of sandals,
and selling the sweepings of the wheat."

[7]The LORD has sworn by the pride of Jacob:
Surely I will never forget any of their deeds.
[8]Shall not the land tremble on this account,
and everyone mourn who lives in it,
and all of it rise like the Nile,
and be tossed about and sink again, like the Nile of Egypt?

[9]On that day, says the Lord GOD,
I will make the sun go down at noon,
and darken the earth in broad daylight.
[10]I will turn your feasts into mourning,
and all your songs into lamentation;
I will bring sackcloth on all loins,
and baldness on every head;
I will make it like the mourning for an only son,
and the end of it like a bitter day.

[11]The time is surely coming, says the Lord GOD,
when I will send a famine on the land;
not a famine of bread, or a thirst for water,
but of hearing the words of the LORD.
[12]They shall wander from sea to sea,
and from north to east;
they shall run to and fro, seeking the word of the LORD,
but they shall not find it.

Genesis 18:1–10a

[1]The LORD appeared to Abraham by the oaks of Mamre, as he sat at the entrance of his tent in the heat of the day. [2]He looked up and saw three men standing near him. When he saw them, he ran from the tent entrance to meet them, and bowed down to the ground. [3]He said, "My lord, if I find favor with you, do not pass by your servant. [4]Let a little water be brought, and wash your feet, and rest yourselves under the tree. [5]Let me bring a little bread, that you may refresh yourselves, and after that you may pass on—since you have come to your servant." So they said, "Do as you have said." [6]And Abraham hastened into the tent to Sarah, and said, "Make ready quickly three measures of choice flour, knead it, and make cakes." [7]Abraham ran to the herd, and took a calf, tender and good, and gave it to the servant, who hastened to prepare it. [8]Then he took curds and milk and the calf that he had prepared, and set it before them; and he stood by them under the tree while they ate.

[9]They said to him, "Where is your wife Sarah?" And he said, "There, in the tent." [10]Then one said, "I will surely return to you in due season, and your wife Sarah shall have a son."

Commentary 1: Connecting the Reading with Scripture

Amos 8:1–12. This text provides opportunities for preachers to explore two very different topics: economic justice and divine communication.

Most people today think of fruit baskets as good things. Who does not love a juicy bite of freshly picked fruit? Who does not feel special when they receive a basket of fruit? Amos's fruit basket, however, is horrifying. It leads to talk of wailing and corpses. Why is fruit connected with death? The Hebrew word for "summer fruit" (*qayits*) is remarkably similar to the word for "end" later in the verse (*qets*). This word *qets* frequently carries deadly overtones (Gen. 6:13; Lam. 4:18; Ezek. 7:2–3).

The text explains why divine punishment draws near. The people have oppressed the poor (8:4). They cannot wait until the Sabbath is over—even though this day of rest served as a reminder that Israel was no longer under Pharaoh's merciless rule (8:5; Deut. 5:15). Meanwhile, business practices reek of dishonesty. Sellers want to make small the "ephah," a unit used to measure goods like flour. They also want to make large the "shekel," a weight and monetary unit often connected with silver (v. 5). The text even talks about purchasing slaves ("buying the poor . . . and the needy," v. 6). It mentions "sandals" perhaps because the needy offered them as a guarantee they would pay back debts, or perhaps because binding transactions could involve exchanging sandals (Ruth 4:7–8). Amos speaks of "selling the sweepings of the wheat," that is, the chaff or worthless part of the plant, left over after the seed was removed (v. 6).

Given the prominent description of Israel's economic sins, preachers can expound on ways that God opposes greed. Like Jesus's God (cf. Matt. 23:23), Amos's God is a God of justice—a God who sides with the poor when no one else comes to their aid (Ps. 12:5; Luke 6:24–25). This God refuses to do nothing while those in need suffer deeply. Even if it means the death of Israel, God will take action against those who harm the least of these.

Indeed, the rest of the passage describes horrible and irreversible punishment on Israel. It is a tragic forecast, much like Psalm 52:5 from the day's lectionary reading. After describing an earthquake (v. 8; cf. 1:1; Zech. 14:5) and mourning practices (v. 10; cf. Ezek. 27:31), the text talks about "a famine . . . of hearing the words of the LORD" (v. 11). God's going silent meant the people were left to their own devices, unable to move in harmony with their savior and protector.

In addition to speaking on God's response to economic injustice, preachers can also use this text for a teaching sermon on how God communicates. The beginning of the passage joins other parts of the Bible in describing dreams and visions that God uses (e.g., Gen. 37:6–9; 41:1–32). These divine messages often use symbolism: there's the wordplay here, while Genesis uses grain (Gen. 37:7; 41:5–7), celestial bodies (37:9), and cows (41:2–4) to represent other things.

How could anyone tell that a dream was an authentic message from God and not a meaningless collection of images while asleep? One clue is that God would often send a series of dreams or visions to reinforce similar messages. So Joseph dreams of both sheaves and stars (Gen. 37:7, 9), similar to how Amos sees not only a fruit basket (8:2) but also locusts (7:1), fire (7:4), and a plumb line (7:7).

Parishioners often ask why God does not seem to speak today the same way that God did in biblical times. Sermons can offer several possible answers. Perhaps God continues to speak, and we simply are not listening. Perhaps the Bible describes very special times in history that merited special messages from God. Perhaps God now speaks more through the written word—the Bible—than in Amos's day, when very little of the Bible had yet been written. Perhaps we—like the people Amos warns—are experiencing a famine of God's word (8:11). Perhaps we want so badly to do things our own ways that God has left us to do just that—a great punishment indeed.

Genesis 18:1–10a. This text easily lends itself to sermons on waiting for God. It also teaches the importance of hospitality. Nearly every congregation is filled with people who quietly wait to see God's promises come true. They want victory over addiction. They want rest from the hectic pace of everyday life. They want healing from disease. They want peace to wash away their persistent worries. Nevertheless, addiction lingers. Craziness erupts. Cancer progresses. Fears wash in anew.

In that sense, people are very much like Abraham and Sarah. Previously, God promised that they would become a great nation (e.g., Gen. 17:4–6, 20), become a blessing (e.g., 12:2–3), have a great name (12:2), have offspring (e.g., 15:4–5), have land (e.g., 13:14–17), have a great reward (e.g., 15:1), and have a long life (15:15).

However, ever since God became involved with Abraham and Sarah, these promises have borne little fruit. Although they have many belongings (13:2), they have no children together. They do not even own land: they live as immigrants (17:8). Later, Abraham will need to purchase land simply to have a place to bury Sarah (23:1–20).

With little more than faith in unfulfilled promises, Abraham sits near "the oaks of Mamre" at the start of our passage. When Abraham sees three men nearby, he leaves his tent and demonstrates the virtue of hospitality. He insists that the visitors rest under the tree so he can bring food and water (18:3–5).

Traveling in the ancient world was extremely dangerous. Those making journeys could easily face robbers, wild animals, thirst, and hunger. Travelers were thus extremely vulnerable and dependent on the kindness of people they encountered. Abraham perceives his visitors' needs. As soon as they agree to stay, he prepares a lavish feast. He tells Sarah to make cakes out of "three measures of choice flour" (v. 6). Just one of these measures would be nearly two gallons: an enormous quantity of meal. Abraham then slaughters and prepares a "tender and good" calf (v. 7), which again would be an extraordinary amount of meat for three persons—more than thirty pounds of meat if the calf were a newborn. He serves the veal with "curds and milk" (v. 8). Abraham then waits on them while they eat in the tree's shade (v. 8).

Abraham and Sarah thus serve as a model of hospitality to strangers for generations to come. They combine the best qualities of both Mary and Martha in the lectionary reading from Luke 10:38–42, where one sister visits with Jesus while the other provides hospitality. Abraham and Sarah's actions moreover provide a sharp contrast to the horrid inhospitality shown by the Sodomites in Genesis 19, who seek to gang-rape visitors to their city. In the NT, Hebrews 13:2 picks up on Abraham and Sarah's generosity and instructs readers to follow in their footsteps: "Do not neglect to show hospitality to strangers, for by doing that some have entertained angels without knowing it." Parishioners might not think of throwing parties or hosting guests as virtues, but the Bible certainly does.

These divine visitors promise that "in due season" (that is, "at a living time"), the elderly couple will have a newborn son. They receive the encouraging word that their hope in God is not in vain. The day of promise rapidly approaches. Soon a baby will be snuggled in their arms.

The NT presents Abraham and Sarah as people of faith who trusted God's promises (Gal. 3:6–9; Heb. 11:8–11). Churchgoers join them when they wait on God to do what previously seemed impossible.

MATTHEW RICHARD SCHLIMM

Commentary 2: Connecting the Reading with the World

Amos 8:1–12. After seeing a disturbing vision (vv. 1–3), Amos proclaims a harrowing word that exposes the corrupt deeds of some Israelite community members and the consequences they are about to suffer on account of their transgressions (vv. 4–12). In this text, we encounter an angry God who will not tolerate injustice and who has no time for celebration and worship that are devoid of ethical praxis. God is angry because the poor and the needy are taken advantage of for economic gain (vv. 4, 6). The injustices are twofold: they are cheated out of money (v. 5), and they are made into bartered goods (v. 6). The text suggests that justice will be a corporate experience and not directed solely at the troublemakers. Looking at the text as a whole, and on a personal note, Amos shows us how power can be used abusively for self-serving purposes that deny others their legal rights and/or human dignity.

Amos's portrait of an angry God, who rails against those who fail at ethical praxis and yet engage in celebration and worship, has profound social and ethical implications for the American culture. Like Amos, who put the religious and political leaders of his day "on notice," student survivors of gun violence have put US government leaders, many of whom are practicing Christians, "on notice" by boldly stating that the prayers and thoughts of elected officials are empty and meaningless, since leaders are not taking the appropriate steps to make policy changes that would protect lives. In the ecclesial context, people who claim to be believers can no longer profess belief and practice their faith without embracing the ethical responsibility of ensuring protection for the most vulnerable among God's people.

Furthermore, heard in the social context of our world today, Amos's words call people everywhere to practice justice—to expose the injustices done to the poor and needy locally, nationally, and globally, and then take steps to eradicate such injustices. The practice of justice is an act and a virtue that hastens the reign of God. In verse 6 Amos accuses the powerful and affluent of his day of buying the poor for silver and the needy for a pair of sandals. Today, those most vulnerable globally are, once again, children. Hundreds of millions of children are denied their childhood because they live in abject poverty or are forced to live with conflict and violence. Many are bought and sold through human trafficking, while others work as child laborers who receive little or no pay. Just recently in Flint, Michigan, city officials who were concerned about higher water rates allowed contaminated water from the Flint River to flow through household pipes; this had catastrophic lead effects for the city's people, especially for children. We know that this situation in Flint is not the only location in the world where water is polluted, causing people to be at risk of sickness and death. The cry of the poor remains constant, and God's people have the responsibility to respond. The preacher can help us see that the prophetic gift is given to all people by virtue of having God's Spirit breathed within them at the time of creation.

Amos's message also has other social and ethical implications for today. Amos foreshadows a time when God will send a famine on the land. This famine will not be of bread, nor thirst for water. The famine will be of hearing the words of the Lord, of hearing words of truth that give hope and direction to life. Today, on the one hand, we do not have a famine of the word, because prophetic voices are speaking out. On the other hand, however, we do have a famine of the word, because many people seem not to be hearing its prophetic aspect. For instance, in her groundbreaking work *Silent Spring*, Rachel Carson exposed the pollution of the environment by the profligate use of toxic chemicals, especially DDT.[1] Even though DDT is now banned, pesticide companies continue to produce chemicals that are harmful to human and nonhuman life. The prophetic word continually goes forth today, but are people hearing it?

Finally, Amos's words continue to shape our personal identity. Amos calls each of us to expose injustice. When we do so, we become beacons of hope for those caught in the web of violence, pain, and suffering.

Genesis 18:1–10a. The story of Abraham and his three guests who are strangers is a lesson in hospitality. Abraham speaks to only one of the guests, and he is quite deferential in his exchange. He refers to himself as a "servant" and his guest as "my lord" (v. 3). Abraham has Sarah whip up a meal quickly, and the food is the finest Abraham could offer: choice flour for cakes, a good and tender calf, and some curds and milk. As host, Abraham did not eat the meal but stood and served his guests. This meal would have been a genuine bedouin meal, lavish and generous, and typical of desert hospitality. Little does Abraham know that he is hosting three divine guests. For his hospitality and generosity, Abraham receives a gift from one of his guests: he is told that his barren wife Sarah will bear a son. Many biblical texts describe the covenant between God and Israel as one of hospitality. Even before God gave Israel the land, God "spread a table for them in the wilderness" (Ps. 78:19).

From an ecclesial perspective, this story about Abraham and his three guests is a call for the people of God today to practice hospitality. This exhortation is found in several NT writings (see Heb. 13:2; 1 Pet. 4:9). The rationale for extending hospitality is multifaceted: first, the recognition that Jews and Christians alike share the same status of resident aliens and exiles (1 Pet. 1; 2:4–10), and second, in offering hospitality to another, one is offering it to Jesus (John 13:20). Throughout the centuries, the church has prized the reception of the stranger and outcast as an important characteristic of Christian life and ministry. Those churches and communities today that have become "sanctuary communities" continue the mission of Abraham, Jesus, and the early Christians. Hospitality to the stranger, the resident alien, is a hallmark of what it means to be "church," which is a community that acts justly, loves tenderly, and lives the gospel authentically.

Abraham's story has social and ethical implications for today, especially with the global concern of immigration. Abraham welcomed the "stranger." Abraham's hospitality that he extended to strangers calls us to view and respond to strangers—to undocumented immigrants—as guests rather than enemies. When we welcome the stranger—the undocumented immigrant—among us, we give witness to the eschatological banquet being realized in the here and now. At

1. Rachel Carson, *Silent Spring* (Boston: Houghton Mifflin, 1962).

this banquet, all have a place at the table. Furthermore, hospitality as a fundamental virtue includes all cultures, races, creeds, and orientations. Especially in today's world, Abraham's story calls us to hasten the reign of God by welcoming the stranger in our midst, especially as we struggle as a global community with the issue of refugees crossing our borders in search of peace and security.

On a personal level, Abraham's story invites us to consider whether or not we have a "hospitality of heart" that welcomes all. Who is welcomed in our lives? Who is welcomed at our tables? Whom do we serve?

CAROL J. DEMPSEY, OP

Psalm 52

[1]Why do you boast, O mighty one,
  of mischief done against the godly?
  All day long [2]you are plotting destruction.
Your tongue is like a sharp razor,
  you worker of treachery.
[3]You love evil more than good,
  and lying more than speaking the truth.
[4]You love all words that devour,
  O deceitful tongue.

[5]But God will break you down forever;
  he will snatch and tear you from your tent;
  he will uproot you from the land of the living.
[6]The righteous will see, and fear,
  and will laugh at the evildoer, saying,
[7]"See the one who would not take
  refuge in God,
but trusted in abundant riches,
  and sought refuge in wealth!"

[8]But I am like a green olive tree
  in the house of God.
I trust in the steadfast love of God
  forever and ever.
[9]I will thank you forever,
  because of what you have done.
In the presence of the faithful
  I will proclaim your name, for it is good.

Psalm 15

[1]O LORD, who may abide in your tent?
  Who may dwell on your holy hill?

[2]Those who walk blamelessly, and do what is right,
  and speak the truth from their heart;
[3]who do not slander with their tongue,
  and do no evil to their friends,
  nor take up a reproach against their neighbors;
[4]in whose eyes the wicked are despised,
  but who honor those who fear the LORD;
who stand by their oath even to their hurt;
[5]who do not lend money at interest,
  and do not take a bribe against the innocent.

Those who do these things shall never be moved.

Connecting the Psalm to Scripture and Worship

Psalm 52. Amos warns of a coming time of repentance for powerful oppressors: feasts into mourning, songs into lamentation, grief, and sackcloth. Yet the psalm sung in response to this reading is no contrite dirge. Instead of taking the perspective of the remorseful oppressor praying for forgiveness, the psalm responds in the voice of a blistering social critic inveighing against such an oppressor. Indeed, while it is noteworthy that this psalm hardly addresses God directly, it is even more unusual that it is hardly recognizable as a prayer. It is a derisive monologue attacking a deceitful person.

The character of the derided "mighty one" in the psalm is similar to the denounced oppressor in Amos. Both trust in wealth and practice deception. Amos describes businesspeople who "make the ephah small and the shekel great, and practice deceit with false balances" (Amos 8:5). The "mighty one" in the psalm is accused of deceit three times (Ps. 52:2–4). Both bring about ruin and destruction.

The psalm uses vivid imagery for the disruptive chain reaction emanating from the deceitfulness of the powerful: slicing, devouring, snatching, tearing, uprooting. In both Amos and the psalm, bodies and landscapes are portrayed as violently riven. However, these images set up the arresting contrast in the penultimate verse of the psalm: "But I am like a green olive tree in the house of God."

The world-disrupting consequences of inequality and injustice are stunning. Scientists tell us that we are likely entering the sixth mass extinction in earth's history, with the most recent one occurring 65 million years ago with the extinction of the dinosaurs—when Australia and Antarctica were joined, before Mount Everest existed. This moment is the first in all of earth's history, however, when a single species—*homo sapiens*—is pushing the others toward extinction. The world's landscape is being—in the words of today's psalm—sliced, devoured, and uprooted as a consequence of systems of wealth acquisition. Especially, given the second reading's hymn to Christ as the firstborn of creation, preachers might address questions of environmental injustice this week, perhaps drawing on the papal encyclical *Laudato Si: On Care for Our Common Home*, which links a critique of social injustice to a vision of God's renewal of creation, or Joseph Sittler's landmark 1961 address to the World Council of Churches, "Called to Unity," an urgent call for theological attention to environmental justice, using this week's Colossians text as an epigraph and touchstone.[1] In the ancient text we sing today, foolishness and evil look like a clear-cut and disrupted ecosystem while wisdom and faithfulness are imaged by a deeply rooted tree.

Sometimes questions of injustice require an unambiguous "Here I stand" moment. In response to a prediction that the world will be shaken by the consequences of social injustice, we sing a sassy, prophetic accusation against a "mighty one" and proclaim ourselves rooted in a contrasting value system: like a green olive tree, we are planted in the steadfast love of God forever. While Amos described an uprooted people in a famine of the word, "wandering from sea to sea . . . seeking the word of the Lord" but unable to find it, we might see an image of holy rootedness in the Gospel text this week: Mary, rooted down before Jesus, attending to the word that sets creation free from bondage.

Psalm 15. Psalm 15 is a call-and-response liturgical catechism that might have been sung in procession into the temple. It begins by calling out questions about who may enter into the presence of God in worship. The answers, comprising almost the entirety of the psalm, describe characteristics of truthfulness, commitment to doing justice, resistance to bribery, and fairness to all—characteristics ascribed to God elsewhere in Hebrew Scriptures. The cadence markedly shifts in the final line of the psalm. There the psalmist makes a declaration that reimagines these characteristics not only as credentials for entering the liturgical assembly but also as profound security for life in a dangerous world: "those who do these things shall never be

1. Joseph Sittler, "Called to Unity," *Ecumenical Review* 14 (1962): 175–87.

moved." Thus, the psalm begins by being set in motion liturgically—a procession moving into the presence of God in worship—and concludes with profound immovability: deep foundations and strong bulwarks that are security against the vicissitudes of life.

The psalm is sung in response to the narrative of Abraham and Sarah being visited by three mysterious strangers. One of the most well-known icons of the Christian tradition, Andrei Rublev's fifteenth-century work *The Trinity* or *The Hospitality of Abraham,* is based on the Genesis text. The icon portrays the three visitors as winged, gathered around a table with a single chalice in the center (the small calf's head in the chalice is a reference to Abraham's calf and an allusion to the sacrificial imagery of the Eucharist), with the visitors apparently blessing the cup as a presider would. The icon is a sort of Christian catechism on meeting face-to-face with the Divine.

The psalm is partly a mirror image of the Genesis text. The psalm asks how mortals may possibly be welcomed by God into the place of worship: *who may be admitted into God's hospitality?* The Genesis text wonders how God may be welcomed by humans into fellowship: *who may admit God into companionship at table?*

These texts in dialogue may invite the preacher to reflect on the paradox of meeting the Holy One in the strange or hungry one. On the one hand, there are cautions sung in the psalm: in order to approach God, one must be blameless. On the other hand, there is the promise in the story of Abraham and Sarah: God draws near to us in mercy, sharing a cup of blessing, offering promises for fruitfulness beyond our power.

The warning and welcome carry a tension embodied in an anecdote shared by Kathleen Norris. An older monk, long schooled in the monastic practice of offering sacred hospitality to strangers who visit the monastery ("receive all guests as Christ," the Rule of St. Benedict admonishes), teaches a younger monk about the weariness that can accompany such welcome: "I have finally learned to accept people as they are. Whatever they are in the world, a prostitute, a prime minister, it is all the same to me. But sometimes I see a stranger coming up the road and I say, 'Oh, Jesus Christ, is it you again?'"[2]

In response to the story of Abraham and Sarah's showing hospitality to strangers—"entertaining angels unawares," as the author of Hebrews puts it (Heb. 13:2)—we sing of the justice and righteousness required of those who would meet God face-to-face. Yet the song prepares us to be surprised by the gospel, where with Mary we are invited to rest, without works, before the face of God. Mary's rest before Jesus may bring preachers back to remember the final line of the psalm, perhaps with a sense of the countercultural resistance that such resting and immovability can involve. The African American spiritual "I Shall Not Be Moved" became in the civil rights era "We Shall Not Be Moved."

BENJAMIN M. STEWART

2. Kathleen Norris, *Dakota: A Spiritual Geography* (Boston: Mariner Books, 2001), 191.

Colossians 1:15–28

[15]He is the image of the invisible God, the firstborn of all creation; [16]for in him all things in heaven and on earth were created, things visible and invisible, whether thrones or dominions or rulers or powers—all things have been created through him and for him. [17]He himself is before all things, and in him all things hold together. [18]He is the head of the body, the church; he is the beginning, the firstborn from the dead, so that he might come to have first place in everything. [19]For in him all the fullness of God was pleased to dwell, [20]and through him God was pleased to reconcile to himself all things, whether on earth or in heaven, by making peace through the blood of his cross.

[21]And you who were once estranged and hostile in mind, doing evil deeds, [22]he has now reconciled in his fleshly body through death, so as to present you holy and blameless and irreproachable before him—[23]provided that you continue securely established and steadfast in the faith, without shifting from the hope promised by the gospel that you heard, which has been proclaimed to every creature under heaven. I, Paul, became a servant of this gospel.

[24]I am now rejoicing in my sufferings for your sake, and in my flesh I am completing what is lacking in Christ's afflictions for the sake of his body, that is, the church. [25]I became its servant according to God's commission that was given to me for you, to make the word of God fully known, [26]the mystery that has been hidden throughout the ages and generations but has now been revealed to his saints. [27]To them God chose to make known how great among the Gentiles are the riches of the glory of this mystery, which is Christ in you, the hope of glory. [28]It is he whom we proclaim, warning everyone and teaching everyone in all wisdom, so that we may present everyone mature in Christ.

Commentary 1: Connecting the Reading with Scripture

The language of the letter changes at the end of the first chapter, moving from a large, cosmic understanding of the God in nature to a clear, practical description of this cosmic entity resting specifically within the life of the believer. This is clearly stated in the sentence toward the end of the section: "Christ in you, the hope of glory" (Col. 1:27).

The Letter to the Colossians, written by Paul or a disciple of Paul, uses language perhaps belonging to Hebrew wisdom tradition, or concepts as seen in the Qumran literature, or maybe even pre-Christian proto-gnostic thought (1:15–20). In this letter, Christ and faith are presented in terms of a cosmic, spiritual event compared to the descriptions given in Romans, for example, which use transactional and even forensic modes of description. The Christ event here is not described as "justification" or "atonement" but rather as "reconciliation" (v. 20).

The first section of this passage, 1:15–20, is known as a Christ hymn. Borrowed words form the core of this section; these verses are most likely a hymn known by the author and readers of the letter. To the first-century reader, this section would have been understood as an inserted hymn or poem. While the words used here, such as "image," "thrones," "dominions," "powers," are not seen in Paul's traditional word usage, this hymn most likely was familiar to the readers, since it was known by various communities in Asia Minor. Where did these words originate? The historical context is almost impossible to determine. However, some scholars have suggested that the words belonged to a pre-Christian, proto-gnostic tradition, where the redeemer is described as the one who breaks into the cosmos to bring redemption. Alternatively, perhaps this Christ hymn originated from the Jewish tradition and is best understood within the context of the Jewish Day of Atonement, the time when the Creator is brought close to all things created, where creation and reconciliation are one. Or maybe the context for the Christ hymn is within the cultural symbols of Hellenistic Judaism and its wisdom tradition.

This section concludes with the theme of reconciliation, which is also the work of the Creator. Presumption of disunity, awareness of chaos, perhaps a rupture in the created order, all create the need for reconciliation, leading creation back to its divine order. Thus the primary focus of the Christ event is that Christ has come to bring peace, to reconcile the created order with the Creator, thereby "making peace" (v. 17).

It is a heavy word for the preacher—*reconciliation.* Perhaps word pictures may help. One strong visual for this word was found in the chapel of the College of Preachers on St. Albans Mound on the grounds of the Washington (DC) National Cathedral. A tall wooden cross stood in the center of the chapel. The face of the Jesus hanging from the cross was not the face of pain and contortion, with blood streaming from the hands and feet, as traditional pictures often reveal. Rather, this cross had Jesus reaching out his arms to wrap around a human figure whose head and shoulders appeared to be pressing deeply into the chest of Jesus—like one big bear hug. This picture of the crucifixion was not atonement, but reconciliation. Jesus was drawing the human form into himself. They were both reconciling to each other. Disunity, chaos, ruptures are now made whole, calmed, and healed.

Colossians moves from big-picture thinking to intimate application. Note the use of the personal pronoun "you" in verse 21. The large literary canvas of cosmic proportion narrows quickly into a personal word, back to the personal connection of author and reader in this intimate literary form, the letter. The section weaves the images from the Christ hymn into the epistolary conversation with exceeding skill. The readers, who have once been alienated (perhaps Gentiles), are now in alignment with this one in whom God dwells (vv. 22–23). The chief aim of the letter may be encased in verse 23: "provided that you continue in the faith." The continuity of the faith may be the particular aim of the correspondence. This letter becomes crucial to the community of believers who are trying to create a community of faith several decades after the death and resurrection of Christ. The community of believers in Colossae is reminded not only of the lofty cosmic vision of Hellenistic Judaism but also of their personal place in this grand cosmic story. The preacher may wish to make these same connections. The contemporary congregation is likewise held in the continuance of this grand cosmic story.

The impersonal tone of this chapter, which at times sounds like a deep, abstract philosophical treatise, more at home in street schools of Athens or Rome, weaves back into a very personal and intimate thought. The personal aim of the author is to make this magnificent story known with the grand words and vast chronological sweep: "I became a minister according to the divine office which was given to me for you, to make the word of God fully known, the mystery . . ." (vv. 25–26 RSV). If the reader has been perplexed by the preceding words of grand cosmic schemes, redeemer myths, and Hellenistic thought, the time has come to bring the message home to the reader narrowed down into a clear, succinct point: the vastness of this cosmic faith is lodged in the individual believer.

"Christ [is] in you, the hope of glory" (v. 27). I was working in China a few years ago, visiting local Chinese high schools, helping students and teacher improve their skills in preparation for university studies in the United States. I spoke the language but was cautioned by personal friends to be careful and not enter into any discussion about the Christian faith, either in Chinese or English. I honored that request. After spending an entire day with a group of young teachers, one of the teachers followed me to the bus and lingered by the door as if to tell me something very important. In Chinese she quietly spoke, "I want you to know that I see the *shen-gwang* in you." I politely thanked her, bowed, and began to leave. Then the Chinese word *shen-gwang* became clear to me. I originally thought that it was just a word that I did not know in that particular dialect or region. As the bus was leaving the parking lot, the meaning became clear. *Shen* means "God," and *gwang* means "light." Although I had never heard those two words placed together before, this new meaning hit me. She has just told me in a quiet, hushed voice that she has seen the God-light in me.

The author of Colossians gives us this simple fact: Christ is *in* you, and that is the hope of glory. Preachers can help listeners know again the cosmic, vast glory of God, the ways that this glory is for the purpose of reconciliation, and how this vast glory with its reconciling character dwells in us, in each of us. The preacher can point to places and situations that need such a word and sign of reconciliation—places of ethical quandary and societal ills. What would it mean to have persons of faith bearing the God-light in ruptured, broken, divided situations? What can it mean to us to see ourselves as ones who are to and do bear God's light in the world?

LINDA MCKINNISH BRIDGES

Commentary 2: Connecting the Reading with the World

Religion in general and Christianity in particular are sometimes critiqued as an exercise in providing answers to questions that nobody is asking. Unfortunately, that critique is occasionally valid. Here, in a letter penned to a tiny Christian community two millennia ago, is a proposal both relevant and bold. It is a response to the one underlying philosophical and theological question people have struggled with since the beginning of time, the one question men and women have asked in every age: Is creation ordered, good, kind, and trustworthy? Human beings in the midst of suffering, caught up in gross injustice, or victimized by cruel forces out of their control have asked: Is creation arbitrary, impersonal, not trustworthy? Are we all, ultimately, on our own, abandoned in a world that is indifferent?

It is a theological quandary as old as the Hebrew exiles in Babylon, who surely concluded that God had forgotten them and lamented, "How can we sing the LORD's song in a foreign land?" (Ps. 137:4); the victims of the Holocaust, herded into the gas chambers; and the uncounted millions of homeless, starving, dying refugees in our own time. There is in human history enough innocent suffering and cruel injustice to make the question inevitable: Is there any sense to this? Is there any hope?

When the Letter to the Colossians was written, early forms of Gnosticism, a quasi-Christian philosophy and movement, believed that the world and creation itself are essentially evil, that God is either ignorant or unconcerned with the affairs of the world and human beings in it, and that the purpose of religion is to deliver people from the world and worldly concerns. This gnostic heresy has lurked around the edges of Christianity and the church ever since, in the lingering suspicion that the world is a nasty, dirty place and that Christians should have as little to do with it as possible, that the world is full of temptation and that faithful Christian discipleship requires denial of the world and of our basic bodily humanity with all its needs and passions and joys.

Thus the ancient writer proposes a radical, sweeping alternative: Jesus Christ, in whom the fullness of God dwells, is Lord of the creation, Lord of the entire cosmos. Jesus, this writer proposes, in what may have been adapted as a hymn in the liturgy of the early church, is not a savior who delivers us from our personal, petty sins to an otherworldly heaven, but the one in whom and for whom the cosmos, our world and everything in it, was created.

Several decades ago British scholar J. B. Phillips wrote a popular bestseller, *Your God Is Too Small.* Phillips challenged Christians to open theological windows and doors, expand the horizons of belief to the far reaches of eternity, to free God from the box most of us keep God in—safe, secure, tame, certainly not challenging or demanding, and not very interesting.[1] God, this Colossians poem/hymn asserts, is creator and Lord of all that is. So the fascinating scientific inquiry into the very nature of reality, scientific research itself, is never a threat to religion, as some fear and teach. Instead, the scientist in the laboratory pursuing and observing the tiniest microscopic elements of life, or through a telescope watching stars form and the universe mysteriously expanding into infinity, is a vital theological resource. The more we learn about the world, the expansive and expanding universe, the profound life force in all animate things, the more we glimpse the reality of God.

Jesus Christ "is the image of the invisible God, the firstborn of all creation . . . in him all things in heaven and on earth were created. . . . He himself is before all things, and in him all things hold together" (Col. 1:15, 16, 17). There is an idea to stir the soul and mind and challenge religious complacency. Creation is in and for Jesus Christ, and so creation is not indifferent at all, but as kind and compassionate as he is. Injustice and cruelty and violence are not inevitable. Instead, as Martin Luther King Jr. memorably reminded us, the long arc of history bends toward justice. Here is good news for suffering, oppressed people. The Lord of creation is not indifferent but as passionately in love with the world and all the people in it as Jesus was. We are safe, ultimately secure in the love of Jesus Christ, in whom all the fullness of God dwells and in whom and for whom the world was created.

This bold hymn pulls us back from exclusivism and the traditional position that our way is the only way. The image of a cosmic Christ invites us to look beyond the boundaries of our own theological tradition and to ponder the proposal that God is attentive to the entirety of creation and humankind. The dynamic generated by a cosmic Christ invites us to respect for and dialogue with other religions and cultures and their traditions and institutional expressions. If creation is in and for Jesus Christ and in him everything holds together, we are compelled to ponder the expansive notion that he is already the Lord and lover of people other than us.

The promise here is that the world and everything in it are infinitely precious to God, and that God will never abandon the world. Neither should we. The moral imperative of a cosmic Christ is that our vocation includes loving care for creation. Suddenly protection of the environment transcends political partisanship and becomes part of what followers of Jesus Christ ought to be about in the world. Carbon emissions into our polluted atmosphere become a moral issue, a religious concern. Sensible emission regulation is now a religious and ethical imperative. Lifting these responsible regulations and withdrawing from international treaties that hold every nation accountable for the health of the planet is sin on a mammoth scale. Observing mountaintops being removed and streams polluted by mine runoff in the name of corporate profit is not only grossly socially irresponsible, but a mammoth sin of both commission and omission. Knowing about the slow death of the Great Barrier Reef and looking the other way is a political sin on a global scale. The world is precious and beloved by the Creator and the Christ in whom the fullness of the Creator dwells.

There is a stunning shift here as well. In a time and environment of diminishing vision and hope for the church, there is an idea here that feels like an electric shock. This cosmic Christ who "was before all things and in whom all things hold together" is also "head of the body, the church." The church! While we engage in ecclesiastical hand-wringing and lament over declines in numbers, prominence, and influence, here is a jolt of hope and purpose:

1. J. B. Phillips, *Your God Is Too Small* (London: Macmillan, 1967).

regardless of where we are and what is happening to us at the moment, God has in mind that the church has a role to play in the redemption of creation.

Clearly major changes are happening all around us. Past certainties are disappearing and the future can be frightening. This ancient hymn is reminder that the church is God's idea—not ours—and it belongs to God and to Jesus Christ and not to us. This should be, as it always has been and always will be, both a judgment and a profound encouragement as we faithfully seek to be obedient in the days ahead. We still have important work to do, the work of redeeming creation.

JOHN M. BUCHANAN

Luke 10:38–42

[38]Now as they went on their way, he entered a certain village, where a woman named Martha welcomed him into her home. [39]She had a sister named Mary, who sat at the Lord's feet and listened to what he was saying. [40]But Martha was distracted by her many tasks; so she came to him and asked, "Lord, do you not care that my sister has left me to do all the work by myself? Tell her then to help me." [41]But the Lord answered her, "Martha, Martha, you are worried and distracted by many things; [42]there is need of only one thing. Mary has chosen the better part, which will not be taken away from her."

Commentary 1: Connecting the Reading to Scripture

As Jesus and his disciples make their way toward Jerusalem (9:51–18:14) and the fate that awaits him there, Jesus is preparing the disciples for mission. In the short term, this mission is aimed at the towns they visit along the way, but Jesus is also preparing them for the mission that will ensue after his death and resurrection, after the Spirit is poured out upon them at Pentecost (Acts 2). Hospitality is a recurrent theme in this material. Jesus also repeatedly stresses the necessity of both attending to his proclamation, which announces the coming of God's empire in both judgment and redemption, and "doing," that is, embodying in their practices the values and convictions that arise from the recognition of God's kingdom. This brief story of Martha and Mary juxtaposes these aspects of discipleship—hospitality, listening and doing, proclaiming the coming of God's empire and the actions that embody this proclamation—but in a surprising way that has long vexed interpreters. Jesus has just turned back a challenge from a lawyer who tests him by asking him what he must "do" to inherit eternal life. Now, however, in the home of two sisters from whom he accepts hospitality, Jesus seems to diminish the importance of "doing," embodied in Martha, in favor of her sister Mary's attention to his word. Does he really mean to pit these two elements of discipleship—and these two sisters—against each other?

Interpretation of this brief story is usually determined by the stereotypes we heap on these two women, which all too often force us to choose one over the other. As a consequence, interpretation has long traded in binary oppositions. Martha welcomes and seeks to serve Jesus through her hospitality, but she is also portrayed here as overwhelmed, frustrated, and even self-righteous, stuck in traditional women's work in the kitchen. Mary, for her part, takes on the role of the more liberated woman, eschewing her domestic responsibilities in order to attend to her own spiritual nurture and theological education. Neither woman comes off well: Jesus chides Martha for her anxiety, even though she seems to embody the ideal of service that Jesus elsewhere clearly affirms (10:40, 41). Mary, despite choosing "the better part" (10:42b), never speaks a word. She has broken free of a traditional female role but remains passive. If we come to this story looking for an unambiguous role model in one of these women, with the other serving as foil, we will be disappointed. While the story seems to invite the reader to take sides between these sisters and the values and roles they represent, it also resists a definitive resolution of these tensions. In the end, it may compel us to abandon our penchant for either/or, exclusive alternatives. How often is our society today riven by binary thinking? Americans are taught to approach virtually every social conflict in either/or, black/white terms. The preacher can help us see this chance to resist it.

A Body Knit Together

We are a body knit together as such by a common religious profession, by unity of discipline, and by the bond of a common hope. We meet together as an assembly and congregation, that, offering up prayer to God as with united force, we may wrestle with Him in our supplications. . . . Though we have our treasure-chest, it is not made up of purchase-money, as of a religion that has its price. On the monthly day, if he likes, each puts in a small donation; but only if it be his pleasure, and only if he be able: for there is no compulsion; all is voluntary. These gifts are, as it were, piety's deposit fund. For they are not taken thence and spent on feasts, and drinking-bouts, and eating-houses, but to support and bury poor people, to supply the wants of boys and girls destitute of means and parents, and of old persons confined now to the house; such, too, as have suffered shipwreck; and if there happen to be any in the mines, or banished to the islands, or shut up in the prisons, for nothing but their fidelity to the cause of God's Church, they become the nurslings of their confession. But it is mainly the deeds of a love so noble that lead many to put a brand upon us. *See*, they say, *how they love one another*, for themselves are animated by mutual hatred; how they are ready even to die for one another, for they themselves will sooner put to death. And they are wroth with us, too, because we call each other brethren; for no other reason, as I think, than because among themselves names of consanguinity are assumed in mere pretense of affection. But we are your brethren as well, by the law of our common mother nature, though you are hardly men, because brothers so unkind. At the same time, how much more fittingly they are called and counted brothers who have been led to the knowledge of God as their common Father, who have drunk in one spirit of holiness, who from the same womb of a common ignorance have agonized into the same light of truth! But on this very account, perhaps, we are regarded as having less claim to be held true brothers, that no tragedy makes a noise about our brotherhood, or that the family possessions, which generally destroy brotherhood among you, create fraternal bonds among us. One in mind and soul, we do not hesitate to share our earthly goods with one another. . . . The Greeks call it *agapè*, i.e., affection. Whatever it costs, our outlay in the name of piety is gain, since with the good things of the feast we benefit the needy; not as it is with you, do parasites aspire to the glory of satisfying their licentious propensities, selling themselves for a belly-feast to all disgraceful treatment,—but as it is with God himself, a peculiar respect is shown to the lowly. . . . Give the congregation of the Christians its due, and hold it unlawful, if it is like assemblies of the illicit sort: by all means let it be condemned, if any complaint can be validly laid against it, such as lies against secret factions. But who has ever suffered harm from our assemblies? We are in our congregations just what we are when separated from each other; we are as a community what we are individuals; we injure nobody, we trouble nobody. When the upright, when the virtuous meet together, when the pious, when the pure assemble in congregation, you ought not to call that a faction, but a *curia*—[i.e., the court of God.]

Tertullian (ca. 160–ca. 225), Apology 39, trans. S. Thelwall, in *Ante-Nicene Fathers*, vol. 3, *Latin Christianity: Its Founder, Tertullian* (New York: Christian Literature, 1885), 47.

While the two sisters seem to represent opposite ends of the discipleship spectrum, between hearing and doing, we should not see in them the embodiment of mutually exclusive patterns of behavior. When Martha welcomes Jesus to her home (v. 38), she fulfills the ideal of the welcoming household that Jesus has affirmed earlier in the chapter (vv. 5–9). At the same time, Luke introduces Mary into the story as listening at Jesus' feet, as the members of receptive households would do. The word Luke uses to describe Mary's hearing often also implies obedient response. By themselves Martha and Mary are each incomplete disciples, but together they embody the listening and service that Jesus has hoped for when he sends his disciples before him in mission. Together, Martha and Mary represent the alternative to those houses that do not welcome Jesus or his disciples (vv. 10–11, 12–15). In the house where Martha and Mary are in partnership, each bringing her "portion" to the table, God's kingdom draws near in both peace (v. 6) and power (vv. 9, 18–20). Just as Martha and Mary need each other, so the church needs diverse, interdependent members. Not everyone in the church has the same gifts or calling. Discipleship in nurtured in community, not within the individual alone. As Paul also suggests in his discussions of unity amid diversity (e.g., Rom. 12:3–8; 1 Cor. 12:12–31; Eph. 4:1–13), we lean on each other in order to be whole.

The problem, of course, is that Martha and Mary are not holding their parts together in partnership. Somehow, the cord that makes these two women "sisters" in the household has become frayed. Luke describes Martha as "distracted by her many tasks" (v. 40). The verb Luke uses here and again in Jesus' response to Martha in 10:41 (*merimnaō*, "to worry or be concerned") carries a sense of having one's attention so monopolized by something, even a necessary thing, that it threatens either to choke or to tear one apart (see 8:14; 12:22–31). The verb is based on the same root (*meris*) that Jesus uses in 10:42, when he tells Martha that "Mary has chosen the better part." Martha's problem is that her "much serving" or "many tasks" are now preventing her from seeing the bigger picture to which her service contributes and in which it has meaning. She sees only her parts, and that exclusive focus now threatens to blind her and to rupture the household. Something similar might also said for Mary, whose sitting and listening cannot go on forever. Martha and Mary's partnership, their sisterhood, is coming apart. They each have parts necessary for the whole, but they are not holding them in concert. Even good and necessary work can become a distraction, just as careful listening can pull us away from necessary "doing."

Most of the interaction in the story is between Jesus and Martha. Martha's words to Jesus, "Lord, do you not care that my sister has left me to do all the work [again *diakonein*, "to serve"] by myself," suggests her sense of isolation and abandonment, as well as resentment. She wants Jesus to intervene: "Tell her to help me." In modern terms, Martha is "triangling" Jesus. Rather than work it out with Mary herself, Martha wants Jesus to fix the problem for her, on her terms. Luke's Jesus persistently resists such triangulation (e.g., 12:13–15). Here he employs three tactics. First, he names the demon: "many things" are worrying (again *merimnaō*, "pulling apart, fragmenting") and distracting Martha. The latter verb in this description (*thorybazein*) carries a sense of confusion, uproar, and bewilderment. Martha's single-minded focus on her service is the cause of tumult rather than concord. Second, he says that "there is need of one (thing)," without indicating what that one thing is. Literally he says, "one is needed/necessary," which may affirm the need for oneness itself, or unity in partnership. Finally, he affirms the legitimacy of Mary's "part"—a "good part," perhaps even the "better part." His saying does not invalidate Martha's part, nor will he let Martha's claims invalidate Mary's part. What are the factors that worry us, distract us, or monopolize our attention? These can become forces that rupture communities. Jesus supplies an effective pastoral model for conflict: name the demons, reassert the ideal of unity, affirm what each party brings.

The early church succeeded in large part because the gospel found adherents among women, like Martha and Mary, who not only worked together in households, but among households that were otherwise usually in competition with one another. The church was successful in mission in such households precisely because their women leaders were so good at both hearing and doing, as well as offering hospitality.

STANLEY P. SAUNDERS

Commentary 2: Connecting the Reading with the World

In the slow-moving months of Ordinary Time, the Revised Common Lectionary offers to the preacher's imagination these five verses from Luke. Luke's portrayal of Martha and Mary may be familiar—too familiar, even—for listeners who have heard countless sermons about the importance of sitting and listening to Jesus, the "better part" of the sisters' choices (Luke 10:42). Yet preachers can question the easy division between sitting at Jesus' feet and serving at the table. Moreover, in this and the other readings of Ordinary Time, preachers can recapture the urgency with which Jesus tries to pull us—Martha, Mary, and contemporary listeners—into the sweep of God's reign.

In this season of Year C, Luke's narrative steadily progresses from 9:51 (Proper 8) when Jesus "set his face to go to Jerusalem," where listeners understand he will be met with desertion and death. That journey takes ten chapters, wherein Luke uses Jesus' parables and teachings to shape disciples preparing for those last days in the Holy City. Jesus' stay with the sisters belongs to that journey.

Listeners encounter Martha first, and preachers should foreground her agency. Martha welcomes Jesus into *her* home (v. 38), exercising ancient codes of hospitality (see 10:5–7, in which Jesus assumes that disciples will stay and eat). Luke's indication that the home belongs to Martha affords us a glimpse into the congregations of his readers, meeting in homes such as Priscilla and Aquila's (Acts 18:2–3; 1 Cor. 16:19). What ministries of hospitality exist in the congregation that the preacher can connect with Martha?

Luke also records that Martha was preoccupied with "her many tasks" or, more accurately, "much table service" (v. 39). "Tasks" and "table service" translate the Greek *diakonia*, an integral word in the church's ministry. In the NT, it often means "ministry," including eucharistic service and proclaiming the word (Acts 6:1–4). So, preachers might wonder, why not here? Listeners already intuitively identify Martha's hospitality and subsequent preparation for the meal as a ministry in its own right; so preachers are warranted to explore the many forms of service the congregation exercises. Since *diakonia* is the root of the office of deacon, this invites reflection on the later role of deacons or diaconal ministers in the congregation or the communion of churches to which it belongs. In a passage that emphasizes the values of Jesus' teachings, it is helpful to remind listeners of the many forms of service that make room for and live out of those teachings.

The trouble begins in verse 40, where Martha is "distracted" in regard to her ministry. Who among us has not been similarly distracted, worrying about details of the service project, the agenda for the meeting, the novelty of the sermon? Who among us has not on occasion opted for passive aggression on par with her complaint: "Lord, do you not care that my sister has left me to do all the work [i.e., to serve, to minister] by myself?" The phrase is reminiscent of a T-shirt printed by the online media platform for Latino/a millennials *We Are Mitú*. Suggested as a gift for mothers, the shirt's curling print reads, "Nadie me ayuda en esta casa." Many responded with laughter, recalling the times their mothers and grandmothers have said the same thing: "No one helps me in this house!" Part of the joke is laughing at our tendency to minimize the outcry while we put off folding the laundry or tidying up. Preachers can invite their people to ponder this scenario. What is happening underneath Martha's pointed question? Where have we diminished the role of various ministries to the chagrin of fellow disciples? When have we used those words ourselves to mask a deeper question: Do you truly see me?

Jesus' words to Martha, "You are worried and distracted by many things" (v. 41), give us pause for more reflection. Can we hear these words spoken with love and care instead of the patronizing way they have been repeated to Christians (and many times, women) over the centuries? When we are engaged in ministry, what pulls us away from the central focus? What worries distract us from what we know is true? Jesus tells Martha that "there is need of only one thing," presumably the central concern beneath all ministry: trust in God. Later on in Luke, Jesus will elaborate on this trust, telling his disciples not to worry (12:22–32). Since this later episode is missing from the Revised Common Lectionary (see Matt. 6:24–34 in Year A, Epiphany 8), preachers may find it a useful conversation partner for today's reading.

Another conversation partner with verse 41 is the prayer Jesus models in the next chapter (11:2–4). Jesus places the petition for daily bread (v. 3) in the dynamic relationship between trust in God's providence (growing grain) and our faithful response (baking bread). Can the preacher imagine Jesus sharing this teaching with Martha, calling her to consider the deeper meaning of her *diakonia* beyond making sure there is food on the table? As Jesus' words concerning Mary suggest, service without the centering of the Word is incomplete.

Listeners hear that Mary "sat at the Lord's feet and listened to what [Jesus] was saying" (v. 39), but since she does not speak, they are left to imagine her perspective. Takes on Mary vary. Some see her as a disciple, a student of Jesus' teachings. Others claim that she is bold to choose study over household service. Still others note her passivity and wonder whether Luke uses the sisters to downplay the role of women deacons in the early church (like Martha) in favor of submissive supporters (like Mary). Regardless of these reconstructions, preachers are left to wrestle with Jesus' words that Mary has "chosen the better part" (v. 42).

Preachers scanning for semantics will notice that Jesus has identified Mary's choice as the "better part" but not the only part. Sitting at the Lord's feet should be not mistaken for the one necessary thing (v. 42); it is only one part of trusting God. Preachers can identify how Christian worship illustrates the relationship of this part to its sister movement, pointing out the many juxtapositions (to use Gordon Lathrop's phrase) that open the congregation to God's surprising presence.[1] The preaching of the Word is central in many Christian traditions, yet its fullness is eclipsed without the table service of the Lord's Supper. The assembly's prayers necessarily include praise for God's faithfulness *and* prayers beseeching God to intercede in the troubles of the world. In the early church and in some traditions still, the offering of gifts to God's glory involved the complementary practice of taking those gifts of money and food to neighbors in need. Christians need to sit and listen, but that is not the only component of discipleship.

Finally, preachers should recall the thrust of Ordinary Time in Year C: to join Jesus on his journey to Jerusalem, to engage his teachings in preparations for their own trials and attempts to live out the gospel. In this context, Mary models the posture we must have toward Jesus, who has urgent teachings to impart about how to live in the kingdom of God. Jesus' urgency counters the slow pace of long summer days (or winter nights in the Southern Hemisphere): the kingdom of God has come near *now*, whether or not children are in school, families are on vacation, or the state legislature is meeting. This is the time for attentive listening so that, when the pace of the year begins to pick up, each of us may practice our *diakonia* with trust in God's presence among us.

HIERALD E. OSORTO

1. Gordon W. Lathrop, *Holy Things: A Liturgical Theology* (Minneapolis: Fortress, 1993), 33–53.

Proper 12 (Sunday between July 24 and July 30 Inclusive)

Hosea 1:2–10 and Genesis 18:20–32
Psalm 85 and Psalm 138

Colossians 2:6–15 (16–19)
Luke 11:1–13

Hosea 1:2–10

[2]When the LORD first spoke through Hosea, the LORD said to Hosea, "Go, take for yourself a wife of whoredom and have children of whoredom, for the land commits great whoredom by forsaking the LORD." [3]So he went and took Gomer daughter of Diblaim, and she conceived and bore him a son.

[4]And the LORD said to him, "Name him Jezreel; for in a little while I will punish the house of Jehu for the blood of Jezreel, and I will put an end to the kingdom of the house of Israel. [5]On that day I will break the bow of Israel in the valley of Jezreel."

[6]She conceived again and bore a daughter. Then the LORD said to him, "Name her Lo-ruhamah, for I will no longer have pity on the house of Israel or forgive them. [7]But I will have pity on the house of Judah, and I will save them by the LORD their God; I will not save them by bow, or by sword, or by war, or by horses, or by horsemen."

[8]When she had weaned Lo-ruhamah, she conceived and bore a son. [9]Then the LORD said, "Name him Lo-ammi, for you are not my people and I am not your God."

[10]Yet the number of the people of Israel shall be like the sand of the sea, which can be neither measured nor numbered; and in the place where it was said to them, "You are not my people," it shall be said to them, "Children of the living God."

Genesis 18:20–32

[20]Then the LORD said, "How great is the outcry against Sodom and Gomorrah and how very grave their sin! [21]I must go down and see whether they have done altogether according to the outcry that has come to me; and if not, I will know."

[22]So the men turned from there, and went toward Sodom, while Abraham remained standing before the LORD. [23]Then Abraham came near and said, "Will you indeed sweep away the righteous with the wicked? [24]Suppose there are fifty righteous within the city; will you then sweep away the place and not forgive it for the fifty righteous who are in it? [25]Far be it from you to do such a thing, to slay the righteous with the wicked, so that the righteous fare as the wicked! Far be that from you! Shall not the Judge of all the earth do what is just?" [26]And the LORD said, "If I find at Sodom fifty righteous in the city, I will forgive the whole place for their sake." [27]Abraham answered, "Let me take it upon myself to speak to the Lord, I who am but dust and ashes. [28]Suppose five of the fifty righteous are lacking? Will you destroy the whole city for lack of five?" And he said, "I will not destroy it if I find forty-five there." [29]Again he spoke to him, "Suppose forty are found there." He answered, "For the sake of forty I will not do it." [30]Then he

said, "Oh do not let the Lord be angry if I speak. Suppose thirty are found there." He answered, "I will not do it, if I find thirty there." [31]He said, "Let me take it upon myself to speak to the Lord. Suppose twenty are found there." He answered, "For the sake of twenty I will not destroy it." [32]Then he said, "Oh do not let the Lord be angry if I speak just once more. Suppose ten are found there." He answered, "For the sake of ten I will not destroy it."

Commentary 1: Connecting the Reading with Scripture

The text from Hosea continues the semicontinuous reading of the prophets. The passage from Genesis is paired with the Gospel reading. Although today's lections from Hosea and Genesis are not related to one another in the lectionary, they point to a common theme: God punishes those who violate the divine purposes.

This theme raises a significant theological issue. Some Christians today assume that God punishes individuals and communities for violating covenant either now or in the future. For these folk, justice demands nothing less. However, this viewpoint faces questions. How do we reconcile divine love and compassion with such violent behavior on God's part? If God has the power to end injustice in a single stroke, and to invoke a world of complete blessing, why does God not do this? Other contemporary Christians believe that God's nature is unconditional love, so that God could not engage in violent punishment. Those who hold this perspective can still claim that sin leads to destruction. While God might not incinerate people, disobedience brings about social collapse. God does not have to destroy us. We destroy ourselves.

Hosea 1:2–10. Hosea spoke after the separation of the one nation into two: Judah (south) and Israel (north). Hosea prophesied in the north, about 750–722 BCE. He spoke both condemnation and hope during a time of social and religious fractiousness. Two issues were paramount. (1) Idolatry: With the blessing of priests, the community sought fertility by worshiping idols while continuing to worship God (e.g., Hos. 2:7–13). (2) Economic exploitation: The ruling class sought peace (and the reinforcing of their own power) by abandoning an alliance with Aram and cooperating with Assyria (e.g., Hos. 5:13–14; 6:8–10; 7:11–12; 12:1). The alignment with Assyria required crushing taxes, with the ruling class exploited the lower classes to pay for them. From Hosea's perspective, these things amounted to a failure of covenant.

In Hosea 1:2–10, Hosea engages in a prophetic symbolic act to dramatize his message about Israel. Hosea uses Gomer's misbehavior and the names of the children as literary figures to represent Israel's violation of covenant.

Hosea named the first child Jezreel, thus referring to the place (Jezreel) where Jehu enacted a bloody coup (2 Kgs. 9–10). God will punish Israel for this bloodshed. The second child is Lo-ruhamah, which in Hebrew means "no mercy." Because of Israel's violation of the divine purposes, God will not immediately have mercy on the community. The third child is Lo-ammi, which means "no people." God would not treat the community as God's own family until punishment was completed. The summary meaning of these symbolic names is that Israel would bear the consequences of its disobedience. The sermon could point to circumstances in our world in which these children still live (figuratively speaking)—that is, where people engage in pointless bloodshed, show no mercy, and violate community.

Verse 10 reminds the reader that condemnation is not God's final word. Beyond judgment, God will restore Israel. Indeed, in just a few chapters the prophet offers one of the most elevated statements in the Bible on God's irrevocable love (Hos. 11:1–11).

Social conditions today resemble those in Hosea's time. Many communities are fractious, abandoning covenantal qualities of life for idolatrous, self-serving, exploitative, and violent behavior. Indeed, the church sometimes acts like a contemporary priest of Baal, blessing these behaviors.

The sermon might help the congregation imagine symbolic prophetic actions it could take to represent God's judgment on culture and church. For example, the congregation might gather in front of a police station with members lying down on the sidewalk, like bodies at a shooting, to protest the brutal treatment of people of color. A preacher might even ask, "What prophetic gestures might I enact *in the sermon* to represent such divine judgment?" For instance, a pastor might lie down in the chancel, again representing a body at a shooting, when preaching prophetically on the conviction that black lives matter.

A sermon might focus on marriage. While the Bible does not directly dwell much on marriage as a covenantal relationship, the church infers that notion from Hosea and others. The preacher might use the appearance of marriage in the text to launch a theological reflection on the civil and religious institutions of marriage in relationship to the fact that so many people today live together without those bonds.

Preachers whose theologies lead them to support same-sex marriages could point out that while the Bible does not directly authorize such unions, many believe that the heart of marriage is covenantal commitment. Such commitment is possible in any relationship.

Genesis 18:20–32. This passage reinforces an important aspect of God's promise to Sarah and Abraham. God chose them as a channel through whom to bless all peoples. "Blessing" includes the full range of things necessary for a secure life: community, land and animals, peace, and mutual support. The sermon could help Christian congregations clarify the notion that God chose Israel not for privilege but for the mission of pointing the way to blessing. For example, a sermon could help the church identify ways it could join in solidarity with people in town who are food insecure.

According to Genesis 18:16–19, the purpose of the story that begins in Genesis 18:16 and continues through Genesis 19:29 is to teach the reader the importance of living in righteousness and justice, that is, in covenantal community (Gen. 18:19). God threatened to destroy Sodom and Gomorrah because of "very grave" sin. The children of Abraham and Sarah can avoid destruction by living in covenant.

The preacher should note that God does not *want* to destroy Sodom and Gomorrah. God will spare the cities if Abraham can find as few as ten righteous people. As an agent of blessing, Abraham sought to prevent the destruction of the cities.

Abraham's actions can guide congregations today in two ways. First, they remind us that the church's mission is to provide a blessing to others in an unrighteous and unjust time, when people are ensnared in a destructive culture. Second, in contrast to religious circles today that encourage people to be resigned to their perception of God's will, this passage authorizes wrestling openly with God. Abraham's debate with God failed; the ancestor could not find ten righteous persons. Nevertheless, the narrative approves of Abraham's challenge. The preacher can help the congregation recognize the validity of wrestling with God.

Genesis 19:1–29 brings this story to climax. Interpreters disagree on whether the sin of Sodom and Gomorrah is homosexual rape or inhospitality or a combination. Given the prominence of this text in the current exploration of sexuality, it is a crime for the lectionary to omit it. The narrative movement from Genesis 18:20–33 to Genesis 19:1–29 gives the preacher a natural opening to consider Sodom and Gomorrah in relationship to contemporary questions of sexual identity and expression. For example, the preacher who concludes that the sin of the ancient cities was inhospitality could raise the question of whether the church today is sufficiently hospitable to persons of diverse sexual orientations.

Beyond the question of the nature of the sin of Sodom and Gomorrah, the narrator of Genesis underlines two things: (1) On the one hand, communities that violate covenant in the manner of the ancient cities can expect similar condemnation. (2) On the other hand, the promises of God will not be destroyed by such destruction. The promise of the possibility of blessing transcends particular acts of judgment, even the most destructive ones.

RONALD J. ALLEN

Commentary 2: Connecting the Reading with the World

The prophet accuses the northern kingdom of Israel of scandalous infidelity to God. Ethical wrongdoing within the community of the people of God constitutes some of this infidelity. Hosea makes reference to these behaviors (e.g., Hos. 4:2). The greatest offense to God, and the central problem of the prophet's book, is Israel's spiritual cheating on God (e.g., 4:1, 17; 8:11; 13:1–2). The gravity of this problem leads Hosea to call Israel a whore, which shocks the listener and grabs our attention.

We can frame this problem of spiritual adultery in at least two different ways. We can look back on the historical infidelity of Israel and then point toward the promise of verse 10 already revealed. When Hosea prophesies about punishing Jehu, abandoning pity, and disowning the people, we understand those words to refer to our past. Israel long ago went into exile under ancient Babylon and Persia. So the infidelity of the prophet's generation has received justice. God's faithfulness appeared in Christ precisely to redeem a future remnant of that disowned people. So the global church celebrates its relationship as "children of the living God." In this historic arc we see God's redemptive scattering and sowing (see the promise of v. 11). We hold up Hosea's words as an affirmation of God's design both to punish infidelity and, in the same stroke, to guarantee new life. Like a fallen tree producing vibrant shoots, or an evicted adolescent turning over a new leaf, God's people are transformed.

The preacher can help the church see contemporary resonance with Hosea's difficult words: individual infidelity, a cultural turn toward consumerism rather than compassion, and the tendency of faith communities to pursue self-interest instead of God's calling. Even so, from the shattered fragments of human sin, God's love empowers new possibility. Infidelity can give way to truth-telling and reconciliation between friends, spouses, and family members. Wealth accrued by avarice can be turned into generosity toward those in need. Congregations focused on their own traditions can wake up to the needs of the changing communities around them.

The church announces this redemptive reality. When we gather for worship, we recognize the power of sin and its effects, but also celebrate God's greater power to bring us into goodness by claiming us as children of the living God. The prophet's words invite liturgical confession and assurances of pardon. They remind us of the necessity of repentance and acceptance of a life transformed by the Spirit. This text might challenge the preacher to celebrate a story in which the congregation or even an individual was turned from a destructive behavior and experienced revitalization. In prayer and song the congregation might be invited to lay bare its own sin and seek the promised forgiveness.

Alternately, we might understand Hosea's words as a warning against a type of sin ever present in human life. Every generation finds new and innovative ways to cheat on God by giving its love, work, and devotion to unworthy things. This infidelity appears in pervasive societal wrongdoing. We might think of individualism, which twists us away from dedicating time to Christian community and Christlike love of neighbor. Materialism might be today's primary sin: investing one's time and money in possessions deprives life of sacrificial generosity. Society-wide lack of commitment—frivolous divorce, absentee parents, exploitative employers and employees—makes the long devotion required by Christ impossible. Systemic racism denies the vision of siblinghood imagined by the NT. Political dogmatism denies the boundary-crossing grace we find in Jesus Christ. In all these ways we show communal infidelity to God.

Idols abound! However, there is good news. With the warning, God offers a guarantee of salvation. Hosea promises that God will take those called "Not my people" and instead name them "children of the living God" (v. 10). In place of rejection God offers belonging; in place of punishment, blessing. The church finds the fulfillment of this promise in Jesus Christ. The Spirit of Christ delivers the church out of sin and retrains it for good. In the church, people learn to love each other. There they learn generosity through the offering plate, the food pantry, and the mission trip. They learn commitment from

The Revelatory Moment

The Christian gospel is God's message of liberation in an unredeemed and tortured world. As such, it is a transcendent reality that lifts our spirits to a world far removed from the suffering of this one. It is an eschatological vision, an experience of transfiguration, such as Jesus experienced at his Baptism (Mk. 1:9–11) or on Mt. Tabor (Mk. 9:2–8), just before he set out on the road to Jerusalem, the road that led to Calvary. Paul had such a vision—"a light from heaven"—as he traveled the road to Damascus (Acts 9:3). Malcolm X, while in prison, had a vision of God, and so too did Martin King hear God speaking to him in his kitchen at a moment of crisis during the Montgomery bus boycott. For all four, the revelatory moment in their lives helped to prepare them to face their deaths, sustained by the conviction that this was not the end but the beginning of a new life of meaning. To paraphrase Eliade, once contact with the transcendent is found, a new existence in the world becomes possible.

And yet the Christian gospel is more than a transcendent reality, more than "going to heaven when I die, to shout salvation as I fly." It is also an immanent reality—a powerful liberating presence among the poor right *now* in their midst, "Building them up where they are torn down and propping them up on every learning side." The gospel is found wherever poor people struggle for justice, fighting for their right to life, liberty, and the pursuit of happiness.

James H. Cone (1936–2018), *The Cross and the Lynching Tree* (Maryknoll, NY: Orbis Books, 2011), 155.

friends who stay with them no matter what. By singing, praying, and studying with people of different skin color, language, and political party, they learn grace and siblinghood. The church is the living testimony that in Christ we are carried into our destiny of glory.

The other OT text appointed for this day illumines one facet of our relationship with this God who redeems. As in the Hosea text, here we are confronted by a problem of great sin—that of Sodom and Gomorrah. In this case, however, the specifics of the sin and its eventual consequence are not the focus of the story. (One finds those details in the following chapter.) Instead the spotlight falls on Abraham as he ferrets out the limits of God's grace. He finds that God's justice always leaves room for mercy. No matter how great the sin of these cities, the righteous will be preserved. For the sake of the righteous, God is patient, desiring salvation rather than punishment (see Matt. 9:9–13 and parallels, and 2 Pet. 3:9).

Our world still has Sodom-and-Gomorrah-sized sinning. Following in Abraham's footsteps, the church hopes for righteousness. Though atrocities abound, the church prays for compassion rather than retribution. Our worship reflects no strident self-righteousness, but a desire for the smallest seeds of righteousness to be preserved and to grow. In our prayers and conversations, Christians recognize that even on the other side of tall political walls there dwell people of good conscience and that to condemn them categorically does not reflect God's loving justice. On a cosmic scale, the church does not insulate itself while the rest of the world goes to hell in a handbasket. In the face of white nationalist trolls, the church will ask: How can they be redeemed? When presented with polarizing and unsatisfactory political leadership, the church resists disengagement and asks: How can we bring light to this darkness? The church is called, in its prayer life, Sunday liturgy, and mission work, to ask God to reveal good in the midst of evil and preserve it. It does so assuming, in the Spirit of Christ, that the entire world is beloved and worth saving. It refuses to accept condemnation as the final word, seeking instead the merciful heart of God.

Abraham learns this lesson about God's grace by asking bold, almost impetuous questions. Because Christians are descendants of Abraham (see Gal. 3:6–7), Abraham's experience informs our own approach to God. The church is hereby encouraged to ask difficult questions about anything, including the proper response to evil. Prayer will present to God both sorrow at human sin and an expectation that God will respond with mercy. Worship songs will open up the liberating truth that God responds to our persistent cries for righteousness to be revealed. Worship and study of this text will invite participants to bring even the most brash, radical questions before God. Jesus' parable of the Persistent Widow (Luke 18:1–8) handily connects this text to the NT, strengthening the message that until righteousness is revealed, persistence is a spiritual virtue.

The Lord declared that Abraham was to "keep the way of the LORD by doing righteousness and justice" (Gen. 18:19). Worship and preaching that empower persistent pursuit of God's mercy and grace, even in the face of widespread evil, will equip the church to keep the same blessed way.

EMRYS TYLER

Psalm 85

[1]LORD, you were favorable to your land;
you restored the fortunes of Jacob.
[2]You forgave the iniquity of your people;
you pardoned all their sin.
[3]You withdrew all your wrath;
you turned from your hot anger.

[4]Restore us again, O God of our salvation,
and put away your indignation toward us.
[5]Will you be angry with us forever?
Will you prolong your anger to all generations?
[6]Will you not revive us again,
so that your people may rejoice in you?
[7]Show us your steadfast love, O LORD,
and grant us your salvation.

[8]Let me hear what God the LORD will speak,
for he will speak peace to his people,
to his faithful, to those who turn to him in their hearts.
[9]Surely his salvation is at hand for those who fear him,
that his glory may dwell in our land.

[10]Steadfast love and faithfulness will meet;
righteousness and peace will kiss each other.
[11]Faithfulness will spring up from the ground,
and righteousness will look down from the sky.
[12]The LORD will give what is good,
and our land will yield its increase.
[13]Righteousness will go before him,
and will make a path for his steps.

Psalm 138

[1]I give you thanks, O LORD, with my whole heart;
before the gods I sing your praise;
[2]I bow down toward your holy temple
and give thanks to your name for your steadfast love and your faithfulness;
for you have exalted your name and your word
above everything.
[3]On the day I called, you answered me,
you increased my strength of soul.

[4]All the kings of the earth shall praise you, O LORD,
for they have heard the words of your mouth.
[5]They shall sing of the ways of the LORD,
for great is the glory of the LORD.
[6]For though the LORD is high, he regards the lowly;
but the haughty he perceives from far away.

[7]Though I walk in the midst of trouble,
you preserve me against the wrath of my enemies;
you stretch out your hand,
and your right hand delivers me.
[8]The LORD will fulfill his purpose for me;
your steadfast love, O LORD, endures forever.
Do not forsake the work of your hands.

Connecting the Psalm to the Scripture and Worship

Psalm 85. In response to a reading filled with images of estrangement from God, we sing of restoration to the land and to God. Even the sometimes-opposed concepts of justice and peace kiss each other. The song prepares us to pray for the mutual forgiveness of sins, for God's dominion to come in its fullness, and for heaven and earth to be reconciled—themes of the Lord's Prayer in this week's Gospel text.

The strange and difficult images of the people's faithlessness and God's judgment in the Hosea text (with only fragmentary promises of mercy) are answered in the psalm by a cascade of sung reminders of God's past faithfulness to the people. God is remembered for having been gracious to the land, restored good fortune, forgiven iniquity, blotted out sins, withdrawn fury, and turned from wrath. Only then does the psalm shift directions to plead for God's restoration and renewal. The final verses of the psalm look to the future fulfillment of God's promises, using vivid and beloved language of reunion, fruitfulness, and completion. The psalm looks forward to the day when the entire cosmos will be enfolded by blessing: "faithfulness will spring up from the ground" below, while "righteousness will look down from the sky."

Walter Brueggemann describes the psalm as "an act of immense hope that is completely assured of God's goodness, which will be established in the earth," refusing "to let present circumstances erode confidence about God's future."[1] From images in Hosea of a marriage disrupted by faithlessness and children named for estrangement, the psalm eventually moves the assembly to sing in anticipation of the kiss between justice and peace and the marriage of heaven and earth. Hosea's images of cheapened relationship give way to the psalm's images of mutuality and enduring partnership. Such a song beautifully imagines what it means to pray with this week's Gospel that God's will be done "on earth as it is in heaven."

A number of phrases in the psalm have been prayed on significant liturgical occasions for centuries. In a form of the intercessions used in morning prayer, verse 7 of the psalm is sung as a daily opening petition for all creatures beginning the day: "show us your mercy, Lord, and grant us your salvation." Some traditions have prayed verse 4 as one of the concluding prayers of the great Ash Wednesday confession of sins, the most extensive confession of the liturgical year: "Restore us, O God, and let your anger

1. Walter Brueggemann and William H. Bellinger Jr., *Psalms*, New Cambridge Bible Commentary (New York: Cambridge University Press, 2014), 369.

depart from us." The final verses of the psalm imagining God's promised future of a reconciled cosmos have long associations with the season of Advent and are currently appointed in the Revised Common Lectionary also for the Second Sunday of Advent (Year B).

The consequences of human infidelity in our relationship with God's creation are becoming increasingly evident. The promises of restoration that we sing in the psalm include multiple images of reconciliation between humans and the land. We remember that God has been gracious to the land in the past (v. 1). We pray that God's glory will dwell in our land (v. 9). We proclaim that earth will be a place of generativity and faithfulness (v. 11), that the living world will be held in a fruitful union of heaven and earth (v. 11), that "our land will yield its increase" (v. 12), and that our earth will be blessed with pathways for God (v. 13). In our experience of broken relationship with the wider creation today—tragically fractured like the marriage in Hosea—we sing of the promise of a land restored by power beyond human faithlessness.

Psalm 138. After hearing a reading in which Abraham is comically persistent in praying for God's mercy, we sing a psalm giving universal praise to God for showing divine mercy, especially to the lowly. Singing this psalm prepares us to intercede persistently for forgiveness in the Lord's Prayer, perhaps just as comically as Abraham—like someone pestering a neighbor at midnight for bread.

Though Abraham's doggedness steals the show in the reading, his repeated appeals for mercy actually function as a savvy literary technique to underscore the mercy of God, rather than the persistence of Abraham. In response to the text, we sing praise for God's initiative. The psalm is bookended by references to God's steadfast love (*hesed*). Between these bookends the psalm intermingles expressions of praise for such steadfast love with remembered examples: God answering calls of need, caring for the lowly, and providing safety from enemies and trouble. This steadfast love, the psalmist declares, will one day be praised across the earth, even by powerful rulers. The prayer of the day explicitly compares the human and divine approaches to mercy in its initial address to God: "you are always more ready to hear than we are to pray, and you gladly give more than we either desire or deserve."

Both the first reading and the psalm invoke an earthy anthropology as part of the plea for God's mercy. Abraham orients himself before God, saying, "I who am but dust and ashes." The psalmist invokes God's creation of humanity from the dust of the earth, pleading, "Do not abandon the work of your hands." With the image of humans as dust formed by God's hands, it is as if God is being offered a reminder of the long arc of divine care for this fragile and beloved creature: God's creation of the earth itself, God's molding of the human creature from the dust and breathing into it the breath of life, God's nurturance of human life among the other flourishing creatures of earth, and then, as Ecclesiastes has it, "the dust returns to the earth as it was, and the breath returns to God who gave it" (Eccl. 12:7). The pleas from Abraham and the psalmist imply that God will be moved to compassion by remembering our earth-to-earth nature. This logic for divine compassion is beautifully articulated elsewhere in the psalms: "for God knows how we were made; God remembers that we are dust" (Ps. 103:14).

The psalm and first reading together allow for homiletical reflection on prayer and worship. The psalm's actions of bowing toward the temple, calling out to God, singing praise, and giving thanks are archetypal actions of Israel's worship. And the theme of persistence in prayer in the first reading—besides being vividly memorable—is echoed repeatedly in the Gospel text. I remember reading (in a long-forgotten source) the story of a Protestant minister praying the weekly intercessions in a predictable liturgical cadence, before pausing and crying out, "Lord, we pray for these same things every single week! Do something!" This minister's outburst embodies a comically poignant dimension of persistent intercessory prayer. The final verse of the psalm acknowledges that intercessory prayer includes confidence in God's enduring goodness along with awareness of profound creaturely fragility: "your steadfast love endures forever; do not abandon the works of your hands."

Preachers might point out how these texts show that praying for mercy offers a challenge to mythologies of independence and self-sufficiency. To pray for mercy in this week's texts involves orienting oneself within a mutual economy of interdependence: naming that we are dust and ashes, that we are made by God's hand and continue to depend on God's care, begging for forgiveness, even as we forgive others.

BENJAMIN M. STEWART

Colossians 2:6–15 (16–19)

[6]As you therefore have received Christ Jesus the Lord, continue to live your lives in him, [7]rooted and built up in him and established in the faith, just as you were taught, abounding in thanksgiving.

[8]See to it that no one takes you captive through philosophy and empty deceit, according to human tradition, according to the elemental spirits of the universe, and not according to Christ. [9]For in him the whole fullness of deity dwells bodily, [10]and you have come to fullness in him, who is the head of every ruler and authority. [11]In him also you were circumcised with a spiritual circumcision, by putting off the body of the flesh in the circumcision of Christ; [12]when you were buried with him in baptism, you were also raised with him through faith in the power of God, who raised him from the dead. [13]And when you were dead in trespasses and the uncircumcision of your flesh, God made you alive together with him, when he forgave us all our trespasses, [14]erasing the record that stood against us with its legal demands. He set this aside, nailing it to the cross. [15]He disarmed the rulers and authorities and made a public example of them, triumphing over them in it.

[16]Therefore do not let anyone condemn you in matters of food and drink or of observing festivals, new moons, or sabbaths. [17]These are only a shadow of what is to come, but the substance belongs to Christ. [18]Do not let anyone disqualify you, insisting on self-abasement and worship of angels, dwelling on visions, puffed up without cause by a human way of thinking, [19]and not holding fast to the head, from whom the whole body, nourished and held together by its ligaments and sinews, grows with a growth that is from God.

Commentary 1: Connecting the Reading with Scripture

What has been lurking below the surface from the opening of this letter suddenly breaks through in our passage: a conflict over teaching. It was at work behind the author's use of "the word of truth" or "the gospel" (Col. 1:5) or the phrase "the knowledge of God's will in all spiritual wisdom and understanding" (1:9) or notion of a life "worthy of the Lord" (1:10), or most especially in the Christ hymn of 1:15–20. What has been lurking behind everything so far written in this letter is the so-called opponents of Colossae who were stirring up questions about the message Epaphras, Paul's coworker and founder of the church at Colossae, had preached (1:7–8; 4:12–13). Those other teachers at Colossae now come into view.

All theology, not least Paul's,[1] is connected to a specific context, and the so-called opponents form some of the context for this letter. They are branded, labeled, and other-ed by Paul. They teach a "philosophy and empty deceit" and "human tradition" and "elemental spirits of the universe"; most especially, their teaching is "not according to Christ" (2:8). In the clarifying paragraph of 2:16–19 it becomes even more obvious that they are Christians who are also Jewish ("food and drink or of observing festivals, new moons, or sabbaths," 2:16); they are mystical ("worship of angels, dwelling on visions"); and they are divisive ("puffed up . . . not holding fast to the head," 2:18–19). Their teachings prompt this letter and Paul's christocentric solution.

1. Debate will continue, but the balance of the evidence, once one appreciates multiple contributors to Paul's letters, favors Pauline authorship.

When our passage opens with the phrase "As you therefore have received Christ Jesus the Lord," it gathers up all that has been taught theologically to this point. Paul's introductory paragraphs from 1:1 through 2:5 have set the stage theologically and christologically for what is said in 2:6. That is, Paul is able to evaluate the theology of the other teachers at Colossae on the basis of one singular event that turns history inside out: the revelation of God's Messiah, Jesus, who is creator and redeemer (1:15–20), the cosmic (1:20) and personal (1:21–23) reconciler. Most importantly in Colossians, God's "fullness" was "pleased to dwell" in him (1:19), and he is the one in whom "the whole fullness of deity dwells bodily" (2:9). What might this mean? The preacher can help us know that who God is can be seen in Jesus and all one needs to flourish in this life derives from Jesus (2:10). What Jesus has done is this: he has reconciled the cosmos to God (1:13–14, 15–20). Paul's entire mission is rooted in Jesus' accomplishment of reconciliation (1:24–29).

The ethical intent of Paul's vision then comes to literary expression in the phrase "As you have therefore received Christ Jesus the Lord." What might this ethical vision look like? To summarize Paul's dense words, the preacher could put it this way: Because God is revealed most fully in Christ himself, and because Christ is the cosmic reconciler, (1) Christians do not need to search out secretive mystical experiences in order to flourish (2:16–19); (2) Christians are to learn the daily art of dying and rising with Christ by putting off sinful living and putting on loving behaviors (3:1–17); and (3) Christians are challenged to reorder their own households under Christ as Lord (3:18–4:1). If God is revealed most completely in Christ, and Christ is the reconciler, then agents of Christ in this world become agents of gracious reconciliations.

Notice *how* Christ has reconciled the world: through the cross (2:13–15). How? God has both liberated us from our sins and debts and conquered evil and systemic forces. At the cross, sin's accusations are silenced and forgiveness dispensed. Behind the code and its accusations are cosmic themes about "rulers and authorities," language that evokes spiritual cosmic battles that become institutionalized in systemic injustices, institutions, and injustices. Here we see the triumph of God in the grace of God revealed in Christ, creator, redeemer, and cosmic reconciler (v. 15). The cross paradoxically appears as the defeat of Christ and goodness but as the victory of God over sin and systemic injustice. At the cross God turns death into life so that the last word is life.

The cross must be understood as the act of God's gracious love toward the entire cosmos. What Paul calls reconciliation, the prophet Hosea calls marriage (Hos. 1:2–10). In one of the Bible's most potent, if also at times disturbing, images, Hosea describes the unfailing, seducing, intimate, and erotic love of God for Israel by sketching Israel as an unfaithful wife or whore and YHWH as the relentless lover. The sinfulness of Israel is painted in horrific tones: Jezreel, an equivalent to Vietnam, Iraq, Syria; and names like Lo-ruhamah and Lo-ammi, that is, "no mercy" and "no people." God makes those who have experienced defeat, no mercy, and exile into God's loved, favored people by a gracious wooing and reconciliation. This theme of the relentless grace of God to reconcile with the people of God runs from Genesis to Revelation, but few passages can match the language of Psalm 85's "you restored the fortunes of Israel" and "You forgave the iniquity of your people" (Ps. 85:1–2), as well God's speaking "peace to [God's] people" (v. 8) because "surely [God's] salvation is at hand" (v. 9). The God of Paul in Colossians is the God of the psalmist; this God eradicates evil and establishes justice through gracious forgiveness. Hence, "righteousness [as God's establishment of justice] and peace will kiss each other" (v. 10), and they do precisely that at the cross of Colossians 2:15 because of the Christ apocalypse (Col. 1:15–20). The preacher can make clear that, at the cross, God both deals with sin and systemic evil and swoops us up into grace, love, and the ministries of reconciliation.

Reconciliation, like forgiveness, is easier to preach than it is to live in embodied ways with those in our community. The God of Hosea and the God of Paul is the God of Jesus, a God of love. This God summons us to pray what we call the "Lord's Prayer" (Luke 11:2–4) and does so because the character of God, unlike sleeping neighbors, will not only awaken to provide the bread for reconciliation and friendship, but even more: our Father God summons us not only to knock on the door but awaits us with the door wide open. This same God who reconciles transcends the gifts of ordinary, good parents, who are not stingy but delighted to provide open doors, provide fish and eggs and all "good gifts" (11:13). Noticeably, the good gifts here are summed up in the greatest gift of all, the good "Holy Spirit" (11:13), who is the distributor of God's reconciling grace.

If in Christ God has revealed the mission of God for cosmic reconciliation, we cannot be surprised that Paul's first imperative in this short letter is "continue to live your lives in him" (Col. 2:6). Paul's letters do not just say or teach; they both *do* and summon the readers to *do*. What are they to do? While the expression of 2:6 sums it up, the "do" of Colossians is spelled out in avoiding the traps of halakhic mysticism (2:16–19), living out one's baptism into the death and resurrection of Christ in the context of the Christian church (3:1–17), and reordering one's household under the lordship of Christ—creator, redeemer, and reconciler (3:18–4:1).

SCOT MCKNIGHT

Commentary 2: Connecting the Reading with the World

Human relationships are often marked by competition, ambition, and acquisitive pursuits for status and respect. This manifests in different segments of society. Capitalist economies, of course, are particularly predicated on competition. Some people use social media as a means to become more famous and influential. People who have the luxury of deciding which school their children attend are often motivated by the desire to see their children get ahead of others. Even pastors are not free from the temptations of ambition and competition and the lure of using ministry as a means for self-advancement.

Paul's Letter to the Colossians indicates competition was alive and well in his time, as some were pursuing God in ways that increased competition among the followers. Apparently, some claimed that they had moved to a higher level religiously, beyond their simple confession of Jesus as Lord and Messiah. Those who had attained this new status engaged elite spiritual practices, such as strict observance of a religious calendar and abstention from certain foods and drinks (2:16–19). Through these practices, this group at Colossae believed they would gain a mystical heavenly encounter in which they would join in worship with the heavenly angels. Paul sees this as both a distraction from their commitment to Christ *and* as resulting in members who are "judging" and "disqualifying" other Christians who did not experience such spiritual ecstasy.

Paul attempts to convince the Colossians of a simple point: The church's confession of Jesus as Messiah and Lord is the ongoing basis for its life, behavior, and identity. In verse 6 Paul appears to have blended together the two earliest creedal confessions of the church—"Jesus is Lord" and "Jesus is Messiah"—in order to remind the church in summary form of their primary confession and allegiance to Jesus as king. This is why Paul's central claim in the entire epistle is what we see in verse 6: "Therefore, as you have received Jesus as Messiah and Lord, so walk in him" (translations by author).

Paul writes to the church to tell them that there is an intrinsic relationship between their initial confession of Jesus as Lord and Messiah *and* their discipleship. We do not confess Jesus as Lord and Messiah and then go looking for some new way to behave or please God. Ethics, behavior, decision-making—all of this is an unpacking of the confession "Jesus is Lord and Messiah." This is why Paul describes "walking in him" with the metaphors of "being rooted and built up *in him*," "being conformed in the faith just as you were taught," and "abounding in thanksgiving" (Col. 2:7).

One of the great but subtle temptations for followers of Jesus is to suppose that Christian maturity consists in adding extra practices, rituals, boundary markers, or beliefs to our Christianity. Then we are often tempted to think that *real* Christianity or those who are really mature are those who do these extra practices. For example, good Christians always pray and read their Bible one hour in the morning. Real Christians are Republicans or are Democrats. Real Christians are Calvinists, or Wesleyans, or Anglicans. Good Christian parents have quiet children who are sent to private Christian schools. Now, in certain settings, some of this *may* be true. The danger is that these second-order beliefs, opinions, and practices are treated as *the definition of what it means to be a follower of Jesus*. The preacher could help a local congregation identify the ways that this occurs today, at a congregational level and at a personal level. How do we confuse primary and second-order beliefs, opinions, and practices?

Paul's response to the Colossians testifies to an inherent temptation in religion to make gradations and distinctions between who is "superreligious" and everyone else. My father is a retired army colonel, and I can remember as a little boy looking at all of those pins, medals, and stripes on his uniform that advertised his rank. That was their function; one quick look at his uniform and you knew whether you were his subordinate or his superior. Paul's point, however, is that Christians are clothed with the person of Christ. That is it. No superior or inferior ranks. The church can certainly grow deeper in knowledge and understanding of who Christ is and what confession of him as Lord means, but there is nothing we add to our faith to give us a superior standpoint over others. The preacher can help us know that our fundamental identity is not found, then, in our gender, age, vocation, or status. It is not to be found in our religiosity, education, good deeds, and zeal for God *or* in our lack of these things. Paul's teaching bears witness to a strong egalitarian foundation for the people of God. Why this is the case for *every Christian* is Paul's focus in 2:9–15.

First, Paul says that "all of God's fullness dwells in Christ in bodily form." This is the obvious reason why our *human* traditions are not on the same level as Christ. "All of God's fullness" does not dwell in our human traditions, wisdom, and worldviews. Second, those who confess Jesus as Messiah and Lord are filled up with God's fullness by virtue of their union with Christ. The preacher can help us discern ways that God's fullness critiques the ways our sights are set too low and we accept human traditions, insights, and views for God's ways. The gospel does critique culture.

In 2:11–15 Paul describes our salvation as consisting in being united together with Christ—this one who is filled with God's fullness. Notice how Paul describes us as joined together with Christ by repeating the prepositional phrases "in him" and "with him." "You were also circumcised *in him*" (v. 11); "having been buried *with him*" (v. 12); "you were raised *with him*" (v. 12b); "He made you alive *with him*" (v. 13). Paul is describing our lives in the closest possible manner *with Christ's life* and the critical events of Christ's human existence: the circumcision of the Messiah (v. 11), his burial (v. 12a), resurrection (vv. 12b, 13b), and victorious enthronement into heaven (v. 15). The preacher can help all of us know again the fullness of life in Christ, which takes up all our social dis-ease and insecurities.

Paul's letter helps the preacher proclaim our identity in Christ. Christ is our life. Christ's identity is our identity. Christ animates our existence. Our identity is that we are in Christ, belong to Christ, are with Christ. Christ is God's beloved Son, and so we are God's beloved sons and daughters. His death to sin is our death to sin. His resurrection is our resurrection. His life is our life. His victory over the evil powers is our victory. If these realities are true, if we all share in the divine fullness of Christ's life and death, then we have no basis for ambitious competition with one another, for God can give no greater gift to his people than sharing in God's own life. As ministers of the gospel, it is our task and gift to creatively and prayerfully look for ways in which we can remind our people of their glorious identity in Christ. This will almost certainly involve evaluating whether there are extra practices, rituals, or pop wisdom that we and our churches are invested in that are not in conformity with Christ and may have the unintended consequence of creating competition and status distinctions.

JOSHUA W. JIPP

Proper 12 (Sunday between July 24 and July 30 Inclusive)

Luke 11:1–13

[1]He was praying in a certain place, and after he had finished, one of his disciples said to him, "Lord, teach us to pray, as John taught his disciples." [2]He said to them, "When you pray, say:

Father, hallowed be your name.
Your kingdom come.
[3]Give us each day our daily bread.
[4]And forgive us our sins,
for we ourselves forgive everyone indebted to us.
And do not bring us to the time of trial."

[5]And he said to them, "Suppose one of you has a friend, and you go to him at midnight and say to him, 'Friend, lend me three loaves of bread; [6]for a friend of mine has arrived, and I have nothing to set before him.' [7]And he answers from within, 'Do not bother me; the door has already been locked, and my children are with me in bed; I cannot get up and give you anything.' [8]I tell you, even though he will not get up and give him anything because he is his friend, at least because of his persistence he will get up and give him whatever he needs.

[9]"So I say to you, Ask, and it will be given you; search, and you will find; knock, and the door will be opened for you. [10]For everyone who asks receives, and everyone who searches finds, and for everyone who knocks, the door will be opened. [11]Is there anyone among you who, if your child asks for a fish, will give a snake instead of a fish? [12]Or if the child asks for an egg, will give a scorpion? [13]If you then, who are evil, know how to give good gifts to your children, how much more will the heavenly Father give the Holy Spirit to those who ask him!"

Commentary 1: Connecting the Reading with Scripture

Luke focuses on prayer more frequently than the other Gospels. Luke begins with prayer (1:13) and ends with prayer (24:53). Jesus receives the Spirit while praying (3:21–22). He prays regularly (5:16) and before crucial events: the call of the disciples (6:12–13), his fateful decision to go to Jerusalem (9:18), the transfiguration (9:28), and the Mount of Olives (22:40–42). Jesus dies praying (23:34, 46), and the risen Lord prays with his disciples (24:30). Here Jesus instructs believers on how to pray (the Lord's Prayer, vv. 1–4) and assures us that God hears and answers our prayers (vv. 5–13).

In Luke, Jesus is a person of prayer, and a sermon could explore how the disciples' request, "Lord, teach us to pray," arises not out of an abstract interest but because they actually saw Jesus praying (11:1). In the previous chapter Luke develops the two great commandments: to love God (Mary's devotion, 10:38–42) and to love one's neighbor (the Good Samaritan, 10:25–37). Here we see another possible sermon trajectory. The prayer Jesus teaches them also moves in two directions: our relationship to God and our willingness to forgive others.

Luke's version of the Lord's Prayer is somewhat different from Matthew's more familiar, more polished form (Matt. 6:9–13). Luke's prayer is briefer and lacks the opening address ("Our . . . who art in heaven"). In Luke, the prayer begins simply "Father" ("Abba"), which highlights the deep relational quality of this prayer.

Claims that this use of "Abba" is without parallel in ancient Jewish prayers[1] are exaggerated. God is addressed as "Father" in Psalm 89:26; 3 Maccabees 6:8; and 4Q372 1:16. Nevertheless, Jesus' use of Abba, expressing the relationship that makes prayer possible, was so striking that it was carried on in the tradition of the early church (Mark 14:36; Rom. 8:15; Gal. 4:6). Preachers may want to emphasize that, before this prayer turns to *our* petitions, it focuses outward, toward God: "hallowed be your name . . . your kingdom come." One's name evokes the whole person (see Ps. 138:2), and the holiness of God's name is rooted in the Decalogue (Exod. 20:7; Deut. 5:11). Therefore, "make your name holy" is tantamount to the added Matthean petition, "Your will be done on earth as it is in heaven" (cf. Ezek. 36:22–23).

The three "our" petitions are for daily bread, forgiveness, and merciful deliverance from (NRSV "the time of") trial. Scholars debate whether the bread petition refers to bread for today, for tomorrow, or for the eschatological banquet (cf. Prov. 30:8). The petition "forgive us our sins" reminds us that prayer for forgiveness requires that we forgive (Sir. 28:2). Forgiveness must flow both from God and toward others, or it cannot flow at all. (The psalm for this day, Psalm 85, is a prayer for forgiveness, and the epistle text declares that God "forgave us all our trespasses, erasing the record that stood against us" [Col. 2:13–14].) The petition for deliverance from trial is climactic, acknowledging that we depend on God not only for sustenance and mercy but also for protection from what threatens our lives and our relationship to God (see Ps. 138:7).

Preachers may want to explore how Jesus' prayer is a part of Scripture's larger portrait of prayer. Abraham's servant prayed for success and for his master, Abraham (Gen. 24:10–15). The classic early prayer is Hannah's (not Eli, the priest's!—1 Sam. 1:9–18). Hannah "poured out her soul before the Lord" (1 Sam. 1:15; cf. Luke 18:9–14), and her prayer was heard (cf. b. Ber. 31). In Matthew, Jesus admonishes the disciples to pray in private, not for show, and "do not heap up empty phrases as the Gentiles do" (Matt. 6:7). Other prayers of Jesus are found in John 11:41–42 and 17:1–26, and the "cry of dereliction" (Matt. 27:46; Mark 15:34; cf. Ps 22:1). The early church practiced "the breaking of bread and the prayers" (Acts 2:42); the plural phrase "the prayers" suggests they prayed the *tefillah* or Eighteen Benedictions daily. The apostles also observed the regular hours of prayer (see Acts 3:1; 10:3; m. Ber 4:1, 3). The prayers of the Gentile Cornelius were heard (Acts 10:1, 4). The rabbis taught that one should follow the example of Hannah, directing one's heart to God before praying, and some of the holy men spent an hour doing so before they prayed (m. Ber. 5:1; b. Ber. 31a–32b).

If the Bible is a book of prayer, and the Lord's Prayer is a model of prayer, the question remains: Does God answer our prayers? Jesus' parable about neighbors in the middle of the night assures us that God indeed answers prayers. If even a sleepy and irritated neighbor would rise in the middle of the night to give aid, then surely God, who "neither slumbers nor sleeps" (Ps. 121:4), will answer our prayers.

The story occurs in a Galilean village, with houses close together, some sharing a common courtyard. The villagers would also have shared the honor-shame conventions of ancient Judaism, including the notion that hospitality requires that a meal—or at least bread—be served to a late-arriving guest.

The parable has two parts: a long question (Luke 11:5–7) that asks whether a neighbor would respond to a request that comes in the most inconvenient of circumstances, and an answer that drives home the point: yes, the neighbor would (v. 8). Does the parable teach that believers should be persistent in prayer or that, since it would be unthinkable for a neighbor to turn away a friend in need (Prov. 3:28–29), certainly God will not turn away our prayers? The question hinges on whether the term *anadeia* in verse 8, which we might translate with the English term "shamelessness," applies to the petitioner outside or the neighbor inside. If the petitioner is the "shameless" one, then the parable urges persistence in prayer. If

1. Joachim Jeremias, *The Prayers of Jesus* (Philadelphia: Fortress, 1978), 11–65, esp. 60, 62. Cf. John Nolland, *Luke 9:21–18:34*, World Biblical Commentary 35B (Dallas: Word, 1989), 613.

the neighbor is "shameless," then the parable emphasizes that prayer appeals to the honor and shamelessness of God. Perhaps both are implied, and the preacher might explore both options. Since Jesus drew his parables from common experience, did he remember a night back in Nazareth when Joseph had gotten up to answer the door? The twin to this parable is the story of the persistent widow in Luke 18:1–8, where again Jesus may have remembered the plight of his widowed mother.

The last unit (vv. 9–13) in this text uses three metaphors about questing: a beggar pleading, a seeker for wisdom searching, and a person knocking at a door (perhaps a homeless person seeking shelter—cf. Luke 13:24–25). Ask, seek, and knock; in each case, the desire is granted. Then Jesus advances a fourth metaphor—a child entreating a parent—and moves the argument from the lesser to the greater: if human beings know how to give to their children, how much more does God. The preacher may want to explore how these four metaphors suggest ways that prayers are answered. For example, the request that the door be opened anticipates the risen Lord's opening the eyes of the two disciples at Emmaus (24:31), opening the Scriptures to them (v. 32), and opening their minds (v. 45). As another example, notice how Luke, for good reason, disrupts the neat parallelism of Matthew (if we . . . give good gifts, certainly the heavenly Father will give good gifts, Matt. 7:11). In Luke, however, Jesus says, "If you then . . . give good gifts to your children, how much more will the heavenly Father give the Holy Spirit." This points ahead to the experience of Pentecost as an answer to prayer.

R. ALAN CULPEPPER

Commentary 2: Connecting the Reading with the World

This reading is about prayer. As the passage begins, Jesus is himself praying, an important and frequent activity of Jesus in Luke's Gospel. One of Jesus' disciples, when he had finished praying, went to Jesus and said to him, "Teach us to pray." The implication here is that prayer can and probably must be learned.

It is sometimes said, however, that there are no atheists in foxholes, implying that prayer is native to humanity under stress, with no instruction needed. Perhaps fear, pain, and desperate need are in fact the first teachers of prayer. If there is a "God-shaped hole" in every human heart, is it natural to cry out to have that hole filled? Such a plea may be inchoate and inarticulate, but does it not count as prayer? It would not be difficult to find stories of people who cry out to God in their pain before they know Jesus and his teaching. Perhaps breathing would make a useful analogy here. We breathe naturally, but people who want to become expert in the use of the voice—singers, actors, and even some preachers—learn painstakingly to breathe in a disciplined and effective manner. Disciplined and developed breathing must be learned by repeated exercise. Closer to the experience of some of our listeners will be a yoga class, where participants are also *taught* to breathe in a certain way. Is prayer like breathing? It may be so, for those who wish to follow Jesus. This passage raises but does not fully answer such questions. While it may be that some form of prayer comes naturally, the main question of this passage is: What does it mean to ask *Jesus* to teach us to pray?

In this passage prayer is a mark of identity. Jesus is asked to teach his disciples not merely to pray, but also to pray in the pattern and manner of their teacher, "as John taught his disciples" to pray. This may partly be a matter of "keeping up with the Joneses" or in this case, "the Johns." If the disciples of John the Baptist have a distinctive prayer or way of praying, then the followers of Jesus ought to have one also. This does not, however, make their request improper. After all, Jesus grants the request and teaches a version of what will become known as the Lord's Prayer. The followers of Jesus will be known by, among other things, their use of this prayer.

The idea of prayer and identity is still important. Sometimes Christian communions are formally identified by their form of government (Episcopalians, Congregationalists), sometimes by their particular practices (Baptists), and sometimes by a relationship to a founding figure (Lutherans). Denominational attachment may be fading today, but these labels still say something about the identity of different Christian communions. A "Blessed Sacrament" parish will be different from a "Bible Church." The preacher can help us know that one value of this text is that it raises the question: What will a church be like that primarily draws its identity from the way it *prays*? Maybe if a church thought of its identity as praying as Jesus prays, then it would also try to live as Jesus lived.

The preacher can guide us to a second insight about what it means to ask Jesus to teach us to pray, that he guides us toward intimacy with God. Prayer is not merely a skill to be learned and practiced or an obligation to be undertaken. No, the most striking thing about the Lord's Prayer is that the believer is invited to call God "Father." Matthew's version ("Father in heaven") strikes a balance between intimacy and transcendence, but Luke's version (simply "Father") moves more closely toward intimacy, even allowing for the paternal authority assumed in a patriarchal society. It is certainly true that a sensitive preacher will address the problem of the gender-specific nature of that title and its effect on human conduct, but it would be a pity to lose the intimacy of the address itself, or the tenderness of the relationship that follows in Jesus' rabbinic-style argument concerning the goodness of God. (Does it help to use the Aramaic term "Abba," which is almost certainly behind Luke's Greek term *patēr* and the English word "Father"? Are there other forms of address that maintain the combination of intimacy and authority in the traditional term? Preachers will have to decide that for themselves in their own contexts.) In any case, the good news is not simply that the follower of Jesus may pray. (Not just must!) The good news lies in the nature of the One to whom we may offer our prayers.

The Lord's Prayer in Luke's version consists of a series of five brief petitions, and preaching on each of them would constitute a good sermon series. As a general observation, though, note how short the Lord's Prayer is. This is true of Matthew's version, but Luke's version is shorter still. What does it mean that the heart of Christian prayer is this very small pile of words? First, the brevity of this prayer befits Jesus' warning in the Sermon on the Mount against piling up words in our prayers. The often windy language of the church caused Scottish poet Edwin Muir to complain, "The Word made flesh is here made word again" (from the poem "The Incarnate One"). Second, this brief prayer is amazingly concentrated and surely deserves our concentrated attention. In praying for an intimate relationship with the holy God, for the coming of God's just and righteous reign, for daily bread, for healed relationships, and for divine protection from evil, this prayer, in short compass, nevertheless spans the breadth of the Christian life.

The Lord's Prayer is followed in Luke with two elements: a parable and a rabbinic-style saying of Jesus, both about prayer. The key to the parable lies in the word the NRSV renders "persistence" (v. 8). Jesus does call for persistence in prayer, in the parable of the Widow and the Unjust Judge. That may not be the focus here. Other translations render that key word as "shamelessness" or "shameless boldness" or the wonderful Yiddish word "chutzpah." Chutzpah is "nerve," what a man has who murders his father and mother and throws himself on the mercy of the court because he is an orphan. Context should rule here. If a neighbor wakes you at 3:00 a.m. to ask for a loaf of bread, do you say, "How persistent!" or do you say, "What nerve!"? What you would actually say on that occasion is what you should preach.

I realize that the only people I would wake at that hour would be my parents. They would welcome me home and give what I need because of who they are. That leads to the rabbinic argument. If earthly fathers know how to give good gifts, how much more will the heavenly Abba give the Holy Spirit. There is no guarantee in Luke that we will get what we ask for. That connects well to our experience of prayer. We do not always get what we ask for, even in loving, generous spirited, nonshopping list prayers. We may not even always sense the presence of the Holy Spirit. There are "My God, my God, why have you forsaken me?" moments. The ultimate gift of prayer is, in the end, the Holy Spirit, God's own presence.

STEPHEN FARRIS

Proper 13 (Sunday between July 31 and August 6 Inclusive)

Hosea 11:1–11 and Ecclesiastes 1:2, 12–14; 2:18–23
Psalm 107:1–9, 43 and Psalm 49:1–12
Colossians 3:1–11
Luke 12:13–21

Hosea 11:1–11

[1]When Israel was a child, I loved him,
and out of Egypt I called my son.
[2]The more I called them,
the more they went from me;
they kept sacrificing to the Baals,
and offering incense to idols.

[3]Yet it was I who taught Ephraim to walk,
I took them up in my arms;
but they did not know that I healed them.
[4]I led them with cords of human kindness,
with bands of love.
I was to them like those
who lift infants to their cheeks.
I bent down to them and fed them.

[5]They shall return to the land of Egypt,
and Assyria shall be their king,
because they have refused to return to me.
[6]The sword rages in their cities,
it consumes their oracle-priests,
and devours because of their schemes.
[7]My people are bent on turning away from me.
To the Most High they call,
but he does not raise them up at all.

[8]How can I give you up, Ephraim?
How can I hand you over, O Israel?
How can I make you like Admah?
How can I treat you like Zeboiim?
My heart recoils within me;
my compassion grows warm and tender.
[9]I will not execute my fierce anger;
I will not again destroy Ephraim;
for I am God and no mortal,
the Holy One in your midst,
and I will not come in wrath.

[10]They shall go after the LORD,
who roars like a lion;

when he roars,
his children shall come trembling from the west.
[11]They shall come trembling like birds from Egypt,
and like doves from the land of Assyria;
and I will return them to their homes, says the LORD.

Ecclesiastes 1:2, 12–14; 2:18–23

[2]Vanity of vanities, says the Teacher,
vanity of vanities! All is vanity.

. . . .

[12]I, the Teacher, when king over Israel in Jerusalem, [13]applied my mind to seek and to search out by wisdom all that is done under heaven; it is an unhappy business that God has given to human beings to be busy with. [14]I saw all the deeds that are done under the sun; and see, all is vanity and a chasing after wind. . . .

[2:18]I hated all my toil in which I had toiled under the sun, seeing that I must leave it to those who come after me [19]—and who knows whether they will be wise or foolish? Yet they will be master of all for which I toiled and used my wisdom under the sun. This also is vanity. [20]So I turned and gave my heart up to despair concerning all the toil of my labors under the sun, [21]because sometimes one who has toiled with wisdom and knowledge and skill must leave all to be enjoyed by another who did not toil for it. This also is vanity and a great evil. [22]What do mortals get from all the toil and strain with which they toil under the sun? [23]For all their days are full of pain, and their work is a vexation; even at night their minds do not rest. This also is vanity.

Commentary 1: Connecting the Reading with Scripture

The text from Hosea is part of the semicontinuous reading of the prophets. The lectionary pairs the passage from Ecclesiastes with Luke 12:13–21. While the lectionary does not intend for Hosea and Ecclesiastes to be read in the same service, a preacher could read them both as the start for a sermon comparing the different theological emphases in Hosea and Ecclesiastes.

Hosea 11:1–11. In Hosea's day, the community had violated the covenant by seeking security through worshiping idols and an alliance with Assyria, who required massive taxes, which Israel's rulers extracted from the lower classes. Hosea 11:1–11 articulates judgment (vv. 1–7) but turns toward restoration (vv. 8–11). Many congregations today are in similar circumstances—entwined in idolatry and injustice.

Some interpreters see the image of God in this chapter as feminine: God cares for Israel like a mother. Maternal compassion moves God to restore Israel. While this interpretation is plausible, it is also true that fathers (and others) shared many of the roles Hosea ascribes to God. With respect to gender, most interpreters today think Hosea speaks in terms of broader familial roles.

God loved Israel as a parent loves a child. God demonstrated that love by liberating Israel from bondage in Egypt. As a tender parent, God taught Ephraim (Israel) to walk, held Israel tenderly in God's arms, led the child safely in the cords of kindness (*hesed*, "covenantal loyalty"), lifted Israel to God's cheeks, and bent down to feed Israel (vv. 1–2a, 3a, 4).

Yet the community worshiped idols (vv. 2b, 3b). In consequence of these violations of covenant, God will hand the community over to Assyria, who will wreak violence on Israel's cities and leaders (vv. 5–6). This judgment will be comparable to bondage in Egypt (v. 5a).

While the parent must discipline the child—to honor the covenant—Hosea 11:8–9 is a poignant statement of the divine nature in relationship to disciplinary action. In an earlier time, God destroyed Admah and Zeboiim because of their sin (Gen. 14:2, 8; 19:24–28; Deut. 29:23). However, the prospect of doing that to Israel again causes God's heart to recoil. In Hebrew symbolism, the heart is less the seat of emotion and is more the operating center of the self.[1] In theological resonance with Exodus 34:6–7, Hosea depicts God's compassion growing warm and tender.

The community can repent and return to God and to covenantal life for real security. The community can come home like lion cubs who have heard the roar of the parent, or like birds returning to the nest (vv. 10–11).

The early twenty-first century is ripe for Hosea's message of God's deep, visceral love, since contemporary conditions resemble those of Hosea's time: in economic life, in relationships among social groups, in international affairs. Life is often anxious, alienated, and painful. While preachers can appropriately speak of God's love for individuals, the prophet has in mind God's fathomless love for Israel as community.

Despite the present raw, destructive fractiousness, God does not give up on human community as sphere for blessing. God seeks restoration. The preacher can help the congregation name resources for social reconstruction that are already present, even though such resources may not be immediately visible to the casual Christian. For instance, after cataloging examples of various personal, social, and environmental destructiveness caused by transnational corporations, a preacher might point to alternative means for goods and services through local workers and minieconomies already present in the congregation's neighborhood, but unnoticed by the household accustomed to big-box stores.

In a different message, the preacher could use verses 8–9 for a broader sermon on the doctrine of God that would focus on the nature and purpose of God. This sermon would identify Hosea's viewpoint, and then bring that perspective into conversation with other understandings of the nature and purpose of God from the Bible, Christian tradition, contemporary theology, and the deepest theological convictions of the congregation and preacher, all with an eye toward positing a comprehensive perspective on God.

Ecclesiastes 1:2, 12–14; 2:18–23. The authors of the Wisdom literature (the sages) rely significantly on observation of life for theological insight. The human family can learn about God and about how to live by paying attention to what happens in life.

Ecclesiastes engages in this experientially based theological method and comes away with the observation that "all is vanity" (1:2). Commentators note that "vanity" (*hebel*) refers to vapor, that is, something that is here one minute and gone the next. Life is ephemeral. It has no substance. When a life is over, it is over, and nothing of importance remains. A human life amounts to "chasing after wind" (1:14).

Ecclesiastes 2:18–23 goes even farther. Here the writer confesses to "hating" life's toil and to giving "the heart up to despair." Life is full of pain, and work is "a vexation." After death, the meaning of one's life vanishes like a vapor. Who knows whether those who inherit the results of one's labor will use it wisely or foolishly?

On the one hand, the presence of this text is a point of identification for people who have such an Eeyore outlook. Such identification can be important for those who encounter religious groups that are irrepressibly—and sometimes oppressively—optimistic. Ecclesiastes is honest about the way many people feel. On the other hand, the preacher should bring Ecclesiastes into dialogue with other voices in the Bible and in Christian tradition who believe that life has more meaning than chasing after wind. Indeed, the Wisdom literature itself offers diverse

1. On the change in the divine self, see the work of my honored colleague, J. Gerald Janzen, "Metaphor and Reality in Hosea 11," *Semeia* 24 (1982): 1–44.

viewpoints on this subject, as we can see in differences among Proverbs, Job, and the Wisdom psalms (e.g., Pss. 37, 49, 78, 112, 127, 128, 133). A preacher might compare these different perspectives so that the congregation can think about which ones they can embrace.

The passage from Ecclesiastes is paired with Luke 12:13–21, perhaps with the idea that the person in the parable who foolishly built greater barns illustrates chasing after wind: "And the things you have prepared, whose will they be?"

While the lectionary does not envision both Hosea and Ecclesiastes in direct interpretive relationship with Luke, the preacher could use them as the basis for a homiletical conversation. The preacher could sketch the worldview of each author. Ecclesiastes presumes that life is a vapor. The prophetic worldview of Hosea assumes that God's purposes can be fulfilled within history through living in covenantal community. Hosea does not assume an apocalypse that brings about a transformation of existence through destruction and re-creation. Luke's worldview is apocalyptic, a viewpoint evident in the moment of judgment in the parable (Luke 12:13–21). In its Lukan setting, the parable assumes that, when Jesus returns, God will condemn those who act greedily. The preacher could also bring into the conversation the epistle for the day, Colossians 3:1–11, where the author contrasts the life before Christ in categories that are existentially similar to those of Ecclesiastes's "chasing after wind" and Hosea's concern for violation of covenant, with the life in Christ, which is noteworthy for its meaning and for its covenantal qualities. After sketching these perspectives, the preacher could then compare the four worldviews with the aim of encouraging the congregation to think about which one(s), if any, make the most theological sense.

RONALD J. ALLEN

Commentary 2: Connecting the Reading with the World

Hosea has indicted the people of God for ten chapters. In chapter 11 comes a turn that opens up a new chamber of the heart of God. Verses 1–8 reveal God as a parent who has invested time, energy, and love in the nurture and care of Israel. Like the parent of an adolescent or adult child who has headed down a horrible path, God laments by calling to mind memories of fondly caring for a child who is young.

All the anger and condemnation built up in the earlier chapters dissolves in the heat of parental compassion. Though the consequences of Israel's infidelity stand (vv. 5–7), their significance pales in the light of divine love. In verse 8, the strain on the divine heart crescendos and then resolves in the decision of verse 9. Unlike human judges and human parents, God will never give up on the children, no matter how bad things get. Here is the pain of a parent who must turn a child over into drug rehab but still returns home to make a room for that child when she returns. Here is the pain of someone who must testify against a friend in court but then readies his calendar to visit that friend in jail. Even the judgment required by sin cannot deprive love of its power.

For generations of Christians taught that the essential attitude of God toward us is anger, Hosea 11 is a breath of fresh air. Without adopting a position that turns a blind eye to the problems of human sin, the text offers a picture of God as a creator-parent heartbroken over wayward humanity and desperate to draw us close. For those who have labored long under the theology of a God filled only with wrath, our study and preaching of Hosea 11 may open the door to the deep and abiding love of God. The deliverance of the woman in John 8:2–11 resonates on a personal level with this message from Hosea for the whole people.

Those of us judged and convicted by family, by the church, or by the legal system may come to believe that there is no love or redemption for us. When we have been cut off by our communities or suffer under the consequences of our mistakes, the veil of rejection can seem impenetrable. Here, precisely, comes the good news from Hosea. The love of God has a stronger bond than that of a mother for her child, and will ensure that the ultimate destination of the children is home.

Many liturgical traditions have a time of confession during worship, a time whose culmination is an assurance of pardon. This turnabout from recognition of wrongdoing to promise of forgiveness and welcome mirrors liturgically the profound shift in Hosea. Theologically, Hosea gives prophetic voice to the surprising love of God expressed physically in Jesus Christ, who came to draw an erring world close to God's bosom (see Luke 13:34–35 and John 12:32).

If Christians are to reflect the character of God, we are to experience the same angst at the condemnation and exile of any part of humanity. So Hosea 11 plants the work of restorative justice in the person of God. The shroud that hangs over a person convicted of a felony, for instance, can hamper employment or even social relationships. The hearts of Christians ought to break over this endless extension of punishment; we should seek to invite those who have completed their terms to return home. The church as a community voice goes further by speaking divinely inspired compassion to the justice system and advocating for sentences that will correct rather than corrupt those who have made grave mistakes. The constant desire of the church is that the world would pursue the compassion of God, and that we would see the world come home, trembling with the relief of forgiveness (v. 10).

Our lectionary text from Ecclesiastes does not strike as hopeful a note as Hosea 11. Yet both the tone and the content of the words from the Teacher deserve thoughtful consideration, because they address perennial problems in the human condition. Pursuit of the difficult philosophical questions of life can lead to rejection of meaning either through philosophical materialism or spiritual exhaustion. Both destinations resonate with the cry that "all is vanity!" The repetitive nature of human toil and the realization that no amount of money earned brings satisfaction to the heart continue to plague our societies. Even if we believe that our earnings have made a positive contribution to the world, nothing guarantees that the next generation will take the fruits of our labor and carry on the good work. Even the wealthiest parents harbor anxiety about whether the inheritance they pass on will be a blessing to their children or the world after they die. Adding insult to injury, faithful human toil sometimes seems to bring no results. Think of the struggles of oncologists, political activists, parents of wayward children, and development workers in unstable communities—just to name a few. The Teacher presses us to consider this ever-present concern: why toil for anything when its effects and enduring value are so far from assured?

Those who come to worship, to study groups, and to service projects often carry a dense set of worries. Acrimony in the daily news cycle and labor disconnected from obvious good purpose conspire to weary the soul. Social media and the endless stream of information coming through digital media overwhelm our spiritual lives with strife and distraction. "Vanity" may be a charitable, if escapist, description of this swollen torrent.

Americans immersed in the great social experiment of democratic capitalism experience on a regular basis "the progress paradox": though by all objective measures our lives continue steadily to improve, our feeling about ourselves continues to degrade.[2] The striving of the Teacher in Ecclesiastes 2 mirrors closely the yearning of American consumers, and the eventual conclusion of each is often the same. Ecclesiastes gives scriptural voice to that weariness. As such, this text provides the opportunity to name a dark elephant in the vault of our life together and banish it by shining the light of hope.

The church in worship and work ought to acknowledge the deep problems of the world but also recognize that these problems will not solve themselves. The person and proclamation of Jesus Christ provide a helpful response to the cry of Ecclesiastes. Proclamation, praise, and prayer in worship answer feelings of despair with

2. For a thorough examination of this phenomenon, see Gregg Easterbrook's book *The Progress Paradox: How Life Gets Better While People Feel Worse* (New York: Random House, 2003).

the promises of resurrection, the sovereignty of God, and the ability of the Spirit to grow good things, even where human ability withers and dies. So, Christians, receive the hope that not all toil is vanity if it is done with and for God (see Col. 3:23–24). Work done out of hope shines much brighter than work done in fatigue and despair. Christian life and worship lives in the tension between the tough experience of Ecclesiastes and the redemptive wisdom of Christ.

These two OT passages together remind us of a central task in preaching. A world weary of its own sin and its well-earned despair can always turn back to God. As we enervate ourselves in contemplation of the darkness, God follows us like a protective parent, ready to take us up and heal us with bandages of love. This message, consonant with the work of Jesus Christ, always comes as good news.

EMRYS TYLER

Psalm 107:1–9, 43

[1]O give thanks to the LORD, for he is good;
for his steadfast love endures forever.
[2]Let the redeemed of the LORD say so,
those he redeemed from trouble
[3]and gathered in from the lands,
from the east and from the west,
from the north and from the south.

[4]Some wandered in desert wastes,
finding no way to an inhabited town;
[5]hungry and thirsty,
their soul fainted within them.
[6]Then they cried to the LORD in their trouble,
and he delivered them from their distress;
[7]he led them by a straight way,
until they reached an inhabited town.
[8]Let them thank the LORD for his steadfast love,
for his wonderful works to humankind.
[9]For he satisfies the thirsty,
and the hungry he fills with good things.
. . . .
[43]Let those who are wise give heed to these things,
and consider the steadfast love of the LORD.

Psalm 49:1–12

[1]Hear this, all you peoples;
give ear, all inhabitants of the world,
[2]both low and high,
rich and poor together.
[3]My mouth shall speak wisdom;
the meditation of my heart shall be understanding.
[4]I will incline my ear to a proverb;
I will solve my riddle to the music of the harp.

[5]Why should I fear in times of trouble,
when the iniquity of my persecutors surrounds me,
[6]those who trust in their wealth
and boast of the abundance of their riches?
[7]Truly, no ransom avails for one's life,
there is no price one can give to God for it.
[8]For the ransom of life is costly,
and can never suffice,
[9]that one should live on forever
and never see the grave.

[10]When we look at the wise, they die;
fool and dolt perish together
and leave their wealth to others.
[11]Their graves are their homes forever,
their dwelling places to all generations,
though they named lands their own.
[12]Mortals cannot abide in their pomp;
they are like the animals that perish.

Connecting the Psalm with Scripture and Worship

Psalm 107:1–9. The God who does mighty acts in history is sometimes portrayed in masculine imagery: God is like a reigning king, a male vineyard owner or warrior, or a divine husband married to a nation-as-wife. This week's reading from Hosea may be read as offering feminine and motherly images of the Divine. God teaches a child to walk, calls lovingly to them when they stray, bends down to feed them, nurses them to health, takes them in her arms and lifts them to her cheek. In describing the inevitable return of the people home to God's nurturing care, the final two verses offer maternal imagery from the wider animal family: the mother lion roars and her children return, or like trembling birds the children return to the nest that nurtured them.

The selection from Psalm 107 is like one stanza of a longer hymn. The complete psalm is comprised of four parallel stanzas, each of which describes people in trouble who cry to God and are rescued. Their perils are varied and vivid: lost and hungry in the wastelands (vv. 4–9), held captive in prison (vv. 10–16), near death with sickness (vv. 17–22), and frightened in storms on the sea (vv. 23–32). The section appointed for today, in response to Hosea's imagery of divine toddler care, recalls God gathering people—hungry, thirsty, homeless—from scattered wastelands and leading them back into safety, nurturance, and community.

The psalm reflects on God providing for those who are homeless, hungry, and thirsty, and associates this pattern with wisdom: "whoever is wise will ponder these things" (*The Book of Common Prayer*). The Gospel echoes wisdom themes in the parable of the Rich Man who plans to build bigger barns. The "You fool!" spoken to the rich man is like Hosea's divine lion's roar calling us, trembling, to our senses. We are warned that such greed is a path leading directly to death. The second reading, from Colossians, in language resonant with baptism, assigns greed and idolatry themselves to burial with Christ so that a new creation may arise. Are there hymns of such wisdom we might sing on this day, especially in contrast to the foolish barn building of dominant North American consumer culture?

In both the first reading and the psalm, the people are imaged as needing guidance in their walking, like toddlers. The Gospel text places in the foreground humanity's need to be led ethically regarding money and riches. Preachers might explore in what ways God is even now still teaching us—living in the richest societies in history—like a toddler to walk. The texts today give space to name both God's patient and tender parental care, and the fierceness of the mother lion's roar of warning against the foolishness of greed that leads to the grave.

The saving action described in the psalm comes in response to the cry of the people in trouble. Worship this week may be in part a cry for deliverance from the deadly burdens of human acquisitiveness. In many of our congregations we are simultaneously trying to build additions to our barns—seeking greater material riches—even as we also suffer the environmental and social consequences of an economic system that privileges the wealthy. Seeking to transcend our compromised commitments and to be saved from their consequences, we sing our psalm to God, who "satisfies the thirsty and fills the hungry with good things" (v. 9 NIV).

From Hosea we hear of our history of being rescued by God—out of slavery, out of injustice—and we hear again God's call like the roar of a mother lion for us to return. In the psalm we sing back to God our mother, singing our gratitude for her steadfast faithfulness. At the conclusion of the song we charge ourselves to meditate on this pattern of divine compassion and rescue as a source of wisdom: "whoever is wise will ponder these things."

Psalm 49:1–12. The Hebrew word *hebel,* translated as "vanity" in Ecclesiastes, connotes a vapor or breath, something insubstantial and ephemeral. This word repeats nearly forty times like a funeral drum through the book: all treasures are vanities eventually left behind in death. This week *hebel* refers not only to human labor and riches, but even to the quest for wisdom and to existence itself: "All is vanity."

While the psalm is thematically related to the reading from Ecclesiastes, the psalmist is, in contrast, full-throated and confident: "Hear this, all you peoples; give ear, all you who dwell in the world, you of high degree and low, rich and poor together; my mouth shall speak of wisdom" (vv. 1–3a [*The Book of Common Prayer*]). The psalm has a more focused purpose than the broader philosophical meditations of Ecclesiastes. This psalm is sung to stir up courage before those who would intimidate or oppress with their wealth, wisdom, or talent. The psalm seeks to sing a reminder to the entire world; the arrogant will be swallowed up in the fierce equality of death. Psalm 49 deconstructs the quest for wealth and status, exposing its trajectory as leading to the grave.

The observation that all of us return to the grave in a dusty equality may have been applied early in human history as a reality check against growing inequality in life. Dorothee Sölle speculates that death may be "the very inventor of equality" in a social critique she wrote as she herself was dying: "Death has no place in the landscape of life for those who are pure doers and winners. . . . We live in a landscape where everyone is young and strong, rich, intelligent, and good-looking—or must appear so. The weak, the old, the dying do not count. . . . It is difficult to die in this landscape of winners who manage without memory."[1]

The book of James similarly sees death as a check against the arrogance of the rich: "For the sun rises with its scorching heat and withers the field; its flower falls, and its beauty perishes. It is the same way with the rich; in the midst of a busy life, they will wither away" (Jas. 1:11).

This psalm of resistance against the oppressions of the wealthy gives us a liberating word to sing in harmony with the Gospel text for the week; we have been set free from the interminable demand of building bigger barns. The second reading too locates this greed-purging power of death in what sounds like the waters of baptism: "For you have died, and your life is hidden with Christ in God. . . . Put to death, therefore, . . . evil desire and greed (which is idolatry)" (Col. 3:3, 5).

The promise at the heart of this spirituality of death is a striking contrast from some visions of a heavenly existence after death. As Walter Brueggemann writes about this psalm, "The alternative to death is here given not as afterlife but only as relationship with God."[2] In response to Ecclesiastes's strong and potentially debilitating word about the inevitability of death for all creatures and the transience of all things, we sing to the entire world a courageous song that embraces a life on earth animated by the wisdom of sacred equality.

BENJAMIN M. STEWART

1. Dorothee Sölle. *The Mystery of Death* (Minneapolis: Fortress, 2007), 10, 15–16.
2. Walter Brueggemann and William H. Bellinger Jr., *Psalms,* New Cambridge Bible Commentary (New York: Cambridge University Press, 2014), 229.

Colossians 3:1–11

[1]So if you have been raised with Christ, seek the things that are above, where Christ is, seated at the right hand of God. [2]Set your minds on things that are above, not on things that are on earth, [3]for you have died, and your life is hidden with Christ in God. [4]When Christ who is your life is revealed, then you also will be revealed with him in glory.

[5]Put to death, therefore, whatever in you is earthly: fornication, impurity, passion, evil desire, and greed (which is idolatry). [6]On account of these the wrath of God is coming on those who are disobedient. [7]These are the ways you also once followed, when you were living that life. [8]But now you must get rid of all such things—anger, wrath, malice, slander, and abusive language from your mouth. [9]Do not lie to one another, seeing that you have stripped off the old self with its practices [10]and have clothed yourselves with the new self, which is being renewed in knowledge according to the image of its creator. [11]In that renewal there is no longer Greek and Jew, circumcised and uncircumcised, barbarian, Scythian, slave and free; but Christ is all and in all!

Commentary 1: Connecting the Reading with Scripture

Early in this letter, the apostle Paul spoke in general terms of the Christian life when he wrote of "faith," "love," and "hope" (Col. 1:4–5, 8) and when he wrote about living a "life worthy of the Lord, fully pleasing to him, as you bear fruit in every good work and as you grow in the knowledge of God" (1:10). He prayed too for their faithfulness (1:11). For Paul, the Christian life is more than ethics or morality. Put differently, it is Christ himself who defines the Christian life, and it is defined by *who Christ is*. The crucified and raised Jesus the Lord redefines what the Christian life is. The best term I know for understanding the Christian life in this way is "Christoformity" or what others call "Cruciformity." If the latter term refers to the Christian's life becoming "formed" by the "cross," the former term expands Cruciformity to being "formed" by the whole life of Christ: his life, teachings, death, burial, resurrection, and glorification.[1]

The story of Christ is presented in Colossians 1:15–20, and because this hymn in some ways echoes the hymn of Philippians 2:6–11, we can describe it in term of a U. Beginning at the throne of God the Father, the Son is sent to earth to become like us in order to effect a cosmic reconciliation; in him "all the fullness of God was pleased to dwell" (Col. 1:19).

The apostle Paul describes himself as "completing what is lacking in Christ's afflictions for the sake of his body" (1:24); under any interpretation he sees his own sufferings in terms of the Lord's passion. Hence, Cruciformity. The Colossians have received this Christ as their resurrected Lord (2:6–7). They are living in him, and what living in him means is spelled out in 3:1–11. In our passage the Christian life is understood in baptismal terms: as death to sin (cf. 2:20; 3:5–11) and being raised for a transformed life (3:1–4).

This *raised life* is sketched briefly in 3:1–4: it means seeking and setting one's mind on things that are above and being confident of one's final victory. Here Paul combines future eschatology (3:4) and present eschatology (3:1–3). What

1. See Michael Gorman, *Cruciformity: Paul's Narrative Spirituality of the Cross* (Grand Rapids: Eerdmans, 2001), esp. 4–5.

is above, and to be our focus, is the enthroned Christ: "where Christ is, seated at the right hand of God" (3:1). The enthroned Christ stands in bold contrast to the Roman Empire, where Caesar rules (3:2, "not on things that are on the earth") and where flesh, the powers, the elemental spirits, and sin rule. Seeking is important in Paul's vision of the Christian life, but we are to seek not our own glory (Gal. 1:10; Phil. 2:21) or our own way (1 Cor. 13:5) but, instead, justification in Christ (Gal. 2:16–17), spiritual gifts (1 Cor. 14:12), and (as is also emphasized in our passage) immortality (Rom. 2:7). Paul's vision of such things reconfigures how he interprets all that occurs on earth. He clearly holds that to seek the things above means to live entirely under the rule of Christ, and this by knowing the promise of Christ's triumphal glory (Col. 3:4).

The *crucified life* is sketched more explicitly in 3:5–11 and has the following two elements: first, in terms of acts not to practice (3:5–9a) and, second, in terms of a theology of conversion (3:9b–11). The Colossians have stripped off the "old self" and put on the "new self" (3:9b–10a). This is a self that transforms into Christlikeness (3:10b). Put together, then, the crucified life is about turning from one way of life to another, the old way of life being marked by desire and disunity and materialism (cf. Gal. 5:19–23; 1 Thess. 4:3–7; Rom. 1:29–32) and the renewed way of life being marked by a unified community. In the renewed life, the former demarcations that ranked a person's high or low status—demarcations shaping every moment of life for those in the Roman Empire—come to a halt in the church, where "there is no longer Greek and Jew, . . . barbarian, Scythian [a stereotype for a hillbilly or ruffian], . . . slave and free." Why? Because Christ "is all and in all" (Col. 3:11). The *crucified* and the *raised life* then is life "in Christ." Once again, all themes in Paul's theology lead to Christocentricity and Christoformity, and these two centers will reshape the gathered community (3:12–17) and the Christian household (3:18–4:1).

The ethics of Paul, however, are not to be separated from the larger theme of God's grace. God's relentless love will not let us go (cf. Hos. 11). God's love is found in Christ's cosmic, reconciling redemption. There is yet an even wider work of God's grace in the world beyond God's activity in Israel and Judah. As our psalm for this Sunday says, "Let the redeemed of the Lord say so." Who shall say this? Those "gathered in from the lands, from the east and from the west, from the north and from the south" (Ps. 107:3). God's love, unlike our faithfulness, is "steadfast" (107:8, 43). In Colossians, there is a witness to the ever-widening and ever-expanding work of God in the world; for Paul rather proudly speaks of the gospel "bearing fruit and growing in the whole world" (Col. 1:6). However exaggerated his language might be, Paul's theology reflects God's own heart: God loves all.

Jesus invites us in his parables to imagine a new, kingdom kind of world, one in which one's status does not derive from the "abundance of possessions" or an increasing number of buildings (Luke 12:13–21). Rather, Jesus tears down such buildings and burns through such possessions to exhort his followers to indwell a world in which richness toward God or status with God—reconciliation, righteousness, love, peace, justice and love—reshapes our every word, deed, and thought. Our Gospel text then brings into clear relief the dangers at work in the earthly and old ways of the believers in Colossians 3:1–11. Seeking things above is about riches toward God, and seeking things on earth is about indwelling opulence as the goal of life.

Yet the Bible's connections between passages on wealth, poverty, blessing, and curse are not as clear as we would at times prefer. If Deuteronomy 28 can offer the promise that obedience produces material blessing while disobedience produces curses, Job invites us to consider that simplistic analysis of a person's value is not determined by one's material blessings. In fact, the ways of God in Job are inscrutable. This kind of thinking reshapes the themes of blessing and curse that we can find in the Psalms, Isaiah, Jesus, James, and even Paul. Their cumulative witness suggests that we can no longer read a person's relation to God and God's plan by their status. In fact, status is subverted in the Bible so much that poverty and generosity for the poor become marks of the Christian life.

The Torah of Moses is explicated, clarified, and expanded in the Sermon on the Mount with Jesus' full exposition of the twin commandments of love (Matt. 5–7; 22:34–40) but also by the apostle Paul's constant teaching of life in the Spirit (as in Gal. 5:22–26). In Colossians, the whole of the Bible's ethical vision comes to expression in two themes: death to sin, self, and systemic evils; life to Christ in the power of the Spirit. Christocentricity leads to Christoformity.

SCOT MCKNIGHT

Commentary 2: Connecting the Reading with the World

Appropriating the Bible's cosmology is no easy task for the contemporary reader or preacher. Many of us do not think that the earth was actually created in six twenty-four-hour days (Gen. 1:1–2:3), that Jesus actually went into the sky above when he ascended "into heaven" (Acts 1:9–11), or that hell is a place of fiery torment beneath our earth (Phil. 2:10). Yet I would venture that most of us do not therefore assume that this language is meaningless drivel of an outdated cosmology. Instead, we believe that Scripture expresses something significant about God, humanity, and our world with poetic and suggestive language.

How are we then to understand Paul's claim *not only* that we will appear one day with Christ in glory *but also* his claim that we have already been coresurrected with the Messiah (Col. 3:1)? Paul has told the church in Colossae that they have died with the Messiah (2:11–12a, 20) *and* been raised together with the Messiah "through faith in the power of God, who raised [Jesus] from the dead" (2:12b). Somewhat famously, E. P. Sanders argued that *participation* or *union with Christ* was at the heart of the apostle Paul's soteriology; he also confessed that he did not know of a contemporary discourse—that is, a "category of perception"—whereby he might signify what such language means to people living in our contemporary world.[2] Yet Paul's claim that we have been resurrected with the Messiah who is seated in the heavens at the right hand of God seems to be foundational to the exhortations he gives to the church in Colossae as he tells them twice, "Seek the things that are above" (3:1) and "set your minds on things that are above" (3:2). Finding contemporary discourses into which we might translate Paul's cosmological and participatory language is necessary if we hope to move from ancient text into our modern world.

How then do Christians live out their heavenly resurrection existence in this world? Preachers might explore at least three ways in which Paul's participatory language holds important meaning for us today.

First, those joined together with Christ are given assurance that their eschatological destiny is safe with God. God has resurrected God's Messiah and seated him at God's right hand above every ruler and power (2:10b). Those who belong to the Messiah "have been hidden with the Messiah in God" (3:3b, my trans.). Therefore, no heavenly or earthly power can separate us from Christ's benevolent rule. Christians need not endlessly worry about their salvation. This is why Paul later says, "Let the peace of the Messiah rule in your hearts" (3:15a, my trans.), for Christ has already reconciled them to God, thereby "making peace through the blood of his cross" (1:20). One is reminded of Paul's triumphant words in Romans 8: "If God is for us, who is against us? He who did not withhold his own Son, but gave him up for all of us, will he not with him also give us everything else? . . . I am convinced that neither death, nor life, nor angels, nor rulers, nor things present, nor things to come, nor powers, nor height, nor depth, nor anything else in all creation, will be able to separate us from the love of God in Christ Jesus our Lord" (Rom. 8:31–32, 38–39).

Second, sharing in Christ's resurrection means sharing in a life that is marked by ethical and moral transformation. Paul makes it clear that the Colossians' heavenly life will be characterized by a rejection of immoral behaviors and

2. E. P. Sanders, *Paul and Palestinian Judaism* (Minneapolis: Fortress, 1977), 522–23.

A Way Opened into Heaven

I hope I have made it clear, by these instances, what is meant by Christian self-denial. If we have good health, and are in easy circumstances, let us beware of high-mindedness, self-sufficiency, self-conceit, arrogance; of delicacy of living, indulgences, luxuries, comforts. Nothing is so likely to corrupt our hearts, and to seduce us from God, as to surround ourselves with comforts,—to have things our own way,—to be the center of a sort of world, whether of things animate or inanimate, which minister to us. For then, in turn, we shall depend on them; they will become necessary to us; their very service and adulation will lead us to trust ourselves to them, and to idolize them. . . . Far be it from us, soldiers of Christ, thus to perplex ourselves with this world, who are making our way towards the world to come. . . . Look up to Christ, and deny yourselves every thing, whatever its character, which you think He would have you relinquish. You need not calculate and measure, if you love much: You need not perplex yourselves with points of curiosity, if you have a heart to venture after Him. True, difficulties will sometimes arise, but they will be seldom. He bids you take up your cross; therefore accept the daily opportunities which occur of yielding to others, when you need not yield, and of doing unpleasant services, which you might avoid. He bids those who would be highest, live as the lowest. . . . So shall self-denial become natural to you, and a change come over you, greatly and imperceptibly; and, like Jacob, you will lie down in the waste, and will soon see Angels, and a way opened for you into heaven.

John Henry Newman (1801–90), "The Duty of Self Denial," in *Parochial and Plain Sermons*, vol. 7 (London: Longmans, Green, and Co., 1908), 97–101.

an embrace of practices fitting for the Christian believer. Thus, Paul commands them to "put to death" sexually immoral behavior (Col. 3:5) and speech that is marked by anger, wrath, and obscenities (3:8). Paul here uses his common rhetorical "once . . . but now" technique (3:7–8; cf. 2 Cor. 5:16–17 and Eph. 5:8).

Once, the Colossians were marked by sexually immoral practices, behaviors that Paul seems to think are problematic because they are greedily preoccupied with the self rather than the other. Paul's demand that Christians reject these vices does not stem from a prudish, self-obsessed moralism. Rather, Paul understands that these vices lead to the destruction of community and stand against human flourishing. Those who are lying and are acting deceptively toward one another cannot participate in a community with trust, love, or humility. Those who are greedily consumed with acting out their sexual desires are not able to love and consider the good of others.

Now, the Colossians have rejected these behaviors. *Now*, they are in the process of becoming conformed to the divine image, namely, Christ, who is the pattern and inaugurator of a new humanity (3:9–10). Paul expects that sharing in Christ's resurrection will be evident in a community that lives within the rule of the Messiah by means of sharing in Christ's own pattern of life in this new humanity. Thus Christians should be marked by merciful compassion, kindness, self-abasement, gentleness, patience, forgiveness, and, most of all, love (3:12–14). In this way, it would seem, Christians demonstrate their already resurrected existence through their particular way of life.

Third, those who share in Christ's resurrection existence participate in a community that has not rejected or eradicated one's individual social identity, but where those social identities are no longer the ultimate or solely defining feature of one's identity. Paul describes this new human existence as a reality wherein "there is no longer Greek and Jew, circumcised and uncircumcised, barbarian, Scythian, slave and free; but Christ is all and in all!" (3:11). God's act in Christ had brought into existence *one new people composed of all kinds of people*. Paul tried to live out his commitments to a new humanity that did not eradicate, but severely qualified, social identity. We see that not only men but also women, not only the free but also slaves, not only Jews but also pagans participated in his planting of churches and were encouraged to participate freely in the common gathering of the Christian assemblies.

This vision stands in marked contrast to what many of us see in our church life—for example, ethnic and cultural sameness, men refusing to share their power with women in leadership, and aversion and fear of difference as a potential polluting or destabilizing of the church. When our social identities are valued above our shared identity in Christ, then inevitably those with less power—usually ethnic minorities, women, the poor, or marginalized—are relegated to a position of subservience within the church. The challenge for Paul is no greater than the challenge we face today. Paul is clear that those who share in Christ's new humanity are one new people.

As preachers, we know that Paul's call to live lives shaped by Christ's resurrection is not easy. Maybe this is because the call is so lofty or because the call comes at a certain cost to our power, our wealth, our very selves. Perhaps this text is among those we can draw from in helping the people of God see how important it is to share consciously in Christ's death and resurrection. Paul calls us to issue reminders to God's people that we are the Messiah's people; we are those who rest secure in Christ's peaceful rule, a rule that assures us of salvation at the final judgment. We are those who are in the process of clothing ourselves with the character of the Messiah, and we are called to share in a new kind of community, a community that embraces and empowers *all peoples*.

JOSHUA W. JIPP

Luke 12:13–21

[13]Someone in the crowd said to him, "Teacher, tell my brother to divide the family inheritance with me." [14]But he said to him, "Friend, who set me to be a judge or arbitrator over you?" [15]And he said to them, "Take care! Be on your guard against all kinds of greed; for one's life does not consist in the abundance of possessions." [16]Then he told them a parable: "The land of a rich man produced abundantly. [17]And he thought to himself, 'What should I do, for I have no place to store my crops?' [18]Then he said, 'I will do this: I will pull down my barns and build larger ones, and there I will store all my grain and my goods. [19]And I will say to my soul, Soul, you have ample goods laid up for many years; relax, eat, drink, be merry.' [20]But God said to him, 'You fool! This very night your life is being demanded of you. And the things you have prepared, whose will they be?' [21]So it is with those who store up treasures for themselves but are not rich toward God."

Commentary 1: Connecting the Reading with Scripture

The parable of the Rich Fool stands in a sequence of teachings in Luke (12:1–13:9) warning the disciples and the crowd to be ready for the coming judgment. What is secret will become known (12:2), so confess Jesus fearlessly and publicly. Fear God, not persecution (12:4–9). Do not worry (12:22–34); be watchful (12:35–48). Judgment will bring division (12:49–53), so watch for its signs (12:54–59) and repent, or you will perish (13:1–9). In the context of these warnings, anyone who is worried about the size of his barn is a fool indeed!

One of Luke's major themes is the danger of wealth. As a corollary to Jesus' blessings on the poor, Luke also adds his woes on the rich (6:24). Mary praises God for looking on her lowliness (1:48), while he has pulled down the powerful and "sent the rich away empty" (1:52–53). In his address in Nazareth, which serves as a keynote in Luke announcing the major themes of Jesus' preaching, Jesus reads Isaiah 61:1–2, "The Spirit of the Lord . . . has anointed me to bring good news to the poor" (Luke 4:18). Later, he tells John the Baptist's disciples that "the poor have good news brought to them" (7:22). In contrast, wealth is dangerous because it can turn a person away from dependence on God and make them insensitive to the plight of the poor. Like thorns and thistles, "the cares and riches and pleasures of life" can choke out the seed of faith (8:14). Lazarus lay at the rich man's gate hungry, while the rich man dined sumptuously every day and never noticed him (16:19–31). Jesus laments how hard it is for those who have wealth to enter the kingdom of God (18:24) and instructs the ruler who is seeking eternal life to sell everything and give it to the poor (18:22; cf. 19:8 and 21:1–4).

This parable finds a number of echoes across the canon. James joins Luke as a champion of Jesus' prophetic warnings against wealth. The rich, who are being brought low, "will disappear like a flower in the field" (Jas. 1:9–11). The church is warned especially about the sin of showing favoritism to the rich, those with "gold rings and fine clothes," while ignoring the poor (2:1–7; cf. Ps. 82:2; Job 34:17–19). Like the parable of the Rich Fool, James castigates those who presumptuously make plans, coming and going, "doing business and making money," while not knowing what tomorrow will bring (Jas. 4:13–14). The rich ought rather to weep and wail; their wealth will rust and eat their flesh like fire: "You have lived on the earth in luxury . . . ; you have fattened your hearts in a day of slaughter" (5:5).

Frequently in Scripture, wealth was interpreted as a sign of God's blessing, but the prophets and sages also warned about the dangers of wealth (Ps. 49:5–6). Hosea charged that "Israel has forgotten his Maker, and built palaces" (Hos. 8:14), and Amos lamented, "Alas for those who are at ease in Zion" (Amos 6:1), "Alas for those who lie on beds of ivory" (6:4), and "The revelry of the loungers shall pass away" (6:7). Qoheleth, the preacher, despaired, "All is vanity" (Eccl. 1:2, 14; cf. Isa. 40:6–8) and, with more self-awareness than the rich fool, laments that those who come after him will have everything for which he toiled (Eccl. 2:18–23; cf. Ps. 49:10). His wealth has only brought anxiety. Like the foolish farmer, Qoheleth too had lain awake worried about what to do with his wealth: "What do mortals get from all the toil and strain with which they toil under the sun? . . . Even at night their minds do not rest. This also is vanity" (Eccl. 2:22–23). Sirach too comments on wealth and insomnia: "Wakefulness over wealth wastes away one's flesh, and anxiety about it drives away sleep" (Sir. 31:1). Wealth does more harm than just deprive one of sleep, however; "one who pursues money will be led astray by it" (31:5; cf. 1 Tim. 6:17–19). The closest parallel to our parable is also found in Sirach. After all his labor, the rich man's reward is this: "When he says, 'I have found rest, and now I shall feast on my goods!' he does not know how long it will be until he leaves them to others and dies" (Sir. 11:18–19).

The parable of the Rich Fool, therefore, stands in a deep, sustained biblical tradition. Its immediate context is a question directed to Jesus about the division of a family's inheritance. The Deuteronomic law specified that the elder brother should receive a double portion of the inheritance (Deut. 21:17; cf. Num. 27:1–11; 36:7–9), a stipulation that no doubt often caused discord. In this case, the man's brother refused to give him his due. Moses may have handled such matters, but Jesus refused to do so. Although the man may have had a legitimate case, Jesus challenged the man to free himself from preoccupation with material things. Even if he gained the whole world, he could lose his soul (Luke 9:25).

The opening of the parable establishes the character—a rich man—and the setting; his land (notice, not he) produced abundantly. The next three verses are a soliloquy, reporting the rich man's thoughts (for other soliloquies in Lukan parables see 12:45; 15:17; 16:3–4; 18:4–5; 20:13). Remember, there is nothing secret that will not become known (12:2–3). Notice four things about his thoughts: (1) the number of times "I" appears, (2) the number of times "my" appears, (3) the confident repetition of what he "will" do, and (4) that there is no mention of God. He will prudently do as Joseph did: build barns and store his bountiful harvest for when lean years come (Gen. 41:35–36). He will store "all" his grain and goods, and then he fantasizes a life of ease, eating, drinking, and making merry (Isa. 22:12–14; Tob. 7:10–11; 1 Cor. 15:32). There is no one else in this picture except the rich man and his goods. Immediately, however, God says, "You fool! This night they will demand your soul of you" (my trans.). Luke often emphasizes immediacy, "this day" (4:21; 19:9; 23:43). The probable meaning of the indefinite, "*they* will demand," is that "*I, God,* will demand." Could it be that his very possessions will demand his soul of him? Then whose will they be?

So, what did the rich man do wrong? Is it his preoccupation with possessions? Is it the greed implied by his plan to store "all" his goods? Is it the presumption of self-sufficiency as he muses about what he will do and how he will ensure a life of ease? Is it his vision of a life of eating, drinking, and making merry? Is it his "practical atheism," living as though there were no God, regardless of what he might say he believed?[1]

A preacher should be cautious about using a text as a club with which to beat the congregation. Especially in a materialistic age, when the gap between the very poor and the very rich is widening every day, how can we be faithful to Jesus' teachings on wealth, neither dismissing nor spiritualizing them, neither reading them literally nor assuming they are absolute commands? The challenge to live faithfully in this respect calls us to reexamine continually our lifestyle and financial choices, while participating in caring communities, providing for those in need, and persistently challenging societal

1. See Peter Rhea Jones, *The Teaching of the Parables* (Nashville: Broadman, 1982), 132–33.

structures that penalize the poor. As the psalmist notes, "Let those who are wise give heed to these things, and consider the steadfast love of the LORD" (Ps. 107:43).

R. ALAN CULPEPPER

Commentary 2: Connecting the Reading with the World

The connection of this reading to contemporary Western culture, with its stark warning against the ultimate folly of greed, is not difficult to perceive. Michael Douglas won an Oscar playing Wall Street buccaneer Gordon Gekko, whose signature line is "Greed is good."[2]

We know we ought to be repelled by the character and the sentiment, but surely there is also fascination in our attitude. It is probably why the film was successful. We know that he is only a dramatic example of a widespread reality in our society. This is nothing new. The only difference might be that there now might be less shame about greed than in the past. Whether or not that is the case, the preacher who wants to refer in the sermon to a more recent film will have little difficulty in finding contemporary illustrative material. A consideration of many of our advertisements might be a fruitful source of illustrations.

We cannot contrast the Christian church with wider society in this respect. There is a stream within the North American church that makes acquisition of yet more possessions our chief end, as seems to be declared by the preachers of the prosperity gospel. This passage might not be a favorite text of a prosperity-gospel preacher, but it is interesting to contemplate what would be the theme of a hypothetical sermon on it. Perhaps the message could say, "Jesus wants you to have bigger barns!" Surely those of us who belong to other theological traditions ought not be content with mockery of the prosperity gospel. Laying aside any evidence of greed among our parishioners and congregants, there is no shortage of clergy who appear to have devoted their lives to building bigger barns or at least to building bigger congregations to fill the barns we already have. The Reverend Gordon Gekko dwells in the hearts of many of us. We must recognize this reality, because our passage is what may be called a "bad news" text. A challenge as firm as the one we find here must speak to the preacher before it speaks to the congregation.

The difficulty in preaching this aspect of the text may lie in not allowing the sermon to descend into a harangue. After all, if the connection of the text to the reality of our society is immediately obvious to the preacher, it is probably immediately obvious to most of the congregation as well. This does not mean that we can evade the plain meaning of the text. If Jesus says, "Be on your guard against all kinds of greed," we cannot speak primarily on, for example, the blessings of wealth and the right use of money. We are required to speak about greed. We are not, however, required to rant.

There is another difficulty. The passage ends with the death and judgment of the rich fool, the main character of the parable. At the end of the parable, his life is required of him, a concept that our contemporaries may find difficult to contemplate. We are, in the first place, a death-denying culture. We hide death away in hospital rooms and nursing homes. We refer to death in a bewildering reality of euphemisms, and our funeral practices may even insulate us from the reality of death. "This very night your life is being demanded of you" is language that is both strange and unwelcome in our ears. However, our listeners are not fools; somewhere inside they do know that all our attempts to deny death are futile. The church may be one place we can speak of the reality of death. If preachers will not say that death cannot be evaded, who will? "Remember that you are dust, and to dust you shall return" (*Book of Common Prayer*) is not a truth for one day in the year (Ash Wednesday) only.

2. Michael Douglas, *Wall Street*, directed by Oliver Stone (Century City, CA: 20th Century Fox, 1987).

The concept of a final judgment may be even more foreign to our ears, however. It rarely seems to be spoken of except in jokes (googling "St. Peter at the gates jokes" produced no fewer than 652,000 hits). It may be, however, that listeners will be able to hear about a final evaluation of their own lives. They may, for example, be able to hear the word of a veteran chaplain who said, "I've sat by hundreds of deathbeds, and I have never heard even one person say, 'I wish I had spent more time at the office.'" Spending "more time at the office" might be a contemporary way of saying spending "more time building bigger barns." It should not be pretended that this self-review is the same as God's judgment, but perhaps it is close enough for homiletical purposes. Perhaps those who are in danger of turning themselves into rich fools will be able to hear it. Even if they do not welcome hearing it, they will have difficulty denying its reality. Perhaps at some future point they may come to understand that they will answer not just to their better self but to their God.

The passage is not merely a warning against greed. There is a positive aspect to the parable as well. It is possible to build not barns but a treasure in heaven. It is possible to be "rich toward God." Getting at this is also homiletically difficult. Perhaps it would be possible to speak hypothetically of our own funerals. What do we hope they will say of us when it comes to the eulogy? Surely, not just that we built for ourselves many barns! It would be sad indeed to hear some version of "She sure spent a lot of time at the office." There are other things, more important things, that we would like to have said about us. Many of those other things will have to do with the people we have loved and, for a Christian, for the God we have loved and who first loved us. That might be the sign of a person who is rich toward God.

All this may also say something about the church. When the church is a sign of the kingdom, it will build not barns but a community with a different orientation than acquisition. It will be a community with a kingdom orientation.

There is a connection with two other texts in the lectionary. Psalm 49 picks up the idea of the inevitability of death and speaks of "those who trust in their wealth and boast of the abundance of their riches." It even uses the epithet "fool" about those who, like the wise, are sure to die. Colossians 3 tells us, "Set your minds on things that are above, not on things that are on earth," which is surely not distant from the word of Jesus in Luke 12. The verse continues, "for you have died, and your life is hidden with Christ in God." This verse will be helpful to preachers who, rightly, want to end with gospel rather than law. The reason it is possible to be rich toward God and to set our minds on things that are above is that our old self has already died. In the eyes of God, we have already passed through the death experience that overthrows the rich fool. What we have been has already passed away, and God looks not at the fool who has died in us but the new life we are granted in Jesus Christ. Now, the preacher may say, "Live as if that were the most true thing about you."

STEPHEN FARRIS

Proper 14 (Sunday between August 7 and August 13 Inclusive)

Isaiah 1:1, 10–20 and Genesis 15:1–6
Psalm 50:1–8, 22–23 and Psalm 33:12–22
Hebrews 11:1–3, 8–16
Luke 12:32–40

Isaiah 1:1, 10–20

[1]The vision of Isaiah son of Amoz, which he saw concerning Judah and Jerusalem in the days of Uzziah, Jotham, Ahaz, and Hezekiah, kings of Judah. . . .

[10]Hear the word of the LORD,
you rulers of Sodom!
Listen to the teaching of our God,
you people of Gomorrah!
[11]What to me is the multitude of your sacrifices?
says the LORD;
I have had enough of burnt offerings of rams
and the fat of fed beasts;
I do not delight in the blood of bulls,
or of lambs, or of goats.

[12]When you come to appear before me,
who asked this from your hand?
Trample my courts no more;
[13]bringing offerings is futile;
incense is an abomination to me.
New moon and sabbath and calling of convocation—
I cannot endure solemn assemblies with iniquity.
[14]Your new moons and your appointed festivals
my soul hates;
they have become a burden to me,
I am weary of bearing them.
[15]When you stretch out your hands,
I will hide my eyes from you;
even though you make many prayers,
I will not listen;
your hands are full of blood.
[16]Wash yourselves; make yourselves clean;
remove the evil of your doings
from before my eyes;
cease to do evil,
[17]learn to do good;
seek justice,
rescue the oppressed,
defend the orphan,
plead for the widow.

[18]Come now, let us argue it out,
says the LORD:
though your sins are like scarlet,
they shall be like snow;
though they are red like crimson,
they shall become like wool.
[19]If you are willing and obedient,
you shall eat the good of the land;
[20]but if you refuse and rebel,
you shall be devoured by the sword;
for the mouth of the LORD has spoken.

Genesis 15:1–6

[1]After these things the word of the LORD came to Abram in a vision, "Do not be afraid, Abram, I am your shield; your reward shall be very great." [2]But Abram said, "O Lord GOD, what will you give me, for I continue childless, and the heir of my house is Eliezer of Damascus?" [3]And Abram said, "You have given me no offspring, and so a slave born in my house is to be my heir." [4]But the word of the LORD came to him, "This man shall not be your heir; no one but your very own issue shall be your heir." [5]He brought him outside and said, "Look toward heaven and count the stars, if you are able to count them." Then he said to him, "So shall your descendants be." [6]And he believed the LORD; and the LORD reckoned it to him as righteousness.

Commentary 1: Connecting the Reading with Scripture

The lection from Isaiah continues the semicontinuous reading of the prophets, but whereas Hosea (Propers 12 and 13) focused on the northern nation (Israel), Isaiah focuses on the southern nation (Judah). The messages of these two prophets are similar. Genesis 15 is paired with Luke 12:32–40, instructions on how to live while awaiting the second coming.

Isaiah 1:1, 10–20. Isaiah 1:1 is a superscription, typical of prophetic writings, establishing the authority of the book (a vision), and identifying the historical setting of the original Isaiah (742–701 BCE). However, the book of Isaiah is likely made up of three parts (Isa. 1–39; Isa. 40–55; Isa. 56–66) composed at different times to different situations (threat from Assyria, Babylonian exile, colony of Persia). The editors of the book of Isaiah placed 1:2–20 at the beginning of the sixty-six chapters as a theological lens through which to interpret the rest of the book.

Isaiah 1:2–20 is in the genre of a *riv* (pronounced "reeve"), a covenant lawsuit. In the presence of witnesses, one party brings an indictment against another party for failing the terms of a covenant and invokes the consequences for the failure. The witnesses here are nothing less than the heavens and the earth: they verify what God says (v. 2a). Taking a cue from this genre, the preacher might set up the sermon as a lawsuit either following the *riv* or adopting a contemporary legal format.

The indictment is that despite God's faithful parenting, Judah has rebelled. The community has forsaken their promises in covenant (vv. 2b–3). The prophet does not specify their violations here, but does so in 1:10–17. The people have persisted in disobedience, and have suffered as a consequence; they are bleeding and sore (v. 6), desolate, and aliens have overcome the land (v. 7). Yet God did not *destroy* the community. Indeed, the community survived only because of divine faithfulness (v. 9). Because the community has survived, it can make the choice set out in Isaiah 1:19–20.

God reveals the underlying problem in verses 10–17: The people violated basic ethical responsibilities for living in covenant, yet sought God's providence through worship. In the Priestly theology of Isaiah, worship is supposed to represent the authentic situation of the people. Verse 17 implies that, day to day, the community practiced evil, lived unjustly, engaged in oppression, and neglected orphans and widows, and then came to worship without a sincere intention to repent and live in covenantal well-being for all. The Priestly God does not object to worship as such. God objects to worship that is not rooted in authentic desire to honor God's purposes by living in mutual support.

When God says, "Come now, let us argue it out" (v. 18), the invitation is not simply to engage in legal give-and-take (in which each side makes its case in court, and rebuts the other), but to engage in critical theological reflection on their situation, and to choose a way forward. By not destroying them (v. 9), God has left the community with the potential to choose a path that can lead to continued curse or one that leads to restoration and blessing (v. 19).

Many congregations—and many wider communities in North America—are in circumstances similar to that of the congregation to which Isaiah directed this prophecy. Such groups often leave behind attitudes and behaviors necessary for the inclusive well-being of covenantal community and, instead, participate in exploitation and repression while engaging in ecclesial and civil rites that assume that God condones and even empowers such repressive behavior. The preacher could help the congregation to consider the distance between covenantal vision and actual circumstances and to posit corrective repentance. For example, many churches bless uncritical nationalism, "America First," even when doing so harms the quality of life of people in other lands, and when doing so will eventually harm the quality of life in the United States. The sermon can name such violation and point the way toward repentance that seeks inclusive well-being for all.

Given the popularity of programs on television that feature courtroom scenes, and the high profile of legal matters in our society, the preacher might cast the sermon in the form of a case for the prosecution. Indeed, the preacher might follow the lawsuit pattern of the text as a structure for a sermon: witnesses, indictment, reasons for the indictment, possible consequences, and urging the congregation toward a verdict in behalf of liberty and justice for all.

Genesis 15:1–6. Although the lectionary appoints only Genesis 15:1–6, the promise of descendants to Sarai and Abram, that story requires Genesis 15:7–11 to capture the fuller meaning. The promise to the couple includes both children as numerous as the stars, "a great nation" (Gen. 12:2a), and the land.

The Priestly editors gave the story its purpose in Genesis in connection with the exile. Defeated by the Babylonians and carried into exile, the exilic community (many of the leaders of Judah) no longer perceived themselves as a great nation. Moreover, they no longer possessed their land, much of which the Babylonians had devastated. The exilic community was in danger of losing confidence in the promises and power of God, of abandoning the faithful life, and, consequently, of turning from the pathway that could lead to restoration and blessing.

A purpose of Genesis 15:1–11 was to offer hope to the exilic community by reminding them that God made the promises of descendants and land to the ancestral couple at a time when the fulfillment of those promises seemed unlikely. God proved powerful and faithful by leading Sarai to give birth to Isaac and by settling their posterity in the promised land.

Isaiah 1:2–20, discussed above, is helpful here as Isaiah interprets divine punishment, such as exile, not as an end but as a means. God intended the exile to prompt the community to repent of idolatry, injustice, and false alliances. After repentance, the way would then be open to restoration. Since God kept the divine promise in the improbable circumstances of Sarai and Abraham, God can do it again.

Many congregations in historic denominations today are in diminishing circumstances and feel exiled. They are in danger of losing confidence in their ability to witness effectively. This text reminds them that God is faithful; blessing is possible, even in circumstances that seem unlikely. During a cold winter, for instance, a struggling urban congregation might take the minimal step of opening its social hall to the homeless at night, and come to think, "If we can do this, we can do something else."

The apparent reason for pairing the reading from Genesis with Luke 12:32–40 seems to be themes of promise, motivation, and assurance. For Luke, God's promises to Sarai and Abram were coming to final fruition through Jesus: the embodiment of the realm of God, the Gentile mission (the great reunion of the human family), and the second coming. Like the people in exile, the congregation to whom Luke wrote experienced disappointment (the failure of Jesus' return). Some were drifting away from faithful witness, and needed motivation. Luke 12:32–40 assures Jesus' followers that, despite its delay, the second coming is ahead, and listeners need to "be ready" by actively witnessing, especially by putting their material resource at the service of the community, especially the needy. Of course, the preacher who goes this route should take care not to portray the Jewish people, institutions, or Scriptures as second-class, or as superseded by Jesus and the church.

RONALD J. ALLEN

What God Has Is Given to Us

Let us offer our complete faith, our devout minds, our obedience, and our continual labors to the Lord that he may be pleased with us. Let us give earthly garments to Christ so that we receive heavenly robes; let us share food and drink in this world so that we may join Abraham, Isaac, and Jacob at the heavenly banquet. . . .

We need to remember what the lives of the first believers were like at the time of the apostles. They were filled with great virtues and burned with the warmth for their new faith. They sold their houses and farms and gladly gave all they had to the apostles for distribution to the poor. By freeing themselves and selling their earthly possessions, they transferred their title to the eternal land and its fruits, homes that would be theirs for eternity. This was the reward for their many good works and their unity in love. . . . Whatever God has is given to us to use, and no person is denied the opportunity to receive God's blessings and gifts. The light of day, the radiance of the sun, the rain, and the wind are given to all. Everyone shares the same sleep and the beauty of the moon and the stars. In the same spirit of equality we on earth share our possessions freely and justly with the community in imitation of God the Father.

Cyprian of Carthage (d. 258), "On the Lapsed," in *Wealth and Power in Early Christianity*, ed. Helen Rhee (Minneapolis: Fortress, 2017), 47–48.

Commentary 2: Connecting the Reading with the World

For several years, a bumper sticker appeared on the vehicles of Christians that read, "Christians are not perfect, just forgiven." Whatever its original intent, this earthy theology might invite the possibility that Christianity offers absolution from sin but has no interest in a cure. Against this ever-present danger of enervating faith, Isaiah rails on behalf of God.

Though few church leaders intend to foster it, an attitude still exists in much of the church that faith guarantees freedom from the guilt of sin without any real expectation that righteousness will be established in us or in the world. This view holds that justice is certainly the aim of the divine historical agenda, but the church does not participate in this redemption. Isaiah's bold poetry against this attitude warns the community of faith not to become a "whitewashed tomb" (see Jesus' words in Matt. 23:27–28). Though Christians must weekly accept the freedom of God's forgiveness from inevitable wrongdoing, we must never expect that acts of atonement—prayers of confession, "sinner's prayers," sacrificial offerings, and so on—can cover over the willful neglect of justice.

Thus, in the liturgy of our worship—whether we use a high or low liturgical form—we must encounter an invitation both to embrace forgiveness and also to follow the divine summons toward greater good. The work of the Holy Spirit accomplishes both ends. The church that goes out from worship emerges not only relieved of sin but also empowered to do the work of justice.

Lest we be tempted to reframe the term "justice" in overspiritualized terms, Isaiah points specifically to the oppressed, the orphan, and the widow. These are not metaphorical or spiritual categories but real groups of people. Because Isaiah includes the poor so often in the rest of the book, we may include them in this survey of those needing justice (see 3:14–15; 10:1–2, among others). As urgent as the need is for Christians to present the good news of Jesus Christ to a world in spiritual darkness, the physical and practical needs of those against whom the sociopolitical deck is stacked call for compassion from the body of Christ.

We must not define the beneficiaries of mercy too narrowly. Though Isaiah may have originally aimed his admonitions at the internal society of Israel, both the expanding scope of the whole book and the fuller context of the Bible indicate that the church must labor for good and justice everywhere (see, e.g., Isa. 60:1–2 and Acts 1:8). The work of redemption, crystallizing in the resurrection, moves outward to encompass all aspects of life, relationships, and society.

Our generation still needs the summons of Isaiah. Too many still need to be rescued from the oppression of racism. The depraved continuation of human trafficking cries out for justice. Refugee crises present new opportunities for the church to pursue good in a world haunted by evil. Violence, disease, and the affluents' abdication of responsibility present an ongoing stream of orphans. Though widows in our American society are not legally powerless, race, poverty, and disability nonetheless regularly place persons in situations of helplessness to which the church must respond. We seek justice in personal relationships, in financial support of assistance programs, and in community action. All three possibilities lay before the congregation that desires not a weekly opiate but the daily bread of Christlike living.

When individuals and congregations heed Isaiah's call to the work of justice—a call echoed by Christ (see Matt. 23:23–24)—then they receive a double promise. Those who do good and seek justice will have both absolution from sin and the bounty of the land. When the call to do justice sounds clearly in the context of worship, the world will truly receive the fullness of the good news.

The reading from Genesis reminds us that trust is a crucial ingredient of life with God. God calls Abraham to trust a seemingly impossible promise. As Paul argues in Romans 4, this capacity to trust God is the singular mark of membership in the family of God.

The family of God trusts in God's ability to fulfill promises, especially promises that elude reason or common experience. Personal authorship of the cosmos, resurrection from the dead, and a just culmination of human history all elude scientific scrutiny and the rigors of reason. Yet these things provide the foundation for our hope and are the core of the good news of Jesus Christ.

Therefore, declarations of faith occupy an essential place in our liturgy and worship. Many Christian traditions include times of reciting the Apostles' Creed or the Nicene Creed. Other traditions encourage times for congregants—through verbal affirmation or embodied signs like approaching the front of the worship space—to voice and embody their trust in God. These means of showing faith anchor us again on the bedrock of the church: God's righteousness to us through Christ.

On the one hand, righteousness is *right standing* with God. Faith confirms for us that we are forever part of the family of God and heirs to the kingdom. Here is an antidote for the anxieties of a culture that believes productivity and acquisition of knowledge determine our value. Here is rest for the soul plagued by data-driven metrics of human worth. Believe in the God who gifts us with an eternal significance granted in Christ. On the other hand, righteousness is also *right conduct.* Faith serves as the font from which the work of the Spirit springs forth. If the church desires to do good and enact justice, it convenes every week to connect with the source of all good and the motivation for all justice: a trustworthy God. Faith will bring about powerful works of good for the world, not because of faith's intrinsic power, but because God is powerful enough and good enough to do it through those who believe.

In a season of world history dominated by nations and nationalism, God's promise to Abraham encourages us to appreciate the global presence and effect of the family of Abraham. This text reinforces the divine word in Genesis 12:2–3 that the descendants of Abraham would bless "all the families of the earth." All those holding faith in the God of Abraham, whether through Moses or Jesus Christ, are spiritual offspring of Abraham and Sarah. Reform Jewish synagogues and temples, Chinese house churches, Orthodox Jewish families in New York, Roman Catholic parishes in Peru, Syrian Christian dioceses—they all manifest the uncountable legacy Abraham was asked to imagine in the starry sky. As the church enacts liturgy, authors confessions, and engages in missions, it does well to unite with sisters and cousins on every continent. Doing so gives glory to the God who took the household of a single shepherd thousands of years ago and brought forth a people that continues to shape history with grace and mercy. It strengthens our affirmation that Christ has called us to be one in faith (see John 17:20–23).

This lectionary pairing of Abraham and Isaiah offers a homiletical opportunity to reflect on the complementary realities that we are saved by grace through faith and not by works (Eph. 2:8–9) and at the same time that "faith without works is dead" (Jas. 2:17). The church needs reminders of the relationship between faith and works so that we avoid the anemic poles of reductionist behavioralism and pietistic disengagement. Every generation of the church must receive both the tools of right conduct in the world and the relationship of trust that gives those tools power.

EMRYS TYLER

Psalm 50:1–8, 22–23

[1]The mighty one, God the LORD,
speaks and summons the earth
from the rising of the sun to its setting.
[2]Out of Zion, the perfection of beauty,
God shines forth.

[3]Our God comes and does not keep silence,
before him is a devouring fire,
and a mighty tempest all around him.
[4]He calls to the heavens above
and to the earth, that he may judge his people:
[5]"Gather to me my faithful ones,
who made a covenant with me by sacrifice!"
[6]The heavens declare his righteousness,
for God himself is judge.

[7]"Hear, O my people, and I will speak,
O Israel, I will testify against you.
I am God, your God.
[8]Not for your sacrifices do I rebuke you;
your burnt offerings are continually before me.
. . . .
[22]"Mark this, then, you who forget God,
or I will tear you apart, and there will be no one to deliver.
[23]Those who bring thanksgiving as their sacrifice honor me;
to those who go the right way
I will show the salvation of God."

Psalm 33:12–22

[12]Happy is the nation whose God is the LORD,
the people whom he has chosen as his heritage.

[13]The LORD looks down from heaven;
he sees all humankind.
[14]From where he sits enthroned he watches
all the inhabitants of the earth—
[15]he who fashions the hearts of them all,
and observes all their deeds.
[16]A king is not saved by his great army;
a warrior is not delivered by his great strength.
[17]The war horse is a vain hope for victory,
and by its great might it cannot save.

[18]Truly the eye of the LORD is on those who fear him,
on those who hope in his steadfast love,
[19]to deliver their soul from death,
and to keep them alive in famine.

[20]Our soul waits for the LORD;
he is our help and shield.
[21]Our heart is glad in him,
because we trust in his holy name.
[22]Let your steadfast love, O LORD, be upon us,
even as we hope in you.

Connecting the Psalm with Scripture and Worship

Psalm 50 describes a shining, burning, storming God who summons Israel to court, enlisting the heavens and the earth to join the cause. For most of the psalm, it is God who does the talking, addressing "the faithful," the ones who dutifully perform the rituals of sacrifice. They are not the people they appear to be, if the psalm is to be believed. God demands a hearing and then offers testimony, but not without an important declaration: I am God, *your* God. This is personal.

What crime have these "faithful" committed? It is not the fact that they worship as instructed, make the sacrifices, burn the offerings, but that they do these (good) things as if God were not *God.* Though the lectionary omits much of the indictment, the missing verses are worth keeping in mind. On the one hand, the people make these sacrifices as if they were doing God a favor, as if God had a hunger only their charred goat could fill, as if every single thing that is—from atoms to galaxies—did not belong to God already. On the other hand, God tells "the wicked" (are they the same as "the faithful"?) that they have no right to recite God's law, no right to take holy words on their lips, since they speak evil the rest of the time.

The final cadences of the psalm could give a hearer whiplash. Pay attention to this rebuke, says the psalmist, "or I will tear you apart" (Ps. 50:22). However, there at the very end comes a more promising alternative: bring *thanksgiving* as your sacrifice, go the right way, and "I will show the salvation of God" (v. 23).

Isaiah's indictment of Israel in chapter 1 also expresses God's intolerance of hypocrites at prayer. There is again the rejection of excessive sacrifice done for all the wrong reasons, the outrage over the liturgical use of bodies that the rest of the time have been engaged in all the wrong things. In Psalm 50, it was mouths that spewed hate speech; in Isaiah 1 it is hands dripping with blood. There is hope that hands can be washed clean and predatory lives transformed, but only if there is a desire to be changed. The psalmist's word for that desire might be thanksgiving. In either case, destruction awaits those who say, "No, thank you." Isaiah, like the psalmist, is convinced of that.

Taken together, these texts comprise a fairly comprehensive jeremiad on the nature of liturgical evil. There used to be much talk about the "worship wars" in the American church, but the real worship war is one that only God can declare. These are serious matters: the relationship between what we do as a gathered community in the presence of God and what we are doing the rest of our lives—no less in the presence of God. The wise preacher will not shy away from the passion that roars from these two witnesses, nor make all of this simply a matter of feeling the right pious feelings. One of the most gripping things about both of these texts is their fleshiness: it is people with bodies who worship, and people with bodies who tell lies and oppress.

The liturgy for the day might acknowledge this reality. Perhaps the prayer of confession names particular parts of the body: eyes blind to the suffering of others, or mouths that voice half-truths. In some settings the confession-forgiveness sequence might include the washing of hands at basins placed around the worship space. Since thanksgiving is the "right way" to worship according to the psalmist, the service might end with a prayer or song of thanksgiving as well.

The psalm appointed for the alternate set of texts, Psalm 33, is about the way God's steadfast love fills the whole world and finds its way to everybody in it. Given that backdrop, dropping in on the action in verse 12 is particularly perilous. A search in Google Images for "Happy is the nation whose God is the Lord" produces hundreds of results, many with verse 12b in the foreground and an American flag waving away in the background. "We need to become one nation under God again," some of the posters say, citing this slogan from Psalm 33, the phrase reduced to a call to action. The psalm. however, is not about human action at all. It is about God's creation and sustenance of the world, and the way God is at work to bring all of it to a good and righteous end. God is our witness, paying attention to every detail. God is the one who chooses the part each nation and person will play in the drama of steadfast love; in contrast to the precariousness of the best-laid plans of human beings, God sees everything and God's "counsel" is forever (Ps. 33:11). It is hardly surprising that we still believe protection comes from the stockpiling of weapons, formed as we are in a violent world; but the psalmist sees beyond the realpolitik of the fearful to the God who can deliver in ultimate, unimaginable ways. God is the only "shield" we need (v. 20). The final cadence of the excerpt (v. 22) is a corporate prayer for God's *hesed* to continue ("let your steadfast love . . . be upon us") and an affirmation of present faith ("even as we hope in you").

Abram's encounter with God in the beginning of Genesis 15 also has to do with the difference it makes to see things through God's wide-angle lens. God appears with a message of encouragement: Do not be afraid, I am your shield (Gen. 15:1). As in Psalm 33, God promises protection, but what sort of protection does Abram need? The nature of his anxiety becomes clear in his complaint: what good is God's reward (v. 1) if he has no child of his own to inherit it (v. 2)? Abram needs protection from oblivion, from the disappearance of his family from the face of the earth.

God responds to Abram's lament by taking him stargazing. "How many do you see?" God asks. Is it the experience of trying and then losing count of those distant suns that changes Abram's mind? Did it remind Abram of the vastness of the universe and the power of the God who dreamed it into being in the first place? The text does not tell us. Psalm 33 can be a useful resource for a preacher in considering why God might have approached Abram in this way. When it is hard to see God at work close by, a preacher might invite hearers to contemplate, even calculate, the magnitude of God's industry in this world: in grains of sand, drops of water, types of beetles and atoms and galaxies, the varieties of human beings and nations and cultures, or the hairs on their very own heads. Psalm 33 sings out that all of this came to be and that all of it is, somehow, related to the steadfast love of the Lord, which fills up everything and will prevail.

When Psalm 33 is read in the course of the liturgy, it is helpful to provide some context before the reading, summarizing the emphases of the first eleven verses. Better yet, read the whole thing. There are some musical settings of the psalm that avoid featuring the misunderstood "Happy is the nation" of verse 12 as the sung or spoken refrain. Verse 22 of Psalm 33 also makes a lovely congregational response for the prayers of the people: "Let your steadfast love, O Lord, be upon us, even as we hope in you."

ANGELA DIENHART HANCOCK

Hebrews 11:1–3, 8–16

[1]Now faith is the assurance of things hoped for, the conviction of things not seen. [2]Indeed, by faith our ancestors received approval. [3]By faith we understand that the worlds were prepared by the word of God, so that what is seen was made from things that are not visible. . . .

[8]By faith Abraham obeyed when he was called to set out for a place that he was to receive as an inheritance; and he set out, not knowing where he was going. [9]By faith he stayed for a time in the land he had been promised, as in a foreign land, living in tents, as did Isaac and Jacob, who were heirs with him of the same promise. [10]For he looked forward to the city that has foundations, whose architect and builder is God. [11]By faith he received power of procreation, even though he was too old—and Sarah herself was barren—because he considered him faithful who had promised. [12]Therefore from one person, and this one as good as dead, descendants were born, "as many as the stars of heaven and as the innumerable grains of sand by the seashore."

[13]All of these died in faith without having received the promises, but from a distance they saw and greeted them. They confessed that they were strangers and foreigners on the earth, [14]for people who speak in this way make it clear that they are seeking a homeland. [15]If they had been thinking of the land that they had left behind, they would have had opportunity to return. [16]But as it is, they desire a better country, that is, a heavenly one. Therefore God is not ashamed to be called their God; indeed, he has prepared a city for them.

Commentary 1: Connecting the Reading with Scripture

Abram and faith are tied so closely in the Bible that it is difficult to think of one without the other. YHWH invited Abram to look into the skies and count the stars to illustrate how numerous his descendants would be. Then, the Bible records, "And he believed the Lord; and the Lord reckoned it to him as righteousness" (Gen. 15:6). This is the beginning of Abram's and Israel's faith journey. It is also the narrative where the apostle Paul anchored his belief in justification *by faith* apart from the works of the law (Gal. 3:6–14). Abram, who is renamed Abraham to anticipate that he will be a "father of many nations" (Gen. 17:5), becomes the model of faith for Paul: his faith disallows boasting (Rom. 4:2), his faith precedes circumcision and diminishes its necessity for salvation (4:9), his faith is independent of Torah observance (4:13), his faith shows the priority of grace (4:16), his faith creates the seed of faith that defines Israel (9:7), and, most especially, Abram shows that justification is by faith through God's promise and grace (Gal. 3:6–9, 14, 18). Paul understands Abraham's faith as a settled relationship with God.

The biblical story of faith is at work in other places in the NT besides Paul's letters, including the famous and seemingly counter-Pauline statement that faith *without works* is dead, which we read in James 2:14–26. The "roll call" of the faithful in Hebrews 11 celebrates faith the way 1 Corinthians 13 celebrates love. Hebrews 11 follows on the heels of a severe warning passage (Heb. 10:19–39), which is connected to other such passages in the book (2:1–4; 3:7–4:13; 5:11–6:12; 12:1–29). These are the negative counterparts to the positive description of faith in chapter 11. For those most fearful of the warning texts, the words and tone of Hebrews 11 can become a source of comfort and hope, even as those most lax in their faith might need the stiff reminders of the warnings.

What is *faith,* then? Genuine faith is made up of various dimensions. Faith is an act of cognition: the "faith" we believe to be true. Faith is an act of volition: faith as an act of "trust." Faith is also "fidelity." One does not choose which of these one prefers, for each of these is enfolded into the others as we can see in Hebrews 11:1–3, where the emphasis is on faith as an act of trust as well as belief in the future kingdom of God (11:1). Faith gives one eyes to see what might not be immediately visible (v. 3) and, as this chapter unfolds, we see "faithfulness" or "fidelity" as central to what faith means. In the Bible's story line, Hebrews teaches, those with faith stand above the others. Hence, in chapter 11 we see a litany of names moving from Abel to Samuel and the prophets. Without names, we hear of "women" (v. 35) and an assortment of others (vv. 35b–38). Each of these died before receiving "what was promised." This promise most likely refers to the fulfillment of the promises in Christ and the church, all leading to the heavenly Jerusalem (11:39–40; 12:22–24).

For Hebrews, then, living faithfully before God now entails looking to the fullness of God's kingdom in the future. Those who have faith now live with their eyes on the future kingdom, not by way of diminishing human and social realities in the present, but by seeing through today's realities to deeper and more lasting realities. That future gives perspective on how to live now. Hebrews produces a virtual phenomenology of faith when the writer says that those who live by faith are those who let their future determine their present (11:13–16). This is how he or she also understands Abraham's near-sacrifice of Isaac in Genesis 22. Though there is not a word of this in Genesis, Hebrews perceives that Abraham—since he trusted in God and God's future—believed God could raise Isaac from the dead if God needed to do so (11:17–19).

A theme arises to the surface with power in Hebrews 11, namely, faith as fidelity or allegiance to God. While faith requires some level of cognitive assent, faith in chapter 11 is about life expressing faith, a whole life and not just the simple act of volitional trust in Christ. In a most non-Pauline (though not anti-Pauline) fashion, the author does not focus so much on Abraham's faith in Genesis 15:6 but on the various acts of faith in and allegiance to YHWH throughout his life. Thus, faith means that Abraham "obeyed" (v. 8), "stayed" (v. 9), "received power of procreation" (v. 11), and "offered up" (v. 17), because he "considered the fact that God is able even to raise someone from the dead" (v. 19). These moments illustrate the theme of this chapter that faith is an *act* of trust that leads to a *life* of trust. Sometimes a one-sided focus on Galatians and Romans can lead to a one-sided emphasis on faith as *trust*; but the discipleship teachings of Jesus to follow him in obedience, the stunning formulas of James 2:14–26, and the importance of ongoing walking in the light in the Johannine letters remind us that faith in the Bible is multifaceted and entails fidelity to God. Faith leads into acts of faithfulness, or it is not genuine faith.

Faithfulness at times turns the people of God into a minority, but God knows the remnant, whoever or wherever they might be, and God has observed their faithfulness and will restore them to their former days (Isa. 11:1, 10–20). Redemption includes judgment against evil, the disestablishment of injustice, and the establishment of God's kingdom. It is not then surprising to read warnings in the Bible against sinfulness and evil, for they must end in God's judgment and redemption (Ps. 50:5, 8, 22–23). Just as Hebrews exhorts us to faithfulness and praises the faithful heroes of the past, so too Jesus summons fellow Israelites to a radical discipleship, including generosity with possessions (Luke 12:32–33). Just like the teaching of Christian faithfulness in Hebrews 11, so Jesus wants his followers to imagine a world in which God approves of God's servants who are faithful, that is, those servants who are found watching and waiting for the return of the master (Luke 12:35–40).

This emphasis on faith as faithfulness makes most sense in the Bible when we recognize the connection God makes with humans in terms of a covenant. The standard formula for the covenant is that God will be our God, and we will be God's people (Gen. 17:7–8; Exod. 6:7; 15:26; Lev. 26:12; cf. Ruth 1:16; Isa. 45:3; Jer. 7:23; 11:4; 30:22; Ezek. 36:28). Both sides of the formula matter; the divine initiative of grace and love, as well as the covenant formation, commitment, and inclusion, requires the response of trust and trust as obedience, which is faithfulness. To be in the covenant by God's grace is to be covenanted to God, to trust God, and to be faithful to God.

We learn about fidelity in our closest relationships as well as in our work spaces. We learn too about fidelity in our choices to stick it out in a local church, in a soup kitchen, or in our theological convictions. We learn through fidelity that the other side of fidelity clarifies or at least shoulders doubts about carrying on, and we learn the need to press on in the Christian faith because it is as the end of our life that our story is written. For Hebrews, no word captures a biography more than "faithful."

SCOT MCKNIGHT

Commentary 2: Connecting the Reading with the World

Those preparing sermons on Hebrews 11 may find themselves nodding along in agreement with the powerful message about the fundamental significance of faith for the people of God. The language of faith permeates Christian discourse, and we often divide people into categories based on whether they are "believers," whether they have "faith." The preacher of this text might want to reflect on what faith is, exactly. Possibilities abound. Is faith a great leap into the unknown, a commitment to something that has no empirical proof or justification? Is it opposed to reason, science, and what we know, based on our own life experiences? Are those who have faith in God no different from the gullible characters we see getting fleeced of their money by the faith healer Jonas Nightengale, played by Steve Martin, in the film *Leap of Faith*?

One approach to this text might emphasize that faith is a nonnegotiable disposition that characterizes the people of God. In this view, while faith is not opposed to rationality and experience, the author is clear that faith in God is possible only for those who believe that our world is sustained by and infused with the very presence of God. In other words, it is by faith that we believe that what we see and experience in our world is rooted in God's creation. That is to say, it is by faith that we understand "that what is seen was made from things that are not visible" (Heb. 11:3b). Faith is the settled conviction that the unseen God is real, and that while God remains hidden from our sight and our touch, this God continues to uphold this world and to commune with God's people. The author of Hebrews, at least, does not seem to think of faith as a great leap into irrationality, for he speaks of his congregation's faith as a pledge or down payment on future realities. In other words, there is a strong overlap between faith and hope.

We know that God's promises and existence do not always seem believable. All who trust in God experience seasons of doubt. All believers will nonetheless question either the reality of God or the presence of God in the world. We may question and doubt the reality of God in times of apathy, in seasons of trials and sufferings, and in moments when the presence of evil and pain in our world overwhelms us. Our author pleads with his audience to maintain their faith in God, to endure in fidelity to God amid their own sufferings and apathy, and to renew their hope in the promises of God (Heb. 10:35–39). Chapter 11 contains the author's homiletical attempt to convince, encourage, and exhort his audience that they are not alone in their attempts to believe and obey the unseen God. What can we learn about our own struggle to believe and act on the basis of an unseen God?

First, while God is unseen, we believe that God speaks. The author of Hebrews begins his sermon with a claim that God has spoken to God's people in many times and in many ways, but now God has spoken through God's Son (1:1–2a). We are those who believe that the world we inhabit was not self-generated but originates in the will and purposes of God. Neither Hebrews nor Genesis tells us *how* or even *when* the world came into existence, but we are told that our world was established by the communicative expression of God. It is "by faith that we understand the universe was created by the word of God" (11:3a, my trans.). I should hasten to emphasize here that faith does not encourage any kind of opposition to scientific exploration of the origins of our universe, but it does require a belief that God is ultimately the creator and sustainer of the world in which we live.

God not only creates the world through God's word; God also enters into relationships with people through the same word. God *calls* Abraham to a new land, and Abraham faithfully responds to God because he trusts in God's *promise* (11:8–9). Sarah trusts God's *promise* that she will have a son (11:11). Faith, then, is not a great leap into irrationality, precisely because it is rooted in the spoken word of God and God's promises to God's people. It is impossible here to ignore the author's earlier statement about the word of God as something that is living, active, and able to penetrate the human soul and spirit (4:12). When we orient ourselves to God's spoken word in the Scriptures, the message of the gospel of Jesus Christ, the proclaimed word in our congregations, and the manifold ways that God continues to speak in the lives of God's people, we are not acting irrationally or foolishly. Instead, we are orienting ourselves to what is truly real, even if it cannot be empirically proved or justified.

Second, we also learn that faith is oriented to God's promise to give resurrection life to God's people. The faith to which Hebrews points is not a mere belief that God is going to reward God's people with worldly status, economic and material prosperity, or freedom from hardship and suffering. In fact, we are reminded that God's own Son "learned obedience through what he suffered" (5:8b). God's Son was not spared from the experience of crying and groaning out to God in the midst of his own trials (5:7). In fact, we are reminded of the great shame and humiliation he experienced on the cross (12:2). That is, Hebrews consistently portrays faith as a hope that is directed toward the future. Abraham and Sarah believed in the God who could give life out of death, in the God who had provided a heavenly city for them. Likewise, Jesus fixed his eyes not on the shame of the cross but, rather, upon the joyful reward of sitting at the right hand of God's throne (12:2). Abraham, Sarah, and Jesus provide us with models that beckon us to trust in God's promise to conquer death and our fear of it (cf. 2:14–15) and that we will, like Jesus (5:7–9; 12:1–2), celebrate a joyous festival in the heavenly Jerusalem where our sufferings, fears, and doubts will have given way to a perfected existence (12:22–23).

Third, our faith in the unseen God who speaks and promises is validated, if not empirically proved, through models and exemplars. Chapter 11 is almost an attempt to overwhelm us with the quality of life that stems from an orientation of faith in the living God. We can continue to find personal models of faith that nourish us and call us forward in our own lives of faith. Perhaps we are encouraged by the heroic faith of someone like a Martin Luther King Jr. He trusted that God was on the side of justice and that the God of the Scriptures cared for the poor, the oppressed, and the marginalized. It is this faith that enabled him to live a life that resulted in martyrdom. Perhaps the model of faith is found in the quiet disposition of an elderly grandparent who faithfully cares for a dying spouse, who generously gives away resources for the good of others, and who quietly volunteers to serve church and community with little recognition. Perhaps it is the very diversity and plurality of these models of faith that is the greatest testimony to us that "faith is the conviction of things not seen" (11:1).

JOSHUA W. JIPP

Luke 12:32–40

[32]"Do not be afraid, little flock, for it is your Father's good pleasure to give you the kingdom. [33]Sell your possessions, and give alms. Make purses for yourselves that do not wear out, an unfailing treasure in heaven, where no thief comes near and no moth destroys. [34]For where your treasure is, there your heart will be also.

[35]"Be dressed for action and have your lamps lit; [36]be like those who are waiting for their master to return from the wedding banquet, so that they may open the door for him as soon as he comes and knocks. [37]Blessed are those slaves whom the master finds alert when he comes; truly I tell you, he will fasten his belt and have them sit down to eat, and he will come and serve them. [38]If he comes during the middle of the night, or near dawn, and finds them so, blessed are those slaves.

[39]"But know this: if the owner of the house had known at what hour the thief was coming, he would not have let his house be broken into. [40]You also must be ready, for the Son of Man is coming at an unexpected hour."

Commentary 1: Connecting the Reading with Scripture

Jonathan Edwards's sermon "Sinners in the Hands of an Angry God" is one of the best expressions of the theology of the Great Awakening in early eighteenth-century New England. Edwards drew heavily from the theology of the prophets and Jesus' warning about the coming judgment. The sermon quotes Luke 12:4–5, "Do not fear those who kill the body. . . . I will warn you whom to fear."

Like Edwards, Isaiah warned the people of Israel in his day, saying that God was tired of their sacrifices. God's commands were simple: "Cease to do evil, learn to do good; seek justice, rescue the oppressed, defend the orphan, plead for the widow. . . . but if you refuse and rebel, you shall be devoured by the sword" (Isa. 1:16b–17, 20a). The week's reading from the Psalms sounds the same note of urgency. The Lord of the heavens will call Israel to testify against them (Ps. 50:1–8). God says to those who forget God, "I will tear you apart," and to those who go the right way, "I will show the salvation of God" (vv. 22–23).

By rightly emphasizing Jesus' preaching of grace, love, and forgiveness, we often neglect the truth that his preaching of grace was always set in the context of the coming judgment. The warnings of the prophets gave rise to apocalypticism, which held that history is moving in a determined fashion toward the last days. In the Bible, we see apocalypticism most clearly in Isaiah 24–27, Daniel 6–12, Zechariah 9–14, and Revelation, but that is just the tip of the iceberg of the apocalyptic literature we find in the Pseudepigrapha (e.g., 1 Enoch, 4 Ezra, 2 Baruch, and the Sibylline Oracles, books 1–2 and 4) and the Dead Sea Scrolls (e.g., the War Scroll and the Temple Scroll).

Most scholars today agree that Jesus stood in these apocalyptic traditions and called his followers to prepare for the restoration of Israel in the coming kingdom of God. Jesus' mentor, John the Baptist, was an eschatological prophet. Jesus referred to himself as Son of Man (Dan. 7:13), called twelve apostles (probably signaling the restoration of the twelve tribes of Israel), acted out God's judgment on the temple, and claimed the power of the Spirit. Paul proclaimed his resurrection as the "firstfruits" of the coming resurrection (1 Cor. 15:20, 23). The theme of many of Jesus' parables and teachings is that the coming of the kingdom is imminent, so preparation is urgent (Mark 13; Matt. 24; Luke 21). The teachings in Luke 12:1–13:9 develop this theme also.

The lectionary text offers a guide for the "eschatologically perplexed" in three easy steps: (1) be generous and so lay up treasure in heaven (12:32–34); (2) like faithful servants expecting their master, get ready (12:35–38); and (3) the Son of Man will come like a thief in the night, so be ready (12:39–40). Each step mixes promise with warning.

Verse 32 serves as a transition from the previous paragraph with its call to trust God for what you need. The coming of the kingdom will be a gift to Jesus' "little lambs," so they need not fear it. The theme of the gift of the kingdom for the lowly runs throughout Luke (e.g., 1:48; 4:18; 6:20–23; 7:22).

The first step in getting ready is to divest yourself of unnecessary baggage: sell what you have and give to the poor. Downsizing can be a liberating experience! Most of us have far more than we need, but Jesus did not take freedom from possessions as far as the Cynics did. After seeing a child drink from his cupped hands, Diogenes of Sinope (fourth century BCE), an early Cynic, threw away his cup, saying, "Fool that I am, to have been carrying superfluous baggage all this time!" (Seneca, *Epistulae Morales* 90.14). Jesus' teaching assumes a forced choice: either grasp or give, either earthly goods or heavenly treasure, either what perishes or what is eternal. Thieves steal, moths eat, and metal rusts. Therefore, invest in treasure that will not wear out and cannot be taken from you. The reason to divest ourselves of material preoccupations is not, as it was for the Cynics, to be able to live freely and without worry; it is because where we put our treasure indicates ultimately where our hearts are.

The second step employs the metaphor of the master and the slave, a comparison drawn from the brutal realities of antiquity. Two parables are echoed in these verses: the parable of the Wise and Foolish Maidens (Matt. 25:1–13) and the parable of the Returning Householder (Mark 13:33–37; Matt. 25:13–15; Luke 19:12–13). The master has left home to celebrate his wedding at the bride's home (a celebration that could take up to a week) before bringing his bride home for the wedding banquet and festivities with his family. The servants need to have everything ready, but they do not know when to expect him. The admonition to "gird your loins" is a quotation from Exodus 12:11, regarding how the Israelites were to observe the first Passover: be ready to leave at any time (cf. 1 Pet. 1:13)! "Be dressed for action" (NRSV) means to tuck your long garment into the sash or belt around your waist.

The image of the returning master knocking on the door (Rev. 3:20) is popular in modern Christian art. "Watching" was a metaphor for eschatological readiness and was often coupled with prayer: "watch and pray" (Mark 14:38; Luke 21:36). The Romans divided the night into four watches of three hours each, from dusk to dawn, so the second watch would be from 9:00 p.m. to midnight and the third from midnight to 3:00 a.m. (see Mark 13:35). The reward for ready servants will be great. Their master will be pleased. He will invite them to his table and serve them (Luke 17:7–10; 22:24–28; John 13:1–17). Behind this picture is the promise of a great banquet in the end times (Isa. 25:6; cf. Luke 13:29; 14:15–24), celebrating a new king (1 Kgs. 1:24–25).

The third step summarizes another parable but makes the same point: be ready. The parable, another story about a householder, envisions a thief coming at night. The comparison of the Son of Man with a thief is not an easy one, but it invites reflection on our concern for earthly security and our neglect of eternal security. The image had become common in the early tradition. Paul warned the Thessalonians not to let the Day of the Lord come upon them like a thief (1 Thess. 5:2, 4). The Matthean version adds a reference to the watch of the night and graphically pictures the thief "digging" into a house made of sun-baked brick or thatch (Matt. 24:43–44). On that day, the heavens will pass away, and everything done on earth will be revealed (2 Pet. 3:10; cf. Luke 12:2–3). John the Seer inserts the saying in the letter to Sardis (Rev. 3:3), which is particularly appropriate because Sardis, which had an impregnable acropolis, had been captured twice without resistance because they were caught off guard, once by Cyrus the Persian in 546 BCE and once by Antiochus the Great in 218 BCE. In Revelation 16:15, the saying is followed by a warning not to be shamed by being caught naked (cf. Rev. 17:16)—probably meaning put on the baptismal robes of the new life in Christ. Luke allows what has been said earlier to suggest what disciples need to do in order to be ready. The purpose of the parable is not to give detailed instructions but to spur the hearer to action: be ready!

R. ALAN CULPEPPER

Commentary 2: Connecting the Reading with the World

There is a fascinating connection between the first verse of our passage and one of the most searing crises ever endured by any part of Christ's church. Luke 12:32 is, in effect, the biblical text of the Theological Declaration of Barmen, the 1934 public statement of the Confessing Church, the group of Christians who resisted the takeover of Germany and of the German Church by Nazi sympathizers of Adolf Hitler. Hitler had been named chancellor of Germany in 1933 as the consequence of a national vote in which the Nazi party had received more votes than any other party but still a minority of the votes of the electorate. Once in power, the Nazis began to take over all the structures of the German state, including the federation of Protestant churches of Germany. The so-called German Christians attempted to make the church a subservient organ of the Nazi state and to an alarming degree also corrupted its doctrine. They preached and taught another gospel, declaring the identity of the nation and the people the supreme good, especially as they were embodied in their Führer. This was idolatry, as the Confessing Church immediately recognized. The culmination of the preamble of the declaration invites the reader to test whether what the Confessing Church declares is founded on the Word of God:

> If you find that we are speaking contrary to Scripture, then do not listen to us! But if you find that we are taking our stand upon Scripture, then let no fear or temptation keep you from treading with us the path of faith and obedience to the Word of God, in order that God's people be of one mind upon earth and that we in faith experience what he himself has said: "I will never leave you, nor forsake you." Therefore, "Fear not, little flock, for it is your Father's good pleasure to give you the kingdom."[1]

This verse may be particularly poignant when we realize that in the Luther Bible, the German translation of "kingdom" is *Reich*. In the face of the looming terror represented by the Third Reich of Hitler and the Nazis, a word both of challenge and, ultimately, of comfort comes. The *Reich*, the kingdom, belongs not to Hitler or his followers in tyranny, but to our God. God's kingdom is a gift to those who trust in that gracious God. That is worthy of emphasis: the kingdom is not primarily an achievement, nor is it something we build. It is, rather, a gift of our God. It is often fear that keeps us from doing what we know is right, and thanks to the gift of God, there is no ultimate reason to fear.

Is all this recounting of the sad story of the Christian church and the Nazis of more than mild interest to a few former history majors? Nationalistic idolatry is not a sin confined to the German church of the Nazi era. The question of the "kingdom" and who rules remains worthy of consideration and of preaching.

"Kin-dom" is often a useful, non-gender-specific paraphrase of "kingdom," but it does not quite fit here. There is a question of authority in this context that is present in the older word "kingdom." The text asks who actually rules in our lives. Scripture frequently presents us with the challenge to commit ourselves to the rule of Christ, to follow him alone, and to receive the promises that come with following him.

The immediate biblical context of the verse suggests that the kingdom is also a gift to those who are ready. Much of Luke 12 as a whole

1. *The Book of Confessions* (Louisville, KY: Office of the General Assembly, 1999), 247–48.

is about the imminence of something new. It is a challenge to live as if something new, the kingdom of God, is about to break into this world. The text uses two different metaphors to describe the newness of the inbreaking kingdom. The first speaks of the return of a master from a wedding banquet. The wise slave is prepared for that return. The second involves the coming of a thief in the night. The assumption is that a householder is unlikely to be ready because the time of the break-in is unknown. The listener, by contrast, should be ready for that advent. This is relatively easy and obvious preaching material. Certainly, there will be little difficulty in finding stories online or in the usual preaching resources on the virtue of preparedness. This is not to suggest that the easy and the obvious should be avoided. After all, the reason this emphasis is easy and obvious is because it is genuinely there in the text. However, a sermon that stops with the wisdom of preparedness risks becoming the pulpit equivalent of the Boy and Girl Scout motto, "Be prepared!" Such a simple conclusion is law rather than gospel and, to be honest, rather banal. The preacher who does *not* stop here, by contrast, is the homiletical equivalent of a wise servant.

There is, however, an unexpected twist that lifts the first metaphor into the realm of gospel in verse 37: "Blessed are those slaves whom the master finds alert when he comes; truly I tell you, he will fasten his belt and have them sit down to eat, and he will come and serve them." This does not happen in ordinary life. Followers of the TV series *Downton Abbey* will know that when the earl and countess return, they do not go into the servants' quarters and serve a meal to the butler, maids, footmen, and cooks! The comfort of the master is paramount, and any meal service will be the other way around. Here, upon his return, the master tightens his belt and serves the servants. That our master is one who takes on the form of a servant is good news.

This brings us to the liturgical context of the text, particularly in those churches in which the preaching of the Word is followed by a celebration of the Eucharist. A colleague once remarked that the job of a preacher is the same as that of a *maître d'hôtel* in a fine restaurant, who says, "Right this way; the table's waiting." This ending to the metaphor of the return of the master, contrary to all social reality as it is, is also the introduction to the representation of the feast at which the master who gave his life for us will serve us bread and wine. The summons is, "Be prepared . . . to be served."

In the church year, this reading is buried in the depths of Ordinary Time. Whether that label is appropriate for any time between resurrection and Parousia is not the question here. Perhaps it is actually fitting that these words about the unexpected arrival of the master, or the thief, are read in the midst of what we are tempted to think is ordinary time. For preachers in the Northern Hemisphere, it may be of further interest that this reading comes in the depth of summer when so many take a vacation from church life and perhaps also from attention to God's work.

The final connection is financial. The use of money is a repeated theme in Jesus' teaching, especially in Luke. See, for example, Luke 12:13–21; 16:1–9; 19:11–27. Money even crops up in parables we think are entirely about other realities, like the story of the Good Samaritan or the Prodigal Son. Perhaps this is because the most prevailing temptation in Luke's church was to build up treasure on earth rather than in heaven. Is it so very different in our church?

STEPHEN FARRIS

Proper 15 (Sunday between August 14 and August 20 Inclusive)

Isaiah 5:1–7 and Jeremiah 23:23–29
Psalm 80:1–2, 8–19 and Psalm 82
Hebrews 11:29–12:2
Luke 12:49–56

Isaiah 5:1–7

[1]Let me sing for my beloved
my love-song concerning his vineyard:
My beloved had a vineyard
on a very fertile hill.
[2]He dug it and cleared it of stones,
and planted it with choice vines;
he built a watchtower in the midst of it,
and hewed out a wine vat in it;
he expected it to yield grapes,
but it yielded wild grapes.

[3]And now, inhabitants of Jerusalem
and people of Judah,
judge between me
and my vineyard.
[4]What more was there to do for my vineyard
that I have not done in it?
When I expected it to yield grapes,
why did it yield wild grapes?

[5]And now I will tell you
what I will do to my vineyard.
I will remove its hedge,
and it shall be devoured;
I will break down its wall,
and it shall be trampled down.
[6]I will make it a waste;
it shall not be pruned or hoed,
and it shall be overgrown with briers and thorns;
I will also command the clouds
that they rain no rain upon it.

[7]For the vineyard of the LORD of hosts
is the house of Israel,
and the people of Judah
are his pleasant planting;
he expected justice,
but saw bloodshed;
righteousness,
but heard a cry!

Jeremiah 23:23–29

[23]Am I a God near by, says the LORD, and not a God far off? [24]Who can hide in secret places so that I cannot see them? says the LORD. Do I not fill heaven and earth? says the LORD. [25]I have heard what the prophets have said who prophesy lies in my name, saying, "I have dreamed, I have dreamed!" [26]How long? Will the hearts of the prophets ever turn back—those who prophesy lies, and who prophesy the deceit of their own heart? [27]They plan to make my people forget my name by their dreams that they tell one another, just as their ancestors forgot my name for Baal. [28]Let the prophet who has a dream tell the dream, but let the one who has my word speak my word faithfully. What has straw in common with wheat? says the LORD. [29]Is not my word like fire, says the LORD, and like a hammer that breaks a rock in pieces?

Commentary 1: Connecting the Reading with Scripture

Isaiah 5:1–7 is part of the set of oracles that begins the final edited form of the book. A heavily redacted book, Isaiah combines prophecies from three separate periods in Israel's history: the time period of the original prophet Isaiah son of Amoz (who lived ca. 760–673 BCE), the exilic prophet known as Second Isaiah (who began his career in Babylon ca. 539 BCE), and the postexilic prophet known as Third Isaiah (who writes from within the community of the returnees ca. 535 BCE). Although the book consists of several strata, the common theme of the final canonical form of the book is the central importance and ultimate fate of the Holy City, Jerusalem, and its population. Many scholars think the first five oracles are arranged as an introduction by a late editor (possibly the final editor of the work), because the call story of the prophet does not appear until chapter 6, after the larger themes of apostasy and the punishment of exile are laid out in broad relief.

Arguing that these oracles appear outside of their original chronological order, however, does not diminish their value. Each oracle of these first five, and particularly chapter 5, spells out the view, continued throughout all sixty-six chapters of the book, that Jerusalem is of utmost importance to God. Accordingly, the city and its people must adhere to God's high standards for righteousness and faithfulness—a divine requirement that they consistently fail to fulfill.

Jerusalem is God's cherished possession, and yet those who live in the Holy City are not the righteous caretakers that God desires. Because of them the vineyard/city does not produce the fruit God intended. Instead of justice, it produces bloodshed; instead of righteousness, an outcry. Because of this basic failure of purpose, God intends to bring destruction to the vineyard/city by tearing down its protective wall and allowing it to be overtaken by enemies. Here in this one parabolic oracle, the history of Jerusalem and with it the entire history of God's people is drawn in miniature. Only after this larger story is laid out in the first five oracles of Isaiah are we then allowed to hear the call story of the original prophet in chapter 6. God demands righteousness. Those who cannot uphold that standard will be exiled from the land. This sets up the history of Jerusalem as paradigmatic for the entire Israelite people, from their original life in the land, through exile, and finally to return.

Psalm 80 also uses the vineyard image, describing Israel as a vine brought by God out of Egypt and planted in the Holy Land. The psalmist laments God's judgment against the "vine," a judgment that resulted in the tearing down of its protective wall. The psalmist then begs God to restore favor to the once-cherished nation. In the NT, the Jewish leaders of Jesus' day are compared, in a similar parable, to unrighteous tenants in God's vineyard, who refuse to give the vineyard owner (i.e., God) the harvest of fruit he is owed. Instead of delivering the fruit, they beat, stone, and kill, not only the prophets who come seeking the harvest, but also the very son of the vineyard owner, who is Jesus (Matt. 21:33–46; Mark 12:1–12; Luke 20:9–19). Perhaps it is just this type of grim expectation that prompts Jesus to teach in Luke 12:49–56 that his coming will not bring peace but rather the sword of conflict.

The second OT lection, Jeremiah 23:23–29, like our first from Isaiah 5, underscores the key role Jerusalem played in ancient Israelite life. Although Jeremiah is often referred to as the weeping prophet, given his negativity and his cynicism about his contemporaries in Jerusalem, a better nickname for him might be the kvetching (or complaining) prophet. According to Jeremiah 1:1, Jeremiah came from a priestly family that had been exiled from the capital city of Jerusalem to the rural backwater of Anathoth in Benjamin since the time of Solomon. They were exiled because their ancestor Abiathar (who was one of two high priests who served King David) backed Adonijah instead of Solomon to succeed David as king (1 Kgs. 2:26). Being removed from Jerusalem, the religious epicenter of Israel, was a cataclysmic fall from grace for Jeremiah's clan and may be seen as the reason he remained so critical of Jerusalem elites even after returning there.

Jeremiah stands in a long line of prophetic tradition that calls out other prophets and religious officials for misleading the people with false prophecy. In Jeremiah 23:23–29, the prophet condemns those who claim to have oracular dreams, which Jeremiah considers to be no more than random products of their own imagination. Just as the story of Elijah on Mount Horeb establishes that the only true medium for divine guidance is the word of God whispered into the prophet's ear (1 Kgs. 19:11–13), Jeremiah rejects any claim to divine authority from those who merely repeat what they have dreamed. "You are just like your ancestors," who forgot me in favor of the Canaanite god Baal, says the Lord. These false prophets' dreams, compared to true words delivered through a true prophet, are no more valuable than straw compared to wheat.

A similar critique is voiced in Psalm 82. Instead of a true prophet criticizing false prophets, YHWH, the true God, criticizes lesser "gods" of the divine assembly. Here the psalmist voices a common Israelite belief that other nations have "gods" whose names are known and who are no doubt worshiped by misguided people, but that these are not true gods. Only YHWH is the true God. Other divine creatures who occupy heaven (like the heavenly hosts, angels, etc.) were created by YHWH and so are not at all equal to God, regardless of how many humans worship them. These "lesser gods" are God's creations, God's children, just as humans are, and so are not genuine gods as YHWH is. Because they do not know how to maintain justice, which is a god's main purpose, God declares that they will be reduced to finitude, no longer immortal.

While this seemingly polytheistic, mythical language of the psalmist may be disturbing to some, both the psalm and the Jeremiah passage reflect a serious issue that confronted ancient Israelite worshipers: Whom should we believe? Whom should we worship? In those days, there was no end to those who claimed to have a message from God. There were omen takers of numerous kinds reading the stars, the livers of sacrificial animals, the signs in nature, to try and discern what the "God far off" was thinking. There was no end to the number of gods that the neighbors of the Israelites worshiped, gods who claimed to have power over rain or disease or war or childbirth. Given this overpopulated supernatural landscape, the lure of the false prophet and the false god was impossible to avoid, much less ignore.

All of these passages are connected by the idea that God has expectations of us. God expects our trust. God has given us the blessings of the earth and of faith and the opportunity to have a relationship with a living God. When we forget that creation, along with this relationship, is a gift, when we refuse to trust God, when we seek our own selfish goals instead of God's goals of peace and righteousness, we lose our way. We lose touch with what is true. We lose the ability to tell fact from fiction, a skill that is always required for the flourishing of human life.

ELIZABETH C. LAROCCA-PITTS

Commentary 2: Connecting the Reading with the World

Divine Judgment as the Bed We Unmake for Ourselves. Inauthentic ways to preach about the prophets abound. One takes place when we preachers cast ourselves as the thundering Isaiah or Jeremiah, with the hapless congregation assigned the role of "faithless Israel." Denunciations of lagging zeal or drooping commitment come easily when we are the ones doing the denouncing. Another happens when we too easily link disaster and divine judgment. From a politician's descent into disfavor to a hurricane's destructive fury, we rush to interpret such events as God's punishment on opinions and behaviors of which we disapprove. Might we be tempted to such inauthentic responses because the prophets speak so often about God's judgment? Is God's judgment simply a hard subject to understand?

Perhaps this passage in Isaiah can help us with that response. It suggests that divine punishment often means arriving at the end of the trail we have blazed for ourselves. We do not often think of Charles Dickens's *A Christmas Carol* during Ordinary Time, but the classic tale might also have some help to offer here. When Marley's ghost appears to Ebenezer Scrooge, more than once he refers to what we might call the truncated heart. Both partners—one dead, one yet alive—have sat alone in their counting house, allowing the circle of their concern to expand no further than its narrow walls. The result for Marley is that when in death his eyes are opened to the suffering and needs of others, the choices he made in life have forged an identity that is incapable of helping. His punishment is to be the person he made himself to be—and to know that he might have been more.

In the story of the vineyard, Israel has in effect decided that it wants to produce wild, sour grapes. To achieve that goal, the vineyard need only revert to uncultivated ground. The actions God promises—removing the hedge, breaking down the wall, ceasing to hoe or prune—are just God's way of seeing to it that Israel gets what it wants. The prophetic word assures us that God will not save us from the consequences of our own folly; often, this is judgment enough.

A Fruitful Future. God has much to lament in these verses. Israel's present injustice to the poor and powerless seems to negate all of God's past labors on Israel's behalf. Worst of all is the loss of an anticipated future in which the vineyard bears fruit worthy of the effort expended on it. Verse 7 (and the verses immediately following) remind us that God expected Israel not simply to refrain from evil but to bear the good fruits of justice and righteousness. God finds Israel wanting when it produces wild and sour grapes, but it seems safe to assume that the same would have happened had they brought forth no fruit at all.

Those preaching on this passage would do well to focus on the *expectation of future outcomes*. One lens through which to look at this comes from the early Christian theologian Irenaeus. Unlike others who conceived of Eve and Adam as fully grown adults, Irenaeus said that God created them as children or, more specifically, adolescents.[1] They were not the fully mature, fully loving individuals God intended them to be, but they could grow into those potential selves. Achieving that goal would mean living into the image of God in which they were created. Irenaeus's interpretation of the Adam and Eve story echoes a deep truth from Isaiah: God created us to bear fruit. Loving more and giving more of ourselves is what it means to be the people of God.

An additional lens comes from another theologian of the early church, the great Augustine. Anyone who was assigned the *Confessions*, his spiritual autobiography, in college or seminary will remember the story of the pear tree (*Confessions* 2, 9). One night, the adolescent Augustine and his hoodlum friends jumped a fence and stole a bunch of pears. They took bites out of a few, but most they simply tossed to some pigs. Why did they do it? Augustine blames it on his not-yet-redeemed state, but clearly more is at work. The pear tree—like Isaiah's grapevine—signified to the theologian his own potential,

1. Irenaeus, *Proof of the Apostolic Preaching*, trans. and ed. Joseph P. Smith, SJ (New York: Paulist Press, 1952), 55.

the fruitfulness for which God had made him. Augustine was (like Israel? like us?) both drawn to that future and afraid of it. Wanting to be that person, yet not knowing how—apart from grace—to achieve the goal, Augustine responded to his own potential the way so many of us do: with (self-)destructive behavior.

God above Us, God with Us. One of the central achievements of the prophetic literature is its sweeping vision of God's sovereignty. When God speaks through the prophet Jeremiah to ask, "Am I a God near by . . . and not a God far off?" (Jer. 23:23), the question is really a statement: we cannot put God in a box. This, it seems, was the mistake of the false prophets Jeremiah denounces in the passage. Their pleasing dreams contained only "the deceit of their own heart" (v. 26), rather than the hard truths Jeremiah knew the people needed to hear. The prophet reminds us that God will not be made a prop in some human stage play.

Divine resistance to domestication and idolatry is a theme worth exploring in this passage. One of the chief ways we try to domesticate God is through civil religion, which equates God's will with the agenda of our own group, tribe, or state. Many in the congregation may not know how effective the Nazis were at religious manipulation of this tribal impulse. This is the background of the Barmen Declaration (1934), written by Karl Barth and his Lutheran colleagues in response to the Nazis' attempts to subsume Christian identity under loyalty to the nation.[2] In simple, yet deeply theological language, the writers and endorsers of Barmen confessed their sole loyalty to Christ. Any attempt to subjugate that loyalty to another—up to and including loyalty to flag and country—is an act of idolatry, they said.

Another approach the preacher might take to Jeremiah's "God far off" is to remember that only the God who *is* God is able to save us; no comfortable idol of our own making can do so. Flannery O'Connor makes this point in her customarily unsettling way in the short story "Parker's Back."[3] The protagonist, O. E. Parker, makes it clear that he has no use for religion,yet throughout the story he is haunted, hunted almost, by Something beyond his understanding. In the end, he surrenders to this reality the only way he knows how: by having the strangest, most alien image of God he can find (a Byzantine painting of Christ) tattooed all over his back. The dark, deep-set eyes of the painting bore through him, looking into his soul and elevating him in an experience of the transcendent. Parker's God, like Jeremiah's, does not bring comfort (at least not immediately). What this God does bring is *authenticity*, an encounter with the truth about the world and himself. In the end, is this not the God the congregation needs to hear about, even when they might not recognize their need?

ROBERT A. RATCLIFF

2. "The Declarations, Resolutions, and Motions Adopted by the Synod of Barmen, May 29–31, 1934," in *The Church's Confession under Hitler*, ed. Arthur C. Cochrane (Philadelphia: Westminster, 1962), 237–42. See also http://www.sacred-texts.com/chr/barmen.htm.
3. Flannery O'Connor, "Parker's Back," in *God: Stories*, ed. C. Michael Curtis (New York: Houghton Mifflin, 1998), 167–85.

Psalm 80:1–2, 8–19

[1]Give ear, O Shepherd of Israel,
 you who lead Joseph like a flock!
You who are enthroned upon the cherubim, shine forth
 [2]before Ephraim and Benjamin and Manasseh.
Stir up your might,
 and come to save us!

. . . .

[8]You brought a vine out of Egypt;
 you drove out the nations and planted it.
[9]You cleared the ground for it;
 it took deep root and filled the land.
[10]The mountains were covered with its shade,
 the mighty cedars with its branches;
[11]it sent out its branches to the sea,
 and its shoots to the River.
[12]Why then have you broken down its walls,
 so that all who pass along the way pluck its fruit?
[13]The boar from the forest ravages it,
 and all that move in the field feed on it.

[14]Turn again, O God of hosts;
 look down from heaven, and see;
have regard for this vine,
 [15]the stock that your right hand planted.
[16]They have burned it with fire, they have cut it down;
 may they perish at the rebuke of your countenance.
[17]But let your hand be upon the one at your right hand,
 the one whom you made strong for yourself.
[18]Then we will never turn back from you;
 give us life, and we will call on your name.

[19]Restore us, O LORD God of hosts;
 let your face shine, that we may be saved.

Psalm 82

[1]God has taken his place in the divine council;
 in the midst of the gods he holds judgment:
[2]"How long will you judge unjustly
 and show partiality to the wicked?
[3]Give justice to the weak and the orphan;
 maintain the right of the lowly and the destitute.
[4]Rescue the weak and the needy;
 deliver them from the hand of the wicked."

[5]They have neither knowledge nor understanding,
they walk around in darkness;
all the foundations of the earth are shaken.

[6]I say, "You are gods,
children of the Most High, all of you;
[7]nevertheless, you shall die like mortals,
and fall like any prince."

[8]Rise up, O God, judge the earth;
for all the nations belong to you!

Connecting the Psalm with Scripture and Worship

We might say the community that prays Psalm 80 has a lot of nerve. The people of Israel directly address the sovereign God with requests that sound an awful lot like demands: listen, shine, stir, come, save, turn, look, regard, give, restore, *do something*! Maybe this is just what desperate people sound like. Not moxie, just panic.

The psalmist begins by pleading with God for an audience, claiming a relationship: Give ear, Shepherd of Israel! Listen, you who lead us! Shine your face on us, that is, come close and do something good. Get up and save (Ps. 80:1–2). The initial series of demands breaks off into the music of parable as the psalm continues. Now Israel is the vine brought safely out from Egypt, replanted in soil that once belonged to others. How do you get God to intervene? Remind God: you were such an excellent gardener, how energetically you made living space for us! Remember how gloriously we grew and spread and covered the land, from the Mediterranean to the Euphrates (vv. 8–11)?

Now all of that has changed. The people know who is responsible when dreams go up in smoke. It is God who ruined everything: broke down the vineyard walls, invited the world to pillage, let the wild things devour. Why? It is an amazing feature of Psalm 80 that the people do not know why God let go, and they say so (v. 12). They ask, expecting God to have an answer.

In the love song Isaiah sings at the beginning of chapter 5, someone else is asking why things went wrong in the vineyard, but from a very different perspective. Like the psalmist, Isaiah also describes the diligence of the gardener: digging, removing stones, planting "choice" vines, building a guard tower, preparing for a fine vintage once the grapes hang sweet (vv. 1–2). The harvest was a terrible disappointment, the grapes fit only for wild things. Why did this happen, especially when the gardener used only best practices?

A wise preacher will not try to harmonize these accounts but give each room to breathe. Psalm 80 raises some hard questions for the God's-eye view Isaiah depicts, if you read closely, and could be deployed as a countervoice in the context of the sermon itself. A preacher might wonder, Is it possible that the people really do not know why God gave up on them? Has God modeled the justice God expects to find in Israel? After all, the people have seen God drive out the nations; blood has been shed, with God's authorization (v. 8). Where is the justice in that? This is dangerous territory, of course, and the preacher will not forget that alongside the confusion in Psalm 80, there is also trust and a bit of bargaining. God is the way to restoration and life, and if God will shine on the garden again, the people will "never turn back" from God (v. 18).

The liturgy that lets Psalm 80 loose is one that acknowledges all is not well, and provides opportunities for worshipers to ask God, "Why?" and "How long?" Worship planners might consider using the haunting responsorial setting of Psalm 80 by Hal Hopson. The

The God Who Never Leaves Us

Christ sits in judgment. That is truly a serious matter. Yet Christ sits in judgment, which also means that we are judged by the Merciful One who lived among tax collectors and sinners, who was tempted as we are [Heb. 4:15], who carried and endured our sorrows, our fears, and our desires in his own body, who knows us and calls us by our names [Isa. 43:1]. Christ sits in judgment, which means that grace is the judge, and forgiveness, and love—whoever clings to them has already been acquitted. Those, of course, who want to be judged by their own works, Christ will judge and pass sentence based on those works. But we should be joyful when we think about that day. We need not tremble and hold back, but give ourselves gladly into his hands. Luther dared even to speak of it as that dear day of judgment. So as we leave worship on the Day of Repentance, let us be not downcast but joyful and confident. Come, Judgment Day, we look forward to you with joy, for then we shall see our merciful Lord and clasp his hand, and he will receive us with open arms.

Turn back, turn back! the whole Bible calls to us joyfully. Turn back—where? To the everlasting mercy of the God who never leaves us, whose heart breaks because of us, the God who created us and loves us beyond all measure. God will be merciful—so come then, Judgment Day. Lord Jesus, make us ready. We await you with joy. Amen.

Dietrich Bonhoeffer (1906–45), "Turning Back," in *The Collected Sermons of Dietrich Bonhoeffer*, ed. Isabel Best (Minneapolis: Augsburg Fortress, 2012), 100.

congregation or choir could chant the "Lord, come soon," while a few verses at a time are read or sung by voices in different parts of the sanctuary. This ostinato refrain could also recur in the context of the prayers of the people, hummed as the intercessions are made, then chanted in response to each one.[1]

In the alternate set of readings for the day, judgment is also a prominent feature. We might call Psalm 82 a backstage pass to the twilight of the gods. It was a common enough idea in ancient times that divine beings gathered every so often in some heavenly boardroom to discuss the fate of the earthly realms they governed, but the psalmist here goes a step further. Israel's God "takes his place" in the divine company (Ps. 82:1), not by joining the conversation but by delivering a jeremiad in the familiar cadences of court proceedings. The "gods" have not governed justly, the Most High God laments; they do favors for villains and fail to protect the most vulnerable in society: the orphan, the poor, the weak (vv. 2–3). In this the gods demonstrate their profound ignorance, and their actions threaten the very heart of the earth. Therefore, they are demoted, God declares, subject to death like everyone else. Then the psalmist takes a breath, a beat, before praying the prayer that ends the psalm: "Rise up, O God, judge the earth!" (v. 8). Take the place of such unjust gods. Be the judge you have every right to be.

In the space between the heavenly council dreamscape and the psalmist's final prayer, the subtext of the psalm bubbles up: What is the God who is God—defender of orphans and beggars and vulnerable souls—waiting for? For judgment does not just mean declaring a verdict but actually declawing the villainous. It means preserving, rescuing, and delivering those who stand in need of saving. We know as well as the psalmist that villains still prowl the earth, and not every tear has been wiped away. Rise up, indeed.

When we turn to Jeremiah's fourth oracle against the false prophets in 23:23–29, we find some of the same themes. Though we are no longer in the mysterious boardroom, God's judgment is again directed against those who claim divine authority and behave badly. Like the gods, the prophets whom Jeremiah lambastes have not done what is good. They have

1. Gary Chamberlain and Hal Hopson, "Psalm 80," in *The Psalter: Psalms and Canticles for Singing* (Louisville, KY: Westminster John Knox, 1993), 70.

lied, led people astray, and dreamed all the wrong dreams for God's people. They have taken advantage of the vulnerable and the gullible. At this crucial time in Israel's history, they chose to comfort, rather than confront, the powerful. The prophets imagined a domesticated God, one close by, manageable, one nap away; but Jeremiah—like the psalmist—knows that Israel's God eludes such control. The God who is God is on the loose, uncontainable, wildfire, and flint. Presuming to speak for this God is a perilous venture, not to be dared without a commission. The word of the Lord is not something a would-be prophet can conjure up, but something that can only be given.

Both Psalm 82 and Jeremiah's oracle remind readers that when it comes right down to it, we can only declare our dependence where divinity is concerned. We can only ask for God's help in doing justice, reading the signs of the times, and speaking the truth—even "gods" do not get it right. Nevertheless we should not neglect to ask often, with urgency, having the nerve: "Rise up, O God!" It is not a thing to ask lightly, when the word is one that burns and shatters (Jer. 23:29). What are we asking, when we ask God to judge the world? To see it; to tell the truth about it; to make it right.

Before the public reading of these verses from Psalm 82, it is critical to provide hearers with a few lines of introduction to help them enter the strange scene of the heavenly courtroom. The liturgy for the day could make use of the last line of the psalm reading as a refrain in the context of prayers of lament and intercession, inviting the whole assembly to plead with God, "Rise up, O God, judge the earth" (Ps. 82:8).

ANGELA DIENHART HANCOCK

Hebrews 11:29–12:2

[29]By faith the people passed through the Red Sea as if it were dry land, but when the Egyptians attempted to do so they were drowned. [30]By faith the walls of Jericho fell after they had been encircled for seven days. [31]By faith Rahab the prostitute did not perish with those who were disobedient, because she had received the spies in peace.

[32]And what more should I say? For time would fail me to tell of Gideon, Barak, Samson, Jephthah, of David and Samuel and the prophets— [33]who through faith conquered kingdoms, administered justice, obtained promises, shut the mouths of lions, [34]quenched raging fire, escaped the edge of the sword, won strength out of weakness, became mighty in war, put foreign armies to flight. [35]Women received their dead by resurrection. Others were tortured, refusing to accept release, in order to obtain a better resurrection. [36]Others suffered mocking and flogging, and even chains and imprisonment. [37]They were stoned to death, they were sawn in two, they were killed by the sword; they went about in skins of sheep and goats, destitute, persecuted, tormented— [38]of whom the world was not worthy. They wandered in deserts and mountains, and in caves and holes in the ground.

[39]Yet all these, though they were commended for their faith, did not receive what was promised, [40]since God had provided something better so that they would not, apart from us, be made perfect.

[12:1]Therefore, since we are surrounded by so great a cloud of witnesses, let us also lay aside every weight and the sin that clings so closely, and let us run with perseverance the race that is set before us, [2]looking to Jesus the pioneer and perfecter of our faith, who for the sake of the joy that was set before him endured the cross, disregarding its shame, and has taken his seat at the right hand of the throne of God.

Commentary 1: Connecting the Reading with Scripture

Hebrews is distinctive in Christian literature for its image of Christ as God's great high priest. The book develops the implication that, as a result of Christ's high priesthood, followers of Christ have access to God's mercy and grace. Hebrews thus urges the reader to endurance and faith. Chapters 11 and 12 are the writer's final exhortation to faithfulness. In the present lection, the writer gradually increases the urgency of that exhortation until it culminates in the eschatological vision of the risen Christ seated at the right hand of God.

After defining faith as "the assurance of things hoped for, the conviction of things not seen" (Heb. 11:1), the writer of Hebrews provides a recitation of exemplars from Israel's sacred story who demonstrate faith by their actions. Each example is a midrash, a brief interpretive comment suggested by elements of the Hebrew Scripture from which it is drawn. Hebrews 11:8–22 focuses on Abraham and Sarah, who trust in God's promise despite their childlessness, and 11:23–28 develops Moses as an exemplar of faith amid hardship. The present lection moves forward through Israel's sacred story, first with the faith of those who crossed the Red Sea in the face of Egyptian pursuit (Exod. 14:1–31), then of Rahab of Jericho (Josh. 2), and finally with a rehearsal of the prophetic figures better known to us through the stories of Judges. As the recitation draws to its conclusion, the references become less precise, although it is possible to discern at least some of them: Samuel "administers justice" (1 Sam. 7:15–17); Daniel, Shadrach, Meshach, and Abednego are likely those who "shut the mouths of lions" and "quenched raging fire" (Dan. 3:8–30 and 6:1–28); David is perhaps the one who "won strength out of weakness" and "became mighty in war, put foreign armies to flight"; the widow of Zarephath (1 Kgs. 17:8–24) and the Shunammite mother (2 Kgs. 4:8–37) both "received their dead by resurrection." Other referents are obscure: the writer lifts up only the implied faithfulness of those who experience various tortures, imprisonments, beatings, and deaths.

As is commonly the case in midrashic exegesis, the writer omits reference to the less savory aspects of the chosen examples, focusing only on the point being made. Here, he omits Abraham and Sarah's incredulity at the promise of Isaac's birth, Israel's grumbling against Moses at the Red Sea and in the wilderness, Rahab's life as a prostitute, Samuel's ambivalence about Saul as king, David's rape of Bathsheba, and Elisha's petulance at Mount Horeb. In each case, he chooses to lift up only their obedience. By omitting these less-than-glowing moments in the lives of his examples, he can make the claim that "the world was not worthy" of them. This last is the ultimate compliment the writer can bestow: all these who have demonstrated a faith that trusts what it cannot see and relies on hope for its survival are too good for the world. This compliment is the apex of this rising chorus of faithfulness begun in verse 8.

And yet.

Verse 39 is the turning point in the writer's exhortation. The key in this exhortation is the "promise" (*epangelia*), a term used throughout Hebrews, moving between generic promises that reward the endurance of the faithful and a specific promise bestowed on individual heroic forebears in faith. Earlier in the epistle, it describes the inheritance of the faithful (6:12) but also God's blessing of Abraham (6:13–14). In 10:23, the "promise" is applied to the community the writer addresses. In 11:8–19, the "promise" is again that given to Abraham, who lived "in the land he had been promised"; Isaac and Jacob are "heirs with him of the same promise" in verse 9. In verses 13 and 17, the "promise" has become "promises," and in verse 33 the prophets "obtained promises."

Even in verse 39, however, the promise in Hebrews remains unfulfilled: "Yet all these . . . did not receive what was promised," awaiting "something better." This "better" something is not specified, but the remainder of the verse makes clear that the long history of faithfulness would not reach its fulfillment without our participation. Together, the writer argues, we are to be "made perfect" (*teleioō*). The Greek term also carries the sense of being completed, fulfilled, or made whole. As used here, it concludes the argument that those in the heritage of faith do not attain fulfillment, nor does their faith achieve wholeness, without the inclusion of the followers of Jesus to whom Hebrews is addressed.

That fulfillment is at last stated in 12:1–2: Jesus Christ, the "pioneer and perfecter of our faith." The writer shifts imagery here, away from the long recitation of the sacred story toward the conclusion of an imagined footrace. The "great cloud of witnesses" is the heritage of faith recited in 11:8–38, now envisioned as a crowd of spectators cheering on the present faithful. The writer urges his audience to shed the "weight" and "sin" that cling to the runner's body like sweat-saturated clothing, so that they might finish the race. Ahead of the racers, the writer sets the vision of Jesus, who has both led the race (*archēgos,* pioneer) and fulfilled its demands (*teleiōtēs,* that is, the one who perfects, fulfills, or completes). Carrying the image further, the writer envisions Jesus himself as a runner who focuses on the "joy that was set before him" and for its sake endures the pain and humiliation of the cross. Rewarded for his faithful "perfection" in completing the race, he now sits at the right hand of the throne of God.

The writer of Hebrews intends this last hortatory section of the epistle as the encouragement to his audience to remain faithful and "not grow weary or lose heart" (12:3). Earlier in the epistle, the author's concern seems to be with his audience's drift away from the essentials of faith: to do so would imperil their salvation (see 2:1–3). As a check against this tendency to drift away from faith, the writer holds up the image of Jesus as the great high priest who, having suffered as one of the faithful, now sits at the right hand of God (4:14–5:14; 8:1–2). Through the offices of the high priest, we are enabled to approach God "with a true heart in full assurance of faith" (10:22).

The Revised Common Lectionary pairs this passage with Isaiah 5:1–7 and Luke 12:49–56, both texts with a strongly eschatological orientation. Isaiah's song of the vineyard connects the impending judgment of God on Israel with Israel's betrayal of its covenantal obligations: "he expected justice, but saw bloodshed; righteousness, but heard a cry!" God, the divine vineyard owner, will uproot Israel, the failed and recalcitrant vine. Luke's "little apocalypse" contains Jesus' declaration that he "came to bring fire to the earth" and his challenge to his hearers that they do not know how to interpret the eschatological moment that is upon them. Both texts are more direct warnings of impending reckoning. By contrast, Hebrews strikes a more encouraging note. Instead of threats, it offers exemplars of faith; instead of dire warnings, it offers promises of hope and joy. That said, we ought not miss the urgency in Hebrews. We are nearing the end of the race, and the crowd of witnesses, those who have lived in faith before us, cheers and urges us not to give up on the race as we approach its culmination. Ahead of us stands the goal, the ultimate apocalyptic image: the risen Christ, seated at the right hand of the divine throne, both to bless and to judge.

PAUL K. HOOKER

Commentary 2: Connecting the Reading with the World

The breathless quality of our reading from Hebrews calls hearers to the edge of their seats. Abraham and Moses were given more space than the other Israelite heroes, but this list of named and unnamed faithful has an urgency that elicits curiosity and focused attention. A preacher preparing a sermon on this text might ask, did the original recipients of this sermon know the details of Barak and Jephthah? Did they get the allusions to the widow of Zarephath and the Shunammite woman? It is unlikely that many twenty-first-century churchgoers will get the nuances of this cloud of witnesses and therein the preacher might find an opportunity. These characters and their respective stories are as engaging and compelling as the epics of ancient Greece, the medieval hagiography of the *Golden Legend,* and even Grimm's fairy tales. This text offers an excuse to take a wild run through the book of Judges and resurrect long-lost ancestors formerly unknown but ready to be claimed and called mentors for our living faithfully.

The recent popularity of television shows such as *Who Do You Think You Are?* and *Finding Your Roots,* which trace the lineage of famous people and others that seek out long-lost family members, reminds us of our very human need to be connected to the past. We long to be part of a longer narrative than just our own life story. DNA testing and databases on websites like ancestry.com enable the curious to discover details, both genetic and historic, about their roots, and often these discoveries transform one's self-understanding. Learning that a great-great-grandmother survived a perilous journey or that a long-ago cousin was a Revolutionary War hero or a slave or a slaveholder shapes the way one views oneself and may even prompt a reevaluation of values and purpose. Knowing the cloud of witnesses of which we are a part helps to frame our present circumstances. Our future hopes and our family tree go all the way back to include Barak and Deborah, Jeremiah, Rahab, Samson, and Shadrach, Meshach, and Abednego. Who knew? Perhaps not many Christians today. Preaching a "who do you think you are?" sermon based on the litany of saints in this text could be not only educational but also a means of strengthening the hearer's sense of Christian identity and purpose.

What more should we say? A great deal, but given the limits of time on any given Sunday, it would be wise to choose one or two of these B-team saints and tell their stories with no less enthusiasm than recounting a personal experience of peril and survival. Dig deep and take the bait of the writer of Hebrews. Figure out which women's dead were resurrected and by whom. Wrestle with the complicated story of Rahab and the carnage that comes later in that story. Question why Barak gets named but Deborah does not. Follow Jeremiah as he is persecuted, imprisoned, and stuck in a cistern. Then ask: So what?

Why are these strange stories more authoritative for us than the stories of the brothers Grimm or Shakespeare's tragedies or the wild accounts of Greek gods and goddesses? First, because they are in our Scriptures, God's authoritative living Word and God's Word to us. Second, because these are *our* ancestors. This is our family, and their courage and perseverance, their faithfulness in the face of persecution and danger, give us strength to run the race before us in our time and place. Their stories remind us that no matter how frightening and tumultuous our context, others have faced no less challenging circumstance and remained steadfast in following the God who remained faithful to the covenant made to Abraham and, through Abraham, to us. Choosing any one of these stories leads the preacher to weave the biblical narrative into that of contemporary Christians.

This litany of Israelite saints invites us to remember other saints too. As we lift up Gideon and remember how the mantle passed from Elijah to Elisha, we should consider more recent members of the cloud that surrounds us. God never stops calling and equipping ordinary people to witness and work in the kingdom; the cloud grows through time. The Lowell Milken Center for Unsung Heroes offers examples of unknown people who have been extraordinarily faithful and courageous.[1] Robert Ellsberg's *All Saints: Daily Reflections on Saints, Prophets, and Witnesses for Our Time* contains 365 short biographies of the faithful, from usual suspects such as Martin Luther to those lesser known like Takasho Nagai and Sister Thea Bowman.[2] A visit to your own church's archives, interviews with current members, and simply offering the space for those present to name their own cloud of witnesses would yield much fruit as well. Preachers could invite members of the congregation to share their own testimonies of saints who have shaped their faith journeys.

The preacher might reflect on how our time seems uniquely difficult and our challenges especially harrowing. Hebrews reminds us otherwise. It looks through a large lens and prompts us to remember the long arc of salvation history, inviting us to remember that we too have a place in the narrative. Reading about the heroes of the faith—biblical, ancient, or contemporary—is not merely an academic exercise or a form of religious entertainment; learning these sagas leads to a real-life response. As Christians, we believe that the sprint through Joshua, Judges, Samuel, and Kings culminates in Christ. Now we must run the race set before *us*.

The preacher can proclaim that Christians know how the promise is fulfilled: through the life, death, and resurrection of God's Son, our Savior Jesus Christ, the one whose sacrifice secured our victory, no matter how challenging the course set before us. We have the benefit of the example of not only those who survived furnace and lions' den, cistern and cave, but of the Messiah who was crucified, dead, and buried, descended into hell, and on the third day rose again from the dead so that nothing can separate us from God's love. Could that knowledge, coupled with the cheering crowd of the communion of the saints, that remarkable cloud of witnesses to whom we are related, spur us to faithful perseverance, no matter the obstacles of our day? The preacher could invite hearers to consider the challenges present in the congregation, community, or world and wrestle in the sermon with what a courageous, steadfast response to those challenges might look like.

While we may never be asked to choose God over persecution, we are daily faced with choosing God over lesser loyalties. We must examine

1. https://lowellmilkencenter.org/unsung-heroes-projects/
2. Robert Ellsberg, *All Saints: Daily Reflections on Saints, Prophets, and Witnesses for Our Time* (New York: Crossroad, 1997).

our budgets and our social-media posts, our relationships and the ones we lack, and question whether or not we are looking to Christ and looking like Christ. Are we imitating the one who emptied himself out for our sakes, or are we full of ourselves? Alternatively, do we recognize our worth, and that of others, as beloved children of God? What are we risking for the sake of the gospel? Looking to Rahab and Zechariah, David and the Shunammite woman, Dorothy Day, Pauli Murray, and those witnesses known only to us, are we moved to follow their example, even as we run the race that only we can? The cloud of witnesses surrounds us. The example of Jesus is ever before us. The past inspires us. All that is left is God's future ahead of us. How we run the race will be our testimony, bearing witness to the next generation—not of *our* faithfulness but of *God's* faithfulness.

JILL DUFFIELD

Luke 12:49–56

[49]"I came to bring fire to the earth, and how I wish it were already kindled! [50]I have a baptism with which to be baptized, and what stress I am under until it is completed! [51]Do you think that I have come to bring peace to the earth? No, I tell you, but rather division! [52]From now on five in one household will be divided, three against two and two against three; [53]they will be divided:

father against son
    and son against father,
mother against daughter
    and daughter against mother,
mother-in-law against her daughter-in-law
    and daughter-in-law against mother-in-law."

[54]He also said to the crowds, "When you see a cloud rising in the west, you immediately say, 'It is going to rain'; and so it happens. [55]And when you see the south wind blowing, you say, 'There will be scorching heat'; and it happens. [56]You hypocrites! You know how to interpret the appearance of earth and sky, but why do you not know how to interpret the present time?"

Commentary 1: Connecting the Reading with Scripture

Like a sign on a teenager's door reading, "Enter at your own risk," this text comes with obvious challenges both for its original audience and for us today. Why did Jesus speak these words? What do we make of his mission? To what signs do we need to pay attention? For what do we need to be prepared?

This text comes in the middle of Luke's Gospel as Jesus is making his way to Jerusalem (9:51–19:48). This particular section (12:1–13:9) is focused on Jesus' instruction to his disciples and the crowds following him. The tension is building for Jesus as he continues to teach, to heal, and to confront those who are following him with the realities of the life to which he is calling them. Conflicts with religious leaders have occurred as Jesus' words and actions have been seen and heard in his ministry in Galilee and now on the road to Jerusalem. Here, Jesus speaks with the voice of a prophet who points to judgment and predictions of the coming days that will demand decision from those who would be his followers. It follows Jesus' teaching to the crowds about being ready for what is to come (12:35–48) and is followed by a warning about repentance (13:1–9). Warnings to friends of Jesus about greed, worry, and being prepared precede this text. The hearer of this reading is prepared to wrestle with Jesus' predictions and warnings about impending conflicts, just as his followers had to do.

There is no clear indication in 12:49–54 whether the audience Jesus is addressing has shifted from the previous discourse, so we can assume he could be speaking to both disciples and the crowd. Notice then how Jesus describes himself in verses 49–51, and recall earlier texts in Luke. Prior to Jesus' baptism, John was baptizing people, asking them to "produce fruit that shows you have changed your hearts and lives" (3:8a CEB). John reminds them that he is baptizing them with water, but that one is coming who will baptize them with "the Holy Spirit and fire" (3:16). John's words of coming judgment are now a named reality in the predictions of Jesus. Here the symbols of fire and baptism function as signs of the destruction and division that will take place in the future coming time of death and resurrection, when Jesus' baptism will be complete.

Jesus continues with the rhetorical question, "Do you think that I have come to bring peace to the earth?" Recall the prophet Simeon, who, after meeting Jesus for the first time, blesses him and his parents and then turns to Mary to tell her he will "be a sign that generates opposition" (2:34b, CEB). Just as Jesus fulfills the prophecy of John, so too questions about his actions and opposition to his teaching have begun to escalate. Jesus' answer to his own question leaves no doubt about his intention. The life he is proposing will not be an easy one. Family members will be separated from each other as households experience division. Jesus' mission has become one of disturbing the orders we know, not merely bringing "peace." These divisions are "created by the diverse decisions made in response to the prophet himself and his message about the kingdom of God."[1]

Jesus turns to the crowds surrounding him with harsh words and penetrating questions (12:54–56). He observes what they pay attention to and what escapes them. They can understand weather patterns but seem unable to grasp other changes going on around them. Addressing them as hypocrites, he asks, "Why do you not know how to interpret the present time?" (12:56). Obviously, Jesus is expecting more from them, the ones who have been listening to him, those who have seen him heal, perform miracles, confront authorities. His voice of prophetic urgency demands more than selective attentiveness if they are to be prepared for what he knows he is facing as he moves closer to Jerusalem.

The other texts for this day circle around the Gospel reading, providing bridges of connection. The poetry of Isaiah describes God as a gardener and the people of Israel as the garden. God will bring judgment on the garden and destroy it, because God "expected justice, but saw bloodshed; righteousness, but heard a cry!" (Isa. 5:7b). The faint image of hope is God's continuing care and love for God's people, "a pleasant planting." Psalm 80 explores the same metaphor of God as gardener, but here the voice of the people is heard. As the vine, they are facing destruction and are asking for God's restoration. "Restore us, O Lord God of hosts; let your face shine, that we may be saved" (Ps. 80:19). Finally, the text from Hebrews reminds the reader of the "so great a cloud of witnesses" (Heb. 12:1a), named and unnamed, whose actions witnessed to their faith. Consider how these lections invite the hearer to hold in tension God's judgment and hope for God's people.

A second connection can be made with Jesus' comment about the division that comes along with following him. When decisions are diverse and divisive, families and faith families struggle. What are the demands of the gospel that are dividing your congregation and families within your congregation? What issues in your community require the response and public action of people of faith? Which issues divide or unite? Are they issues around gender, health care, gun violence, economic justice and fair wages, or public education? The school-to-prison pipeline? Ecological issues threatening the environment? Racism and white privilege? Where does your congregation stand in solidarity with Muslims and Jews when their houses of worship are desecrated or targeted for violence? Is your congregation wrestling with changes in immigration laws and considering their role as places of sanctuary? Living with diverse responses to issues is never easy, always risky, always an act of faith.

Finally, consider connecting this text with contemporary "signs." In the context of your ministry, what are the cultural signs to which people pay attention? Which go unnoticed? In his question to the crowd, Jesus assumed they had been paying attention to his teachings and to the actions they had witnessed. They should have been able to discern both the trajectory of Jesus' mission and his expectations of transformation.

This Gospel text challenges our comfortable faith and our expectation that members of our faith communities will always agree. The other lections from Isaiah and the Psalter are equally challenging in their judgment. We are left to wrestle with Jesus' announcement that divisions even among family are inevitable among his followers. Together, these texts remind us of the

1. Luke Timothy Johnson, *The Gospel of Luke*, Sacra Pagina (Collegeville, MN: Liturgical Press, 1991), 209.

work we are called to do in response to these realities. Divisions are real and how we respond is important. As the writer of Hebrews reminds us, there is a cloud of witnesses whose lives of faith surround us and remind us how we are to live.

John prepared the way for Jesus, inviting people to be baptized and to emerge out of those waters with changed hearts and lives. In this season after Pentecost, we recall that the fire Jesus brought also whipped through the early church on Pentecost. The fire was energizing, filling people with God's Spirit. Fire as judgment and fire as spiritual energy: two very different images for God's work among God's people.

ELIZABETH F. CALDWELL

Commentary 2: Connecting the Reading with the World

As the religious landscape of the United States becomes increasingly pluralistic, a growing group of scholars consider interreligious conversation an essential piece of Christian theology. The belief that God is creator of all and that everything and everyone dwells in God's creative presence means that Christians may understand God anew and afresh by thinking carefully about different expressions of religious belief. This passage from Luke offers an opportunity to experiment with such an idea by using a text from the Hindu tradition as a point of reference.

A Hindu friend once offered me a bit of advice that has helped me think about my faith in a new light. In Hinduism, she said, the goal of life is completion, not perfection. Moreover, human flourishing is tied to being complete, and being complete entails wisdom gained through experience and through hardship. Similar themes are explored in our passage when Jesus talks about division.

To illustrate her point further, my friend relayed a story about how Ganesha, a Hindu deity, is portrayed in iconography. Ganesha has an elephant head and one broken tusk. He holds that broken, imperfect tusk in one of his hands. Hindu tradition teaches that it is with the broken tusk that Ganesha wrote down, at Vyasa's dictation, the *Mahabharata*, one of the most beloved texts in Hinduism. Only with brokenness is completion found. Only through suffering do truth and beauty emerge.[2]

This particular notion of brokenness that offers humanity a step closer to completion is one that offers us a unique vantage point from which to consider Jesus' words. Luke's Jesus speaks harsh words in this passage, words that are passionate and urge action. Jesus says that the kingdom of God has been inaugurated on earth; we are fools if we do not see it. Seeing the kingdom should be as apparent as predicting the weather. However, the kingdom Jesus brings is one of division and hardship, not peace. That division will reach us at a very personal level. It will be felt within our most private spaces and in intimate relationships. Such division can cause us great suffering as families are broken and divided. Can beauty and completion emerge from such division, conflict, and suffering?

The familial relationships that Jesus mentions—father and son, mother and daughter, mother-in-law and daughter-in-law—were all duty-based relationships in the ancient world. Relationships based solely on affection were more likely to be mother-son and brother-sister relationships, because these relationships entailed a freedom not as accessible in the ones mentioned by Jesus.[3] The relationships Jesus identifies could, of course, involve affection, but they always involved duty and obligation.

These family relationships involved obligations for a number of reasons. In the first century, it would be expected that the eldest son in the household would eventually inherit his father's position and property. Thus the eldest son would remain in the household, while younger brothers would move nearby as they came of age. The eldest son would be expected

2. Royina Grewal, *The Book of Ganesha* (New Dehli: Penguin, 2003), 17–39.
3. Bruce J. Malina, "Honor, Shame, and Social Status Revisited," *Journal of Biblical Literature* 128 (2009): 591–611.

to learn the details associated with his future position and would naturally feel both the honor and burden of birth order. The mother and daughter relationship mentioned in the text most likely refers to an unmarried daughter while she still lives in her father's house. The unmarried daughter would be especially obligated to keep her honor, and while a woman could bring shame upon her family in a number of ways throughout her lifetime, an unmarried daughter had a specific duty to remain chaste, not only to bring honor to her family, but also to maintain her worth as a potential wife. A mother would feel the responsibility of ensuring the chastity of her daughter. As for a daughter-in-law, in the first-century world, it was also common for a new wife to move into the family home of her husband. The marriage was viewed as a union created to serve the interests of the kinship group, and the new wife was obligated to maintain her marriage contract in a manner that edified the whole. The new wife would rarely be fully integrated into the family unit. She would most likely always remain on the fringes, and her best hope of becoming a figure of value would be to give birth to a son.[4]

These duty-based relationships are the ones that are the target of Jesus' impassioned warning about impending division. The particular relationships he mentions are structured in such a way that tension may be expected, but there is also anticipation that obligations inherent in these relationships will be met and given expectations fulfilled. In this particular passage, Jesus problematizes the idea of peace and appears to yearn for something different, referencing the "stress" he feels as he anticipates a time of completion. Perhaps Jesus is urging listeners to move beyond the duty that is a focal point of these relationships. Yet these were the very relationships that, even if tension might be involved, kept society in order. When the members of the generations, both younger and older, fulfilled their duties to their families, societal expectations were met, and balance was maintained.

Why would Jesus suggest that what he brought to the earth would destroy such order? The message Jesus brings upsets order. It is meant to disquiet and disturb. Keeping with the theme of upheaval present throughout the Gospel of Luke and found in Jesus' attention to the poor (e.g., 4:18; 16:19–31; 19:8–10) and even in stories of seating arrangements at banquets (14:7–24), duty-based relationships are being torn apart. This leaves broken families, but it also makes space for another kind of order to emerge; here we may find something beautiful growing out of and from the suffering that accompanies being broken. A new freedom is possible when obligations associated only with dutiful action are cast aside and thrown off.

Another Lukan theme, the theme of liberation, is coupled here with the idea of upheaval. Individuals willing to throw off obligations associated with the relationships Jesus mentions are now free to follow him in a way that was not previously possible. A new and much more important sense of duty emerges in the context of this freedom: the duty to do the work of God. This liberating step away from broken family structures and toward completion occurs because a sense of duty shifts in such a significant way. The new focus on the work of the kingdom of God is work moving in the direction of completion.

Christians tend to equate completion and perfection. When the kingdom is complete, perfection is achieved. From the vantage point of Ganesha's story, it may be possible to explore additional options. Completion may hold all the imperfections and experiences of suffering and brokenness that are a part of our lived realities in all their beauty. In this passage, Jesus' sense of urgency is compelling. He works for and in the direction of completion, and the completion he outlines leaves a trail of destruction. As we ponder this text, we may also contemplate the duties and obligations present in our own contexts that prohibit us from the doing the work of the kingdom of God, and we might also consider the broken pieces of our lives that enable us to move in the direction of Jesus' calling.

SALLY SMITH HOLT

4. Bruce J. Malina, *The New Testament World: Insights from Cultural Anthropology*, 3rd ed. (Louisville, KY: Westminster John Knox, 2001), 141–45.

Proper 16 (Sunday between August 21 and August 27 Inclusive)

Jeremiah 1:4–10 and Isaiah 58:9b–14
Psalm 71:1–6 and Psalm 103:1–8
Hebrews 12:18–29
Luke 13:10–17

Jeremiah 1:4–10

[4]Now the word of the LORD came to me saying,

[5]"Before I formed you in the womb I knew you,
and before you were born I consecrated you;
I appointed you a prophet to the nations."

[6]Then I said, "Ah, Lord GOD! Truly I do not know how to speak, for I am only a boy." [7]But the LORD said to me,

"Do not say, 'I am only a boy';
for you shall go to all to whom I send you,
and you shall speak whatever I command you.
[8]Do not be afraid of them,
for I am with you to deliver you,
says the LORD."

[9]Then the LORD put out his hand and touched my mouth; and the LORD said to me,

"Now I have put my words in your mouth.
[10]See, today I appoint you over nations and over kingdoms,
to pluck up and to pull down,
to destroy and to overthrow,
to build and to plant."

Isaiah 58:9b–14

[9]If you remove the yoke from among you,
the pointing of the finger, the speaking of evil,
[10]if you offer your food to the hungry
and satisfy the needs of the afflicted,
then your light shall rise in the darkness
and your gloom be like the noonday.
[11]The LORD will guide you continually,
and satisfy your needs in parched places,
and make your bones strong;
and you shall be like a watered garden,
like a spring of water,
whose waters never fail.
[12]Your ancient ruins shall be rebuilt;
you shall raise up the foundations of many generations;
you shall be called the repairer of the breach,
the restorer of streets to live in.

[13]If you refrain from trampling the sabbath,
from pursuing your own interests on my holy day;
if you call the sabbath a delight
and the holy day of the LORD honorable;
if you honor it, not going your own ways,
serving your own interests, or pursuing your own affairs;
[14]then you shall take delight in the LORD,
and I will make you ride upon the heights of the earth;
I will feed you with the heritage of your ancestor Jacob,
for the mouth of the LORD has spoken.

Commentary 1: Connecting the Reading with Scripture

What catches most readers' attention about the call story of the prophet Jeremiah is that, unlike other prophets, he appears to have been called prior to being born. In other ways, however, Jeremiah 1:4–10 has the familiar structure of a biblical call story. First, God states that an individual has been chosen for a specific purpose. Next, the person to whom God speaks demurs, giving the reason why God must be mistaken, because the person chosen feels either unworthy or unable to fulfill the mission or both. Then God reaffirms the call and promises to equip the person with whatever is needed to fulfill the mission. Often at this point, call stories recount some mechanical means of putting the word of God in the chosen person's mouth. Isaiah has his lips touched with a coal from the heavenly altar (Isa. 6:1–7). Ezekiel is given a scroll to ingest (Ezek. 2:1–3:4). In other call stories, another person helps the prophet fulfill his or her mission. Samuel has Eli to help him overcome his inexperience by advising him to go back and listen for God's word (1 Sam. 3:1–14). Moses, who demurs more than any other prophet and whose call story stretches over two chapters (Exod. 3:1–4:17), is eventually given Aaron to speak for him (4:14). The key point of all these stories, however, is that only a humble person—one who is surprised to be chosen by God—is worthy of prophetic power.

Another common biblical theme in these stories of prophetic calling is the idea that God chooses an unlikely person. Jeremiah is young, as is Samuel. Saul is from an obscure clan in the smallest tribe in Israel (1 Sam. 9:21). David is the youngest of Jesse's sons (1 Sam. 16:11). This theme of beginning one's walk with God early in life is also echoed in Psalm 71. Similarly, Jesus of Nazareth is lifted up as one who seeks God at an early age (Luke 2:49). He is also an unlikely choice for messiah, according to some: a person of humble origins (Matt. 13:55) from an obscure rural backwater (John 1:46).

One can see this theme of Jesus defying expectations repeatedly in the Gospels. When Jesus gives a ruling of law or heals someone on the Sabbath, as he does in Luke 13:10–17, there is no doubt that he strikes many as an unlikely person to have such power. Authorities are often offended by him. His view of rabbinic laws of the Sabbath, while not unique among Jewish interpreters, must have looked unusual, coming from someone others considered untrained and lacking authority. The fact that he spoke as someone with authority of his own, even though he was the son of a tradesman, is often remarked on in the Gospels (Matt. 21:23; Mark 1:27; Luke 5:24; John 8:28).

The readings this week from both Jeremiah and Luke pose a similar question. Will we claim the ministry God has given to us, whether or not we feel worthy or others consider us worthy? Will we acknowledge that all ministry belongs to God and that those of us entrusted with a ministerial task have been so entrusted because God is willing to equip us? Humility is a vital quality in any who would do the will of God. However, one must ultimately accept the call of God if one is to be of service. Only those who are willing to take up the task, regardless of obstacles placed in the way, will fulfill the destiny God has for them. Humility is essential, but so also is courage. One must accept a gift from the hand of God before that gift can be shared with others. Those who are humble realize that no gift of God is meant only for the person to whom it is first given. Gifts of God are meant to be shared.

Like reluctant prophets, the Israelites who first heard Isaiah 58:9b–14 had a hard time accepting that God had real expectations of them. This passage comes from the opening chapters of Third Isaiah (Isa. 56–66), which dates to the time during which Israelites have returned from exile to live in the land but have not yet mastered obeying the laws of God. They have rediscovered the old Canaanite gods and the traditions of their worship (Isa. 57:7). They have not learned to do justice for the poor, something with which they struggled from the earliest days of the Israelite prophets (Amos 2:6–8). They have not learned to practice holiness in a way that is pleasing to God. In fact, other biblical books from this time period show the community more concerned with who will and will not be allowed to remain in their new society than with how the community as a whole can please God (Ezra 9:1–4; Neh. 13:23–31; Isa. 56:3–5).

One way that Israelite religion changed during the exile and in the years just after the return was the emergence of the Sabbath as a central feature of the faith. Though the command to honor the Sabbath was always a feature of Israelite religion (especially during the years when there was no temple to which the people could go to worship), the Sabbath became a holy *time* that substituted for the holy *place* that had been destroyed. These historical realities gave Sabbath laws and practices a much more important role in postexilic Judaism than they appear to have had in preexilic Israelite religion. Discussions of how one should honor the Sabbath are swirling around in the time of Third Isaiah.

The Sabbath should be a time to honor God, not a time simply to take off from work, declares the prophet. In the first eight verses of Isaiah 58, the people are instructed to center their religious practices on doing works of mercy and justice. They should not go out of their way to do purportedly "holy" things like fasting if they cannot do justice at the same time. God values justice and mercy more than such religious gestures, warns the prophet. As Psalm 103:6 states, "The Lord works vindication and justice for all who are oppressed." Those who would be holy as God is holy would do well to remember this and attempt to emulate it.

Although the theological practice of subordinating the OT to the New was rejected by the early church as heresy, this tendency, known as supersessionism, is fully embraced by the book of Hebrews. Throughout Hebrews a contrast is set up between what the author considered the rigid practices of OT covenant law and the new, more merciful covenant instituted by Christ (Heb. 12:18–24). To some extent, the teaching of Third Isaiah foreshadows this trajectory of biblical interpretation by contrasting older, narrower ways of interpreting the law with newer understandings more in keeping with life among those who had returned from exile and were reshaping Judaism for that future.

By the time Jesus begins his ministry, the debate about correct Sabbath observance is in full swing. We see the hard-liners insisting on ever more restricted activities on the Sabbath while others, like Jesus, employ the Pharisaic principle of waiving Sabbath law for the purpose of preserving life. By healing a disabled woman on the Sabbath (Luke 13:10–17), Jesus shows that he prefers the principle voiced by Third Isaiah: God desires that we center our religious observances on "satisfying the needs of the afflicted" (Isa. 58:10), not on "pursuing your own interests on God's holy day" (v. 13). By healing her, Jesus places himself squarely in the tradition of Isaiah, advocating that all religious life should seek to produce justice.

ELIZABETH C. LAROCCA-PITTS

Commentary 2: Connecting the Reading with the World

"Call" stories in the Bible arrest our attention. Direct conversations between God and human beings are not, after all, so numerous that we get to treat them lightly. A sermon on these readings might begin by admitting the dual sense of dread and fascination such stories awaken. "What," we ask ourselves, "if God told *me* to do that?"

The Ambiguity of the Divine Call. Ambiguity might seem an odd word to highlight in relation to our reading. After all, how much plainer could God make things? While nothing but certainty greets us on the divine side of this equation, the same cannot be said of the human side. One need only look at Jeremiah's reaction—and that of so many of the other biblical characters similarly commissioned by God—to understand this. For every Isaiah saying, "Here am I, Lord, send me," there is at least one Moses saying, "Have you thought about my brother Aaron?" So often, the divine call is received not as a joy but as a burden.

In Arthur C. Clarke's novel *Imperial Earth,* the future leaders of the planet are chosen by computers from a select list of qualified candidates, rather than anything like popular elections.[1] The reason? No one perceptive enough to do the job well is ever going to want it, for she or he will realize the hardships and sacrifice it is going to impose. Those who are chosen work especially hard to excel, knowing this is the only way to win early release from their responsibilities.

So it is with the prophets. They are smart enough to know what is about to happen to them. Might one reason for their reluctance be how hard it is to distinguish the genuine voice of God from that which one's audience wants to hear? Jeremiah's own experience with other prophets offering Judah false hope certainly points in this direction. So too does the little book from the early Christian era known as the Didache. Part of that text celebrates the ministry of prophets in the early church. These early leaders itinerated from town to town, delivering the Holy Spirit's message. Dissimilar in many ways to the biblical prophets, they did share with them the idea that their words came directly from God.

Unless, of course, they did not, which is the problem with which the Didache struggles. Strongly drawn to these early Christian prophets, the anonymous writer nonetheless displays an ambivalence toward their message, recognizing how hard it is to authenticate what they say. Does this dynamic partially explain Jeremiah's reluctance? Does it explain yours and mine? Perhaps this passage offers an opportunity to lay bare the absurdity of preaching, to step out from behind the curtain, stand with the congregation, and admit that we, like the prophets, sometimes cannot be sure where God is in all of this. Placing ourselves on this side of the divine-human conversation (instead of always on God's) is the only way for the people, and not just the prophet, to hear God's word of assurance: "Now I have put my words in your mouth."

God's No and God's Yes. Verse 10 offers a poetic outline of Jeremiah's ministry: to pluck up and to pull down, to destroy and to overthrow, to build and to plant. Obvious in this outline is its dual nature: the prophetic word is negative and positive, God's no and God's yes. How do we relate the two?

Karl Barth proposed a solution that was essentially linear: before we can hear God's yes, we must first hear God's no.[2] Until God's no informs us that we are not the fully loving people God created us to be, then the only yes we are capable of hearing is simply hollow self-congratulation. The problem, of course, is how often we preachers get stuck on the no part and never make it to the yes. Better, in that case, to lean toward Martin Luther's understanding, in which God's no is God's yes by another name. When he came to his breakthrough understanding of Romans 1:16–17, Luther realized that

1. Arthur C. Clarke, *Imperial Earth* (New York: Ballantine, 1976).
2. Karl Barth, *The Word of God and the Word of Man* (Gloucester, MA: Peter Smith, 1978), 169.

God's righteousness (in which he could hear only God's no, the condemnation for his own sinfulness) was best displayed in the gospel (the yes of God's gracious forgiveness in Christ).

Holy Restlessness. Whether negative or positive, the prophetic message to which God calls Jeremiah is the same: *things are gonna change around here.* Jeremiah's discomfort with being called by God is a pale shadow of God's dissatisfaction with the society built by human hands. That dissatisfaction infects Jeremiah, who comes to be known for his bitter denunciations of the people's blindness to their situation. This "disease" with the way things are made Jeremiah an outcast, landing him in personal exile, even as Judah headed toward its communal version of the same.

Many pastors know Marilynne Robinson's Pulitzer Prize–winning novel *Gilead*, yet I suspect fewer have read her haunting first novel, *Housekeeping*.[3] The novel follows two daughters, Ruth and Lucille, whose paths diverge after the death of their mother. Lucille is drawn into a more sedentary and conventional life. Ruth, following the example of her loving yet unreliable aunt Sylvie, finds herself enticed by the unbounded and open road. To those like Lucille, Ruth and Sylvie's footloose wandering probably appears as simple irresponsibility. Might it be grounded in something more? Might it reveal a yearning, however inarticulate, for the new thing God is about to do? Might not such "holy restlessness" define the prophets?

Turning to our reading from Isaiah 58, we find what at least seems like ambivalence and restlessness on God's part toward that most troublesome corner of creation: us.

Toward God, toward One Another. The section of Isaiah 58 that precedes our reading, taken on its own, crowns a clear winner in the ancient tug-of-war between personal and social holiness. It speaks of those who "delight to draw near to God" through conspicuous acts of religious observance like fasting, even as they "forsake the ordinance of their God" by oppressing their neighbor. The prophet has nothing but scorn for such empty displays of religiosity. What good does a fast do us if all the while we quarrel, fight, and "strike with a wicked fist"?

When we turn the corner into verses 9b–14, we encounter a different perspective on this question. In the first part of the passage, if Israel ceases to oppress and accuse and instead chooses to feed the hungry, then the Lord will make of it a "watered garden." Similar results are promised in the second part if the people observe the Sabbath properly. Huh? What happened to the contrast between meaningless religious ritual and meaningful social action?

What happened is that this dichotomy, like so many others, is false. An ancient monk named Dorotheos illustrates why this is so.[4] He tells us to think of God and humans as the center and circumference, respectively, of a circle. Any time two of us humans out here on the edge move toward God in the center, we will of necessity be moving toward one another. Likewise, if we are moving away from one another in ways such as the prophet describes, then we *cannot* be moving toward God. Perhaps Dorotheos provides the preacher with an additional picture of the solidarity of the divine call. It is a call to hear "thus says the Lord" alongside those whose brokenness is only as great as our own.

ROBERT A. RATCLIFF

3. Marilynne Robinson, *Gilead* (New York: Picador, 2004); idem, *Housekeeping* (New York: Pan, 1980).
4. E. Rozanne Elder, ed., *Dorotheos of Gaza: Discourses and Sayings* (Kalamazoo, MI: Cistercian Publications, 1977), 138–39.

Psalm 71:1–6

[1]In you, O LORD, I take refuge;
let me never be put to shame.
[2]In your righteousness deliver me and rescue me;
incline your ear to me and save me.
[3]Be to me a rock of refuge,
a strong fortress, to save me,
for you are my rock and my fortress.

[4]Rescue me, O my God, from the hand of the wicked,
from the grasp of the unjust and cruel.
[5]For you, O Lord, are my hope,
my trust, O LORD, from my youth.
[6]Upon you I have leaned from my birth;
it was you who took me from my mother's womb.
My praise is continually of you.

Psalm 103:1–8

[1]Bless the LORD, O my soul,
and all that is within me,
bless his holy name.
[2]Bless the LORD, O my soul,
and do not forget all his benefits—
[3]who forgives all your iniquity,
who heals all your diseases,
[4]who redeems your life from the Pit,
who crowns you with steadfast love and mercy,
[5]who satisfies you with good as long as you live
so that your youth is renewed like the eagle's.

[6]The LORD works vindication
and justice for all who are oppressed.
[7]He made known his ways to Moses,
his acts to the people of Israel.
[8]The LORD is merciful and gracious,
slow to anger and abounding in steadfast love.

Connecting the Psalm with Scripture and Worship

It came as a shock to many some years ago when Mother Teresa's private letters and journals were published and the evidence of her decades-long struggle with doubt was there for all to see.[1] What did we expect? That someone called to serve God in a particularly dramatic way would never worry, never question, never be afraid again? Like Mother Teresa's life, Psalm 71 is a joyful, anxious, confident, bewildered, praising, pleading masterpiece.

On the one hand, we can assume that the psalmist writes from a place of need. This is someone who needs a refuge and is worried about being shamed by others (v. 1); someone who cries out to God for deliverance, rescue, salvation, and a hearing (v. 2); someone who is subject to the whims of people who are unfair and vicious (v. 4). The psalm is laced with lament and punctuated by petitions. On the other hand, Psalm 71 also testifies to a deep and unshakable awareness not only of God's presence from the very beginning of life, but also of God's trustworthiness, in spite of the fears, doubts, and needs that crowd in on all sides. The God described here is the midwife who pulls the psalmist into the world and the one who has been there—a rock of refuge, a strong fortress—ever since. The psalmist does not try to solve the puzzle of how this affirmation of God's constancy and present experiences of threat and anguish fit together. Both dimensions just *are*. What the psalmist does know is that God is the only one who can help, and there is no need to hold back in a relationship as intimate and enduring as this one.

The call of Jeremiah also lets us eavesdrop on someone in the midst of a panic attack, this time in anticipation of the difficulties sure to come for anyone bearing God's unwelcome message. God's reassurances sound familiar to readers of Psalm 71: God has been there from the beginning for Jeremiah, even before the beginning, and God will be there, always, to deliver (vv. 5, 8). On the basis of this promise, there is no need to be afraid.

Is it the case for Jeremiah that these early talking points do the trick? That he will never again worry, question, or be afraid as he prophesies the end of a dynasty? Psalm 71 can be a useful resource for preachers who recognize that Jeremiah's life of faith, like the rest of ours, is not without its moments of doubt and anxiety—sometimes more than moments. It is good to be reminded that those who have responded to God's call before us have been joyful, anxious, confident, bewildered, praising, pleading, and, in all of that, beloved.

Psalm 71 poses something of a liturgical challenge because of the blessed schizophrenia described above. One could minimize these complexities by using a repetitive musical setting of the psalm, for example, but there is another, more provocative, option. It is illuminating to highlight the distinct postures of verses 1–6 by using two different voices when the psalm is read in worship—one voicing the "trust," the other making the petitions. The two voices could then come together in the testimony of the final line: "My praise is continually of you" (v. 6).

The alternate set of readings features an excerpt from Psalm 103 that is treasured by many, and understandably so. It is so familiar that we can miss the strangeness of its opening phrase: "Bless the LORD, O my soul" (v. 1a). It is an exhortation from the self to the self, uncommon enough, but the idea that "blessing" is something humans rightly do in relation to God is more unusual still. Many commentators dissolve any provocation away by equating "bless" with "praise." Maybe it is as simple as that, or maybe there is an intimacy to blessing—acknowledging the blessedness of another—that makes it a more fitting word when "all that is within" a person is involved (v. 1b).

In the second verse, the self urges itself to "bless the LORD" again, and not to lose track of all the things God does to promote well-being. The psalmist then proceeds to recite God's actions over the next several verses. Some of the

1. Mother Teresa and Brian Kolodiejchuk, *Mother Teresa: Come Be My Light; The Private Writings of the "Saint of Calcutta"* (New York: Doubleday, 2007).

things named seem personal, and may be evidence that the writer of this psalm—like many who have loved it over the centuries—is recovering after a time of struggle or suffering. God's activities are wide-ranging: forgiving, healing, redeeming, satisfying, renewing, revealing, and making justice for those who need it most. All of this demonstrates that God is "abounding in steadfast love" (v. 8).

The passage from chapter 58 of Isaiah may also resonate with people recovering from a time of trial, though it is less about naming what God has done and more about imagining what God promises to do if the community can start again, differently: doing justice and loving mercy and delighting in God's affairs. Like Psalm 103, Isaiah tells of God's power to heal and nurture: making bones strong, satisfying every thirst. The Gospel reading for the day (Luke 13:10–17) also has healing at its heart: Jesus heals the bent-over woman, prompting an argument about what it means to observe the Sabbath.

It might be fruitful for a preacher to consider the differences in the tone of Isaiah and the psalmist: Isaiah's promises are conditional: if you shape up, then God will change everything. The psalmist knows nothing of conditions, but sings with abandon of a merciful, gracious, patient, steadfast God, who "works vindication and justice for all who are oppressed" (v. 6).

Could this be the root of the difference in perspective between them? God's complaint against the people Isaiah addresses repeatedly points out their relentless oppression of the poor, their bullying, slander, and corresponding hypocrisy. They do not live as those who worship a God abounding in steadfast love. Perhaps the psalmist writes from the point of view of one among the oppressed, one who now knows liberation, maybe someone like the woman Jesus heals in Luke 13. In this way, the psalm may be an example of what it *feels* like to live in the watered garden Isaiah describes, where relationships have been transformed, bones once crushed grow strong, everyone rejoices in God's benefits, and the work of reparation can begin. A preacher could make the most of the fact that it is good news that there is room in this garden for reformed and reforming oppressors as well.

Psalm 103:1–8 works very well as a responsive call to worship, and there are many hymns and songs that take up the language and function of these verses. "Praise to the Lord, the Almighty," is one well-known example. There is also liturgical potential in the little phrase "do not forget" in verse 2. This might be used intermittently throughout the service, every time one of God's gracious actions is mentioned. For example, after the declaration of forgiveness the congregation may say something to the effect of "thanks be to God!" and then a voice from somewhere in the room urges, "Do not forget!" A couple of relatively confident liturgists seated in different parts of the worship space can be enlisted to do this, and eventually others around them may catch on and join in.

ANGELA DIENHART HANCOCK

Hebrews 12:18–29

[18]You have not come to something that can be touched, a blazing fire, and darkness, and gloom, and a tempest, [19]and the sound of a trumpet, and a voice whose words made the hearers beg that not another word be spoken to them. [20](For they could not endure the order that was given, "If even an animal touches the mountain, it shall be stoned to death." [21]Indeed, so terrifying was the sight that Moses said, "I tremble with fear.") [22]But you have come to Mount Zion and to the city of the living God, the heavenly Jerusalem, and to innumerable angels in festal gathering, [23]and to the assembly of the firstborn who are enrolled in heaven, and to God the judge of all, and to the spirits of the righteous made perfect, [24]and to Jesus, the mediator of a new covenant, and to the sprinkled blood that speaks a better word than the blood of Abel.

[25]See that you do not refuse the one who is speaking; for if they did not escape when they refused the one who warned them on earth, how much less will we escape if we reject the one who warns from heaven! [26]At that time his voice shook the earth; but now he has promised, "Yet once more I will shake not only the earth but also the heaven." [27]This phrase, "Yet once more," indicates the removal of what is shaken—that is, created things—so that what cannot be shaken may remain. [28]Therefore, since we are receiving a kingdom that cannot be shaken, let us give thanks, by which we offer to God an acceptable worship with reverence and awe; [29]for indeed our God is a consuming fire.

Commentary 1: Connecting the Reading with Scripture

In many ways, Hebrews 12:18–29 is the grand conclusion of the book and certainly of 11:1–12:29. Hebrews 11:1–12:2 lays out the great exhortation to faith and endurance in the metaphor of the footrace of faith, calling the reader to complete (*teleioō*) the race, as Jesus has already done. In 12:3–17, the writer expands the theme, encouraging endurance to obtain grace, echoing in 12:12 the metaphor of the footrace ("lift your drooping hands and strengthen your weak knees") from 12:1.

Our passage continues this appeal to images of faithfulness. Verses 18–29 develop the theme of inheriting divine grace in two sets of contrasting images. The first contrast (vv. 18–24) is between two mountains prominent in Israel's story: Sinai and Zion. Sinai (not explicitly named) is where Moses received the Torah (Exod. 19–20); the mountain serves as a figure for Israel's earliest encounters with God. Mount Zion is the location of Jerusalem and where Jewish and early Christian eschatological expectation anticipated the arrival of the heavenly city, the new Jerusalem (Dan. 7; Rev. 21). The two mountains thus bracket Israel's sacred story. Each half of the contrast begins by using forms of the verb *erchomai*, "to come": "you have *not* come" (v. 18) and "you *have* come" (v. 22, italics added).

Believers in Christ "have *not* come" to Mount Sinai, which is seen in threatening terms. It is a place of terror, "blazing fire," "darkness and gloom," "tempest," and the blast of a trumpet. Most of these references are drawn from Exodus 19:16–25, the theophany and the giving of the Decalogue. The writer of Hebrews, however, is not interested in the law so much as in Israel's response of fear, rejection, and withdrawal at the sound of the voice of God. He draws attention to the people's demand of Moses—"Let not God speak to us, lest we die" (Exod. 20:19 RSV)—and to the warning that no one from Israel—not even an animal (Exod. 19:13)—approach

Cherish the Desire of God

The mind that is the prisoner of conventional ideas, and the will that is the captive of its own desire cannot accept the seeds of an unfamiliar truth and a supernatural desire. For how can I receive the seeds of freedom if I am in love with slavery and how can I cherish the desire of God if I am filled with another and an opposite desire? God cannot plan His liberty in me because I am prisoner and I do not even desire to be free. I love my captivity and I imprison myself in the desire for the things that I hate, and I have hardened my heart against true love. I must learn therefore to let go of the familiar and the usual and consent to what is new and unknown to me. I must learn to "leave myself" in order to find myself by yielding to the love of God. If I were looking for God, every event and every moment would sow, in my will, grains of His life that would spring up one day in a tremendous harvest.

Thomas Merton, "Seeds of Contemplation," in *New Seeds of Contemplation* (New York: New Directions Books, 1962), 16.

or touch the mountain on pain of death. Both are measures of the fear and dread associated by Hebrews with the Sinai experience.

In verses 22–24, "you *have* come" to Mount Zion, now explicitly named as "the city of the living God" and "the heavenly Jerusalem." To arrive there is to come to the eschatological moment toward which Hebrews has been reaching. Again, the writer draws on Hebrew Scripture for the theme of Zion as the locus of the eschatological event (Pss. 2:6; 46:4; 99:2–5; 122; Isa. 8:18; 9:7; 10:12; Ezek. 40–48; Joel 2:32; Mic. 4:1–4). Hebrews itself refers to the desire for the eschatological "better" city (Heb. 11:10, 16; 13:14). "Innumerable angels in festal gathering" is likely a reference to the apocalyptic vision of the heavenly throne of the "ancient of days" in Daniel 7:10 before which stand "ten thousand times ten thousand." This reference probably recalled for early Christians the "one like a son of man" (Dan. 7:13), a figure of the eschatological Christ. The assembled "firstborn" recalls the references of Hebrews 11:4–22 to the patriarchs who passed the promise of God from generation to generation through the firstborn male. It also refers to the followers of Jesus, whom the writer describes as the "firstborn of the world" (Heb. 1:6; also Col. 1:15). These are "enrolled in heaven"—an image consonant with being recorded in the "book of life" (Dan. 12:1; Mal. 3:16; Luke 10:20; also Exod. 32:32; Ps. 69:28; Rev. 13:8; 17:8; 20:12–15). These "firstborn" are gathered before God, along with the "spirits of the righteous made perfect" (*teleioō*). As in Hebrews 11:40 and 12:2, the writer evokes the sense of "completion" or "fulfillment" of a race, connecting the spirits gathered before God with the "great cloud of witnesses" who encourage the endurance of his readers.

Finally, we meet Jesus, the "mediator" whose "sprinkled blood speaks a better word than the blood of Abel." Behind this reference lie two scriptural traditions. First, in Leviticus 4:1–7, a worshiper atones for sin with a sin offering, in which the blood of the sacrifice is sprinkled on the altar and sanctuary veil. Christian tradition associates the blood of Christ—offered at the eucharistic table and on the cross—with the same expiation from sin. Hebrews will return to this theme in 13:12. Second, the "blood of Abel" is that spilled on the ground by Cain (Gen. 4:8–10); according to Hebrews, it seems, Abel's murder results from the jealousy of Cain that Abel's sacrifice was acceptable to God, while his own was not. The writer connects Abel's blood with acceptable sacrifice, anticipating the fuller and "better" sacrifice of Christ.

The second contrast is Hebrews 12:25–29, between that which is "shaken" and that which is unshakable. Once again, the writer draws on the language of the Sinai theophany. The warning to "not refuse the one who is speaking" (v. 25) returns us to Exodus 20:19 and the demand of Israel that God not speak directly to them again. Those who did refuse to hear God's word "did not escape," which may refer to any of a number of punitive events, from reversals in the wilderness (e.g., Num. 14:26–45; 16:1–50; 21:4–9) to the destruction of Jerusalem in 587 BCE (2 Kgs. 25). Hebrews has relied on this theme from the outset of the letter, reminding the reader that "long ago God spoke to our ancestors" (Heb. 1:1) and asking, "How can we escape if we neglect" the salvation offered in God's words (2:3)? The God whom the faithful dare not ignore "shook the earth"—most likely not a reference to the Sinai narrative in Exodus directly but to poetic treatments of it such as Psalm 68:8 or to other theophanies like the Isaiah call narrative (Isa. 6:4).

At the center of this section is a quotation from Haggai 2:6–7. Hebrews relies not on the Hebrew but the Septuagint for the wording, omitting the second half and inserting the words "not only" and "but also" (v. 26). These changes lead to a shift in emphasis away from Haggai's promise of wealth and splendor for the new temple in Jerusalem toward an eschatological shaking (the verb in v. 26 is *seisō*, from which we derive "seismic") in which not only earth but even heaven will quake at the sound of the word of God. Verse 27 provides the pivotal point in the comparison. Hebrews explains that "Yet once more" means that what is shaken is "removed." Encompassed within what is shaken and removed is the created order ("what has been made"), leaving behind that which "cannot be shaken." The effect is to contrast the temporality of creation with the endurance and stability of the "unshakable" heavenly city, in which dwell God and Christ.

"Therefore," the writer urges readers to "give thanks" (v. 28). This thankful worship is grounded in the gift of a kingdom, in all likelihood the eschatological kingdom of Daniel 7:10, which has figured in the background of much of this section. Note the present tense of the participle, "we are receiving" (*paralambanontes*), perhaps an indication that the eschatological arrival of the kingdom is an ongoing event. The kingdom is in the process of coming, and for this, we "give thanks" in a worship of "reverence and awe."

The Revised Common Lectionary pairs this text with Jeremiah 1:4–10, the call narrative of Jeremiah. Verse 10 sets the prophet "over nations and kingdoms, . . . to destroy and to overthrow, to build and to plant," an apocalyptic commission that comports well with the eschatological themes of Hebrews of promise. One cannot fairly be heard without the other.

PAUL K. HOOKER

Commentary 2: Connecting the Reading with the World

Why do contemporary worshipers come to church?

What if the preacher proclaims real presence, real unmediated access to God? In other words, to what can we point that will enable the congregation to experience the presence of God? The preacher of Hebrews is on a roll, admonishing the gathered faithful to live as the holy people they are as a result of Christ. Just prior to our appointed verses came paraenetic instructions: pursue peace, do not let bitterness grow, do not be like Esau, immoral and godless as he was. That is, you know better, so do better. There is no excuse for practicing idolatry, no excuse for wrangling and grumbling. Why? Real presence. Real unmediated access to God. You know better. You know Jesus. Do better.

Prior to the coming of Jesus, God's people experienced the awesome presence of the Divine through smoke and fire, tempest and trumpet, Moses' shining face and the commandments. Despite such pyrotechnics, sound, and light, the Israelites built a golden calf, grumbled against Moses, and otherwise failed to hold up their end of the covenant. Enter the prophets and exile and return and more prophets. However, with the coming of Jesus, the mediator of the new covenant, God's people have come face-to-face not with a human intermediary but with the heavenly Messiah. Will they dare not follow the will of God now? Questioning Moses' authority is one thing; refusing to follow the Son of God a whole different matter. Cue fire and brimstone from the pulpit. Maybe weeping and gnashing of teeth. Shake the seats as they do on theme-park rides. That would get people's attention! Given, however, the unavailability of such special effects, how are preachers to engender such a response?

The writer of Hebrews seems intent on garnering awe and fear. He wants hearers on the edge of their seats, attention focused, at the ready to ask with eagerness and earnestness, "What should we do?" Chapter 13 will answer that question, revealing that today's reading is flanked by instructions for ethical living, and therefore at least one of the goals of these verses is to motivate the faithful to act. Why? Because of real presence. As frightened as the Israelites were at the booming voice from heaven and the blazing fire on Sinai, how much more ought we to be overwhelmed by the presence of Jesus Christ in our midst! How much more should we be motivated to do the will of God! How much more should we be moved to worship, praise, and wonder!

Motivating those assembled to act could include a sermon focus on real presence. Invite hearers to sit with the reality of real, unmediated access to the triune God. Really, though, how many modern-day people in the pew (or pulpit) have an acute sense of the Divine when they enter a sanctuary or go out into their day-to-day world? How often are any of us conscious of Christ in our midst when two or three are gathered or being lifted into the presence of the ascended Christ, gathered with the whole communion of the saints, when we celebrate Communion? How many of us are keenly aware that when we go to our Galilee our risen Lord meets us there? The reality of which we are most aware is not the Divine but the mundane: bills to pay, meals to cook, work to do, family to tend, bathrooms to clean. No wonder the writer of Hebrews resorts to conjuring up old-school images of fire and brimstone, trumpets and terror. How else can he prod people from complacency and a tendency to forget that daily living—how we treat those next to us in the pew, those next door to us, and those the next ocean over—are connected to the covenant, old and new? There is a "do this or else" feel to these verses, a sort of finger-wagging that does not play well in postmodern, pluralistic, individual-rights-loving contexts today.

Will it preach in our contexts? Yes. Because of real presence. Not ours but that of the Holy Spirit. Conjuring up the holy is not the job of the preacher, but calling people's attention to the reality of it is. For Hebrews, the images of Moses and Mount Sinai resonated with the audience. For those attempting to get the attention of twenty-first-century people, maybe not so much. In an age of virtual reality and other hauntingly real digital effects, fire on a mountain and trumpet blasts from above may engender a shoulder shrug instead of a soul-disturbing shudder. So, what does open us to the real presence of the Holy One, who is no less present today than on Mount Sinai or Mount Zion or in the upper room or in Galilee?

Jaded to the transcendent though many contemporary Christians may be, hunger for mystery has not abated. Miraculously, congregations do gather week after week for worship, perhaps not expecting much, but their real presence is a decision that communicates hope that another real presence will show up too. Why else come to worship in an age when other options abound and no cultural pressure compels attendance? Given that, how much more ought the preacher boldly to proclaim the gospel, directing attention to the consuming fire of our God within and without? These verses from Hebrews should compel preachers to discern what images, biblical and otherwise, will move their hearers to the edge of their seats in anticipation of experiencing God.

Likely, there are experiences unique to each community and congregation that would be as moving for them as the OT stories were for the first audiences of Hebrews. One small church I served came together in the wake of Hurricane Katrina to welcome a family displaced by that tempest. Watching the news, hearing the scope of the disaster, and seeing the helplessness of those suddenly rendered homeless compelled the congregation to ask, "What should we do?" The flooding had rendered those a few states over refugees. The manse was unoccupied. The answer was clear. In short order, the manse was cleaned and stocked with food, clothing, and furniture. Days later, the church welcomed a family of four, the real presence of that small congregation combined with the real presence of that beleaguered family to make undeniably manifest the real presence of God. Praise, thanksgiving, and worship ensued.

Heaven and earth get shaken up, pressed down, and overflow to and through us in many forms. Sometimes like a burning bush, at other times like heartburn (or as I once heard, "discernment through nausea"). A word comes to consciousness while in prayer, a stranger's request upends our busy self-importance, a close friend challenges our prejudices through sharing her story, a hymn from our childhood undoes us in worship, taking the bread and the cup transports us to a scene of the heavenly banquet and the communion of the saints. Suddenly, we are consumed with a passion to reconcile with one long estranged from us. In these ways, we know the real presence of God. We know God with us, not far off, obscured by clouds or relayed to us through another, but unmediated, our friend and Master and Messiah right before us.

The preacher's job is not to conjure up the real presence of God but rather cast a vision rich with images that invite those gathered to see the consuming fire already there, present and at work and worthy of worship. No pyrotechnics or shaking pews required.

JILL DUFFIELD

Proper 16 (Sunday between August 21 and August 27 Inclusive)

Luke 13:10–17

> [10]Now he was teaching in one of the synagogues on the sabbath. [11]And just then there appeared a woman with a spirit that had crippled her for eighteen years. She was bent over and was quite unable to stand up straight. [12]When Jesus saw her, he called her over and said, "Woman, you are set free from your ailment." [13]When he laid his hands on her, immediately she stood up straight and began praising God. [14]But the leader of the synagogue, indignant because Jesus had cured on the sabbath, kept saying to the crowd, "There are six days on which work ought to be done; come on those days and be cured, and not on the sabbath day." [15]But the Lord answered him and said, "You hypocrites! Does not each of you on the sabbath untie his ox or his donkey from the manger, and lead it away to give it water? [16]And ought not this woman, a daughter of Abraham whom Satan bound for eighteen long years, be set free from this bondage on the sabbath day?" [17]When he said this, all his opponents were put to shame; and the entire crowd was rejoicing at all the wonderful things that he was doing.

Commentary 1 Connecting the Reading with Scripture

Luke is the only Gospel writer who tells the story of Jesus healing a disabled woman in the synagogue on the Sabbath. She is not noticed. We do not know her name. She is someone to whom no one wants to talk, because she is different.

This is the second story in Luke of a Sabbath healing by Jesus. The first (Luke 6:6–11) can be imagined in a series of unfolding scenes. As the story opens, we see Jesus encountering the man with the withered hand, religious leaders hovering nearby to see what will happen next. These religious leaders know about Jesus' challenge of laws forbidding the picking of grain on the Sabbath (6:1–5). The scene changes, and as readers we witness Jesus challenging these religious ones with their concerns. "Here's a question for you," he says, "Is it legal on the Sabbath to do good or to do evil, to save life or to destroy it?" (6:9 CEB). The scene shifts again and Jesus moves in closer to the man whose hand is stretched out. His hand is healed. The last scene shows the backs of the religious leaders, huddled together in their anger, trying to decide what to do about Jesus.

In the second story (13:10–17), a panorama shot reveals the inside of the synagogue. Gathered on the Sabbath, worshipers are listening to Jesus' teaching. A close-up reveals the image of a woman so disabled that her vision can take in only what she sees on the floor at her feet. Jesus sees her, invites her to approach him, and the scene shows her bent over in front of him with his hands on her shoulder. Next, she is shown standing straight, her arms in the air, her mouth open and praising God. The synagogue leader is pictured engaging Jesus with questions and Jesus responding to him. The last image is a final panorama shot showing Jesus, the bent-over woman now standing up straight, the synagogue leader looking at Jesus, and the worshipers expressing their joy at what they have just seen.

Notice some of the details of the text that the camera might have missed.

- This is the fourth Lukan story about Jesus in a synagogue (2:41–52; 4:16–21; 6:6–11). Here, the emphasis—mentioned three times!—is on teaching in the synagogue on the Sabbath (13:10, 14, 16).
- As in the Sabbath healing story in chapter 6, the woman does not ask to be healed. Jesus invites her to come to him. This woman, perhaps invisible to the community because of her illness and lack of status, is invited in by Jesus.

- Acting with God's power, Jesus sets her free from the spirit that has afflicted her body. Recall that Jesus began his ministry by reading from the scroll of Isaiah. In choosing a text that twice mentions the work of releasing those who are captive or oppressed (4:18), he makes clear the focus of his work. His healing act is also an act of deliverance, freeing her from that which had bound her for eighteen years.
- Jesus lays his hands on her (13:13). The use of these words in this particular action of Jesus occurs in healing stories or the times when Jesus gives new names to the disciples. In this story, she is both healed and restored to the wholeness of her community.
- Sabbath laws are emphasized and worthy of our full attention. Notice how the word "ought" is used. The leader of the synagogue points out that healing is considered to be work, and there are six days when work "ought [*dei*] to be done." After responding with the example of caring for animals on the Sabbath, Jesus asks "ought not [*edei*] this woman" be "set free from this bondage on the sabbath day?" Jesus' act of healing was obviously a problem for the synagogue leader, who was responsible for the faithful reading of the law in worship, but it was not a problem for the majority of persons who were there. As Amy-Jill Levine points out, the Jewish worshipers that day would not have had a problem with the healing: "They would have recognized his [Jesus'] argument to be a standard form for discussion of legal matters. He argues on the basis of what is called in Hebrew a *qal v'homer*, or 'from the lighter to the greater,' model."[1] So, if you feed and care for oxen and donkeys on the Sabbath, then you should also be able to heal someone in need. Jesus shifts the argument from what is legally permissible on the Sabbath to the obligations of Sabbath.[2]
- Sabbath was a joyful day for remembering Israel's release from slavery in Egypt. Frances Taylor Gench writes that since freedom and liberation are at the heart of Sabbath worship, "the release of a captive woman, then, is a highly appropriate way to make the day holy, representing the very fulfillment, rather than a violation, of the sabbath."[3] Rather than viewing the story as Jesus' correcting the synagogue leader, see it as Jesus acting consistently within his tradition. In setting her free on the Sabbath, Jesus also sets free those who are there. In healing her on a Sabbath, a day of rest, they are freed from too narrow an understanding of what rest looks like.
- Jesus addresses the woman as "a daughter of Abraham," a designation unique in the Bible. Luke addresses Zacchaeus as a "son of Abraham." Zacchaeus is a tax collector, despised by most, but called out and loved by Jesus. She is a disabled woman, walking bent over for eighteen years, seen by Jesus and healed. What an interesting pair! Both are on the fringes of their communities, invited by Jesus to the center. Perhaps like Abraham, they have important roles in modeling faithful lives in response to God's call.

Consider two connections that might be made in your ministry context. Connect with the disabled woman. She did not approach Jesus and ask to be healed. He chose her, and in the act of healing, he challenged a synagogue leader's understanding of Sabbath work. Jesus' healing is holy Sabbath work (see Exod. 31:14). In calling her "daughter of Abraham," he names her, heals her, restores her health, and delivers her to her community, visible and named.

Who are the "daughters of Abraham" in your community in need of a ministry of healing presence? Who are the ones who cannot look up and see anything because they are held down by

1. Amy-Jill Levine, *The Misunderstood Jew: The Church and the Scandal of the Jewish Jesus* (San Francisco: Harper, 2006), 32.
2. Natalie K. Houghtby-Haddon, *Changed Imagination, Changed Obedience: Social Imagination and the Bent-Over Woman in the Gospel of Luke* (Eugene, OR: Pickwick, 2011), 41.
3. Frances Taylor Gench, *Back to the Well: Women's Encounters with Jesus in the Gospels* (Louisville, KY: Westminster John Knox, 2004), 89.

experiences of violence? Who are the ones whose backs are bent from caring for others? Who are the ones that nobody notices? Like Jesus, we are involved in healing when we invite those on the edges of our faith communities into the center.

Consider for yourself and for those in your congregation, Jesus' reframing of what Sabbath looks like: Sabbath rest as a practice of faith, Sabbath as a day of holy work. Then challenge your listeners to consider what it might look like for their lives. To what holy work are we called? To what kind of Sabbath practices might God be drawing us?

ELIZABETH F. CALDWELL

Commentary 2: Connecting the Reading with the World

The bent woman in Luke 13 was most likely unable to participate in normal social interaction, yet she made her way to synagogue on that Sabbath. Maybe her posture was similar to that of the animals Jesus mentions when critiquing his opponents in verse 15. In the ancient world, was she considered no more than a beast of burden, forever in the servile position of an ox or a donkey? Jesus reminds the reader that even livestock had the right to Sabbath rest. The synagogue leaders are concerned with preserving the order of the law, a worthy endeavor, but their concern seems to preclude them from understanding the compassionate perspective offered by Jesus. This text provides us with an opportunity to reflect on what factors may limit our own perspectives and capacities to understand and empathize with others in our own communities who are marginalized.

Because of her physical condition, the bent-over woman could not have a face-to-face conversation with others in her community; we can imagine how this condition would have led to some sense of marginalization and isolation. Her experience of such conditions had lasted eighteen long years (v. 11). Thus, we suspect that she may not have been fully included in her community for quite some time. Then, she showed up at the synagogue and met Jesus.

Two relatively new concepts—*cripping* and *intersectionality*—may help in our consideration of the bent-over woman's encounter with Jesus, a miracle of healing found only in the Gospel of Luke.

The term "cripping" is one broadly used in disability studies. Cripping is a process that seeks to promote bringing the contributions of people with disabilities into the so-called mainstream. The term is representative of all types of disabilities and advances inclusion of the perspectives of people with disabilities as valued and unique contributions to human diversity.[4]

For an example of how cripping might be understood, let us consider the notion of "cripping time." Scholars specializing in disability studies suggest that cripping time may be more appropriate to our understanding of a holy pace. Whether because of a physical condition or because of how long it takes to navigate in a world set up for able-bodied people, some people with disabilities necessarily move at a slower pace than others. A slower pace in no way indicates that people with disabilities are behind others in a negative sense. Rather, cripping time provides a way to experience a pace where holy moments and spaces, not readily available in a culture that moves quickly and prioritizes the speed of so many things, might be realized. How fast is your computer, your car, or your rise up the pay scale? The pace of the world in which Jesus lived was not like our fast-paced society. What if the pace of Jesus' world had more in common with the steady and slower one observable in some places within the crip community?[5] What do we fail to notice as we rush from one task to another during hurried days, and did the pace of Jesus in Luke 13 provide him with an opportunity to notice someone who might be overlooked more easily today?

4. See Wright State University, "Breaking Silences: Crip Theory," https://www.wright.edu/event/sex-disability-conference/crip-theory.
5. Cf. John Swinton, *Becoming Friends of Time: Disability, Timefullness, and Gentle Discipleship* (Waco, TX: Baylor University Press, 2016).

"Intersectionality" is another concept appropriate to our consideration of this passage. A term first coined nearly three decades ago, intersectionality refers to the way multiple oppressions are experienced.[6] No person has just one identity marker, and when multiple identity markers are considered, the ways in which we experience the social constructs under which we live seem increasingly complex and interconnected.

In this passage, the bent-over woman possesses multiple, intersecting identities. She is female, a daughter of Abraham, a person with a disability, and a person bound by Satan, according to Jesus (v. 16). When Jesus heals her on the Sabbath, he comes under the immediate criticism of the leader of the synagogue for violation of Sabbath law, yet he has done so much more than this.

By transgressing several boundaries in his interaction with the bent-over woman, Jesus highlights that laws and rules are best interpreted through the lens of mercy. Additionally, the actions of Jesus push the reader to consider the intersecting identity markers at play in this scene. The narrative is already fraught with tension. Jesus' opponents call into question his fealty to the callings and obligations of the Sabbath. Indirectly, might they also be challenging the bent-over woman's identity? Further, Jesus interacts with a woman, calling her over to an area of the synagogue that may have been reserved specifically for men. He also touches her, a woman, and one who has a disability and is bound by Satan. This closeness could render him unclean, but instead of letting the identity markers of the woman limit him, he accepts and works with and through each marker.

Jesus proclaims that Satan has bound this woman; notice that he does not name her a sinner. Instead, his words and touch liberate her from satanic bondage. Her liberation results in her praise of God. How then might we think of being bound by Satan? Perhaps we are all bound by the limitations of our bodies but simply in different ways. Since we are created beings bound to our physical contexts, our freedom may be realized by acceptance of our limitations, and we may attain liberation through our loving relationships. Jesus saw a woman excluded from normal, everyday interaction, and his understanding of and connection with her humanity was transformative.

The bent-over woman's identity as a female and a daughter of Abraham intersected with her state of bondage and the physical repercussions of that bondage. She experiences intersecting oppressions of gender and disability, and her liberation, while a result of Jesus' willingness to transgress boundaries and prioritize mercy over rule keeping, also causes us to wonder who else may be in need of liberation in this passage. What if the woman, even before her healing, has more freedom than the leader of the synagogue? He may be experiencing his own kind of bondage. Her status, even though Satan has bound her, does not incapacitate her. She is able to see and respond to Jesus as he sees her and meets her needs. In contrast, the leader of the synagogue may feel the burden of obligation connected to his role in the community. Perhaps the leader's sense of duty prevents him from authentically participating in the freedom that Jesus is offering. Jesus offers harsh words of condemnation, and the reader is informed that his opponents feel shame. We feel shame when we are confronted with a truth and realize we have been in the wrong.

This passage offers us hope that all who witnessed the transformation of the bent-over woman experienced similar transformations when confronted with the truth offered by Jesus. When we become obstacles to ourselves or when institutionalized religion becomes a force that prohibits us from experiencing and worshiping God, it becomes exceedingly clear that each of us requires the mercy and healing power that Jesus displays in this passage, no matter our intersecting identities.

SALLY SMITH HOLT

6. Kimberle Crenshaw, "Mapping the Margins: Intersectionality, Identity Politics, and Violence against Women of Color," *Stanford Law Review* 43 (1991): 1241–99.

Proper 17 (Sunday between August 28 and September 3 Inclusive)

Jeremiah 2:4–13 and Proverbs 25:6–7
Psalm 81:1, 10–16 and Psalm 112
Hebrews 13:1–8, 15–16
Luke 14:1, 7–14

Jeremiah 2:4–13

[4]Hear the word of the LORD, O house of Jacob, and all the families of the house of Israel. [5]Thus says the LORD:

What wrong did your ancestors find in me
that they went far from me,
and went after worthless things, and became worthless themselves?
[6]They did not say, "Where is the LORD
who brought us up from the land of Egypt,
who led us in the wilderness,
in a land of deserts and pits,
in a land of drought and deep darkness,
in a land that no one passes through,
where no one lives?"
[7]I brought you into a plentiful land
to eat its fruits and its good things.
But when you entered you defiled my land,
and made my heritage an abomination.
[8]The priests did not say, "Where is the LORD?"
Those who handle the law did not know me;
the rulers transgressed against me;
the prophets prophesied by Baal,
and went after things that do not profit.

[9]Therefore once more I accuse you,
says the LORD,
and I accuse your children's children.
[10]Cross to the coasts of Cyprus and look,
send to Kedar and examine with care;
see if there has ever been such a thing.
[11]Has a nation changed its gods,
even though they are no gods?
But my people have changed their glory
for something that does not profit.
[12]Be appalled, O heavens, at this,
be shocked, be utterly desolate,
says the LORD,
[13]for my people have committed two evils:
they have forsaken me,
the fountain of living water,
and dug out cisterns for themselves,
cracked cisterns
that can hold no water.

Proverbs 25:6–7

[6]Do not put yourself forward in the king's presence
or stand in the place of the great;
[7]for it is better to be told, "Come up here,"
than to be put lower in the presence of a noble.

Commentary 1: Connecting the Reading with Scripture

This first suggested OT passage is a classic prophetic critique of Israel's tendency toward apostasy. No matter what the Lord does for them—bringing them up from the land of Egypt, leading them through the wilderness, giving them a rich new land filled with good things—they still insist on going after "worthless things," that is, idols and the gods of other cultures. Even those priests and prophets who are charged with teaching the right practice of Israelite religion are corrupted, for they teach foreign practices dedicated to foreign gods. This is a common complaint of Jeremiah, due to certain desperate actions taken by the last few kings of the southern kingdom of Judah. Knowing that it was only a matter of time before the Babylonians wiped them off the map completely, the people of Judah turned to pagan practices, hoping that if YHWH would not rescue them, perhaps some other god would. They even revived the ancient and abominable practice of child sacrifice in an effort to secure the attention of a god, any god, who might rescue them (Jer. 7:16–33).

To Jeremiah, Israel's abandonment of YHWH is something that not even the most ignorant foreigner would do to their own gods. Who has ever heard of a nation abandoning their gods? Even those cultures who have puny ineffectual gods remain true to them! God offers us fresh running water, yet we prefer to dig cracked and decaying holes in the ground to hold stagnant water. The contrast between the living God of Israel and the dead, dormant gods of the nations is clear to Jeremiah, and he seeks to make it clear to his contemporaries.

If Judah wishes to be heard and rescued, says Jeremiah, all they need to do is return to the Lord, do justice, and love mercy (7:5–7). This is also the message of Psalm 81. If God's people would listen to God, then God would quickly subdue their enemies and turn God's hand against their foes (81:13–14). Sirach also repeats this theme by stating that the first act of human pride is to forsake the Lord, and pride is the beginning of human sin (Sir. 10:12–13). It is that sin of pride that causes God to drive humanity away from God's presence.

Although the Gospel lesson from Luke 14:1, 7–14, does not deal directly with apostasy as the primary sin of humanity, it does advocate for abandoning pride and serving the lowly as a means of pleasing God. In this passage, Jesus gives the same wise counsel of Proverbs 25:6–7 by advising those who wish to be exalted to first humble themselves in the presence of others. He goes on to urge those who offer hospitality to offer it to those who cannot repay it, namely, the poor.

All of these teachings share the view that God is less pleased with grand human gestures that seek to communicate piety and instead communicate pride. Instead, God seeks simple humble gestures that promote justice and mercy (see Amos 5:15–27). If only people would turn to God with their whole heart, the prophets declare over and over again, instead of trying out exotic rituals and grand gestures of their own design, hoping for validation from God (Mic. 6:1–8). God validates the faithful and the just and the humble, but somehow that lesson is hard for human beings to absorb.

The second recommended OT lection comes from Proverbs, a cornerstone of biblical Wisdom literature. Like other collections of proverbial sayings known in the ancient Near East (such as the Instructions of Ani and the Instructions of Amenemope from Egypt or the proverbs preserved by Ashurbanipal in Assyria), the biblical book of Proverbs purports to preserve the proverbs of Solomon (of which he is said to have written three thousand, according to 1 Kgs. 4:32). However, the book is not simply made up of proverbial sayings of Solomon. It also includes instructions to young people on how to choose Wisdom over Folly (both personified as female characters), as well as collections of proverbs and poems by wise ancients other than Solomon (e.g., Prov. 31).

The heading "Proverbs of Solomon" occurs at the beginning of chapter 10 and continues until another heading ("Proverbs of the Wise") appears in the middle of chapter 22, even as more "Proverbs of the Wise" continue through chapter 24. At the beginning of Proverbs 25, however, a new heading appears: "Other Proverbs of Solomon That the Officials of King Hezekiah of Judah Copied." This heading returns us to those sayings attributed to the great king. The first four proverbs in the chapter are clearly those that would have been valued by a royal court, because they deal with kings and how one should relate to them. We find the assigned passage under this final heading.

The message of Proverbs 25:6–7 is that humility is a virtue for which all courtiers should strive. One who wishes to be promoted should not put himself or herself forward but take a lower place, hoping to be moved up by the king. This passage seems to be the foundation of Jesus' teaching in the Gospel lesson (Luke 14:1, 7–14). In this passage, Jesus advises those who are invited to a banquet not to seek the highest seats next to the host but, rather, to seek the lower seats in order perhaps to be moved up and not back when catching the host's attention. He also advises that those who show hospitality by inviting others to a banquet should not invite those whose social status will trigger a reciprocal invitation; rather, one should invite those who have no favors to offer in return. This takes the teaching of humility beyond what is done out of self-interest and into the subject of what God expects of the righteous person, namely, justice and mercy. This message of justice and mercy as the virtues of the righteous is also the subject of the psalm for this Sunday, Psalm 112.

Proverbs typically holds fast to the teaching of Deuteronomy that virtuous actions bring a reward from God, while unvirtuous actions bring divine condemnation and retribution. Unlike other parts of the Wisdom literature such as Job or Ecclesiastes, Proverbs does not seem to contest this assumption. Those who fail in life, according to Proverbs, are either wicked, stupid, or lazy. However, Proverbs does include the concept that the poor can be righteous—rejecting the more extreme version of this philosophy, which would assume that anyone who is poor has lost the blessing of God and must be in the midst of punishment for some unknown evil action or character flaw. Rather, Proverbs seems resigned to the fate of the poor who are not said to have reached that condition through fault of their own. Proverbs 13:23 says, "The field of the poor may yield much food, but it is swept away through injustice." Proverbs 14:31 states, "Those who oppress the poor insult their Maker, but those who are kind to the needy honor him." These statements do not portray poverty as a punishment but rather as a sad fact of human life. Those who have a tendency to carry Deuteronomistic theology to absurd lengths regarding what might be understood as divine punishment for human sins would do well to read Proverbs carefully in order to understand the subtleties of OT thought on this subject.

ELIZABETH C. LAROCCA-PITTS

Commentary 2: Connecting the Reading with the World

The reading from Jeremiah 2:4–13 is particularly rich in possibilities for preaching. Its passionate, intimate tone, heavy with the weight of memory and the suggestion of betrayal, reveals a God deeply entwined in relationship with Israel.

1. Look for the Analogy. Thomas Aquinas reminds us that all speech about and knowledge of God happens by way of analogy. Because God lies beyond our senses, everything we say about God is in some way a comparison to the physical world: God is *like* x, *bigger than* y, or *unlike* z. Simile and metaphor are our only tools to name the Divine.

Perhaps no one understood this truth better than the prophets. Even as they described YHWH as the sovereign Lord of all that is, they grounded their language about God in day-to-day experience. Our reading is one of many times the prophets draw on the image of a lawsuit to communicate Israel's fractured relationship to God.[1] The passage, which begins with a deceptively neutral calling of the court into session, quickly shifts into accusations of idolatry, cast in the form of a question in verse 5 that is repeated as an outright declaration in verse 9. Verses 6–8 gather evidence, and verse 10 calls nonexistent witnesses whose absence testifies to the outrageous fact that no other nation has ever before behaved this way. The lawsuit concludes in verse 13 with an indictment that is at the same time a passage of judgment: having forsaken the source of living water, Israel has condemned itself to cracked cisterns that will quickly leak out.

The analogy of the lawsuit rings with God's passion for justice. The divine plaintiff struggles on behalf of those to whom justice has been denied. A fruitful homiletical use for this analogy might be an invitation to align ourselves with that struggle.

2. Rejection and Grief. Metaphors are layered; one can easily lie beneath another. Remembering this fact equips the preacher to explore the passage further. Another recurring metaphor in the prophets, and indeed the whole OT, is Israel as YHWH's spouse.[2] Surely the lawsuit's underpinning of emotion presumes just such an intimacy between the plaintiff and the defendant. Look at the verbs that show up in the NRSV: "defile," "transgress," "accuse," "forsake." This is not the language of a dispassionate legal dispute but, rather, the recriminations of a bitter lovers' quarrel. God's heart is broken by our choice of that which is less than God, because God's love for us is so steadfast.

Much folk wisdom has been expended on the question of which is greater, the grief of loss or the grief of rejection. Those who go through the dissolution of a long-term relationship say that the lack of finality adds to their pain and that they sometimes wish for the irrevocability of loss. The end of a relationship means someone has turned away from another. To be the one thus rejected is to know a deep and abiding grief. We hear that grief in God's words through the prophet.

This passage employs the convention of the courtroom but assumes a context far more intimate. It provides a good opportunity to remind the congregation that we impoverish ourselves when we fail to see the breadth of biblical metaphors for the divine-human encounter. Most of the time, for example, parental love is the best way to describe God's care for God's people. However, as the Song of Solomon demonstrates, sometimes bringing to mind the wild recklessness of physical intimacy is the only way to do justice to the love of God. In the same way, the language of a ruined love affair invests the legal imagery of covenant with more textured and affecting meaning. A sermon on this passage might remind congregants of those times when they have suffered rejection and betrayal. Being in relationship with us means that God has become open to just that same heartbreak when we, through negligence or ill will, reject God and God's children.

3. Twilight of the Idols. At the heart of God's complaint against Israel in this passage is the sin of idolatry, a subject that presents the preacher with a particular challenge. On the one hand, the subject is unavoidable in Scripture. On the other, practically no one in the congregation believes they have any personal investment in the practice of idolatry. Rare is the pastoral visit to a congregant's home that uncovers a secret shrine to Moloch or Baal. Jeremiah's distinctive approach to idolatry alongside the work of

1. See, for example, Isa. 41:21–29 and 5:3–30.
2. For example, Hos. 1–3; Jer. 3:1–4:4; and Ezra 10.

a renowned twentieth-century theologian may allow us to gain some homiletical traction here.

Verse 8 summarizes Israel's idolatry by claiming that God's people "went after things that do not profit." Verse 11 clarifies further: the gods of the other nations "are no gods." Nothing was to be gained by Israel's idolatry, because the object of their idolatrous worship was nothing. The prophet's harshest criticism expresses incredulity at Israel's choice to betray YHWH. Even idolaters do not trade their old idols in for new ones.

Jeremiah indicts Israel for assigning ultimate worth to that which is less, even least. As it turns out, this is precisely how H. Richard Niebuhr explains the common human experience of faith.[3] The beginning of faith, Niebuhr tells us, lies in "centers of value," those realities from which we derive a sense of our worth and identity. Anything can be a center of value, but for most of us the list is pretty standard: home, family, tribe, occupation, religion, nation. These values tell us who we are and what we are worth, and for this reason we devote ourselves to them, which Niebuhr defines as faith. The problem here, of course, is that all of these realities are temporal, transitory, and thus bound to fail us. They are our idols; the faith we invest in them is rightfully reserved for that which is ultimate. Realizing this truth is what opens to us the possibility of a real and radical monotheism: devotion to the God who alone is worthy of that devotion.

4. The Heart Follows the Hands and Feet. A good way to approach Proverbs 25:6–7 is to locate it along the following progression: Proverbs 25:6–7 → Luke 14:7–10 → Luke 14:11 → Luke 14:12–14. Our reading from Proverbs introduces a brief bit of sage advice: it is better to be invited up the social ladder than kicked down it. When Jesus tells his semiparable in Luke 14 about guests seated at a banquet, he seems to say much the same. When he gets to verse 11, that advice has deepened into another example of Jesus' oft-repeated reminders that priorities under the reign of God are upside down from those of the world. Finally, verses 12–14 tell how to embody this principle (which we might summarize as *invite the marginalized to dinner*) and then assign eschatological importance to doing so.

Note that this all starts with a tip for how to get ahead in this world but winds up with matters of eternal significance. Proverbs says nothing about why one should choose the lower position; the implication is simply that it is shrewder to do so. When Jesus gives the same advice, though, it promises more: to humble oneself is to be exalted. Could the two readings taken together signify that attitudes follow actions? Could they say that the difference between the slick operator and the saint means little as long as we help people?

ROBERT A. RATCLIFF

3. See esp. H. Richard Niebuhr, *Radical Monotheism and Western Culture* (Louisville, KY: Westminster John Knox, 1993); idem, *Faith on Earth* (New Haven, CT: Yale University Press, 1991).

Psalm 81:1, 10–16

[1]Sing aloud to God our strength;
shout for joy to the God of Jacob.

. . . .

[10]I am the LORD your God,
who brought you up out of the land of Egypt.
Open your mouth wide and I will fill it.

[11]"But my people did not listen to my voice;
Israel would not submit to me.
[12]So I gave them over to their stubborn hearts,
to follow their own counsels.
[13]O that my people would listen to me,
that Israel would walk in my ways!
[14]Then I would quickly subdue their enemies,
and turn my hand against their foes.
[15]Those who hate the LORD would cringe before him,
and their doom would last forever.
[16]I would feed you with the finest of the wheat,
and with honey from the rock I would satisfy you."

Psalm 112

[1]Praise the LORD!
Happy are those who fear the LORD,
who greatly delight in his commandments.
[2]Their descendants will be mighty in the land;
the generation of the upright will be blessed.
[3]Wealth and riches are in their houses,
and their righteousness endures forever.
[4]They rise in the darkness as a light for the upright;
they are gracious, merciful, and righteous.
[5]It is well with those who deal generously and lend,
who conduct their affairs with justice.
[6]For the righteous will never be moved;
they will be remembered forever.
[7]They are not afraid of evil tidings;
their hearts are firm, secure in the LORD.
[8]Their hearts are steady, they will not be afraid;
in the end they will look in triumph on their foes.
[9]They have distributed freely, they have given to the poor;
their righteousness endures forever;
their horn is exalted in honor.
[10]The wicked see it and are angry;
they gnash their teeth and melt away;
the desire of the wicked comes to nothing.

Connecting the Psalm with Scripture and Worship

In Psalm 81, Israel has disappointed God again—but there is good news. The sonorous convocation of verse 1 calls for the inclusion of women in the next verse (not included in the lection). The "tambourine" of verse 2 is actually an ancient hand drum primarily played by women (Exod. 15:20; Judg. 11:34; 1 Sam. 18:6).[1] A feminine pulse drives God's declaration to Israel. Good news appears in the reintroduction of the First Commandment in verse 10, "I am the Lord your God, who brought you up out of the land of Egypt," and knits it together with an allusion to the beneficence of quails that filled the land to sustain the wandering Israelites: "Open your mouth wide and I will fill it" (Exod. 20:2; Deut. 5:6; Num. 11:31–34; Exod. 16:12–13). When Moses delivers the Decalogue in Deuteronomy, he cries, "Hear, O Israel, the statutes and ordinances that I am addressing to you today." Jeremiah 2:4–5 calls out in a similar register. The complaint of God voiced in Psalm 81 resonates in Jeremiah 2 as well, "I brought you into a plentiful land to eat its fruits and its good things. But when you entered you defiled my land, and made my heritage an abomination" (Jer. 2:7). In Jeremiah 2, however, the sting of God's rebuke does not give way to the honey of Psalm 81:16.

It may be preferable to lift up Psalm 81 as a counterpoint to Jeremiah 2, as an opening toward hope in God not yet enunciated in Jeremiah. The abstraction of connecting with the disobedience of the house of Jacob and Israel can be made concrete in a sermon by framing disobedience now with an inverse, ethical expansion of what is implied in the opening verses of Psalm 81. Without women, the decrees of God do not happen. Making this kind of exegetical leap is worth considering, because what is as vital as digging into the circumstances undergirding a biblical text is to sort out and, if possible, show how the writing still speaks to our particular situation today. Reception of the text matters.

On the one hand, preaching for the empowerment of women in ministry entails shaping a message of humility for a still-male-dominated American Christianity. The number of female students in theological education has grown. Female leadership in churches at voluntary and associate staff levels has increased. More communities of faith find female leadership acceptable. Yet, as of 2015, the actual number of females leading congregations has not risen in a generation, since 1998.[2] While women comprise over half of the workforce in the United States, and receive more undergraduate and graduate degrees than men, women make only 80 cents on the dollar that every male earns. Women earn less in nearly every profession. For African American women, equal pay will not be attainable at the current rate of "progress" until 2119. Hispanic women will have to wait until 2224.[3] My mother would call that **很奇怪** *Hěn qíguài*—"very strange."

On the other hand, preaching a sermon that links American patriarchy with the disobedience of the Israelites in the Psalter and Jeremiah entails crafting a message fueled by spiritual confidence. Women, call the assemblies under your care to heed the word of God. Men and friends who identify differently from those gendered identities, preach about how God demands the free and equal distribution of God's mercy, God's provision, and God's commands that we love the Lord our God with all of our hearts, souls, and minds, and our neighbors as ourselves.

If the advice here seems remote from the Psalter, it merely picks up on what it takes to achieve happiness in God as shared by psalm from the complementary stream of the lectionary, Psalm 112:1, "Happy are those who fear the Lord, who greatly delight in his commandments." Psalm 112 is a Wisdom psalm. The Hebrew word for wisdom, *hokma*, is a feminine noun. Psalm 112 also unfolds with a structure

1. Nancy R. Bowen, "Psalm 81," in *Psalms for Preaching and Worship: A Lectionary Commentary*, ed. Roger E. Van Harn and Brent A. Strawn (Grand Rapids: Eerdmans, 2009), 212–13.
2. National Study of Congregations, *NCS Wave III Report*, released 2015, p. 12.
3. See "Pay Equity and Discrimination," Institute for Women's Policy Research, 2019; https://iwpr.org/issue/employment-education-economic-change/pay-equity-discrimination/.

that indicates comprehensiveness. It is written in acrostic, meaning in its case that each line begins with a successive letter of the Hebrew alphabet from beginning to end. It shares the wisdom of God from *aleph* to *tav* or what we in English would call from A to Z. A kind of complete theological knowledge can be gleaned from contemplation of its verses.

In Psalm 112, the one who delights in God's commands receives divine favor that enables a merciful, generous, and joyful lifestyle in God, and models the sharing of God's generosity effortlessly and continuously. "Wealth and riches are in their houses, and their righteousness endures forever," the psalmist proclaims (Ps. 112:3). "They have distributed freely, they have given to the poor; their righteousness endures forever; their horn is exalted in honor" (v. 9). What Psalm 112 describes is far more profound than prosperity, but economic justice established through personal piety to God.

Embracing the lifestyle of reverence and economic justice portrayed in Psalm 112 requires the kind of humility Proverbs 25:6–7 recommends. Although most of us do not live in monarchies, we can still understand the admonition not to "put yourself forward in the king's presence or stand in the place of the great; for it is better to be told, 'Come up here,' than to be put lower in the presence of a noble." Jesus, in Luke 14:7–11, universalizes the instruction of Proverbs 25:6–7 and makes it good news: "For all who exalt themselves will be humbled, and those who humble themselves will be exalted." It does not take much of a leap to see how the transmission of that advice applies to the inequality in the professional, economic, ministerial, and overall social positions of women and men today.

How might a worship service address the inequality of women? Perhaps it could begin with a procession of female tambourine or hand drum players to set the liturgical tone. Perhaps female congregants could be invited to testify to injustice in their lives or to speak words of affirmation for the gifts that God has given them to share, or how they have been affirmed by fellow Christians. Perhaps the different associations of women and men and other nonconforming gender identities as caretakers could become disrupted, nuanced, deepened, challenged, and situated with respect to the God who promises to provide if the children of God would only listen. Following that God means that we too must engage in economic justice for all. Otherwise, we risk unhappy lives and lives unfaithful to Jesus. Whatever liturgical direction we choose, it will be important to remember the implicit declaration of Psalm 81, that how we worship together determines who we are and will become in God.

GERALD C. LIU

Hebrews 13:1–8, 15–16

[1]Let mutual love continue. [2]Do not neglect to show hospitality to strangers, for by doing that some have entertained angels without knowing it. [3]Remember those who are in prison, as though you were in prison with them; those who are being tortured, as though you yourselves were being tortured. [4]Let marriage be held in honor by all, and let the marriage bed be kept undefiled; for God will judge fornicators and adulterers. [5]Keep your lives free from the love of money, and be content with what you have; for he has said, "I will never leave you or forsake you." [6]So we can say with confidence,

"The Lord is my helper;
I will not be afraid.
What can anyone do to me?"

[7]Remember your leaders, those who spoke the word of God to you; consider the outcome of their way of life, and imitate their faith. [8]Jesus Christ is the same yesterday and today and forever. . . . [15]Through him, then, let us continually offer a sacrifice of praise to God, that is, the fruit of lips that confess his name. [16]Do not neglect to do good and to share what you have, for such sacrifices are pleasing to God.

Commentary 1: Connecting the Reading with Scripture

The final chapter of Hebrews is distinct from the preceding two chapters in that the writer leaves behind the exegetical detail and eschatological vision of that material in favor of a series of moral imperatives (13:1–19) and a ringing charge familiar to many Christians as a liturgical benediction (vv. 20–21). Distinct as these chapters may be in style, however, they are not discontinuous in intent, significance, or meaning. In 13:1–21, the writer seems focused on grounding both exegesis and eschatology in a series of behaviors that bear witness to the presence of the kingdom of God in the community of faith.

Verses 1–19 characterize the life well-lived in the unshakable kingdom of 12:28. The opening rubric—"Let mutual love continue"—may be intended as a governing theme for the section, although the relationship between mutual love and the specific imperatives grows fainter as one proceeds. More likely, "mutual love"—*philadelphia*—is intended to be paired with "hospitality"—*philoxenia,* "love of strangers"—in verse 1–2. The first focuses on love within the community; the second requires the practice of the same love (*philia*) toward those beyond the community. Perhaps by "hospitality" the writer means receptivity to the visits of other Christians from distant places (see Rom. 12:13, but also 1 Tim. 3:2 and 1 Pet. 4:9); certainly, this meaning would comport with the writer's expectation of hospitality in his visit to the community (Heb. 13:23).

In any case, "hospitality" to the stranger captures the writer's attention. Unlike the undeveloped imperative to "continue" sibling love (*philadelphia*), the love of strangers (*philoxenia*) is amplified by a reference to "entertaining angels" unknowingly. This likely points to Genesis 18:1–15. There, Abraham and Sarah receive three visitors at the oaks of Mamre, a narrative long regarded in Christian tradition (especially in Orthodox communions) as an appearance of the Trinity. Hebrews may also be referring to other angelic visitations: to Lot in Genesis

19:1–14 (Lot's hospitality spares the angelic visitors from harm; they in turn save Lot and his family); to Gideon in Judges 6:11–18 (the angel persuades Gideon to lead the Manassites against Midian, resulting in Israel's liberation from oppression); to Samson's mother in Judges 13:3–22 (she bears and rears Samson after an angel promises that he will deliver Israel from the Philistines); or to Tobit in Tobit 5–12 (an angel's many interventions save Tobit's life and mission). In each case, an angelic visit prompts a response by the visited, often resulting in powerful consequences.

Verse 3 requires remembering the imprisoned and tortured. This is no mere intellectual act; rather, the writer encourages a sort of spiritual embodiment of the conditions of imprisonment and abuse. The response to others' mistreatment is particularly striking. We can translate the phrase as "just like being in the same body." In an era when we commonly respond to the suffering of others with vague promises to "pray for" them, the near-physical assumption of those sufferings is a powerful reminder of the requirements of mutual love.

Verse 4 turns to the subject of marriage and sexual relations. The command to "honor" marriage leads to the heart of the matter: that the "marriage bed" as the place of sexual relations must remain "undefiled." This concern for sexual morality reflects Judaism's commitment to appropriate sexual behavior as essential for the integrity of the community before God. Sexual integrity is commanded in the Decalogue (Exod. 20:14) and the Holiness Code in Leviticus (Lev. 18:1–30). Both ground the commandment in the divine claim: "I am the LORD your God." Sexual integrity is essential to Israel's identity as the people of God. This is not explicit in Hebrews 13:4, but the writer is clear that "God will judge" the fornicator (*pornos*, that is, one who engages in forbidden sexual relations) and the adulterer (*moichos,* that is, one who violates the marriage covenant). Some use this text to condemn homosexual relations, but this goes further than the reference will support. The text does, however, call for consideration of the relationship between individual sexual morality and the overall health of the faith community.

Verses 5–6 turn to the place of money and greed in the community. Those who inherit the unshakable kingdom must keep free of greed (that is, they must not be "silver-loving") and be content with what they have. The writer includes two quotations in support of these imperatives. The first is Deuteronomy 31:6, Moses' encouragement to Israel upon entry into Canaan that God "will not fail you or forsake you." The writer of Hebrews offers the same encouragement to his readers that God will not abandon them amid economic straits. The second is Psalm 118:6, a hymn to God's steadfast goodness to Israel. In the midst of distress (v. 5) the psalmist cries to God and is saved, prompting the confident exultation that "with the LORD on my side I do not fear; what can mortals do to me?" In the immediate context of economic privation, but also against the larger background of Hebrews' call for endurance in faith, these citations provide comfort and offer a measure of trust.

Verses 7–8 encourage the reader to "remember your leaders" who "spoke the word of God." The language recalls 12:25, where readers are warned not to "reject the one who warns from heaven." In that context, the speaker is God; here they are those who speak "the word of God." Their lives are worthy of consideration, and the reader is encouraged to consider their "outcome." The writer does not say what that outcome is. It may be martyrdom or suffering of some other sort, in which case the assurances of verses 5–6 are particularly appropriate; it may also simply be a life well lived. In any case, readers are to "imitate" their leaders' faith, adopting it as their own.

Verse 8 is perhaps best translated, "Jesus Christ, yesterday and today the same, and into eternity." The language is almost hymnic, even though no ancient hymn bearing this wording is extant. The eternal stability of Jesus Christ is the point; it is the same trustworthy divine presence mentioned in the Deuteronomy citation (v. 5).

The Revised Common Lectionary omits verses 9–14 from the lection. These verses contain a warning against "strange doctrines" and a reminder that strength comes from grace and not from ritual obedience (v. 9). The writer develops the metaphor of Jesus as the atoning sacrifice whose blood is spilled within the tabernacle but whose body dies outside (cf. Lev. 16:1–34). In the metaphor, the tabernacle of Leviticus becomes a figure for Jerusalem, and readers are called to "go to [Jesus] outside the camp" (Heb. 13:13). This metaphor becomes the foundation for the imperative in verse 15 to "continually offer . . . praise to God, that is, the fruit of lips that confess his name." Sacrifice and verbal praise have a long history in Judaism as paired modes of praise (Pss. 34:1; 50:14, 23; 71:8; 107:22; 145:21); their presence here recalls the "acceptable worship" believers are to offer in 12:28.

Verse 16 returns to the theme of the daily life (cf. vv. 1–8). Doing good and sharing one's possessions are commended as sacrifices "pleasing" (*euaresteō*) to God—the same term used to describe worship as "acceptable" to God in 12:28. "Sharing" (*koinōnia*) evokes the mutuality and hospitality commanded in verses 1–4. Worshiping God acceptably is also living in mutual love and generosity toward others.

PAUL K. HOOKER

Commentary 2: Connecting the Reading to the World

Hebrews 13 could have been titled "Discipleship 101." Right on the heels of otherworldly descriptions of trumpets and clouds in chapter 12 come "rubber meets the road" instructions to these early Christians and to us. Love one another. "Let mutual love *continue*" (13:1). This would suggest that the Hebrews are loving one another. Either that or it is aspirational language that invites those nascent believers to live into that love, even if they are not yet as Christlike as their teacher would hope. Let mutual love continue. The preacher might note that this is instruction number one from which all the others flow.

Extend hospitality to strangers. This ought not to be a surprise to the assembled audience. If in fact these are Jewish Christians, then the practice of hospitality to strangers is well known. Abraham and Sarah welcome and feed three strangers who turn out to be angels, angels bringing remarkable news about a soon-to-be-born son (Gen. 18:1–15). Lot strongly urges two angels to stay, and when they do he makes them a feast (19:1–3). Gideon has an angelic encounter, as does Samson's mother, and, of course, we know about Mary's unexpected annunciation. Hospitality given without the hope of reciprocity is dutiful and faithful. Sometimes it leads to a dinner party with heavenly guests. You never know when and where this might happen, although oak trees seem especially likely places (see 18:1–15). A sermon focus could be the Christian responsibility to extend hospitality, noting ways the congregations may already do so through serving meals at the local homeless shelter or regular church suppers.

Love one another and care for those outside the flock. Go even further: remember those in prison *as though you were in prison with them*, those who are being tortured *as though you yourselves were being tortured.* In other words, when one part of the body hurts, the entire body is wounded. The unity won for us in Christ has real-world consequences and costs. Each member of the body is not only a brother or sister but our own flesh. The implications of this truth are myriad and demanding. In *The Cross and the Lynching Tree*, James Cone begins his concluding chapter with this very verse from Hebrews. Cone argues that white Christians failed to remember those being tortured and lynched as if they themselves were being tortured and lynched. He writes about white theologians and laypeople alike failing to connect the crucified Jesus with the enslavement, segregation, and lynching of black people. He says, "It takes a lot of theological blindness to do that, especially since the vigilantes were white Christians who claimed to worship the Jew lynched in Jerusalem."[1]

1. James H. Cone, *The Cross and the Lynching Tree* (Maryknoll, NY: Orbis Books, 2011), 159.

A fruitful question that a sermon could explore is this: How are Christians still failing to act not only as brothers and sisters but as a unified, indivisible body, heartbroken and hurting when one part suffers and therefore relentlessly seeking justice for the whole?

The list of expectations for followers of the servant and sacrificed Lord continue moving from the larger community to the immediate household. Honor marriage, and do not love money. Even the most intimate details of our lives are bound to the rule of love and the reign of Jesus. Contemporary believers might quickly acknowledge that nothing good can come from adultery or the sexual exploitation of other human beings. The harder mandate to execute in our daily living may be the one regarding money. American consumerism relentlessly beats the drum of discontent. Being content with what you have is downright unpatriotic, or so the message has been proclaimed. Go shopping, help the economy, help the country. Never mind the overflowing landfills and the stockpiles of used clothing. Christians are called to contentment, not the relentless acquisition of partners or products. The preacher might lift up the hopeful word that comes in the wake of these warnings and admonitions, the promise of Christ's neverfailing presence and help. Release from relentless consuming comes as a gift of Jesus Christ, akin to the peace that passes understanding (John 14:27). Contentment is to be received as a gift, not sought out as one more thing to be acquired.

Finally, remember your leaders. This is a curious admonishment to keep on the short list of discipleship musts. Why remember your leaders? Perhaps because mentoring matters. It matters a great deal for a community that is small, new, and facing persecution from without and the challenges of communal living from within. Learning to be a disciple happens best with an apprentice model. Watching a skilled artisan create a plate or a bowl, a quilt or a cake, imparts more than knowledge; not only is the information shared, but relationships are built. Relationships of trust allow for honest questions, shared struggles, and loving accountability. Leaders in the faith, the ones who have passed it on to us, are invaluable teachers of mutual love that can be emulated in tangible ways like hospitality, prison visits, advocacy work, generosity, and more.

Willie James Jennings in his theological tour de force, *The Christian Imagination: Theology and the Origins of Race*, writes about the disconnect that occurred between the colonial West's teaching of Jesus' salvation and tangible acts of care between the evangelists and those they proselytized. Those sharing the good news of the gospel continued to enslave their brothers and sisters in Christ. Jennings writes,

> A theological isolationism in which God's providential care had to substitute for communal care. There is a difference as well as a connection between providential care and the care of others performed as ecclesial community. However, when providential care is deployed in substitution it indicates an absence, a kind of recapitulation of Gethsemane, of isolated agony where Jesus' disciples failed to help him.[2]

In other words, it is Discipleship 101 that we must worship in spirit and in truth, in word and deed. The prophets' resounding and repetitive cry of God's disgust at sacrifices without mercy, worship without justice, praise without compassion put into practice, is echoed in Hebrews. God's care for us and our care for one another, fellow Christian and stranger alike, cannot be separated if we are to be faithful to the gospel of Jesus Christ. How, the preacher might ask, are our faith communities keeping God's care for us and our care for one another connected and obvious?

The reading ends with a call to continual worship *and* ongoing good works. Those good works do not save us; Jesus has done that. Doing good and sharing what we have define us, demonstrating that the God who loves us is also Lord over us and over every aspect of our lives. Mutual love, hospitality, faithfulness, contentment, humility to remember our

2. Willie James Jennings, *The Christian Imagination: Theology and the Origins of Race* (New Haven, CT: Yale University Press, 2010), 183.

leaders and learn from them: these things are Discipleship 101. They are simple but far from easy. The good news is that Jesus prays for us, the Spirit intercedes for us, and the community holds us accountable, standing with us in our suffering and our joys. Two verses not to miss in this reading are verses 6 and 8. We can say with confidence, "The Lord is my helper; I will not be afraid. What can anyone do to me?" "Jesus Christ is the same yesterday and today and forever." Therefore, we can boldly practice discipleship, knowing grace abounds as we mature in Christ, however haltingly.

JILL DUFFIELD

Luke 14:1, 7–14

[1]On one occasion when Jesus was going to the house of a leader of the Pharisees to eat a meal on the sabbath, they were watching him closely. . . .

[7]When he noticed how the guests chose the places of honor, he told them a parable. [8]"When you are invited by someone to a wedding banquet, do not sit down at the place of honor, in case someone more distinguished than you has been invited by your host; [9]and the host who invited both of you may come and say to you, 'Give this person your place,' and then in disgrace you would start to take the lowest place. [10]But when you are invited, go and sit down at the lowest place, so that when your host comes, he may say to you, 'Friend, move up higher'; then you will be honored in the presence of all who sit at the table with you. [11]For all who exalt themselves will be humbled, and those who humble themselves will be exalted."

[12]He said also to the one who had invited him, "When you give a luncheon or a dinner, do not invite your friends or your brothers or your relatives or rich neighbors, in case they may invite you in return, and you would be repaid. [13]But when you give a banquet, invite the poor, the crippled, the lame, and the blind. [14]And you will be blessed, because they cannot repay you, for you will be repaid at the resurrection of the righteous."

Commentary 1: Connecting the Reading with Scripture

It is a familiar scene: Jesus being invited to dinner at the home of a Pharisee. What is Jesus going to do this time? What conflict is provoked? What practice is he criticizing? What kind of table is he envisioning?

Here, Jesus teaches in three ways. Luke 14:1–6 begins with Jesus' Sabbath healing. Verses 7–14 include a parable as well as his instruction to the host. Verses 15–24 recount Jesus' parable of the Dinner Party. The chapter concludes with Jesus' comments to those who are following him about the demands of discipleship.

On this occasion, the invitation comes from a leader of the Pharisees, a group active in Judaism in the first century and committed to interpreting the laws of the Torah in order to understand God's intentions for God's people. They not only invite Jesus into their homes for meals and conversation; they also later warn him about Herod's desire to question him (13:31). They are both curious and concerned about how Jesus is interpreting issues like who is acceptable at this or that table and what constitutes work on the Sabbath.

In Luke's first account of Jesus' dining with a Pharisee, Simon wonders who this Jesus is who allows a woman to wash and anoint his feet and then forgives her sins (7:36–50). At the conclusion of the second story (11:37–54), when Jesus is accused of not properly washing before the meal, the response is even more critical. After the dinner conversation, the experts in law and some of the Pharisees are "plotting against him trying to trap him in his words" (11:54 CEB). The third dining story begins with a note of concern. Some of the Pharisees are "watching him closely" to see what he will say or do at this dinner. Jesus does not disappoint when he immediately heals one of the guests, provoking them with the now-familiar question about the legality of Sabbath healing.

Having experienced dinner parties on previous occasions, Jesus knows what to expect. In antiquity, meals in homes had great social value.

Consider What We Are

You must know that no man ever left himself so much in this life, but he could find more to leave. There are few who are truly aware of this and who are steadfast in it. It is really an equal exchange and barter: just as much as you go out of all things, just so much, neither more nor less, does God enter in with all that is His—if indeed you go right out of all that is yours. Start with that, and let it cost you all you can afford. And in that you will find true peace, and nowhere else.

People should not worry so much about what they have to do; they should consider rather what they are. . . . Do not think to place holiness in doing; we should place holiness in being, for it is not the works that sanctify us, but we who should sanctify the works. However holy the deeds may be, they do not sanctify us in the least insofar as they are deeds, but rather, insofar as we are and have being, just so far do we hallow all that we do, whether it be eating, sleeping, waking, or anything else. Those in whom being is but slight, whatever deeds they do amount to nothing. Therefore note that all our endeavors should be devoted to being good, not caring so much about what we do or what kind of works, but how the ground of our works is.

Meister Eckhart, *The Talks of Instruction*, no. 4, in *The Complete Works of Meister Eckhart*, trans. Maurice O'C. Walshe (New York: Crossroad, 2009), 489.

Invitations by the wealthy to a meal were a measure of one's cultural status. Servants were sent in advance with a reminder for the guests. U-shaped tables defined the social order. The closeness of your place to the middle of the U indicated your importance to the host, since there was the most coveted seat. If you were seated at the ends of the table, your place in the social order was immediately obvious. Guests reclined at the table as food was served; they ate and conversed. The teaching and dialogue that occurred at table was like that of the Greco-Roman symposium, where dining and learning were combined. Such occasions were the privilege of the male upper class. To be invited to such a meal carried with it the social obligation to respond in kind.

Jesus immediately observes how the guests are trying to get the best seats at the table. The advice in the parable that one should sit in the least honorable place first would have been easily understood by the original audience hearing this story (14:8–11). They were familiar with the advice of Proverbs 25:6–7. They also understood the honor of being asked to move up near the center, as opposed to the shame of being moved to the edges of the table and conversation. The moral Jesus adds to the story—"For all who exalt [*hypsōn*] themselves will be humbled [*tapeinōthēsetai*], and those who humble [*tapeinōn*] themselves will be exalted [*hypsōthēsetai*]" (14:11)—echoes the words of Mary's song of praise to God in 1:52: "He has brought down the powerful from their thrones, and lifted up [*hypsōsen*] the lowly [*tapeinous*]."

First-century readers would have seen the action of God in this reversal of cultural practices of status. Jesus offers the parable, but the reader is left to wonder what happens if the host does not call the person to the better seat. Jesus invites his hearers to rethink their places at the table and to imagine new ways of being in relation to those with whom they share a meal.

Jesus then turns his attention to the host of the dinner in verses 12–14 with specific instructions about his guest list. Again, Jesus reverses the cultural norms for dining etiquette. Instead of inviting those who can invite you back, Jesus tells him to invite those who are different from his usual dinner guests. "But when you give a banquet, invite the poor, the crippled, the lame, and the blind. And you will be blessed [*makarios*], because they cannot repay you, for you will be repaid at the resurrection of the righteous" (vv. 13–14). Recall the Lukan Beatitudes and the Sermon on the Plain in 6:20–26, when Jesus says that God's realm belongs to the poor, who are blessed (*makarioi*). Jesus' comments to the host about an alternative guest list invited hearers then and readers today to imagine a table in God's realm where the socially stratified world of rich and poor is upended, a table where all are welcomed.

Who is invited? Who is welcome at the table? Who is missing? All of these questions are provoked by this text. Where the original audience of this text needed help was in seeing how Jesus' reframing of power and status required continual reviewing of the guest list. A preacher might ask listeners to consider the tables at which they have eaten, to recall lunchtime in middle school. Were they seated with the powerful or popular? Were they seated at the edges, looking in, hoping to be included?

What is the table etiquette Jesus is inviting us to consider today? What parables are evident in our practices of welcoming others into God's realm? Are Meals on Wheels just delivered, or are meals shared at table together? Are guests at Room in the Inn fed in a separate room apart from the church night supper, or is bread broken, given, shared, and blessed together—children, teenagers, adults at table? Children and youth could be encouraged to think about the school lunchroom and social orders in place at those tables.[1]

Other lectionary texts open up possibilities for our reading of the Gospel text. God's words to Jeremiah in 2:4–13 are a reminder of how people have not just forgotten God's acts on their behalf; they have failed to remember God. Neither God's people nor the priests ask, "Where is the Lord?" In Psalm 81, God laments, "O that my people would listen to me, that Israel would walk in my ways!" (Ps. 81:13). Hebrews reminds us to show hospitality to strangers, to remember those in prison, and to focus not on wealth but to be happy with what we have.

Jesus invites diners to think about their table guest list, whom they include, whom they exclude, where the guests will sit—all important considerations if they are to live into a new communal social order that demonstrates how they remember his teaching, walk in his ways, and sit at table with strangers and friends.

We know that one of the dinner guests got it. "Blessed is anyone who will eat bread in the kingdom of God!" (Luke 14:15). How are we changed as we break bread and share in conversation with those whom Jesus invites to our table? Hopefully we leave these tables full of hope to share in God's world, where hunger abounds.

ELIZABETH F. CALDWELL

Commentary 2: Connecting the Reading with the World

Luke narrates a social context quite different from our own. In one way, it is strikingly similar, however. In antiquity and today, communities tend to neglect too many of their neighbors. Imperial contexts privilege the power and rights of certain people over those of others. Under Rome, elites—those who were part of the wealthy class or who held a military or political position of note—were valuable, and the poor, the disabled, slaves, and those of lower status were relegated to the category of unimportant. These were the nameless and expendable masses.

Our own context is one shaped by the ideas of Western individualism, a mind-set that makes central the individual and her needs; it can encourage us to be self-interested or even selfish. This philosophical system may contribute positively to the structures under which we live by emphasizing the value of individual rights. Whether its effects are negative or positive, it is a way of thinking deeply embedded in our culture, and we cannot escape its influence.

Published in 1859, John Stuart Mill's *On Liberty* has shaped ideas of Western individualism.[2] Mill promoted utilitarianism, the notion that we should determine how to act by considering what would bring about good for the greatest number of people. Such utilitarianism might seem to

1. Check out "We Dine Together," a club started by teenagers in a high school in Florida so no one has to eat alone at lunch, or Mix It Up at Lunch Day (Teachingtolerance.org).
2. John Stuart Mill, *On Liberty* (London: John W. Parker and Son, 1859).

conflict with other ideas about liberty or individualism. Why should individuals be granted as much liberty as possible if we are interested in the good of the community? Mill concludes that expanding the limits of individual liberty as much as possible is actually the best way to promote utilitarianism. Liberty gives human beings the opportunity to be creative, distinct, even entrepreneurial. When people are given such freedom, we have the potential to be great, and the greatness of individuals benefits the community as a whole. Mill further suggests that in societies that fail to promote individual liberty, a status quo of mediocrity would take hold.

As we read Luke, we might be tempted to point out the ways that the ancient world failed to consider the potential of every person. For instance, in Luke 8, we learn the narrative of the Gerasene demoniac who appears to have lived naked among the tombs and apart from society. In our own social context, we are heavily influenced by the belief that each person matters and that each one of us may contribute significantly to the whole of society. It may appear that we are considering two worlds vastly removed from one another. How are we to make connections between the ancient world depicted in Luke and our own?

In many ways, this passage may serve to remind us of how similar our own context is to the ancient one depicted by Luke. Social status and wealth are still markers that identify our importance. We remain preoccupied with how we might distinguish our social status and our level of wealth from those around us. The clothes we put on our bodies, the vehicles we choose to drive, and the neighborhoods in which we live all serve as reminders to us and those around us of our social status and our level of wealth (see Jas. 2:1–7). While we adhere to an ideology that suggests all have inherent worth, in reality we tend to assign worth based on someone's accumulation of resources and wealth. What Jesus communicates about status and wealth in these verses should cause us to worry and wonder about an alternative way to live and ascribe value to others.

We may ponder why it is so significant, in this passage, that a meal is to be eaten on the Sabbath. Sabbath is the day set aside to worship and honor God and, according to Deuteronomy 5:15, is also a day to remember a time when Israel experienced the sting of slavery. All who remember Sabbath in the context of the meal Jesus is about to eat at the house of the Pharisee would also know that they are instructed to remember that they are part of a people who were once slaves in Egypt; they were once a people relegated to the lowest position in society. If Sabbath has become an opportunity to display higher status, then its true meaning has been lost.

The ancient cultural context around meals is another important connection to note. In the Roman Empire, much like today, meals were typically shared among persons of similar social status.[3] The presence of Jesus as a guest at this meal is already an irregularity for someone of his social ranking, and the teaching of Jesus in this passage only furthers Lukan themes of upset. The accepted status quo will be turned aside in the kingdom Jesus describes; the irregular will become normative. Since meals were typically shared among persons of the same social class, there was also an expectation of reciprocity. If invited to participate in a meal, it was understood that an invitation must be offered in return. To accept an invitation to eat with another and fail to reciprocate would bring shame and invite speculation that resources to provide a meal in return were inadequate. Thus social status would be jeopardized.

In Luke, the themes of social status and the reversal of social status are constantly present. Luke's Jesus is one who comes to turn the present world upside down. In the world Jesus brings, social status and wealth are not the markers by which we judge ourselves and others, because these are not the markers that God utilizes to determine our importance. Those who are exalted in this world will not be in such positions under God's standards, and those who are humbled in this world will be exalted in a system that belongs to God and not to Rome.

3. Amanda C. Miller, "Bridge Work and Seating Charts: A Study of Luke's Ethics of Wealth, Poverty, and Reversal," *Interpretation* 68 (2014): 416–27.

What markers does Jesus determine are important for us to consider? In this passage, Luke's Jesus highlights humility as a virtue. In a social context where humiliation and shame are to be avoided, the idea of voluntarily humbling oneself is unusual. To take a seat of lower position at a table made up of one's peers is the opposite of what is expected. Further, in a world that expects reciprocity, the virtue of giving freely without expectation is radical. Inviting the dispossessed, disabled, and marginalized to share a meal brings true honor and blessing, because these are the people who are unable to provide reciprocity. In short, the practice of inclusion and habit of extending hospitality are markers that matter to God.

In some ways, our world may not be so very different from the one depicted in the Gospel of Luke. If our context is built on the notion that individuals matter simply because of how they might contribute to the whole, Luke's Jesus proclaims that individuals matter simply because all are included and invited to participate in the communal banquet offered by God. In both worlds, the illusions of worth based on wealth and social status distort what is truly significant according to the teachings of Jesus. However, distinct differences obviously exist. The greatest good for the greatest number of people in the Gospel of Luke does not match up to the ideas promoted by John Stuart Mill and that still have such firm roots in our cultural context. In the Gospel, liberty offered for the benefit of the whole is certainly not the focus. Rather, the good is found in our care and concern for others, freely offered.

SALLY SMITH HOLT

Proper 18 (Sunday between September 4 and September 10 Inclusive)

Jeremiah 18:1–11 and
Deuteronomy 30:15–20
Psalm 139:1–6, 13–18 and Psalm 1
Philemon 1–21
Luke 14:25–33

Jeremiah 18:1–11

[1]The word that came to Jeremiah from the LORD: [2]"Come, go down to the potter's house, and there I will let you hear my words." [3]So I went down to the potter's house, and there he was working at his wheel. [4]The vessel he was making of clay was spoiled in the potter's hand, and he reworked it into another vessel, as seemed good to him.

[5]Then the word of the LORD came to me: [6]Can I not do with you, O house of Israel, just as this potter has done? says the LORD. Just like the clay in the potter's hand, so are you in my hand, O house of Israel. [7]At one moment I may declare concerning a nation or a kingdom, that I will pluck up and break down and destroy it, [8]but if that nation, concerning which I have spoken, turns from its evil, I will change my mind about the disaster that I intended to bring on it. [9]And at another moment I may declare concerning a nation or a kingdom that I will build and plant it, [10]but if it does evil in my sight, not listening to my voice, then I will change my mind about the good that I had intended to do to it. [11]Now, therefore, say to the people of Judah and the inhabitants of Jerusalem: Thus says the LORD: Look, I am a potter shaping evil against you and devising a plan against you. Turn now, all of you from your evil way, and amend your ways and your doings.

Deuteronomy 30:15–20

[15]See, I have set before you today life and prosperity, death and adversity. [16]If you obey the commandments of the LORD your God that I am commanding you today, by loving the LORD your God, walking in his ways, and observing his commandments, decrees, and ordinances, then you shall live and become numerous, and the LORD your God will bless you in the land that you are entering to possess. [17]But if your heart turns away and you do not hear, but are led astray to bow down to other gods and serve them, [18]I declare to you today that you shall perish; you shall not live long in the land that you are crossing the Jordan to enter and possess. [19]I call heaven and earth to witness against you today that I have set before you life and death, blessings and curses. Choose life so that you and your descendants may live, [20]loving the LORD your God, obeying him, and holding fast to him; for that means life to you and length of days, so that you may live in the land that the LORD swore to give to your ancestors, to Abraham, to Isaac, and to Jacob.

Commentary 1: Connecting the Reading with Scripture

Jeremiah 18 and Deuteronomy 30 both reflect the theological conviction that with obedience comes blessing and with disobedience comes curse. The majority theory advanced by scholars is that the Torah as we have it came together during the exile in Babylon.[1] Walter Brueggemann writes, "The book of Jeremiah is reflective of and responsive to the historical crisis of the last days of Judah, culminating in the destruction of Jerusalem and the temple in 587 B.C.E. This crisis is the dominant and shaping event of the entire Old Testament."[2] The operating questions were "How did we get here?" and "How could this happen to the people of God?" Those shaped by Deuteronomic thought answered the question by saying, "Because we did not abide by the covenant." They tended to understand exile to be a consequence of their sin. Something about that is refreshing—to admit that the challenges we face in life are often a consequence of our own unfaithful decisions. Rarely in our world do people conclude *their own* sin landed them in trouble. More often we explain the suffering of *another* as a consequence of *their* sin. When *we* suffer, we wonder, "Why us?" The voice of Deuteronomic thought speaks clearly through the ages in these two passages. To quote Jimmy Buffett, "It's my own damn fault" (from his song "Margaritaville"). Such moral calculus is no doubt appealing to many in a world where moral ambiguity seems to define the day.

The problem is that life seldom works this way. Within the biblical witness, such theology is held in tension with other voices like that of Job, who, though described as "blameless and upright" (Job 1:1), suffered inconceivable loss. Such texts also must be held in tension with a theology of grace undergirding the Hebrew Scriptures. God delivered Israel from slavery because of God's righteousness, not because the slaves in Egypt demonstrated any particular faithfulness (Exod. 3:7–8). The prophet Hosea stands as a witness to God's unfathomable grace (see Hos. 11:8–11). In the NT, Paul asserts we are justified by grace through the faith of Jesus Christ and not by any works of our own (Rom. 5:1–10). Within the Scriptures, these are some of the many witnesses who affirm that God does not give us what we deserve but what we need, which is grace. If God's actions are dependent on our behavior, then who really is in charge? Is that not the beginning of a slippery slope toward idolatry? This tension need not be resolved. Rather, it may be employed to generate homiletical energy.

The assigned reading from Jeremiah is the first of three sections making up chapter 18. Verses 1–11 pronounce God's warning to Judah. Verses 12–18 offer Judah's objection, God's response, and Judah's plot against Jeremiah. Verses 19–23 provide Jeremiah's prayer to God in response to the people's condemnation, which is the fourth lament found in Jeremiah. These laments echo those of Moses throughout the exodus (see Exod. 5:22; Num. 11:11–15). In chapter 19, what is malleable clay in this reading has become an earthenware jug to be shattered as a sign of God's judgment.

Our reading, however, begins with Jeremiah's call to go to the potter's house. Obediently he goes, doing exactly what God tells him to do. This is the mark of the faithful prophet throughout Hebrew Scripture. There he watches the potter work a vessel at the wheel. The vessel spoils, so the potter reworks it. To this point, we hear a potential message of grace. If we head in the wrong direction, God has a way of reworking us into a vessel pleasing to the Lord.

There is a problem with the metaphor. Clay is a passive object in the process of being turned on the potter's wheel. The potter drives the process. Pots being turned on the wheel generally spoil because the potter exerts too much force on the clay or because the clay is not properly centered on the wheel. This creates some challenges with the metaphor but also some possibilities, from a preaching perspective. Might God share some responsibility in Judah's unfaithfulness? It was God who brought Israel into being in the first place. Can the potter blame the clay for its shape?

1. Leander E. Keck, "Introduction to the Canon," in *The New Interpreter's Bible*, ed. Leander E. Keck, 10 vols. (Nashville: Abingdon, 1994), 1:9.
2. Walter Brueggemann, *To Pluck Up, To Tear Down: Jeremiah 1–25* (Grand Rapids: Eerdmans, 1988), 1.

Perhaps the key to understanding the text is *malleability*. While on the wheel, clay must remain malleable in the potter's hands. The clay's shape changes as the wheel turns. To use the Reformed mantra, it is "reformed and always being reformed" by the potter. In Jeremiah 19:1–11, the clay hardens into a jug that is shattered as a sign of God's judgment. What if that is what happens when we harden? When our shape becomes fixed, we leave little room for God's grace to reshape us.

Even the metaphor itself proves malleable as it shifts in verse 11. There the clay changes from being Judah to being the plans God is devising for Judah. God's plans are shaped by Judah's faithfulness. God's plans are malleable. This concept is not without its own tensions. According to question 4 of the Westminster Shorter Catechism, "God is a Spirit, infinite, eternal and unchangeable." Yet in this text, God is malleable, willing to change God's plans in response to Judah's faithfulness or lack thereof. There is possibility in such a declaration. In the end, the prophet makes it clear that faithfulness to God, regardless of circumstance, is Judah's best hope.

The reading from Deuteronomy offers the best illustration of the book's vision of a world defined by God's justice and righteousness born of Israel's faithfulness. Brueggemann writes, "Israel's speech witnesses to profound hope, based in the promise-maker and promise-keeper for whom all things are possible."[3] This God calls God's people to keep their promises and so know promised blessings of justice and righteousness. The hope of this vision is inspiring.

The problem comes when life does not work this way: when bad things happen to good people or, worse, when good things happen to people who are so clearly bad. While we may long for the moral clarity of the Deuteronomist, life seldom submits to such simple formulas. In addition, life's moral decisions are seldom as black and white as Deuteronomy 30 might suggest. There is so much gray in the ethical conundrums of our day that we cannot even agree on how to spell "grey"! Again, without offering resolution, such tensions can provide energy for the sermon.

The other passages assigned for this day speak to this ambiguity. The Gospel lection has Jesus suggesting that hating family is a prerequisite for discipleship. Is that not in direct conflict with the commandment to honor father and mother? Philemon presents the troubling scenario of Paul sending a slave back to his master. How does that square with the God of exodus, who frees the enslaved? Perhaps in the end, our only comfort is found in Psalm 139, in the God who searches us and knows us better than we know ourselves, the God who hems us in behind and before, the God whose thoughts are weighty and vaster than the sands of the earth. We come to the end of our struggle, and we are still with God.

JOSEPH J. CLIFFORD

Commentary 2: Connecting the Reading with the World

Sometimes we have to open our eyes to hear the Word of God. Such is the case for the prophet Jeremiah in today's reading. It seems that Jeremiah needs to see the potter at work, shaping and reshaping the clay vessel, so he can hear and understand God's word concerning the house of Israel. This passage challenges us to broaden the ways we think about our knowledge of God. We habitually experience God through hearing; we listen for the Word of God and we hear a Word proclaimed. Are there other ways to engage the Creator? We know God differently when we experience God with multiple senses, smell and touch and sight.

The words Jeremiah hears from God are harsh; they are words of judgment against the people of Israel. These words convey a God who will pluck up, break down, and destroy in one moment but, in another, graciously build up and plant. Through the prophet, God speaks

3. Walter Brueggemann, *Theology of the Old Testament: Testimony, Dispute, Advocacy* (Minneapolis: Fortress Press, 1997), 561.

words of warning: change your ways or you will suffer the consequences.

We do not like to hear such harsh words. They do not make us feel good. We crave reassurance of our goodness and God's goodness toward us. Jeremiah's reassurance comes with the sights, sounds, and smells of the potter's house. The smell of the clay reminds us of Genesis and the way God formed humanity from the dust of the earth. Seeing and feeling the supple texture of the clay, being told we are like this clay, helps us know in our hearts that we can still change and be transformed. God's words of judgment and warning soften as we see the potter, with great care and patience, shape and reshape her vessel. God's words of judgment and warning are important, but they have to be placed in the context of the potter's house. There, God's judgment is good news, because of God's great love for us; God takes great care to mold us into God's people.

God is like a potter, and so too are we; God empowers and emboldens us to be shapers and molders of people. We should long to deliver the Word of God to the people in a way that is engaging and accessible. We should strive for embodied worship and preaching that engages the mind and the senses. We must act as prophets, sharing the thrum in our ribcages as we sing a hymn, the sobering taste of Jesus' body broken, the sight of those who come to the clear waters of baptism, or the powerful cadence of a prayer spoken as a community. The potter in today's Scripture is another prophet of the Lord, a person who embodies the Word of God so that others can know God more fully.

We can also make a connection to this idea of embodiment as we think of the mission of the church in and for the world. What actions accompany our proclamation? How are we showing people the Word of God? There is sometimes a discrepancy between our aspirations to be people of God and our behavior. We *want* to do good, to show love and care to others, but we so often fail. We fail because, like the people of Israel in Jeremiah's prophecy, we tend to turn away from God and our neighbor. We find ourselves in places of pain and sorrow, feeling plucked up, broken down, or destroyed. Even in these times, though, we are graciously built up and replanted. We rest in the hands of God, the potter, who is working to shape and reshape us into vessels.

We also have a tendency to want to be the judge of others. We forget the work of the potter, and we stand in front of the clay ready to criticize with every breath. One challenge for us is to learn God's way of judgment, starting from an intense love for our neighbor. Together, we shape and reshape life until it becomes a vessel for God, a vessel to nourish an emaciated world.

The Soul in Whom God Reposes

God dwells secretly in all souls and is hidden in their substance, for otherwise they would not last. Yet there is a difference, a great difference, in His dwelling in them. In some souls, He dwells alone, and in others He does not dwell alone. Abiding in some, He is pleased; and in others, He is displeased. He lives in some as though in His own house, commanding and ruling everything; and in others as though a stranger in a strange house, where they do not permit Him to give orders or do anything.

It is in that soul in which less of its own appetites and pleasures dwell that He dwells more alone, more pleased, and more as though in His own house, ruling and governing it. And He dwells more in secret, the more He dwells alone. Thus in this soul, in which neither any appetite nor other images or forms nor any affections for created things dwell, the beloved dwells secretly with an embrace so much the closer, more intimate, and more interior, the purer and more alone the soul is to everything other than God. His dwelling is in secret, then, because the devil cannot reach the area of this embrace, nor can one's intellect understand how it occurs. . . .

Oh, how happy is this soul that ever experiences God resting and reposing within it!

John of the Cross, "The Living Flame of Love," in *John of the Cross: Selected Writings*, ed. Kieran Kavanaugh, OCD, Classics of Western Spirituality series (New York: Paulist Press, 1987), 314–15.

The text from Jeremiah tells us of the way God shapes and reshapes our lives, while the text from Deuteronomy reminds us that the shape of our lives also depends on decisions we make. We can choose life, or we can choose death. Sometimes this choice is obvious. At other times, particularly in times and places of abundance, it becomes more difficult to choose between life and death. The things that we think will be life-giving can easily become idols, idols we may not even notice. In the wilderness, idols may be easier to spot; a golden calf clearly does not belong in the desert. In the land of milk and honey, however, idols can be more difficult to identify. The struggle to discern between God and idol, between life and death, is connected to the social systems in which we live.

Perpetuated by mass media and reflected in social media, consumer culture and individualism create a culture of scarcity, a culture rooted in a myth. This culture traps us into thinking we need material things and excess money to lead happy and successful lives. Worse, this culture of scarcity convinces us that there are not enough materials to go around. We find ourselves thinking that choosing life for one person means choosing death for another. If we help the refugee, we will not be able to help the veteran. Leaning into this myth of scarcity puts us in the business of weighing the value of one life against another and feeling as if we must decide who prospers and who suffers. It seems the land of milk and honey enables us to be just self-sufficient enough that we begin to believe that we do not need others. We begin to believe that we do not need God. In doing so, we create our own isolation. We begin to choose death, not even realizing what we are doing. The text challenges us to choose life, to choose relationship.

Another way to connect with this text is to think of it in an ecclesial context as a text addressing a community that is working to make sense of their collective history and identity. They wonder, "How did we get here? How did our ancestors fail? Where was and where is God?" Care should be taken in answering these questions. After all, we *can* choose life, *do* all the "right" things, *say* all the "right" things, *believe* all the "right" things, and still end up in exile. Seeking understanding of their situation led them to judge their own faithfulness to God and God's ways.

Like the Israelites, we often find ourselves in tumultuous political climates. People fight for power and wealth. People feel displaced or exiled. People weigh the value of each other's lives and liberty. As the people of God, we ask, "How did we get here?" Moving forward, we should be reminded to ask, "How do we choose life?"

As individuals and communities, we are called to choose life. Every day and with every decision, we are called to choose life! The choice is not always easy; it is not always clear. Life and death, joy and grief, praise and lament, maybe even blessing and curse can be dangerously intertwined. Sometimes—arguably more often than not—life is ours to discover in the wilderness, in exile, or even in death.

ALLIE UTLEY

Proper 18 (Sunday between September 4 and September 10 Inclusive)

Psalm 139:1–6, 13–18

[1]O LORD, you have searched me and known me.
[2]You know when I sit down and when I rise up;
you discern my thoughts from far away.
[3]You search out my path and my lying down,
and are acquainted with all my ways.
[4]Even before a word is on my tongue,
O LORD, you know it completely.
[5]You hem me in, behind and before,
and lay your hand upon me.
[6]Such knowledge is too wonderful for me;
it is so high that I cannot attain it.
. . . .
[13]For it was you who formed my inward parts;
you knit me together in my mother's womb.
[14]I praise you, for I am fearfully and wonderfully made.
Wonderful are your works;
that I know very well.
[15]My frame was not hidden from you,
when I was being made in secret,
intricately woven in the depths of the earth.
[16]Your eyes beheld my unformed substance.
In your book were written
all the days that were formed for me,
when none of them as yet existed.
[17]How weighty to me are your thoughts, O God!
How vast is the sum of them!
[18]I try to count them—they are more than the sand;
I come to the end—I am still with you.

Psalm 1

[1]Happy are those
who do not follow the advice of the wicked,
or take the path that sinners tread,
or sit in the seat of scoffers;
[2]but their delight is in the law of the LORD,
and on his law they meditate day and night.
[3]They are like trees
planted by streams of water,
which yield their fruit in its season,
and their leaves do not wither.
In all that they do, they prosper.

[4]The wicked are not so,
but are like chaff that the wind drives away.
[5]Therefore the wicked will not stand in the judgment,
nor sinners in the congregation of the righteous;
[6]for the LORD watches over the way of the righteous,
but the way of the wicked will perish.

Connecting the Psalm with Scripture and Worship

As a youth minister in Atlanta, I led a group of adolescents to a pottery studio where we learned how to "throw" clay, which is more like cradling an unwieldy mound until it resembles an object worth keeping. That is goopier and trickier than one might expect. A lot can go wrong. The clay is heavy. Contact and moisture matter for its malleability. It must be smacked a few times for it to have the right density (young people can get a kick out of doing that), and it must be centered on a potter's wheel. The clay and the "bat" or surface of the wheel must have the right amount of water absorbed. Not enough and the clay will slip and slide all over the place. Too much and the clay can become wobbly, mushy, and riddled with air bubbles. In either situation, and many permutations of them, the clay must either be reworked, or scraped, or both, and recentered—or it is time to start over with a new chunk.

Once the clay is sealed or smacked into place, and the wheel is in motion, the right amount of pressure must be applied through the foot to the out-of-sight pedal that controls the speed of the wheel's rotation, and through the hands as the clay is coaxed into more than a blob. Learning how to massage, squeeze, pull, push, brace, flatten, and lift the clay is not an easy task. It requires patience, practice, and vision.

We may have never thrown clay. It may be worth a try and be a more helpful exercise for developing a sermon from today's passages than, say, biblical form criticism. Even watching a video about pottery making or reading someone else's account of it on a page would open the homiletic imagination in very helpful ways for contemplating and bringing to sermonic life the pottery-making imagery of Jeremiah 18:1–11 and the complementary poetry of Psalm 139 found in verses 15–16: "My frame was not hidden from you, when I was being made in secret, intricately woven in the depths of the earth. Your eyes beheld my unformed substance. In your book were written all the days that were formed for me, when none of them as yet existed." The tactile language of Jeremiah and the psalmist makes clear how God reached into existence in order to manifest the will of God during the times of those Scriptures, and the poetry still suggests how God touches our lives now.

Hopefully, we do not feel as if God is smacking us like a potter to clay when we hear Jeremiah's words; he does not hold back in his warning toward Judah and the inhabitants of Jerusalem: "At one moment I may declare concerning a nation or a kingdom, that I will pluck up and break down and destroy it" (Jer. 18:7). (It is worth noting that scholars question the authenticity of Jeremiah 18:1–11. Some believe that perhaps verses 1–6 constitute original material, but verses 7–11 seem like an addition by a Deuteronomistic editor.[1]) In any case, if we are honest, God's calling in our lives can sometimes feel like a dizzying centrifugal force. Reading Jeremiah together with Psalm 139:13–18 introduces stabilizing liturgical language.

The psalmist proclaims that the formation of God has deeper reasoning than our understanding. God knows him in every movement and aspiration, in every way (Ps. 139:1–4). Like the potter's hands, God cradles the psalmist, "You hem me in, behind and before, and lay your hand

1. William L. Holladay, *Jeremiah 1: A Commentary on the Book of the Prophet Jeremiah (Chapters 1–25)*, Hermeneia (Philadelphia: Fortress, 1986), 514.

upon me" (v. 5). That holy touch overwhelms him. It is "too wonderful," and unattainably high. It feels both tender and terrifying. Yet abiding in the place of being stressed, torqued, molded, and massaged by God produces intimate and unstoppable euphoria in God. "How weighty to me are your thoughts, O God! How vast is the sum of them! I try to count them—they are more than the sand; I come to the end—I am still with you" (vv. 17–18). When we are in the thick of service and ministry and feel real discomfort and associate it as *from God*, we can reflect on the difficulty of our situation by peering through biblical ultimatums and contemplating instead the wonder of God. We can ponder God's wonder and proclaim it as the psalmist did, to invigorate faithful work that can often seem goopier and trickier than at first expected.

The reading from Deuteronomy also voices a sentiment similar to that of the prophet: "But if your heart turns away and you do not hear, but are led astray to bow down to other gods and serve them, I declare to you today that you shall perish; you shall not live long in the land that you are crossing the Jordan to enter and possess" (Deut. 30:17–18). Here God poses a life-and-death choice. The decision for life has already been made for the Israelites with the covenant previously established at Horeb (Deut. 5:2). The first chapter of the Psalter, which declares those "happy" who "delight in the law of the Lord, and on his law they meditate day and night," can be positioned as a kind of echo of reassurance that God ultimately desires life. Of course, the Law here in Psalm 1 refers to the Torah.

If Psalm 1 serves as a preamble to the entire Psalter, then the Law codifies the mysterious, searching, and ungraspable knowledge of God, who understands and encounters the deepest depths of the human condition and watches over those who love God. Indeed, the petition for protection from the wicked way and guidance into the "everlasting way" of Psalm 139 clearly recapitulates the promise of Psalm 1:6, "for the Lord watches over the way of the righteous, but the way of the wicked will perish." Critical for setting Psalms 139 and 1 in worship today is to weigh how the wicked can appear pious and transgress the righteous. What do we pray, preach, and sing when clergy abuse the young people entrusted to them? God forbid, maybe we were those young people, or worse, maybe we have perpetrated such evil.

How can a worshiping assembly together communicate the intimacy of God (as scary as it may seem) as that which heals, even when we are hurt or when we harm in the most unforgivable and unspeakable ways? God produces awe and renews the psalmist spiritually and psychologically, from "the womb" (Ps. 139:13) and forevermore, even when the psalmist feels done for or "at the end" (v. 18). That seems to contrast with the God of Deuteronomy and Jeremiah, who is treacherous if folks do not straighten up.

How might we, who represent God in the flesh, rethink the judgmental and sinful actions of our communities of faith? How can we craft moving, mourning, repenting, and redeeming worship that is capable of reaching and receiving the majority of adolescents who do not participate in the ministries of the church at all, much less youth ministry? How might we lead worship with an eye toward those adults who long ago outgrew or rightfully fled from our witness? God may be tugging or nudging us to come up with liturgical responses, or to start over with new chunks of doxological clay.

GERALD C. LIU

Proper 18 (Sunday between September 4 and September 10 Inclusive)

Philemon 1–21

[1]Paul, a prisoner of Christ Jesus, and Timothy our brother,

To Philemon our dear friend and co-worker, [2]to Apphia our sister, to Archippus our fellow soldier, and to the church in your house:

[3]Grace to you and peace from God our Father and the Lord Jesus Christ.

[4]When I remember you in my prayers, I always thank my God [5]because I hear of your love for all the saints and your faith toward the Lord Jesus. [6]I pray that the sharing of your faith may become effective when you perceive all the good that we may do for Christ. [7]I have indeed received much joy and encouragement from your love, because the hearts of the saints have been refreshed through you, my brother.

[8]For this reason, though I am bold enough in Christ to command you to do your duty, [9]yet I would rather appeal to you on the basis of love—and I, Paul, do this as an old man, and now also as a prisoner of Christ Jesus. [10]I am appealing to you for my child, Onesimus, whose father I have become during my imprisonment. [11]Formerly he was useless to you, but now he is indeed useful both to you and to me. [12]I am sending him, that is, my own heart, back to you. [13]I wanted to keep him with me, so that he might be of service to me in your place during my imprisonment for the gospel; [14]but I preferred to do nothing without your consent, in order that your good deed might be voluntary and not something forced. [15]Perhaps this is the reason he was separated from you for a while, so that you might have him back forever, [16]no longer as a slave but more than a slave, a beloved brother—especially to me but how much more to you, both in the flesh and in the Lord.

[17]So if you consider me your partner, welcome him as you would welcome me. [18]If he has wronged you in any way, or owes you anything, charge that to my account. [19]I, Paul, am writing this with my own hand: I will repay it. I say nothing about your owing me even your own self. [20]Yes, brother, let me have this benefit from you in the Lord! Refresh my heart in Christ. [21]Confident of your obedience, I am writing to you, knowing that you will do even more than I say.

Commentary 1: Connecting the Reading with Scripture

The lessons for this Sunday provide guidelines for making difficult decisions that require us to "sit down and count the cost" (Luke 14:28). Each lesson presents the reader with a consequential choice: shall we live with or without God? What we decide determines whether we live into a grace-formed partnership with God (Deut. 30:19; Ps. 1). We are to be cautious about what pitfalls to avoid and costs to anticipate; we are encouraged to embrace the Lord's instruction, which draws us forward on a pathway toward a blessed life.

The NT lesson, Philemon 1–21, includes most of Paul's briefest canonical letter.[1] Although a personal letter written with rhetorical skill, it plots the unwritten story of two interpenetrating relationships. The relationship introduced first is between Paul, who writes this letter as

1. See Robert W. Wall, *Colossians and Philemon* (Downers Grove, IL: IVP Academic, 1993), 178–216.

a Roman prisoner (vv. 1, 9–10, 13, 22), and Philemon (v. 1), the leader of a house church that has supported Paul's mission (vv. 2, 7). The opening thanksgiving (vv. 4–7)—a standard feature of a personal letter in antiquity—testifies to Philemon's reputation for generosity (v. 5): he has "refreshed" Paul (v. 7) and, Paul hopes, will "refresh" him once again in the future (v. 20). This happy prospect is grounded in Paul's sensibility that they are "partners" (vv. 6, 17) in a shared mission.

Philemon's kindness toward Paul is personified by Onesimus (v. 10), Philemon's slave (v. 16). He cared for an elderly Paul in prison (v. 9) and, while there, became Paul's convert to Christ (v. 10) and a close friend (v. 16). How one understands their relationship, taking into account Onesimus's status as Philemon's slave, determines how this letter is read. This is a carefully crafted letter that seeks to persuade a difficult decision from Philemon: to grant Onesimus his freedom at some unspecified financial cost (vv. 18–19).

Little is said about the circumstances that prompt Paul's decision. Nothing is said, for instance, that clearly indicates Paul is interceding for Onesimus on a legal matter. Some scholars think that Onesimus has departed from Philemon's employ without his permission, which is punishable by death under Roman law. Whatever the cause, when earthed in the social world of this letter, the reader should understand that Onesimus's relationship to Philemon is precarious. Even though slaves made up roughly 25 percent of the Roman world, they were offered little protection under Roman law. As members of Rome's lowest social class, people like Onesimus had no civil rights. The owner's rights, by contrast, were assiduously protected to ensure the productivity of a slave institution that made the empire's economic engine run smoothly. Slaves were not allowed to have intimate relationships with another that might distract them nor own property of their own that might divide their loyalty. Onesimus was himself the owned property of Philemon, who would have placed a value on him commensurate with his work as Philemon's slave. Indeed, an important element of Paul's rhetorical elegance is his appeal for Philemon to reimagine how the name Onesimus ("useful" in Greek) denotes his slave's real value, no longer as a slave but as "a beloved brother" (v. 16).

This conception of Roman slavery is challenged by Israel's Scripture, which was undoubtedly read aloud in Paul's diasporic congregations (see Acts 15:21). For example, the radical practice of the manumission of Israelite slaves during the jubilee year (Lev. 25:39–46 and Deut. 15:13–15) supports Paul's reversal in how Philemon's Christian community should envisage its own social diversity. Scripture's witness is strengthened by Jesus' proclamation that his messianic mission inaugurated this "year of the Lord's favor" (Luke 4:19), especially since Paul himself argued that slaves and free are "all one in Christ Jesus" (Gal. 3:28). This social solidarity in Christ marks out a congregation's "partnership [*koinōnia*] of the faith" (v. 6, my trans.).

In any case, Paul's "appeal" to Philemon on Onesimus's behalf begins with irony. Rather than assert the apostolic authority due him (v. 8), he makes his request "on the basis of love" as an "old man" who is presently jailed as a "prisoner for Christ Jesus" (v. 9). That is, Paul's personal predicament makes an apostolic "command" (v. 8) imprudent. Even so, his appeal's intention is clearly collaborative, not coercive, as implied by his prior thanksgiving for Philemon's resume of refreshing hospitality (vv. 6–7).

The repetition of Paul's "appeal" to Philemon cues his introduction of Onesimus into the letter, not as his slave but as "my child," a convert to Christ. Paul's radical transformation of Onesimus is subsequently deepened by personifying him as "my own heart" (v. 12), a source of compassion to Paul, and then by averring that he is "no longer . . . a slave but . . . a beloved brother" (v. 16). While nothing is said of the circumstances that brought the two together in a Roman prison, Paul's purposeful resetting of Onesimus's public identity is strategic.

Onesimus's transformation is envisaged in two wordplays. Onesimus's name means "useful" in Greek. Paul's claim that Onesimus was previously "useless" (*achrēstos*) to Philemon is ironical, since he is now "useful" (*euchrēstos*). Moreover, he now "serves" Paul in prison as Philemon's proxy (v. 13) thereby benefiting both (v. 11). Strikingly, this verb for "serve" (*diakoneō*) is the same one often used for the practice of ministry (Acts 6:2)—not one we would typically associate with a slave's actions.

A second wordplay may be even more illuminating. The word for "useless" (*achrēstos*) sounds the same as the Greek word for "without Christ" (*achristos*). Perhaps Paul is referring here not to a breakdown in Onesimus's working relationship with Philemon and the legal fuss it may have provoked but to the uselessness of their spiritual relationship when Onesimus was still a nonbeliever (so v. 10). In this case, the happy prospect of Onesimus's return to Philemon or of Philemon's manumission of Onesimus is not predicated on Roman or biblical law about slavery but on their transformed relationship initiated by Onesimus's conversion to Christ.[2]

Almost certainly, his conversion would have made an impression on a Christian like Philemon, whom Paul earlier greeted as a "*beloved* coworker" (v. 1). It may even explain Paul's optimism that Philemon would freely choose to act kindly toward his slave, since he no longer is a slave but "a *beloved* brother" (v. 16). Just as Paul calls Philemon "beloved" (v. 1) and "brother" (vv. 7, 20), so also Onesimus's conversion to Christ has elevated his status to this same high bar.

According to Paul, this transformed relationship between slave and master in Christ also harbors implications about Onesimus's future. He should be received as an equal "partner" (v. 17) in the fellowship that now includes Paul and Philemon (v. 6). Moreover, any debt he owes should be charged to the apostle's account (v. 18). Even if this is taken literally, Paul's reminder that Philemon owes Paul his life (v. 19) implies a quid pro quo: Philemon's spiritual debt to Paul forgoes any compensation that he may rightfully expect when freeing a slave. In this setting, Paul's use of the Greek verb for "owe" may also allude to its use in LXX Deuteronomy 15:2, which stipulates that creditors forgive the debts of fellow Israelites during the year of "the LORD's remission" (see 15:12; Exod. 21:1–11).

Philemon's difficult decision, framed by Paul's opening prayer that he refresh the hearts of God's people (v. 7), is repeated at the letter's end by the apostle's emphatic request for a personal "benefit" (*onaimēn*, another play on Onesimus's name, whose freedom from slavery is the requested benefit): "Refresh my heart in Christ" (v. 20).

ROBERT W. WALL

Commentary 2: Connecting the Reading with the World

The letter from Paul to Philemon demonstrates just how disruptive God's grace can be. Jesus had warned his disciples of this, telling them that the gospel might bring division rather than peace. In Philemon, we witness how true Jesus' words turned out to be in the context of the relationship among three primary players: the slave owner Philemon, his slave Onesimus, and their mutual friend Paul. Paul's letter portrays a real-life, real-time story of the power of the gospel to unsettle and ultimately reset both our interpersonal relationships and our wider cultural and social systems.

At first glance, the preacher might find it difficult to find relevant connections between the context of this letter and today's world. Even with the constant presence of racial tensions and institutionalized prejudice, we live in a time when slavery is no longer the law of our land. The story of returning a former slave to his master might seem like too archaic a narrative.

Our ability to make a contemporary connection to the book may be aided by its short length. Sometimes, when a text has a gap in its narrative, it is the Spirit's way of inviting us to fill it with our own contextual experiences and to make connections that affirm both scriptural truth and present-day relevance. Philemon's mere twenty-one verses might invite the preacher to explore (1) the context of Paul's appeal, (2) the method of that appeal, and (3) the impact of that appeal on the way we live.

2. Cf. Sara Winter, "Paul's Letter to Philemon," *New Testament Studies* 33 (1987): 1–15.

The Context of the Appeal. We are not told much about the background of how Onesimus crossed paths with Paul. What we do know is that in the time that Paul and Onesimus were together, Paul introduced him to faith in Jesus (v. 10). This conversion posed a dramatic change not only for Onesimus but for each of his relationships.

Family-systems theory suggests that a dysfunctional family can operate with stability when everyone in the family participates and contributes to the dysfunction. The moment one person in the family decides to become healthy and ceases to contribute to the unhealthiness, that decision threatens to destabilize the entire system. Often the system places tremendous pressure on that individual to go back to their former life so that the system can return to stability. The conversion of Onesimus is an example of such a transformative destabilization of established social order.

The preacher might explore such connections with real-life examples from ministry with people whose decisions to live healthy and free lives are disruptive to their families, workplaces, or communities. Such examples might include a family member who decides to name addictive behavior in the rest of the family, a person in an abusive relationship who decides to seek refuge, a whistle-blower at work who walks the unpopular path of integrity.

Popular culture may offer other narratives that illustrate how personal transformation can upend conventional social order. Many recent films and novels portray dystopian settings in which the central character experiences a new freedom and subsequently threatens to undermine social systems. In *The Hunger Games*, the nation of Panem is controlled by the Capitol and its brutal gladiatorial combats involving teenagers until heroine Katniss Everdeen decides to break free of the Capitol's control. In *The Giver*, an enclosed world is sterilized of all emotions, convinced that emotional displays are too unpredictable and irrational until a mentor introduces a young boy to the capacity to feel. In *Divergent*, young people are predetermined for separate factions in an ordered, postapocalyptic world until a young woman named Tris and her band of divergents decide to fight the system. The protagonists in each of these three novels choose to translate their newly found independence into resistance of the established social order. Other novels, such as Ben Winters's *Underground Airlines* and Colson Whitehead's *Underground Railroad*, may offer more direct connections between the reality of slavery in America and Philemon's message of transformative freedom.

The preacher might find many other narratives to illuminate this central aspect of the background of Philemon. The conversion of Onesimus to Christianity not only transforms his life; it also impacts both his relationships with Paul and Philemon and his entrapment in slavery. His decision to live free in Christ consequently impacts his relationship with Philemon, in particular, and the wider social order in general. His story points to God's power and initiative to be a "resistance fighter" against society's systemic sinfulness.

The Method of Paul's Appeal. In this letter, Paul is persuasive but not confrontational. The tone of the letter is one of respect, love, and admiration for Philemon rather than coercion or condescension. That motif is most directly expressed in verses 8 and 9, in which Paul acknowledges that while he may have the power to "command" Philemon to act, he would much rather appeal to him on the basis of love.

The way Paul chooses to make this appeal illuminates a profound approach to discernment. The preacher might acknowledge that much of twenty-first-century American culture is conditioned by what Richard Rohr has characterized as binary thinking: either/or, winners/losers, conservative/liberal, creation/evolution.[3] The result is that our culture is polarized, divided, and so entrenched in our ideologies that dialogue is rare and shouting matches are the rule of the day.

This letter challenges us to look for ways to appeal to each other—even those with whom we disagree—on the basis of love rather than one-upmanship and competition. The driving

3. See examples of Richard Rohr's meditations at https://cac.org/.

impulse for the Christian should not be to prove herself to be right but to remind herself of the love of Christ that connects us. Therein lies both the convicting challenge of this letter and its hopeful word of liberation. When we decide to interact with others out of love, then the gospel can fully transform the cultures and systems of the world into the likeness of the kingdom.

The Impact of Paul's Appeal. How did Philemon respond to Paul's appeal? We would like to think that Philemon welcomed Onesimus back as a beloved brother and that Paul's intervention shaped a new relationship between the master and the former slave. It could also be that Philemon turned down that request, walking away from Paul's entreaty much as the rich young ruler walked away from Jesus (Mark 10:17–22). It could be that the situation was resolved easily, or it may have introduced a different level of complexity that required more hard work. We simply do not know.

It may be better not to know, for the letter refuses to make a false promise that things will always work out when we choose to follow Jesus and our conversion disrupts our established relationships and social systems. It chooses not to discourage us by reminding us of the difficulties in doing so. The uncertain resolution to the letter's request is a reminder that the gospel introduces an array of possibilities beyond the brokenness and dysfunction of the world. The choice to follow Jesus will not always be easy, and healing may not come in the ways or the timing we expect. Surrendering to Jesus means yielding our need to see the fruit of our commitments according to our own desired schedule. "God does not call us to be successful," Mother Teresa is attributed as saying, "God only calls us to be faithful." Regardless of how Philemon ultimately responds to this letter, Onesimus is faithful in saying yes to Jesus, and Paul is faithful in making the appeal.

MAGREY R. DEVEGA

Proper 18 (Sunday between September 4 and September 10 Inclusive)

Luke 14:25–33

[25]Now large crowds were traveling with him; and he turned and said to them, [26]"Whoever comes to me and does not hate father and mother, wife and children, brothers and sisters, yes, and even life itself, cannot be my disciple. [27]Whoever does not carry the cross and follow me cannot be my disciple. [28]For which of you, intending to build a tower, does not first sit down and estimate the cost, to see whether he has enough to complete it? [29]Otherwise, when he has laid a foundation and is not able to finish, all who see it will begin to ridicule him, [30]saying, 'This fellow began to build and was not able to finish.' [31]Or what king, going out to wage war against another king, will not sit down first and consider whether he is able with ten thousand to oppose the one who comes against him with twenty thousand? [32]If he cannot, then, while the other is still far away, he sends a delegation and asks for the terms of peace. [33]So therefore, none of you can become my disciple if you do not give up all your possessions."

Commentary 1: Connecting the Reading to Scripture

In this reading, Jesus teaches about the cost of discipleship. He speaks in radical terms of the total commitment needed by those who would be his true followers. This commitment is to the person of Jesus and to following him without reservation or entanglements. The need for perseverance in daily cross-bearing is highlighted by the scenario of a king who began a tower that could not be finished and one who began a war without the resources to win. In both cases, persistence in commitment is needed. A commitment to the person of Jesus is required for Jesus' followers, marked by willingness to give up all possessions (Luke 14:33).

Immediate Literary Context. Jesus' teaching context shifts from a dinner with a Pharisee (vv. 1–24) to his continuing journey to Jerusalem, a journey that begins with his resolute commitment "to go to Jerusalem" (9:51). With this verse, Jesus begins a specific journey in obedience to what he believes is the will of God, a journey that will involve his suffering and rejection (9:22).

Jesus connects discipleship with the "cross" his followers will carry by denying themselves and following him: "If any want to become my followers, let them deny themselves and take up their cross daily and follow me" (9:23). In our passage, this theme is accentuated by Jesus' admonition that "whoever does not carry the cross and follow me cannot be my disciple" (14:27). Such cross-bearing is a condition of genuine discipleship.

Immediately before our passage, Jesus tells the parable of the Great Dinner. where an invitation to enter God's kingdom is extended far and wide (vv. 15–24; cf. Matt. 22:1–14). The desire of the owner is that his "house may be filled" (v. 23). Turning to the demands of discipleship, Jesus speaks to those who would enter the kingdom. These demands include a primary love for Jesus over family relationships and anything else that would hinder commitment to Jesus—even "life itself" (v. 26). In this sense, there is an "antithetic parallelism" between the Great Dinner parable and our passage.[1] At the dinner, the invitation to enter God's kingdom

1. See Joseph A. Fitzmyer, *The Gospel according to Luke X–XXIV*, Anchor Bible (New York: Doubleday, 1985), 1060.

is proclaimed all around. In our passage, Jesus stipulates that those who would enter must be willing to give up all else—all lesser loyalties—to do so. The widening focus of the Great Dinner parable is narrowed to those who are willing to "carry the cross and follow me" (v. 27).

Larger Literary Context. This passage fits into the larger literary context of Luke's Gospel by focusing on key dimensions of Christian discipleship. Basic here is discipleship as following Jesus. If Jesus' determination "to go to Jerusalem" in 9:51 is a narrative hinge in the narrative, then "to be a disciple of Christ one has to follow him along the road that he walks to his destiny in Jerusalem, his *exodus*, his transit to the Father."[2] Jesus' sharp sayings to "follow me," here and in other places, give pointed specificity to the nature of this following (see 14:27 along with 9:23; 5:27; 18:22). Discipleship is a process of commitment, not a one-time statement of intention. Earlier, Jesus says disciples must "take up their cross daily" and "follow me" (9:23). This befits the nature of the journey of following in the way of Jesus, since following is an ongoing manner of moving through life and not one single step.

The decisive nature of this daily following is stressed by Jesus' sayings to three would-be followers (9:57–62; cf. Matt. 8:18–22). In these cases, the command to "follow me" was not followed by those who found excuses to reject the invitation of Jesus. He then notes the unvarnished commitment that following him requires: "No one who puts a hand to the plow and looks back is fit for the kingdom of God" (9:62).

In short, for Luke, "the disciple must walk in the footsteps of Jesus." For Luke, "Christian discipleship is portrayed not only as the acceptance of a master's teaching, but as the identification of oneself with the master's way of life and destiny in an intimate, personal following of him."

The Larger Thematic Context. The larger thematic context of this passage is Luke's emphasis on Jesus as the one who brings salvation and the arrival of God's kingdom as the revelation of a Way. This "Way" is the path of discipleship for those who will follow Jesus. Following Jesus means walking after Jesus. For Luke, Jesus' command to follow him involves a daily self-denial. No human relationships must interfere with following Jesus on his way. This self-denial and following Jesus' Way mean "one no longer lives for oneself but for the kingdom of God"; to take up one's cross means "the death of self, of personal ambition and self-centered purpose."[3] Discipleship means following Jesus along his way as the way of the cross. This entails the subordination of all relationships to following Jesus (14:26); the self-denial that is total in commitment to the person of Jesus (v. 27); and the radical renunciation of "all your possessions" (v. 33) so they do not hinder following Jesus on the way.

The theme of "following Jesus on his way" is further amplified when we see Luke's use of "the Way" as a corporate description for the early Christian community in the book of Acts (9:2; 19:9, 23; 22:4; 24:14, 22). This is a distinctive Lukan usage of "the Way" in the NT. Individual disciples joined in following the Way of Jesus. Christian communities themselves became designated as the Way as their members lived out their journeys of self-denial and identification with their risen Lord.

This recognition of the importance of the Way as a designation for early Christian communities shows the impact of this concept for early Christian notions of discipleship. An added element of the seriousness with which early disciples took Jesus' words is found in the description of life among the early believers and how those in the earliest church "had all things in common" and "would sell their possessions and goods and distribute the proceeds to all, as any had need" (Acts 2:45). These "people of the Way" obeyed Jesus' prescription that "none of you can become my disciple if you do not give up all your possessions" (v. 33). They enacted it as an expression of what it meant to be followers of Jesus who were following Jesus along his way—which had become their way, as well. They realized the impact of the cost of discipleship when it meant giving up their material possessions. They did this not only as an

2. Fitzmyer, *Luke X–XXIV*, 241. The quote two paragraphs below is from the same source.
3. George Eldon Ladd, *A Theology of the New Testament*, rev. ed. (Grand Rapids: Eerdmans, 1993), 130.

act of obedience and an expression of following Jesus but also as an outward expression of their self-denial and the death of self, rejection of personal ambition, and end of self-centered purpose in life that sought only personal gain. The cost of discipleship for "followers of the Way" was social as well as spiritual.

Today, Jesus' words about possessions and leaving families point us toward a radical vision of commitment to Jesus. They challenge us to engage our whole selves in the ministries to which we are called. In the church and beyond, we are called to make costly sacrifices and have a single-minded devotion to enacting Jesus' way in the actions we take. These entail our social and political commitments as well as the personal love and care we give to others—all others.

DONALD K. MCKIM

Commentary 2: Connecting the Reading with the World

In a time when church membership is declining in many communities, it may seem odd that Jesus would discourage potential followers. In the previous lectionary text (14:15–24), Jesus announces the radical truth that everyone is welcome in the kingdom of God. His parable opens the door of the great banquet to the poor, outsiders, sinners, and strangers. In 14:25, many of these people follow Jesus. He acknowledges them as human beings in ways they may have never experienced. He speaks a powerful and gracious truth through his down-to-earth manner and accessible style. They want to be in his presence.

Instead of celebrating the growing number of followers, however, Jesus engages in tough talk about the cost of discipleship. Perhaps he recognizes that some of them are primarily interested in material benefits; others may expect Jesus to overthrow the Roman Empire. They may not realize yet that the journey to Jerusalem will be difficult, and it will not end well. So, Jesus speaks bluntly to them. If you do not hate your parents and spouse and children and siblings, he says, you cannot be my disciple. If you will not carry a cross and be ready to die, do not waste my time. If you need your possessions, go home.

The text does not report whether this sermon thinned the ranks of followers, but it must have diminished some of the superficial enthusiasm. Jesus may have been a captivating figure with a powerful message, but he also asked for a significant commitment. How many people could leave their families and possessions behind? Were these wannabe disciples ready to die? That was a lot to ask. Jesus advised his followers to count the costs. Know what you are in for. Be prepared for loss and poverty and suffering. Perhaps a few stayed, but some must have gone home.

Those drawn to Jesus have been wrestling with the meaning of discipleship ever since. What does it mean to follow Jesus?

In the early centuries of the church, some Christians took up the cross and died as martyrs. Some lived alone in the desert. Some joined communities of monks or nuns. Some flagellated themselves or deprived themselves of food and sleep. In various ways, they left their families, disposed of their possessions, and took up the cross. We might dismiss these disciples as the overachievers of Christian devotion. They may evoke awe, admiration, and respect, but their actions do not seem realistic to many of us in the twenty-first century; their actions probably did not seem realistic to others in their own settings either.

This advice from Jesus is difficult to interpret, even more difficult to preach. Imagine asking potential church members to renounce their families and possessions. That would not be an effective church-growth strategy. Typically, prospective followers are told instead that they do not have to hate their families as long as they put Jesus first. They do not have to give away all their possessions if they love Jesus more than money. They do not have to carry a cross, although they might be ridiculed for being a Christian. This is a kinder, gentler version of discipleship. Is this version perhaps exactly what Jesus discouraged? Has following Jesus become too easy?

In the United States in the 1950s, some religious leaders proclaimed that faith offered peace of mind, peace of soul, peace with God.[4] Being a Christian was socially acceptable and might aid one's rise in the workplace or community. President Dwight Eisenhower even encouraged Americans to go to church for the good of the nation. Perhaps not surprisingly, church membership reached an all-time high in the United States. More recently, some religious leaders have proclaimed that God wants Christians to be rich. As this Lukan text makes clear, this prosperity gospel is an oxymoron that could hardly be further from these words of Jesus.

In contrast, other Christians have responded to the words of Jesus by intensifying the requirements for church membership. The first generation of Puritans in the 1630s demanded that their children recount a dramatic conversion experience in order to become church members. Some churches expect members to abstain from drinking, dancing, movies, and premarital sex. Some churches ask for a specific commitment of time and money. Some demand obedience to the authority of the pastor and other leaders. These high-demand policies are sometimes effective in producing deeper commitments, but they can also become legalistic, shaming, and authoritarian. The children of the Puritans, for example, did not always have the same dramatic conversion experiences that their parents did and thus did not feel worthy to join the church. The Puritans finally had to develop a halfway membership to accommodate children and grandchildren who otherwise might not have attended church at all.

Contemporary disciples might consider what they are called to give up or add to their lives in order to follow Jesus. We may not necessarily be called to live alone in the desert, but we might consider the inordinate power that social media has over our lives. We are not called to self-punishment but to replace greed, privilege, and entitlement with justice and compassion.

Jesus did not want his followers to think that discipleship was easy, but neither was it open only to spiritual overachievers. He wanted his followers to know what they were in for, so he told two parables about the value of preparation and planning ahead. Do not build a tower or wage war without knowing what is required, he said. Do not follow me if you think it will be easy.

In her book *Wild*, Cheryl Strayed describes the summer she spent hiking the Pacific Crest Trail.[5] She purchased all the necessary equipment and mailed boxes of food, so she could be resupplied on the trail. Even so, she set off to hike with a pack that was too large and boots that were too small. Because she did not practice hiking with a full pack, she spent her first weeks with aching muscles, open sores from the pressure of the pack, and battered feet. She considered quitting in the first week because she was so ill-prepared for the rigors of the trail. She found, though, that the challenge brought out the best in her. She developed calluses and stronger muscles. She learned to push through when she was tired and to appreciate the kindness of strangers.

The words of Jesus in this text seem so difficult and unrealistic that we are often tempted to soften them. The point is that they *were* and *are* challenging. If it is too easy and attractive to follow Jesus, maybe we do not fully understand Jesus or the gospel. Jesus asks his followers, then and now, to do something so difficult that they will doubt their abilities. They are surprised to find that the challenge often brings out the best in them. They are forced to build muscle and develop calluses. They get dirty. They learn to push beyond their limits and rely on the kindness of strangers. Most importantly, they learn that in the end it is not their hard work or sacrifice or obedience that matters. They are given the grace to do what is hard.

We will never be fully prepared for hiking, for marriage, for parenting, for life, for discipleship. We will never know what we are in for. We will never get it all right. We will never earn God's approval by what we give up—but we can trust in the grace of the one we follow.

LYNN JAPINGA

4. Three best-selling books during the 1950s were *Peace of Mind: Insights on Human Nature That Can Change Your Life*, by Rabbi Joshua Liebman (New York: Simon & Schuster, 1946); *Peace of Soul*, by Archbishop Fulton Sheen (New York: McGraw-Hill, 1949); and *Peace with God: The Secret of Happiness*, by evangelist Billy Graham (Garden City, NY: Doubleday, 1953).

5. Cheryl Strayed, *Wild: From Lost to Found on the Pacific Crest Trail* (New York: Knopf, 2012).

Proper 19 (Sunday between September 11 and September 17 Inclusive)

Jeremiah 4:11–12, 22–28 and
Exodus 32:7–14
Psalm 14 and Psalm 51:1–10
1 Timothy 1:12–17
Luke 15:1–10

Jeremiah 4:11–12, 22–28

[11]At that time it will be said to this people and to Jerusalem: A hot wind comes from me out of the bare heights in the desert toward my poor people, not to winnow or cleanse— [12]a wind too strong for that. Now it is I who speak in judgment against them. . . .

[22]"For my people are foolish,
they do not know me;
they are stupid children,
they have no understanding.
They are skilled in doing evil,
but do not know how to do good."

[23]I looked on the earth, and lo, it was waste and void;
and to the heavens, and they had no light.
[24]I looked on the mountains, and lo, they were quaking,
and all the hills moved to and fro.
[25]I looked, and lo, there was no one at all,
and all the birds of the air had fled.
[26]I looked, and lo, the fruitful land was a desert,
and all its cities were laid in ruins
before the LORD, before his fierce anger.

[27]For thus says the LORD: The whole land shall be a desolation; yet I will not make a full end.

[28]Because of this the earth shall mourn,
and the heavens above grow black;
for I have spoken, I have purposed;
I have not relented nor will I turn back.

Exodus 32:7–14

[7]The LORD said to Moses, "Go down at once! Your people, whom you brought up out of the land of Egypt, have acted perversely; [8]they have been quick to turn aside from the way that I commanded them; they have cast for themselves an image of a calf, and have worshiped it and sacrificed to it, and said, 'These are your gods, O Israel, who brought you up out of the land of Egypt!'" [9]The LORD said to Moses, "I have seen this people, how stiff-necked they are. [10]Now let me alone, so that my wrath may burn hot against them and I may consume them; and of you I will make a great nation."

[11]But Moses implored the LORD his God, and said, "O LORD, why does your wrath burn hot against your people, whom you brought out of the land of Egypt with great power and with a mighty hand? [12]Why should the Egyptians say, 'It was with evil intent that he brought them out to kill them in the mountains, and to consume them from the face of the earth'? Turn from your fierce wrath; change your mind and do not bring disaster on your people. [13]Remember Abraham, Isaac, and Israel, your servants, how you swore to them by your own self, saying to them, 'I will multiply your descendants like the stars of heaven, and all this land that I have promised I will give to your descendants, and they shall inherit it forever.'" [14]And the LORD changed his mind about the disaster that he planned to bring on his people.

Commentary 1: Connecting the Reading with Scripture

Patrick Miller writes, "The great crisis of Israel's history in the OT period involved the destruction of the Temple, the dwelling place of the Lord of Israel, and the exile of God's people."[1] Jeremiah details what happened and, more importantly, why. The prophet proclaims that this destruction is the consequence of Judah's unfaithfulness. In Jeremiah 3:21–4:4, the prophet calls the people to repent, promising blessing that will come in response to repentance. Jeremiah apparently doubts Judah's capacity to repent, as what follows is a sweeping promise of destruction, called by one scholar, "the fullest, most drastic articulation of Yahweh's deathly judgment on Jerusalem."[2] Though the lectionary offers only a taste of the text, one must engage the whole section—Jeremiah 4:5–28—to grasp the comprehensive nature of the judgment. It is unrelenting in scope, moving from earthly metaphors of judgment, to forces of nature, to a disrupted cosmos.

Judgment begins with images of an invading army (Jer. 4:5–6). The metaphor shifts to a devouring lion, "a destroyer of nations." After an interlude of acknowledgment of the coming judgment on the part of leaders in verses 9–10, the onslaught continues at the opening of the lectionary reading. Now the metaphor becomes a hot wind, "too strong for" winnowing or cleansing, and we are called to behold the onset of "chariots like the whirlwind." After another indictment in verse 22, the metaphor moves to all creation. Jeremiah's vision of the earth as "waste and void" in verse 23 invokes the Hebrew words in Genesis 1:2, *tohu wa bohu*, "formless and void." According to Walter Brueggemann, the aim is "to express the resurgence of chaos and disorder that is experienced by the poet in every dimension of life."[3] The lights of the heavens have been extinguished, mountains shake, people are gone, birds have fled, vegetation is nowhere to be found. This is the cleaning of the slate of creation, an incredibly disturbing image void of hope—until 4:27b.

The Hebrew text of 4:27b is more ambiguous than the phrasing provided by the NRSV: "yet I will not make a full end." Scholars have offered a range of possibilities. Some say this represents a later edit to Jeremiah's original pronouncement. Others interpret the Hebrew to imply the destruction is not yet complete. A third approach suggests it is an emphatic statement of total destruction: "You ain't seen nothing yet!" The preacher must choose. Perhaps this represents a lone speck of light in the impenetrable darkness of Jeremiah 4, but the overall text seems to be a sweeping indictment, and the

1. Patrick D. Miller, "The Book of Jeremiah: Introduction, Commentary, and Reflection," in *The New Interpreter's Bible*, ed. Leander E. Keck, 10 vols. (Nashville: Abingdon, 2001), 6:555.
2. Walter Brueggemann, *Theology of the Old Testament: Testimony, Dispute, Advocacy* (Minneapolis: Fortress, 1991), 542.
3. Walter Brueggemann, *Jeremiah 1–25: To Pluck Up, To Tear Down*, International Theological Commentary (Grand Rapids: Eerdmans, 1988), 56.

clause in 4:27b seems out of place when interpreted this way.

God's response to the golden calf and Moses' response to God's oracle of judgment in Exodus 32 offer a different perspective. In both Jeremiah and Exodus, the people have sinned before the Lord. In both, God has resolved to wipe out the people because of their sin. It could be argued that both texts call for a reboot with a remnant—the lack of "a full end" in Jeremiah 4:27 and starting over with Moses in Exodus 32:10. However, Moses' response to God's oracle of judgment is quite different from Jeremiah's.

While Jeremiah is resigned to be the prophet of doom, Moses negotiates with God to ease the pain of judgment. In Moses' exchange with God, Moses seems to be the mature party. He begins by correcting God. At the opening of the reading, YHWH identifies Israel as "your people, whom you brought up out of the land of Egypt." In verse 11, Moses reminds God that they are *God's* people, whom *God* brought out of the land of Egypt. Then Moses becomes a public relations agent for the Divine. "What will the Egyptians say about you, Lord?" he wonders aloud to the Almighty. It is as if Moses suggests God has a reputation to keep, and destroying Israel would look bad, especially after delivering them from Egypt.

In verse 12, Moses engages God in stunning rhetoric. The Hebrew term often translated "turn" is a theologically loaded word that is often understood as carrying the sense of "repent." Does Moses really call God to repent? This is a bold imperative to proclaim to the Almighty. The offense is not eased when Moses calls God to remember the covenant established with Abraham. This is typically God's role, to call the people to remember. Moses calls *God* to remember—this is stunning. Even more stunning, however, is that Moses' intercession changes God's mind. While punishment is still meted out for their rebellion (Exod. 32:20, 25–29, 32), God does not follow through with the intended destruction.

Considering the texts in conversation with one another, Jeremiah and Exodus offer two contrasts in how God's servants respond to a sinful people. There are similarities in context and in God's response. In both texts the people have rebelled against God. In both texts, God's wrath burns hot. In both, God has resolved to destroy the people as a consequence of their sin. Both texts involve repentance. In Jeremiah, the people face destruction because they refuse to repent. In Exodus, however, Moses calls *God* to repent. Therein lies the amazing contrast. One servant of God is resigned to the ensuing judgment; the other refuses to accept destruction as a faithful option. The results could not stand in more stark opposition. In Jeremiah, judgment comes and exile ensues. In Exodus, in response to Moses' intercession, God relents, perhaps even repents from the destruction that had been resolved.

Are God's servants in the world called to proclaim the unrelenting judgment of God? Are we called, instead, to negotiate with God on behalf of God's people? Is now the time for the proclamation of judgment, or is now the time for the plea for mercy? This is a fundamental question to face. In conversation with one another, these two passages provide challenging possibilities for response. In considering an answer to the question, it is important to remember that these passages are not directed at the wider world; they are directed at, and on behalf of, the people of God. Jeremiah is not prophesying against the nations in this text but against Judah. Moses is not negotiating with God to spare the Egyptians; he is negotiating on behalf of God's own people.

This calls forth a more challenging question. What is the character of God? Is God the unrelenting judge, preparing to start over with a new creation? Is God willing to show mercy? While the passages from Hebrew Scriptures stand on their own, the NT lections for the day provide a different response to the character of the Divine. The Gospel lection from Luke offers the parables of the Lost Sheep and the Lost Coin that reveal the God who seeks until all are found and rejoices upon reclaiming what has been lost. The epistle lection from 1 Timothy 1 proclaims the saying that is "sure and worthy of full acceptance, that Christ came into the world to save sinners."

JOSEPH J. CLIFFORD

Commentary 2: Connecting the Reading with the World

In this reading, God is not dealing only with the nation of Israel but with the whole cosmos. God brings destruction to the whole of creation. The reader must wrestle with the idea that when the people of God do not *know* God, all of creation will suffer. This week we investigate connections between the people and God and the connection between the people of God and the earth.

There is an important connection between the text and the church's call to care for and protect God's creation. We are reminded that the God of Israel is the God of all creation. We can use this week's text as a lens to think about eco-justice. Our human actions have a direct impact on the earth, both in our local communities and on a global scale. As a human race we face issues such as global warming, disposing of toxic waste, urban sprawl, and threats to wilderness preservation. As Christians, we look to our faith and to the Scriptures to discern how we respond to environmental concerns. How does knowing God help us to address these issues? How does knowing God help us to live in harmony with all the creatures and creations of God? The text invites us to reconsider the church's emphasis in the modern era on a personal relationship between the individual and God.

The text does not minimize this personal relationship, but calls us beyond it. It connects us to the cosmos, making the consequences of the practice of our faith far more significant than preserving our right relationship with God and reserving our place in heaven. Because of the people of the tribes of Israel, a hot wind will blow across the desert. The dust will fill the air, blocking the light, suffocating life. The actions of a few will have implications for many. The text is clear: desolation will come, but it will not be the end. As the Lord looks over the desolated land, there is no light, no life, only waste and void. However, dust eventually settles and God is relentless; out of nothing and out of the dust God creates life. Jeremiah's depiction of a land "formless and void" (v. 23) calls to mind the story of creation, reminding us of God's creative potential as well as our formation from and connectedness to the earth.

A primary concern of this pericope is that the people do not know God. What does it mean to know God? How do we know we know God? How do others know we know God? The author writes that the people of Judah are skilled in evil-doing, but God requires us to do good. Perhaps this is an indication that knowing has something to do with doing. There is a connection between what we know and what we practice. The ancient Greeks called this *phronēsis*: a kind of knowledge or wisdom grounded in practice. What is the church practicing? Are our liturgical and ecclesial practices helping us know God and cultivate the skill to do good? We learn something from doing things over and over again. A pianist becomes skilled by practicing the music scales. Basketball players become stars by shooting the same shot over and over again. The church becomes faithful people of God when they practice doing the good work of God.

Finally, this text has implications for how we understand our relationship to God, how we connect to God. It is difficult to hear and understand such harsh words from God: "my people are foolish, they do not know me; they are stupid children, they have no understanding" (v. 22). Hearing this admonition, we may be tempted to turn from God, to run away. We can turn, instead, toward God and hear these words as a message of love and grace. We are like children and so God is like a parent. Parents have moments of frustration with children. Can we not acknowledge humbly that God must feel that way about God's children? God loves us so much that God anguishes over us.

Exodus 32:7–14 is the story of a passionate God. The people of Israel have done just the thing they were told not to do; they have built an idol to worship. Seeing their betrayal, God, whose wrath burns hot, hastily declares that the people shall be destroyed. God, whose entire being is about relationship, says to Moses, "Leave me alone!" Fortunately, Moses appeals to God on behalf of the Israelites, and God changes God's mind.

We are also guilty of creating idols. We are all worthy of God's wrath. Who is on top of the mountain interceding on our behalf? We may not even be aware that someone is pleading to God on our behalf. For what people and places do we ask for intercession? This passage invites us to take seriously the power of intercessory prayer, and thinking about prayer requires us to ponder how we understand God to be working in our lives. Does God intervene in our daily lives? Do we believe prayer actually matters, that it might actually work? If so, what do we do with unanswered prayers? How do we carefully explain or investigate unanswered prayer so as not to inflict harm on Christian communities? These are the questions that today's passage forces us to reckon with. Our answers to these questions will connect with the way we relate to others in our ecclesial and cultural communities.

Prayer has both a vertical dimension, connecting us to God, and a social dimension, connecting us to one another. In both dimensions, prayer demands vulnerability. Prayer requires us to share our brokenness with one another and God. In prayer we share our pain and our burdens. Sometimes we even allow ourselves to be touched, to have hands laid on us as prayers are lifted up. In prayer we are intimately present to each other, and we believe that God is intimately present and active in our lives. To know and believe this is powerful. Perhaps it will lead us to gather together around prayer instead of working together to build idols.

Some may find it difficult to make a connection between the unmoving and unchangeable God they believe in and the changing, emotional God conveyed in this passage. Emotions themselves are often viewed as suspect and disconnected from intellect or reason. In various times and places, the church has separated the head and the heart, the mind and the body. God teaches us by example that it is okay to feel deeply and passionately. Anger, even rage, can be a part of our lives and need not lead to rash decisions. God feels an intense wrath toward the people of Israel, but in the end it does not inform his action. Rather, Moses persuades God to act out of love and mercy. God's intense wrath is connected to God's love and mercy. God would not feel so angry if God were not deeply in love with God's people. Where is our passion as a people of God? Whom and what do we love deeply? How do we show this love and passion to the world?

ALLIE UTLEY

Proper 19 (Sunday between September 11 and September 17 Inclusive)

Psalm 14

[1]Fools say in their hearts, "There is no God."
They are corrupt, they do abominable deeds;
there is no one who does good.

[2]The LORD looks down from heaven on humankind
to see if there are any who are wise,
who seek after God.

[3]They have all gone astray, they are all alike perverse;
there is no one who does good,
no, not one.

[4]Have they no knowledge, all the evildoers
who eat up my people as they eat bread,
and do not call upon the LORD?

[5]There they shall be in great terror,
for God is with the company of the righteous.
[6]You would confound the plans of the poor,
but the LORD is their refuge.

[7]O that deliverance for Israel would come from Zion!
When the LORD restores the fortunes of his people,
Jacob will rejoice; Israel will be glad.

Psalm 51:1–10

[1]Have mercy on me, O God,
according to your steadfast love;
according to your abundant mercy
blot out my transgressions.
[2]Wash me thoroughly from my iniquity,
and cleanse me from my sin.

[3]For I know my transgressions,
and my sin is ever before me.
[4]Against you, you alone, have I sinned,
and done what is evil in your sight,
so that you are justified in your sentence
and blameless when you pass judgment.
[5]Indeed, I was born guilty,
a sinner when my mother conceived me.

[6]You desire truth in the inward being;
therefore teach me wisdom in my secret heart.
[7]Purge me with hyssop, and I shall be clean;
wash me, and I shall be whiter than snow.
[8]Let me hear joy and gladness;
let the bones that you have crushed rejoice.
[9]Hide your face from my sins,
and blot out all my iniquities.

[10]Create in me a clean heart, O God,
and put a new and right spirit within me.

Connecting the Psalm with Scripture and the Word

We have all met fools who say in their heart, "There is no God" (Ps. 14:1). Maybe we see one every time we look in the mirror. Glancing at the day's news—or reflecting on the pain, disappointment, and loss staining our lives—it seems quite sensible not to believe in God. It is easier to surrender our faith than it is to believe.

Jeremiah 4 does little to present a God in which we would want to believe. The prophet warns of a "hot wind" that will come from YHWH, and God instructs the prophet to warn Judah and Jerusalem against an "evil from the north" (Jer. 4:6), brought by God. When read alongside Psalm 14, God's frustration seems even worse. Yet the cosmological combat of Jeremiah 4 is mythic.[1] While intent to rouse faithfulness is sincere in both passages, the rhetoric is more sizzle than steak. It is mostly hot air.

Because the prophet and the psalmist mean what they say, but do not really mean it, liturgical appropriation of their furious words must also be prayerfully and carefully balanced. We have to even out the spice of Psalm 14 and Jeremiah 4 with pinches of truth about God from elsewhere.

Within a worship service today, verses from each passage could be alternated in a congregational reading that enunciates the Lord's fury but indicates a glimmer of hope. For example, consider the following sequence: Psalm 14:2; Jeremiah 4:22; Psalm 14:3; and Jeremiah 4:23–26; ending with Psalm 14:7. The last verse closes with hope for the deliverance of the Lord, and assurance that when it comes, "Jacob will rejoice; Israel will be glad." Then follow with Psalm 51 to round out the turn to the redemption of God:

Reader 1: Have mercy on me, O God, according to your steadfast love; according to your abundant mercy blot out my transgressions.
Reader 2: Against you, you alone, have I sinned, and done what is evil in your sight, so that you are justified in your sentence and blameless when you pass judgment.
Reader 1: Create in me a clean heart, O God, and put a new and right spirit within me.
Reader 2: Do not cast me away from your presence, and do not take your holy spirit from me.
Reader 1: Restore to me the joy of your salvation, and sustain in me a willing spirit.
Reader 2: Then I will teach transgressors your ways, and sinners will return to you.
Psalm 51:1, 4, 10–13

What began as a congregational reading of God's wrath shifts to a shared prayer for God's grace. In these verses, the purported author of the Psalm 51, David, repents of his despicable

1. Kathleen M. O'Connor, "Jeremiah," in *The New Interpreter's Study Bible: New Revised Standard Version with the Apocrypha*, ed. Walter Harrelson (Nashville: Abingdon, 2003), 1059.

infidelity with Bathsheba and his murder of Uriah. While we do not repeat Psalm 51 for the same reasons, we can pray David's prayer because we need the same mercy from God that he did for all kinds of reasons. With the psalmist, we know that no matter how angry God seems, God desires human redemption.

That knowledge has a long tradition. In the Exodus reading, which is paired with Psalm 51 in the complementary stream of the lectionary, Moses eases the temper of a God warring with the children of God. After discovering that they have been worshiping a golden calf, God wants to consume the Israelites and start over. Moses reminds God of the divine promises to Abraham, Isaac, and Israel, "and the LORD changed his mind about the disaster that he planned to bring on his people" (Exod. 32:14). Notably, what is rendered in English as LORD—YHWH—can be rendered as "eternal" or "existing One." For Moses, God is present in every circumstance—including situations where God seems ready to destroy everyone and everything—but God does not desire destruction. What is translated as "changed his mind"—in Hebrew, *nacham*—can also mean "repented." In every circumstance, the God of Moses, Jeremiah, the psalmist, and of us wants forgiveness, no matter what. Furthermore, the Hebrew word for "wrath" (Exod. 32:12)—*'aph*—concerns nostrils, infering something like seething through a flared nose.[2] In Exodus 32:14, *nacham* can also be rendered as something like heavy sighing or exhaling. Figuratively, the God of Moses exhaled hot air and returned to a composure and ministry of mercy.

The word for "air" in Jeremiah does not directly relate to *nacham*. It does, however, harmonize like a neighboring tone of the same scriptural key. In Jeremiah, the word for "air" is *ruach*, the term for the Spirit of God that moves over the formless water before animating all of life. Redemption always whispers in the tirades and chaos associated with the Eternal One.

With the understanding that God always desires redemption, we cannot let the foolishness of disbelief get the best of us, no matter how reasonable it seems. In the face of widespread addiction, unconscionable violence, political and ecological turmoil, and so many other maladies, traumas, and transgressions in our lives, it becomes all too easy to lose sight of who God is. Worse, we may want to give up on the very idea of God altogether. Feeling that depth of doubt is healthy. Expressing it has its benefits. Developing pastoral patience for it is absolutely crucial. Yet we cannot permit ourselves to get carried away.

We can find spiritual stamina to sustain us through the nihilism of disbelief by remembering that even God gets carried away by the cruelty and capriciousness of life and humankind. God spews vitriol that threatens to annihilate it all. Yet ultimately God desires to redeem. God hears us when we intercede on behalf of others. God holds us when we grasp for mercy ourselves. As children of God and portraits of the Eternal One, we can express our rage against the world and look evil in its eye. Yet our passion and gaze cannot end there. We must see past what debilitates our faith and remember that "there is joy in the presence of the angels of God over one sinner who repents" (Luke 15:10). We must reenvision, receive, and reenact that joy again and again. Even when Scripture itself disappoints us with imagery such as being cleansed "whiter than snow" (Ps. 51:7), we must ultimately maintain hope in the salvation of God.

GERALD C. LIU

2. Brian Rainey, email exchange with author, October 26, 2017.

Proper 19 (Sunday between September 11 and September 17 Inclusive)

1 Timothy 1:12–17

> [12]I am grateful to Christ Jesus our Lord, who has strengthened me, because he judged me faithful and appointed me to his service, [13]even though I was formerly a blasphemer, a persecutor, and a man of violence. But I received mercy because I had acted ignorantly in unbelief, [14]and the grace of our Lord overflowed for me with the faith and love that are in Christ Jesus. [15]The saying is sure and worthy of full acceptance, that Christ Jesus came into the world to save sinners—of whom I am the foremost. [16]But for that very reason I received mercy, so that in me, as the foremost, Jesus Christ might display the utmost patience, making me an example to those who would come to believe in him for eternal life. [17]To the King of the ages, immortal, invisible, the only God, be honor and glory forever and ever. Amen.

Commentary 1: Connecting the Reading with Scripture

The lessons for this Sunday give expression to what stands at the epicenter of the church's proclamation of the gospel: the one and only God, immortal and invisible, graciously encounters even the "foremost" of sinners to "create a clean heart within us" (Ps. 51:10). What is clear from these lessons is that the Creator's action on our behalf because of Christ Jesus requires a humble response that recognizes a sinner's profound need for forgiveness. God, who desires to deliver us from the nasty effects of our sins, simply will not act to restore us without our earnest response.

Despite its importance during the church's history, 1 Timothy has become one of the NT's most neglected books, mostly because its Pauline authorship is disputed by modern scholarship. Such decisions are not only indeterminate and irrelevant for establishing the spiritual authority of a biblical book; they are typically distracting of a sermon's performance in forming a faithful congregation.[1] Focus instead on the heart of this lesson: the transforming effects of a sinner's reception of God's mercy.

Expressions of thanksgiving for others is the standard, although not uniform, manner by which Paul introduces his letters. The literary function of these epistolary notes of praise is to sound the core beliefs of Paul's theological grammar that organize most of what follows. For Paul, praise is the prelude to proclamation. This passage concludes in doxology (1:17) that sizes up the character of the Deity who has the capacity to make good on the gospel's stunning promise to save sinners for eternal life through Christ Jesus. Moreover, it complements another doxology found at the end of this letter (6:15b–16) to frame the ecclesial instructions found between. The proper conduct of the "household of God" (3:15) and its spiritual leaders is grounded in the worship of God, the immortal Sovereign for the ages, who is worthy of honor and glory.

Most of Paul's letters begin with a thanksgiving that reads like a pastoral prayer with a petition for the well-being of its recipients. In this case, however, Paul thanks "Christ Jesus our Lord" for saving *him* from ignorance and unbelief (1:13) and for calling him to a ministry of the "glorious gospel" entrusted to him (v. 11). The pattern of conversion and then a commissioning of the converted is typological of God's

1. For a fuller exposition of this passage, see Robert W. Wall, *1–2 Timothy and Titus*, Two Horizons New Testament Commentary (Grand Rapids: Eerdmans, 2013). For discussion of the letter's authorship, see pp. 4–7, 70–75.

way of recruiting partners for the work of salvation (e.g., Moses in Exod. 3). A close reading of Scripture's antecedent story of Paul's conversion and commissioning told in Acts 9 fills out the clipped retelling of it here. He is the "foremost" of sinners because prior to his conversion to Jesus he publicly insulted him ("blasphemer") and violently persecuted his followers (v. 13). Paul's turn to the risen Jesus is reimagined as the "overflowing" of divine grace "for me" (v. 14a) in demonstration that "Christ Jesus came into the world to save sinners" (v. 15).

The irony presented by this autobiography is that these snapshots from an apostle's life are not to secure his apostolic authority but serve to illustrate the nature of the "faith and love that are in Christ Jesus" (v. 14b). Paul's conversion story personifies the transforming effect of God's grace in all of life (see v. 17); a former enemy of Christ Jesus, the foremost of sinners, becomes his champion, an exemplar of Christ's "utmost patience" for all who come to faith (v. 16).

The catchphrase, "this saying is sure and worthy of full acceptance" (v. 15a), is routinely used in the Pastoral Epistles (see 1 Tim. 1:15; 3:1; 4:9; 2 Tim. 2:11; Titus 3:8; cf. Titus 1:9) to introduce a distinctively Pauline formulation of God's way of salvation. In this instance, "Christ Jesus came into the world to save sinners" serves as a "creedal cameo"[2]—a memorable yet dense phrase that helps converts to Jesus conceptualize their experience of being initiated into Christian faith. Conversions of Paul's kind—a personification of salvation's apocalypse—remind us of the powerful, transformative effects of God's way of dealing with sin.

This lesson also illustrates a particular kind of spiritual crisis that requires conversion of the sinner's imagination: Paul says God acted mercifully toward him because he "had acted ignorantly in unbelief" (v. 13). This too is thematic of Paul's story in Acts (cf. Acts 9:5; 3:17; 17:3). According to Acts God gives second chances to those whose prior rejection of Christ is due to their ignorance of God's messianic way of salvation. Paul's ignorance is not for lack of intelligence or knowledge of God. He was well schooled and well informed. His ignorance was the result of unbelief. For this reason, the attentive hearing of and turn toward God's gospel in faith dispels such ignorance and opens one's heart to knowledge of God's truth (cf. 1 Tim. 2:4; Acts 3:26)—hence, the essential meaning of repentance is a "change of mind."

Even though "Christ Jesus" is the name used for Jesus in this letter, Paul adds "our Lord" here. The public profession that the risen Jesus is the church's Lord is a principal identity marker of Pauline congregations in the public square (Rom. 10:9). By this public profession of faith, sinners admit their agreement with the central claims of Paul's gospel about Christ's atoning death, bodily resurrection, heavenly exaltation, and triumphant return (see 3:16). That is, all believers share with the apostle the same core beliefs about Christ and experience the same realization that Jesus "came into the world to save sinners . . . for eternal life."

The exegetical question facing today's preachers is how to use this Pauline "sound bite" to form a congregation of faithful readers. Its deep logic is that readers should aim God's word at a redemptive result. Those preaching on this passage should strive, not only to overturn people's ignorance or misinformation about the messianic mission of Jesus, but more critically to proclaim the effect of taking what is learned about him to heart, which results in the sinner's converting experience of God's transforming grace. The presumption, of course, is that when a community is reformed by its experience of gospel truth, it will be compelled by the Spirit of this same Christ to continue to preach, parade, and practice it in the world for his sake.

Hardly anywhere in the Pauline letters does the reader find a clearer expression of the apostle's understanding of God's way of salvation than in this lesson. Clearly, the principal source of Paul's claims about Christ Jesus is his conversion experience of being saved from ignorance for a ministry of the gospel. The careful reader should recognize that this lesson's subtext explores what might be called an epistemology of theology. Paul learned God's gospel by his conversion experience, rather than by catechesis. Surely his theological grammar remained deeply Jewish:

2. Raymond F. Collins, *I and II Timothy and Titus*, New Testament Library (Louisville, KY: Westminster John Knox, 2002), 43.

the covenant-keeping God of the exodus, who is faithful to promises made, mercifully liberates God's people, here personified by Paul, from their ignorance and insults to become agents of God's liberating mercy for others. Now Paul's slant toward Israel's biblical story is radicalized by his encounter of the risen One and the forgiveness he experienced as a result.

ROBERT W. WALL

Commentary 2: Connecting the Reading with the World

This section of Paul's letter to Timothy is part memoir and part testimonial, brimming with gratitude for what God has done in Paul's life. It is also self-deferential, as Paul acknowledges his weaknesses, his imperfections, and the blemishes from his past. He also offers himself as an example for Timothy and others to follow, not for his own glory but for the glory of God.

Were it not for these verses, the entire first chapter would otherwise read like a doom-and-gloom report to his young protégé about the shadowy side of ministry. The rest of the chapter resonates with the disheartening state of spirituality in today's culture: spiritual stagnation among the membership, the rise of both agnosticism and civil religion, the "false teachers" of moral therapeutic deism and the prosperity gospel, and the prominent presence of some church members who live less out of love and more out of power and self-preservation.

First Timothy 1:12–17 can therefore offer hope to the brokenness in our world today by (1) affirming the strength that can come from God, (2) rekindling our flames of passion and devotion, and (3) encouraging personal testimony.

God Gives Strength. Paul is not interested in sugarcoating the realities of ministry; in fact, he feels it necessary to give Timothy ample warning to ensure he works with eyes wide open. None of that message, though, deters the central conviction that Paul maintains, which is that despite the ugliness and messiness of life in the real world, God grants strength, mercy, and grace for even a sinner like himself.

There are numerous stories in popular culture that display profound human resilience amid abject darkness and desperation. In Cormac McCarthy's *The Road*, a father and son travel through a desolate, postapocalyptic wasteland, enduring one calamity after another. Toward the end of the book, as the father recognizes his old age is drawing him closer to death, he offers encouraging words in a dialogue with his son, in similar fashion to Paul's words to Timothy:

> "You have to carry the fire."
> "I don't know how to."
> "Yes you do."
> "Is it real? The fire?"
> "Yes it is."
> "Where is it? I don't know where it is."
> "Yes you do. It's inside you. It was always there. I can see it."[3]

Rekindling the Flame. That "fire" for the apostle Paul is the grace of God, which overflowed for him in faith and love (v. 14). That fire would enable Timothy to endure the struggles of ministry in the real world. In fact, that theme would continue more directly in Paul's Second Letter to Timothy, in which he reminds Timothy to "rekindle the gift of God that is within you through the laying on of my hands" (2 Tim. 1:6). The Greek word for "rekindle the gift" can also be translated as "fan the flame" or even "wake up the fiery beast" within you.

The fire of God's patience and mercy enabled Paul to live with a freedom that he knew he did not deserve, for he readily acknowledged that his life was much more like the sinners elsewhere mentioned in this chapter. Before the preacher even begins to exegete the congregation and make homiletical connections for the sermon, it would be good to pause, even for a moment, to embrace that same gratitude that Paul describes

3. Cormac McCarthy, *The Road* (New York: Vintage Books, 2006), 278–79.

Empty Our Hearts of Hatred

Finally, we petition that forgiveness come to us, "as we forgive our debtors" [Matt. 6:12]: namely, as we spare and pardon all who have in any way injured us, either treating us unjustly in deed or insulting us in word. Not that it is ours to forgive the guilt of transgression or offense, for this belongs to God alone [cf. Isa. 43:25]! This, rather, is our forgiveness: willingly to cast from the mind wrath, hatred, desire for revenge, and willingly to banish to oblivion the remembrance of injustice. For this reason, we ought not to seek forgiveness of sins from God unless we ourselves also forgive the offenses against us of all those who do or have done us ill. If we retain feelings of hatred in our hearts, if we plot revenge and ponder any occasion to cause harm, and even if we do not try to get back into our enemies' good graces, by every sort of good office deserve well of them, and commend ourselves to them, by this prayer we entreat God not to forgive our sins. For we ask that he do to us as we do to others [cf. Matt. 7:12]. This, indeed, is to petition him not to do it to us unless we ourselves do it. What do people of this sort gain from their petition but a heavier judgment?

Finally, we must note that this condition—that he "forgive us as we forgive our debtors" [Matt. 6:12]—is not added because by the forgiveness we grant to others we deserve his forgiveness, as if this indicated the cause of it. Rather, by this word the Lord intended partly to comfort the weakness of our faith. For he has added this as a sign to assure us he has granted forgiveness of sins to us just as surely as we are aware of having forgiven others, provided our hearts have been emptied and purged of all hatred, envy, and vengeance. Also, it is partly by this mark that the Lord excludes from the number of his children those persons who, being eager for revenge and slow to forgive, practice persistent enmity and foment against others the very indignation that they pray to be averted from themselves. This the Lord does that such men dare not call upon him as Father.

John Calvin, *Institutes of the Christian Religion*, book 34, chap. 20, par. 45, ed. John T. McNeill (Philadelphia: The Westminster Press, 1960), 912.

in verse 12. With gratitude, the preacher might wonder at the ways they too have received the warm fire of God's forgiveness, and acknowledge how they have received this amazing gift despite their own flaws and shortcomings. It is out of that grateful remembrance that a very different sermon might emerge: not a "doom and gloom" assessment of what is wrong with the world, but a hopeful vision of what the world *can become* because of the faithful love of God at work in the world.

It is that sense of hope that thus becomes the prevailing theme of 1 Timothy, despite the dire warnings of false teachers. How timely is that message of hope for the people of God today. It is far too easy to be focused on all the wrong things that are happening: violence, polarization and division, the decline of commitment to organized religion, the diminishing of the church's significance in society at large, the steady shrinking of worship attendance, membership, and financial giving, and so much more. To be sure, much of the rest of 1 Timothy 1 would affirm that diagnosis.

The Power of Personal Testimony. This text offers a hopeful counternarrative, in the form of Paul's personal testimony. Even though he lived a life antithetical to the gospel, God "poured out favor all over him." Because of what God has done in him, God can do the same in the world through Christ.

The preacher might consider ways that he or she might simply offer testimony, bearing witness in similar fashion to Paul. How has the preacher also experienced God's transforming love in his or her own life? What is the evidence that God has been merciful to the preacher, even though she or he did not deserve it? Are there stories from the preacher's past, either personally or in the practice of ministry, that illustrate God's "utmost patience," so that these stories might be "an example to those who would come to believe in him for eternal life" (v. 16)?

Then there are stories to consider from people within the congregation itself. Who are those who might characterize themselves as having been "the foremost" of sinners, whom God has transformed through the power of Christ Jesus? Who are the ones who have received mercy, in whom Jesus has "displayed utmost patience"? Paul describes the power in sharing such testimonies as an "example to those who would come to believe in him for eternal life."

The preacher might then remind the congregation of how the simple act of sharing testimony can offer good news to others. He or she might invite people to consider what stories of hope within their own past might be of comfort to those who are facing similar challenges. What stories of transformation might inspire someone who feels outside the reach of God's love because of mistakes they have made? What stories of courage and fidelity to the Christian faith might encourage a person who is struggling against pressures in the workplace, family, or culture at large to compromise their convictions? Rather than instruct or reprimand, this passage can underscore that personal narrative can be the most powerful counternarrative to the destructive influences around us.

Verse 17 concludes this passage with a doxology, describing God in cosmic, supernatural terms. Paul wants to remind Timothy that no matter how bogged down one might become in the traumas of life on earth, God is much bigger than problems that ultimately become insignificant in light of God's glory. When viewed from the high altitude of God's limitless power and infinite love, all the struggles of life and all the "doom and gloom" forecasts of the world around us pale in comparison to the hope that one can claim in God.

A sermon built largely on personal testimony might then conclude with doxology: attestations of the majesty and grandeur of God, beyond our comprehension and larger than our troubled obsessions. Closing hymn possibilities would include "Immortal, Invisible, God Only Wise," "Praise to the Lord, the Almighty," "God of Grace and God of Glory," and other songs with similar emphases.

MAGREY R. DEVEGA

Proper 19 (Sunday between September 11 and September 17 Inclusive)

Luke 15:1–10

[1]Now all the tax collectors and sinners were coming near to listen to him. [2]And the Pharisees and the scribes were grumbling and saying, "This fellow welcomes sinners and eats with them."

[3]So he told them this parable: [4]"Which one of you, having a hundred sheep and losing one of them, does not leave the ninety-nine in the wilderness and go after the one that is lost until he finds it? [5]When he has found it, he lays it on his shoulders and rejoices. [6]And when he comes home, he calls together his friends and neighbors, saying to them, 'Rejoice with me, for I have found my sheep that was lost.' [7]Just so, I tell you, there will be more joy in heaven over one sinner who repents than over ninety-nine righteous persons who need no repentance.

[8]"Or what woman having ten silver coins, if she loses one of them, does not light a lamp, sweep the house, and search carefully until she finds it? [9]When she has found it, she calls together her friends and neighbors, saying, 'Rejoice with me, for I have found the coin that I had lost.' [10]Just so, I tell you, there is joy in the presence of the angels of God over one sinner who repents."

Commentary 1: Connecting the Reading with Scripture

Luke 15 features three parables of Jesus: the Lost Sheep (15:1–7), the Lost Coin (15:8–10), and the Lost Son (15:11–32). This trilogy, which has been called "the heart of the Third Gospel," shows God's love and mercy for sinful persons. Jesus' call for repentance and conversion strikes a strong note of joy—applied to God when the "lost" are recovered. The paired parables of our passage show that in Jesus' preaching, God's initiative and grace are widely and freely given to all.

The parables are part of Luke's account of Jesus traveling toward Jerusalem to face his passion and death. These opening parables of Luke 15 begin a large unit within Luke's account of Jesus' travel narrative, extending to 18:14 or 19:27.

These initial parables were told in the context of "tax collectors and sinners" coming to listen to Jesus (15:1). This upset the Pharisees and scribes who were "grumbling and saying, 'This fellow welcomes sinners and eats with them'" (15:2; cf. 5:30; 7:34). The leaders felt this association with sinners was inappropriate behavior for Jesus. They exhibited no "hospitality" or generous attitudes toward those regarded as "lost."

Jesus' parables counter this attitude and its restrictiveness. In them, he demonstrated God's care for those who are despised and rejected by society. In the parables, God is the active participant in seeking to save the lost. This gives the parables their urgency and power as expressions of the nature of God enacted in the midst of everyday human life. God's purpose is to restore the lost. God's way of work is to seek and save through merciful love. These parables offer testimony to the depths of God's compassion and the width of God's concern.

It is interesting to note the parables of the Lost Sheep and the Lost Coin share a similar structure and plotline. This can be summarized as follows:

> Which man/woman . . . having 100 sheep/10 coins. If he/she loses one . . . does not leave/sweep . . . go after/and seek . . . until he/she finds it? When he/she has found it . . . he/she calls together his/her friends and neighbors, saying, 'Rejoice with me, for I have found my sheep/the coin . . . . which was/I had

> lost.' Just so, I tell you, there will be more joy/is joy in heaven/before the angels of God over one sinner who repents.[1]

The movement here is from a full community to the loss of a member or part of that community. God, represented by a man and then a woman, diligently searches and scours for what is lost. When it is found, the community is called together to rejoice and celebrate. The lost has been found! This mirrors the divine joy "in heaven" over "one sinner who repents"—or over those who are brought into the community and thus receive new life.

I once spoke with a seminary student from another culture. He pointed out that when reading these parables, North American culture tends to focus its attention on the single lost sheep or coin. The joy comes when it is found. The student said that his culture finds joy in the corporate dimension of the stories, in the fact that the community can now be complete. Those who preach these parables can explore both personal and communal aspects, discovering joy both on behalf of the sinner who is found and the church community that now receives fullness through the addition of another member.

The context of these parables—Jesus' address to religious leaders who showed no compassion for "sinners"—is reminiscent of Ezekiel 34, where there is a contrast between Israel's false shepherds, who will not seek the lost sheep of Israel in the wilderness (Ezek. 34:7–8), with God, the true shepherd who says, "I myself will search for my sheep, and will seek them out" (v. 11). This background, along with the Lukan parables and the actions of Jesus, points to the images of Jesus, the Messiah, as the "good Shepherd" (John 10:1, 11, 14).[2]

The two parables in Luke 15:1–10 point to the larger literary context of Jesus' teachings, composed of sayings, parables, and actions, throughout Luke's Gospel. In both parables, the theme revolves around the compassionate, searching God who desires to restore the lost and heaven's delightful joy when repentance occurs. This theme shows up in other episodes in Luke. The "younger" or prodigal son who fell into degradation and disobedience (15:11–32) was welcomed home with joyful celebration. The ten lepers (17:11–19), forced to live outside the community because they were unclean, were made clean by Jesus so they could participate in the community. The tax collector Zacchaeus, who would have been regarded as a traitor to the Jewish people by working for the occupying Romans (Luke 19:7), is featured in the memorable story of Jesus' table fellowship at Zacchaeus's house (vv. 1–10), where Jesus says he has come "to seek out and to save the lost" (v. 10). All these highlight the rescue of societal outcasts by Jesus and his call, "Rejoice with me, for I have found my sheep that was lost" (15:6).

The parables of the Lost Sheep and the Lost Coin provide connections to themes in Luke concerning those who are rejected, marginalized, or hated by the prevailing religious and social cultures of Jesus' day. Through Jesus' teachings, these "outsiders" or "others" are said to be recipients of God's love and mercy for sinful persons.

In the parable of the Lost Sheep, the shepherd scoured the countryside to bring back a sheep that was lost. When he returned home, friends and neighbors were called to share in rejoicing. The woman who lost one of her ten coins searched carefully to find it. On finding it, she gathered her friends and neighbors to rejoice together. In both parables, Jesus speaks of "joy in heaven" (v. 7) and "joy in the presence of the angels of God" (v. 10) when the lost is found. In both parables, God takes the initiative to find and restore the lost.

The divine initiative in seeking and saving the lost is inherent in the whole of Luke's Gospel. God sends Jesus Christ into the world to restore the divine/human relationship disrupted by sin (John 3:16; Rom. 5:8; 2 Cor. 5:19, etc.). Luke's Gospel is an especially appropriate book to convey this repeated message, since it tells of the birth of Jesus (Luke 2:1–20) and "the good

1. David L. Tiede, *Luke* (Minneapolis: Augsburg, 1988), 274.
2. See further, David H. Johnson, "Shepherd Sheep," in *Dictionary of Jesus and the Gospels*, ed. Joel B. Green and Scot McKnight (Downers Grove, IL: InterVarsity Press, 1992), 751–54.

news of great joy for all the people." Jesus is the "Savior" (vv. 10, 11) who saves, rescues, and restores humanity to a loving God.

The determination of the shepherd to find the lost sheep and the woman to find the lost coin is the determination of God, who, in Jesus Christ, has come "to seek out and to save the lost" (19:10). This is God's divine initiative. Salvation, reconciliation, forgiveness of sin, and peace with God come through what God has done for humanity in Christ, taking the initiative to do for humans what we cannot do for ourselves. The parables of the Lost Sheep and the Lost Coin present scenes from the lives of ordinary people to convey an extraordinary message.

DONALD K. MCKIM

Commentary 2: Connecting the Reading with the World

"Lost, found, party." This is a popular preaching outline for the parables of the Lost Sheep and Lost Coin. These feel-good stories demonstrate the length and depth of God's searching love. There are other ways of approaching the stories, not initially comfortable and inspiring, that offer insight into the human condition and the nature of divine grace. Each of the following questions offers the preacher a different approach to the familiar stories.

Why Did Jesus Tell These Parables? The Pharisees and scribes were grumbling about the riffraff who were drawn to Jesus. Why did they grumble? Why do people resist God's searching love? Why do they claim to have experienced grace, and yet resent grace offered to others?

The Pharisees and scribes despised the tax collectors and sinners who came to Jesus. Tax collectors worked for the Roman government and were considered traitors who sold themselves to the Romans. The sinners might have committed a serious crime, but the term was also applied to those who had broken ritual purity laws and to women whose husbands divorced them. Tax collectors and sinners were unacceptable because they did not believe and behave properly. The scribes and Pharisees were quick to condemn but slow to recognize the hollowness of their own righteous behavior.

In our contentious, polarized society, there are many groups that evoke similar disdain. People grumble about Republicans, Democrats, Muslims, immigrants, poor people, homeless people, panhandlers, people of other races, liberals, conservatives, advocates of gay marriage, and critics of gay marriage. Almost everyone can find a reason to grumble about somebody. The reason for disapproval is not ritual purity, but identity and beliefs. Who is a real American? Who is a real Christian? Who belongs? Who should be allowed to live in the United States? Who is worthy of health-care benefits? Who gets to decide the answers to these questions?

People with long memories sometimes tell stories of the good old days when members of Congress disagreed over a bill but ate dinner together after the debate ended. In church assemblies, a liberal and a conservative might have disagreed over women's ordination but had a beer together at the end of the day because they had been friends since seminary. Such tolerance and goodwill have largely disappeared. Mean-spirited rhetoric in political and religious debates makes it difficult to recognize the legitimate concerns of the other, much less to trust or compromise with them. In church assemblies, conservatives and progressives form private Facebook groups for strategizing. Denominations fracture after hotly contested debates and decisions. Especially in national politics, Democrats and Republicans find it difficult to cooperate for the good of the whole nation. Disagreement escalates. One side threatens to leave or exclude or filibuster. Little is accomplished for the good of the whole.

Sometimes the grumbling is directed not to political and religious opponents, but to those whose "sin" is being different. They have brown skin, or call God Allah, or speak Spanish. "Different" often seems to mean "inferior" or "dangerous," or both. The grumblers may resent the "lost" when they receive citizenship or welfare benefits or attention that they do not "deserve." The preacher might ask: What is it about human nature that makes us grumble when something good happens to someone else? Do we believe in merit rather than mercy? Do we believe that we have to earn God's grace, so we begrudge others who seem to receive grace as a gift? Can we celebrate God's goodness to others? Do we resent God's energetic seeking of those we prefer to avoid?

Who Is Lost? In other words, who is in and who is out? Who is present at the dining table? The corporate boardroom? Denominational leadership? The elite university? Who is absent? Who is missing from the decision-making, policy-setting tables? Do the people who are present *want* to find those who are missing? This question encourages those with privilege to consider their relationship with those who are marginalized.

Congregations are often composed of people who look and think alike. This may be unintentional if the congregation is located in a homogeneous area or has developed a particular identity or niche. However, sometimes a congregation sends a blatant or subtle message that those who are not white and middle-class are not welcome. This could be an unspoken dress code or worship style or repeated reference to a particular ethnic identity. It is true that churches cannot always be all things to all people, but it is worth asking: Who comes? Who does not? Why?

At times churches are tempted to seek "the lost" for all the wrong reasons. A church seeks out a token family of another race in order to appear multicultural. A church invites people because it counts decisions or conversions. A church seeks young families to do the work and pay the bills. These strategies are not seeking the lost for their sake. How might a congregation demonstrate God's passionate love for all people, even those whom society has marginalized? How does the church demonstrate its commitment to love all those that God loves, not out of self-preservation, but because that is the gospel?

Who Is Seeking the Lost? In these parables, God is imaged as a shepherd and a woman, and both images would have offended Jesus' followers. Shepherds were often considered uncouth, perhaps thieves or vagrants. A shepherd did not seem to be a suitable metaphor to say something true about God.

Comparing God to a woman would have been even more offensive. How could the powerful, all-knowing God be imaged as a weak and powerless woman? Jesus, however, chose to compare God to a diligent woman who shined a light to illuminate the dark room and swept until she found the coin. It might be said of her, "Nevertheless, she persisted." The preacher might ask why there is resistance to seeing God in feminine terms. What insights and meaning might be gained from thinking of God as a woman? How might this challenge or expand traditional images of God?

Are You Lost or Found? Many Christians automatically identify with the ninety-nine sheep or the nine coins. The point of the story then is how we, the found, treat the other who is lost. This approach can potentially encourage paternalism and superiority.

The real point of the story is to recognize that we are all the lost who need to be found. Even if we have been obedient sheep for decades, we were at one point found by God. God still seeks. When shame makes us wander away from others into isolation, God comes looking for us. When we fail or hurt someone or say the wrong thing, God comes looking for us.

Margaret Wise Brown's book *The Runaway Bunny* illustrates this loving, seeking, persistent God.[3] The little bunny is trying to escape his mother. He offers numerous scenarios of escape. He will be a bird and fly away. His mother says she will be the tree that he comes home to. The bunny says he will become a sailboat and sail away. The mother bunny says she will be the wind and blow where she wants him to go.

Barack Obama tells a story about Senator Robert Byrd, who was a member of the Ku Klux Klan in his youth. Byrd acknowledged regret over the foolishness of youth. Obama responded, "We all have regrets, Senator. We just ask that in the end, God's grace shines upon us."[4]

Nevertheless, God persists, shining the light and seeking the lost.

LYNN JAPINGA

3. Margaret Wise Brown, *The Runaway Bunny* (New York: Harper & Row, 1942).
4. Barack Obama, *The Audacity of Hope* (New York: Crown Publishers, 2006), 100.

Proper 20 (Sunday between September 18 and September 24 Inclusive)

Jeremiah 8:18–9:1 and Amos 8:4–7
Psalm 79:1–9 and Psalm 113
1 Timothy 2:1–7
Luke 16:1–13

Jeremiah 8:18–9:1

[18]My joy is gone, grief is upon me,
my heart is sick.
[19]Hark, the cry of my poor people
from far and wide in the land:
"Is the LORD not in Zion?
Is her King not in her?"
("Why have they provoked me to anger with their images,
with their foreign idols?")
[20]"The harvest is past, the summer is ended,
and we are not saved."
[21]For the hurt of my poor people I am hurt,
I mourn, and dismay has taken hold of me.

[22] Is there no balm in Gilead?
Is there no physician there?
Why then has the health of my poor people
not been restored?
[9:1]O that my head were a spring of water,
and my eyes a fountain of tears,
so that I might weep day and night
for the slain of my poor people!

Amos 8:4–7

[4]Hear this, you that trample on the needy,
and bring to ruin the poor of the land,
[5]saying, "When will the new moon be over
so that we may sell grain;
and the sabbath,
so that we may offer wheat for sale?
We will make the ephah small and the shekel great,
and practice deceit with false balances,
[6]buying the poor for silver
and the needy for a pair of sandals,
and selling the sweepings of the wheat."

[7]The LORD has sworn by the pride of Jacob:
Surely I will never forget any of their deeds.

Commentary 1: Connecting the Reading with Scripture

These OT readings offer two distinct trajectories for the preacher. The reading from Jeremiah is a lament filled with angst and passion, while the passage from Amos represents an unflinching oracle of judgment defined by righteous indignation. They represent two different views of God's character that must be held in tension with one another, regardless of the trajectory the preacher takes.

Jeremiah is often referred to as the Weeping Prophet. No text affirms this title more than Jeremiah 8:18–9:1. His lament is without qualification. Such grief is not to be explained, but experienced and expressed. While lament is seldom the focus of Christian worship, it is powerfully present in Hebrew Scriptures. In addition to the unqualified cries of this text, parallels are found within the psalms of lament. Of the hundred fifty psalms, fifty are laments. The typical structure of these psalms is lament, followed by remembrance of God's saving power in the past, concluding with a statement of faith to endure the current situation that evoked the lament. Psalm 88 stands apart among the laments as it contains no remembrance of God's saving power in the past, or any affirmation of faith in the end. It is pure lament, ending in despair. So it is with this lament from Jeremiah.

In Jeremiah, it is difficult to discern whether the lament is uttered by God or by Jeremiah. Both voices seem present in this passage. In the end, it is not necessary to distinguish them, as the ambiguity reveals an important theological point. That the prophet's sadness is so intertwined with God's speaks to the character of the Divine. The suffering of God's people profoundly saddens God. As the mouthpiece for God, the prophet reflects this sadness. God's sadness is the prophet's sadness. Neither God nor the prophet relishes judgment or its consequences.

The text begins with a threefold assertion: joy is gone, grief has descended, hearts are broken. The spectrum of English translations of 8:18 reflects the difficulty of translating this grief. In Hebrew it is only six words. The NIV offers an honest comment on the first word, *mableegeeth*: "The meaning of the Hebrew for this word is uncertain." That the first-person-singular pronoun is attached to each lamentation intensifies the pathos. Again, it is difficult to discern whether these are God's words or Jeremiah's. In the end they are intertwined, which is a homiletic possibility in and of itself. If this is the voice of God, then it is a profound contradiction to the idea of a passionless or impassible God. As this passage opens, God's joy is gone; God's very heart is broken.

After declaring the depth of the despair, the lament continues. The cries of the people have been heard by God, paralleling the cries in Egypt heard by YHWH, related in Exodus 3:7–10, which began Israel's relationship with God. God heard the cries of the slaves and responded by delivering them from bondage. In Jeremiah, the cries are offered in the wake of judgment, and no response is given. Deliverance is denied. That does not mean the pain of the people is not acknowledged. God feels their pain in a profound way and hears their longing for the divine presence in Zion (Jer. 8:20–21).

In verse 21, the voice of the passage seems to change to that of the prophet. If verses 18–19 are God's lament, verses 21–22 could be understood as Jeremiah's lament. It follows the same structure as the initial cry, beginning with a declaration of despair that is subsequently enhanced by three questions, and concludes with a pronouncement of sadness in 9:1. As with the opening lament, the prophet's questions go unanswered.

While the temptation is to resolve the lament in some way, the text does not do this. Despite the words of the familiar hymn asserting, "There is a balm in Gilead," the text leaves this question unanswered. In fact, the third question implies that there must *not* be a balm in Gilead, as the people are not healed. Despite the temptation to resolve this lament, to go to the good news that "there is a balm in Gilead to heal the sin-sick soul," that is not where the passage goes. Instead, the prophet acknowledges the pain of a present circumstance affirming the often-unresolved questions born from pain. He stands with the people in that pain, waiting for a future as yet undisclosed. Such solidarity with those who suffer offers a profound witness and potential for faithful proclamation.

The Things That Have Power to Save

The man who is truly and nobly rich, then, is he who is rich in virtues and able to use every fortune in a holy and faithful manner; but the spurious rich man is he who is rich according to the flesh, and has changed his life into outward possessions which are passing away and perishing, belonging now to one, now to another, and in the end to no one at all. Again, in the same way there is a genuine poor man and also a spurious and falsely-named poor man, the one poor in spirit, the inner personal poverty, and the other poor in worldly goods, the outward alien poverty. Now to him who is not poor in worldly goods and is rich in passions, the man who is poor in spirit and is rich towards God says, "Detach yourself from the alien possessions that dwell in your soul, in order that you may become pure in heart and may see God, which in other words means to enter into the kingdom of heaven. And how are you to detach yourself from them? By selling them. What then? Are you to take riches for possessions, to make an exchange of one wealth for another by turning real estate into money? Not at all. But in place of that which formerly dwelt in the soul you long to save, bring in another kind of wealth that makes you divine and provides eternal life, namely, resolves that are fixed in accord with God's commandment; and in return for these you shall have abundant reward and honor, perpetual salvation and eternal incorruption. In this way you make a good sale of what you have, of the many things that are superfluous and that shut heaven against you, while you receive in exchange for them the things that have power to save. As for the first, let the fleshly poor who need them have them; but you, having received in their stead the spiritual wealth, will now have treasure in heaven."

Clement of Alexandria, "The Rich Man's Salvation," 19, in *Clement of Alexandria*, trans. G. W. Butterworth, Loeb Classical Library 92 (Cambridge, MA: Harvard University Press, 1919), 309, 311.

To be sure, this text is born of a unique situation, God's judgment on a sinful people. Therefore, there is danger in comparing Jeremiah's grief to those suffering pain in the present. This is not the pain of a parent who has lost a child, or a spouse who is widowed too early, or a community devastated by disaster, or a nation suffering at the hands of tragedy. One would not want people suffering losses like these to link their pain to God's judgment on their lives for some undisclosed sin. Yet pain is pain, whether a consequence of circumstance or sin. There is power in the raw expression of grief expressed in this passage, and that grief is something all who suffer share in common. The questions posed in the text express the pain of many who suffer, regardless of the cause. Where is God in all this? Is there no balm in Gilead? Is there no physician there? Unresolved pain is a reality of life; this passage reflects this reality.

Amos offers a very different preaching trajectory. This is the powerful prophet of Tekoa at his best. Amos speaks for the God whose unrelenting eye sees all, even the dishonest practices of the world of commerce. This oracle of judgment is pronounced against all who "trample on the needy, and bring to ruin the poor." This passage represents the fourth indictment of Israel in Amos for oppressing the poor (see 2:6–7; 4:1; 5:11–12). It is a theme not only for Amos; it is found throughout the indictments of many prophets, including Micah (2:8–9; 3:1–4), Zechariah (7:9–10), Isaiah (1:12–17; 10:1–2; 25:4–12; 58:6–11; 61:1–4), Jeremiah (22:13–17), and Ezekiel (16:49; 18:7, 16; 22:27). At the heart of their injustice lies a greed that is incapable of enjoying seasons of rest like the new moon and the Sabbath, but instead longs to get back to the pursuit of unrighteous gain. Given God's judgment on the consumerism of Amos's day, it is impossible to imagine the scope of judgment in our day.

A parallel narrative to illustrate God's omniscient vision can be found in 1 Kings 21, the story of Naboth's vineyard. Naboth, the victim of Jezebel and Ahab's lust for land, is framed on false charges and executed. In the wake of it all, Elijah confronts Ahab, convicts him of his crime, and sentences his descendants. God saw it all, and God did not abide such injustice. For congregations that typically focus on the grace of God, this text illumines an important aspect of God's character, justice. To those who are guilty of injustice in this world, this text offers a word of warning. To those who are wronged, it offers an assurance of an ultimate judgment.

Lest the preacher find too much pleasure in proclaiming the prophet's warning in the contemporary context, one must not forget that these prophets' oracles are born of God's pain, which is a product of God's love.

JOSEPH J. CLIFFORD

Commentary 2: Connecting the Reading with the World

How painful it must be for the one whose joy is gone, whose heart is broken, to hear the cries of the people. It is a seemingly endless circle of pain and grief, the people bound together by suffering. Endless debate attempts to determine whether this text is God's or Jeremiah's lament. Maybe we do well not to concern ourselves with who voices the lament. Maybe it is good and right when the voice of God and the voice of the people become one.

The text opens with a painful description of the author's state, then invites the recipient to hear the cries of the people, the people far and wide (Jer. 8:19). What does this listening look like in a global, technology-savvy world? Through technology and commerce we are more connected to people across the globe than ever before. We are able to hear the cries in new and effective ways. On social-media platforms such as Facebook we change our profile pictures or respond to posts in order to grieve globally over terrorism. We learn about and cry over the experiences of Syrian refugees fleeing bombs and watching loved ones die. Open your social media after a local or global tragedy, and you will hear the cries of the people.

The same tools that connect us also distance us. We scroll over videos, articles, and memes, all vying for our attention. Changing our profile picture or "sharing" an article only poses for authentic connectivity. Seeing unending lamentation from around the globe may nurture some empathy, but it does not always birth action. Social media give us a false sense of participation when it comes to the outcry of others. We do not truly lament with our brothers and sisters in Christ, at least not in the way we are called to lament.

We should lament. Things are not the way they are supposed to be, yet we have what we need for healing and wholeness. There *is* a balm in Gilead. There *is* a physician. Still, suffering exists. How do our ecclesial communities proclaim healing and wholeness in the midst of suffering? How do we, as individuals, make connections between the struggles of our daily lives and the proclamation we hear on Sunday mornings? We struggle to lament, to emulate the great prophets of our faith, because of cultural and social pressure to be strong. This text invites the reader to consider the fullness of life in Christ, the connection between joy and grief, healing and suffering.

If we can use the text to learn to lament, we then must learn to sustain the lament, to live through seasons of grief. When someone is sick or loved ones die, there is an initial outpouring of support, tears, and empathy. Casseroles are made. Cards are sent. The sense of urgency is not lost on us. As the weeks go by, the grief and pain continue, but the community of the faithful fails to be present. We slip into routines. We forget the pain of others. Our attention is diverted to the next tragedy, the next need. We allow our lament to become listless, and those in pain and in grief are left to suffer alone.

When human rights are violated, the people of God become outraged; they hit the streets in protest. There is a call for action. Speeches are written and proclaimed in the public square. Money is raised. Hearts are moved. As weeks go by, the injustice persists but the outrage fades, and the people of God return to their routine lives. Without action, without lament, the injustices of the world begin to feel normal, part of the status quo. Those suffering injustice are silenced.

Perhaps the voice of lament in today's text teaches us to narrow our focus so that we might learn to sustain our efforts, to weep night and day for the slain people (Jer. 9:1) until that time when God wipes away all tears. Perhaps our best focus is on the people God has called *us* to serve, the community with which we have the ability to act effectively, trusting that God will call prophets for all people in all places. It is then that lament and the action it spurs hold the potential to bring about the kingdom.

No one likes to be the bearer of bad news, but that is God's call to Amos in today's reading (Amos 8:4–7). One of the rhetorical tools used by the prophet Amos is the coupling of a vision with a report. The lectionary utilizes only the report. Some reports, like a report card, are personal. Clearly, the recipient of the report card is the one being evaluated or judged. Other reports are grander in scale, addressing a large group or corporation, a social entity.

In an initial reading, we are not likely to hear or identify ourselves as the subject of this text from Amos. We likely do not self-identify with the one who tramples the needy or brings ruin to the poor (v. 4). However, if we want to hear the word of God in this passage, we must stop looking for the other to blame and look inward to seek and mend the fault in ourselves. Amos may be critiquing individual behavior, but he is also concerned with the systems people have created, systems that would oppress or harm the poor and the needy. God hopes and calls for a world in which systems will be just and fair, helping all people to prosper. Amos's report card calls both individuals and systems to account.

Regardless of good intention, our systems fall short of this ideological goal. We divide people according to difference—race, religion, class, sexual orientation. We intentionally and unintentionally arrange ourselves on a hierarchical plane. When inequality exists on a personal plane, it can be easy to identify, but we struggle to identify inequality when it is systematic or structural. The inequality in *systems* and *structures* is addressed in today's text. The "you" is all of us who participate in systems and structures of inequality; *we* are the "you" God addresses.

What kind of systems does God ordain? We are called to discern what is just in the eye of God and work toward participation in those systems and structures, systems like the year of jubilee. In contrast to these biblical systems that intend to bring prosperity to all, we have created social and economic systems in which a minority of people on the globe consume a majority of the world's resources. If we are on the side of God, we have to be on the side of the poor and the needy. How can we stand with the poor and the needy when we are so dependent on the economic and social systems that keep the poor and needy in their place at the bottom of a hierarchy?

We stand with the poor and needy when we work toward dismantling systems of oppression. This is a complex and difficult task but one to which we are called by God. At the end of the book of Amos, we find hope for the people of Israel, a vision of redemption. God's destruction will not be complete, and Israel will be rebuilt from the ruins. What does a vision of hope and restoration look like for our current context? How might our nations be a place of justice and equality? We will find our hope and our redemption only when both individuals and systems reflect justice for all people.

ALLIE UTLEY

Proper 20 (Sunday between September 18 and September 24 Inclusive)

Psalm 79:1–9

[1]O God, the nations have come into your inheritance;
they have defiled your holy temple;
they have laid Jerusalem in ruins.
[2]They have given the bodies of your servants
to the birds of the air for food,
the flesh of your faithful to the wild animals of the earth.
[3]They have poured out their blood like water
all around Jerusalem,
and there was no one to bury them.
[4]We have become a taunt to our neighbors,
mocked and derided by those around us.

[5]How long, O LORD? Will you be angry forever?
Will your jealous wrath burn like fire?
[6]Pour out your anger on the nations
that do not know you,
and on the kingdoms
that do not call on your name.
[7]For they have devoured Jacob
and laid waste his habitation.

[8]Do not remember against us the iniquities of our ancestors;
let your compassion come speedily to meet us,
for we are brought very low.
[9]Help us, O God of our salvation,
for the glory of your name;
deliver us, and forgive our sins,
for your name's sake.

Psalm 113

[1]Praise the LORD!
Praise, O servants of the LORD;
praise the name of the LORD.

[2]Blessed be the name of the LORD
from this time on and forevermore.
[3]From the rising of the sun to its setting
the name of the LORD is to be praised.
[4]The LORD is high above all nations,
and his glory above the heavens.

[5]Who is like the LORD our God,
who is seated on high,
[6]who looks far down
on the heavens and the earth?
[7]He raises the poor from the dust,
and lifts the needy from the ash heap,
[8]to make them sit with princes,
with the princes of his people.
[9]He gives the barren woman a home,
making her the joyous mother of children.
Praise the LORD!

Connecting the Psalm to Scripture and Worship

Psalm 79:1–9. This psalm is read in synagogues on the fast day Ninth of Ab to mourn and commemorate the destruction of the temple, first by the Babylonians and then by the Romans. It is a communal prayer for divine deliverance accompanied by requests that God punish Israel's enemies (vv. 6, 10) and those who taunted the community as it stumbled through ashes and shame (v. 12). While it is possible that the context for these desperate appeals is Hasmonean (second century BCE), the explicit reference to the ruin of Jerusalem favors the Babylonian devastation of 587 BCE as the presenting historical circumstance.

Verses 1–4 liturgically associate the suffering community intimately with its God. These verses feature the possessive pronoun "your" suffixed to the nouns "inheritance," "temple," "servants," and "faithful (ones)" in the context of a cry before and complaint to and against YHWH. What the community has endured is not only a national and personal catastrophe. It is also a personal affront to YHWH. The setting is worship. The logic is covenantal: the community belongs to YHWH. What happens to it implicates YHWH, particularly YHWH's standing in the world. (V. 12 boldly blurs any distance between the community and YHWH's fate; mocking the community is tantamount to mocking YHWH personally.)

The atrocities visited on YHWH's community are morally and ritually obscene. They include not only mass murder, but covenant-violating defilement of the temple (v. 1b, hence the liturgical setting Ninth of Ab), the slain, (v. 2) and Jerusalem itself, within whose sanctified precincts the blood of the dead has been splashed "like water" (v. 3). The reference to blood may allude ironically and bitterly to its proper disposal during temple sacrificial rites (Deut. 12:27) and in food preparation (Deut. 12:15–16). Covenant practices by which YHWH upholds the order of the created world on its sacred foundations, and the place of YHWH's community in that order, have been turned on their head, and chaos has spilled out.

The list of crimes declared to God begins with "the nations," who are where they are not supposed to be. YHWH's affection may be focused on the covenant people, the "apple" of YHWH's eye (Deut. 32:10), but YHWH's governance extends to all nations (Deut. 32:8). In verse 4 the recitation shifts from third and second persons to the direct, first-person (plural) address "we." This turn connotes exasperation, revealing suddenly and perhaps desperately the full pathos of the situation. The worshipers who now cry out are in fact, liturgically speaking, the same people who were violated and who can no longer cry out. In this worship, murdered voices ask to be heard.

Verse 5 constitutes a turning point in the prayer, in the form of a searing question: How long? This question constitutes the primary emotional location of the psalm, one that rings often throughout the Psalter (6:3; 13:1, 2; 35:17; 62:3; 74:10; 79:5; 80:4; 82:2; 89:46; 94:3; 119:84). How long will this desecrating state of affairs continue? The question is punctuated with a cry of devotion, "O LORD." It is nevertheless also a complaint-accusation hardly capable of greater feeling, because YHWH, who alone is God, has the divine prerogative of answering, "[F]orever" (v. 5a). The theological import of the possessive pronouns "your" in verses 1–3 is now fully revealed. It is YHWH, and no other, who has in divine rage (v. 5) ordained the atrocities of the noncovenantal nation(s). Their manifestly cruel ignorance of YHWH, which ignorance is the common root of their violence, is grotesque.[1] Yet these nations are but the instruments of the "jealous wrath" of YHWH, a description that may technically allude to idolatrous relations between YHWH's community and other gods (Deut. 32:16). The blood of the community now poured out (Ps. 79:3, 10) is recalled as a figure of judgment in a raft of petitions requesting that YHWH deliver *and* avenge YHWH's people (vv. 6, 9, 10). As for taunting neighbors (v. 4), their recompense is requested last and without mercy. Hopefully their punishment will be "sevenfold," that is, as complete and utter as *divinely* possible (v. 12).

What is at stake in this prayer is nothing less than YHWH's "name" (v. 9), a cipher for the effective presence of YHWH's saving power among the people of YHWH. Reference here to "your name" also appeals to the divine reputation. YHWH's character, YHWH's honor, can be questioned if chaos for YHWH's people should turn out to know no end. At the same time, reference to the "name" further maintains liturgically YHWH's transcendence, while simultaneously beckoning YHWH to be redemptively immanent.

YHWH's sovereign decision to use "the nations" as the agents of divine wrath is inexplicable. The appeal to YHWH cannot now be simply to save the community. YHWH's salvation must recreate the community, restoring it to its ordained vocation of praise beyond every loss and beyond even divine judgment itself: "Then we your people . . . will give thanks forever" (v. 13). *The community has in prayer turned to YHWH in the midst of flames, even though YHWH is in fact the fire.*

Psalm 113. Sung before and after Pesach, Psalm 113 introduces a larger unit (Pss. 113–18) known as part of the Hallel of Egypt. It is immediately followed in Psalm 114 by praise to YHWH for YHWH's mighty deliverance from Egypt through "wonders" (Exod. 3:20): the natural world did unnatural things at YHWH's bidding for YHWH's purposes (Ps. 114:3–8). Psalm 113 is hymnic in structure, beginning with an extended threefold introduction calling for the praise of YHWH by the "servants of YHWH," that is, those who by their participation in the liturgy are counted among the faithful descendants of the people delivered from Egypt. This includes the worship leaders and almost certainly all assembled before them (v. 1). The call now is to YHWH's servants, but it will be extended in Psalm 117 to include the postexilic lesson (cf. Gen. 12:1–3) that the call is finally to all nations and peoples. Neither all time nor all space (Ps. 113:2–3) can contain this praise. YHWH, at a divine distance, is "seated," suggesting royal power and ease (v. 5b). This transcendence and power are no impediment to divine attention and concern (v. 6).

Verses 7–9 provide in poetic parallel form quintessential examples of YHWH's attentive care and reflect mandates to the people of God from both Torah and the prophets. The parallelism of verse 7 may be understood as additive. "Poor" corresponds to "needy" and "dust" to "ash heap" (literally "dung heap"). Neither the oppressed nor the despicable are beyond YHWH's care. Likewise, in a social hierarchy in which the status of women was deeply rooted in childbearing, YHWH, who remains "seated," will "cause to be seated" (*Hofal*) the childless woman. The intertextual allusion brings to mind Sarah, Rachel, and Hannah, among others.[2] The attribute of YHWH that inspires endless praise, and endless wonder, is divine reversal of estate. YHWH elevates the lowly. It is they who "sit" with YHWH. The faithful answer to the rhetorical "*Who is like YHWH our God?*" (v. 5a) is, as the inclusio framing this psalm indicates (vv. 1, 9), praise.

E. CARSON BRISSON

1. Marvin E. Tate, *Psalms 51–100*, Word Biblical Commentary 20 (Dallas: Word, 1990), 300.
2. James Luther Mays, *Psalms*, Interpretation (Louisvillle, KY: Westminster John Knox, 2011), 362.

Proper 20 (Sunday between September 18 and September 24 Inclusive)

1 Timothy 2:1–7

[1]First of all, then, I urge that supplications, prayers, intercessions, and thanksgivings be made for everyone, [2]for kings and all who are in high positions, so that we may lead a quiet and peaceable life in all godliness and dignity. [3]This is right and is acceptable in the sight of God our Savior, [4]who desires everyone to be saved and to come to the knowledge of the truth. [5]For

there is one God;
there is also one mediator between God and humankind,
Christ Jesus, himself human,
[6]who gave himself a ransom for all

—this was attested at the right time. [7]For this I was appointed a herald and an apostle (I am telling the truth, I am not lying), a teacher of the Gentiles in faith and truth.

Commentary 1: Connecting the Reading with Scripture

Paul's initial instruction to Timothy seeks to bring clarity to the theological motive and public manner of Christian worship. In this regard, prayer is introduced as the quintessential worship practice, and the community's prayers are for everyone (1 Tim. 2:1–2), because God's desire is to save everyone (vv. 3–7).

Two different and often competing human families are mentioned, the one comprising a political household led by "rulers and all those in positions of authority" (v. 2 [my trans.]; cf. Titus 3:1–2), and the other a sacred household led by God. Paul's instructions give partial recognition of the tension often provoked by competing loyalties between these rival households in which believers hold joint membership. In this case, the stability embodied by a congregation's political relationships serves the *missio Dei* rather than the empire: if God wants to save everyone from death (2:4) for eternal life (1:16), and Christ Jesus enters the world to realize God's redemptive plan (so 1:15; cf. 2:5–6), then the congregation's worship practices should purpose what God does.

Paul's instruction regarding prayer is noteworthy, not only because he grants it priority (2:1) but because of its sheer length; it is the longest discussion of prayer in the NT. The "therefore" that begins these instructions (2:1) may well assume that Timothy has in mind the vivid contrast made between the false teachers (1:3–11, 19–20) and the apostle, whose own conversion from falsehood is mimetic of prophetic ministry (1:12–17; cf. 2:7). There may be other divisions within the congregation as well, whether precipitated by the presence of false teachers or its cultural surroundings. The plain sense of this passage indicates no such threat, and Paul's emphasis on the practice of congregational prayer is a means of grace for peacekeeping within the neighborhood (2:2).

I would not make too fine a distinction between the four general terms used to describe the congregation's prayers—"petitions, prayers, intercessions, and thanksgivings" (2:1). What seems more important is the catholic scope of the church's concern, reflected by the phrase, "rulers and all those in positions of authority." This entire letter is bracketed by the claim for God's sovereign rule (1:17; 6:15), which doubtless challenges the implicit political tenet of any empire: the sovereignty of its rule. Surprisingly, friction between church and state is found everywhere in the NT (e.g., Acts 22–28; 1 Pet. 3:13–17; Rev. 13). Scripture's sentiment to support those who lead the secular household was widely shared in antiquity. Paul's Judaism practiced praying for one's pagan rulers, following the example of Daniel, who used prayer to ensure peaceful relations with hostile pagan powers.

In any case, Paul does not view worship as a political practice, as though the church's mission is complicit in a program of social domestication. His motive is clearly theological. Prayers for rulers, whether emperor or president, are offered to God in prospect of their conversion to the truth and salvation from their sins. Moreover, the expressed purpose to "lead a quiet and peaceable life in all godliness and dignity" (2:2b) should be read by the following formula of the *missio Dei*, which suggests that prayers target the sanctification of the public square. Civil religion, no; missional church, yes.

This lesson turns on one of the most important theological summaries found in Paul's canonical letters. Its gravitas is his explanation of the final catchphrase of verse 4, which understands conversion as a coming to "the knowledge of the truth." The implied question this formula occasions is: Which narrative of the truth saves people from self-destructive sin and death? Which narrative dispels ignorance (cf. 1:13) and puts us on a track to God? Paul sets out the theological agreements of a grammar that orders his teaching of "faith and truth" to the nations (2:7)

1. "There is one God" (2:5a). This affirmation of the OT Shema (Deut. 6:4) held special importance in Paul's Diaspora Judaism, where Israel's God had competition from rival deities, both local and national. Paul's lack of interest in naming the empire's kings or its rival deities implies they offer no realistic alternative to God's way of salvation through Christ Jesus. There is one God, whose single desire is to save everyone and everything.

2. "There is also one mediator between God and humankind" (2:5b). Paul's insistence that there is but one mediator, Christ Jesus, could have communicated a political message that rejected the king's role as the sole medium of the gods. One God, one Messiah, Christ Jesus, who together proffer a single salvation for everyone to receive. This exclusive conception of "the truth," even though offered to everyone, remains exceedingly challenging to offer today's postmodern world in which such claims are typically relativized according to personal preference.

3. "Christ Jesus, himself human" (2:5c). This reference to Jesus' humanity seems awkward at first. Some suggest that it goes best with the next phrase that speaks of Jesus' death, since Paul's Adam-Christology requires a connection to the Lord's humanity and his self-sacrificial death (cf. Phil. 2:6–8). I doubt any of this is in play here, where Paul extends his reference to Jesus' humanity as a messianic broker of God's promised blessing for all the families of earth (cf. Gen. 12:1–3). If an expansion of the prior claim that God desires every person to come to a knowledge of truth, then Christ's humanity includes an epistemological role: God's self-revelation in one of us makes crystal clear God's desire to save every one of us.

4. "[Christ Jesus] who gave himself a ransom for all" (2:6). In Paul's social world, payment of a ransom freed slaves from indenture. Mention of it alludes to the most important biblical typology of God's way of salvation: God's liberation of an enslaved Israel from their captivity to a pagan power to live in *their* land and freely worship *their* God. The reader may well have expected a more traditional Pauline dogmatics: "who gave himself a ransom *for sin*" (cf. Titus 2:14). Instead, Paul repeats "for all" ("everyone," 2:1, 4) because here he presses for the global scope of God's salvation as the principal theological motive why the congregation should pray even for their pagan rulers.

Paul's mention of the Lord's payment of a ransom would have had special currency in Ephesus with its huge slave population, where it would evoke images of a ransom price paid to set a slave free. Further, the prefix of the distinctive word Paul uses for ransom (*antilytron*) implies a substitution is made; Jesus exchanged his life as one human on behalf of every other human. The idea of a person sacrificing his or her life for another often defines covenant loyalty in Scripture (see 4 Macc. 6:29; 17:21–22; 2 Macc. 7:37–38; cf. Deut. 32:36; Mark 10:45).

5. Paul was "appointed a herald and an apostle . . . a teacher of the Gentiles in faith

and truth" (2:7). Paul's teaching authority is a central feature of his canonical profile, whose memory and message endures through his NT letters and biography in Acts. Nowhere else is found this stunning claim that Paul's apostolic appointment is to teach faith and truth to Gentiles (i.e., "the nations"). The prior reading of Paul's story in Acts would incline the reader to understand "nations" in its most inclusive sense. The Paul of Acts, a consecrated teacher of Israel and missionary to Gentiles, aims his mission in the same direction as the community's prayers: at bringing knowledge of the truth about God's salvation "before Gentiles and kings" (Acts 9:15). So here Paul is herald of the good news about Christ so that everyone may "come to the knowledge of the truth" and be saved.

ROBERT W. WALL

Commentary 2: Connecting the Reading with the World

Paul's words to Timothy read like rubrics for worship, a set of instructions that order and balance the devotional life of individuals and the corporate worship of the community. It begins with guidelines for prayer (2:1), a directive to pray for political leaders (vv. 2–4), a creedal statement about the oneness of God (vv. 5–6), and a testimonial to Paul's calling (v. 7). Any one of these streams provides rich content for the preacher to explore.

First, he calls for "supplications, prayers, intercessions, and thanksgivings to be made for everyone." He reminds Timothy that prayer is the foundation for one's commitment to Christ, and such prayer must be directed toward the needs of others rather than solely for one's own. The human tendency is to pray egotistically, praising God on the basis of what God has done for us, neglecting to be thankful, and offering petitions only for our own needs. The kind of prayer that Paul describes, however, is "for everyone." It is a prayer that pushes our perspectives beyond ourselves to include others, even those with whom we are in conflict.

This kind of prayer sets the tone for the remainder of this passage. The rest of the text explores different ways that the worship of God and the affirmation of God's nature ought to transcend the kinds of divisions we experience in our individual relationships and society at large. His words echo the call of Jesus in the Beatitudes to pray for one's enemies and to bless those who curse one. There ought to be no room for bias or discrimination in the way a person prays. It surpasses all boundaries that would otherwise divide us.

It is then reasonable for Paul to follow with a command to pray for people in power, for "kings and all who are in high positions." This might immediately strike the preacher as a minefield to traverse delicately in a time when many people are quite reluctant to mix faith with politics, and where divisive partisanship often governs our interactions with others. In the words of Linus Van Pelt to his friend Charlie Brown, "There are three things I have learned never to discuss with people: religion, politics, and the Great Pumpkin."

Paul's command may therefore be difficult for people who wonder whether Christians ought to have a voice in matters of politics and public policy. There are some who believe that the separation of church and state means that preachers should not talk about politics, and that faith and politics should have nothing to do with each other. There are those who believe that Jesus' teaching dwelt entirely in the realm of the spiritual, the individual, and the interpersonal—not the political.

How then might we interpret Paul's command to pray for kings and all who are in high positions? We might remember that praying for our leaders need not be either an endorsement or an indictment of them. It can be an appeal to God that their actions fall in line with God's purposes for the world.

Such prayer can therefore still be prophetic, in a way that is consistent with many of the Bible's strongest and clearest stories of the relationship between faith and religion. Nathan confronted King David. Elijah took on Ahab and Jezebel. Jesus questioned Pilate about truth. In the words of Martin Luther King Jr., the church is neither the master nor the servant of the state, but the conscience of the state.[1]

This text can then serve as an energizing reminder of the necessity of the church, particularly in politically polarizing and difficult times. It is good to be the church, for we can lead the way in creating a "quiet and peaceable life in all godliness and dignity."

Having called Christians first to pray for everyone, and then to pray for secular leaders with whom one might have political and partisan differences, Paul shifts the tone of his message to a kind of creedal formulation about the oneness of God and the oneness of Christ's work as mediator. He reminds us that God transcends all boundaries that may divide us from each other.

Edwin Markham's poem "Outwitted" describes our human tendency to draw circles that encamp those that think and act like us, and shun those who are different from us:

> He drew a circle that shut me out –
> Heretic, rebel, a thing to flout . . .

But Markham's poem then shifts to a hopeful word about the expansiveness of love, echoing Paul's urge to draw that circle wider, by the grace of God:

> But Love and I had the wit to win:
> We drew a circle that took him in.[2]

Because of the vastness of God's reign and the pervasiveness of God's love, we can transcend our divisions. There is one God, Paul says with conviction, and Jesus is the sole mediator for all humanity and the ransom for all. Frederick William Faber's hymn "There's a Wideness in God's Mercy" underscores the importance of this truth about the nature of God and God's love:

> For the Love of God is broader / Than the measure of our mind;
> And the heart of the Eternal / Is most wonderfully kind.
> If our love were but more simple / We should rest upon God's word;
> And our lives would be illumined / By the presence of our Lord.[3]

Ultimately, Paul identifies these theological claims as the basis for his own call to ministry. Because there is one God, and because of the redeeming work of Jesus, Paul not only can be appointed as a "herald and an apostle"; he can also fulfill that role unapologetically. The parenthetical "I am telling the truth, I am not lying" may be as much a reminder to himself amid his personal turmoil as it is a personal encouragement to young Timothy. This verse may be a helpful reminder for us to reclaim a sense of calling to ministry for clergy and laypeople alike, and to reaffirm our unswerving commitment to the gospel.

There would be a clear connection to the sacraments, should either baptism or Communion be observed on this Sunday. In baptism, the congregation renews its commitment to faithfully participate in the life of the church and advance the mission of God. In Communion, the congregation unites and commits to ministry to all; to be the body of Christ offered to the world. In both liturgical acts, we recognize that the extraordinary grace of God can be made real through the ordinariness of our lives if we will submit ourselves in obedience and surrender to Christ. We can all therefore be "heralds and apostles."

The final phrase is a fitting conclusion to this passage: "a teacher of the Gentiles in faith and truth." What does it mean for *faith* and *truth* to be held together? Truth is a conviction that is based on evidence, on proof that has been verified with experience. Faith is a conviction that is based on one's belief in the trustworthiness of God, regardless of the evidence. Truth can be gauged with our senses, and faith covers the gap beyond the empirical. Together, they ground the Christian in faithful discipleship, guide our obedience to the God who is sovereign above all, and unite us despite our divisions. Paul is a teacher of this gospel, and his lesson to us can be a liberating one.

MAGREY R. DEVEGA

1. Martin Luther King Jr., "A Knock at Midnight," Stanford University, June 5, 1963, https://kinginstitute.stanford.edu/king-papers/documents/knock-midnight.
2. Edwin Markham, *The Shoes of Happiness and Other Poems* (Garden City, NY: Doubleday, Page & Co., 1915), 1.
3. *United Methodist Hymnal* published in *Hymnody.org*, https://hymnary.org/hymn/UMH/121.

Proper 20 (Sunday between September 18 and September 24 Inclusive)

Luke 16:1–13

[1]Then Jesus said to the disciples, "There was a rich man who had a manager, and charges were brought to him that this man was squandering his property. [2]So he summoned him and said to him, 'What is this that I hear about you? Give me an accounting of your management, because you cannot be my manager any longer.' [3]Then the manager said to himself, 'What will I do, now that my master is taking the position away from me? I am not strong enough to dig, and I am ashamed to beg. [4]I have decided what to do so that, when I am dismissed as manager, people may welcome me into their homes.' [5]So, summoning his master's debtors one by one, he asked the first, 'How much do you owe my master?' [6]He answered, 'A hundred jugs of olive oil.' He said to him, 'Take your bill, sit down quickly, and make it fifty.' [7]Then he asked another, 'And how much do you owe?' He replied, 'A hundred containers of wheat.' He said to him, 'Take your bill and make it eighty.' [8]And his master commended the dishonest manager because he had acted shrewdly; for the children of this age are more shrewd in dealing with their own generation than are the children of light. [9]And I tell you, make friends for yourselves by means of dishonest wealth so that when it is gone, they may welcome you into the eternal homes.

[10]"Whoever is faithful in a very little is faithful also in much; and whoever is dishonest in a very little is dishonest also in much. [11]If then you have not been faithful with the dishonest wealth, who will entrust to you the true riches? [12]And if you have not been faithful with what belongs to another, who will give you what is your own? [13]No slave can serve two masters; for a slave will either hate the one and love the other, or be devoted to the one and despise the other. You cannot serve God and wealth."

Commentary 1: Connecting the Reading to Scripture

The parable of the Dishonest Manager is one of the most baffling of Jesus' parables, leading to varieties of interpretation that have to be carefully constructed. Exegetical questions relate to the scope of the parable, with most interpreters seeing it as Luke 16:1–8, with further wisdom about wealth and possessions added in verses 9–13. The parable itself presents a steward or manager who has been dishonest by squandering his master's money. Faced with the dire consequences for his actions, the manager devised a plan and had a portion of his master's debt recovered from his debtors. Then "the master commended the dishonest manager because he had acted shrewdly" (v. 8). Jesus used the parable to comment on the use of material possessions and urge followers to act faithfully and give primary allegiance to serving God rather than riches. Said Jesus: "You cannot serve God and wealth" (v. 13).

This parable follows those of the previous chapter, Luke 15, where a dominant note was joy in the lost being found. Now the focus is on the proper use of material possessions. There is a connection here with the parable of the Prodigal Son, where the younger son took his goods, went to a distant country, and "squandered his property in dissolute living" (15:13).

Immediately following the Dishonest Manager parable, Jesus reproved the Pharisees, gave two sayings about the Law (16:14–17), and made a statement about divorce (16:18). Then comes the parable of the Rich Man and Lazarus (16:19–31). Here is portrayed a reversal of fortunes in the afterlife, when the rich man who died suffers agony in Hades (16:23–24) and the beggar Lazarus, who lay sore and hungry at the rich man's gate in the present life, died and was carried away "to be with Abraham" (16:20–21, 22). Here too the ways that wealth and material possessions are used in this life are significant.

The current parable proceeds in several steps:

1. Rich man has a manager. (v. 1)
2. Problem: Manager is accused of mismanagement, must account for his accounting. (v. 2)
3. Manager considers options. (v. 3)
4. Manager establishes a strategy. (vv. 4–7)
5. Rich man evaluates manager's strategy. (v. 8a)

There is a similar structure in the parable of the Rich Fool (12:16–20), but the outcomes of the parables are direct opposites.

In the parable of the Dishonest—or Cunning—Manager, the manager summoned the boss's debtors and had each reduce the amount they owed. Some have suggested this entailed his excluding interest, in accordance with Deuteronomy 23:19–20, or that the manager may have reduced the amounts to cover what his own profit would have been, thus forfeiting his commission. The boss commended the manager because he "acted shrewdly" (Luke 16:8). This was commendation in the face of the potential loss of revenue entailed by the reduction of the amounts owed by the debtors.

Jesus' comments—to his disciples (v. 1)—contrast the shrewdness of a child of "this age" (the manager), who was concerned with finding a place to land after potential dismissal (being welcomed into homes—v. 4), with those who are focused on the age to come, marked by "eternal homes" (v. 9). Jesus said, "The children of this age are more shrewd in dealing with their own generation than are the children of light" (v. 8b). In effect, Jesus was saying, What if disciples who seek God's reign would exhibit the kind of intelligence and shrewdness of the cunning manager?

Should we too urge those who use their intellects and astuteness in their daily work to bring their same aptitudes to bear in living as disciples who serve the reign of God? Use the abilities you have to deal with your "own generation" (v. 8) for the purposes of the age to come and its "eternal homes"—God's purposes and reign. Use your abilities to live as "children of light" (vv. 8, 9).

The theme that no one can "serve two masters," and thus "you cannot serve God and wealth" (v. 13), is Jesus' comprehensive summary statement at the end of the dishonest manager passage. Will you live as "children of this age" or as "children of light"? Will you use your shrewdness to serve only yourself, or others?

This points to the broadest question of discipleship posed by Jesus: Will you follow me? This was at stake in Luke's account of the calling of Jesus' first disciples (5:1–11, 27–28). When Peter, James, and John responded to the call to follow Jesus, Luke says, distinctively, that they "left everything and followed him" (5:11). The same language is used with Levi's action: "He got up, left everything, and followed him" (v. 28). These responses show the committed loyalty of Jesus' disciples to the person of Jesus himself and not to the bonds of life as they had known them. In Luke, "answering the call to follow Jesus means detaching oneself from one's former life: family, home, livelihood and, as will become increasingly clear, possessions (e.g., 12:33; 14:26, 33; 18:22, 28–29)."[1]

Jesus, as Luke presents him, taught that "the domain ruled by wealth is a dangerous habitat, for attachment to wealth entangles one in concerns that run counter to the values and commitments of the realm of God (8:14; 12:22–34; 14:18–20; 16:13; 17:26–30)."[2] Jesus warned the wealthy about the dangers of attachments to outward possessions (6:24; 12:13–21; 18:24–25) and spoke of an ultimate reversal of power and social location between rich and poor (1:51–53; 6:20–21, 24–25; 16:19–31). This means one's relationship to wealth can have ultimate consequences.

1. John T. Carroll, *Luke: A Commentary*, New Testament Library (Louisville, KY: Westminster John Knox, 2012), 125–26.
2. Carroll, *Luke*, 374.

As contemporary Christians, we all have to come to terms with our relationship to the wealth we have been given, in various forms. Our issues are not whether or not we will have any wealth, but in what ways the wealth we do have can serve the purposes of God's reign rather than be loved for what it brings to us.

Luke's account of the rich ruler (18:18–30) is poignant. When the rich ruler inquired how to inherit eternal life, Jesus told him that, despite obedience to the commandments, he still lacked one thing: "Sell all that you own and distribute the money to the poor, and you will have treasure in heaven; then come, follow me." This was too much for the ruler. When he heard it "he became sad; for he was very rich." Then Jesus said, "It is easier for a camel to go through the eye of a needle than for someone who is rich to enter the kingdom of God" (18:25). Here, love of riches was stronger than love of Jesus. In terms of the Dishonest Manager parable, the ruler could not serve two masters: God and wealth.

For Jesus' disciples, Peter spoke and said the disciples have "left our homes and followed you" (18:28). To these disciples, Jesus promised, "There is no one who has left house or wife or brothers or parents or children, for the sake of the kingdom of God, who will not get back very much more in this age, and in the age to come eternal life" (18:29–30). Being a disciple of Jesus Christ demands a full loyalty to Jesus. We must sit loose with whatever wealth we are given and never let it lessen our love and commitment to Jesus.

DONALD K. MCKIM

Commentary 2: Connecting the Reading to the World

Jesus was not a big fan of financial planning, at least not as we know it today. He advised a potential disciple to sell his possessions and give the proceeds to the poor (Luke 18:18–30). He told would-be disciples not to worry about their lives, the future, or what they will eat or drink or wear (12:22–31). He chastised the rich fool for building bigger barns to store his belongings (12:13–21). Perhaps this lack of material concern for the future was viable in a family-oriented culture where children cared for their elderly parents. However, in the twenty-first century, when many parents support their adult children and face the possibility of living thirty years beyond retirement, Jesus' advice seems unrealistic. We are anxious about the stock market, anxious about retirement funds, and anxious about being anxious. We also realize that while some people worry about their nest eggs for the future, many other people cannot feed and house their families in the present.

In part because of these instructions from Jesus, Christians have had an uneasy relationship with money. Monks and nuns took vows of poverty because they thought money was seductive, dangerous, and best avoided. They dressed modestly, gave up personal property, and lived simply in their communities. Some monastic orders sold hand-crafted bread or wine or books to support themselves, but became wealthy when their industries were successful. They then had to restart their communal lives and make a conscious effort to live in poverty. The followers of Francis of Assisi were so adamant about avoiding the contamination of "filthy lucre" that they refused to touch money at all.

At the other extreme some Christians have attained millionaire or even billionaire status, sometimes through morally ambiguous means. Wealthy people may see their success as divine blessing on their virtue and effort (Deut. 8:12–16); they may be uncomfortable with excess wealth and give some of it away.

Most Christians live somewhere in between these extremes of poverty and wealth. They are caught in the midst of multiple realities: they need money to survive, they may have more than their fair share, and they know many other people do not have enough. It would be helpful to have some clear guidance from Scripture as to exactly how much money followers of Jesus can keep for themselves and how much they should give away.

The text about the shrewd steward provides no such clarity. It does talk about money, but in such an ambiguous way that commentators draw different conclusions about the meaning and application of the story.

At first glance, Jesus appears to agree with the master's praise of the steward. He concludes the story by telling the disciples to "use your wealth to win friends for yourselves." The steward exemplifies ingenuity, street smarts, and thinking outside of the box. Naiveté and passivity are not Christian virtues. A sermon might note the value of creative problem solving as a way to prepare for an uncertain future. Christians should be astute and smart. They should be willing to take risks. They should use money wisely to do good works and gain security.

This interpretation makes some sense, especially given the proverbs that Luke's Jesus adds to the end of the parable in verses 10–13. The logical conclusion, however, is that Jesus praised the steward's blatant dishonesty. Some commentators attempt to justify the steward's behavior by giving it a more positive spin. Perhaps a commission was included in the amount the tenants owed. When the steward reduced their bills, he did not cheat the master but declined the money that was owed to him. Perhaps an interest charge was included in the final bill, though it was not identified as such because Jews were forbidden to charge interest. The master could not protest when the steward removed the interest, because it would prove that he had committed the sin of usury. Perhaps the steward was actually a very generous man, like Robin Hood, who stole from the rich and gave to the poor.

This approach to the text might inspire a sermon focused on the virtues of the steward. He sacrificed his commission to build a new community for himself. He reversed his master's sin of usury, an action that benefitted the master, the debtors, and the steward himself. He took money from his wealthy manager and gave it to the poor. In these ways, he used money for the good of others.

Another interpretation of the parable insists that the steward was simply dishonest. He did not give away his own money. He did not seek justice for the poor. He falsified accounts for his own benefit. What if the master and Jesus grudgingly admired the steward's creative thinking but objected to his actions? The proverbs in verses 10–13 about the use of money can be read as an indictment of the steward. He was dishonest in a little. He was not faithful with the resources of another. He served the wrong master. He was not a role model!

If Jesus did praise the steward, he was contradicting his other teachings about money. As noted above, Jesus does not usually encourage anxious preparation for the future. Is it possible that Jesus did not agree with the master's praise of the steward and was instead being sarcastic? Perhaps Jesus believed that the shrewd steward did the wrong thing for the wrong reason. After all, whatever security the steward found with his "friends" would be no more effective in securing a future than the stuff in the rich fool's barns.

The steward resembles a politician who tries to win votes with promises of lower taxes. Of course he or she will make friends! It does not matter that the promises are impossible to fulfill. The politician is thinking about his or her own interests, not the interests of the whole.

The steward certainly had moxie; he had the courage to take a big risk. Those skills are often admired in certain public figures who appear strong and decisive and free of traditional moral restrictions. Consider famous criminals such as Al Capone, Bonnie and Clyde, or the Godfather in the movies—criminals, yet they are admired for their audacity and intelligence, for escaping capture and punishment, for getting away with murder. Consider some famous politicians and world leaders who lied or cheated while in office, and yet continue to receive grudging respect or even outright approval because they were tough and decisive.

Perhaps Jesus is advising his listeners *not* to idolize and emulate the shrewd master. The kingdom operates with different values. Wealth and resources are not primarily for personal benefit, but a way to care for the whole community. Wealth and resources should not be used to manipulate and earn favors to be called in later. The means of making money are as important as the ends. The shrewd steward and people like him might appear worldly wise and impressive. They might be "players" in business or politics or even religion. They might get what they want in the short term, but are they demonstrating kingdom values? Are they using wealth and power to bring more wealth and power to themselves?

The preacher in search of a text for Stewardship Sunday may not find a clear moral imperative in this parable, but it certainly raises a number of important questions about how Christians gain, use, and give away their money. How can wealth and power be used to serve God's purposes?

LYNN JAPINGA

Proper 21 (Sunday between September 25 and October 1 Inclusive)

Jeremiah 32:1–3a, 6–15 and
Amos 6:1a, 4–7
Psalm 91:1–6, 14–16 and Psalm 146
1 Timothy 6:6–19
Luke 16:19–31

Jeremiah 32:1–3a, 6–15

[1]The word that came to Jeremiah from the LORD in the tenth year of King Zedekiah of Judah, which was the eighteenth year of Nebuchadrezzar. [2]At that time the army of the king of Babylon was besieging Jerusalem, and the prophet Jeremiah was confined in the court of the guard that was in the palace of the king of Judah, [3]where King Zedekiah of Judah had confined him. Zedekiah had said, "Why do you prophesy and say: Thus says the LORD: . . .

[6]Jeremiah said, The word of the LORD came to me: [7]Hanamel son of your uncle Shallum is going to come to you and say, "Buy my field that is at Anathoth, for the right of redemption by purchase is yours." [8]Then my cousin Hanamel came to me in the court of the guard, in accordance with the word of the LORD, and said to me, "Buy my field that is at Anathoth in the land of Benjamin, for the right of possession and redemption is yours; buy it for yourself." Then I knew that this was the word of the LORD.

[9]And I bought the field at Anathoth from my cousin Hanamel, and weighed out the money to him, seventeen shekels of silver. [10]I signed the deed, sealed it, got witnesses, and weighed the money on scales. [11]Then I took the sealed deed of purchase, containing the terms and conditions, and the open copy; [12]and I gave the deed of purchase to Baruch son of Neriah son of Mahseiah, in the presence of my cousin Hanamel, in the presence of the witnesses who signed the deed of purchase, and in the presence of all the Judeans who were sitting in the court of the guard. [13]In their presence I charged Baruch, saying, [14]Thus says the LORD of hosts, the God of Israel: Take these deeds, both this sealed deed of purchase and this open deed, and put them in an earthenware jar, in order that they may last for a long time. [15]For thus says the LORD of hosts, the God of Israel: Houses and fields and vineyards shall again be bought in this land.

Amos 6:1a, 4–7

[1]Alas for those who are at ease in Zion,
and for those who feel secure on Mount Samaria.
. . . .
[4]Alas for those who lie on beds of ivory,
and lounge on their couches,
and eat lambs from the flock,
and calves from the stall;
[5]who sing idle songs to the sound of the harp,
and like David improvise on instruments of music;

[6]who drink wine from bowls,
and anoint themselves with the finest oils,
but are not grieved over the ruin of Joseph!
[7]Therefore they shall now be the first to go into exile,
and the revelry of the loungers shall pass away.

Commentary 1: Connecting the Reading with Scripture

A short poem by an anonymous author reads: "Two men looked through prison bars. One saw the mud; the other, the stars." In a simple way, the poem serves as a reminder that hope and joy are not *necessarily* the result of fortuitous events in a person's life; they also arise, especially during trials, through adopting a peculiar perspective on the events themselves. The first lectionary text, Jeremiah 32:1–3a, 6–15, invites exiles living in Babylon around 587 BCE to adopt a peculiar perspective concerning Jeremiah's decision to buy a field in Anathoth. As Israel's defeat by the Babylonians moves toward its inevitable conclusion, the purchase of the field encourages exiles to "see the stars," especially in uncertain times.

As chapter 32 begins, Jeremiah finds himself "confined in the court of the guard" in the royal palace. This scene connects with a larger theme: Jeremiah suffers for carrying an unpopular prophetic word. He survives a plot against his life by his own family (Jer. 11:13–23), a priest puts him in stocks in public (20:1–2), he faces death threats (26:7–9) and imprisonment (37:11–16), people throw him in a cistern (38:6–13), and he faces false accusations (43:1–3). In this chapter and the parallel account in chapter 37, Jeremiah suffers because of the judgment he pronounces on Zedekiah king of Judah (32:3b–5).

Even so, the word of the Lord comes to him (32:1, 6) and reveals that his cousin Hanamel will ask him to buy his field in their hometown of Anathoth. Hanamel not only visits him "in accordance with the word of the Lord" (v. 8); he also fulfills the prophecy when he says, "Buy my field." While it is possible that Hanamel already had lost hope, it is more plausible that war had brought about poverty. Hanamel needed a relative to buy his land for the family in accordance with the provisions set forth in Leviticus 25:23–28.

In verses 9–15, Jeremiah does more than help his cousin. He reminds exiles in Babylon *and* war-torn citizens in Jerusalem to cling to hope. Jeremiah purchases the field, signs and seals the deed of purchase, and gives it to a scribe named Baruch in the presence of several witness including "all of the Judeans who were sitting in the court of the guard" (v. 12). Notice the public nature of the purchase. He commands Baruch to put both the sealed and unsealed deed in an "earthenware jar" in order to preserve them (v. 13). In so doing, he turns a business transaction into a "sign act" designed to demonstrate that God has not abandoned the land or the people. The scroll and the jar symbolize the greater promise that "houses and fields and vineyards shall again be bought in this land" (v. 15). The sign act of chapter 32:10–15 and the subsequent prayers and promises connect to a larger theme of holding onto hope in chapters 30–31. God has promised not only to restore and rebuild Israel (30:16–18); God will do nothing less than establish a new covenant with them (31:31–34).

While the first lection resounds with hope concerning Israel's future, the second lection, Amos 6:1a, 4–7, resounds with judgment against Israel's leaders for failing to abide by righteousness and justice in the world. Although the book begins with judgment oracles against foreign nations, Amos 6 makes clear that eighth-century-BCE leaders in the northern and southern kingdoms, those in Zion (v. 1a) *and* Samaria (v. 1b), cannot escape indictment.

The word "Alas" in verse 1 comes from the word "woe" in Hebrew (cf. 5:18) and sets the stage for a larger sevenfold woe oracle (vv. 1a, 1b, 3, 4a, 4b, 5, 6a). The prophets used woe oracles to lament the sorry spiritual-moral state of a nation in decay whose leaders were in disarray (cf. Isa. 28–30). Divine judgment, prophetic anger, and deep lament come together in a woe oracle. In the NT, Jesus pronounces woe oracles against the wealthy (Luke 6:24–25) and against religious leaders (Matt. 23:13–29). The "notables" (v. 1b) whom Amos rebukes do not lead with valor, uprightness, and loving-kindness. Their leadership looks more like ease (v. 1a), revelry (vv. 4–6a), and hypocrisy (v. 6b).

Those "at ease" (v. 1a) are oblivious to the plight of their suffering neighbors (cf. Isa. 32:9–11). They have lost themselves in opulence, lying on ivory beds and lounging on beautiful couches (v. 4a), while people in close proximity struggle and their nation languishes. They refuse to acknowledge the way things really are.

Verses 4–7 display features of what OT scholars refer to as an ancient Near Eastern *marzēaḥ* feast. In fact, *marzēaḥ* appears in verse 7 as "loungers." All three elements of the feast show up here: (1) wealthy participants, (2) religious-cultic feasting, and (3) excessive drinking. Only the superrich can afford beds adorned with ivory, couches (v. 4a), and the finest oils (v. 6a). Regarding the cultic significance of verse 4b, Francis I. Andersen and David Freedman point out that "meat was rarely eaten in ordinary life, and for most people it was available only on the most cultic and sacramental occasions."[1] The musical improvisations of verse 5 reinforce the idea of ease and even arrogance. Somehow, these leaders believe they sound "like David." Drinking wine from bowls rather than glasses in verse 6 communicates excess as well as religious shamelessness. To illustrate the offense itself, R. Reed Lessing offers a helpful modern analogy: "These partiers had taken wine that had been reserved for Holy Communion and were drinking it, not even from glasses, but straight from the bottle."[2]

Leaders filled with a warped understanding of reality have no space in their souls to be "grieved by the ruin of Joseph" (v. 6b). In other places in the OT, the word "grieved" means "to be sick, to be made sick." The imagery is striking. Complacency, opulence, and hedonism have inoculated the nation's elites against feeling sickened by the downfall of their nation. What are the consequences for such attitudes and behaviors? Their feasting will surely pass away, and they will be the "first to go into exile" (v. 7).

When the two lections come together, it appears as if they have little in common: different prophets, different centuries, and different messages: Amos with a message of judgment and Jeremiah with a message of hope. However, the connections should not go unnoticed. Exile serves as the more obvious thematic connection. Even as Jeremiah lifts up the promise of return, he makes it clear that the earthenware jar must last for a "long time" (Jer. 32:14) while the nation suffers in exile for its disobedience. Different exiles in different centuries have the same root cause: disobedience to Torah through failing to love God and neighbor. Also, notice the common theme of leadership. Remember that the primary instigators of Jeremiah's imprisonment in Jeremiah 32:1–3a and his suffering elsewhere (20:1–2; 38:6–13; 43:1–3) were leaders who refused to acknowledge reality. They were not "feasting" like those in Amos 6, but their resistance to God and to God's messenger, Jeremiah, blinded them to reality. They had no space in their souls to receive the word of the Lord, and much less to grieve the ruin of the nation. On account of their disobedience, they suffered the same fate as those warned in Amos 6:7. The *leaders* were the first to go into exile (Jer. 29:1–2).

JARED E. ALCÁNTARA

Commentary 2: Connecting the Reading with the World

The Hebrew prophets not only engaged in prophetic witness through their words; they also engaged in prophetic witness through their actions. Jeremiah is foremost among them. When he wants to signal that God's covenant people have become defiled and good for nothing,

1. Francis I. Andersen and David Noel Freedman, *Amos*, Anchor Bible (New York: Doubleday, 1989), 563.
2. R. Reed Lessing, *Amos: A Theological Exposition of Sacred Scripture*, Concordia Commentary (St. Louis: Concordia, 2009), 405–6.

Jeremiah wears a loincloth that he had worn and then buried for a while (and thus ruined) to signal their demise (Jer. 13:11). When he wants to signal Judah's coming subjection to Babylonian rule, he fashions a yoke like that worn by oxen, and wears it around his own neck (Jer. 27).

Ordinarily, Jeremiah's prophetic actions are meant to indict Judah for its faithlessness and disobedience and to forecast a judgment that is to come. However, in this text, judgment is already hammering at the door. The Babylonians are laying siege to Jerusalem, and Jeremiah is under house arrest for having prophesied its demise. This might be the perfect time for the prophet to say, "I told you so. I warned you."

That is not what Jeremiah does. Instead, he engages in another prophetic action. He arranges to purchase a piece of land in his home territory of Anathoth. He pays good money for land that will soon be worthless—both to him (given his imprisonment) and to his relatives (given the imminent fall of Judah). He engages in what, for the entire world, looks like an incredibly foolish act, and he does so in a very public manner.

Why this public sign-act from the prophet? Because Jeremiah believes with all his heart that Judah is still in the hands of a God who loves the people despite their disobedience. He believes that redemption, not judgment, will be God's last word. He proclaims, "For thus says the LORD of hosts, the God of Israel: Houses and fields and vineyards shall again be bought in this land" (32:15).

Walter Brueggemann has said that prophetic witness involves not only "criticizing" the old order that is to die, but "energizing" the people with the hope of a new order God will yet bring into being.[3] Here we witness Jeremiah—at a time when the spirits of the people are at their very lowest—engaging in an energizing act of prophetic promise and hope.

What does it mean to "buy a field in Anathoth" in today's world?

Perhaps, on a personal level, it means to follow the example of Father Gregory Boyle, who, instead of throwing up his hands in despair over the gang violence in Los Angeles, started a business in the heart of the city that employs gang members as its workers and embraces a vision that seeks to help both the community and its young people become all God created them to be.[4]

Perhaps, on a more communal level, it means that instead of simply throwing up hands in despair over the unjust racial profiling of young black men for arrests, imprisonment, and brutality, we invest in fields of hope like "Black Lives Matter," or we encourage our churches to become centers of hope and advocacy and antiracism training.

Perhaps it means that when it seems that all the power politics in a geographical area is going in a direction that is antithetical to what we believe the gospel requires of us, we start having Moral Mondays in our local communities, as the Rev. William Barber did in North Carolina, planting our little fields of hope and protest right on the town green outside the halls of power.

Perhaps it means that when we witness children caught in a spiraling cycle of poverty and low school performance, we advocate for investing more resources in the poorest school districts in our areas, rather than in the wealthiest.

It is often easier in prophetic witness to criticize the old order than it is to come up with creative avenues for purchasing and planting fields of hope in the very communities where we live and work. Jeremiah calls us to do both—even if our hope-filled acts seem absolutely foolish to the rest of the world.

If Jeremiah's words inspire hopeful action in places where hope seems futile, Amos's words are meant to light a fire under all those who are complacent and are "lounging on their couches" (Amos 6:4b) in the face of rampant poverty and economic injustice. These prophetic words are clearly addressed to the affluent and privileged—to those who prosper most when the economy of a nation flourishes.

In verses 1–3 the sin Amos addresses is that of having too much national pride, namely, a hubris that views one's own nation as "the first of the nations" (v. 1b), that looks down on and

3. See Walter Brueggemann, *The Prophetic Imagination*, 2nd ed. (Minneapolis: Fortress, 2001), 3–5.
4. See Gregory Boyle, *Tattoos of the Heart: The Power of Boundless Compassion* (New York: Free Press, 2011).

demeans the nations around it, and that puts its faith in its own national security. "Are you better than these kingdoms?" Amos asks. "Or is your territory greater than their territory"? (v. 2b). The prideful attitudes and actions of Israel and Judah, he seems to imply, are going to bring "near a reign of violence" (v. 3b)—perhaps the coming Day of the Lord he has already described in the previous chapter as being "darkness, not light" (5:20a).

In verses 4–6 Amos turns his attention to a second sin: that of indifference and apathy. Throughout this book Amos speaks a great deal about the plight of the poor, the needy, the oppressed, those who are mistreated in the courts and swindled in business practices, and who long for a justice that never seems to come their way. Here Amos contrasts their plight with the indifferent and callous conspicuous consumption of the privileged who feast on the finest foods, drink their wine from bowls, lounge on beds of ivory, anoint themselves with the finest oils and cosmetics, and amuse themselves with "idle songs." Their sin (at least in this passage) is not one of intentional mistreatment of the poor. Their sin is that *they "are not grieved over the ruin of Joseph*" (v. 6b; emphasis added). They are complacent, self-satisfied, and too apathetic to notice or to mourn the plight of the oppressed in their midst. Their party music is playing so loudly that they cannot hear the pleading cries for justice. Their bodies are so sated they cannot even imagine being hungry. Their houses and neighborhoods are so opulent they are sheltered from having to witness the poverty in which others live. As a result, they avert their eyes and their ears, and they fiddle (or play the harp) while immense suffering goes on all around them.

It does not take much stretch of the imagination to hear our own culture, our own nation, and some of our own practices indicted here as well. What Amos decries is patriotism gone awry, national pride that has fallen prey to a self-centered and destructive arrogance, apathy that has given way to inaction at best, and callous indifference at worst. It is clear that God is not pleased. In an ironic twist Amos says that those who consider themselves "first of the nations" will be the first to go into exile. Those who consider themselves the consummate partiers will find themselves without any revelry. Those who put their ultimate trust in their nation's security will find themselves delivered up, along with all that they have, into the hands of others. It is a troubling and indicting judgment—but one that we too ignore at our own peril.

LEONORA TUBBS TISDALE

Psalm 91:1–6, 14–16

[1]You who live in the shelter of the Most High,
who abide in the shadow of the Almighty,
[2]will say to the LORD, "My refuge and my fortress;
my God, in whom I trust."
[3]For he will deliver you from the snare of the fowler
and from the deadly pestilence;
[4]he will cover you with his pinions,
and under his wings you will find refuge;
his faithfulness is a shield and buckler.
[5]You will not fear the terror of the night,
or the arrow that flies by day,
[6]or the pestilence that stalks in darkness,
or the destruction that wastes at noonday.

. . . .

[14]Those who love me, I will deliver;
I will protect those who know my name.
[15]When they call to me, I will answer them;
I will be with them in trouble,
I will rescue them and honor them.
[16]With long life I will satisfy them,
and show them my salvation.

Psalm 146

[1]Praise the LORD!
Praise the LORD, O my soul!
[2]I will praise the LORD as long as I live;
I will sing praises to my God all my life long.

[3]Do not put your trust in princes,
in mortals, in whom there is no help.
[4]When their breath departs, they return to the earth;
on that very day their plans perish.

[5]Happy are those whose help is the God of Jacob,
whose hope is in the LORD their God,
[6]who made heaven and earth,
the sea, and all that is in them;
who keeps faith forever;
[7]who executes justice for the oppressed;
who gives food to the hungry.

The LORD sets the prisoners free;
[8]the LORD opens the eyes of the blind.

The Lord lifts up those who are bowed down;
the Lord loves the righteous.
[9]The LORD watches over the strangers;
he upholds the orphan and the widow,
but the way of the wicked he brings to ruin.

[10]The LORD will reign forever,
your God, O Zion, for all generations.
Praise the LORD!

Connecting the Psalm with Scripture and Worship

Psalm 146. Psalm 146 leads into the concluding doxological section of Book V of the Psalms, signaling the approaching conclusion of the Psalter itself. Its inclusive "Hallelujahs" (Ps. 146:1a, 10c) fittingly and liturgically frame the psalm's interior antithetical structure, the content of which is not praise but instruction. The psalmist contrasts human help, which must not be trusted, given its ephemeral nature, with divine help, which is to be trusted because, in addition to its benefits, it never ends (vv. 4, 6; cf. Ps. 118:8–9).[1]

Before a final call to praise, which signals no ending at all but rather a refreshed summons to the worshiping community to continue its vocation (v. 10), the psalmist recalls the familiar biblical image of the "path of the wicked" as a journey to ordained ruin, a note sounded at the foundation of the Psalter itself (Ps. 1:1, 6). It is a word to those who would be wise (Ps. 1:2–3). The oblique divine sanctioning of the wicked characteristic of Psalm 1 (vv. 4–6) has now become a straightforward and sobering announcement of judgment: *"the way of the wicked he brings* [Piel] *to ruin"* (Ps. 146:9c).

In Psalm 146:1 the psalmist addresses in hymnic form his or her own soul in the presence of the congregation, calling the psalmist and, by extension, the worshiping community to join in the praise of YHWH. The psalmist's desire is that YHWH will accept this song of praise, and that it would never end, as would befit the enduring goodness of God (v. 2).

Verses 3–4 implicitly continue the praise of YHWH by negatively characterizing royal authority; the psalmist likely remembers the foreign rulers of the exile, but may also have in mind the leaders who have failed their own community. The personal transience ("breath," v. 4a) of rulers is an obvious foreshadowing (to the wise) of the accelerated transience ("that very day") of political power ("plans," v. 4b).

In contrast to the fleeting reign of human rulers, it is YHWH who in truth rules. YHWH's reign is endless, concentrated in Zion (v. 10). YHWH alone can be trusted. The state of those who trust in YHWH, translated "happy" (NRSV; cf. Ps. 1:1) in verse 5, is not to be understood as the emotional condition of pleasure, but as the emancipation from anxiety YHWH alone grants the worshiper—including freedom from the fear of any mortal power.[2]

In a motif typical of a song of Zion, and perhaps reflecting a cultic setting for this hymn, YHWH's reliability is grounded in YHWH's power and prerogative as creator (v. 6). Unlike human rulers, whose end is "dust," and unlike the gods (of foreign pontiffs and peoples), whose jurisdictions are limited (cf. Jonah 1:5–10), YHWH has "made" (NRSV v. 6; better "is Maker of") the world and its nations. This is the undeniable foundation of YHWH's universal jurisdiction, the reliability of which is an endless and immutable extension of nothing less than YHWH's character ("faithfulness," v. 6).

1. James Luther Mays, *Psalms*, Interpretation (Louisville, KY: Westminster John Knox, 2011), 440.
2. John S. Kselman and Michael L Barré, "Psalms," in *The New Jerome Biblical Commentary*, ed. Raymond E. Brown, Joseph A. Fitzmyer, and Roland E. Murphy (Englewood Cliffs, NJ: Prentice-Hall, 1990), 551.

Open Our Hearts to the Poor

Brothers and sisters . . . accept my words on love of the poor, not in a mean spirit but generously, that you may be rich in God's Kingdom; and pray that we may bestow these words on you richly, and nourish your souls with our discourse, breaking spiritual bread for the poor. Perhaps we may make nourishment rain from heaven, as Moses did in ancient times, lavishing on you the bread of angels; or perhaps we may feed many thousands in the desert with a few loaves, and leave them satisfied, as Jesus later did, who is the true bread and the source of true life. . . . We must open our hearts, then, to all the poor, to those suffering evil for any reason at all, according to the Scripture . . . "rejoice with those who rejoice and weep with those who weep" (Romans 12:15). Because we are human beings, we must offer the favor of our kindness first of all to other human beings, whether they need it because they are widows or orphans, or because they are exiles from their own country, or because of the cruelty of their masters or the harshness of their rulers or the inhumanity of their tax-collectors, or because of the bloody violence of robbers or the insatiable greed of thieves, or because of the legal confiscation of their property, or shipwreck—all are wretched alike, and so all look towards our hands, as we look towards God, for the things we need.

Gregory of Nazianzus, *Oration 14*, in *Gregory of Nazianzus*, trans. Brian E. Daley, Early Church Fathers (London: Routledge, 2006), 76, 78.

YHWH's character is directly revealed in YHWH's actions on behalf of the covenant community, with the particular and emphatic emphasis that YHWH, whose creative power is celebrated in the physical realm, can be trusted to ensure the moral reliability of the universe. YHWH is now described (praised) in a cascade of clauses that celebrate YHWH as the preeminent (and tireless) agent of justice and help (vv. 7–9c) for the needy and oppressed. The language is characteristic of biblical expressions of concern (Deut. 10:18; 24:19–21; Zech. 7:10; Prov. 22:22–23; Jer. 7:5–7; 22:3; Isa. 10:1–3; 33:14–15; Amos 5:11; Pss. 9:9; 68:5; 72:4; 82:3–4). While individual forms of loss and oppression are cited, they also reflect YHWH's and the community's concern for the suffering of disadvantaged and displaced groups ("sets the prisoners free"; cf. Exod. 3:7–8; Isa. 61:1–4).[3]

The generation of exile and the generation now singing praises in worship are united by YHWH's covenant concerns and mandates for justice, which are to be nourished, but never replaced, by praise rising out of remembering, and vouchsafed in the vigilant absence of trust in any save YHWH alone (Exod. 20:3; Deut. 6:4).

Psalm 91:1–6, 14–16. Psalm 91 begins with the poet addressing in implied second person "the dwelling one" (NRSV "You who live"), who enters the sanctuary of *Elyon* or *Shaddai* (v. 1), both divine names used in poetic parallelism to build toward the use of *YHWH* in verse 2 (cf. Gen. 17:1; 28:3; 35:11; 49:25; Deut. 32:8 for *Elyon* and *Shaddai* in the Yahwist's tradition). All that is provided with respect to the identity of this one who enters YHWH's sanctuary is the individual's first-person exclamation of trust in verse 2, a threefold acclamation with perhaps each image in additive relationship building from the familiar biblical metaphors of a protected space for the afflicted or pursued, "refuge" (cf. Pss. 14:6, 46:1; 71:7; 94:22), to a more secure dwelling "fortress" (Pss. 31:3; 59:9, 17), to a final and insurmountable declaration of the complete security provided by "my God" (v. 2c). No more information is offered *from* this worshiper. No more information is needed. The liturgical cry of verse 2 expresses completely the core and unshakable identity of this "dweller" and "abider." Verses 3, 5, and 6 feature a storm of troubles and afflictions from which the worshiper is safe. In addition to standard threats cast in dramatic genitives ("the snare of the fowler," "the terror of the night"), these verses include divine protection against "pestilence" (vv. 3, 6; cf. v. 10), a malady often associated in

3. Mays, *Psalms*, 441.

biblical texts with YHWH's judgment against enemies and against YHWH's own people (cf. Exod. 5:3; 9:3; 9:15; 23:28; Lev. 26:25; Num. 14:12; Deut. 28:21; 2 Sam. 24:15; Jer. 14:12; 15:2; 21:6–8).

Lodged at the eye of this tempest, verse 4 combines two images of YHWH as protector. The first is the figure of YHWH as an alarmed bird protecting its young by covering them with its "pinions" and "wings." This figure may extend the reference to "the shadow of the Almighty" in verse 1 (cf. Ps. 17:8; 36:7).[4] The second reference deepens the sense of danger and protection by employing a figure of speech known as a merism, the use of parts to refer to the whole—in this case, "shield and buckler" for "military." With "his faithfulness" as subject, this merism connotes a sense of complete protection as in verse 2c. YHWH is sufficiently with the community *amid* every danger, not the absence of danger.

Verses 14–16 conclude the psalm with an oracle of salvation. YHWH has been listening and now responds, albeit through the liturgist, in first person. Seven clauses, each collapsing subject, verb, and object into a single term (vv. 14a, b; 15b, d, e; 16a, b), bespeak the intimate proximity of YHWH with the community that in "trouble" (v. 15) cries out in trust, as exemplified in the confession of the otherwise anonymous worshiper welcomed into the sanctuary (v. 1).

E. CARSON BRISSON

4. Mays, *Psalms*, 297.

1 Timothy 6:6–19

[6]Of course, there is great gain in godliness combined with contentment; [7]for we brought nothing into the world, so that we can take nothing out of it; [8]but if we have food and clothing, we will be content with these. [9]But those who want to be rich fall into temptation and are trapped by many senseless and harmful desires that plunge people into ruin and destruction. [10]For the love of money is a root of all kinds of evil, and in their eagerness to be rich some have wandered away from the faith and pierced themselves with many pains.

[11]But as for you, man of God, shun all this; pursue righteousness, godliness, faith, love, endurance, gentleness. [12]Fight the good fight of the faith; take hold of the eternal life, to which you were called and for which you made the good confession in the presence of many witnesses. [13]In the presence of God, who gives life to all things, and of Christ Jesus, who in his testimony before Pontius Pilate made the good confession, I charge you [14]to keep the commandment without spot or blame until the manifestation of our Lord Jesus Christ, [15]which he will bring about at the right time—he who is the blessed and only Sovereign, the King of kings and Lord of lords. [16]It is he alone who has immortality and dwells in unapproachable light, whom no one has ever seen or can see; to him be honor and eternal dominion. Amen.

[17]As for those who in the present age are rich, command them not to be haughty, or to set their hopes on the uncertainty of riches, but rather on God who richly provides us with everything for our enjoyment. [18]They are to do good, to be rich in good works, generous, and ready to share, [19]thus storing up for themselves the treasure of a good foundation for the future, so that they may take hold of the life that really is life.

Connections 1: Connecting the Reading with Scripture

The immediate context of this passage stirs up trouble. Possibly to avoid the issue of slavery, the editors of the Revised Common Lectionary begin this lection with 6:6 rather than the beginning of chapter 6. In these overlooked verses the author of 1 Timothy exhorts slaves to obey unbelieving masters lest they bring shame on the gospel, and to respect believing masters because they are, according to the Greek text, brothers. The church lives in the wake of American white supremacy on full display in Charlottesville, global racial tensions like the Burmese treatment of the Rohingya people, and a flourishing worldwide sex trafficking industry that demonstrates that the evil of slavery is alive and well. While tempting to sidestep this difficult issue, as the Revised Common Lectionary allows, there are many possibilities for the preacher seeking to offer a word that is faithful and relevant.

A preacher might consider focusing on the dissonance between exhorting slaves to treat their masters with respect and the fact that precious few in the church today would affirm that slavery is anything but an odious practice at odds with the gospel. The text clearly not only affirms slaves' respecting their masters for the sake of marketing but also affirms without question the reality that early Christian believers themselves owned slaves. The preacher might wade into the rich, problematic question of what thoughtful believers are to do when we encounter scriptural claims that contradict what the contemporary church affirms. A preacher might point to denominational statements on scriptural interpretation or cite readings from abolitionists to offer a more nuanced interpretive framework than the folksy slogan "The Bible says it. I believe it. That settles it."

Moving beyond the immediate context, the larger framework of the letter raises at least two issues. First, there is the question of how Paul views wealth. Those seeking a simple answer will be disappointed. While it is tempting to think that Paul, or the early Pauline community, is positing a dualism between worldly wealth and holiness, the larger context shows us that Paul actually makes a more moderate case allowing for the possibility of wealthy believers. Within the reading itself (6:17) Paul admonishes the rich not to be haughty but to trust in God. Paul could have told the rich that in order to be faithful they needed to sell all they have and follow after Jesus—but he does not. Rather, the assumption behind this statement is that it is possible to be wealthy and Christian. This question of focus is similar to Paul's earlier words against extreme asceticism in 4:3. Some were apparently advocating extreme fasting and chastity, but Paul pushes back on this near-Docetism in 4:4, writing, "Everything created by God is good." With food and sexuality the issue is about focus: are we focused on our abilities and ourselves, or are we striving toward God? In the same way with money, Paul is less concerned with how much a believer has than with the believer's focus: are we focused on God or gain?

In terms of preaching, one could compare the actual Pauline phrase asserting that the love of money is the root of all evil with the popular version stating that money itself is the root of all evil. The popular version of the phrase makes it sound as if money in and of itself is problematic and should just be avoided. Paul allows for the possibility of wealth, lifting up instead the question—not whether it is okay to be wealthy—whether a believer is remaining fixed on God. A preacher could bring in the text just preceding the reading in 6:5, in which Paul calls out those seeing godliness itself as a means of gain. Clearly, if Paul allows for the possibility of faithful people being wealthy, he would also speak strongly against any kind of prosperity gospel that sees faithfulness as something to be used for gain.

A second interesting connection between the reading and the larger context of the letter is the way Paul frames keeping the faith as a kind of fight. In the reading itself in 6:12 Paul exhorts the young Timothy to "fight the good fight of the faith." This is not the only time Paul writes like this. In 1:18 Paul sets up the entire letter as a set of instructions such that Timothy can "fight the good fight." Given the truth behind Marshall McLuhan's phrase "the medium is the message,"[1] what does it mean that Paul frames his message using a metaphor of a fight? Is this inherently violent language that cannot help but lead us toward more violence? This is an important question at a time when we continue to ask questions about violence in our media, and one I know stirs passion. I witnessed a pastoral colleague pose a question to other colleagues regarding whether the language of "prayer warrior" is appropriate or whether we should seek a way to talk about our effort that is not rooted in conflict. The response was emotional, charged, and the question generated an engaged and productive discussion.

Within the context of the wider lectionary the preacher might consider a couple of different possibilities. Both the reading from Jeremiah (Jer. 32:1–3a, 6–15) and the Lukan passage (Luke 16:19–31) raise the issue of wealth, but they offer strikingly different views. The Luke passage tells the familiar story of the rich man and poor Lazarus. Luke, with his characteristic invective against the rich, portrays the rich man as so consumed with his pleasure he is blind to the suffering of others. For Luke, wealth itself seems to be a problem. The Jeremiah text offers a completely different view. This text centers on Jeremiah's buying the field at Anathoth in the midst of the Babylonian destruction. In this text wealth is used to express faith that God will return Israel to the land.

A preacher could explore the seemingly divergent view of wealth found in Luke's story and in 1 Timothy. Whereas Paul can conceive of the possibility that believers can have wealth if they are sufficiently focused on God, Luke's

1. Marshall McLuhan, *Understanding Media: The Extensions of Man* (New York: McGraw-Hill, 1964), 7.

story questions whether wealth itself might make a person more selfish and less able to see and empathize with the plight of others. The preacher could pair Paul's word with the Jeremiah text to emphasize the importance of stewardship. The point in both texts is not how much money people have, but if they are using it to the glory of God. Of course a preacher might also weave together all three. One way to do this might be to start with Jeremiah's faithful use of wealth, create a Lowery loop with Luke's cautionary tale, and resolve with Paul's wise word about money not itself being evil but the love of money that is problematic.

When this text is considered against the backdrop of the rest of the canon, there are even more possibilities to consider. Much of Paul's wisdom here rests in learning how to be content, rather than seeking happiness through the vain promise of "more." This thread runs throughout the Bible. Proverbs 16:8 and 28:6 lift up how it is better to be righteous with less than to be rich and have more. Qoheleth views wealth and striving as vanity, but in Ecclesiastes 9:7–10 he affirms enjoying the little things in life, like eating one's bread and marriage. Paul himself may offer the best statement on learning how to be content. In Philippians 4:12–13 he writes that he has learned how to be content in every situation life has offered.

KEN EVERS-HOOD

Commentary 2: Connecting the Reading with the World

From its inception, the church has embraced seasonal Jewish feasts and adapted certain pagan celebrations for its own liturgical purposes. Yet Christian life is lived not in perpetual celebration or ecstasy but amid Ordinary Time, with feet firmly planted in the mundane, negotiating matters of food, clothing, wealth, and power. Suspended between the backward glance to Easter and the forward glance to the Advent of God's ever new coming, the first Christians were responding to the call to order their lives in response to this story and vision. If Easter inscribes in us a joyous hope for the world's redemption, then the liturgical season of Ordinary Time commences the hard work of discerning how we may participate with God's Logos hidden in the ordinary things of life. Evangelization in the book of Acts gives way to the task of ordering local communities of the faithful as extension and completion of God's work in Jesus Christ. Hence, the Pastoral Epistles constitute a crucial interval between the conversion and systematization of the church's polity. This is not incidental but determinative for its life and thought.

In 1 Timothy 6, the apostle Paul instructs Timothy, his "loyal child in the faith," in the handling of practical concerns affecting the church, especially as it pertains to ordering its corporate life and issues regarding wealth and possessions. He instructs the church not to conform to prevailing cultural habits and attitudes concerning wealth and possessions and to bear witness to Christ its head by being formed in the way of Christ.

Paul recommends the virtue of simplicity, employing an oft-repeated proverb, "We brought nothing into the world, so that we can take nothing out of it" (v. 7). The implication here is that simplicity is a secondary virtue that relies first on the faithfulness of God to provide what is needed. Trust in God's faithfulness is to be the secure foundation for our lives. Paul's case is strengthened by warnings about the negative consequences of loving money and possessions. He states that those who love money—those having a disordered relationship with money—risk serious harm. He uses terms such as "pierced with pains," "ruin," and "destruction" to describe their fate. The "love" of money is a form of idolatry, an inordinate attachment to those things that are not worthy of love and cannot love us back.

Isaiah 44:15 helps illustrate this point: "It [a wooden log] can be used as fuel. Part of it he takes and warms himself; he kindles a fire and bakes bread. Then he makes a god and worships it, makes it a carved image and bows down before it." While Paul does not specify personal consequences, we may assume that love of unworthy objects results in spiritual, psychic, relational, and physical disorders. In other words, those things we love form us most deeply. We were created for love of God and neighbor; in these we flourish, and apart from such love we become less than human.

For Paul, it matters a great deal how the church addresses the prevailing cultural attitudes and habits that privilege the wealthy and the arrogance and access associated with wealth. Contrasting these habits with the ethics apparent in Jesus' life and teachings strengthens Paul's warning regarding wealth. Paul evokes the model of Jesus, when his testimony before Pilate made the good confession (see John 18:28–38). Jesus' confession—that his kingdom was not of this world and that he came to bear witness to the truth of that reign—confounds Pilate. Perhaps unable to understand or not wanting to deal with Jesus' confession, he seems to dismiss his claim with a question that, even today, steers the conversation away from the content of that truth, Jesus the Christ, to a debate about "what is truth" or whether any truth can be truly known. By focusing on whether anything is knowable, real, or absolute, for instance, we can avoid being confronted with the responsibility of committing to truth and, most importantly, living by it. The author sees the struggle between these two orientations as a matter of "fighting the good fight of faith" (v. 12).

Paul contrasts material self-seeking and "the treasure of a good foundation for the future, so that they may take hold of the life that really is life" (v. 19). This passage has often been interpreted as an affirmation of the spiritual realm and a denial of the material realm. Without question, a nascent form of Gnosticism prevailed in Paul's day, making a world-denying dualism one possible reading of these texts. However, when viewed through the lens of Jesus' own practices and the whole of the Christian canon, we see an admonition centered around an ethic of generosity—not denying the good creation that God "provides for our enjoyment" (v. 17)—but sharing in joyful feasting with all.

When we look at the corpus of Paul's letters, it seems clear that he is concerned about the risk not only for individuals, but especially for the impact on the body of Christ, the church. The "upside-down kingdom" Jesus inaugurated rejected the human tendency to privilege the wealthy and powerful. Christian life is to be lived corporately, neither hierarchical or uniform, nor chaotic or atomistic, but as a unified and harmonious body knitted together in mutual service, as was the pattern of Christ. We are to put our faith in God, who "alone . . . has immortality and dwells in unapproachable light, whom no one has ever seen or can see; to him be honor and eternal dominion" (v. 16). It asserts the ultimate power of God as manifested in the self-giving servant, Jesus. Paul suggests that the church should not embrace a theology of scarcity. Instead, it should model a theology of generosity that negates the urgency of storing up wealth and power, while expressing gratitude for God's grace by sharing God's gifts with all. Unlike Rome, which ruled by means of wealth and power, the church compels its followers by the beauty of self-giving love in communities unified by the Spirit.

It is difficult for us today to imagine how radical were these thoughts for people whose place in the world was dictated by their poverty or political marginality. With the inauguration of Christ's church, the doors to God's kingdom were thrown open to all. Now, in this upside-down kingdom, people were valued not for their might or wealth but because they were proclaimed good by the Creator, redeemed by Christ, and equipped and empowered by the Spirit. These affirmations have enormous significance for the church today. The church is called to resist hierarchies based on wealth and power and to embrace all those redeemed and gifted by the Spirit.

This means engaging in practices such as simplicity, welcoming the stranger, and charity and justice on behalf of the least in our midst. For Christians, the practice of living as church in community is not a mere coincidental gathering of like-minded individuals; it demands rhythms of mutual love, support, and prayer so that even the "least of these" find their place in God's community of redemption. While the church has lived into these commitments only ambiguously, nevertheless we struggle to implement policies and practices that foster such mutual care. Culturally inscribed prejudices that inhibit community are rooted deep beneath our conscious awareness and require more than social practices or education. "Fight[ing] the good fight of the faith" calls for practices of self-study, contemplation, confession, loving accountability, and forgiveness.

DAVID F. WHITE

Luke 16:19–31

[19]"There was a rich man who was dressed in purple and fine linen and who feasted sumptuously every day. [20]And at his gate lay a poor man named Lazarus, covered with sores, [21]who longed to satisfy his hunger with what fell from the rich man's table; even the dogs would come and lick his sores. [22]The poor man died and was carried away by the angels to be with Abraham. The rich man also died and was buried. [23]In Hades, where he was being tormented, he looked up and saw Abraham far away with Lazarus by his side. [24]He called out, 'Father Abraham, have mercy on me, and send Lazarus to dip the tip of his finger in water and cool my tongue; for I am in agony in these flames.' [25]But Abraham said, 'Child, remember that during your lifetime you received your good things, and Lazarus in like manner evil things; but now he is comforted here, and you are in agony. [26]Besides all this, between you and us a great chasm has been fixed, so that those who might want to pass from here to you cannot do so, and no one can cross from there to us.' [27]He said, 'Then, father, I beg you to send him to my father's house— [28]for I have five brothers—that he may warn them, so that they will not also come into this place of torment.' [29]Abraham replied, 'They have Moses and the prophets; they should listen to them.' [30]He said, 'No, father Abraham; but if someone goes to them from the dead, they will repent.' [31]He said to him, 'If they do not listen to Moses and the prophets, neither will they be convinced even if someone rises from the dead.'"

Commentary 1: Connecting the Reading with Scripture

Even in an environment of increasing biblical illiteracy, this parable will likely be familiar to many contemporary hearers. Rich in imagery, we find that Lazarus, the unnamed rich man, Abraham the foreparent of faith and exemplar of righteousness, the sore-licking dogs, the hope of water on a fingertip, and the tormenting flames of Hades play key roles in fashioning this parable of reversals. It is tempting to take the Revised Common Lectionary's cue and by its limited parameters allow the parable to remain addressed to no one in particular, but that is not the case for Luke. As part of Jesus' long, winding journey to Jerusalem, Luke frames this episode as part of a conversation with the Pharisees (Luke 16:14). Up to this point this group of Pharisees has apparently been eavesdropping on his conversation with the disciples (16:1). Reaching even further back, Jesus has been alternating between addressing the Pharisees and scribes (15:1), and the disciples. Now the Pharisees have turned to ridiculing him (16:14), because, Luke comments, they "were lovers of money," and Jesus has just informed them, following the parable of the Dishonest Manager, that no one can "serve God and wealth" (16:13). Jesus follows the direct (albeit somewhat thematically disconnected) aphorisms of 16:15–18 with the more indirect, narrative speech of the parable. Both are connected to the preceding conversation with the disciples from the beginning of chapter 16. Preachers should be careful to situate the parable in this context, since the addressees greatly inform our interpretive practice.

Preachers should also note that the parable is open ended. Luke provides no summary statement from Jesus informing the Pharisees and disciples what to make of the story. There is no narrative resolution to what happens to the rich man's five brothers. Do they listen to Moses and the prophets (v. 29)? Jesus holds open the possibility of repentance (v. 31), a theme deep at the heart of Luke's Gospel. Readers are left to make their own conclusions, about how they will use their wealth, should they be like the rich man or his brothers, or if they can look forward to the comforting promise of reversal, should they be like Lazarus.

There is no doubt that as readers hear the drama of Lazarus and the rich man, Jesus' first-sermon promises of "good news to the poor" (4:18) are at work here. Jesus also unfolds how in the realm of God, interconnected relationships of community and economy are of utmost importance. This web of interconnection also stretches into the life beyond this life. Jesus will make another judgment about what will happen beyond this life when he promises the God-fearing thief at his side during the crucifixion, "Truly I tell you, today you will be with me in Paradise" (23:40–43). This open-endedness in narrative design allows preachers to invite response from multiple points of entry.

In making their way to Luke, preachers may want to point to the variety of ways the Bible discusses relationships of wealth and neighbor. Taken as a whole, the Bible provides a "multiple learnings styles" approach for guidance. Jesus' narrative, open-ended, indirect speech fills out the variety of speech types or genres by which the canon addresses the larger theme of humanity's relationships with wealth and neighbor. For this Sunday in the lectionary alone, other types of speech present a larger picture of instruction. The prophetic declaration of Amos 6:1a, 4–7 cries out, "Alas for those who are at ease in Zion, and for those who feel secure on Mount Samaria. . . . Alas for those who lie on beds of ivory, and lounge on their couches, and eat lambs from the flock, and calves from the stall." It is not difficult to see the rich man through the eyes of Amos.

At the same time, Psalm 146 sings praise to the God "who keeps faith forever; who executes justice for the oppressed; who gives food to the hungry" (Ps. 146:6–7). Here we might see God's care for Lazarus and God's hand in the rich man's undoing: "The LORD lifts up those who are bowed down; the LORD loves the righteous. The LORD watches over the strangers; he upholds the orphan and the widow, but the way of the wicked he brings to ruin" (vv. 8–9). If the five brothers know this—and according to Abraham they should—and if they live accordingly, they will avoid the torment their brother endures.

Rounding out the canonical chorus, the lectionary complements the other readings with 1 Timothy 6:6–19, which champions contentment with the basic necessities of life and the pursuit of godliness. Here we find the aphorism that has made its way into the cultural lexicon: "For the love of money is a root of all kinds of evil" (1 Tim. 6:10). Oddly enough, and certainly worthy of note, like the Lukan parable this verse is also often divorced from its context. Indeed, the verse continues, "and in their eagerness to be rich some have wandered away from the faith and pierced themselves with many pains." Surely the rich man's self-inflicted pain can be seen here too. Wandering away from the faith means wandering away from the one who was positioned right outside his gate. The rich man has no one to blame but himself for the position in which he finds himself.

These texts speak in concert with one another, yielding themselves to a rich interplay, especially given the perspective of some of the characters in Luke's story. Canonically speaking, the biblical witness speaks univocally about the dual, integrally related dangers wealth presents: the temptation to ignore neighbor, and the possibility of opening a chasm between ourselves and God by that inaction. The canon also speaks of God's perpetual care (or, "preferential option," to use the language of liberation theology) for those who are economically and socially disadvantaged. The Lukan Jesus does not deviate from the path set by the witness of the Hebrew Bible. The early-church witness of 1 Timothy continues to build on these foundations. There is a thematic unity regarding the relationships between how humanity negotiates relationships with wealth, neighbor, and God.

Homiletically speaking, the multiple genres of speech in this week's lectionary context (parable, prophetic declaration, song of praise, aphorism) might indicate to us that there is no one way that the preacher must speak about the sticky subject of wealth and related issues of materialism, abundance, and care for neighbor. Jesus' introduction of indirect, parabolic speech suggests the freedom to go beyond aphoristic, direct speech, markers by which many preachers might characterize what constitutes "prophetic preaching." Through carefully chosen narrative structure, rounded characters, and detail, even in its brevity the parable moves toward speech that humanizes those who are disadvantaged, evokes human pathos, and allows listeners to inhabit the kind of narrative space that encourages their participation (with whom do we identify in this story, if anyone?). It is also speech that intentionally seeks to provoke further thought and action by way of narrative as well (what do we do now?). This is part of what makes this parable so powerful and why we return to it so often: it demands continual conversion. It narrates the twists and turns of discipleship in the context of Luke's unfolding narrative of Jesus' journey to Jerusalem, where he faces torment at the hands of the powerful elite and, ultimately, vindication by God.

RICHARD W. VOELZ

Commentary 2: Connecting the Reading with the World

In many respects, the parable in Luke 16:19–31 is quintessentially the message of Jesus directed to the rich and poor alike. Luke's Gospel is a political message, like those of the prophets. The parables told by Jesus are continuations of the wisdom of the prophets (see Luke 4:14–30). Jesus' parables are invitations to deeper, more expansive faith with a keen awareness of the cultural and political complexities of being faithful followers in community. The parable of the Rich Man and Lazarus is a tale of caution and foreboding to those with wealth, societal privilege, and affluence. Equally, it is a tale of comfort for those who have been forsaken by their neighbors. The parable is a reinscription of the Golden Rule: do to others as you would have done to you (Luke 6:31).

The parable of the Rich Man and Lazarus opens with Jesus describing the rich man. The wealthy man wears fine clothes and dines sumptuously every day. Living in a gated house, the man has enough real estate and possessions to necessitate security. One would assume that a man of such status would have a name worth articulating. Jesus, however, gives the rich man no name. The rich man, in the eyes of the storyteller, is a nobody. Juxtaposed to the unnamed rich man is a man named Lazarus. While this is not the Lazarus of the Fourth Gospel, the listener is given the impression of Jesus' personal knowledge of the man because of the vivid description of his body and his day-to-day torment. Lazarus is introduced in the story as a sickly, poor man so downtrodden that he lies begging for food at the property gate of the rich man. The storyteller makes Lazarus's plight more vivid by describing the painful sores that cover Lazarus's ailing body. As a man stricken by poverty, the starving man is tormented by dogs who would lick his sores—surely a ghastly and excruciating situation to endure! Lazarus's name is familiar to Jesus, and his situation is empathically known by Jesus.

Interpreting the parable requires attention to both what is said and what is not said. Jesus, the storyteller, spins a tale with exaggerated characters and an overly simplified, dichotomized situation to make the message clear. Like many good storytellers, Jesus invites the listener to consider the plight of both characters and then decide for himself or herself the "why" of the result—in this case, damnation. The conversation between the rich man and Abraham reveals that the rich man, even though he chose to ignore Lazarus while languishing at his gate, knows Lazarus. While the rich man is tormented in Hades, his conversation with Abraham and his request of Lazarus reveal that he still feels entitled to ask for service, care, and consideration from those of the lower class. Even in Hades, the rich man wants the labor of the poor to support his family. Their fates on earth have been reversed in the afterlife, yet the rich man believes he, even from Hades, has more privilege than Lazarus, in heaven. The arrogance is astounding and skillfully portrayed by the storyteller.

Furthermore, the story does not tell us what Lazarus would tell the brothers, were he to be dispatched. We must read between the lines. Would Lazarus tell the brothers to be more generous and kind to the poor? Would Lazarus inform the brothers to get rid of their wealth? Perhaps Lazarus would tell the brothers that the kind of privilege provided by money is not the kind of privilege that merits eternity with Abraham. Using our sanctified imaginations helps to see the many lessons of the parable.

Our imaginations can also help us see the storyteller's use of irony. No doubt, the rich man had a lavish and extravagant "homegoing" or funeral where the family and neighbors made a huge showing of their grief for the dearly departed—only for the rich man to go to Hades. The storyteller helps us see the distorted values of society, the oppressive systems that keep these values in place, and the ironic ways Christians portend faithfulness.

The fact that the rich man ends up in Hades while Lazarus is with Abraham in paradise is an indication of judgment of both men. The story does not explicitly identify the rich man's wrongdoing or the goodness of Lazarus. We do know that the villain of the story is the man who possessed status, wealth, and power, but ignored the plight of the needy. His societal values left him so bereft that even in Hades, he does not understand the notions of compassion, equity, or justice. Lazarus, in heaven, was likely not blessed simply because he was poor, but because he was mistreated by his neighbor, who could have relieved his suffering. In this parable, heaven is for those who are forsaken by others.

The message of this parable was radical in Jesus' time and is radical in this digital age. God is on the side of the oppressed, poor, marginalized, and downtrodden. God judges those with means, wealth, privilege, and social status who ignore the poor and who make invisible the voiceless, marginalized, and minoritized. The liberation struggle of the poor is the clear mandate of this narrative. God is the God of rich (wo)men and the Lazaruses of this world and the next world. The interconnectedness of our social existence is profound. Those with wealth are cautioned to end their isolation from the poor and to develop ways to work with and on behalf of the poor or risk torment.

This story is a chilling caution to those who place confidence in financial security over a life of service to neighbor. The parable teaches that divine judgment is concerned with our use of resources, wealth, and finances in this life, as these have consequences for the next life. Our task is to use wealth for ministry—for relieving suffering and edifying the marginalized. Actions other than compassion and openheartedness put persons in jeopardy of an afterlife of misery.

The sorrow songs of the African American tradition can help illumine the lesson(s) of this parable. In a chapter devoted to sorrow songs in *The Souls of Black Folk*, W. E. B. Du Bois describes sorrow songs as folk songs remembered by those who survived North American chattel slavery. Du Bois wrote that sorrow songs are "the most beautiful expression of human experience born this side the seas. It has been neglected, it has been, and is, half despised, and above all it has been persistently mistaken and misunderstood; but notwithstanding, it still remains as the singular spiritual heritage of the nation and the greatest gift of the [African American] people [to the United States]."[1] Examples of sorrow songs are "Rock-a My Soul in the Bosom of Abraham," "Soon-a Will Be Done," "No Hidin' Place," "Steal Away," "Deep River," "Go Down, Moses," "Ezekiel Saw the Wheel," "I Got a Home in the Rock," and "Lay This Body Down." Sorrow songs seek to expose the injustices of the world and hold to the hope of divine vindication and liberation in this life as well as the next.

You probably will not be teaching and preaching to persons who resonate only with the rich man or only with Lazarus, because your community will have a diversity of persons. The gospel instructs the faithful to attend to those less fortunate in our midst. Jesus, in telling this story, hoped that the people might repent before death and judgment. The judgment of the Divine is not capricious or arbitrary but squarely connected to faithfully living committed to justice.

NANCY LYNNE WESTFIELD

1. W. E. B. Du Bois, *The Souls of Black Folk; Essays and Sketches* (Chicago: A. C. McClurg & Co., 1903), 537.

Proper 22 (Sunday between October 2 and October 8 Inclusive)

Lamentations 1:1–6 and Habakkuk 1:1–4; 2:1–4
Lamentations 3:19–26 and Psalm 137, Psalm 37:1–9
2 Timothy 1:1–14
Luke 17:5–10

Lamentations 1:1–6

[1]How lonely sits the city
that once was full of people!
How like a widow she has become,
she that was great among the nations!
She that was a princess among the provinces
has become a vassal.

[2]She weeps bitterly in the night,
with tears on her cheeks;
among all her lovers
she has no one to comfort her;
all her friends have dealt treacherously with her,
they have become her enemies.

[3]Judah has gone into exile with suffering
and hard servitude;
she lives now among the nations,
and finds no resting place;
her pursuers have all overtaken her
in the midst of her distress.

[4]The roads to Zion mourn,
for no one comes to the festivals;
all her gates are desolate,
her priests groan;
her young girls grieve,
and her lot is bitter.

[5]Her foes have become the masters,
her enemies prosper,
because the LORD has made her suffer
for the multitude of her transgressions;
her children have gone away,
captives before the foe.

[6]From daughter Zion has departed
all her majesty.
Her princes have become like stags
that find no pasture;
they fled without strength
before the pursuer.

Habakkuk 1:1–4; 2:1–4

[1]The oracle that the prophet Habakkuk saw.
[2]O LORD, how long shall I cry for help,
  and you will not listen?
Or cry to you "Violence!"
  and you will not save?
[3]Why do you make me see wrongdoing
  and look at trouble?
Destruction and violence are before me;
  strife and contention arise.
[4]So the law becomes slack
  and justice never prevails.
The wicked surround the righteous—
  therefore judgment comes forth perverted.

. . . .

[2:1]I will stand at my watchpost,
  and station myself on the rampart;
I will keep watch to see what he will say to me,
  and what he will answer concerning my complaint.
[2]Then the LORD answered me and said:
Write the vision;
  make it plain on tablets,
  so that a runner may read it.
[3]For there is still a vision for the appointed time;
  it speaks of the end, and does not lie.
If it seems to tarry, wait for it;
  it will surely come, it will not delay.
[4]Look at the proud!
  Their spirit is not right in them,
  but the righteous live by their faith.

Commentary 1: Connecting the Reading with Scripture

In 1983, the son of well-known theologian Nicholas Wolterstorff died in a tragic climbing accident in Austria. Like most parents who lose a child, Wolterstorff passed through a deep sorrow that consumed and almost devoured him. Years later, in *Lament for a Son,* he catalogued the doubts and questions that plagued him after his son's death, asking, "Will my eyes adjust to this darkness? Will I find you [God] in the dark—not in the streaks of light which remain, but in the darkness. . . . And are there songs for singing when the light has gone dim? Or in the dark, is it best to wait in silence?"[1] *Lament for a Son* modernizes an ancient Hebrew practice. Biblical writers brought their laments to God, even when their questions and doubts brought them to the brink of unbelief.

In the first lection, Lamentations 1:1–6, the writer laments over the darkness that has befallen Zion. Lamentations 1, twenty-two verses long, is an alphabetic acrostic poem in the same vein as chapters 2–4. It can be divided into two main

1. Nicholas Wolterstorff, *Lament for a Son* (Grand Rapids: Eerdmans, 1987), 15.

sections. In verses 1–11, the writer laments over Zion in the third person with an occasional interjection (e.g., v. 9c), and, in verses 12–22, Zion "speaks" in the first person to bear witness to its suffering. Traditionally attributed to Jeremiah in the sixth century BCE, a time when most of Israel's leaders had been carried into exile, the book of Lamentations functions as a prolonged lament. Where is God? Does God care? Has God abandoned us? What do we do when all we see is darkness?

Verse 1 describes the swift fall of Zion, the symbol of the kingdom and its people. The city that once burgeoned with inhabitants is now "lonely" (v. 1a). This word means "desolated" or "deserted" (see Isa. 27:10). At one time, Zion ruled as a "princess among the provinces"; now it is a vassal to foreign enemies. It was "great among the nations" but is now a widow: vulnerable, unsafe, in mourning. Like a widow, Zion weeps bitterly at night and has "no one to comfort her," a refrain that appears also in verses 9, 16, 17, and 21. The lovers and friends described in verse 2b represent the foreign nations whose shallow allegiances have shifted from friend to foe, now that the political tide has turned in their favor. Consequently, Judah has been carried into exilic servitude. Its enemies pursue it like a hunter, an image that occurs in verses 3c and 6c. Instead of finding rest in the promised land, Judah "finds no resting place" in exile (v. 3b; cf. 5:5).

Verses 4–6 reveal that the darkness touches everyone and everything: priests groan (v. 4b), young girls grieve (v. 4c), children are carried into captivity (v. 5), and princes flee like stags from their hunters (v. 6b–c). Even the roads mourn for want of the festivals that once adorned them (v. 4a). The majesty of Zion has departed (v. 6); only questions remain. The writer does not so much assign blame as acknowledge God's role in punishing the nation's disobedience. Darkness covers Zion because God has made it "suffer for the multitude of [its] transgressions" (v. 5; cf. 1:14, 15, 21).

In the second lection, Habakkuk 1:1–4 and 2:1–4, the writer uses lament to express anger toward God (Hab. 1:1–4), and God responds with a revelation (2:1–4). The historical situation of these verses—and the entire book, for that matter—confounds biblical scholars. The book of Habakkuk offers little-to-no description of its author, setting, and referent. Even the meaning of the name Habakkuk remains unclear. The majority view is that the Chaldean enemies spoken of in 1:6 are the Babylonians and that the book was written sometime around the fall of Jerusalem in 597 BCE. Despite these uncertainties, the book still speaks powerfully to people of various ages, races, and cultures on account of its raw subject matter. The writer wrestles through some of the fundamental questions of human existence. Why do the wicked prosper and the righteous suffer? Why is God inactive and even absent in the midst of profound injustice and wickedness? Remember Wolterstorff: "Will I find you in the dark?"

Habakkuk 1:1–4 asks two big questions and then laments the lack of answers: How long? and Why? (vv. 2–3). How long must I cry out for help to God with no revelation and no rescue? Why would a good God allow such violence and wickedness without doing anything? The consequences of God's inactivity reveal themselves in verse 4: Torah becomes "slack" (that is, "numb"), justice never wins, the wicked attack, and justice is perverted. Both questions are common in Scripture. How long? recurs in various forms in the Psalms (Pss. 13:1–2; 35:17; 89:46) and also in the heavenly vision of Revelation 6:10. Why? threads its way through several books of the Bible, especially the Psalms and Job. Even Jesus asks, "Why?" when he quotes from Psalm 22:1 in his cry of dereliction from the cross: "My God, my God, why have you forsaken me?" (Mark 15:34).

Habakkuk waits for an answer to How long? and Why? In 2:1, he stands at his watch post (cf. Ezek. 33:7; Hos. 9:8) to see what answer God will give to his complaint. The Hebrew word for "complaint" often occurred in the context of lawsuits. In a sense, Habakkuk has taken God to court and is waiting for God's counterargument. The answer finally comes through a vision (Hab. 2:2). The Lord instructs Habakkuk to write the revelation down so that a runner may read it, that is, deliver it to others. Verses 3b–4 lift up a series of contrasts: God's trustworthy vision will surely come and will not lie;

the vision may be slow in coming, but wait for it; and, the unrighteous have a spirit that is not right ("a crooked soul"), but the righteous will live by their faith.

To be sure, the final phrase in verse 4 merits a book-length treatment, especially because of how important it is to the theology of the apostle Paul (cf. Rom. 1:17; Gal. 3:11) and, much later, the Reformer Martin Luther. The LXX version of this verse also appears in Hebrews 10:38. Some of the debates surround translation issues: Is it "faith" or "faithfulness"? Is it "his faith" or "their faith"? The answers actually raise more questions. Key questions of this verse in its context include: Faith in what? Faith in whom? The answers come a few verses earlier: faith in a vision that does not lie and faith in a God who answers our complaints. In the end, the promise comes to those who believe in a trustworthy revelation from God: "There is still a vision!"

The cries of anguish in Habakkuk 1 and Lamentations 1 remind readers that, when faced with a choice between denying their tears and despairing in their tears, the prophets choose neither. Instead, they pray their tears. As Francis I. Andersen reminds us, "The freedom with which the prophet has the matter out with God shows how deep is the bond between them. His agony is caused by the very strength of his theological convictions."[2] To lament is to bring one's agony before God, to trust that God is big enough to handle unanswered questions, and to hang on to hope that somehow a vision is still possible in the darkness.

JARED E. ALCÁNTARA

Commentary 2: Connecting the Reading with the World

Words of true prophets work on multiple levels and convey a variety of meanings and interpretations. At every level, these words *convict*, a concept meaning "to prove guilt or responsibility." Throughout Lamentations and Habakkuk, the authors hold up a mirror that reveals the painful and powerful truth that actions have consequences.

On a personal level, the city of God is compared to a lonely widow, one who once enjoyed honor, glory, reverence, and admiration from all the nations. Now she sits in desolation, abandoned and bereft, unable to completely understand what has happened to her. How many of us experience situations where we feel left out or left behind, forgotten and alone? In such circumstances, it is common to become resentful and bitter, feeling victimized and ill treated. The sense of injustice and mistreatment can become overwhelming. When we wallow in victimization, we lose objectivity and the ability to see ways we contribute to our own condition. The prophets remark that the city suffers "for the multitude of her transgressions." Actions have consequences. The desolate city is not without blame. As with any of us at the darkest and most despairing times in our lives, rarely are we without responsibility for what we feel and experience. If our relationships turn sour, generally we play some part in their decay. How often are we punished for the things we do not do? How often do we feel put upon when the consequences of our actions come home to us?

On another level, these Scriptures speak across the centuries to entire cultures where taking responsibility becomes anathema, where whatever happens is always someone else's fault or failing. We are living in such times. Persons in politics and government constantly play a blame game, accusing opposing parties and individuals of malicious intent, corruption, and conspiracy. Our courts are filled with nuisance claims that assign guilt while abdicating responsibility. A student, punished by his parents for not doing his homework, sues them for emotional trauma—and wins. A young woman hears a sermon on responsibility to the poor and marginalized that she claims made her so

2. Francis I. Andersen, *Habakkuk*, Anchor Bible (New York: Doubleday, 2001), 109.

uncomfortable that she had to leave the church. A professor is fired for using terminology that a student finds objectionable. "The wicked surround the righteous—therefore judgment comes forth perverted." We live in a time of "fake news" and "alternative facts," and many people are deeply offended when they are asked to be accountable for their words and actions. The writers of the prophetic Scriptures clearly proclaim that such actions have consequences, and until we are ready to accept responsibility, things cannot change for the better.

There is also an ecclesial level of interpretation to these passages. The church is as guilty as the dominant culture for the current state of affairs. Faithfulness to God gives way to squabbles and controversies within the fellowship. Those core values that unite us—love of God, devotion to Christ, baptism in water and the Spirit—lose focus as we debate gender identity, inclusiveness, and carpet color. We have important decisions to make, but lesser matters displace ultimate concern.

What then is our witness to the world? Are we a faithful spouse or a desolate widow? Do we rejoice in the potential for blessing that is ours, or do we mourn bitterly losses of money, prestige, power, and honor? Are we more focused on being faithful to the work and will of God, or are we angry and afraid because fewer people are coming to see what we might have to offer? If Protestant Christianity is suffering, do we seek a cause to blame, or do we accept responsibility for the ways we have created our own reality? The words of the prophet are clear: where we find ourselves today is in a destination of our own making and design.

Throughout Lamentations, there is a pervasive sense of despair. Not only has the relationship to God been broken; there is fear that it is broken beyond repair. This is an important message at every level—personal, cultural, within the fellowship, and beyond to our communities. The prophet's words challenge the listeners to wake up to the steps that brought the people to this forsaken state. Beyond guilt, the writer is inviting hearers to own their shame. The reality is that we have done this to ourselves. This was a devastating admission for the "people of God." God's people are protected, special, and holy. Nothing bad can happen to God's people. This was the myth created by the priests to define and describe the Hebrew children.

When people live under a beneficent mythology like this, they come to take for granted their elevated and superior position. The artificial divisions between "us" and the multitude of "thems" take on a quality all their own. We are too good for this to be our own doing.

At a personal level, we should take a hard, honest, and painful look at all we have thought, said, and done. At a communal level, we should be down on our knees apologizing to God and one another for our unfaithfulness and selfish behavior. We should confess every way we have been unkind, unfair, unfeeling, unthinking, and unfaithful. At a global level, we should ask forgiveness for apathy in the face of suffering, comfort in the face of violence, and indifference in the face of injustice. We should acknowledge any and all ways we look to our own means and devices to live lives of security and luxury, instead of trusting in the providence of God. Contrition in the face of guilt and shame is not to be an occasional occurrence, but the ongoing process for faithful humility, individually and communally.

On a more universal level, Lamentations and Habakkuk describe a situation of exile and estrangement where there is simply no reasonable or rational expectation for forgiveness or restoration. Yet God is so much greater than our human hopes or expectations. Our God is a unifying force of reconciliation and peace. Beyond justice defined as what is deserved, the justice of God is one of wholeness, harmony, and grace. Unfaithful Jerusalem, scorned by her many "lovers," has no right to ask to be forgiven and taken back—but God's ways are not our ways. Jerusalem can be restored to her former glory, if only she repents and renews her covenantal vow. We may feel that our politics is too corrupt and that government is the problem, not the solution, but God is merciful and there is always hope.

Each individual is guilty of sin and should feel a certain shame at failing to be the person God calls us to be. As a people of God, a congregation of faithful believers, we should remember that we are made one in Christ, and the failing of one impacts us all. God wants and needs us as members of our global household to be a loving, caring, obedient, and just people. This is true individually, relationally within and beyond the congregation, and in every encounter we have in the world. Together, we can be the witness for God that is beyond any one of us individually. By God's grace, we will each day become more than we were the day before. This is the power and mercy of God at work in the world—helping us to become together that which is impossible on our own.

DAN R. DICK

Proper 22 (Sunday between October 2 and October 8 Inclusive)

Lamentations 3:19–26

[19]The thought of my affliction and my homelessness
is wormwood and gall!
[20]My soul continually thinks of it
and is bowed down within me.
[21]But this I call to mind,
and therefore I have hope:

[22]The steadfast love of the LORD never ceases,
his mercies never come to an end;
[23]they are new every morning;
great is your faithfulness.
[24]"The LORD is my portion," says my soul,
"therefore I will hope in him."

[25]The LORD is good to those who wait for him,
to the soul that seeks him.
[26]It is good that one should wait quietly
for the salvation of the LORD.

Psalm 137

[1]By the rivers of Babylon—
there we sat down and there we wept
when we remembered Zion.
[2]On the willows there
we hung up our harps.
[3]For there our captors
asked us for songs,
and our tormentors asked for mirth, saying,
"Sing us one of the songs of Zion!"

[4]How could we sing the LORD's song
in a foreign land?
[5]If I forget you, O Jerusalem,
let my right hand wither!
[6]Let my tongue cling to the roof of my mouth,
if I do not remember you,
if I do not set Jerusalem
above my highest joy.

[7]Remember, O LORD, against the Edomites
the day of Jerusalem's fall,
how they said, "Tear it down! Tear it down!
Down to its foundations!"

[8]O daughter Babylon, you devastator!
Happy shall they be who pay you back
what you have done to us!
[9]Happy shall they be who take your little ones
and dash them against the rock!

Psalm 37:1–9

[1]Do not fret because of the wicked;
do not be envious of wrongdoers,
[2]for they will soon fade like the grass,
and wither like the green herb.

[3]Trust in the LORD, and do good;
so you will live in the land, and enjoy security.
[4]Take delight in the LORD,
and he will give you the desires of your heart.

[5]Commit your way to the LORD;
trust in him, and he will act.
[6]He will make your vindication shine like the light,
and the justice of your cause like the noonday.

[7]Be still before the LORD, and wait patiently for him;
do not fret over those who prosper in their way,
over those who carry out evil devices.

[8]Refrain from anger, and forsake wrath.
Do not fret—it leads only to evil.
[9]For the wicked shall be cut off,
but those who wait for the LORD shall inherit the land.

Connecting the Psalm to Scripture and Worship

Psalm 37:1–9. Has YHWH ceased to be YHWH? This question, and nothing less, confronts YHWH's community, through the words of Habakkuk: "How long shall I cry for help, and you will not listen? Or cry to you 'Violence!' and you will not save?" (Hab. 1:2). The question in Habakkuk is expressed in the classic parallel fashion characteristic of Hebrew poetic form. Repetition adds emphasis to the text and may serve as a mnemonic and liturgical device of considerable power. The negation of divine attentiveness ("not listening") is a reversal of the hard-won insight at the heart of the community's hope (Gen. 21:17–20). The suggestion that YHWH "will not save" is a thought beyond the known experience of the God whose name itself is synonymous with deliverance (Ps. 68:20). Has YHWH ceased to be YHWH? (cf. Pss. 22:1–2; 88).

Psalm 37, an acrostic psalm lodged within the first of the five sections or "movements" of the Psalter, may be viewed as an answer to Habakkuk's cry (Hab. 1:2) arising out of the gathered community in the midst of worship and prayer.

The psalm is a poem of instruction, a Wisdom psalm in which those whose relationship with YHWH locates them among the "righteous" (Ps. 37:16, 17, 21, 25, 28, 29, 30, 32, 39) will eventually flourish, while the "wicked" will certainly and with shocking suddenness come to bad ends (vv. 1–2, 9–10, 12–15, 20–22, 36, 38). A sense of the "short run" compared to the "long haul" soaks the poem in references to age (v. 25), offspring (v. 26), patience (vv. 7, 9, 34), and YHWH's sovereign knowledge of the ordained (ethical) direction of time itself (vv. 13, 18–19, 27).

The psalm underscores that success is fleeting and the wicked will "fade like the grass" (v. 1), a striking image in a region of the Near East where vegetation quickly perishes at the end of the rains each spring. YHWH "loves justice" and "will not forsake" those who are faithful (v. 28). The righteous are not to "fret" (NRSV; better Robert Alter's translation: not to become "incensed"[1]), which "leads only to evil" (v. 8). As for the wicked (vv. 2, 7, 8), their "sword shall enter their own heart" and their "bows shall be broken" (v. 15). They will vanish "like smoke" (v. 20). "The righteous," though, "shall inherit the land, and live in it forever" (v. 29), as YHWH has promised.

The community wonders and asks: Has YHWH ceased to be YHWH? While the answer makes its way toward them, it is not to "fretting" that the community is called (vv. 1, 8) but to "keeping" YHWH's just and merciful way (v. 34), and to the worship of YHWH alone, *regardless of the answer.*

Lamentations 3:19–26. Habakkuk's individual anguish takes communal voice in Lamentations 1. These verses struggle eloquently with the overwhelming suffering and grief of Zion as survivors stagger through the experience and memory of the Babylonian destruction of Jerusalem (the "Zion" tradition—Lamentations 1:4, 5, 17—underscores the chosen status and religious/cultic significance of the city, hence the amplification of horror at its ruin).

Where will the community now turn? Consolation is unavailable from any source (1:2); restoration is not on its blessed way, so even the paths to Jerusalem mourn (1:3–4). Have these roads become again the footpaths of alien gods? The triumph of enemies over Zion's priests and princes is total (1:4, 6). Worst of all, YHWH's covenant promises of "rest" (2 Sam. 7:11) in a secure land and of protection against enemies (Deut. 28:7) appear to have been vacated as a consequence of the people's covenant disobedience (1:5; cf. Deut. 28:15–19). The non-chosen, forbidden to enter YHWH's house, have done so (1:10). Zion has ceased to be Zion. YHWH is now "like an enemy" (Lam. 2:5a). Has YHWH ceased to be YHWH?

The canticle in Lamentations 3:19–26 begins with the summary statement of a different, and new, voice compared to the forlorn voices that have admitted and explored disastrous guilt in chapters 1 and 2 (1:6, 20; 2:4). Old words return new again in this chapter ("steadfast love" and "mercies," v. 22; "portion," v. 24; "good," vv. 26–29; "you heard my plea," v. 56; "You came near," v. 57). They rise out of a declaration of suffering (vv. 1–20), but they imagine a new day.

There is a "call to mind" (or "heart") that begins to allow hope in the future. The community has experienced divine retribution to the fullest extent, and for this speaker, it is *from* YHWH: "He has filled me with bitterness, he has sated me with wormwood" (v. 15; cf. Ruth 1:20; Ps. 119:25). Yet this condition is not forever (Lam. 3:31). The basis for the speaker's hope is none other than YHWH. While YHWH punishes (2:1–9), YHWH limits punishment (3:31). Even in punishment, YHWH's commitment to covenant promises never expires (v. 22a), and YHWH's "mercies" (from the noun for "womb"; cf. Jonah 4:2) "never reach an end" (v. 22b). This is the wisdom waiting in the ruins to lead to a future. In an echo of the "good" first pronounced over creation (Gen. 1:4, 10, 12, 18, 21, 25, 31) and possible to see only as shimmering hope in the fire of the moment (Lam. 2:3, 4), the adjective "good" returns to the narrative and takes first position in the next two clauses (Lam. 3:25, 26, also 27), evoking themes of wisdom, not as a justification

1. Robert Alter, *The Book of Psalms* (New York: W. W. Norton, 2007), 129.

or explanation for loss, but nevertheless rising out of that loss: "Good is the Lord to those who wait for him, to the soul that seeks him. Good it is that one should wait quietly for the Lord" (3:25–26, my trans.). The speaker's hope has finished its search; it will rest in YHWH alone, YHWH of covenant fidelity and womb-love. When Zion and the land were new and YHWH granted to each tribe its share, the priests were not allotted a share and were sustained only by what is offered to YHWH. They had to depend on YHWH alone. That is the situation now for the devastated community. YHWH, nothing else, is their only true "portion" (v. 24).[2]

Psalm 137. Psalm 137, a lament song of the community in memory of Babylonian exile, continues the theme of Lamentations' bitter, ruined, and lonely city. Their captors assume the music of their captives (Zion tradition) may now be enjoyed as entertainment. The verbs translated "forget" and "wither" (NRSV, Ps. 137:5), from the same Hebrew root, create a play on sound that deepens the pathos of their individual clauses. The musician poets do not simply refuse to entertain; they call down a curse upon themselves if they should be tempted to any vocation other than their covenantal destiny, which is bound to lost Zion. To that curse they add an invective wishing revenge upon their enemies, perhaps remembering the terrors of their own losses, perhaps even within the legal range of talion, not explicitly but obliquely (v. 9) raising the specter of sacralized violence and its crimson stain.[3] Has YHWH ceased to be YHWH?

E. CARSON BRISSON

2. Duane Garrett and Paul R. House, *Song of Songs, Lamentations*, Word Biblical Commentary 23B (Nashville: Thomas Nelson, 2004), 415.
3. James L. Crenshaw, *The Psalms: An Introduction* (Grand Rapids: Eerdmans, 2001), 68.

Proper 22 (Sunday between October 2 and October 8 Inclusive)

2 Timothy 1:1–14

[1]Paul, an apostle of Christ Jesus by the will of God, for the sake of the promise of life that is in Christ Jesus,

[2]To Timothy, my beloved child:

Grace, mercy, and peace from God the Father and Christ Jesus our Lord.

[3]I am grateful to God—whom I worship with a clear conscience, as my ancestors did—when I remember you constantly in my prayers night and day. [4]Recalling your tears, I long to see you so that I may be filled with joy. [5]I am reminded of your sincere faith, a faith that lived first in your grandmother Lois and your mother Eunice and now, I am sure, lives in you. [6]For this reason I remind you to rekindle the gift of God that is within you through the laying on of my hands; [7]for God did not give us a spirit of cowardice, but rather a spirit of power and of love and of self-discipline.

[8]Do not be ashamed, then, of the testimony about our Lord or of me his prisoner, but join with me in suffering for the gospel, relying on the power of God, [9]who saved us and called us with a holy calling, not according to our works but according to his own purpose and grace. This grace was given to us in Christ Jesus before the ages began, [10]but it has now been revealed through the appearing of our Savior Christ Jesus, who abolished death and brought life and immortality to light through the gospel. [11]For this gospel I was appointed a herald and an apostle and a teacher, [12]and for this reason I suffer as I do. But I am not ashamed, for I know the one in whom I have put my trust, and I am sure that he is able to guard until that day what I have entrusted to him. [13]Hold to the standard of sound teaching that you have heard from me, in the faith and love that are in Christ Jesus. [14]Guard the good treasure entrusted to you, with the help of the Holy Spirit living in us.

Commentary 1: Connecting the Reading with Scripture

Second Timothy stands in the tradition of a farewell discourse. Many biblical figures offer words of wisdom as they depart: think of Moses offering his blessing before he was allowed to see, but not enter, the promised land; Elijah granting Elisha a double portion of his blessing before rising up on the fiery chariot; Jesus' long discourse in John 13–17 giving the disciples the new commandment and promising the gift of the Holy Spirit. Few farewell discourses are as personal and as touching as Paul's farewell here in 2 Timothy. Paul remembers Timothy's tears and the gift of faith handed down to him through his mother and grandmother, and vulnerably shares his own suffering as well.

The immediate context bears fruit when it comes to understanding the nature of Paul's suffering. While Paul alludes to his incarceration in verse 8, the immediate context sheds more light on the full scope of Paul's pain. Just after the pericope, in 2 Timothy 1:15 Paul writes: "You are aware that all who are in Asia have turned away from me, including Phygelus and Hermogenes." We do not have any other information about Phygelus and Hermogenes other than that they have turned on Paul along with all of Asia, he writes. Given his quick acknowledgment of Onesiphorus and his household's care for him, this is likely Pauline hyperbole. This kind of overstatement points to the depth of Paul's grief. Even if all of Asia had not rejected him, it clearly feels like it to him as he writes this. Not only imprisoned, Paul is rejected by those with whom he lived and to whom he preached.

The preacher might consider the incredible strength that stems not only from Paul's faith, but also from the power Paul draws from his place in God's grace and the tradition in which he finds himself. Unlike our individualist culture, Paul's is a collectivist milieu. Community, tradition, and God define Paul's understanding of himself. When Paul introduces himself, he does so by claiming his place in relationship to the apostles. When Paul articulates his faith, he claims his heritage proudly: "I am grateful to God—whom I worship with a clear conscience, as my ancestors did" (1:3). When he addresses Timothy, Paul does not just speak to this young man as an individual but recognizes Timothy as standing firmly in the faith of his mother and grandmother, Eunice and Lois. Paul thinks of God's grace as something that has been given to us "before the ages" (v. 9), and he considers this grace and the teachings about it to be a kind of treasure that should be carefully guarded (v. 14). Paul does not imagine himself or Timothy as fearless individuals, heroically choosing the faith as an expression of their free will. Rather, the faith summons them. This understanding of the faith as something that summons rather than something we heroically choose—so counter to our individualistic age—is worth preaching again and again today.

In terms of the larger context of the letter, as well as the larger Pauline context, preachers would do well to notice the prominence Paul places on the women in Timothy's life. In the larger context of the Pastoral Epistles, Paul lifts up women by name several times. Later in 2 Timothy, along with Lois and Eunice, Paul mentions Prisca and Claudia by name (4:19, 21). Drawing on the enatic relationship between Paul and the churches to whom he gave birth, in *Our Mother Saint Paul*, Beverly Roberts Gaventa champions Paul's maternal imagery for himself. Especially in 1 Thessalonians 2:7, Galatians 4:19, and 1 Corinthians 3:1–12, Gaventa notes Paul employs maternal imagery to describe himself.[1] The preacher could effectively draw out the connection Lois and Eunice have with Timothy to elevate the often underappreciated role women have played in the church.

The lectionary readings introduce other interpretive possibilities. Grief hangs over this text. We are not sure exactly what tears Paul remembers Timothy shedding, but we know him in the context of sadness and a failing faith. The other lectionary readings amplify this theme. Lamentations 1:1–6, the OT lection, imagines Jerusalem as a widow with no one to comfort her. Psalm 137, set during the exile, asks how to sing the songs of Zion while living in a foreign land. In a world where few have direct experience with death, and grief is swept under the rug, preachers could connect these readings and explore the power of lamentation with their congregations.

Luke 17:5–10 is entirely different. In the Luke reading we find a problematic text. While Luke mentions the well-known proverb about having faith the size of mustard seed moving mountains, Luke also shares a troubling story from the lips of Jesus about slaves. Jesus asks us to imagine being a slave owner. Jesus tells us a slave owner does not thank the slave when their work is done, but rather simply expects the work to be done. Similarly, in response to the disciples asking Jesus to increase their faith, Jesus says they should just think of themselves as unworthy slaves who are just doing their job. This is an extremely difficult reading. In the same way Jesus is telling the disciples they do not require extra faith but simply need to work hard without considering their own merit, Paul exhorts Timothy to apply himself to the work of the gospel regardless of his personal feelings of sadness, of failure. This is not an easy word to preach, but in a hyperindividualistic age it can be liberating to imagine ourselves not as individual consumers and earners but part of something much greater than ourselves.

The wider canon brings other avenues of exploration. I was struck by Paul's writing about laying hands on Timothy. The laying on of hands is a common practice today, but its biblical roots are somewhat mysterious. In many instances, Jesus and the apostles lay hands on people to heal them. Jesus exclusively lays hands on people to heal them. In Acts 6:6 the apostles also lay hands on the Greek-speaking

1. Beverly Roberts Gaventa, *Our Mother Saint Paul* (Louisville, KY: Westminster John Knox, 2007).

disciples who, moving forward, will practice leadership in the church's mission. The OT is even more interesting. In Numbers 27:18 God instructs Moses to lay hands on Joshua as a way of ordaining his leadership. Throughout Leviticus priests are called to lay hands on animals being offered to God as a sacrifice. A preacher could consider reading this text as a jumping-off point to explore the biblical meaning of the laying on of hands.

Another possibility to explore is the unusual reference to immortality. In 2 Timothy 1:10, Paul discusses how Jesus brings life and immortality through his death. The Greek understanding of immortality, the belief in a preexisting soul that endures physical death, is quite distinct from the biblical understanding of immortality as eternal life in which our bodies are renewed in resurrection. While Paul references immortality three times in Romans and once in 1 Timothy, the vast majority of occurrences of this notion are found in the Wisdom of Solomon and other books in the Apocrypha.

Given the incredible multicultural exchanges taking place in the ancient world and in our own, preachers could explore how the word "immortality" is variously understood by some cultures. A preacher could discuss different biblical views of the afterlife and how these views made sense within those contexts. Using this as a springboard, preachers could consider how our own backgrounds and contexts shape and color our understanding of the world.

KEN EVERS-HOOD

Christ This Day Calls and Invites

You have a better opportunity than many others. You have the gospel preached to you. You are instructed in the way of salvation by him. And many others have no such privilege. Christ in his Word calls you to come to him. He invites, he bids you come, and welcome. . . . Christ calls all, men and women, young and old, and little children. All are invited to look to him that they may be saved. Christ gave directions to preach the gospel to every creature under heaven. Christ has provided a great feast. He has set his door wide open. Whosoever will, may come. You may come and eat without money. Come for nothing. Christ has paid the price, and you may come for nothing. Nothing is required of you for your escaping eternal burnings and having all the glory of heaven, but only to come to Christ for it with all your heart. You may have Christ for your Savior and may have all heaven, only if you will give Christ your hearts. Christ stands at the door and knocks. If you will open the door, he will come in and will give himself to you, and all that he has. Now is your opportunity, while life lasts. Christ never will invite you and offer himself to you anymore after you are dead. . . . Christ this day calls and invites you. I am his servant, and I invite you to come to him. Therefore make haste. Delay not. Give your heart to Christ and he will save you from hell, and all heaven shall be yours.

Jonathan Edwards, "He That Believeth Shall Be Saved," in *The Sermons of Jonathan Edwards: A Reader*, ed. Wilson H. Kimnach et al. (New Haven, CT: Yale University Press, 1999), 119–20.

Commentary 2: Connecting the Reading with the World

While this passage appears in the lectionary within Ordinary Time, it represents the importance of perceiving the extraordinary in the fabric of the ordinary—of ordering life in response to the extraordinary gift of God in Christ. Christians must remain alive to the wonder of God's ongoing redemption. Paul reminds Timothy to "fan the flame" (NRSV "rekindle," 2 Tim. 1:6), the gift of God. Only when we understand that our lives are lived before the eternal God, and that each day is a gift, can we truly engage in our human vocation, worship. There is nothing we can do to merit the grace of Jesus Christ. We are "saved and called" only "because of his own purpose and grace" (v. 9). This grace is none other than a glimpse of God's own gracious inner life issuing forth in creation and its redemption. Worship is a response of wonder to God's gift. In fact, all of ordinary life is to be lived in worshipful wonder, emulating God's own beauty, the love of God's own love, even unto suffering. None of this is possible without keeping the gift of God alive in our hearts and minds. This is one of the tasks of ordinary time to which Paul urges Timothy and the church of Ephesus.

Another recurring theme in this passage concerns the significance of family in passing on the faith from one generation to the next. Paul gives thanks to God whom he serves, as did also his Jewish ancestors. He reminds Timothy of his faith legacy handed on from his grandmother Lois and mother Eunice. This emphasis on intergenerational nurture points to several important realities for the church. We can grasp the importance of this legacy and intergenerational nurture points through Jesus' direct relationship with the apostles, to Paul, whose calling was justified by his Damascus-road encounter with Jesus, to the manifold spiritual baptism at Pentecost, to the passing down of Christian faith through the family, as in the case of Timothy. These variegated means of passing on the faith have one thing in common; they are relational. Here Paul points to a significant theological conclusion, that although faith in Christ cannot finally be limited to the work of family or other social structures, it is nevertheless possible for such relationships to transmit faith. When Paul refers to Timothy's mother and grandmother, he is not pointing to any random social practice but specifically highlights the mother-child dyad as a medium for faith. Christian faith is not commonly transmitted by just any random, exploitative, or oppressive sociocultural practice; a loving nurturing family can be a vessel exemplifying in form and content the self-giving love of God in Christ. It is no accident that parts of the Christian church in recent decades have emphasized the family, especially as cultural conditions across many institutions have excluded an ethic of care.

In addition to Paul's acknowledgment of the importance of family, his remedy for fanning the flames of a waning faith is also embodied through "the laying on of hands" (v. 6). Laying hands on a fellow seeker or ordinand was for early Christians a means of imparting the Spirit. Modern Christians have sadly viewed such practice as symbolic only and have abandoned it in many quarters. Essentially, the laying on of hands as a means of conveying God's Spirit is a reminder that Christian truth is not "gnosis"—that is, it is not the passing on of knowledge alone. God's truth is incarnational—mediated through the incarnate Christ, who calls us to be mediators of his truth through who we are, what we do and through our corporate entities.

Some scholars believe that Paul may have written this letter while suffering from an illness (vv. 6–12) and possibly nearing the end of his life. This would make his stress on passing on the gospel tradition all the more important. Erik Erikson suggests that the end stages of human life involve generativity and integrity—making a positive contribution and having the confidence that one's life has mattered.[2] Arguably, this is one way to characterize, in psychological terms, Paul's instructions to Timothy as a concern for ensuring that his work has mattered and will live after him.

Here we can grasp an important theological point about suffering. Paul suffers, whether through illness or persecution, as a herald and apostle of Jesus Christ. He urges the church in Ephesus to suffer along with him for the sake of the gospel. Always, Paul's model is the life, death, and resurrection of Jesus. Paul's (and the church's) suffering is transformed by the suffering Christ, who did not surrender but conquered death. Christian faith is faith in the incarnate, loving God who suffered in his human body through his life and death on the cross; therefore, Christian suffering is identified with our hope in the resurrected Christ. Hope in the face of suffering—whether in the pain and degradation of illness and death, the friction of family and community, or persecution for bearing witness to Christ, is a clear mark of the church. A church that avoids suffering is not

2. See, for example, Erik H. Erikson, *The Life Cycle Completed* (New York: Norton, 1982).

comprehensible. In Christ's resurrection we are promised our own redemption.

As the church turns its face toward the world, it matters greatly how we bear witness. The church must seek ways to suffer on behalf of the least, those suffering poverty, sickness, or injustice of all sorts. Bearing witness to Christ is not simply declaring right theology. The church's ministry amid the social sphere must include making suffering manifest, not for its own sake but out of love on behalf of others.

We live in an era that assumes that suffering of all sorts is both avoidable and to be avoided. Living a good life means denying death and suffering, our own and others. We create walls of youthful images, narratives of power, technological devices, and politics of fear that serve to remove us from the friction of relationships with the earth, strangers, ourselves, and God. Cloistering ourselves away from those with whom we disagree has become a social possibility. Christians have long understood that our hearts do not become more loving apart from the friction involved in suffering on behalf of the stranger or God. These others cannot be discovered rummaging through the cellars of our egos, but require Christian practices. As Paul asserts, "the Spirit God gave us does not make us timid, but gives us power, love and self-discipline" (v. 7, my trans.). Paul understands suffering not as redemptive in itself, but in the context of the promise of resurrection "revealed through the appearing of our Savior, Christ Jesus, who has destroyed death and has brought life and immortality to light through the gospel" (v. 10).

We have lived through a modern era in which the assumption was that right knowledge issued forth right behavior. Here at the far end of modernity, most have come to understand that embodied social practices more effectively change behaviors and make us who we are. We are far more likely to develop good theology if we consistently practice worship, living as community, hospitality to strangers, forgiveness, prayer, seeking justice, or singing. From the ground of these embodied social practices come our theological and ethical ideas. This is the sort of embodied faith that Paul seems to be affirming in this passage: a faith that is lived in families, in social bodies, and across generations in their habits and practices; a faith that suffers, even as Paul did, and does not avoid the messiness of love for others. Such a faith is not primarily compelled by romantic notions of love or random acts of kindness, but by love that participates with Christ's love.

DAVID F. WHITE

Luke 17:5–10

[5]The apostles said to the Lord, "Increase our faith!" [6]The Lord replied, "If you had faith the size of a mustard seed, you could say to this mulberry tree, 'Be uprooted and planted in the sea,' and it would obey you.

[7]"Who among you would say to your slave who has just come in from plowing or tending sheep in the field, 'Come here at once and take your place at the table'? [8]Would you not rather say to him, 'Prepare supper for me, put on your apron and serve me while I eat and drink; later you may eat and drink'? [9]Do you thank the slave for doing what was commanded? [10]So you also, when you have done all that you were ordered to do, say, 'We are worthless slaves; we have done only what we ought to have done!'"

Commentary 1: Connecting the Reading with Scripture

Although this section of loosely connected sayings of Jesus begins a new chapter, it ends the second stage of Jesus' journey to the cross in Jerusalem. If the Gospel lections are preached continuously, the first thing that may present itself about this week's reading is the gap between the previous week's ending (16:19–31) and this week's beginning (17:5–10). Listeners will miss Jesus' address to the disciples about stumbling, little ones, and community discipline/forgiveness, moving directly to the words in verses 5–6 about faith, to a word about slave-master relationships in verses 7–10, two discrete units.

Unlike other occurrences of the content of verses 5–6, there is not much literary context that helps the preacher interpret the passage. It is worth noting that verses 5–6 appear also in Matthew 17:20 (which does not appear in the Revised Common Lectionary cycles), following the transfiguration and immediately after the episode of Jesus curing the epileptic boy when the disciples ask Jesus privately, "Why could we not cast it out?" (v. 19). Matthew's version connects the saying to the disciples' inability to perform the kind of miracle for which they believed they were empowered. Alternatively, a version of this text occurs in Matthew 21:18–22 (which also does not appear in the Revised Common Lectionary cycles). There Jesus curses the fig tree, it withers, and Jesus comments on the role of faith to lift mountains and throw them into the sea (vv. 21–22). Verses 5–6 also have extracanonical parallels in the Gospel of Thomas (§48 and §106), focusing on reconciliation, peacemaking, and unity.

Without help from the immediate narrative context as in Matthew and the Gospel of Thomas, Luke's version perplexes. The audience for the saying shifts away from the "disciples" (v. 1) to the "apostles" (v. 5). So, faith for what purpose? Held in comparison with the versions noted above, Luke's version seems to be somewhat of an absurd conflation of the version in Matthew 21. If an apostle commands a mulberry (sycamore) tree to be moved, it will be replanted in the sea! Why would anyone want to do that? What would it accomplish? Luke did not pen a clumsy or hastily written Gospel (1:1–4). Although it is clear that this episode was important for early Christian communities to tell and retell in one form or another, the question of its role in Luke's narrative remains.

It may serve preachers well to recall the broader context of Luke's Gospel and the second volume, Acts. Luke's two-volume account traces the path of the good news of Jesus Christ and the beginning of the church, complete with its growing pains of Jewish-Gentile relationships, house churches, growth beyond Jerusalem, and its witness within the seemingly all-powerful Roman Empire. In other words, Luke's Gospel accounts for how the fledgling church met the many challenges it was facing. A word on the power of what faith can accomplish, even to the point of absurdity, serves to encourage disciples of Jesus in the midst of challenge. Here, then, is a pastoral word from Luke to the communities that received it then—and receive it still. With perhaps little symbolic, cultural, or political capital among early Christian communities, how significant it must have been—and indeed is—to repeat the promises of world-altering power for those living into the reign of God.

Another preaching possibility for these verses focuses on the audience. As noted, Luke suggests a small difference in the audience for this saying. In the Synoptics, "apostles" indicates the group of Twelve (see Luke 6:13), and Luke uses this term with more frequency with regard to the Twelve (6x) than do Mark (2x) and Matthew (1x). The Twelve are the focus for this teaching, and it is they who have legends that spring up around their faithful work in the apocryphal literature of early Christianity. These accounts are atypical and interesting accounts for congregants to hear. While there is no direct link between this saying and the apocryphal literature that emerges, it does indicate the significance of what the church believed to be true. By faith, disciples of Jesus find world-altering power.

Verses 7–10, unique to Luke, certainly present the more puzzling, if not difficult reading. Like the previous sayings, they come without narrative scaffolding or Gospel parallels. Luke places this "Who among you . . ." scenario on Jesus' lips. Despite contemporary readers' sensitization to the horrors of chattel slavery, Jesus is no stranger to telling stories about slaves and masters as part of the Greco-Roman social world. Slaves and masters appear in Jesus' teachings at 12:35–48; 14:15–24; 15:11–32; 19:11–27; and 20:9–19. The stories of these relationships serve not as social commentary but rather to illustrate relationships of faith. That seems no different here. The master expects the slave to complete the extra request as part of the slave's duty. The slave should not expect to receive special reward for complying with what was required of their household status.

It is unclear if Jesus is still speaking to just the apostles as in verses 5–6 or if this camera lens has widened back to the larger group of disciples addressed in verse 1. The preacher will need to decide. If just to the apostles, they are the analogue to the slave, receiving instruction about the power they have just been promised in verses 5–6. In this reading, the apostles are warned not to expect a reward for their faithful work. This is a moment in which Jesus encourages humility in faithful service, perhaps to counter the tendency of the Twelve to argue about greatness (9:46–48; 22:24–30). In 22:26b–27, Jesus says that "the leader [must become] like one who serves. For who is greater, the one who is at the table or the one who serves? Is it not the one at the table? But I am among you as one who serves."

As a possible partner for intertextual interpretation, Fred Craddock points to Romans 3:27.[1] Though not a correlated lectionary text, Paul unpacks the relationship between law, humanity, and Jesus. He unequivocally states that in the life of those who are justified by faith, there is no room for boasting. So it is with those who follow Jesus in Luke. No further reward is merited, and no boasting is warranted for those who follow Jesus.

Still, there is some tension here. Jesus' radical table practice and teaching in Luke suggests that in the commonwealth of God, social relationships are reversed. This is a dominant theme in Luke. Those who feast at the table of God are those who *seem* least entitled and expected to do so (e.g., 14:15–24). So, is the answer to Jesus' rhetorical question on the apostles' striving for greatness, "Well, no one, of course, Jesus! We should expect no reward for our faithful work"? This is the dominant interpretation, and with good reason. Jesus characterizes the right response of slaves in verse 10. Might this disconnected saying also continue to question the assumptions about who is welcome at God's great banquet feast in Luke's Gospel? Informed by the wider context of Luke, the answer to Jesus' rhetorical question might also be: "Well, everyone, of course, Jesus! In the kingdom of God, this is standard operating procedure!" Admittedly, the larger

1. Fred Craddock, *Luke*, Interpretation (Louisville, KY: Westminster John Knox, 1990), 200.

context and verse 10 make this alternative reading significantly less plausible, but it is worthy of considering this story in the wider context of Jesus' words and actions regarding social relations throughout Luke.

RICHARD W. VOELZ

Commentary 2: Connecting the Reading with the World

Luke 17:5 opens with an imperative statement punctuated by an exclamation mark. "Increase our faith!" said the apostles to Jesus. While the punctuation mark does not appear in the original language, the English translation uses the exclamation mark to underscore the mood of the verb and clues the reader that this request is not a mere declaration by the disciples to Jesus, but an imperative marked by excitement, emotion, and intensity. "Increase our faith!" is a demand. This moment further develops Luke's portrayal of the disciples as persons who sometimes lack faith. Luke paints the disciples as men who are struggling to follow Jesus. They are challenged by him and are too often confused by his values and tenets. Their demand for Jesus to increase their faith is an appeal for what they know they need but lack, even in the very presence of Jesus.

Faith is an innate human yearning. The disciples suspect Jesus to be someone in whom to have faith, but their human frailty creates a moment of insistence rather than persistence. "Increase our faith!" is the insistent plea by those who know their faith is flawed and inadequate. We do not know if the disciples were demanding of Jesus because they knew he would willingly provide what they needed. We can only speculate on what event or experience prompted the request. It is not clear if the disciples were anxious because Jesus might choose to withhold and not provide their request. The request indicates a moment that was emotionally charged with anticipation for satisfying their hunger for faith.

Rather than magically increasing the faith of the disciples, Jesus' response is to teach them about the nature of faith. A liberative teacher, Jesus employs commonplace elements of nature and familiar cultural structures so the disciples will easily make new meaning and have a more expansive understanding. In other words, Jesus used what they knew to teach them what they did not know.

In the first response, Jesus squarely says, "If you had even the tiniest amount of faith, you *would have* said to a deeply rooted mulberry tree. . . . C'mon guys, this is the easy stuff." The emotional demand by the disciples is met by Jesus' annoyance and dissatisfaction. Succinctly, Jesus tells the disciples they have failed. The Greek syntax in 17:6 infers that Jesus' answer is one of irritation. For the disciples, these words by Jesus are not easy. Jesus uses dramatic and meaningful metaphors so that his rebuff is not misconstrued.

Jesus said, should you possess an infinitesimal amount of faith, you would have mighty power, but you do not possess even a little bit of faith. The mustard seed and mulberry tree, and their respective natures, were well known and well understood by the disciples. Although a mustard seed is minuscule, it grows into something gigantic. Mustard seeds are typically 0.039 to 0.079 inch in diameter. The disciples were acquainted with the mulberry tree's having extraordinarily deep root systems and hard wood, making it nearly impossible to uproot or harvest. Beyond the invitation to new understanding, Jesus' illustration serves as a rebuke against their demand; it illustrates their failure and inadequacy. Jesus' harshness infers that with the tiniest amount of faith comes power enough to speak change into existence. This is a reference to the creation story, where God spoke the world into existence and commanded the natural elements. It is also a reference to the fig tree in the Gospel of Mark (Mark 11:12–14) and to the kind of faith in God that moves a mountain into the sea (11:20–25). As readers of Luke, we have to wonder if the disciples regretted their demand for increased faith.

In Jesus' second response in verse 7, the teaching about faith turns to expectations for the disciples to act with faith and allegiance to

God. The second illustration provides a description of the nature of faithfulness. Jesus employs an illustration using the master-slave relationship. Disciples would be knowledgeable about the system of slavery and the life of a slave.

Today, this kind of metaphor is too regularly misconstrued as a way to approve of slavery, or the message underneath the illustration is lost to those for whom institutional slavery is deemed ethically problematic. For the children of enslaved ancestors, this reference to the tradition of slavery in the ancient Near East can be upsetting and off-putting. In the ancient world, an enslaved person was a socioeconomic entity confined to codes of obedience and docility. Luke was writing to a Greco-Roman audience where slavery was also widespread, thus creating a multiple-layered metaphor.

Wrongly, preachers and teachers will compare the chattel slavery of the United States with the system of servitude of biblical times and assert that the slavery of biblical times was "friendlier" or "more humane"—as if models of slavery can be calibrated for tolerability by the enslaved. Comparing systems of enslavement is imprecise and crass. Slavery in any period was and is a work of evil. Slavery of every kind creates untold suffering, degradation, and humiliation. Regardless of the modern-day problem this illustration creates, we must grapple with what is in the text.

Like the first response, Jesus' second response to the disciples is not a crowd-pleasing one. In a story steeped in slave culture, Jesus indicts the disciples for expecting any reward, even the reward of increased faith. With this metaphor, Jesus teaches the disciples that the reward for ministry well done is simply the opportunity to do more work. The reward for doing well is having done it, and that is all there is to say. In the twenty-first century, the expectations for having done well are assumed to be instant gratification, feedback, praise, and reward through such social transactions as salary increases, bonus points in games, or cultural gestures of gratitude. What Jesus calls for, however, is a drastically countercultural virtue. Do not expect reward or praise.

In the mustard seed example and the slave illustration, Jesus' response to the demand for increased faith results in a double dose of scolding of the disciples. The gospel message is that even a little bit of faith is all that is needed to perform great ministry, miracles, exorcisms, and healings. The illustrations stand in direct criticism and indictment of the current-day prosperity gospel. Prosperity gospel holds to the belief that material wealth is a sign of God's favor. Greed and competition are flaunted and rewarded as the highest values. Those who lack material wealth are somehow thought to be deficient in faith. This passage completely negates that belief. It denounces the theology of prosperity gospel. We must question the pervasiveness of such theology.

This harsh yet precise message from Jesus about the nature of faith and the need for faithfulness seems fitting for the season of Lent, when the Christian community is in a time of reflection, contemplation, and preparation for new life. The Lenten season is a time when we especially strive to be mindful of our purpose, focus, and obligations as disciples of Jesus in the twenty-first century. In the digital age, what does it mean to have minuscule faith? In what ways can we be more aware of, and more faithful to, our allegiance to Jesus? What would it mean, in tangible ways, for our faith communities to be accountable for our faithfulness?

NANCY LYNNE WESTFIELD

Proper 23 (Sunday between October 9 and October 15 Inclusive)

Jeremiah 29:1, 4–7 and 2 Kings 5:1–3, 7–15c
Psalm 66:1–12 and Psalm 111
2 Timothy 2:8–15
Luke 17:11–19

Jeremiah 29:1, 4–7

[1]These are the words of the letter that the prophet Jeremiah sent from Jerusalem to the remaining elders among the exiles, and to the priests, the prophets, and all the people, whom Nebuchadnezzar had taken into exile from Jerusalem to Babylon. . . .

[4]Thus says the LORD of hosts, the God of Israel, to all the exiles whom I have sent into exile from Jerusalem to Babylon: [5]Build houses and live in them; plant gardens and eat what they produce. [6]Take wives and have sons and daughters; take wives for your sons, and give your daughters in marriage, that they may bear sons and daughters; multiply there, and do not decrease. [7]But seek the welfare of the city where I have sent you into exile, and pray to the LORD on its behalf, for in its welfare you will find your welfare.

2 Kings 5:1–3, 7–15c

[1]Naaman, commander of the army of the king of Aram, was a great man and in high favor with his master, because by him the LORD had given victory to Aram. The man, though a mighty warrior, suffered from leprosy. [2]Now the Arameans on one of their raids had taken a young girl captive from the land of Israel, and she served Naaman's wife. [3]She said to her mistress, "If only my lord were with the prophet who is in Samaria! He would cure him of his leprosy." . . .

[7]When the king of Israel read the letter, he tore his clothes and said, "Am I God, to give death or life, that this man sends word to me to cure a man of his leprosy? Just look and see how he is trying to pick a quarrel with me."

[8]But when Elisha the man of God heard that the king of Israel had torn his clothes, he sent a message to the king, "Why have you torn your clothes? Let him come to me, that he may learn that there is a prophet in Israel." [9]So Naaman came with his horses and chariots, and halted at the entrance of Elisha's house. [10]Elisha sent a messenger to him, saying, "Go, wash in the Jordan seven times, and your flesh shall be restored and you shall be clean." [11]But Naaman became angry and went away, saying, "I thought that for me he would surely come out, and stand and call on the name of the LORD his God, and would wave his hand over the spot, and cure the leprosy! [12]Are not Abana and Pharpar, the rivers of Damascus, better than all the waters of Israel? Could I not wash in them, and be clean?" He turned and went away in a rage. [13]But his servants approached and said to him, "Father, if the prophet had commanded you to do something difficult, would you not have done it? How much more, when all he said to you was, 'Wash, and be clean'?" [14]So he went down and immersed himself seven times in the Jordan,

according to the word of the man of God; his flesh was restored like the flesh of a young boy, and he was clean.

[15]Then he returned to the man of God, he and all his company; he came and stood before him and said, "Now I know that there is no God in all the earth except in Israel."

Commentary 1: Connecting the Reading with Scripture

The roots of nonviolent resistance predate Mahatma Gandhi, Martin Luther King Jr., and even Jesus. They extend to an exilic community living in Babylon in the sixth century BCE. The first lection, Jeremiah 29:1, 4–7, the Letter to the Exiles, lifts up a radical, countercultural strategy of "nonviolent social resistance" in the face of opposition and oppression.[1] Instead of instructions for revolution, these verses call on *everyone* from the least to the greatest to build houses, plant gardens, raise families, and increase rather than decrease (Jer. 29:4–6). When faced with the dichotomy "Should we run from Babylon or raze it to the ground?" an unexpected answer comes: Reside in Babylon! Verse 7 raises the stakes. Seek the *shalom* of the place that brought you into exile, and pray to the Lord for *shalom* to come to it, so that *shalom* will come to you. This is the *only place in the OT with an explicit command to pray for enemies and unbelievers.* When Jesus says, "Pray for those who persecute you," bear in mind that he draws on a mandate that had been issued before (Matt. 5:44; Luke 6:27–28).

Jeremiah had to contend with false prophets who sought to distract and dissuade Israel from fulfilling God's vision for life in exile on two fronts: those in Jerusalem like Hananiah (Jer. 28:10–17) and those in Babylon who prophesied lies and deceived those who listened (29:8–9). In both cases, the temptation came to short-circuit the plans of God. The chapter shows that God will judge not only Jerusalem (vv. 15–19); God will also judge Babylon (vv. 20–23). The first half of the letter discusses *shalom* and the second half judgment. The charge to "reside in Babylon" does not mean that the oppressive regime evades God's justice. God's justice *will* come, but in God's time rather than their time line. While they wait, the counsel to them sounds much like Jesus' teaching to his disciples: they are the salt of the earth and the light of the world (Matt. 5:13–16). The charge is to actualize the vision of God in the place where they reside, a reminder that is just as important today as it was in the sixth century BCE. Eldin Villafañe puts it this way: "Against the false prophets who might call for 'assimilation,' 'revolution,' or 'escapism,' Jeremiah called for 'critical engagement'—for presence."[2]

The second lection, 2 Kings 5:1–3, 7–15c, in which Naaman is healed of leprosy, overturns worldly values by humbling the exalted and exalting the humble. Naaman occupied a position of power (v. 1). He was the commander of a foreign king's army, a "great man" held in "high favor" by his superior, who was also a "mighty warrior." It appears that God showed him favor by giving victory to Aram (rather than Israel) under his leadership. Even so, his prestige could not change his predicament. He suffered from leprosy.

Deliverance came to Naaman from an unexpected place (v. 2). The Arameans had captured a young girl (that is, a "little girl") from Israel who then served the wife of Naaman. Not only did she remember Elisha, the "prophet who is in Samaria"; she also told Naaman that the God of Elisha had the power to heal him. The writer of 2 Kings does not reveal her name, family, tribe, or hometown. Nevertheless, it is no accident that God worked through a little girl from Israel who crossed over barriers of status, class, gender,

1. See Daniel L. Smith, *The Religion of the Landless: The Social Context of the Babylonian Exile* (Bloomington, IN: Meyer-Stone, 1989), 137.
2. Eldin Villafañe, *Seek the Peace of the City: Reflections on Urban Ministry* (Grand Rapids: Eerdmans, 1995), 2.

and ethnicity in order to effect real change in the world.

The healing of Naaman occurs only after a political detour (vv. 4–7) and personal humbling (vv. 8–13). Naaman seeks healing through a political route. The king of Aram writes a letter to the king of Israel requesting that his commander be healed (vv. 4–6) and Naaman arrives with plenty of money and clothing, presumably a bribe for an exchange of services. After the king of Israel reads the letter (v. 7), he tears his robes because he believes the king of Aram wants to "quarrel" with him by means of an impossible request. Both kings must come to a place of humble dependence. The king of Aram has to send his commander outside his kingdom, and the king of Israel has to realize that only God can "give death or life" (v. 7).

Elisha enters the scene in verse 8, and his ministry of healing humbles Naaman. Through an intermediary, he instructs him to wash seven times in the Jordan River. In verse 11, Naaman becomes angry with Elisha for various reasons: sending an intermediary, refusing to "wave his hand over the spot" to cure him, and forcing him to wash in the Jordan rather than the rivers of Damascus, which were far "better than all the waters of Israel." As he departs in a rage (v. 12), notice that those who speak truth to him are his servants. It is they who convince him to change his mind. In order to be healed, Naaman must heed the counsel of so many that are beneath him: a servant girl, a backwoods prophet, and his own servants. He even has to dip in a lesser body of water. The reward is worth the risk. After the waters restore his flesh to flesh like that of "a young boy" (v. 14), Naaman stands before Elisha again, this time with a new attitude. In verse 15, he exclaims, "Now I know that there is no God in all the earth except in Israel."

This story contrasts with the subsequent account in verses 20–27. Right after the miracle, Elisha's servant Gehazi exploits Naaman's wealth by trying to profit from his healing despite Elisha's refusal to accept payment (v. 15d). When Elisha discovers Gehazi's deception, he informs him that the leprosy that afflicted Naaman will now afflict him and his descendants (v. 27). This story is also part of a larger literary unit, 2 Kings 2–13, comprising the Elisha stories.

Other themes emerge in 2 Kings 5 besides those of humbling and exaltation. For instance, Elisha heals a Shunammite woman's son in chapter 4 and a foreign army commander in chapter 5. God's compassion and healing extend beyond Israel to include the foreigner whom Israel is commanded to love (e.g., Deut. 10:19). In Luke 4:27, Jesus points to *this* miracle as a shining example of the culture-crossing ministry for which he came into the world.

In many ways, the healing of Naaman in 2 Kings 5 actualizes many of the same values that are lifted up in the first lection, Jeremiah 29. Naaman is the enemy, the commander of a foreign army. Although the Israelites are not in exile, they too must decide how to engage their enemies. As for the servant girl and Elisha, do they seek the *shalom* of Naaman, or do they seek his destruction? Do they run, raze, or reside in the place where God has called them to serve?

"Minor characters" effect real change in both accounts. In 2 Kings 5, God uses nameless servants to accomplish supernatural purposes in the life of Naaman. In Jeremiah 29, God reminds those in exile that the simple and anonymous tasks of laying down roots, raising families, praying, and seeking peace are actually part of a larger plan to enact God's vision in the world.

JARED E. ALCÁNTARA

Commentary 2: Connecting the Reading with the World

God's instructions, at times, seem suspiciously simple. Build houses, live in them, get married, raise children, settle down, go to work, hope, and pray for your community. Endure. So God commands the exilic Israelite community through the prophet Jeremiah in Jeremiah 29:4–7. Sounds easy enough, but it is the simple things that are at times the most challenging. Indeed, most of us have a natural aversion to easy instructions. They seem too good to be true and, as a result, they require a kind of trust and faith that believes God can find solutions, maybe even simple ones, to problems that to us are difficult and complex.

Like the Israelites of Jeremiah 29, we too have difficulties with God's simple instructions. A possible sermon might ponder what requests God is making of us. Might it include not dismissing God's response as too ordinary and prosaic? Perhaps such requests entail a reminder to simply treat those around us with love, kindness, and respect. To be aware of and empathetic to the poor, sick, hungry, and hopeless. To just love God and live as best as we can.

It is especially easy to forget God's simple instructions during times of chaos—a context with which the audience of Jeremiah was well acquainted. At the moment Jeremiah was prophesying, the population of Judah was being exiled and removed to a foreign land. These series of deportations would climax with the destruction of the temple in Jerusalem built by King Solomon. In the end, the world as the Israelites knew it was utterly destroyed.

By telling a community that had been dispersed and displaced that it ought to try to live a good life, God is not simply requesting a lifestyle shift but a radical adjustment of their theology. By telling the exiled Israelites to build houses, go to work, marry, and pray for their new communities, God is, in fact, telling the Israelites to resist the allure of succumbing to their feelings of despair, dismay, depression, and numbness. To make the best of a bad situation. To try to move forward and survive.

Jeremiah, in essence, is calling on the exiled Israelites to sustain their faith in God. Indeed, the devastation of the exile was in part ideological. It directly contravened a popular theology in Judah called Zion or royal theology, which maintained that Zion (Jerusalem) and the rule of Davidic dynasty would never be abolished (Jer. 7:1–15). The destruction of Jerusalem and the exile that followed strongly hinted that the Israelites had been foolish to trust in their God. In the face of this religious upheaval, Jeremiah encourages the community to continue to have faith in God's larger plan—a plan that seems utterly impossible, but which Jeremiah hints is possible for God. They are to hope and know that God can and will bring God's promises to pass.

Jeremiah's message evokes questions that the church needs to hear and address. In what ways has the church faced situations of injustice, chaos, and horror with passivity and hopelessness? When and in what ways have we equated acceptance with doing nothing and feeling nothing? How might we both accept our place in an unjust world and also sustain our belief that the "arc of the moral universe" does indeed "bend towards justice"?[3]

This kind of faith demands not just a heavenly insight, but also a subjugation and suppression of human pride—the kind of pride that claims that we know what is best and, therefore, only we can fix it. This kind of pride believes that we are the only ones who truly see and understand. It proclaims our limited vision as the best and thus the only one that matters.

Pride, acting as an impediment to the acceptance and faithful execution of simple divine instructions, connects Jeremiah 29 with the second pericope of our lection, 2 Kings 5. Hearing from his wife's Israelite slave girl that an Israelite miracle worker can cure him of his troubling skin ailment, Naaman, a Syrian general, journeys to Israel to seek out this healer named Elisha. When the general arrives, instead of meeting him in person, Elisha sends a messenger to tell Naaman to do something that sounds suspiciously easy: wash in the river Jordan seven times (2 Kgs. 5:10).

Like the Israelites in Jeremiah 29, Naaman too is incensed at these simple commands and nearly returns home. How dare this foreign prophet give him such an elementary solution—a solution that could have been easily done at home? As is so often the case, however, it is those on the margins who are able to detect with quicker clarity the divine truthfulness underneath Elisha's unfussy instructions. Lacking the pride of his master, Naaman's servant raises a simple point: "So what if the instructions are simple, what might it hurt to try?" It is

3. These words paraphrase Martin Luther King Jr., "Statement on Ending the Bus Boycott," https://kinginstitute.stanford.edu/king-papers/documents/statement-ending-bus-boycott.

only our pride that prevents us from acknowledging and indeed seeing this fact.

Like Naaman, we too find it challenging to follow God's simple directives. Moreover, like the Israelites in Jeremiah 29, many of us also resonate with the feeling that the world we live in is increasingly chaotic, insecure, unfamiliar, and foreign; that our country or town is no longer recognizable; that we need complicated maneuvers to survive in such a place. God's command to the Israelites simply to accept and make do, despite feelings of bitterness, hopelessness, depression, and disorientation, is also a call to us and to the church as a whole to endure, try our best, and hope amid our own metaphoric exiles.

Jeremiah's message is also a call for the church to recognize the role it has played and continues to play in the exile of others. As is evident in poems such as Langston Hughes's "Let America Be America Again," with its haunting refrain of "It never was America to me," there are communities that have long experienced exile as a result of their gender, skin color, belief system, or sexual orientation.[4] A wise preacher would do well to challenge the audience to consider the ways the church has upheld and indeed benefited from oppressive systems that create exile for others.

God in Jeremiah 29 commands that the Israelite exiles, despite feelings of depression, isolation, and anxiety, look beyond their personal well-being and prosperity. Rather, God states that they should also seek "the welfare of the city where I have sent you into exile" because "in its welfare you will find your welfare" (Jer. 29:7). God thus demands that the Israelites pray for the well-being and success of the Babylonian cities into which they were forcibly relocated and, by extension, the Babylonian oppressors who live in them.

In so doing, Jeremiah 29 reminds us that we too must seek the best for the "Babylonians" in our midst—that is, those with whom we disagree and those who may be directly or indirectly responsible for our "exile" or pain—as our success is incumbent on and directly correlated to theirs. In these times of bitter social and political division, both Jeremiah's call to the exiles and the narrative of Naaman's healing remind us of our connection to one another. That healing, success, and endurance come from faith and hope, and the constant reaffirmation of that faith and hope in community—a community that consists not just of those whom we like or are similar to us, but those with whom we dissent, diverge, and differ.

SONG-MI SUZIE PARK

4. Langston Hughes, "Let America Be America Again," in *The Collected Poems of Langston Hughes* (New York: Knopf, 1994), 189–91.

Psalm 66:1–12

[1]Make a joyful noise to God, all the earth;
[2]sing the glory of his name;
give to him glorious praise.
[3]Say to God, "How awesome are your deeds!
Because of your great power, your enemies cringe before you.
[4]All the earth worships you;
they sing praises to you,
sing praises to your name."

[5]Come and see what God has done:
he is awesome in his deeds among mortals.
[6]He turned the sea into dry land;
they passed through the river on foot.
There we rejoiced in him,
[7]who rules by his might forever,
whose eyes keep watch on the nations—
let the rebellious not exalt themselves.

[8]Bless our God, O peoples,
let the sound of his praise be heard,
[9]who has kept us among the living,
and has not let our feet slip.
[10]For you, O God, have tested us;
you have tried us as silver is tried.
[11]You brought us into the net;
you laid burdens on our backs;
[12]you let people ride over our heads;
we went through fire and through water;
yet you have brought us out to a spacious place.

Psalm 111

[1]Praise the LORD!
I will give thanks to the LORD with my whole heart,
in the company of the upright, in the congregation.
[2]Great are the works of the LORD,
studied by all who delight in them.
[3]Full of honor and majesty is his work,
and his righteousness endures forever.
[4]He has gained renown by his wonderful deeds;
the LORD is gracious and merciful.
[5]He provides food for those who fear him;
he is ever mindful of his covenant.
[6]He has shown his people the power of his works,
in giving them the heritage of the nations.

[7]The works of his hands are faithful and just;
all his precepts are trustworthy.
[8]They are established forever and ever,
to be performed with faithfulness and uprightness.
[9]He sent redemption to his people;
he has commanded his covenant forever.
Holy and awesome is his name.
[10]The fear of the LORD is the beginning of wisdom;
all those who practice it have a good understanding.
His praise endures forever.

Connecting the Psalm with Scripture and Worship

Psalm 66:1–12. Psalm 66 is a composite—a medley, if you will—beginning with a communal hymn of praise (vv. 1–12) and then moving into a personal song of thanksgiving (vv. 13–20). The sudden shift from "we/us" to "I/me" after verse 12 makes this transition clear. While the lectionary for Proper 23 employs only the first half of the psalm, it is helpful to remember its larger shape, which may reflect the psalm's use in the postexilic temple liturgy as a congregational hymn followed by a priestly prayer.[1]

The hymn of praise (vv. 1–12) featured in the lectionary consists of three stanzas. The first (vv. 1–4) is a call to worship for the whole creation; this is praise on a grand and cosmic scale. The second (vv. 5–7) is an invitation to bear witness to God's mighty acts in history; now the hymn makes particular reference to the root event of Israel's history, the exodus. The third (vv. 8–12) expresses gratitude for redemption; these verses suggest the more recent trauma of exile, framing that ordeal as a time of testing by God.

Paired with the prophet Jeremiah's call to the people in exile, "seek the welfare of the city where I have sent you" (Jer. 29:7), Psalm 66:1–12 offers a hopeful refrain. It comes as a hymn from the other side of exile, a proleptic song of praise. These are hard-won hallelujahs, tempered by the anxiety and alienation of the immigrant experience and redolent of the prophet's lamentations. Indeed, verse 10 bears a strong resemblance to Jeremiah's complaints: "For you, O God, have tested us; you have tried us as silver is tried" (see Jer. 9:7). The prophet now urges the people to make a home and a new life for themselves: "Build houses and live in them; plant gardens and eat what they produce" (Jer. 29:5). They may do so in the expectation of singing with the psalmist, "you have brought us out to a spacious [or abundant] place" (Ps. 66:12).

The psalm offers two insights to the preacher. First, it suggests that the complementary practices of lament and gratitude may have something to do with surviving and thriving in the midst of adversity. Remember that, in the spirituality of the psalms, deep lament and genuine gratitude are not contradictions, but vital counterparts in the context of an authentic relationship with God.[2] Psalm 66:1–12 demonstrates this profound connection, as pangs of suffering exist alongside shouts of praise. Second, the larger context of the psalm reveals the way individual well-being and the common good are intimately related, as a congregational hymn (vv. 1–12) is followed by a personal song of praise (vv. 13–20). Thus, the psalm forms an answer to Jeremiah's surprising counsel that the people should pray for the city of their exile, for "in its welfare you will find your welfare" (Jer. 29:7).

Worship leaders might make good use of the strong phrases that begin each stanza of the psalm. "Make a joyful noise to God" (v. 1) would be a fitting call to worship. "Come and

1. James Luther Mays, *Psalms*, Interpretation (Louisville, KY: John Knox, 1994), 221–24.
2. Claus Westermann, *Praise and Lament in the Psalms* (Louisville, KY: Westminster John Knox, 1987).

see what God has done" (v. 5) would be an excellent introduction to the proclamation of the Word. "Bless our God, O peoples" (v. 8) would be an appropriate invitation to the Lord's Table.

The theme so prevalent in these texts—that of praise for God's providence, even in a time of discouragement or distress—is perhaps best summarized by a beloved passage that appears just a few verses after the first reading. "For surely I know the plans I have for you, says the LORD, plans for your welfare and not for harm, to give you a future with hope" (Jer. 29:11).

Psalm 111. Psalm 111 is an alphabetical acrostic—one of several such poems that may be found throughout the book of Psalms and elsewhere in the Hebrew Scriptures. Each poetic line starts with a letter of the Hebrew alphabet, following in order from A to Z (or *aleph* to *tav*). Its next-door neighbor, Psalm 112, is another alphabetical acrostic; answering the final line of Psalm 111, it lists the attributes, blessings, and conduct of those who "fear the LORD" (Ps. 112:1; cf. Ps. 111:10). Together they form a picture of faith and faithfulness—what it means to live a life of gratitude for God's grace.

Indeed, as the opening verse of Psalm 111 makes clear, its primary theme is great thanksgiving: "I will give thanks to the LORD with my whole heart" (v. 1). Subsequent verses of the psalm seek to proclaim—in an alphabetically exhaustive way—the gracious works of the God who inspires such gratitude. The psalm's content is broad and generalized, praising God's goodness, grace, and glory, God's justice, righteousness, and faithfulness. Specific references to God's mighty acts in history are discernable only through a cluster of subtle allusions to the manna in the wilderness, the covenant at Sinai, and the conquest of Canaan (vv. 5–6). For this reason, this brief psalm is widely accessible and applicable to a variety of situations.

Psalm 111 is presented as the prayer of a person who has been healed of leprosy. Its primary point of reference is the first reading (2 Kgs. 5:1–3, 7–15c), in which the Aramean warrior Naaman is cured of his leprosy by the prophet Elisha after the gracious intervention of a servant girl, an Israelite prisoner of war. However, this psalm would serve equally well as the prayer of the "tenth leper," the Samaritan who returned to thank Jesus in the Gospel reading for the day (Luke 17:11–19). In both cases, the one praying is an outsider, a Gentile or a Samaritan who has come to know and worship the Lord through the experience of God's healing grace. Given this context, the psalm's opening and closing verses also seem to suggest a sense of welcome and belonging in a new community of faith.

The one proclaiming the good news on this day should not miss the opportunity to explore the themes of grace and gratitude in Christian faith, life, and worship. (Look up Martin Luther's famous reflection on the "tenth leper turning back."[3]) These Scriptures challenge us with their insistence that the best examples of gratitude come from unexpected people and places. These texts also offer a chance to connect Word and sacrament by exploring the significance of "Eucharist" (Greek for "thanksgiving"). The first verse of Psalm 111 could almost be a paraphrase of the presider's words in introductory dialogue at the Lord's Supper: "The Lord be with you. Lift up your hearts. Let us give thanks to the Lord our God."

The poetic structure of the psalm offers a good excuse to play with the alphabet in worship: to use an alphabetical litany of names or attributes of God, or to include a word search in the children's bulletin. Another idea might be to borrow or adapt the alphabetical Jewish prayer of confession known as the *Ashamnu*; various English versions can be found online. Beyond the service itself, it might be interesting to challenge worshipers to compose their own acrostic psalms of thanksgiving as a spiritual discipline in the following week—making an alphabetical list of things for which they are grateful.

Psalm 111 teaches us that the Lord is merciful and faithful, from beginning to end, Alpha to Omega, A to Z. Thanks be to God!

DAVID GAMBRELL

3. Martin Luther, "The Ten Lepers," http://www.lectionarycentral.com/trinity14/LutherGospel.html.

2 Timothy 2:8–15

[8]Remember Jesus Christ, raised from the dead, a descendant of David—that is my gospel, [9]for which I suffer hardship, even to the point of being chained like a criminal. But the word of God is not chained. [10]Therefore I endure everything for the sake of the elect, so that they may also obtain the salvation that is in Christ Jesus, with eternal glory. [11]The saying is sure:

If we have died with him, we will also live with him;
[12]if we endure, we will also reign with him;
if we deny him, he will also deny us;
[13]if we are faithless, he remains faithful—
for he cannot deny himself.

[14]Remind them of this, and warn them before God that they are to avoid wrangling over words, which does no good but only ruins those who are listening. [15]Do your best to present yourself to God as one approved by him, a worker who has no need to be ashamed, rightly explaining the word of truth.

Connections 1: Connecting the Reading with the Scripture

This passage contains something of a mystery for which the context offers some help in understanding. Some congregations will politely nod their heads as Paul exhorts us to be "good soldiers" (2:3) and to "remember Jesus Christ" (2:8); but many will raise an eyebrow when Paul quotes what some argue is a saying or a hymn fragment. The saying opens in a comfortable fashion: "If we have died with him, we will also live with him; if we endure, we will also reign with him" (2:11–12). We hear in these verses familiar baptismal language of dying and rising with Christ. Then, however, in 2:12 we read: "If we deny him, he will also deny us." Few like to think about God denying anyone. Yet texts such as Jesus saying he came to bring not peace but a sword and the parable of the Foolish Bridesmaids come to mind. We are uncomfortable with this threat of judgment, but it at least makes sense. Confusing is what follows in verse 13: "If we are faithless, he remains faithful—for he cannot deny himself."

The honest preacher may find herself wondering, "Okay, which is it, Paul? Denial or no denial? You can't have it both ways." Some may leap to the hope that the passage should be read in light of 2:13, arguing Christ will be faithful to us regardless of our faithfulness to him. Others may hold that the two verses are less connected. It is one thing to falter in faithfulness and quite another to deny Christ. Still other preachers may choose to maintain the tension between Christ denying us and Christ remaining faithful, pairing grace and judgment in such a way as to show their mutual necessity. All preachers should note that in places like 2:25, Paul himself holds out hope even for seeming enemies of the gospel that, if corrected with gentleness, even they may return to the fold.

Suffering plays a significant role not only in this passage but in the immediate context as well. In the first verse we hear Paul encouraging Timothy to share in Christ's suffering. Before this, in the previous lectionary reading, Paul invites Timothy to join Paul himself in suffering. The preacher might consider exploring this theme of suffering. On first blush this might seem problematic—as if Paul is encouraging Timothy to seek out suffering for its own sake. A closer reading confirms that Paul's exhortation here is not to seek out suffering so much as to accept the fact that suffering comes with the territory when following Christ. In 1:11–12 Paul makes clear this connection between championing the gospel and suffering. The preacher might note that while it is often tempting to assume that faithfulness leads to greater peace and purpose, the reality is that faithfulness can also lead to painful experiences. Also, in concert with this, faith does not shield believers from failure, tragedy, and loss. Faith is not what guarantees protection from pain but what helps us through it.

In the larger context Paul's warning against "wrangling" over words in 2:14 resonates with similar instruction elsewhere in the Pastoral Epistles. In 1 Timothy 6:3–4 Paul excoriates leaders who confuse others with "disputes about words" and "wrangling." In Titus 1:10 Paul warns Timothy about people with nothing better to do than stir up controversy with idle talk. Preachers might consider lifting up this theme as a way of prompting congregants to wonder about the difference between speaking the truth in love and causing needless disputes by wrangling over words. It might be particularly interesting for preachers to apply Paul's teaching to appropriate Christian behavior on social media. When is it right to challenge the opinion of another? How should this be done to maintain both the purity and the integrity of the body of Christ?

In the context of Paul's entire corpus, the analogy to an athlete represents a rich theme beginning to garner more and more interest. Paul frequently employs athletic or gaming imagery. In Galatians, Paul meets with the other disciples in order to ensure he has not run his race in vain (Gal. 2:2). In Philippians, Paul describes living into his sense of call as a goal and a prize (Phil. 3:13–14). Most significantly, in 1 Corinthians 9:24–27, Paul likens his ministry to the games:

> Do you not know that in a race the runners all compete, but only one receives the prize? Run in such a way that you may win it. Athletes exercise self-control in all things; they do it to receive a perishable wreath, but we an imperishable one. So I do not run aimlessly, nor do I box as though beating the air; but I punish my body and enslave it, so that after proclaiming to others I myself should not be disqualified.

This connection between Paul and what scholars refer to as gameful thinking provides fresh insight into Paul's work, especially timely for a generation of gamers. Preachers might consider reading works like Jane McGonigal's *Reality Is Broken*, as well as digging into rich theological resources like Moltmann's *Theology of Play*, Hugo Rahner's *Man at Play*, and Harvey Cox's *Feast of Fools*.

Another theme present in the full body of Paul's work is his experience of incarceration. In verse 9 Paul personalizes the suffering metaphor noting that he himself suffers "to the point of being chained like a criminal." Paul writes about being in chains in several letters, including Ephesians, Philippians, and Colossians: "Remember my chains" (Col. 4:18). The book of Acts records multiple incarcerations for Paul and his traveling companions. This shared prisoner theme provides a rich possibility for homiletic departure.

Preachers might take this opportunity to speak to the importance of ministering to those currently in prison as well as those attempting to return to society. As someone in and out of jail himself, Paul humanizes the prisoner for whom many in our congregations may feel fear and revulsion. Given Jesus' injunction to clothe the naked, care for the sick, and visit the imprisoned, helping Christians connect with the incarcerated is not only good for those marked by the criminal justice system but should be considered a spiritual discipline for all believers.

The other lectionary reading in Jeremiah 29:1, 4–7 offers an interesting possibility. In the Jeremiah reading the exiles receive a word that they are to make their peace in the land of Babylon. They are to build houses, marry, and, most intriguingly, they are to pray for the welfare of their new city. This strikes a chord with Paul's word here regarding athletes competing according to the rules and a greater sense of cultural accommodation in the Pastoral Epistles. Paul in Galatians and Philemon can imagine a church of radical equality where slave and free are one in Christ and slave owners like Philemon might consider free Onesimus as a fellow believer.

The more conservative household codes in the Pastorals show a practical adaptation to first-century cultural norms. Both Jeremiah and

Paul in 2 Timothy seem to be making some concessions to the realities on the ground they are facing. Preachers could explore when it is appropriate for the church to accept cultural norms and when believers might consider resistance. The courageous preacher might consider exploring historic civil disobedience movements as well as such controversies as National Football League players kneeling in protest against racism during the US national anthem.

KEN EVERS-HOOD

Commentary 2: Connecting the Reading with the World

This letter comes as instruction to the church of Ephesus by means of Paul's junior colleague, Timothy, upon the occasion of Paul's sickness and likely impending death. Second Timothy prescribes the attitudes and behaviors of followers of Christ, especially as incorporated into that unique social expression the church, and hence is an appropriate text for Ordinary Time. More specifically, this passage seems to focus on attitudes appropriate for followers of Jesus. In spite of his own bondage (v. 9), Paul asserts that he is confident in the gospel, which is not bound but is free and freeing (v. 10). He understands his bondage as in some mysterious way involved in the paschal rhythm of Jesus' life-death-resurrection; his suffering will be redeemed, just as Christ's was redeemed. For Paul, the promise of resurrection is the good news of the gospel that God is faithful and will deliver on his promise to redeem.

To contemporary readers, such terms may be common expressions, and we risk becoming desensitized to their radical nature. Especially in the context of Roman occupation in the first century, pride was unquestionably associated with wealth, status, and power. It is difficult to imagine how impossible it would sound to original hearers of Paul who, like Jesus, disavowed power and embraced suffering and hope in God. Trust in God's faithfulness and unashamed rejection of power over others is to be the foundational attitude of the church, the ordering principle for our lives. Not only is Christian hope forever tied to Christ's resurrection, but this promised redemption gives hope and mitigates the sting of suffering. Paul's own confidence is so profound as to provide comfort amid his own hardship, captivity, and humiliation.

A related theme involves Paul's characterization of language vis-à-vis the Word. Paul warns the church "to avoid wrangling over words, which does no good but only ruins those who are listening" (v. 14). Paul is speaking against those who claim secret knowledge and various forms of sophistry. Paul's remarks must also be interpreted in the context of his own thought, much of which is, itself, quite "wordy," even systematic. We must not therefore imagine that Paul is opposed to reason or rhetoric. Instead, he seems to be warning against those who pronounce doctrines that are not disciplined by Christlike long-suffering and hope, especially those who like to refine their arguments and "weaponize" them against others. Paul's challenge, "Do your best to present yourself to God as one approved by him, a worker who has no need to be ashamed, rightly explaining the word of truth" (v. 15), seems to contextualize our "words" in relation to our "work," which is our ethical response to the death and resurrection of Jesus Christ (the Word).

Paul's confidence in Christ's death and resurrection is so profound that his entire theology can be viewed as an attempt to elaborate its universal significance, not only for individuals but also, especially, for the church. Although Paul's ecclesiology is fleshed out in other epistles, its outline can be glimpsed here. The church must not be seen merely as an affinity group, a group of individuals convened by their collective interests. The church is the widening circle of God's loving inclusion in imitation of Christ's own suffering hope, in which our redemption is perfected and our lives enlarged for each other. Its politics counters those regimes that grasp power and exclude the weak. For Paul, the death and resurrection become the organizing principle of God's kingdom, an ethic that invites solidarity with those suffering on a journey toward redemption.

In other epistles (1 Cor. 1:10; Eph. 2:19–21; 3–4; Rom. 12:4–6; Gal. 3:28; Phil. 1:27) Paul makes the unity of the church a key witness against the coercive power of regimes. Apart from an ethic of suffering hope, unity can be only an impossible ideal, or worse, it can be distorted into mere uniformity. Only a social body disciplined by fellow-suffering can be attentive to the diversity of gifts that Paul describes and the peace that Christ promises. Only a social body hopeful of God's redemption can find something beyond their egos to bind them.

Especially in the Western world, our lives are mediated by the market and the power of the state, against which the gospel continues to be as radical as it was to first-century Romans and Palestinians. Market ideology is built around the sovereignty of individual choice. What is supplied, we are told, is based on what individuals demand. We have been trained by the market economy that desire is self-validating, and so we become incapable of escaping the confines of the self. Since the Middle Ages, the nation-state has diminished the power of communities and intermediate groups of care in order to take on more power for itself. At the hands of the nation-state there is a kind of fragmentation and atomization of social life. It is a reality that pastors confront on a daily basis, a reality that threatens the coherence of the body of Christ.

We live in a society of strangers, where interpersonal relationships are mediated by claims of formal rights against one another. These two forces constitute a training ground for individualism hostile to self-giving love to which the gospel bears witness. We celebrate those who garner power, wealth, or attention but obscure those whose gifts are not comprehensible in these terms, including gifts that enhance the quality of our love. Into such a world, the church has a special role of rendering visible the truth of the cross—of suffering with others in the hope of the faithfulness of God to redeem.

Suffering on behalf of others is a theme that can be glimpsed in many different forms in cultural life. Certainly, we see this vividly in the self-giving love of a parent for a child and in common acts of care. A teacher commits numerous small acts of sacrifice in order to empathize with students and enhance their life together. Those who provide hospitality through food, shelter, and care for strangers make space in their hearts, meanwhile finding themselves enlarged by the gifts of the stranger. These paschal rhythms are found abroad in culture in art, in other religions, and in our most deeply held values, norms, and laws. The church has a responsibility to highlight these paschal rhythms wherever they may be, within and beyond the walls of the church.

These few verses in 2 Timothy can be seen as a rather complex vision of human knowing. As expressed above, Paul holds several things in relationship: the passion of Christ, human words, human work, suffering, and the church. Paul's testimony concerning his confidence in the crucifixion and resurrection of Jesus Christ is not merely a personal belief, but a rule for ethical corporate life. In other words, his warning about "wrangling over words" (v. 14), along with his admonition to be a "worker . . . rightly explaining the word of truth" (v. 15), seems not to indicate a rejection of language, rhetoric, or dialectic—these are forms of communicating that truth. Rather, it posits the Christ event as the foundational principle to all we say and do. Mere unbounded speculation or sophistry is rejected. This flies in the face of modern rationalism or positivism, which prioritizes reason as an abstraction. Here, on the far side of modernity, attention to the importance of Christian practices is consistent with Paul's emphasis on paschal rhythms as grounded in the incarnation and manifested throughout the daily ministry of the church.

DAVID F. WHITE

Luke 17:11–19

[11]On the way to Jerusalem Jesus was going through the region between Samaria and Galilee. [12]As he entered a village, ten lepers approached him. Keeping their distance, [13]they called out, saying, "Jesus, Master, have mercy on us!" [14]When he saw them, he said to them, "Go and show yourselves to the priests." And as they went, they were made clean. [15]Then one of them, when he saw that he was healed, turned back, praising God with a loud voice. [16]He prostrated himself at Jesus' feet and thanked him. And he was a Samaritan. [17]Then Jesus asked, "Were not ten made clean? But the other nine, where are they? [18]Was none of them found to return and give praise to God except this foreigner?" [19]Then he said to him, "Get up and go on your way; your faith has made you well."

Commentary 1: Connecting the Reading with Scripture

At the beginning of this passage, Luke reorients readers to a new section of the narrative journey begun back in chapter 9. In verse 11, Luke describes this new path: "On the way to Jerusalem Jesus was going through the region between Samaria and Galilee." Despite this narrative marker indicating a new phase in Jesus' final journey to Jerusalem, we would do well not to disconnect the story of Jesus and the ten cleansed lepers from the sayings material that immediately precedes it in verses 5–6. There Jesus addresses faith and its power to accomplish amazing feats. The apostles, who request an increase in faith, are promised that even mustard-seed faith is powerful enough to uproot a mulberry tree and plant it in the sea.

Luke's narrative of the lepers bears out this pronouncement but expands it, demonstrating not only the power of faith but also the range of people who can possess it. Indeed, Jesus attributes the leper's faith—and a Samaritan leper at that—as that which has made him well (noting that "made well" is alternately translated elsewhere as "saved" and "healed"). The spatial arrangement of the characters in the narrative is intriguing. Like a stage play, Luke has arranged the "blocking" of this scene to carry out part of the theological intention. As Jesus enters the village, the lepers approach him, but remain at the socially accepted distance. On Jesus' words, they depart to go in proximity to the priests. Of course, one turns back, praising God, and lays himself at Jesus' feet. The physical barriers of distance evaporate, and Jesus tells the leper, "Get up." At that command, Jesus reaches beyond a simple spatial instruction. The Greek here is the same word used for "resurrection." Indeed, it must have been nothing less for the now former leper.

This story does not appear in any of the other Gospels, but it conjures echoes that remind us of other places in Luke's Gospel and beyond, and the Lukan theme of what John T. Carroll calls "salvation by reversal: inside-out transpositions."[1] Consider how Jesus interacts with lepers and Samaritans, characteristic outsiders who find themselves included as members of the realm of God. In Luke 5:12–14, immediately after calling the first disciples, Jesus similarly heals a leper "in one of the cities" (v. 12). This healing serves to increase Jesus' popularity, apparently contrary to his instructions to the leper not to share the report of his cleansing at the touch of Jesus. As Luke's readers journey with Jesus to the inevitable cross in Jerusalem now, we find a stunningly similar healing as Jesus' public popularity begins to turn downward.

In Luke 9:51–56, as Jesus begins to "set his face toward Jerusalem," he is not received in

1. John T. Carroll, *Jesus and the Gospels: An Introduction* (Louisville, KY: Westminster John Knox, 2016), 171.

All Creatures of Our God and King

Most high, omnipotent, good Lord,
Praise, glory and honor and benediction all, are Thine.
To Thee alone do they belong, most High,
And there is no man fit to mention Thee.
Praise be to Thee, my Lord, with all Thy creatures,
Especially to my worshipful brother sun,
The which lights up the day, and through him dost Thou brightness give;
And beautiful is he and radiant with splendor great;
Of Thee, most High, signification gives.
Praised be my Lord, for sister moon and for the stars,
In heaven Thou has formed them clear and precious and fair.
Praised be my Lord for brother wind
And for the air and clouds and fair and every kind of weather,
The which Thou givest to Thy creatures nourishment.
Praised be my Lord for sister water,
The which is greatly helpful and humble and precious and pure.
Praised be my Lord for brother fire,
By the which Thou lightest up the dark.
And fair is he and gay and mighty and strong.
Praised be my Lord for our sister, mother earth,
The which sustains and keeps us
And brings forth diverse fruits with grass and flowers bright.
Praised be my Lord for those who for Thy love forgive
And weakness bear tribulation.
Blessed those who shall in peace endure,
For by Thee, most High, shall they be crowned.
Praised be my Lord for our sister, the bodily death,
From the which no living man can flee.
Woe to them who die in mortal sin;
Blessed those who shall find themselves in Thy most holy will,
For the second death shall do them no ill.
Praise ye and bless ye my Lord, and give Him thanks,
And be subject unto Him with great humility.

Francis of Assisi, "Canticle of the Sun," in *The Writings of St. Francis of Assisi*, ed. Paschal Robinson (Philadelphia: The Dolphin Press, 1905), 152–53.

a village of the Samaritans to which Jesus has sent messengers to prepare the way. Rather than allowing James and John to "command fire to come down and consume" the city, Jesus rebukes the zealous disciples and goes to another village. This merciful response characterizes Jesus' consistent attitude toward Samaritans, despite challenge from his inner circle and socioreligious precedent to act otherwise.

In Luke 10:25–37, Jesus tells the story of the faithful, neighborly Samaritan who "had mercy" (v. 37) when others, who ostensibly knew better, failed. The Samaritan's merciful action parallels Jesus' own action in this story as he heals those who meet him at the edge of the village crying, "Jesus, Master, have mercy on us" (v. 13). Again, despite the narrative reorientation of verse 11, Jesus seems to be fulfilling the role of servant, doing "only what we ought to have done" (v. 10).

Jesus heals leprosy in Matthew 8:1–3; Mark 1:40–42, and he empowers the disciples to do so in Matthew 10:8. The curing of leprosy is part of what Jesus tells the followers of John the

Baptist to report back to him in Luke 7:21–23 and its parallel in Matthew 11:4–6. In short, curing leprosy is a significant part of Jesus' ministry that commands attention and becomes a significant component of the disciples' ministry as well.

With a wider canonical aperture, the lectionary pairs the healing of the ten lepers with that of Naaman in 2 Kings 5:1–3, 7–15c. Elisha heals Naaman, commander of the army of the king of Aram, but only after his protest at the supposed substandard quality of the Jordan to the waters of Naaman's home, claimed by him to be "better than all the waters of Israel" (v. 12). Luke references this story more explicitly in the hometown sermon gone bad of 4:27.

Not unrelated to the healings, note how the lepers call out to Jesus (v. 13), "Jesus, Master, have mercy on us!" This address, "Master," is used only six times in the NT, all for Jesus, all in Luke, and all previous to this usage. This is more than interesting trivia for preachers to share with congregants. The previous occurrences all come from the lips of disciples: Simon Peter before the miraculous catch of fish (5:5); the disciples in the storm-rocked boat (8:24); Peter during the exchange with Jesus about who touched him (8:45); Peter again at the transfiguration (9:33); and John reporting a person exorcising in Jesus' name (9:49). Now it appears on the lips of the lepers. Given what we know about the boundary-transgressing Jesus at this point in Luke's narrative, that the lepers call out to Jesus with the title previously only used by Jesus' inner circle should come as no surprise (or perhaps it is intended to surprise us!).

While the title they ascribe to Jesus has limited use, the way they phrase their request enjoys wider expression. The appeal for "mercy" is a common cry throughout both testaments. In the OT, the cry goes to God, and in the Gospels to Jesus. It also functions as a way of describing God's work or disposition. In both verb and noun form, there are too many occurrences to list. The recognition of God's mercy is important for this reason: Jesus stands in continuity with and embodies God's ongoing work in the world. In his ministry, Jesus functions as God's agent of mercy.

In all this, a composite picture of interrelated issues begins to emerge for preachers. Luke sees in Jesus that faith has the power to heal (save), but neither faith nor healing is limited by borders and boundaries, whether those boundaries are geographical, religious, social, combinations of these, or otherwise. Who may have faith? Anyone. Who can act in faith? Anyone. Who can acknowledge Jesus' identity as God's agent? Anyone. Who can receive healing (salvation)? Anyone. Anywhere; from any background. This Lukan picture of Jesus continues to surprise. Luke's account in this story and elsewhere is provocative: Jesus' actions may scandalize those interested in guarding socioreligious boundaries. Nevertheless, Jesus acts with mercy toward outsiders, lauds their faith, eats at a variety of tables, and crosses a variety of boundaries. He is a living parable of the realm of God. So it is worth leaning into Luke's literary design to ask in a sermon: How do this narrative and Luke's Gospel as a whole help communities of faith think about and act in relationship with those who might be seen as outside the household of faith? Though this is a hard sermonic question, the text can bear the weight.

RICHARD W. VOELZ

Commentary 2: Connecting the Reading with the World

This pericope upholds two reoccurring themes in Luke. In the first theme, Jesus cares deeply about those who are outcast and oppressed. Jesus, repeatedly, is attentive to those who are forsaken and judged inferior. The second theme has to do with the unlikely persons who recognize him as a healer, prophet, and extraordinary person. In the recollections of Luke, persons who are marginalized and deemed underclass seem well placed to see Jesus for who he is, as he too has seen them for who they are, and how they are. We can recognize the Divine amid suffering and distress as much as in redemption, restoration, and exhortation.

As we consider the details provided by Luke, we see that Luke's description of the ten lepers begins with their approaching Jesus. The suffering men recognize Jesus as he enters the village. Again, the text does not tell us how they recognize Jesus, just that they do. Perhaps the men recognized Jesus because one or two, before their illness, had been a member of one of the large crowds that gathered to hear Jesus' preaching and teaching. Perhaps, while begging on the outskirts of the village, they had heard gossip about a great healer who was traveling in the region. Maybe they recognized Jesus as an answer to prayer after long years of suffering, shame, and misery. It is important to Luke that Jesus be portrayed as recognized especially by those who are considered "other."

It is important to curb an impulse to read the Lukan stories of Jesus as if they were lessons about the mundane and trivial. In this instance, it would be easy to assume that the nine healed men were unappreciative while the one man is a hero for returning to give thanks. On the contrary, the text does not say the nine lepers lacked common courtesy or gratitude. It is entirely possible that the healed men were simply exuberant to return home to their lives and families after years of disease and shame. Running to return home after a liberative moment would be a very human response to a divine encounter. We do not know why the nine made the decision they made, nor do we know why the Samaritan returned to give thanks. We do know that the themes of Luke are more profound than the promotion of social etiquette and pleasantries of appreciation.

This healing story of the ten lepers comes after the story of Jesus' having admonished the disciples who did not recognize him (17:5–10). The positioning of this story after the story of the rebuked disciples supports Luke's theme of the otherness of those who recognize Jesus. While those who live with Jesus go unknowing and unaware of Jesus' identity and power, the ones who are shunned most by the community recognize him. Those with social status do not recognize him, yet those with social stigma look to him for mercy and healing. Recognizing Jesus, the leprous men initiated the encounter asking for mercy, a clear indication of their shame. We know that leprosy in that time meant being outcasts from family, home, and village. Leprous persons were thought to be sick as punishment for wrongdoing or wrong thinking. Sickness was a social disgrace that often led to death after sustained neglect and disenfranchisement from community. The ten lepers could not enter any village, any home, or approach anyone who was not also sick. They were displaced vagabonds at the mercy of the environment and, often, cruel people. It is amazing that even in their pain, humiliation, and regrets, they recognize Jesus.

Once made clean, one of the healed men finds Jesus and thanks him. Luke identifies the returning man as a Samaritan, even though the ethnic identities of the other nine go unnamed. Jews and Samaritans had shared tensions between them due to their common subjugation and servitude in the identity politics of the region. In identifying this man as a Samaritan, Luke is ensuring we know this man is an "other" in the eyes of the Jews. Jesus calls the one who showed gratitude a "foreigner." In calling him a foreigner, Jesus identifies him as a person of a different race, a person who is not one of the kindred, a person who is not Jewish and is thought not to belong or to matter. In giving mercy to someone beyond the familial and familiar, Jesus models that his mission is not relegated only to a singular ethnic group. His mission is meant for all peoples. Jesus' good news is for all the nations; it is a far-reaching appeal to the entire world.

The radical message of this story is not only that Jesus is a merciful person and healer. The radical message is that Jesus says that difference is to be honored. By having deliberately identified the healed man as a foreigner, Jesus is saying that difference is not to be ignored but respected. This naming cuts across any impulse to say that being a Samaritan did not matter to Jesus. On the contrary, Jesus identifies the Samaritan as a foreigner to make the point that it was a foreigner who recognized him, asked for mercy, was healed, and now returns to worship and give thanks. The good news of Jesus is that foreignness is included, incorporated, part of the whole; it is not ignored. The salvation and restoration for this foreign, Samaritan man was not in making him someone he is not. Rather, his healing restored him to his family as a Samaritan. The salvation of Jesus provides mercy and healing, and honors the differences of identity politics, both then and now. The good news of this encounter is Jesus' modeling and instruction for people to step across social biases, xenophobia, and bigotry. We are to share mercy with outsiders without asking them to assimilate to our ways or melt their differences into our pots.

Who matters to Jesus should matter to us. What matters to Jesus should matter to us. In contemporary time, we must ask: Whom are we pushing out of our village? Who is a pariah now? Who are the lepers and the Samaritans of the twenty-first century?

The #BlackLivesMatter movement slogan is used to raise consciousness about police violence against people of color and to protest the injustices against those considered by many to be the lepers or Samaritans in the United States. The movement's name and mission, however, has been ignorantly countered by the rhetoric of "all lives matter." This is not a semantic difference but a theologically critical difference that is counter to the gospel message. The message of #BlackLivesMatter is analogous to the message of this passage. #BlackLivesMatter does not say black lives matter *more*. Akin to what Jesus said of the foreigner, despite the politics of discrimination, racism, and injustice, the lives of black people are equally valuable to the lives of all other people, including the lives of white people. Jesus said, in showing mercy and healing the foreigner, #SamaritanLivesMatter. For those who recognize Jesus, understanding that he cares deeply for our particularity, our identities, and our differences is at the heart of the gospel message. At the end of the passage, Jesus tells the healed Samaritan man that his faithfulness has made him well. It is a faithfulness that grew in him as a Samaritan, not in spite of being Samaritan.

NANCY LYNNE WESTFIELD

Proper 24 (Sunday between October 16 and October 22 Inclusive)

Jeremiah 31:27–34 and Genesis 32:22–31
Psalm 119:97–104 and Psalm 121
2 Timothy 3:14–4:5
Luke 18:1–8

Jeremiah 31:27–34

[27]The days are surely coming, says the LORD, when I will sow the house of Israel and the house of Judah with the seed of humans and the seed of animals. [28]And just as I have watched over them to pluck up and break down, to overthrow, destroy, and bring evil, so I will watch over them to build and to plant, says the LORD. [29]In those days they shall no longer say:

> "The parents have eaten sour grapes,
> and the children's teeth are set on edge."

[30]But all shall die for their own sins; the teeth of everyone who eats sour grapes shall be set on edge.

[31]The days are surely coming, says the LORD, when I will make a new covenant with the house of Israel and the house of Judah. [32]It will not be like the covenant that I made with their ancestors when I took them by the hand to bring them out of the land of Egypt—a covenant that they broke, though I was their husband, says the LORD. [33]But this is the covenant that I will make with the house of Israel after those days, says the LORD: I will put my law within them, and I will write it on their hearts; and I will be their God, and they shall be my people. [34]No longer shall they teach one another, or say to each other, "Know the LORD," for they shall all know me, from the least of them to the greatest, says the LORD; for I will forgive their iniquity, and remember their sin no more.

Genesis 32:22–31

[22]The same night he got up and took his two wives, his two maids, and his eleven children, and crossed the ford of the Jabbok. [23]He took them and sent them across the stream, and likewise everything that he had. [24]Jacob was left alone; and a man wrestled with him until daybreak. [25]When the man saw that he did not prevail against Jacob, he struck him on the hip socket; and Jacob's hip was put out of joint as he wrestled with him. [26]Then he said, "Let me go, for the day is breaking." But Jacob said, "I will not let you go, unless you bless me." [27]So he said to him, "What is your name?" And he said, "Jacob." [28]Then the man said, "You shall no longer be called Jacob, but Israel, for you have striven with God and with humans, and have prevailed." [29]Then Jacob asked him, "Please tell me your name." But he said, "Why is it that you ask my name?" And there he blessed him. [30]So Jacob called the place Peniel, saying, "For I have seen God face to face, and yet my life is preserved." [31]The sun rose upon him as he passed Penuel, limping because of his hip.

Commentary 1: Connecting the Reading with Scripture

Jeremiah 31:27–34. The people of Judah were facing a grim time as the integrity of their nation slowly unraveled under the pressure of the Babylonian Empire. Within an anthology of material majoring on the failings of the people, a new block of material begins at 30:1, often called the Book of Consolations (Jer. 30–33). The refrain "the days are surely coming . . ." indicates the change in tone and focus. The two sections in today's reading are each prefaced by that hopeful phrase, meaning that "what has been need not continue to be" (vv. 27, 31).

The opening metaphor is of a people and their animals being planted on the land God has given them. The text then reaches back to the language of the prophet's commissioning: "to pluck up and to pull down, to destroy and to overthrow, to build and to plant" (1:10). After much plucking up and pulling down, destroying and overthrowing, the reader now hears the Lord's promises "to build and to plant" (31:28) a people on their own land, united as "the house of Israel and the house of Judah" (v. 27). This picture is reminiscent of other moments of prophetic hope (e.g., Amos 9:15; Hag. 2:19).

Jeremiah's reference to the proverb on sour grapes anticipates a day of blessing where there will be no sin for which a subsequent generation must bear the cost, nothing to set their teeth on edge. Perhaps the later promise of pardon in Jeremiah 50:20 reflects this. It also echoes Ezekiel's application of the metaphor that "it is only the person who sins that shall die" (Ezek. 18:4). In that respect it looks forward to the new covenant.

This new covenant will be in radical discontinuity with the covenant associated with the exodus from Egypt (Jer. 31:32). The characteristic of this new covenant is that the ways and will of God will be "[written] on their hearts" (v. 33). (The NSRV's reference to "law" fails to capture the sense of the Hebrew word *torah.*) Sin will no longer be engraved in the heart (17:1). Instead, there will be a time when the hope of Deuteronomy will finally be realized (Deut. 11:18–21), and the ways and will of God will be fully known and lived.

When the new covenant is realized, the need to teach God's ways (Deut. 11:20) becomes obsolete; the law given at Mount Sinai as intermediary is no longer required. The people on whose hearts has been written the ways of the new covenant "shall all know me" (v. 34). The knowledge of God written in the hearts arises from their experience of God's forgiving and not remembering their sins.

In contrast, the earlier covenant at Mount Sinai when the Lord mastered them as a husband (v. 32) evokes a troubling image earthed in patriarchal assumptions of marriage and power relationships. Is it possible that when forgiveness prevails, when "[God] will be their God, and they shall be [God's] people" (v. 33), we catch a glimpse of a more egalitarian future when the relationship between God and humanity is familial rather than political, and when humanity is unencumbered by the mastery of man over woman?

Luke reports that Jesus understood the shedding of his blood as constituting "the new covenant" uniquely referred to in this passage (Luke 22:20; see also 1 Cor. 11:25; 2 Cor. 3:1–6). The disruption of old inequities, typified by those between men and women, and anticipated by Jeremiah and his editors, begins in the ministry of Jesus and continues in the participation of Christians in the life of Christ. That sustains our proclamation (2 Tim. 4:2) and our prayers (Luke 18:7–8) "until he comes" (1 Cor. 11:26).

Genesis 32:22–31. This elusive story takes place within the long history of antagonism between Jacob and his slightly older twin brother Esau. After a lifetime of shrewd, borderline unethical, dealings with his kin, Jacob is now a wealthy nomad. So is Esau, and in the mind of Jacob at least, Esau has a score to settle.

When the strands of his complicated life threaten to engulf him, Jacob wrestles through the night with a stranger (32:24). The central point of this story is the brief dialogue between Jacob and his antagonist (vv. 26–29). Therein Jacob's identity is transformed from the deceiver (Jacob) to the ancestor of a people (Israel), and he is blessed. Somehow this wrestling lies at the heart of Jacob's vocation as Israel and therefore of his and Israel's experience of God's blessing.

It is impossible to determine with whom or with what sort of being Jacob wrestles. The narrator is not interested in answering the question. As is typical of the Hebraic mind-set, the narrator is comfortable blurring the distinction between the tangible and the unseen world; Jacob has "striven with God and with humans" (v. 28). At the end of this night of wrestling, Jacob knows that he has "seen God face to face" (v. 30). It turns out that the God who has blessed Jacob is the very God who has opposed him—and left him with a limp. The limp and the blessing are inseparable. In the words of Walter Brueggemann, "Israel is not formed by success or shrewdness or land, but by an assault from God. Perhaps it is grace, but not the kind usually imagined."[1]

Gerhard von Rad calls Jacob's near defeat of the heavenly being in verses 25–26 a "monstrous conception."[2] This detail is surely more than the relic of an ancient saga underlying the text. It expresses the startling risk that God has taken to allow humanity to express God's image. God's very self is drawn into the struggle that this entails.

So, for a brief moment in the wider patriarchal narrative, the story has slowed, the focus has shifted, and the looming crisis with Esau has faded from view. Now, as he limps away, "Jacob looked up and saw Esau coming" (33:1). Esau, the one so wronged by his brother, initiates reconciliation. Jacob, who has seen the face of God in his wrestling, now recognizes "the face of God" (33:10) in Esau's actions. Jacob's personal struggles and God's blessing coalesce at the encounter at Jabbok.

However, this moment of turning in his life has not yet perfected Jacob. Having agreed with Esau that the brothers' two nomadic clans travel together, Jacob lets Esau get ahead and then turns aside to Shechem (33:17–18). Yet he is changed.

There is an element of struggle in the life of the new covenant glimpsed by Jeremiah. Jesus understands prayer at least partly in those terms as he encourages his hearers to "pray always and not lose heart" (Luke 18:1) in the face of difficulty. Prayer includes striving with God.

Later, the author of the letters to Timothy encouraged his young protégé to persist in the midst of difficulty: "be persistent, whether the time is favorable or unfavorable" (2 Tim. 4:2). For Timothy, it is in that persistence, in the endurance of "suffering" (2 Tim. 4:5), that he works out his call as an evangelist and preacher.

As the story of Jacob's struggle is nestled within the wider story of God's blessing in the new covenant, the believer's story nestles within the story of God. We too limp in the footsteps of the one who wrestled with the face of God to the point of despair on the Mount of Olives (Luke 22:42–46). Foreshadowed by Jacob, he discovered within that struggle his vocation afresh as the Son of Man.

TIM MEADOWCROFT

Commentary 2: Connecting the Reading with the World

Genesis 32:22–31 and Jeremiah 31:27–34 can both be read as preparing the way for the annunciation, the birth of God, and the new covenant we know in Jesus Christ. Both passages describe a close encounter with the Divine and ready us for a wholly different kind of divine encounter in which we see God not under the cover of darkness but as the light of the world, not in a strictly interior fashion but in the human face of Jesus Christ.

It is easy to read the story of Jacob and picture the scene in our minds. Go further. Imagine being in Jacob's place. He is filled with fear because all his life he has been concerned only

1. Walter Brueggemann, *Genesis* (Atlanta: John Knox, 1982), 269.
2. Gerhard von Rad, *Genesis* (London: SCM, 1961), 316.

for his own welfare. Time after time he has put himself first. At some point, his past will catch up with him. Someone he has wronged will succeed in evening the score. On the night before meeting his brother after years apart, he encounters a bigger opponent.

One approach to preaching this text is to ask when fear of facing a deserved rebuke, an undeniable guilt, stalks us. Repentance is not a popular pursuit, but it is preferable to being haunted by wrongs we have not set right. Self-doubt is also pervasive. Probe what makes it so difficult for us to accept that we, like Jacob, are forgiven and blessed by God. Question why we are so reluctant to accept love from God and from those around us. We do push back against God, stubbornly doubting the blessings of faith and wanting God and others around us to prove their love time and time again. Cite examples of how we push people away, work against our self-interest, and throw up barriers to peace. Our patterns are nothing new. Part of the relevance of biblical stories is the unchanging nature of humankind.

Another tack is to point to Jacob's greatest strengths that are visible in this encounter. Lift up his determination and temerity. The field of positive psychology seeks to cultivate and build on an individual's strengths to maximize productivity and life satisfaction. We find strength in our faith, an unwavering trust in God. Jacob pushes back and wrestles with God. He locks himself in a one-way battle for acceptance, determined not to relent until he wrests a blessing from one he sees as an opponent, but who actually is his strongest supporter.

We must admit we have wrestled with God and encountered God in deeply personal and life-changing ways—when yearning, fighting, clawing for an outcome different from the reality unfolding before us, when arguing that God's justice differs from our sense of fairness, when debating the advantages of advancing our will instead of God's will. Experience proves that God is not afraid to contend with us. God welcomes our engagement. We will not outwit God. We cannot triumph over God. We can be thankful that God always is gracious and God is patient with us.

Another idea is to cite examples of metamorphosis from literature. Charles Dickens gives us Ebenezer Scrooge. Franz Kafka contributes Gregor. There is Disney's adaptation of *Beauty and the Beast*. Engaging with God changes us far more profoundly. Like Jacob, after wrestling with God we know God's blessings. Like Jacob, experiencing the presence of God means our lives are never again the same.

In our pride, we struggle against God. It takes more courage to trust God, although God always works to bring good from the mess we make of our relationships and our lives.

We also see God's steadfast love and faithfulness in the consolation and hope the prophet Jeremiah offers. The sinfulness of humankind is named without flinching. It requires the hard work of acknowledgment and repentance. We cannot pretend to deserve God's blessing. We have abused God's creation and used the world's resources selfishly and without regard for their care or protection. We have exerted power over the weak and allowed evils like greed and corruption to grow unchecked. We have flaunted the advances of technology and ignored the interconnectivity of all of life. But God's love for us is so great that God does not step away and leave us to complete our demise. God continues to open the way for redemption. We cannot bring on the eschaton, but we can hope for a better future, a future no longer defined by the past of our ancestors or by our own past (or current) waywardness. Jeremiah promises that God will take a new tack. God will renew us from the inside out by performing cardio inscription, not a medical procedure but a spiritual process, a divine encryption that cannot be hacked by temptation or overcome by weakness, an encryption that is not vulnerable to fear or subject to selfishness.

God will incorporate within us—literally allow us to embody—God's will, God's desire for humankind. The will of God is for us to no longer be separated from God. God seeks to be integral to us, as central to our being as our flesh and blood. Far from giving up on us, God implants the amazing forgiveness and grace of God into our very beings, writing on our hearts, going to our deepest core. We will be stamped indelibly as God's own, and inspired by a will greater than our own to live as God's people: deeply concerned about those around us and

Our Only Wisdom

The two cities then were created by two kinds of love: the earthly city by a love of self carried even to the point of contempt for God, the heavenly city by a love of God carried even to the point of contempt for self. Consequently, the earthly city glories in itself while the other glories in the Lord. For the former seeks glory from men, but the latter finds its greatest glory in God, the witness of our conscience. The earthly city lifts up its head in its own glory; the heavenly city says to its God: "My glory and the lifter of my head." In the one, the lust for dominion has dominion over its princes as well as over the nations that it subdues; in the other, both those put in charge and those placed under them serve one another in love, the former by their counsel, the latter by their obedience. The earthly city loves its own strength as revealed in its men of power; the heavenly city says to its God: "I will love thee, O Lord, my strength."

Thus in the earthly city its wise men who live according to man have pursued the goods either of the body or of their own mind or of both together; or if any of them were able to know God, "they did not honor him as God or give thanks to him, but they became futile in their thinking and their senseless minds were darkened; claiming to be wise," that is, exalting themselves in their own wisdom under the dominion of pride, "they became fools, and exchanged the glory of the immortal God for images resembling mortal man or birds or beasts or reptiles," for in the adoration of idols of this sort they were either leaders or followers of the populace, "and worshipped and served the creature rather than the creator, who is blessed forever." In the heavenly city, on the other hand, man's only wisdom is the religion that guides him rightly to worship the true God and awaits as its reward in the fellowship of saints, not only human but also angelic, this goal, "that God may be all in all."

Augustine, *City of God*, book 14, par. 28, in *Augustine, The City of God against the Pagans,* trans. Philip Levine, Loeb Classical Library 414 (Cambridge, MA: Harvard University Press, 1966), 405, 407.

willing to sacrifice ourselves for them; empowered to show strength through kindness, and to be great in genuine humility. To live as God's people is to live lives counter to the culture around us, lives that to outsiders seem oxymoronic, lives defined by the teachings and example of Jesus Christ, who exalts above the mighty and the powerful those who are meek and poor in spirit.

Core strength is touted as a key element in every exercise program. Strengthening one's core contributes to balance, stability, energy, and power and is an elixir for many of the ills of aging. It helps us withstand multiple assaults to our well-being. So does strengthening our spiritual core, developing the deep strength of faith conditioning, practicing exercises like prayer and humility, focusing on the wisdom, love, mercy, and habits of the Lord. When these core strengths undergird our decision-making and are imprinted on our priorities, we are transformed beyond anything we are capable of on our own. We are made new as only God can remake us. We are moved from sinner to saint, set free and given a new identity. We face a future that is full of possibility.

Think of the difference it makes in the life of a troubled youth when an adult believes in him and sees him no longer as a stereotype but as a young person with limitless potential. In gaining hope through a new self-image, he essentially is given new life. Through the new covenant, God gives this new life to us all.

The prophet Jeremiah paints a picture of God's relationship with us as deep and intimate and personal. It is an indwelling relationship of intense, self-giving love. It redefines us, lifting us from a self-centered realm to a higher plane, where we consider the needs of others and elevate them above our own.

A Benedictine monk preached, "Our hope is that when Christ receives us, he will recognize his own image in our hearts."[3] May it be so.

FAIRFAX F. FAIR

3. Kathleen Norris, *Acedia and Me: A Marriage, Monks, and a Writer's Life* (New York: Riverhead Books, 2008), 211.

Psalm 119:97–104

[97]Oh, how I love your law!
It is my meditation all day long.
[98]Your commandment makes me wiser than my enemies,
for it is always with me.
[99]I have more understanding than all my teachers,
for your decrees are my meditation.
[100]I understand more than the aged,
for I keep your precepts.
[101]I hold back my feet from every evil way,
in order to keep your word.
[102]I do not turn away from your ordinances,
for you have taught me.
[103]How sweet are your words to my taste,
sweeter than honey to my mouth!
[104]Through your precepts I get understanding;
therefore I hate every false way.

Psalm 121

[1]I lift up my eyes to the hills—
from where will my help come?
[2]My help comes from the LORD,
who made heaven and earth.

[3]He will not let your foot be moved;
he who keeps you will not slumber.
[4]He who keeps Israel
will neither slumber nor sleep.

[5]The LORD is your keeper;
the LORD is your shade at your right hand.
[6]The sun shall not strike you by day,
nor the moon by night.

[7]The LORD will keep you from all evil;
he will keep your life.
[8]The LORD will keep
your going out and your coming in
from this time on and forevermore.

Connecting the Psalm to Scripture and Worship

Psalm 119:97–104. Psalm 119, the longest of the psalms and the longest chapter in the Bible, is an alphabetical acrostic poem; each of its twenty-two eight-line stanzas features a different letter of the Hebrew alphabet. This demanding poetic structure betrays a labor of love; indeed, Psalm 119 is a love song to the law (or *Torah*) of God. It draws on numerous synonyms for the law—"commandments," "decrees," "ordinances," "precepts," "word"—in order to "spell out" the psalmist's devotion to the way and teaching of the Lord.

The stanza in the lectionary today (vv. 97–104) is brought to us by the letter M—or the Hebrew letter *mem*. The psalmist boasts of a surpassing love of God's law, yielding more wisdom than enemies (v. 98), more understanding than teachers (v. 99), more insight than elders (v. 100). In a couplet echoed in the baptismal liturgy, the psalmist renounces "every evil way" (v. 101), turning instead to the teaching of God (v. 102). Echoing the related Psalm 19, the psalmist declares that God's words are sweeter than honey (v. 103), the source of all understanding and the antithesis of falsehood (v. 104). God's way of life is the psalmist's "pride and joy."

Such sentiments have clear resonance with Jeremiah 31:27–34, the first reading for Proper 24. This passage—the final installment in a long series of readings from the prophet in the semicontinuous track of the Revised Common Lectionary—is taken from Jeremiah's Book of Consolations (Jer. 30–33). The prophet announces the good news of God's new covenant: "I will put my law within them, and I will write it on their hearts; and I will be their God, and they shall be my people" (Jer. 31:33). Those who have the word of God inscribed in their hearts will be able to exclaim with the psalmist, "Oh, how I love your law!" (v. 97).

What does it mean to have such affection for the word of God—to know God's way "by heart" and to delight in the fulfillment of God's law? The Reformed theological tradition offers some insights for preachers considering these questions. John Calvin taught of "three uses of the law": as a mirror, a fence, and a guide. As a mirror, the law convicts us of our sin in contrast to the holiness of God. As a fence, the law promotes order and restrains evil in society. As a guide, the law leads us in the paths of righteousness and teaches us to follow God's way. Calvin emphasized this "third use of the law," as a gift of God's grace and source of guidance for faithful living.[1] Jeremiah's vision of the people of God redeemed and restored—now rejoicing in the way of God—seems to suggest a similar understanding of the law.

A good way to reflect this kind of enthusiasm for God's law would be to sing a musical setting of the Decalogue (Ten Commandments) after the declaration of forgiveness. Indeed, this is a practice that would have been familiar to Calvin's congregations and other churches of the Reformed tradition. A summary of the law, as found in Luke 10:25–28 (and parallels) or John 13:34–35, would be another way to celebrate God's way of life in worship. At a more basic level, love for God's teaching can be embodied through careful attention to the reading of Scripture—a good practice any time the word is proclaimed.

Psalm 119:97–104 demonstrates that there is always *more* for us to discover in God's word—more goodness, more truth, more beauty; more wisdom, more joy, more life—if we only take it to heart.

Psalm 121. Psalm 121 is one of the Songs of Ascent (Pss. 120–34), a collection of fifteen psalms associated with pilgrims traveling to the Jerusalem temple at the time of a festival. This beloved psalm describes the sheltering presence of God on a treacherous journey, accompanying pilgrims night and day and protecting them from danger. OT scholar Robert Davidson proposes that this psalm might have served as a blessing for pilgrims at the conclusion of the festival, its words of comfort and strength meant to encourage and sustain the homeward-bound travelers.[2]

1. John Calvin, *Institutes of the Christian Religion*, 2.7.6–12.
2. Robert Davidson, *The Vitality of Worship: A Commentary on the Book of Psalms* (Grand Rapids: Eerdmans, 1998), 407–9.

In the complementary track of the Revised Common Lectionary, Psalm 121 is offered as the response to Genesis 32:22–31. The Genesis story finds Jacob alone in the valley of the Jabbok River; the psalm promises that our help will come not from the surrounding hills, but from the maker of heaven and earth (v. 2). Jacob wrestles all night with a mysterious stranger; the psalm promises that the protector of "Israel" (soon to be Jacob's new name) will never slumber or sleep (v. 4). Jacob is struck on the hip and left with a limp; ironically perhaps, the psalm promises that the sun and moon will *not* strike us (v. 6), and that God will not let our feet be moved (v. 3). Jacob receives a blessing through this encounter, and this the psalm delivers in abundance: "The LORD will keep your going out and your coming in from this time on and forevermore" (v. 8).

Psalm 121 also finds resonance with the Gospel reading for Proper 24, Jesus' parable of the Persistent Widow and the Unjust Judge (Luke 18:1–8). As the widow exemplifies ceaseless prayer in the face of adversity, the psalm itself provides a model of such prayer. As the figure of the judge demonstrates the weakness and corruption of earthly authorities, the psalm directs us to trust in the almighty and eternal Creator of the cosmos. As God grants justice to the faithful who cry out day and night, the psalm says that the Lord will never slumber or sleep (v. 4).

Where do we find blessing in our darkest hours? From whom do we seek help in times of trouble? How do we pursue justice in a corrupt and callous world? The stories of Genesis 32 and Luke 18 suggest that God meets us in the struggle; the song of Psalm 121 promises that this is so. A sermon on the texts of Proper 24 might begin with the question posed by this psalm and end with the good news of its closing verse; in between, the preacher might consider the examples of Jacob's wrestling and the widow's demand for justice as illustrations of faithful struggle.

As for its use in worship, notice that the second verse of Psalm 121 echoes the classic Reformed call to worship (sometimes called the "votum"), derived from another Song of Ascent: "Our help is in the name of the LORD, maker of heaven and earth" (Ps. 124:8). The final line of the psalm (Ps. 121:8) would make a fitting benediction on this day, particularly if spoken from the door of the church. Musical settings of Psalm 121 include the venerable Scottish Psalter paraphrase "I to the Hills Will Lift Mine Eyes," Felix Mendelssohn's soaring trio and chorus from *Elijah*, and Richard Smallwood's powerful anthem "Total Praise."

Psalm 121 has inspired confidence and hope for generations of the people of God. In times of trouble, this ancient pilgrim's prayer continues to call us to lift our eyes and put our trust in the steadfast love of God.

DAVID GAMBRELL

2 Timothy 3:14–4:5

[14]But as for you, continue in what you have learned and firmly believed, knowing from whom you learned it, [15]and how from childhood you have known the sacred writings that are able to instruct you for salvation through faith in Christ Jesus. [16]All scripture is inspired by God and is useful for teaching, for reproof, for correction, and for training in righteousness, [17]so that everyone who belongs to God may be proficient, equipped for every good work.

[4:1]In the presence of God and of Christ Jesus, who is to judge the living and the dead, and in view of his appearing and his kingdom, I solemnly urge you: [2]proclaim the message; be persistent whether the time is favorable or unfavorable; convince, rebuke, and encourage, with the utmost patience in teaching. [3]For the time is coming when people will not put up with sound doctrine, but having itching ears, they will accumulate for themselves teachers to suit their own desires, [4]and will turn away from listening to the truth and wander away to myths. [5]As for you, always be sober, endure suffering, do the work of an evangelist, carry out your ministry fully.

Commentary 1: Connecting the Reading with Scripture

In the last half of 2 Timothy, Paul passionately admonishes Timothy to be strong, for bad times are coming. He reminds Timothy to take courage in what he has firmly believed, mindful of the authority of the source: his own family, Lois and Eunice, his ancestors in the faith, and Paul himself. One can sense the urgency in Paul's voice as he challenges Timothy to be strong, keep the faith, and diligently carry out his ministry to the fullest. Chapters 3 and 4 explain both the power of faith and the nature of the bad times to come.

Paul sets two patterns of ministry before Timothy. The first is himself: the teaching, conduct, aim in life, faith, patience, love, and steadfastness that Timothy observed as Paul endured many persecutions and suffering for his witness (2:8–13; 3:10–11). Through it all, Paul reminds him that God's grace, and the fortitude that comes from serving a faithful God, delivered him. Paul admonishes Timothy to the same kind of love, patience, endurance, and consistency for the sake of the ministry to which they have been called (3:10). Deceivers, by way of constrast, seek to destroy the work of the gospel with their counterfeit faith (3:8). They are to be avoided (3:5b). This passage reminds us of Jesus' own words in John 10:10 concerning the thief that comes "only to steal and kill and destroy." Like Jesus, God's true witnesses proclaim and live out a gospel that gives abundant life.

The centrality of Scripture in Christian formation, the danger of novel teachings, and the importance of Timothy's carrying on his evangelical work stand out in this passage. The implication, made explicit in 4:6–8, is that Paul's ministry is coming to an end, so Timothy must be prepared to carry on the work. In 1 Timothy, the emphasis of such preparation was on church order. Here, it is on doctrine; Timothy must resist the novel false teachings that arise with steadfastness and patience.

Timothy has a solid foundation through his learning in Scripture. It is important to note that the Scripture in question was the Greek translation of the Hebrew Bible known as the Septuagint. Certain of the documents that would form the future NT canon, such as the undoubtedly authentic letters of Paul, had acquired a measure of authority. However, there was no NT as we know it today (i.e., the twenty-seven books). This, at the very least, underscores the importance of the Hebrew Scriptures for understanding, interpreting, and affirming the message, life, and witness of Jesus the Christ (Luke 24:27). They are consistent with Jesus' call to faithfulness to God and therefore also Paul's admonition (e.g., Isa. 5:20; Zeph. 3:13; Pss. 5:6; 24:3–4; 32:2; Prov. 12:17; Jer. 9:8–9; et al.).

Scripture provides the standard by which humans are to be judged. To live in accordance with Scripture is to live rightly. To live in contradiction to Scripture is to betray the Lord and invite judgment. The indication that a disciple is living rightly is persecution. Paul regards his persecutions as evidence of his faithfulness, and says flatly that it will be so for all followers of Christ.

The ultimate goal is for Timothy to be formed into the kind of apostle that Paul himself exemplifies. Paul is both teacher and example of how to behave as a true apostle in the face of inevitable persecution and suffering. Thus, he urges Timothy to keep on doing what he, Paul, has been doing.

Verses 16–17 are often used as proof texts to establish the paramount authority of Scripture. In the context of this passage, though, these verses specify more the *function* of Scripture; It imparts knowledge and teaches how that knowledge is to be used. Thus, Paul's admonition to Timothy in 4:1–5 is the result of the application of Scripture. The novelty that stems from unnamed myths is contrary and deceitful.

In the lectionary readings there is a tension between the letter and the Spirit. As we have seen, the reading from 2 Timothy stresses the importance of Scripture for shaping the lives of Christians. The reading from Jeremiah speaks of a new covenant marked by a new law written on the heart. The implication is that there will be no more need for an external written law.

The Psalter reading from Psalm 119 heightens this tension. Its theme is praise for the law and the psalmist's success in following that law. God's judgment, as expressed in Jeremiah, is that the people as a whole were not as successful as the psalmist in observing the law, so something else—a law written on the heart—must replace it.

It is important to note that, with regard to Scripture, the tension between letter and Spirit is not a flat contradiction. First, "Scripture" in the Timothy passage is more than the law. More importantly, there is no suggestion in the Timothy passage that attending to Scripture precluded being led by the Spirit. However, the term "Holy Spirit" is used only once in the entire epistle, and it is easy to let the stress on conduct overwhelm the sense of the necessity of the Spirit's presence. The passage in Jeremiah is an important counter to this.

Paul is a figure of authority throughout the NT canon. This is perhaps inevitable, given that he was the author of a majority of the NT epistles, as well as being a major figure in the Acts of the Apostles. In many of these epistles he was forced to defend either his teaching or his authority. This is certainly the case in the Pastorals, but the basis of that authority lay in his suffering as he carried out his apostleship and his fidelity to the teachings of Scripture. In Galatians, however, his claim to authority derived from his direct commissioning from the risen Lord. That direct commissioning enabled him to proclaim his independence from all the other apostles—notably Peter in the Antioch incident recounted in Galatians 2:11–14. In 2 Timothy, Paul does not set himself against other apostles or distinguish his authority from theirs. He is part of the old guard. His (and therefore Timothy's) opponents are the ones with a new message, and that is precisely why they are to be resisted.

Second Timothy clearly reflects a time of transition in the life of the NT church. On the one hand, the church has been in existence long enough to have a multigenerational tradition; Timothy's teachers go back to his grandmother. On the other hand, Paul seems to consider his ministry finished, and Timothy represents one of those who will carry on the work. The Epistles to Timothy are a sort of handbook for the ministry of a new generation.

Many scholars have questioned whether 2 Timothy, and indeed all the Pastorals, were written by Paul or by a later writer using Paul's name. Neither alternative affects the epistle's usefulness as an instructional handbook for the coming generations of church leadership.

Finally, this section of 2 Timothy is in direct opposition to the so-called gospel of prosperity. It is almost a gospel of adversity. Furthermore, we note that this adversity is as likely to come from inside the church as from outside. Timothy, who in this respect symbolizes all Christians, must be strong in respect to both danger from without and hypocrisy within. In approaching this text, preachers must guard against presenting the gospel as a means of material reward. The reward is oneness with Christ and his body, the church—nothing less and nothing else.

DAVID W. JOHNSON

Commentary 2: Connecting the Reading with the World

In 2 Timothy 3:14–17 we find one in a series of exhortations to Timothy instructing him how to live and conduct himself as a Christian in the midst of open and sometimes painful opposition. In essence, Paul is urging young Timothy to be steadfast in what he had learned and continues to firmly believe. Moreover, he urges him to remember from whom he learned these beliefs. Remembering from whom he learned speaks of the importance of traditions. It is not only Timothy's own convictions gained in the past that are to galvanize him, but also the knowledge of the generational source of that teaching, the character and reliability of those who taught him. This would include Timothy's mother and grandmother (2 Tim. 1:5) and, of course, Paul himself.

Our first connection relates to culture and society and holding fast to our traditional faith in an ever-changing world. While our opposition may not stem from false teachers, in today's highly secularized society, those who profess faith in Jesus Christ face opposition and criticism from those who believe our faith to be antiquated and anachronistic. Societal norms have changed, we are told, and only verifiable scientific facts are acceptable to intelligent, rational human beings. Such criticism notwithstanding, what we believe matters, and how we live out what we believe can be and is a powerful testimony to that which enriches and deepens our everyday lives. Faith matters! Faith is lived out, not just in our personal lives but also in the public square.

Paul also calls on Timothy to remember the importance of tradition in his faith journey. Godliness encompasses respect for the traditions of one's ancestors. For those of us who live in a posttradition era, what does it mean to pass this faith from generation to generation? In days past, churches thought it important to pass on kinship ties, nationality, language, racial heritage, denominational loyalties, as well as particular doctrinal stances. In more recent times people have claimed that what is most important is not so much the handing down of past tribal/cultural traditions but, rather, the passing on of that which gives vibrancy and dynamism to their personal and spiritual journey. They also desire quality in all aspects of ministry and integrity in those who offer themselves for leadership. They seek to have their faith shaped by congregations that practice what they preach. These things take priority over traditional cultural ties that sometimes lose their power and purpose. As we seek to build up the body of Christ in contemporary times, we have to adjust to new ways of holding fast to what is good and healthy from our past, while at the same reaching for what will sustain and nurture us in the days ahead. Empty ritual and cold ceremony are no substitute for a dynamic faith respectful of past traditions but not imprisoned by them.

Paul next appeals to Timothy to remember the importance of Scripture in his faith formation. He does this by pointing to the "sacred writings" or the Scriptures as able to give Timothy understanding and instruction for salvation through faith in Jesus Christ (2 Tim. 3:15). A possible connection for the contemporary listener is for the preacher to speak of the importance of Scripture in our contemporary expressions of personal faith and public witness. What role should the Scriptures play in our everyday lives? What are some of the ways they continue to be meaningful to our formation in the faith community and to the wider world? In the last third of the twentieth century, James Smart, in *The Strange Silence of the Bible in the Church*, observed that the voice of Scriptures was falling silent in the preaching and teaching of the church and in the consciousness of Christian people.[1] Smart laid some of the blame at the feet of historical-critical scholarship. Does critical scholarship necessarily lead to the diminution of the importance of Scripture in our lives?

For some faith traditions the Bible continues to be their final source of authority in all matters of faith and practice. For others the Bible is one of any number of sources they consult when seeking direction on how to live a life with purpose and meaning. Still others in this postmodern era, where we celebrate otherness and difference, no longer believe in the one-size-fits-all grand metanarrative of Scripture. For them the Bible is a reliable source but not their final source. Some scholars even go so far as to suggest that Martin Luther King Jr.'s "Letter from a Birmingham Jail" could be included at some future date into a reopened biblical canon. King's epoch letter exemplifies for them the social teachings of Jesus Christ in a revelatory way.

For Paul, Scripture leads to a deep and profound faith in Jesus Christ. It attests to who God is and what God has done for us and for our salvation, especially as that witness is manifested in Jesus Christ. Though we may be inclined to get at that understanding of faith in Jesus Christ through different paths, if those paths lead to deeper faith and a solid commitment to Christ, then they should be regarded as viable and fitting paths to faith for contemporary times.

Paul further states that all Scripture is inspired by God. Before he writes about the different uses to which the Scriptures may be put, he wants Timothy to understand their importance. Thus, Paul uses the term "inspired" to affirm the authoritative and foundational nature of Scripture to authenticate the gospel message and provide a pastoral tool for ministry. The term "God-breathed" also allowed Paul to communicate his adherence to the Jewish tradition that the OT Scriptures are divinely inspired. Not only are the inspired Scriptures authoritative for Paul because of their intimate connection with God; they are also beneficial for teaching, reproof, correction, and training in righteousness. The ecclesial connection here is that fidelity to the Scriptures enables the minister to serve the needs of the people in the church. Paul assures Timothy that Scripture equips and provides a more than sufficient base from which to minister. As 2 Timothy 3:17 reads, "So that everyone who belongs to God may be proficient, equipped for every good work."

In 2 Timothy 4:1–5, we have a final charge from Paul to young Timothy as Paul nears what many scholars believe to be the end of his Christian race. The chapter has a solemn tone, both in the final charges that Paul brings to Timothy and in Paul's statements concerning his own impending death. Some have described this charge as Paul's last will and testament, while others believe he is simply looking beyond the time of his Roman imprisonment. What is important to remember is that our ministries are not our own; they belong to God. Many in Christian ministry could save themselves lots of heartache and worry if they could only remember that the work they are involved in is in God's hands. So we are not ultimately accountable to churches, denominations, or judicatories but to the One who will judge us on the last day. The knowledge that we must ultimately answer to God should encourage our hearts in times of despair and weariness. With five terse imperatives we are instructed to preach the word, be persistent whether the time is favorable or unfavorable, convince, rebuke, and encourage. We do this always mindful that the One who called us is faithful and will see our work to its fitting conclusion.

CLEOPHUS J. LARUE

1. James D. Smart, *The Strange Silence of the Bible in the Church* (Philadelphia: Westminster, 1970), 15.

Luke 18:1–8

[1]Then Jesus told them a parable about their need to pray always and not to lose heart. [2]He said, "In a certain city there was a judge who neither feared God nor had respect for people. [3]In that city there was a widow who kept coming to him and saying, 'Grant me justice against my opponent.' [4]For a while he refused; but later he said to himself, 'Though I have no fear of God and no respect for anyone, [5]yet because this widow keeps bothering me, I will grant her justice, so that she may not wear me out by continually coming.'" [6]And the Lord said, "Listen to what the unjust judge says. [7]And will not God grant justice to his chosen ones who cry to him day and night? Will he delay long in helping them? [8]I tell you, he will quickly grant justice to them. And yet, when the Son of Man comes, will he find faith on earth?"

Commentary 1: Connecting the Reading with Scripture

The parable of the Unjust Judge and the Persistent Widow is found only in the Gospel of Luke (18:1–8) and is situated within the traveling narrative (9:51–19:27). In the passage just before this parable, Jesus speaks about the coming of the Son of Man and acknowledges that, before the end comes, people will grow impatient for it (17:20–37). References to the Son of Man in 17:22, 24, 26, and 30 connect with Jesus' question at the end of the parable: "But when the Son of Man comes, will he find faith on earth?" (18:8). The answer to Jesus' rhetorical question, an affirmative yes, thus links this parable with the parable of the Pharisee and the Tax Collector that immediately follows (18:9–14). The question regarding the delay of the second coming seems to be a major concern for the Lukan community. Luke emphasizes that the period before the Parousia has been extended indefinitely; furthermore, he acknowledges that in this interim period it will be easy for people to lose confidence in God and to quit praying. So Luke recalls Jesus telling "a parable about their need to pray always and not to lose heart" (18:1). The parable encourages the disciples to keep on praying with conviction, in spite of the dark and difficult days ahead. The context of this parable provides an important clue to its multifaceted meaning. The parable revolves around two starkly contrasting characters: a judge and a widow.

The judge is described as one who "neither feared God nor had respect for people." Biblical judges were considered wise and reputable individuals (Deut. 1:15) and commissioned by God to "shepherd God's people" (1 Chr. 17:6). Furthermore, they ought to know that "fearing the Lord" is the beginning of wisdom (Prov. 1:7) and is an essential characteristic of the pious person (Pss. 14:4; 22:23). In the Magnificat, Mary already acclaimed, "God's mercy is for those who fear him from generation to generation" (Luke 1:50). In 12:4–7, Jesus told his disciples not to fear their future persecutors but to fear only God. In the light of OT expectation of a judge and Luke's emphasis on fearing God, there is obviously something wrong with the character of this judge. He is completely unfit for his position.

Standing opposite the judge is a widow who has neither power nor authority. In the Bible, widows almost always symbolize powerlessness and vulnerability (Exod. 22:22–24; Acts 6:1; 9:41; Jas. 1:27; 1 Tim. 5:3–15). Consequently, the Torah demands special care for them, as well as for orphans and strangers (Deut. 10:18; 14:29; 16:11, 14; 24:19–21; 26:12–13). There is even a specific command: "You shall not pervert the justice due the sojourner or to the fatherless, or take a widow's garment in pledge" (Deut. 24:17 RSV). Those who do so are even cursed (Deut. 27:19). The prophets considered rendering justice to widows as being loyal to the covenant (Mal. 3:5; Isa. 1:17, 23; 10:2; Jer. 49:11; Ezek. 22:7). The psalmists depict God as the judge who will come to help widows (Pss. 68:5; 146:9).

Widows had an honorable place in the early church. There might have been an "order" of widows whose ministry was to perform charitable works. The author of 1 Timothy states, "Honor widows who are really widows. . . . The real widow, left alone, has set her hope on God and continues in supplications and prayers night and day" (1 Tim. 5:3, 5). Luke gives an added prominence to widows both in his Gospel and in Acts. Anna, the widow who blessed the infant Jesus, is described as one who "never left the temple but worshiped there with fasting and prayer night and day" (Luke 2:37). The story of Jesus raising the son of the widow of Nain is found only in the Gospel of Luke (7:11–17). Luke's Jesus praises a widow for putting two copper coins in the treasury (21:1–3) and condemns those who "devour widows' houses" (20:47). Widows are also featured prominently in the book of Acts, namely, at the daily distribution of food (Acts 6:1–6) and in Peter's raising of Tabitha (9:39, 41).

Though vulnerable and a victim of injustice, the widow in our parable is bold and relentless in her demand for justice. Although biblical judges were charged with the responsibility of hearing complaints fairly and impartially, this judge refused to hear her case. Still, the widow "kept pressing him" (the imperfect verb should be translated as iterative). In other words, the standoff seemed to have continued for some time, but she did not give up. We are not told the specifics of her grievance. It was probably something to do with property or possession that, without due process, would leave the widow even more impoverished and defenseless. The judge finally gave in. In his soliloquy or interior monologue (vv. 4b–5), the judge states that he will render her justice because he is afraid of "being punched under the eye" (NRSV "wear me out," v. 5). The language of "a black eye" is a boxing metaphor that adds a bit of exaggerated humor. Interestingly, to outmatch the powerful and unjust judge, the widow used the only weapon she possessed, namely, her audacious persistence.

The parable does not end with the judge's words of relenting due to the widow's persistent pleading or "mighty punch" but, rather, with what Jesus says in verses 6–8, that God will render swift justice to God's "chosen ones who are crying out to him day and night." The repeated use of the word "justice" (vv. 3, 5, 7, 8) flashes like neon lights, highlighting Luke's central message both in the parable itself (vv. 2–6) and its interpretation (vv. 7–8). At the heart of this whole passage (18:1–8) is the plea for justice, which the widow tenaciously and audaciously fights for with every fiber of her being. It is the widow who is cast in the image of God, not the judge. Since God is a God of justice, God will not delay in bringing forth justice for God's chosen ones if they persist in their cause and stay the course. Notice that Jesus concludes the parable about justice and prayer with the question, "And yet, when the Son of Man comes, will he find *faith* on earth?" (v. 8b).

For Luke, it is *prayer with faith*, which is another name for persistence that will help overcome any injustice and wrong. Recall how Luke introduces the parable: "Then Jesus told them a parable about their need to *pray* always and not to lose heart" (18:1). In Luke's view, prayer is the essential medium to strengthen faith and undo injustices and evil acts in the world. In Luke's Gospel, Jesus prays often: at his baptism (3:21); in "deserted places" (5:16); on the mountain (6:12; 9:28); alone (9:18); in "a certain place" (11:1); on the Mount of Olives (22:41, 44); and hanging on a cross (23:34). It is in prayer that Jesus is transfigured with heavenly glory (9:29), and it is through prayer that he receives the strength to face his passion and death (22:43). Jesus often teaches and encourages his disciples to pray (6:28; 11:1–13; 18:1–8, 9–14; 22:40, 46). He warns his disciples that it is only through prayer that they can overcome the trials that lie ahead (22:46). Consequently, the parable of the Unjust Judge and the Persistent Widow provides another lesson in the power of prayer that helps overcome all obstacles.

VANTHANH NGUYEN, SVD

Commentary 2: Connecting the Reading with the World

This reading reminds us of the inexorably future-oriented nature of faith. The Christ-focused life allows for no comfortable contentment with the present. If the long season of Pentecost has lulled us into a sense of the reassuring regularity of life's rhythms, the widow's cry alerts us to unfinished business and unresolved pain. Verse 8 rounds off the teaching about the coming of the Son of Man, which Jesus has been giving since 17:22. With a jolt, we realize that Advent is just around the corner—as in fact it always is.

As Christians we naturally hear the parable as addressed to ourselves, but it offers as a model an oppressed widow, a classic representative of "the poor" to whom God's kingdom is promised (6:20). Jesus' encouragement to the disciples is set within the horizon of God's purpose to bring fullness of life for all, and his special care for the weak and vulnerable, manifest throughout Scripture. It is precisely as those who need to depend completely on God that Israel herself can be called the "chosen ones," the objects of his special love.[1] So when Jesus promises that God will "grant justice to his chosen ones" (18:7), the church should not take this as applying only narrowly to itself. God's purpose to restore equilibrium to the whole human race is in view (cf. Mary's Song, 1:46–55).

How exactly is the story meant to encourage us "to pray always and not lose heart" (v. 1)? If the widow's persistence with the judge is a model for us, what does that imply about the nature of God? Those who read this as a parable of comparison must face the awkward fact that (in this reading) God seems to be compared to a godless functionary. Those who read it as a parable of contrast must face the awkward fact that even though God may be completely different from the reluctant judge, Jesus still seems to urge us to pray as if he were not.

We need to feel the force of Jesus' brief anecdote as a realistic vignette from his world. It suggests that, notwithstanding the general godlessness of a judicial regime, justice is possible *now* for those who persistently seek it. The widow's action, then, is not a mere metaphor for prayer as inward communion with God. She does not stay at home on her knees, but goes to the one who can deliver justice, and demands it. Thus, we should not draw a sharp distinction between asking God to act and taking action ourselves to bring about just ends. We might even see pursuing justice as a form of prayer. God acts on the widow's behalf through, and despite, the godlessness of the human authority figure.

Widows were archetypally vulnerable in a society where the individual family unit was usually the sole source of social support and identity. In keeping with the biblical tradition of not only affirming God's care for them, but also identifying heroic faith among them (e.g., Naomi and Ruth; the widow of Zarephath in 1 Kgs. 17:8–24), Luke presents this widow who confounds any stereotype of helplessness (Anna in 2:36–38). In making imaginative connections between the story and our own societies, we will wish to find authentic examples of those who in the midst of extreme vulnerability assert their power as responsible agents. Heroines and heroes of justice-seeking prayer are often those who overturn expectations of how they should behave, and thus cause discomfort to settled social patterns.

The judge in the story also seems to be an archetype but not a stereotype. The godlessness of rulers was well nigh proverbial, as Psalm 82 reveals. Thus, he stands for all those heartless individuals and regimes, both then and now, who have power to effect the righting of wrongs but do not do so. Yet he is not a stereotype, since—without any real conversion of heart—he resolves in the end to deal with the widow's case. Hence, contemporary stories of hope that echo this one will point not only to the potential of the poor, but also to the weakness of the powerful. Changing their attitudes may be beyond what anyone can attain, but changing their behavior can be enough to give someone a taste of God's kingdom.

1. See Jonathan Sacks, *Not in God's Name: Confronting Religious Violence* (London: Hodder & Stoughton, 2015), 198–200.

What, though, is the "justice" the widow seeks? We are probably not meant to see this as mere personal vindictiveness, as the KJV's "avenge me" may suggest. The cultural assumptions that widows were liable to be exploited and authorities were liable to be callous lead us to presume a just cause. We are left to imagine the nature of her dispute with her "adversary" and what a "just" outcome might be. In the first instance, perhaps, she simply wants her case to be heard, a desire that will certainly resonate with, for example, many asylum seekers and people falsely imprisoned.

This desire for justice in one's own cause may make some Western Christians with an aversion to litigation a little squeamish—maybe reflecting the fact that they have not been on the receiving end of the harsh realities of oppression. Yet those realities are close to home, since the structures that keep many living in a perpetual state of marginality and risk are not just local or national, but international. Today's "widow" seeking justice against her opponent may perhaps be the coffee grower in a developing nation unable to gain a reasonable price for her crop because the international trading system keeps prices artificially low to feed the demands of the rich West.

Justice, biblically understood, goes far beyond blind tit-for-tat retribution, vengeance craved by the embittered, or any narrowly legal setting. Justice or righteousness is that state of harmony reflecting God's created order in which all that God has made can flourish as God intended. It also has the specific force of "vindication" for those with whom God has aligned himself, "his chosen ones" (v. 7). The widow sought it as it applied to her personally, but in Luke justice is surely a key element of the universal kingdom of God that Jesus said was "among" his hearers (17:21), if not an actual synonym for it. Paul would claim that God's righteousness has been revealed and restored through Christ and is now manifested through his people (Rom. 1:16–17; 2 Cor. 5:16–22). Contemporary hearers of the story will benefit from clarification of this biblical perspective on justice, in the light of the varied connotations of the word today.

What encouragement then does this story give individual disciples in their prayer? It points, in the oblique manner suggested above, to prayer as being long-term, whole-life perseverance in faith, both yearning and working for the coming of God's just kingdom (cf. Luke 11:2) for all. The story affirms the reliable mercy of God for all who labor under the oppression of earthly "kingdoms" of any type but is realistic in picturing the tough endurance needed. It maintains a clear ultimate focus on the consummation of that kingdom when the Son of Man comes (v. 8), while holding out hope that surprising glimpses of it are to be seen now. James Montgomery's hymn "Lord, teach us how to pray aright"[2] captures the spirit of the text (with an echo also of Job 13:15 KJV) when it asks for

> Patience to watch, and wait, and weep,
> Though mercy long delay;
> Courage our fainting souls to keep,
> And trust thee, though thou slay.

STEPHEN I. WRIGHT

2. See "The English Hymnal #78." Hymnary.org. https://hymnary.org/hymn/EH1906/78.

Proper 25 (Sunday between October 23 and October 29 Inclusive)

Joel 2:23–32 and Jeremiah 14:7–10, 19–22
Psalm 65 and Psalm 84:1–7
2 Timothy 4:6–8, 16–18
Luke 18:9–14

Joel 2:23–32

[23]O children of Zion, be glad
and rejoice in the LORD your God;
for he has given the early rain for your vindication,
he has poured down for you abundant rain,
the early and the later rain, as before.
[24]The threshing floors shall be full of grain,
the vats shall overflow with wine and oil.

[25]I will repay you for the years
that the swarming locust has eaten,
the hopper, the destroyer, and the cutter,
my great army, which I sent against you.

[26]You shall eat in plenty and be satisfied,
and praise the name of the LORD your God,
who has dealt wondrously with you.
And my people shall never again be put to shame.
[27]You shall know that I am in the midst of Israel,
and that I, the LORD, am your God and there is no other.
And my people shall never again be put to shame.

[28]Then afterward
I will pour out my spirit on all flesh;
your sons and your daughters shall prophesy,
your old men shall dream dreams,
and your young men shall see visions.
[29]Even on the male and female slaves,
in those days, I will pour out my spirit.

[30]I will show portents in the heavens and on the earth, blood and fire and columns of smoke. [31]The sun shall be turned to darkness, and the moon to blood, before the great and terrible day of the LORD comes. [32]Then everyone who calls on the name of the LORD shall be saved; for in Mount Zion and in Jerusalem there shall be those who escape, as the LORD has said, and among the survivors shall be those whom the LORD calls.

Jeremiah 14:7–10, 19–22

[7]Although our iniquities testify against us,
act, O LORD, for your name's sake;
our apostasies indeed are many,
and we have sinned against you.
[8]O hope of Israel,
its savior in time of trouble,
why should you be like a stranger in the land,
like a traveler turning aside for the night?
[9]Why should you be like someone confused,
like a mighty warrior who cannot give help?
Yet you, O LORD, are in the midst of us,
and we are called by your name;
do not forsake us!

[10]Thus says the LORD concerning this people:
Truly they have loved to wander,
they have not restrained their feet;
therefore the LORD does not accept them,
now he will remember their iniquity
and punish their sins.

. . . .

[19]Have you completely rejected Judah?
Does your heart loathe Zion?
Why have you struck us down
so that there is no healing for us?
We look for peace, but find no good;
for a time of healing, but there is terror instead.
[20]We acknowledge our wickedness, O LORD,
the iniquity of our ancestors,
for we have sinned against you.
[21]Do not spurn us, for your name's sake;
do not dishonor your glorious throne;
remember and do not break your covenant with us.
[22]Can any idols of the nations bring rain?
Or can the heavens give showers?
Is it not you, O LORD our God?
We set our hope on you,
for it is you who do all this.

Commentary 1: Connecting the Reading with Scripture

The people of the southern kingdom of Judah were facing a perfect storm: drought compounded by a plague of locusts. Anybody who has lived through such a plague knows the terror of the actual swarm: an anticipated harvest ruined and the new season's planting compromised. Adding to the catastrophe, Joel also mentions invading armies (2:20, 25). Perhaps this is a metaphor evoked by the invasive locusts, or perhaps Joel speaks of both environmental and political disaster.

Joel is not all woes and horrors. Rather, there is a marked shift in focus at Joel 2:28 from judgment to hope. Though this shift seems initially discordant, this makes sense in the context of Joel as both halves of the book gather around a vision of the Day of the Lord, a theme shared with Amos and Isaiah of Jerusalem. As imagined by the Hebrew prophets, the Day of the Lord, a time of anticipated intervention by the Lord, would be a day both "great" and "terrible" (v. 31), of both judgment and salvation.

The recipients of the prophecy are addressed as "children of Zion" (v. 23). As well as referring to Jerusalem, the term "Zion" evokes a powerful strand of thought around the cosmic rule of YHWH from Jerusalem, a rule that would eventually be characterized by a flowing river and fertility (Ezek. 47:1–12; Zech. 14:8). Addressing the nation as Zion anticipates this hope, which comes to fruition later in Joel's vision at 3:18–21, when the prophet announces the blessings that the Lord will bestow on Zion.

This vision is deeply connected to contemporary circumstances of drought caused by the failure of rains critical for the harvest (2:23–24). In an environment where every drop of water is a gift, promised abundance (v. 23) followed by overflowing harvests (v. 24) is a blessing indeed. This promise also foreshadows the cosmic reign of YHWH from the hill of Zion (3:17), with unimaginable fertility and abundance of water (3:18; see also Amos 9:13).

Though the drought and locust have stolen and stripped, God "will repay" the people for those lost years (2:25). The verb translated as "repay" stems from the same word group as the noun *shalom*, with its implication of wholeness and restoration. God here promises much more than monetary replenishment, more than the restoration of a reliable crop cycle. Rather, verses 26–27 speak of release from shame. The repayment of God means that the people will be secure, not only in their food supply (v. 26), but also in their identity as the covenant people of God (v. 27).

The Day of the Lord is normally viewed as a time of both salvation and judgment, but with the shimmer of a promise of more to come (Ezek. 30; Amos 9:11–15; Zech. 14:4). Accordingly, in verse 28 Joel turns to a time "afterward." The satisfaction and security promised in preceding verses will further express itself by an outpouring of God's spirit, understood primarily as a spirit of prophecy. This experience will be characterized by access for all to the word of the Lord through the regular means of prophecy: visions and dreams. Normally impregnable boundaries in ancient society will break down as everyone—slaves and free, men and women, old and young—will experience the outpouring of God's spirit. This coming day, accompanied by portents deployed from the book of Exodus (vv. 30–31), will bring salvation for those who "[call] on the name of the Lord" (v. 32).

Peter on the day of Pentecost saw the fulfillment of verses 28–32 in the coming of the Spirit on the gathered believers (Acts 2:17–21). However, for Peter, the coming of the Spirit inaugurates a new era for all of humanity. If Joel has foreseen the democratizing of the spirit of prophecy, Peter universalizes it: "everyone who calls on the name of the Lord shall be saved" (Acts 2:21).

As with Joel, a sustained period of drought (Jer. 14:22) compounded with the rising threat of Babylon might have set the context for Jeremiah's oracle (14:7–10, 19–22). Jeremiah begins by both acknowledging the sins of the people (v. 7) and protesting God's silence as dishonoring God's own name. In doing so, Jeremiah echoes a common strategy of the lamenting psalmist, that God should act on behalf of the lamenter, so that God's name might be honored (Pss. 25:11; 79:9; 109:21). The name in Hebrew thought is considered to reflect the essence of the name-bearer's character, and so the prophet is appealing to the covenant-keeping nature of God to act on behalf of his covenant people. The sentiment is repeated in verse 21. In verse 9 the prophet reminds God that God's identity is inextricably bound up with that of his people. God's "name is called upon us"; God is "in the midst of us" (v. 9).

Another of YHWH's names is "hope of Israel" (v. 8), which sounds similar to the Hebrew term for pool or reservoir (Isa. 22:11). The double entendre again hints of the need for hope in drought-stricken Israel. This "hope" is in poetic parallelism with "savior." The people look to the Lord to save them from both the drought and an encroaching Babylonian army, but God is worse than silent or absent. In a series of metaphors Jeremiah depicts God as uncaring and helpless: a stranger who cannot be approached; a traveler who fails to see the urgency and turns aside to sleep; somebody who is confused; or a beaten warrior (vv. 8–9). God states that the failure lies with the people (v. 10), who have "loved to wander" to the wrong places for help: to Assyria and Egypt to be exact (Jer. 2:18). The judgment is unyielding; they will be remembered (v. 10), but in the wrong sort of way.

Jeremiah then responds with a further lament (vv. 19–22). There are two significant shifts in this lament, however. The first is a more explicit questioning of YHWH's disapproval along with a poignant longing for healing. "Healing" includes the notion of restoration and recovery from disaster (see Isa. 53:5). For the moment, though, this longing is met only by God's implacability. A second shift is a more explicit allusion to the physical circumstances that occasion the lament. Rather than restoration and healing, there is terror, a visceral fear (v. 19). It is hard to know wherein lies the greater terror: in invasion and drought or in the implacability of God (see 1 Sam. 16:14; Dan. 8:17; Job 7:14).

Alongside the reprisal of the honor of God's name is another curious phrase: "do not dishonor your glorious throne" (v. 21). The verb translated as "dishonor" carries the sense of holding something in contempt. The prophet pleads for God to "remember" the covenant (v. 21), rather than the people's "iniquity" (v. 10); to do otherwise is tantamount to holding his own name in contempt. Finally, as the last bargaining chip, Jeremiah reminds God of their utter dependence on him for rain in a time of drought, perhaps in implicit acknowledgment of the people's "apostasies" (v. 7). God remains unyielding: "send them out of my sight, and let them go" (15:1).

The challenge to preachers is to hold the unyielding silence of God with God's forgiveness and pouring out of the spirit anticipated by Joel. Part of the journey of faith is thus to be fortified by Peter's declaration from the book of Joel that "everyone who calls on the name of the Lord shall be saved."

TIM MEADOWCROFT

Commentary 2: Connecting the Reading with the World

Both Joel and Jeremiah speak into periods of deep national travail. During good times Jeremiah's people pay God no mind. They chase after other gods. Similarly, we pursue false divinities such as wealth, power, or influence, idols that lure us away from the one true God. Those Jeremiah addresses admit that their iniquities testify against them, that they have not been faithful or attentive to God. Why should any of us expect God to show us charity when we are disrespectful toward God or ignore God and God's claims on our lives?

We are less inclined as a society to link our actions to God's punishments—and less inclined to admit our iniquities—but there is no doubt that our abuses of self, others, and God's creation have far-reaching ramifications. In response to the consequences of our actions, some of us rail at God, alleging divine injustice rather than acknowledging our complicity. Some sink into the depths of despair, convinced that our dire straits are deserved because of something we have done or left undone. Some turn bewildered to God and raise issues of theodicy while displaying no compunction to approach God before a personal situation becomes desperate. Others use traumatic events as reason to claim that a loving God does not exist and to assert that there is nothing to be gained in appealing to God. Into all these realities, the preacher is called to preach a word that is both prophetic (naming our waywardness) and pastoral (proclaiming our basis for hope). We are called by God's name (Jer. 14:9b) and set our hope on God (v. 22).

Self-justifying behavior is timeless. We are quick to dodge culpability and eager to blame another. We have a great capacity to cry out to God, and then turn on our heels and dismiss God when our circumstances ease. We confess our complete dependence on God in one breath and brag about our self-sufficiency in the next. We lack the humility to admit that, despite our scientific and technological advancements, we are powerless before God.

Abundant life comes from living in right relationship with God and one another. We cannot expect of others what we do not expect of ourselves. Lift up the hypocrisy of claiming to be obedient to God while demanding for ourselves privileges we do not afford others. Explore and expand on Jeremiah's references to drought, which frame this passage.

The vast majority of scientists agree that humankind is disrupting the earth's rhythms and harmonies and compounding the effects of natural disasters. Literature gives us graphic pictures of our vulnerability. Poet Wendell Berry, a child of the agricultural South "born in a drouth year," writes, "Fear of dust in my mouth is always with me."[1]

Drought is a universal human predicament sometimes dressed in different clothing. Our lives provide travails analogous to those referenced by the prophets. People in various parts of the world experience times of literal drought. Others know metaphorical drought: serious illness, job loss, home foreclosure, loss of faith, loss of hope, infidelity, or other hardship. Droughts may come on us suddenly and leave us crying desperately to God to intervene. Alcoholism, drug addiction, or huge gambling debts may develop over years and be of our own making. There are spiritual as well as physical droughts. There are parallels in the degradation of human dignity we allow by tolerating disrespect, misogyny, and bullying. We mirror Jeremiah's first hearers when we are blind to our complicity in the earth's devastation and the oppression of God's children, yet we persist in crying out to God for mercy.

Opposite drought are devastating floods and broken levees that sweep lives away and wildfires that rip through swaths of the country. Humans are complicit in such catastrophic losses. Images sear our souls and elicit our identification, giving way for the preacher to tie an ancient text to the very real sufferings of our times.

After a period of immense suffering indicative of a broken relationship with God, the prophet Joel invites the reader into a new relationship with God that is both humbling and necessarily reciprocal. Joel's people endured a period of crippling drought and a plague of locusts that ravaged the land as effectively as an invading army. Anyone who has lived where periodical cicadas emerge by the thousands has some knowledge of the aptness of the invasion metaphor. To those in an ancient agricultural context and in the less-developed world today, the consequences of locusts are not an inconvenience but devastating. Despair grips Joel's people. Drought and plagues mean famine, disease, and death due to malnutrition or starvation.

Against this, the prophet paints a high-stakes reversal of circumstances. God offers hope where there was despair. According to Joel 2:25–3:21, God turns from punishment, promising to repay "for the years that the swarming locust has eaten" (2:25). God relents from chastening the children of Zion and reasserts covenantal faithfulness. God's plan is for the earth to bloom with plenty.

Our abuse of the physical world is at cross-purposes with God's call for us to be stewards of creation. The effects of a supercharged atmosphere are not limited to the natural world but bleed into a raft of social issues and tensions pitting people against profits, the prosperous against the poor, population growth against limited land and resources. This text gives the preacher an opportunity to speak prophetically to worshipers. Where are we derelict as stewards of the planet and of human relationships? Point out the tension between God's desire that the earth bloom with plenty and our remaining silent while the rich get more and the poor sink, where our effects on the earth are ignored and island nations are subsumed by rising waters.

The most familiar verses in the Joel passage are echoed in Acts: God will pour out blessings on all equally (Acts 2:17–21). The preacher can lift up examples of humankind's continual resistance to this, our continual efforts to elevate ourselves at the expense of others.

Nearing the end of the liturgical year and approaching the celebration of the reign of Christ, this reading offers a reset for worshipers. Because of the unchanging nature of God, the prophet's ancient words are simultaneously a wake-up call for the entitled and a balm for the

1. Wendell Berry, "Water" (1970), in *The Ecopoetry Anthology*, ed. Ann Fisher-Wirth and Laura-Gray Street (San Antonio, TX: Trinity University Press, 2013), 176.

downtrodden, a cautionary note and refreshment for the dry and barren earth. God's pledge to shield all from future shame, to rain down blessing and power, and to live out the righteousness of God by renewing the relationship between God and humankind are offerings of hope. This passage concludes with a promise for all who call on the Lord. Here is an action step that does not change God but changes us. Those whom the Lord calls are those who call on the Lord (Joel 2:32). This promised grace is effected through God's working in humankind and working for us.

Like the prophet, the preacher appeals to the people. How might we work with God to know God's presence and seek the restoration of the environment, the health of crop-producing soil, the protection of polar icecaps, the return of civil discourse? God calls us. In that calling we have a choice: to step up emboldened, empowered, and freed to call on God, or to shrink back and shirk responsibility. We are much more able to accept the invitation to partner with God if we already have a relationship with God.

FAIRFAX F. FAIR

Proper 25 (Sunday between October 23 and October 29 Inclusive)

Psalm 65

[1]Praise is due to you,
  O God, in Zion;
and to you shall vows be performed,
  [2]O you who answer prayer!
To you all flesh shall come.
[3]When deeds of iniquity overwhelm us,
  you forgive our transgressions.
[4]Happy are those whom you choose and bring near
  to live in your courts.
We shall be satisfied with the goodness of your house,
  your holy temple.

[5]By awesome deeds you answer us with deliverance,
  O God of our salvation;
you are the hope of all the ends of the earth
  and of the farthest seas.
[6]By your strength you established the mountains;
  you are girded with might.
[7]You silence the roaring of the seas,
  the roaring of their waves,
  the tumult of the peoples.
[8]Those who live at earth's farthest bounds are awed by your signs;
you make the gateways of the morning and the evening shout for joy.

[9]You visit the earth and water it,
  you greatly enrich it;
the river of God is full of water;
  you provide the people with grain,
  for so you have prepared it.
[10]You water its furrows abundantly,
  settling its ridges,
softening it with showers,
  and blessing its growth.
[11]You crown the year with your bounty;
  your wagon tracks overflow with richness.
[12]The pastures of the wilderness overflow,
  the hills gird themselves with joy,
[13]the meadows clothe themselves with flocks,
  the valleys deck themselves with grain,
  they shout and sing together for joy.

Psalm 84:1–7

[1]How lovely is your dwelling place,
O LORD of hosts!
[2]My soul longs, indeed it faints
for the courts of the LORD;
my heart and my flesh sing for joy
to the living God.

[3]Even the sparrow finds a home,
and the swallow a nest for herself,
where she may lay her young,
at your altars, O LORD of hosts,
my King and my God.
[4]Happy are those who live in your house,
ever singing your praise.

[5]Happy are those whose strength is in you,
in whose heart are the highways to Zion.
[6]As they go through the valley of Baca
they make it a place of springs;
the early rain also covers it with pools.
[7]They go from strength to strength;
the God of gods will be seen in Zion.

Connecting the Psalm with Scripture and Worship

Psalm 65 (Joel 2:23–32). It is hard not to think of Pentecost when we hear the words, "I will pour out my spirit on all flesh" (Joel 2:28). The juxtaposition of Joel 2 and Psalm 65 gives us the opportunity to consider this image in a different season.

Psalms scholar Sigmund Mowinckel called Psalm 65 "the thanksgiving psalm of the harvest feast" (Tabernacles or *Sukkot*), giving "a magnificent picture of all the blessings promised and granted by [God's] new victory over the powers of chaos."[1] Indeed, the psalm has a cosmic scope—praising God as the "hope of all the ends of the earth and of the farthest seas" (v. 5), who makes "the gateways of the morning and the evening shout for joy" (v. 8). The psalmist blesses the Lord for the gift of the rain upon which the harvest depends (v. 9) and depicts the whole creation singing praise to God, with humanity joining in the joyful song. A reference to God "crown[ing] the year with . . . bounty" (v. 11) seems to reflect the turning of the year at Rosh Hashanah, prior to the time of harvest.

The first reading, from Joel, underscores the psalm's connection to the harvest festival, with its references to abundant rain (Joel 2:23), threshing floors filled with grain (v. 24), relief from destructive plagues (v. 25), and a bountiful crop for the people of God (v. 26). In Joel, God promises, "I will pour out my spirit on all flesh" (v. 28); the psalm responds, "O you who answer prayer! To you all flesh shall come" (Ps. 65:2). In Joel people everywhere will "dream dreams" and "see visions" (Joel 2:28), and the psalmist exclaims: "Those who live at earth's farthest bounds are awed by your signs" (Ps. 65:8). The grand, cosmic imagery in Joel takes a more foreboding turn with "portents in the heavens

1. Sigmund Mowinckel, *The Psalms in Israel's Worship* (Grand Rapids: Eerdmans, 2004), 162.

and on the earth, blood and fire and columns of smoke" (Joel 2:30) "before the great and terrible day of the LORD" (v. 31). Just as Joel suggests that "everyone who calls on the name of the LORD shall be saved" (Joel 2:32) the psalmist bears witness to God's mighty acts of redemption: "By awesome deeds you answer us with deliverance, O God of our salvation" (Ps. 65:5).

This appearance of Joel 2 (with its companion, Psalm 65) in the waning weeks of the Christian year helps us remember that God pours out the Spirit in all seasons, and on the whole earth—not just on the church or even the human race. Psalm 65 challenges us to broaden our horizons, to consider the universal scope of God's love for the world, including care for creation, feeding the hungry, and delivering the oppressed. These are critical themes for preaching in our time. With the many vivid images of creation in this psalm, worship planners may wish to think about how liturgical space interacts (or does not interact) with the rhythms of nature.

Psalm 84:1–7 (Jeremiah 14:7–10, 19–22). Perhaps you picture yourself surrounded by stained glass and organ pipes, singing "How Lovely Is Thy Dwelling Place" from the *German Requiem* of Johannes Brahms. Perhaps you have fond memories of being in a crowded auditorium at a youth conference, belting out "Better Is One Day" by Matt Redman. Regardless, Psalm 84 transports us to a place of worship—the dwelling place of the Lord of hosts, the courts of the Holy One, the very house of God.

Psalm 84 is a pilgrim song, reflecting a worshiper's fervent desire to be present at the Jerusalem temple on a festival day: "My soul longs, indeed it faints for the courts of the LORD" (v. 2). Like a sparrow or swallow, the pilgrim yearns to find shelter in God's house (v. 3). Liturgical scholar Irene Nowell suggests this psalm may be associated with the Day of Atonement (Yom Kippur) or the Feast of Tabernacles (*Sukkot*), observed around the time of the first rains of autumn. This would explain the psalm's reference to springs, pools, and early rain (v. 6). Nowell also points out that Psalm 84 includes three "beatitudes" (the first two within the bounds of this lectionary pericope): "Happy are those who live in your house" (v. 4), "Happy are those whose strength is in you" (v. 5), and "Happy is everyone who trusts in you" (v. 12).[2]

Psalm 84 might be understood as the prayer of the repentant tax collector in Luke 18:9–14, the Gospel reading for the day. The tax collector humbles himself before the Lord, confessing his sin and calling on God's mercy. By contrast, this proud Pharisee praises his own righteousness and pities his fellow worshipers. Which would stand awe-struck in the temple, singing, "How lovely is your dwelling place" (v. 1)? Which would say, "I would rather be a doorkeeper in the house of my God" (v. 10)?

The first reading is thematically tied to the Gospel in the complementary track of the Revised Common Lectionary. Jeremiah 14:7–10, 19–22 is a communal prayer of confession and lament—acknowledging the people's transgressions and imploring God to be gracious, much like the tax collector's more personal cry: "God, be merciful to me, a sinner!" (Luke 18:13). In either case, Psalm 84:1–7 expresses the wonder and gratitude of one who—in spite of everything—has been invited to stand in the presence of the Holy One. The watery imagery of Psalm 84:6 seems especially well suited to the closing verse of the Jeremiah passage, praising God as the giver of rain (Jer. 14:22).

A sermon on the texts for Proper 25 might focus on the way in which God extends mercy to saints and sinners alike—just as God "sends rain on the righteous and on the unrighteous" (Matt. 5:45). Taking a cue from Psalm 84, the preacher might consider the remarkable gift of deep intimacy and honest relationship with the living God in worship. Worship planners might wish to study the 2010 World Communion of Reformed Churches document "Worshiping the Triune God." Like Psalm 84, this description of faithful worship is interwoven with "beatitudes" on liturgical life. Through Psalm 84, God calls us to worship, and we respond: "Happy are those who live in your house, ever singing your praise" (v. 4).

2. Irene Nowell, *Sing a New Song: The Psalms in the Sunday Lectionary* (Collegeville, MN: Liturgical Press, 1993), 279.

Finally, note that almost all of the readings for Proper 25—in both the semicontinuous and complementary tracks—include the image of "pouring out." The Gospel reading, Luke 18:9–14, is the only one in which this image is not explicitly stated, and even here the tax collector's effusive outpouring of prayer is contrasted with the Pharisee's carefully measured offering.

If worship in your congregation does not ordinarily include the pouring of water into the baptismal font, this would be an excellent day to consider the practice. Appropriate times to pour water into the font include the opening of worship, the call to confession, and the declaration of forgiveness, the call to discipleship, and the invitation to offering. Wherever or whenever it happens, the evocative gesture of pouring water vividly conveys the extravagance of God's grace, the generosity of Christ's self-offering, and the abundance of the Spirit's gifts.

DAVID GAMBRELL

2 Timothy 4:6–8, 16–18

[6]As for me, I am already being poured out as a libation, and the time of my departure has come. [7]I have fought the good fight, I have finished the race, I have kept the faith. [8]From now on there is reserved for me the crown of righteousness, which the Lord, the righteous judge, will give me on that day, and not only to me but also to all who have longed for his appearing. . . .

[16]At my first defense no one came to my support, but all deserted me. May it not be counted against them! [17]But the Lord stood by me and gave me strength, so that through me the message might be fully proclaimed and all the Gentiles might hear it. So I was rescued from the lion's mouth. [18]The Lord will rescue me from every evil attack and save me for his heavenly kingdom. To him be the glory forever and ever. Amen.

Commentary 1: Connecting the Reading with Scripture

Second Timothy 4:6–8 forms the conclusion of the paraenetic discourses that characterize the entire epistle. The subject alternates between "I" and "you" throughout. Paul recounts his own experiences and his manner of ministry and interposes his analysis of the dangers and problems Timothy is going to face. He then focuses on what Timothy must do and how he must do it. The final "But as for me" of verse 6 recounts what is likely to await him. The phrase "crown of righteousness" is associated with martyrdom in the early church.[1] In this case, the implied martyrdom is both the culmination of his ministry and the reward for his faithfulness.

The verses that come later in the passage (vv. 16–18) make Paul's situation more concrete. He has faced a trial alone and feels deserted. God, though, was with him, and even in such circumstances Paul was able to continue his proclamation. Somehow Paul endured the trial, although 1 Timothy 1 suggests that he is still imprisoned in Rome, and it is clear throughout the epistle that he expects to be put to death very soon.

The specifics of Paul's situation, as depicted in 2 Timothy, are maddeningly unclear. If he is in fact in Rome, there must be some connection with the conclusion of the book of Acts, which has Paul under guard in Rome, but with considerable freedom of movement. If the biographical details of 2 Timothy are accurate, Paul in chains and subject to examination must have occurred at a later time. Whether a convincing reconstruction of the events surrounding the end of Paul's life can be made is a moot point. What is clear is that 2 Timothy depicts the situation of a person in captivity facing execution. His major concern is to prepare those who will come after him for their own ministry. In this context, "Timothy," who was undoubtedly a real person, also can symbolize any successor of Paul, from that day to this, who is undertaking service to the gospel.

If 2 Timothy is genuine, these verses represent Paul's own judgment on his ministry. If they are from another hand, they form the judgment of Paul's successors on his ministry. In a sense, this passage constitutes his obituary, and it is congratulatory: Paul has done all that he has been asked to do thus far, and all that remains is his death, which he anticipates will be at the hand of others.

Paul often refers to his own ministry in the letters. Sometimes this is in reference to a particular situation, as in Galatians. In other

1. See Martin Dibelius and Hans Conzelmann, *The Pastoral Epistles: A Commentary on the Pastoral Epistles*, Hermeneia (Philadelphia: Fortress, 1972), 121.

instances, he gives more general characterizations of his ministry (cf. 2 Cor. 4:8–11). Often in such accounts he is paradoxical: "I, but not I" (e.g., 2 Cor. 12:5–10). In this case, however, there is no paradox. Paul's parallel phrases, "I have fought . . . , I have finished . . . , I have kept . . ." are without qualification or paradox. This lack of qualification might strike some as self-congratulatory or even boastful. Indeed, in his commentary on 2 Timothy, John Calvin felt it necessary to defend Paul against a charge of works righteousness.[2]

If the letter is not authentically Pauline, this aspect is more understandable and easier to accept as posthumous praise. It is an obituary in the first person. If the letter is from Paul's own hand, one does find something of a qualification in verse 17, in which Paul states that God's strength was working through him as he faced his judgment abandoned and alone.

In some sense, this is reminiscent of Jesus before Herod and Pilate. He also stood alone, abandoned by his disciples. It is impossible to say whether Paul intended this resemblance, but surely it occurred to him. It is important not to claim too much of this. Paul surely does not intend to present himself as a Christ figure, but at least it can be said that followers of Jesus, including Paul himself, might be called on to face what Jesus faced.

The lectionary omits verses 9–15 from this reading. There is a reason for this exclusion, but there is a rather significant loss as well. This list of instructions for Timothy and people known to Paul gives 2 Timothy the flavor of an actual letter. Such lists are prominent parts of letters such as Romans and 1 Corinthians, but are absent in 1 Timothy. The whole passage humanizes Paul. He is in prison but he is keeping busy. He is also thinking about people he knows. Most of them he values, but he does have some anger and resentment. The triumphant saint of verses 6–8 is actually very human when these details are presented, and consequently more endearing.

Moving from Timothy to other passages for this lection, the common thread of these readings is rather elusive. The passage from Joel 2:23–32, an apocalyptic prophecy, might be well known because it is substantially repeated in Peter's Pentecost speech in Acts 2, which does harmonize with the apocalyptic elements in this passage. In both, there is an element of universalism. Paul's concern during his trial is that the Gentiles hear the gospel, and the Joel passage from Joel promises that God's spirit will be poured out on all flesh. Both passages also appear to affirm the hope of divine salvation in face of a harsh reality filled with sufferings, failures, and possibly death.

The parable from Luke 18:9–14, also well known, focuses on the individual. The sinner who acknowledges his sin is justified; the righteous Pharisee is not. Paul in verses 6–8 sounds somewhat more like the Pharisee than the tax collector, but Paul also (in v. 17) acknowledges that it is God's strength that brings about the victory. In the undoubtedly authentic letters, Paul might boast of his accomplishments then immediately say he is acting like a fool (2 Cor. 11–12).

Psalm 65 has a different tone altogether. It is a straightforward and detailed celebration of the goodness of God's creation. In this psalm, we are rather far away from Paul facing death in prison and Joel's vision of what is to come, but it is certainly possible to reconcile all this. The God who created all things good is in the process of redeeming that creation and summons people to share in the work of creation.

Despite the consensus (but by no means unanimous) of contemporary scholars that 2 Timothy is the product of a later hand, the usefulness of the book is evident. It is a handbook for ministry, particularly for ministry in times of transition. The book is a reminder that when the work of a single individual—in this case, Paul—is done, the work itself is not done, and others must assume their own tasks. Furthermore, the epistle warns, the work will not be easy. It will involve trial and suffering and might lead to death. Even that death will be a part of God's triumph and will come with a crown.

DAVID W. JOHNSON

2. John Calvin, *Commentary on 1 and 2 Timothy, and Titus* (Wheaton, IL: Crossway, 1998), 163.

Commentary 2: Connecting the Reading to the World

Paul declares that he has "fought the good fight," that he has "finished the race," and that he has "kept the faith" (v. 7). These words, which will bring the apostle Paul's ministry to a close, are written in the face of death and, in a sense, in defiance of death. Paul writes these words for Timothy's sake to inspire him by the grace of God to duplicate them in his life with the same courage, assurance, and joy. He is in effect saying to Timothy, "I have done what was necessary in my time; now you must do what is necessary in your time."

These are words of stamina and endurance that we so desperately need to hear in contemporary times. We live in a stressful time, when untold numbers of ministers are walking away from ordained ministry after only a few years of service. Many say they simply cannot contend with the stress, long hours, low pay, and lack of appreciation on the part of the membership. Studies show that the salaries of ministers in general are considerably below those of other professionals. Others cite family concerns as the reason for their early exit from ministry. Paul would have resonated with this feeling of isolation (v. 16).

Even those who remain in ministry may suffer severe burnout as they go about their work. For some, the joy and hopefulness they experienced in the early days of their ministry are now gone. They feel trapped in the routinization and ho-hum of ministry. Many say they feel that organized religion is no longer where the action is when it comes to making a difference in the world. They find themselves unable to answer positively Jürgen Moltmann's burning questions about the significance of the church: Who are we? Does it matter? Some ministers and laypeople alike hang on, counting the days until they can claim their retirement benefits and head off to a life that no longer includes the daily grind of ministry.

Paul clearly saw his ministry in a different light—even when faced with persecution and the threat of death. In fact, as he looks back over his life, he seems to accept with conviction and assurance the fact that his life is already to the point of being poured out in sacrifice (v. 6). These words of Paul to young Timothy should be heard by us today, not in terms of concluding our ministries but in terms of patient endurance and determination to continue on with our ministries. What Paul is asking of Timothy is no more than Paul has done himself. The valiant runner who is close to the goal is beckoning the others on to win the laurel crown (v. 7). The two metaphors that dominate this passage are sacrifice and departure. There is no sense of giving up or giving in, but Paul seems driven by the conviction that though the fight may be hard, it is a fight he has been called to by none other than God. He seems to possess the confident assurance that God will lead him to his purposeful end in ministry (v. 18).

This is not a word just for ministers. This is equally a word to all people of faith. At the heart of this charge is the admonition for Timothy to live a life with purpose and meaning. Paul sees himself as having lived a purposeful life, and now living out a purposeful death. So this passage raises important questions worthy of address: How can we live a purposeful life? What should a purposeful life entail?

Every Christian ought to desire to have his or her life brought to its purposeful end or telos. Though we are not imprisoned like Paul, we are nonetheless expected to live a life that is pleasing and acceptable to God. In the black church, elders who had given themselves in service to God would often close their prayers by saying, "And now, Lord, when I have done all that you have assigned my hands to do, I pray that you would receive me into your heavenly abode, where every day will be Sunday and Sabbath shall have no end." There is much to be said for finishing well, to which all the people of God should aspire. Paul is here encouraging Timothy to finish well the course he has now taken up, and he does this by pointing to his own life and his impending death (v. 8).

There is also a word in this charge for the community of faith in our times. We live now in an age of deep mistrust of ecclesiastical authority. Coupled with this distrust is the steep decline of Christianity in parts of the world.

The Embrace of God's Maternal Love

"By this the charity of God has appeared toward us: that God has sent His Only-Begotten Son into the world, that we may live by Him. In this is charity, not that we have loved God, but that He has loved us, and sent His Son to be a propitiation for our sins" [1 John 4:9–10]. What does this mean? That because God loved us, another salvation arose than that we had had in the beginning, when we were heirs of innocence and holiness; for the Supernal Father showed His charity in our dangers, though we deserved punishment, in sending by supernal power His Holy Word alone into the darkness of the world for the people's sake. There the Word perfected all good things, and by His gentleness brought back to life those who had been cast out because of their unclean sins and could not return to their lost holiness. What does this mean?

That through this fountain of life came the embrace of God's maternal love, which has nourished us unto life and is our help in perils, and is the deepest and sweetest charity and prepares us for penitence. How?

God has mercifully remembered His great work and His precious pearl, Man, whom He formed from the mud of the earth and into whom He breathed the breath of life. How? By devising the life of penitence, which will never fail in efficacy. For through his proud suasion the cunning serpent deceived Man, but God cast him into penitence, which calls for the humility the Devil did not know and could not practice; for he knew not how to rise up to the right way.

Hence this salvation of charity did not spring from us, and we were ignorant and incapable of loving God for our salvation; but He Himself, the Creator and Lord of all, so loved His people that for their salvation He sent His Son, the Prince and Savior of the faithful, who washed and dried our wounds. And He exuded the sweetest balm, from which flow all good things for salvation. Therefore, O human, you must understand that no misfortune or change can touch God. For the Father is the Father, the Son is the Son, and the Holy Spirit is the Holy Spirit, and these Three Persons are indivisible in the Unity of the Divinity.

Hildegard of Bingen, *Scivias*, trans. Mother Columba Hart and Jane Bishop, Classics of Western Spirituality (New York: Paulist Press, 1990), 162–63.

Andrew Walls, the European missiologist from Aberdeen, Scotland, observes that Christianity is in recession in Western countries, and in Europe it has dwindled out of recognition. The number of those who identify with no religious organization is on the rise. Paul's charge encourages the community of faith to faithfulness and endurance in an age of increasing secularization. Even though the epicenter of Christianity has now moved to the Global South, and Christianity is not as strong in some places as it once was, we are still charged to fight the good fight and to carry out our ministry fully. Moreover, Paul's message also demands that the church reflect and think about ways in which it has been complicit in its own decline and, more importantly, what church can do now to more accurately reflect Christ.

Socially and ethically, Paul's dedication and commitment to the cause of Jesus Christ also has something to say to what culture and society deem a successful life. We are too inclined to judge one another by net worth, employment, material gains, and worldly favor. Paul, for his part, touts his willingness to sacrifice his life for what he believes to be the nonnegotiables of the Christian faith: love, service, sacrifice, and devotion to others. Martin Luther King Jr. said it is not how long a person lives, but how well a person lives that really matters. To stand in defiance of the values the culture holds dear is not always easy, yet this God who loves us and claims us in Jesus Christ is a God who often traffics in paradox and reversals. It would seem foolish to some to give one's life so completely and fully to the things of God, even when death is near, but Paul willingly offers his life to this more excellent way, and he urges young Timothy to do the same. May we be so inspired by Paul's heroic example.

As for the personal connection, service to Jesus Christ often comes at a cost. Paul notes that during his times of trial no one came to support him, but the Lord stood by him and gave him strength. It was the Lord who helped him on his journey and strengthened him on his way (v. 17). Today we are called to stand firm in that glorious conviction that, come what may, we are never left alone to fight this good fight on our own. Paul looks toward the end of his life with great confidence that the God who called him to this work will rescue him from every attack and save him for his heavenly kingdom (v. 18). We too can take comfort in Paul's assurance of divine aid at life's most difficult passages. God has promised never to leave us, never to leave us alone.

CLEOPHUS J. LARUE

Luke 18:9–14

[9]He also told this parable to some who trusted in themselves that they were righteous and regarded others with contempt: [10]"Two men went up to the temple to pray, one a Pharisee and the other a tax collector. [11]The Pharisee, standing by himself, was praying thus, 'God, I thank you that I am not like other people: thieves, rogues, adulterers, or even like this tax collector. [12]I fast twice a week; I give a tenth of all my income.' [13]But the tax collector, standing far off, would not even look up to heaven, but was beating his breast and saying, 'God, be merciful to me, a sinner!' [14]I tell you, this man went down to his home justified rather than the other; for all who exalt themselves will be humbled, but all who humble themselves will be exalted."

Commentary 1: Connecting the Reading with Scripture

The parable of the Pharisee and the Tax Collector (Luke 18:9–14) comes after the parable of the Unjust Judge and the Persistent Widow (18:1–8). These two Lukan parables are often interpreted side by side because of the apparently shared theme of prayer. In addition, the passage that follows this Sunday's parable is about the disciples' not allowing the children to come to Jesus, causing Jesus to rebuke them, saying, "Whoever does not receive the kingdom of God as a little child will never enter it" (18:17). The narrative setting of the parable of the Pharisee and the Tax Collector fits nicely within the general theme of dependence on God's graciousness rather than a reliance on one's self. While Jesus might have directed the parable at the Pharisees in its original context, Luke seems to have a wider audience in mind, addressing anyone who is just as vulnerable to pride and self-righteousness as the Pharisee is in our parable.

The actual parable is sandwiched between two interpretive statements spoken by Jesus (vv. 9 and 14). Verse 9 introduces and gives the context of the parable, stating that Jesus "told this parable to some who trusted in themselves that they were righteous and regarded others with contempt." "Being righteous" is an important theme in the Gospel of Luke. Elizabeth and Zechariah were said to be "righteous before God, living blamelessly according to all the commandments and regulations of the Lord" (1:6). Simeon was "righteous and devout" (2:25). The descriptions of the prophetess Anna, who "never left the temple but worshiped there with fasting and prayer night and day" (2:37), fit the profile of one being righteous. Having witnessed the death of Jesus, the centurion declared, "Certainly this man was righteous" (23:47). Joseph of Arimathea is described as "a good and righteous man" (23:50). Obviously, Luke offers his readers many examples of genuine righteousness. These individuals are righteous because they obey God's commandments and completely trust in God's mercy. To those who are self-righteous, in other words, trusting only in themselves, Jesus declares, "I tell you, there will be more joy in heaven over one sinner who repents than over ninety-nine righteous persons who need no repentance" (15:7). He also states, "I have come to call not the righteous but sinners to repentance" (5:32). Jesus also warns about those who despise others because they think of themselves as better. According to 18:9, Jesus' parable targets those who regard others "with contempt." Luke uses the same verb to describe Herod's mockery of Jesus (23:11). When we treat people with disrespect, we deny their human dignity before God.

The parable depicts two contrasting figures, a Pharisee and a tax collector, praying in the temple. The description of both "going up" fits the geographical location of the temple in Jerusalem. Since the temple is situated at the highest point in the city, people always go up to Jerusalem, whether they come from the north, south, east, or west. For Luke, the temple is a special place of prayer where righteous folks and early disciples went to pray (1:9; 19:46; 24:53; Acts 2:46; 3:1). To see a Pharisee in the great temple praying is nothing unusual, but a tax collector praying in the temple is indeed a bit odd and possibly shocking. Furthermore, the Pharisee and the tax collector appear to be standing close enough to see each other.

Contrary to the often-negative caricatures of the Pharisees in the Gospels, the Pharisees in the time of Jesus were respectable religious leaders who zealously preserved God's covenant by practicing holiness as dictated in the Torah: "You shall be holy, for I the LORD your God am holy" (Lev. 19:2b). In their view the best way to keep that covenant relationship with God and be holy was by separating themselves from all that was unclean. Consequently, the word "pharisee," from which their name derived, means "separated one." So the Pharisee boasted in his prayer that he has rigorously kept the law of holiness by separating himself from anything that might have made him unclean. He is unlike thieves, rogues, adulterers, and the tax collector standing nearby, who are always in an unclean state, as they constantly break the law and remain unholy. Furthermore, the Pharisee has not only kept the law but has even gone above and beyond the law's requirements.[1] While fasting was required only on the Day of Atonement (Lev. 16:29–31), this Pharisee fasted twice a week. While tithing was required only for some items (Deut. 14:22–29), he was tithing a portion of everything he obtained. Clearly this Pharisee practiced "an asceticism beyond the norm" and had "a very high standard of observance beyond the legal requirements."[2] This Pharisee was apparently beyond reproach.

At the other end of the spectrum stands the tax collector. Tax collectors accumulated personal wealth by demanding tax payments in excess of what Rome levied. The Jews in the time of Jesus despised them because of their apparent greed and collaboration with the Roman occupiers. Nevertheless, the tax collector in the parable demonstrates a surprising attitude of humility by standing far off and keeping his eyes lowered. Moreover, by beating his breast, he shows genuine repentance (23:48). While the Pharisee is confident of his own righteousness and therefore "gives thanks" that he is not like the rest, the tax collector sincerely confesses that he is a "sinner." He boasts of nothing before God but unassumingly pleads for God's "mercy." His prayer echoes the opening words of Psalm 51: "Have mercy on me, O God."

There is little doubt about which of these men has lived a righteous life and which has not. Yet Jesus' evaluation in the parable turns the normal order of things upside down. The tax collector was the only person who went home "justified." Once again Jesus sympathizes with sinners and tax collectors (5:30; 7:39; 15:2). To drive home the point even further, Jesus concludes saying, "For all who exalt themselves will be humbled, but all who humble themselves will be exalted" (18:14b). The theme of divine reversal, whereby God takes what we place first and suddenly flips it upside down to be last, is a repeated motif in Luke's Gospel (for example, 1:51–53; 6:20–26; 14:11; 15:11–32; 16:19–31).

The surprising twist of Jesus' conclusion challenges us to examine anew the values and standards by which we live and practice our faith. The parable teaches that having a high standard of observance of the law and practicing asceticism beyond the norm are not enough if we remain self-centered and disdain others. As Paul clearly states, "And if I have prophetic powers, and understand all mysteries and all knowledge, and if I have all faith, so as to remove mountains, but do not have love, I am nothing" (1 Cor. 13:2). In other words, our religious observances and asceticism should make us humble before God and more loving toward others. Furthermore, it should not push us away from other people but rather draw us closer to them, whether they are saints or sinners.

VANTHANH NGUYEN, SVD

1. Stephanie Harrison, "The Case of the Pharisee and the Tax Collector: Justification and Social Location in Luke's Gospel," *Currents in Theology and Mission* 32, no. 2 (2005): 101.
2. Luke Timothy Johnson, *The Gospel of Luke*, Sacra Pagina (Collegeville, MN: Liturgical Press, 1991), 272.

Commentary 2: Connecting the Reading with the World

This parable of Jesus depicts the condition of two men, a tax collector and a Pharisee, as they pray in the temple. Like so many parables, contrast is used for a didactic purpose: the repentant prayer of the tax collector is starkly contrasted to the self-righteous declaration of the Pharisee. Just as Jesus comes to Zacchaeus's house "today" (Luke 19:5) and promises the bandit on the cross that he would be with him in paradise "today" (23:43), so there is no postponement or uncertainty in the tax collector's "justification" (18:14); unlike the "vindication" of the elect in the previous parable (18:7, 8), it happens immediately. The story thus challenges its hearers/readers to seize the present as the time of God's salvation, and presses us to ask just what it was about the tax collector's stance, as opposed to that of the Pharisee, that enabled him to go home in the right with God.

How do Christians hear this story against the backdrop of church tradition? We labor under the difficulty of having, for centuries, so stereotyped the Pharisees as self-righteous opponents of Jesus that we find it difficult to hear the story's challenge afresh. The long history of anti-Semitism in Christianity stems, in part, from such stereotypes of these early Jewish leaders. Indeed, it still remains all too easy for Christians to hear the story as a vindication of "our" humble way of doing things over against "their" complacency, legalism, or pride (whether "they" are generalized as adherents of another religion, another cultural grouping, or another Christian tradition). As we do so, we come perilously close to being ensnared in the very trap we proclaim we are avoiding.

Yet surely Luke, like his fellow evangelists, recorded such stories, not to cement the smug identity of an "us" over against a "them," but to warn the churches against falling into the complacency to which some of Jesus' contemporaries had fallen victim. The fact that the scene of the story is the temple should alert us to the possibility that the stark divisions of attitude that Jesus exposes may occur in the very midst of the community of faith (cf. Luke 2:34–35). Perhaps we will avoid the risk of such thinking only if we are perpetually alert to how close and vulnerable we are to it.

Identifying the original social resonances of the story enables us to connect it more sensitively to the present. Its setting is the Second Temple or Herod's temple in Jerusalem, at once the symbolic heart of Judaism and, at the time of Jesus, the main religious validator of an oppressive social order. Both Pharisee and tax collector had a role in that order—the Pharisee in his insistence on tithes that would maintain the temple cult, and the tax collector in his blatant involvement in the Roman exploitation of Jewish people. Both are Jewish, which is unsurprising, considering the context and ethnicity of Jesus and his audience. Both are caught up in an imperial system much larger than they. This reminds us that Jesus does not speak of individual moral choices as if they take place in a vacuum but in a realistic, ethically ambiguous setting.

The question of this passage concerns how honest these two characters will be in the face of the truth about that system. The Pharisee seems comfortable in the conviction that his personal acts of piety—in contrast to the behavior of the tax collector and his like, who have given up all pretence of careful Torah observance—are sufficient to ensure his acceptability before God. The tax collector has reached the recognition that no such acts of piety can whitewash the evil of the system in which he is implicated. The only realistic plea one can make to God is for mercy, not for acknowledgment of one's religious endeavors.

The parable's challenge in today's culture thus concerns the willingness of any—in the church or outside it—to face up to the truth of their part in structures of evil, and recognize the impossibility of evading that truth by concealing it beneath pious enthusiasm. It is perilous to make direct equations between either the Pharisee or the tax collector and particular groups in the present. Occasionally we may be granted the prophetic insight to do so, but we are bold indeed if we think we can make such equations without unfair stereotyping or becoming self-righteous ourselves. What must be named are the attitudes, wherever they are found, which reflect those of these two characters.

The tax collector's prayer might be interpreted as indicating despair over the human incapacity to perform genuinely righteous acts, that all we can hope for is God's forgiveness for our sin. Some Reformation and post-Reformation teaching may—unwittingly perhaps—have contributed to that sense. Indeed, a famous echo of the tax collector's cry for mercy is A. M. Toplady's great hymn "Rock of Ages" (*English Hymnal* 477). This hymn, which requests divine mercy, says nothing, however, of the effects of its reception; for this reason, it should be used in contexts where the consequences of that mercy are elucidated.

Indeed, Luke forbids the attitude of perpetual despair. He is clear that restoration of relationship with God, as the tax collector finds in the story, leads naturally to a restoration of relationships. For example, the very next chapter portrays a tax collector, Zacchaeus, who instead of going to God's house, has Jesus come to his, bringing with him "salvation" (19:1–10). The divine mercy that Jesus communicates through his willingness to associate with Zacchaeus, and Zacchaeus's willingness to receive him, thus leads to concrete action. Generosity replaces grasping, and restitution is made for wrong (19:8). So the story in 18:9–14 suggests that much can indeed be done by the "forgiven" about injustice.

The live-and-let-live mores of much of the world today may make it difficult to empathize with either the Pharisee or the tax collector. The Pharisee with his contemptuous dismissal of the less pious may seem a repugnant character to all who embrace the tolerance and diversity of liberal cultures. The tax collector's self-abasement also seems excessive to those who value the need of self-esteem for human flourishing. It thus requires an effort on our part to sense the continuing pertinence of the choice presented, but it is an effort that needs to be made as we penetrate beneath the surface of their postures in the temple to discover the attitudes that will, or will not, lead to liberating rightness with God today.

The aphorism of Jesus that concludes the story (v. 14) invites us to look out on the world to see how this reversal is played out. There is a humbling of the proud and an exaltation of the humble that is visible even in the present, as in various places dictators are toppled and the helpless find power. The fact that these things occur does not in itself offer justification for any particular geopolitical action, military or otherwise. Jesus is offering an observation about the working of God, not an exhortation to take the humbling and exalting process into our own hands. Nor, of course, does it mean that those who are exalted will not themselves need to be humbled again one day. Rather, it is an assurance that ultimately human beings will learn to see themselves and their world in true perspective, as their relationship to one another and to God as the one true authority is finally rebalanced.

STEPHEN I. WRIGHT

All Saints

Daniel 7:1–3, 15–18
Psalm 149

Ephesians 1:11–23
Luke 6:20–31

Daniel 7:1–3, 15–18

[1]In the first year of King Belshazzar of Babylon, Daniel had a dream and visions of his head as he lay in bed. Then he wrote down the dream: [2]I, Daniel, saw in my vision by night the four winds of heaven stirring up the great sea, [3]and four great beasts came up out of the sea, different from one another. . . .

[15]As for me, Daniel, my spirit was troubled within me, and the visions of my head terrified me. [16]I approached one of the attendants to ask him the truth concerning all this. So he said that he would disclose to me the interpretation of the matter: [17]"As for these four great beasts, four kings shall arise out of the earth. [18]But the holy ones of the Most High shall receive the kingdom and possess the kingdom forever—forever and ever."

Commentary 1: Connecting the Reading with Scripture

There are moments when we simply do not understand what is going on, we cannot see the end from the beginning, and we have a sense of foreboding and even terror in the face of global uncertainties. That was the experience of the people of God in the 160s BCE, the probable date for the final compilation of the book of Daniel. The Jewish community was enduring the tyranny of the invading Greek Seleucid king Antiochus IV Epiphanes. His oppression would culminate in the desecration of the Jerusalem temple in 167 BCE—the event referenced by the phrase "the abomination that makes desolate" or "the abomination of desolation" (Dan. 11:31)—when he infamously sacrificed a pig in the temple. As made evident by the Maccabean revolt, the great Jewish rebellion during the time of Antiochus's reign, uncertainty and fear gripped the nation.

Reflective of this chaos and uncertainty, Daniel 7 occupies a liminal space. Like the preceding chapters (Dan. 1–6), Daniel 7 is written in Aramaic. However, unlike those chapters, Daniel 7 consists not of a court tale, but an apocalyptic vision. In this, it aligns with the succeeding chapters of Daniel, which, though written in Hebrew, also entail visions and prophecies. In short, Daniel 7 functions as a hinge between the Aramaic, narrative section (Dan. 1–6) and the section of apocalyptic visions composed in Hebrew (Dan. 8–12). As such, it captures and speaks into this pervasive uncertainty.

Befitting the genre of apocalyptic literature (apocalypse means "revelation"), Daniel has a vision that leaves him confused, troubled in spirit, and indeed "terrified" (7:15). Given what he sees, however, Daniel's terror is not surprising. Four winds stir up the great sea (7:2). Immediately we know from the "four winds" that there are universal forces at work, larger than any human ability to feel a sense of control or personal discretion over them. At the same time these winds are stirring "the great sea." At one level, this evokes the Mediterranean, which dominated the westerly thoughts of Daniel's people. More importantly, though, at a mythic level it bespeaks an ancient understanding of the sea as a source of chaos. That is why the book of Revelation, filled as it is with visions deeply reminiscent of those in Daniel (see Rev. 13), announces a time when the forces of chaos will finally be defeated, when "the sea [will be] no more" (Rev. 21:1).

For the moment, though, these beasts both bear and embody chaos. When the "four great beasts" emerge from this restless sea, each is different from the other. Though these beasts can generally be designated as a lion, a bear, a leopard, and an unidentifiable creature with iron teeth and ten horns, it is apparent that each bears category-bending features. This presentation of the monsters culminates in the "terrifying and dreadful and exceedingly strong" (7:7) fourth and last beast. The sequence in chapter 7 alludes to the four-elements dream in Daniel 2, which also culminates in judgment against the last, fourth member. These variegated forces of chaos refuse to shape themselves into manageable or recognizable categories.

Once he has seen the vision, Daniel turns to "one of the attendants" (7:16), probably an angelic figure, for help. Typical of biblical apocalyptic literature, the transcendent visions experienced by the prophet require an external interpretation by a divine interpreter. The attendant confirms what Daniel, the onetime senior official in great empires, would have suspected, that these four strange beasts from the chaotic sea represent earthly powers (v. 17) and that his vision relates to current geopolitical events. The impervious line that the Western mind-set draws between vision and reality, and hence between heaven and earth, is more porous in the apocalyptic mind-set; heaven and earth bleed into one another.

Daniel 7, though strange, has familiar resonances. There are many moments in history when the people of God are subject to the terrifying coercions of political and social forces, alongside an inability to discern just what is going on. To this uncertainty, Daniel 7 offers hope. According to Daniel's interpreter, in the face of these forces "the holy ones of the Most High" will receive the kingdom forever (v. 18). Though the identity of these "holy ones" is debated, there is a strong argument that they refer to the people of God. Though there is no process detailed by which power shifts toward the holy ones, Daniel 7 offers the promise that this is their heritage. Though for the moment this promise is all that is available to those who are subjected to the actions of the fourth beast, or fear for what the

The Eternal Shore

Come, let us join our friends above
who have obtained the prize,
and on the eagle wings of love
to joys celestial rise.
Let saints on earth unite to sing
with those to glory gone,
for all the servants of our King
in earth and heaven are one.

One family we dwell in him,
one church above, beneath,
though now divided by the stream,
the narrow stream of death;
one army of the living God,
to his command we bow;
part of his host have crossed the flood,
and part are crossing now.

Ten thousand to their endless home
this solemn moment fly,
and we are to the margin come,
and we expect to die.
E'en now by faith we join our hands
with those that went before,
and greet the blood-besprinkled bands
on the eternal shore.

Our spirits too shall quickly join,
like theirs with glory crowned,
and shout to see our Captain's sign,
to hear this trumpet sound.
O that we now might grasp our Guide!
O that the word were given!
Come, Lord of Hosts, the waves divide,
and land us all in heaven.

Charles Wesley, "Come, Let Us Join Our Friends Above," Hymnary.org: https://hymnary.org/text/come_let_us_join_our_friends_above.

fourth beast might bring, Daniel 7 confirms that this is enough.

Daniel's vision in chapter 7 culminates in the throne room, a central point physically and conceptually in the message of the book of Daniel. In this scene, situated between the vision of the four beasts and their interpretation, "one like a human being" or "one like a son of man" is ushered into the throne and seated next to "the Ancient One" (7:13–14). When the power of the fourth beast is destroyed, this figure is granted "dominion and glory and kingship" (7:14), the same result promised for the holy ones of the Most High, the saints, in the angelic interpretation. Astonishingly, it is the saints who, in the face of chaotic geopolitical powers and of their own uncertainties and fears, are destined to rule from alongside the Ancient One in the throne room of heaven. As we celebrate All Saints' Day in the life of the church, they refer to those very saints whom we recall and among whom we number ourselves.

While in Daniel's vision the figure in the throne room is a representative human being, the term "son of man" came to take on messianic significance during the years leading up to the appearance of Jesus. The early church identified the one like a son of man in Daniel's vision as Jesus. Arguably, for Jesus himself the genius of his self-ascription "Son of Man" was that it captured both his messianic vocation and his essential humanity. In the Son of Man, heaven and earth meet, and the saints are invited into the mission of God. The early church sometimes explained this dynamic as "[participation] in the divine nature" in the face of a corrupt world (2 Pet. 1:4), a participation made possible by the one like a son of man's place in the throne room of God.

For the writer to the Ephesians, there was no doubt that the promised power and authority of Daniel's vision reaches its culmination in Christ (Eph. 1:20–21). Believers are in some way caught up with Christ into this new reality by means of their participation in the church as the body of Christ (Eph. 1:22–23). This is still the hope of the church in confusing times. However, Luke reminds the followers of Jesus in his record of the Sermon on the Plain that power is found in weakness and reversal (Luke 6:20–31). The road to the one like a son of man's attainment of dominion was to be through the crucifixion. The road to the inheritance of the saints lies still through suffering.

Like Daniel and his fellow Jews, the saints today occupy this liminal space between earth and heaven, between the faithful exercise of vocation and the anticipation of a glorious inheritance. Still today we face category-busting fears and confusing world geopolitical circumstances. In the face of these fears and circumstances, Daniel 7 reminds the faithful of their destiny as "the saints of the Most High," and so encourages perseverance.

TIM MEADOWCROFT

Commentary 2: Connecting the Reading with the World

Why is an apocalyptic text, set in an era of persecution, the lectionary's suggestion for a day when we celebrate saints, those who "from their labors rest"? A little digging suggests it is actually a nice match. This text starts in a dark place. All Saints starts with the pain of loss in the remembrance of the deaths of those we love. Daniel's vision also begins in a place of great fear.

Many among us have a fear of the process of dying. Most of us push apocalyptic texts to the side. Similarly, our society pushes the dying to the margins, removed from our homes and other places of everyday life. This text transforms fear into hope. It gives us a powerful and reassuring vision of God's ultimate triumph over death and other challenges. All Saints points to a life beyond this world, a life where darkness is as light. This first of Daniel's visions provides an opportunity for the preacher to offer hope to the grieving and hope to the living in the proclamation of God's ultimate victory.

No era is without strife. The setting of the book of Daniel is during the reign of Antiochus IV Epiphanes, who is described in 1 Maccabees as "a sinful root." There always are people opposed to others, conflicts that endanger peace, and circumstances that try our resolve. Some of our concerns are different from those in Daniel's time, but some are as old as humankind. We battle political corruption, forces of injustice, the misuse of power, oppression, and despair. We face climate change, pandemics, and income inequality. We encounter obstacles too steep to overcome on our own. We question the power of God, the promise of a future better than our present, and the validity of faith. In this we are not different from Daniel. We too meet great chaotic, frightening beasts arising in the world around us. Ours have names like Tyrant, Poverty, and Discrimination.

Our need for hope is also no different from that of Daniel. We know challenges: physical pain, the frustration of feeling powerless to effect change, disappointment, and sorrow. We know the loneliness that comes from losing a life partner and the death of promise that comes with the loss of a child. Like Daniel, our spirits too are troubled. We have sleepless nights when fearsome scenarios fill our thoughts. We struggle against fear of what may be, fear of wild fires or powerful storms, of discord between family members or nations, of threats to an orderly life so severe that it descends into a free-for-all of values or even anarchy. What we see also at times terrifies us. With all the trials that are part of life, how can we remain people of hope? How can we endure years of travail like Daniel and join him in proclaiming at the end that "the holy ones of the Most High shall receive the kingdom and possess the kingdom forever—and forever and ever" (Dan. 7:18)?

The book of Daniel initially seems foreign to our experience. It is set in a specific period of history but cannot be read simply as an account of actual past events. There is no time we can point to when four beasts mysteriously emerged from the sea. Rather, Daniel's collection of visions—creatures symbolizing blasphemy and violence in the reign of Antiochus IV Epiphanes—links metaphorically to people of every era who live through times of great strife and persecution. As Daniel's head fills with visions of four great beasts that rise from a stormy sea, fearsome creatures with mixed-up features of various wild animals—tusks and teeth and stamping feet—creatures with horns dotted with eyes, Daniel himself is terrified. Each of us can identify with our own real or imagined beasts. Daniel's vision also includes an Ancient One who ascends to a throne of fiery flames to rule over the thrashing, devouring beasts. It is here that we find what qualifies as gospel—good news that gives reason for hope—and that speaks to All Saints' Day and to a broader swath of our current realities. This is the opposite of escapist literature. The book of Daniel is poetic prose that names the pain and terror that confronts us by whatever name—a terrorist's attack, a family member struggling with opioid addiction, a stage-four-cancer diagnosis—and ends with reason to persevere.

In pointing forward to God's perfect reign, consider including the sacrament of Communion in a commemoration of All Saints' Day that includes this text. Communion, as a foretaste of the heavenly banquet that awaits us, fuels us to press on to the hope of Daniel's vision. As worshipers join one another at Table to proclaim Jesus Christ Lord of all and sovereign over all, we make a bold statement against the powers of this world. When we eat together, we also demonstrate a oneness that is given us in Christ, a unity strong enough to heal human brokenness.

When we proclaim that Christ will come again, that we will dwell with Christ, that we are his people and that we will know in him and through him life that defies reason and expectation and human limits, we engage in a defiant act that breaks down barriers erected because of demographics, political allegiances, or any of the other hundreds of specifics we human beings use to divide ourselves. Receiving Communion, we step into God's kingdom. Separations between the living and the dead, separations seared in grief and compounded by pettiness, separations that come from insecurity or greed or fear or envy, even separations that come from judging one another, are overcome.

In God's anticipated world, trial is replaced by peace. Saints we have known and loved have entered this realm. God's kingdom is not yet fulfilled for the rest of us. Even now, when we replace Daniel's vivid visions of beasts with the concerns that keep us up at night or cause us to binge on food or alcohol or to thrash about at others, when we are challenged by apostasy, changing mores, and great uncertainty, when threats to world peace are casually thrown around and violence breaks out, when despair seems to reign in individuals' hearts and comfort seems unattainable, Daniel's words inspire us. God dwells with us. Our trust in God allows us to push the beasts aside and begin living the better life now.

Use this All Saints' Day text to reshape perspectives on life and death and all the many factors and influences that make up both. Seize its vision—hope with substance—a vision that acknowledges painful realities and reaffirms God's promise to us that hope wins, God's goodness prevails, love triumphs, and our future—even if it does not feel secure in the short term—is assured at the last. God does not promise us a smooth path but promises to accompany us along the way. Our communities of faith offer companionship and perspective as we journey forward, conversation partners to help interpret and make sense of what we are seeing and fearing, people with whom to organize against oppressive and destructive forces, avenues to provide sanctuary, fellow marchers to force doors open for all, and opportunities to testify to God's love that is so great that it includes us each one, on All Saints' Day and every day. This is Daniel's vision. This is God's promise. Thanks be to God.

FAIRFAX F. FAIR

Psalm 149

[1]Praise the LORD!
Sing to the LORD a new song,
his praise in the assembly of the faithful.
[2]Let Israel be glad in its Maker;
let the children of Zion rejoice in their King.
[3]Let them praise his name with dancing,
making melody to him with tambourine and lyre.
[4]For the LORD takes pleasure in his people;
he adorns the humble with victory.
[5]Let the faithful exult in glory;
let them sing for joy on their couches.
[6]Let the high praises of God be in their throats
and two-edged swords in their hands,
[7]to execute vengeance on the nations
and punishment on the peoples,
[8]to bind their kings with fetters
and their nobles with chains of iron,
[9]to execute on them the judgment decreed.
This is glory for all his faithful ones.
Praise the LORD!

Connecting the Psalm to Scripture and Worship

The life of a saint is a double-edged sword—at least that's the metaphor Psalm 149 might suggest for All Saints' Day in Year C. The psalm depicts the faithful (*hasidim*; see vv. 1, 5, 9) with "two-edged swords in their hands" (v. 6), executing the righteous judgment of God against the rulers and peoples that defy God's will. It is a fierce and fearsome image and (let us be honest) a somewhat troubling one—a seemingly sour note so near the grand finale of the book of Psalms and, in the context of the lectionary, the Christian year. Psalm 149, one of the Laudate Psalms that close the Psalter, is also framed with exuberant joy, beginning and ending with the word "hallelujah" ("praise the LORD!"). The psalm describes those same faithful ones rejoicing in glorious song, dancing and making music with the harp and tambourine (a scene evocative of the song of victory at the sea; see Exod. 15). The word "hallelujah" itself seems to begin with laughter. As Paul Westermeyer has observed, regarding the Laudate Psalms: "From laughter to song is a small step. To praise God, the highest form of joy, is to make music."[1]

Implements of violence and instruments of praise: what are we to make of this polarity? On the one hand, we must not romanticize or spiritualize the trouble in this text. Whatever the historical context, theological convictions, or literary intent of the psalmist might have been, so-called religious violence is to be condemned. On the other hand, we must not romanticize or spiritualize the lives of the saints. Faithfulness to God *does* put us at odds with the powers and principalities of the world, and *will* lead us into the fray—figuratively speaking or otherwise. We believe that Christ *will* come again to judge and rule the world, destroying the reign of sin

1. Paul Westermeyer, *Te Deum: The Church and Music* (Minneapolis: Augsburg Fortress, 1998), 28.

and death forever. This is good news to celebrate with songs of joy.

Here Psalm 149 is offered as a response to a disturbing and apocalyptic reading from the seventh chapter of Daniel. The lectionary spares us the gory details, describing the opening of Daniel's dream (Dan. 7:1–3) then jumping forward to disclose its interpretation (7:15–18). To summarize what happens in between: Daniel envisions four mighty rulers, depicted as great beasts, arising from the chaos of the sea to terrorize the earth. Just when it seems that all is lost, Daniel sees the ancient and eternal God ascend to the throne, handily defeating and deposing the earthly kings. Then one like a human being (that is, "Son of Man") approaches the throne to receive "dominion and glory and kingship" (v. 14) forever; for Christian readers, this sounds like the Lord Jesus Christ. One of the throne room attendants in the vision then explains to Daniel that "the holy ones of the Most High" (v. 18) will share in this royal inheritance forever. As a companion to Daniel's dream, Psalm 149—a hymn with some kinship to the enthronement psalms—underscores the sovereignty of God over the powers of evil and promises the faithful a place of honor in God's holy realm.

The second reading for All Saints' Day, Ephesians 1:11–23, picks up this theme: "In Christ we have also obtained an inheritance" (Eph. 1:11). The opening of this letter to "the saints who are in Ephesus and are faithful in Christ Jesus" (v. 1) describes how these faithful ones have received the gospel of salvation and have been sealed with the promise of the Holy Spirit. The apostle explains that this mark of the Spirit "is the pledge of our inheritance toward redemption as God's own people" (v. 14). This is why the saints will, in the words of Psalm 149, "sing to the Lord a new song" (Ps. 149:1), and "rejoice in their King" (v. 2). The apostle prays that the people of God in Ephesus will know their "glorious inheritance among the saints" (Eph. 1:18) and the "immeasurable greatness of [God's] power for [those] who believe" (1:19). Some have drawn on an image from the end of Ephesians—the "sword of the Spirit" (Eph. 6:17), a metaphor for the word of God—to address the violence of Psalm 149:6–9. While this was surely not the intent of the psalmist, it does offer one resource for interpretation.

In the book of Luke, even the Beatitudes are a double-edged sword: note that the Gospel reading, Luke 6:20–31, includes both blessings ("Blessed are you") and curses ("Woe to you"). Jesus describes the trials and consequences of a faithful life—poverty, hunger, sorrow, exclusion, revulsion, defamation—all for the sake of the realm of God (vv. 20–23). In this lesser-known version of the Beatitudes, however, Jesus also calls to account those who fail to follow God's way—the rich and renowned, the smug and satisfied (vv. 24–26). These latter statements certainly resemble the judgment of Psalm 149 (vv. 6–9). Jesus makes it clear that the lives of the saints lead them directly into conflict and struggle: loving your enemies, blessing those who curse you, turning the other cheek, and giving away your earthly goods (Luke 6:27–30). In summary, Jesus says, "Do to others as you would have them do to you" (Luke 6:31). This is how the faithful seek and find the glory of God (see Ps. 149:9).

In the face of all adversity, animosity, and antagonism, saints are those who nevertheless praise God, exclaiming, "Hallelujah!" In the hope of what shall be, saints are those who envision the fulfillment of God's promise, singing, "Praise the Lord!" As the beloved hymn for All Saints' Day so eloquently puts it: "And when the strife is fierce, the warfare long, steals on the ear the distant triumph song, when hearts are brave again, and arms are strong. Alleluia! Alleluia!"[2]

DAVID GAMBRELL

2. William Walsham How, "For All the Saints," in *Glory to God: The Presbyterian Hymnal* (Louisville, KY: Westminster John Knox, 2013), no. 326.

Ephesians 1:11–23

[11]In Christ we have also obtained an inheritance, having been destined according to the purpose of him who accomplishes all things according to his counsel and will, [12]so that we, who were the first to set our hope on Christ, might live for the praise of his glory. [13]In him you also, when you had heard the word of truth, the gospel of your salvation, and had believed in him, were marked with the seal of the promised Holy Spirit; [14]this is the pledge of our inheritance toward redemption as God's own people, to the praise of his glory.

[15]I have heard of your faith in the Lord Jesus and your love toward all the saints, and for this reason [16]I do not cease to give thanks for you as I remember you in my prayers. [17]I pray that the God of our Lord Jesus Christ, the Father of glory, may give you a spirit of wisdom and revelation as you come to know him, [18]so that, with the eyes of your heart enlightened, you may know what is the hope to which he has called you, what are the riches of his glorious inheritance among the saints, [19]and what is the immeasurable greatness of his power for us who believe, according to the working of his great power. [20]God put this power to work in Christ when he raised him from the dead and seated him at his right hand in the heavenly places, [21]far above all rule and authority and power and dominion, and above every name that is named, not only in this age but also in the age to come. [22]And he has put all things under his feet and has made him the head over all things for the church, [23]which is his body, the fullness of him who fills all in all.

Commentary 1: Connecting the Reading with Scripture

Though Ephesians presents itself as a letter, it lacks the specificity of other Pauline epistles. No recipient is mentioned by name, and no specific situation is discussed. It thus seems closer to Hebrews or James as a general summation of the gospel, not directed to any particular church or issue, than it is to other letters of Paul. This lack of particularity is one of the factors that has led many scholars to question the Pauline authorship of the letter. Theologically, Ephesians is unquestionably Pauline, whether or not it was written by Paul himself.

Ephesians 1:11 occurs in the middle of a rather convoluted sentence in the original Greek, in a section in which Paul enumerates the blessings that have been bestowed already, and those that are still to come in Christ (vv. 3–14). To best understand this passage, preachers ought to begin with verse 3, instead of with verse 11, to discern Paul's exposition.

Throughout this passage, Paul alternates between what God has accomplished and what is yet to be done. The eschatological element is clear; there is an age that has not yet come (v. 21) but is surely coming. The future redemption is more than a hope; it is a certainty, based on the "inheritance" that is guaranteed by the "seal of the Spirit." The seal might refer to baptism, or a more general designation of the various gifts of the Spirit.[1] The distinction between past and future here is not between past actuality and future possibility, but between two aspects of one actuality: that which has been given and that which is yet to be given—or that which is seen and that which has yet to be seen (Rom. 8:24–25). Those who preach on this text must

1. Markus Barth, *Ephesians 1–3*, Anchor Bible 34 (Garden City, NY: Doubleday, 1974), 135–43.

be careful to respect the eschatological emphasis without diminishing its certainty. What Christ has done is continuous with what Christ will do. The "not yet" cannot be reduced to a "perhaps."

In the first half of chapter 1, Paul speaks in the first person plural, "we." Beginning in verse 15, he switches to the second person, "you." This raises the issue of whom Paul is addressing. On the basis of chapter 2, it becomes clear that the "you" are Gentile converts, while the "we" seems to oscillate between Jews and the totality of the people. There is a logic to this. Chapter 2 speaks of the two peoples, Jews and Gentiles, having become one through Jesus Christ. This reflects Galatians 3:28. It also echoes the principle theme of Romans 11. Whereas the unification in Romans 11 is eschatological, in Ephesians (and Galatians) it seems to be fully realized, at least in principle, because of the work of God in Christ.

In verse 15, Paul turns to his prayer for the Ephesians. This prayer has a double purpose. It is, of course, a prayer, but it is also didactic. It teaches the Ephesians how they should pray, especially on their own behalf. They need the wisdom to understand that which they have received, not simply intellectually, but with their entire being, "the eyes of their hearts."

In terms of the larger thematic context, being "in Christ" (a phrase that, with its cognates, occurs eight times in this chapter) could be said to characterize the entire NT. Here it is connected to being chosen for a divine purpose, the proof of which is demonstrated by the seal of the Holy Spirit, likely a reference to baptism. The notion that this constitutes an inheritance is related to Galatians 4:7, where Paul speaks of members of the church as children and heirs. It is this idea of people who will receive an inheritance as children that marks off members of the church. This is related to Paul's discussion in Romans 4 of believers as children of Abraham.

The close connection, and occasional duplication, between Ephesians and Colossians, has often been explored by commentators. The so-called cosmic Christ of Ephesians 1:20–23 is closely related to Colossians 1:15–20. Both maintain that God has placed the resurrected Christ above all things, although in Colossians there is an emphasis on Christ as the agent of creation that is not in the Ephesians passage. The idea of the church as the body of which Christ is the head is present in both, and receives considerable elaboration in 1 Corinthians 12. The idea that Christ is both ruler and reconciler of all can also be found in 1 Corinthians 15:25–28, although in that passage the rule of Christ will finally be returned to God. All three passages agree that God working through Christ will accomplish the unification of the cosmos.

Ephesians 1:11–23 is the reading for All Saints' Day, with Daniel 7:1–3, 15–18; Luke 6:20–31; and Psalm 149 as accompanying texts. Of these readings, the passage from Ephesians is the most directly applicable to All Saints' Day. It speaks of the church's election as the first recipient of God's promises, and the church's participation in the work of Christ as his body. Psalm 149, one of the so-called Laudate Psalms, is a hymn of praise to God, albeit with a somewhat bloodthirsty moment in verse 7. A possible connection between Daniel and Ephesians might be the emphasis on the contrast between fleeting worldly powers and the true, everlasting power of God, which is, by extension, promised for the followers of God (Dan. 7:18; Eph. 1:21–23). Moreover, the eschatological note in Daniel 7:18 points to the triumph of God—a triumph that is given specificity in Ephesians. In this, all three passages look forward to Christ the King Sunday.

The Gospel reading is Luke's version of the Beatitudes. This is much less well known than the Beatitudes of Matthew 5, and also rather more grim. It contains condemnations as well as blessings. It is certainly possible to regard the blessings as a description of the authentic church, and the warnings as characterizations of the church that has abandoned its mission and its Lord. Such an approach could at least mute the triumphalism that can creep into ecclesiological sermons. It is important for Christians to remember that their lives are not simply blessings. There are warnings as well. The church must behave in certain ways if it is not to betray the blessings it has received.

All Saints' Day is often swamped by its proximity to Reformation Sunday in Protestant churches, but the theme of Reformation Sunday runs counter to All Saints' Day. All Saints' Day is a celebration of the ultimate unity of the church, especially the church on earth and the church in heaven, the church militant and the church triumphant. Reformation Sunday, while acknowledging the undoubted importance of Martin Luther's publication of the Ninety-five Theses as the beginning of the Reformation, recalls the division of the Western church into Roman Catholic and Protestant, a division that remains unhealed.

Ephesians has a crucial place in the NT canon as a summation of the gospel message in general, and Paul's distinctive interpretation of that message in particular. This particular passage emphasizes all that Christ has given and continues to give to the church—gifts that enable the church's ministry. Those who preach on this text must emphasize both the reality of the gifts and the tasks to which the saints are called. If they are to be truly enjoyed, the gifts must be employed, for that is how the work continues.

DAVID W. JOHNSON

Commentary 2: Connecting the Reading with the World

Paul opens the passage from Ephesians by stating that the church should be viewed as God's heritage: God has not only ordained a uniting of all things in Christ, but believers are God's inheritance through Christ (Eph. 1:11). This heritage has a purpose. God works his purposes for this ultimate glorification—those who are chosen by God exist for God's praise and God's glory (v. 14). Concerned as Ephesians is with unity and Jewish Christian and Gentile relations, these purposive acts of God, where the saints are to be viewed as God's heritage, also include the Gentiles. In Christ and through his mediation, Gentiles are included in God's great plan and purpose for his people. They too are part of God's heritage. Hence, everyone, one and all, has a stake in the redemptive purposes of God. Our lives are to reflect our inclusion into God's grand scheme of redemption. We are also counted among those saints, and our connection to them is through Jesus Christ. Those who have expressed a hope in Christ Jesus exist now to honor and praise God.

Liturgically, this passage from Ephesians is fitting for All Saints' Day, as this day is a time to remember the ongoing sanctification of the whole people of God. While we may give thanks for the lives of particular individuals of ages past, we must also remember that God is glorified by the ordinary holy lives of believers in this and every age. Right now we are a part of God's heritage (1:11). Thus, while this day is indeed an appropriate time to give thanks to members of the community of faith who have died in past years, it is also a time to pray a prayer of thanksgiving that we too, irrespective of race, ethnicity, or gender, are counted among the company of the faithful in this present world and in God's eternal realm.

It is also the case that All Saints' Day is a fitting time to remember that God is a big-tent God when it comes to those who have been included in his purposive acts on behalf of humankind. Although the apostle to the Gentiles and the champion to the uttermost of their equality in the church, Paul never ignores the priority of God's revelation to Israel. However, Paul sees God's purposive acts in Israel also revealed at a further stage through the birth of the church of which the Gentiles are a part.

This idea of Paul's inclusion of Gentiles has implications for how we see the modern context. Sociologists tell us that the United States, like many other places in the world, is fast becoming a nation where no single racial/ethnic group will have a majority. Those who have found unity in Christ Jesus and in the purposive acts of God do not fear this fast-approaching diverse world. Rather, we must celebrate it, for in this wonderful coming together of humanity from everywhere and everyplace we can see the furtherance of the redemptive purposes of God and praise God's name for the oneness found in Christ Jesus. Paul reminds us that regardless of race and ethnicity, Christians are members of the same body, a worldwide church, though we come into that body from different cultures.

What a timely message for our multicultural world. All people from every nation, kindred, and tongue are included in God's great plan and purpose for his people. The unifying factor which identifies us as God's own people is our faith placed in Christ Jesus through the preached word. A wise preacher might therefore remind the church of the miraculous joy that is found in the diversity and unity of the Christian body. A sermon on the difficulties facing the unity of the church and the fears that underlie such divisions might also be appropriate and timely.

Although God has a big tent when it comes to identifying and naming his saints and his purposive acts on behalf of those saints, Paul also calls our attention to the fact that the way to Christ for all the saints is the same. The first step is to hear the word of truth. It is then followed by a trustful acceptance of the one who speaks this word (1:13). The third step is the seal of the Holy Spirit, which for some refers to baptism as the outward attestation of the Christian's resolve to follow in the way of Christ and in the fellowship of his church (1:14). The ground is level at the foot of the cross, but it is the cross that is the central focus of the people we have been called to be.

There are ecclesial ramifications to Paul's vision. Not only is there a big tent for the saints, but the tent is wide and inclusive. From his prison in Rome, Paul has heard of the spiritual health of the churches of Asia Minor that sprang up through his influence. Because of this he overflows with gratitude, giving thanks to God. Paul, even in his Roman imprisonment, has learned the secret of joy, to look not at one's own circumstances but, rather, to the welfare of others as the source of peace and happiness. If the saints of the churches of Asia Minor are well in the Lord, then Paul is content.

The ecclesial connection here is for the church to recognize that it must have a commitment to the welfare of all of the people in this world that God so loves. In an age of increasing secularization, some would circle the wagons and seek to minister only to those of the household of faith. Though our care and concern begins with those in the household of faith, we must never forget that we have been called to minister to the whole of God's created order. The spiritual health of the people in Asia Minor consisted not only of their faith in the Lord Jesus but also of their love for all the saints. Paul wants the Christians in Asia Minor to understand that their love was not to be a narrow, provincial love, encompassing just those of their own community; rather, theirs was to be a love that extended beyond all boundaries. A prudent preacher might therefore speak on the need for the church to reflect Christ's love for the entire world by ministering to or empathizing with those outside the boundaries of their own communities, especially those on the margins, such as the poor, elderly, immigrant, and disabled.

Paul no doubt received information about the spiritual progress of the Ephesians from Tychicus and Epaphras, but also from others. Though not unaware of the believers' flaws, he finds something for which to give God thanks and make it the reason for his praise of those saints. Paul tells the Ephesians that he had heard of their faith in the Lord Jesus and also of their love for all the saints (1:15).

Socially and ethically, this means that genuine faith in Jesus Christ always focuses on Christ and emanates in love to others. Firm faith and fervent love are necessary Christian virtues, but they are not the sum and circumference of the Christian life. Our prayer, like that of the apostle Paul, should be for God to give us the wisdom and revelation to come into an even greater understanding of the faith and the inclusive God who has made us a part of his wondrous actions (1:17). Indeed, on this day we give God thanks for all of those who have put their trust in almighty God.

CLEOPHUS J. LARUE

Luke 6:20–31

[20]Then he looked up at his disciples and said:

"Blessed are you who are poor,
for yours is the kingdom of God.
[21]"Blessed are you who are hungry now,
for you will be filled
"Blessed are you who weep now,
for you will laugh.

[22]"Blessed are you when people hate you, and when they exclude you, revile you, and defame you on account of the Son of Man. [23]Rejoice in that day and leap for joy, for surely your reward is great in heaven; for that is what their ancestors did to the prophets.

[24]"But woe to you who are rich,
for you have received your consolation.
[25]"Woe to you who are full now,
for you will be hungry.
"Woe to you who are laughing now,
for you will mourn and weep.

[26]"Woe to you when all speak well of you, for that is what their ancestors did to the false prophets.

[27]"But I say to you that listen, Love your enemies, do good to those who hate you, [28]bless those who curse you, pray for those who abuse you. [29]If anyone strikes you on the cheek, offer the other also; and from anyone who takes away your coat do not withhold even your shirt. [30]Give to everyone who begs from you; and if anyone takes away your goods, do not ask for them again. [31]Do to others as you would have them do to you."

Commentary 1: Connecting the Reading with Scripture

The Gospel reading for the feast of All Saints is taken from the Sermon on the Plain found in Luke's Gospel. Luke's Sermon on the Plain (6:17–49) is noticeably shorter than Matthew's Sermon on the Mount (5:1–7:29). Luke's sermon contains only thirty-three verses while Matthew's sermon has one hundred eleven. In Luke's Gospel, Jesus delivers the sermon after having chosen the Twelve (6:17–19) and after having come down from a mountain (6:17). In Matthew's Gospel, however, Jesus does not choose his disciples until much later in the narrative (10:1–4), and the whole sermon takes place on a mountain (5:1).

Our reading from Luke's Gospel may be divided into three units: (1) blessings (6:20–23); (2) woes (6:24–26); and (3) love of enemies (6:27–31). The unit on love of enemies extends to verse 36, but our Gospel lection shortens it to end at verse 31. The audience of this whole sermon appears to be "his disciples" (6:20), intending "to shape their conduct." Jesus' powerful words deal with the concerns of poverty, hunger, grief, and persecution, which might "reflect the situation in the early church in the time of Luke."[1]

Jesus in the Gospel of Luke declares four beatitudes instead of eight as found in the Gospel

1. Joseph A. Fitzmyer, *The Gospel according to Luke I–IX*, Anchor Bible (New York: Doubleday, 1970), 629–30.

of Matthew. The usual translation of the Greek *makarios* is "blessed." The sense of the Greek word implies "a person's inner happiness"[2] due to some good fortune that the person has received. The first obvious difference between the Lukan Beatitudes and Matthew's is that Jesus in Luke spoke in the second person ("you, yours") rather than in the third person ("they, theirs"). Second, Jesus in Luke does not spiritualize the conditions of the Beatitudes. Rather, those who are actually poor and hungry are blessed, in contrast to Matthew's poor "in spirit" and hungry "for righteousness" who are blessed. The third notable difference is that the Lukan Beatitudes stress the immediacy or "here and now" of the promises of consolation. The word "now" is used repeatedly (twice in v. 21 and twice in v. 25).

Beatitudes are like congratulations, which are often found in Jewish Wisdom writings (Pss. 1:1; 41:1; Prov. 14:21; Sir. 31:8). Their purpose is to affirm, encourage, and hold up an example of those qualities for which the person is recognized and praised. Jesus first and foremost congratulates those who are poor. The Greek word *ptōchos*, used here, may suggest a person who has been reduced to the condition of a beggar. The Gospel of Luke shows special concern for the poor (7:22; 14:13, 21; 16:20, 22; 21:2, 3). Jesus came "to bring good news to the poor" (4:18), to feast with the poor (14:13, 21), to seek restitution for the poor (19:8), and to praise the poor (21:1–3). Jesus himself is poor, since he depended on others for food (8:1–3) and shelter (9:58).

In the second beatitude, Jesus promises that the hungry will be fed. This promise alludes to the eschatological banquet for the elect found in the OT (Ps. 107:9; Isa. 25:6; 49:10; Jer. 31:12) that will be fulfilled by Jesus (cf. Luke 9:12–17). As for those who are weeping and being persecuted "on account of the Son of Man," they will experience laughter and joy. Joy is a common theme in Luke's Gospel (1:14; 2:10; 8:13; 10:17; 15:7, 10; 24:41, 52). To those who are poor, hungry, weeping, and being persecuted for Christ belongs the kingdom of God, which for Luke is both a present reality and a future one. Consequently, the arrival of Jesus ushers in the presence of the reign of God and initiates a reversal of fortunes.

The four woes (6:24–26) that follow the four blessings heighten the great turnaround that the reign of God will bring. Only Luke has these four woes, which match the Beatitudes precisely in form and content. The blessings and woes are set in opposing parallelism. The Greek word for "woe" "does not denote a mere misfortune, but a deep and inconsolable misery, in contrast to the 'blessings' of the previous verses."[3] The rich who have their rewards now stand in antithesis to the poor who belong to the kingdom, and those who now laugh but later will weep stand in antithesis to those who now weep but later will laugh. Noticeably, Mary in the Magnificat had already announced the following reversal: "[God] has brought down the powerful from their thrones, and lifted up the lowly; [God] has filled the hungry with good things, and sent the rich away empty" (1:52–53).

Following the four woes is the unit on "love of enemies" (6:27–31), which is the heart of Jesus' ethical teaching. Jesus' commandment to love one's enemies as God has loved Israel is so radical that his teaching on the subject is probably scandalous. The meaning of love is elaborated by the following three imperatives: "*do good* to those who hate you, *bless* those who curse you, *pray* for those who abuse you." All the imperatives, including to love, are in the Greek present tense, connoting continual actions that are not temporary or occasional activities but rather habitual behaviors. In a nutshell, the love commandment challenges the disciples to not even seek vengeance or retribution; rather we ought to return hatred with acts of kindness, mistreatment with charity, and abuse with deeds of mercy.

Jesus' radical love commandment does not stop there. Jesus gives four concrete examples about how one should act when he or she is maltreated: "If anyone strikes you on the cheek, offer the other also; and from anyone who takes

2. Fitzmyer, *Luke I–IX*, 632.
3. James E. Edwards, *The Gospel according to Luke* (Grand Rapids: Eerdmans, 2015), 195.

away your coat do not withhold even your shirt. Give to everyone who begs from you; and if anyone takes away your goods, do not ask for them again" (6:29–30). These four examples of nonretaliation are not passive responses but are actually provocative responses to preclude further cause for aggression. Again, the teaching of Jesus is radical, since it goes against our natural human response to retaliate when we are maltreated. The passage concludes with the well-known Golden Rule: "Do to others as you would have them do to you" (v. 31).

It is no coincidence that the Gospel reading for the feast of All Saints is taken from Luke's Sermon on the Plain. Several themes of the feast stand out. First, Christians are encouraged to live holy lives so that we too might be "blessed," like those countless holy women and men who have faithfully lived the teachings of Jesus and therefore are now truly blessed. Second, Christians are ambassadors of peace and reconciliation, even when we are maltreated and ridiculed. Finally, the Scripture reading and today's feast share an invitation to live a radical faith in God. It is a call from a life of self-absorption to holy simplicity, meekness, and charity. Let us therefore honor those "great cloud of witnesses" (Heb. 12:1) by running the race and persevering to the end so that one day they too will join us in the march singing, "Oh, when the saints go marching in . . ."

VANTHANH NGUYEN, SVD

Commentary 2: Connecting the Reading with the World

The danger of this passage's being assigned to All Saints' Day is that the connection may feed two common misunderstandings: first, that only radically holy people are "saints," and second, that Jesus' Beatitudes are moral commands about what such saints are to be like. These misunderstandings may generate sermons that either hold up seemingly impossible ideals to imitate or burden hearers with guilt-inducing demands.

In Paul's letters (e.g., Rom. 1:7; Eph. 1:1), "saints" is a common term for Christian believers. In the Gospels, the normal term for the followers of Jesus is "disciples"; here it is the disciples whom Jesus is addressing (Luke 6:20). The term "saints" echoes the OT notion of Israel as a "holy people," set apart by God for himself and his purposes, the object of God's freely bestowed love prior to any moral behavior. In a similar way, Luke portrays Jesus pronouncing blessing on his disciples before he gives them any commands. This is the "gospel" order: by grace we are saved, so that we may do good works (Eph. 2:8–10).

In Matthew, while some of the Beatitudes have more moral overtones (for example, the pure of heart are regarded as blessed in 5:8), they remain blessings, rather than commands. Saints should be defined primarily as those who receive God's blessing, not as the especially virtuous. Hence, one connection offered by this biblical text is that when used on All Saints' Day, it redefines or sharpens how we imagine saints and saintliness. The focus shifts from our own virtuous deeds to the freely offered grace of God.

There is an added layer of complexity because those pronounced blessed by Jesus are further defined as "you who are poor . . . are hungry . . . weep" and are hated (6:20–22). Conversely, he pronounces woes over "you who are rich . . . are full . . . are laughing" and spoken well of (6:24–26). Those addressed are identified by their social status and success, as well as their adherence to Jesus. That "you" is used in both blessings and woes implies that both groups are represented among the listening "disciples," as they may be among sermon listeners today.

So being identified as a disciple is no cause for smugness. In the great upheaval when God's kingdom is established, there will be a radical social realignment that will cause pain to some. Wealthy disciples (Western Christians certainly among them) must be prepared for that, and preachers are called to be fearless in warning them against the insidious temptation to rely on their wealth. In addition, in the process of God's kingdom coming about, all who side with Jesus can expect the same kind of rejection that the prophets received (6:22–23). Hence, prophetic preachers inspired by this passage will remind hearers that they too, like the prophets, should expect rejection for speaking out, as Jesus did, for the poor and the disenfranchised.

Many may balk at the stark contrast Jesus draws between the poor and the rich, because many of us, by comparison with the majority of the world, are wealthy. Moreover, we are subtly influenced by the idea that the wealthy are blessed. Unlimited economic growth has been an assumed and unchallenged goal. Jesus challenges this idea, but this does not mean that the rich cannot be saved—just that entry to the kingdom will require a radical, perhaps painful, rethink of priorities (Luke 18:24–27). The story of Zacchaeus (Luke 19:1–10) shows what may happen when the rich repent: oppressive appropriation of others' goods can cease, and new openheartedness brings rich and poor closer together.

Though the church can rejoice in being the "saints of God," we should think of this neither as a badge of achievement and virtue, nor as a passport to security in God's forthcoming rule. Like his first disciples, we may be those who gather round him most closely, but his message continues to be for the "great multitude" from far and wide (6:17) who had come "to hear him and be healed" (v. 18), not merely for our own benefit. Our privilege as disciples is to hear this message and pass it on. As saints we proclaim a just and peaceable kingdom that is not only for ourselves, but for the world.

The commands that Jesus gives in verses 27–31 match the radical quality of the blessings and woes. The latter speak of God's intention to vindicate the poor (Ps. 12:5)—without distinction on grounds of morality, faith, ethnicity, or any other marker—and the lifestyle Jesus urges has an exuberance consonant with that purpose of restoration. It entails the beginning of a new future order.

These commands, like the blessings and woes, have particular resonance on All Saints' Day. We rightly remember as saints those who have caught on to the spirit of Jesus as expressed in Luke 6:27–31: Those who have loved their enemies, prayed for their persecutors, turned the other cheek to their attackers, been generous to their oppressors, and given to those in need display particularly clearly the richness of the blessing they have received. Such people often seem eccentric to the more conformist majority, and thus stand out in history. We hold this in tension with the fact that "all saints" includes many whose response to Christ is unremembered, and many who have, for reasons often beyond their own control, struggled to respond to his blessing with the faith, hope, and love he encourages here.

We miss the point of Jesus' commands if we treat them as a list of rules. Rather, they encapsulate an attitude to life, a joyful way of wisdom, that recognizes how good it is to be treated thus oneself (v. 31). Jesus' vision and outlook should not be identified with stoicism. In calling the poor "blessed," he is not saying that they should think of themselves as "happy" or their suffering as "good." He is simply giving hope, and then urging those who have grasped it to become themselves reasons for others to hope. As has often been pointed out, verses 27–29 are not instructions simply to lie down under oppression, but to engage in positive, nonviolent resistance to abusive ways. Preachers can use them to encourage people to assert their dignity in the face of bullying or abuse, in the home, in the workplace, or anywhere else: refusing to return evil for evil, while demonstrating courage and creativity in seeking to overcome it.

The situations in which we are called to live out these commands today are very different from those under the Roman Empire in Jesus' time. Christians today who do live under hostile regimes or in conditions of poverty can often set a vivid example to the more comfortably off of what the Jesus lifestyle looks like. For saints who enjoy greater security, and live in societies partly shaped by centuries of Jesus' influence, living out that way can be more complex.

For example, how should we apply Jesus' words, addressed to individuals, to the question of how nations should respond to the aggression or violence of others? Presumably, loving one's enemies does not mean either merely succumbing to such aggression, or mirroring its spirit in one's response. What of Jesus' words "Give to everyone who begs from you"? It may not always be in the best interests of a beggar to give them immediately what we happen to have on us (v. 30), but we may be able to throw in our lot generously with organizations working to house the homeless and restore self-worth to those who have lost all sense of it. In such ways the saints of God, those who know his blessing, become agents of his blessing in the midst of a messy and ambiguous world.

STEPHEN I. WRIGHT

Proper 26 (Sunday between October 30 and November 5 Inclusive)

Habakkuk 1:1–4; 2:1–4 and
  Isaiah 1:10–18
Psalm 119:137–144 and Psalm 32:1–7
2 Thessalonians 1:1–4, 11–12
Luke 19:1–10

Habakkuk 1:1–4, 2:1–4

[1]The oracle that the prophet Habakkuk saw.
[2]O LORD, how long shall I cry for help,
  and you will not listen?
Or cry to you "Violence!"
  and you will not save?
[3]Why do you make me see wrongdoing
  and look at trouble?
Destruction and violence are before me;
  strife and contention arise.
[4]So the law becomes slack
  and justice never prevails.
The wicked surround the righteous—
  therefore judgment comes forth perverted.

[2:1]I will stand at my watchpost,
  and station myself on the rampart;
I will keep watch to see what he will say to me,
  and what he will answer concerning my complaint.
[2]Then the LORD answered me and said:
Write the vision;
  make it plain on tablets,
  so that a runner may read it.
[3]For there is still a vision for the appointed time;
  it speaks of the end, and does not lie.
If it seems to tarry, wait for it;
  it will surely come, it will not delay.
[4]Look at the proud!
  Their spirit is not right in them,
  but the righteous live by their faith.

Isaiah 1:10–18

[10]Hear the word of the LORD,
  you rulers of Sodom!
Listen to the teaching of our God,
  you people of Gomorrah!
[11]What to me is the multitude of your sacrifices?
  says the LORD;

I have had enough of burnt offerings of rams
and the fat of fed beasts;
I do not delight in the blood of bulls,
or of lambs, or of goats.

[12]When you come to appear before me,
who asked this from your hand?
Trample my courts no more;
[13]bringing offerings is futile;
incense is an abomination to me.
New moon and sabbath and calling of convocation—
I cannot endure solemn assemblies with iniquity.
[14]Your new moons and your appointed festivals
my soul hates;
they have become a burden to me,
I am weary of bearing them.
[15]When you stretch out your hands,
I will hide my eyes from you;
even though you make many prayers,
I will not listen;
your hands are full of blood.
[16]Wash yourselves; make yourselves clean;
remove the evil of your doings
from before my eyes;
cease to do evil,
[17]learn to do good;
seek justice,
rescue the oppressed,
defend the orphan,
plead for the widow.

[18]Come now, let us argue it out,
says the LORD:
though your sins are like scarlet,
they shall be like snow;
though they are red like crimson,
they shall become like wool.

Commentary 1: Connecting the Reading with Scripture

Justice and righteousness are main topics for the passages of this lection. While Psalm 119:137–44 describes God as righteous in God's nature, Habakkuk 1:1–4; 2:1–4 points out the contradiction of a righteous God who allows destruction. Isaiah 1:10–18 shows God's response to a lack of justice: confrontation, warning, an invitation to repentance and transformation. The NT readings give examples of justice and righteousness through a community living in righteousness (2 Thess. 1:1–4, 11–12) and the transformation of a man by the message of Jesus that moved him to do justice (Luke 19:1–10).

The prophet Habakkuk, like other Hebrew prophets, laments the absence of justice in Judah. He complains that God has failed to respond in the face of abounding violence, wrongdoing, and strife whereby the "wicked surround the righteous" and thereby pervert justice (Hab. 1:3–4). Justice to Habakkuk is a theological matter. He directs his complaints to the source of justice: God. He questions God's silence and inaction regarding Judah's conduct, using language characteristic of psalms of lament: "how long?" (1:2; cf. Pss. 13:1–2; 79:5). Indeed, when one considers the ubiquity and longevity of violence, contention, and injustice (1:2–4), "how long?" is a perpetual query.

In this case, however, God responds to Habakkuk's question. The answer is not one that he expects. God states that he too cannot ignore Judah's conduct. As a result, the country will be punished, for the Lord has appointed the Chaldeans as agents of punishment (1:5). The description of this foreign nation is bone-chilling: bitter-tempered (Heb. *mar*, NRSV "fierce") and violent, submitted to no other authority, sweeping away everything that they find on their way. The Babylonians, an all-consuming whirlwind, who "advance like a desert wind and gather prisoners like sand"—this is God's answer to the violence and injustice amid Judah (1:9 NIV).

Habakkuk, unsurprisingly, does not like God's answer. Indeed, the prophet points out a contradiction: How can a just God appoint a violent and arrogant nation to destroy unrighteous Judah (1:16–17)? Should God answer injustice with more injustice, and violence with more violence? In asking such questions, Habakkuk joins the list of figures such as Moses and Job who question God's decision of destruction, in light of God's character and nature (e.g., Exod. 32:7–14).

Ever determined, the prophet presses God for an answer. He waits vigilantly like a watchperson. The answer comes as God orders Habakkuk to write down a vision. The pride and arrogance of the Chaldeans will also eventually cause their downfall (2:4a, 5). God will balance the scales of justice over time. Justice, though not immediately forthcoming, will win out at the end. The prophet's message will act as proof that God's promises are true.

In the meantime, however, justice depends on the individual actions. In a famous verse, Habakkuk 2:4b, the prophet states that "the righteous live by their faith." The character of the invading nation and, indeed, the unjust nation of Judah as a whole stand in contrast to the person committed to justice. The word "faith" in this text corresponds to the Hebrew word *emuna*, which has connotations beyond mere belief. It conveys the sense of "loyalty, perseverance, and reliability." Thus, a fitting translation would be "the righteous live by their faithfulness." In this light, Habakkuk affirms that while the proud Chaldeans (cf. 2:5) do not act correctly, their violence will not last forever. The duty of those committed to justice is to wait faithfully for the fulfillment of Habakkuk's more just vision of the future.

Habakkuk 2:4 had a profound impact on the writings of the apostle Paul and the history of the Christian church. Paul cites this passage in Romans 1:17 and Galatians 3:11, and the verse is the foundation of the doctrine of justification by faith. The verse also played a key role in the Reformation. Martin Luther understood that we are justified by God's justice, and not by any works or religious practice. The faithful then respond to God through acts of justice. This idea has powerful sermonic potential: What does it mean that acts that promote justice are a faithful response to our salvation?

Prior to Habakkuk's ministry, the prophet Isaiah addressed the same issues of violence and lack of justice in Judah (Isa. 1:21, 27; 5:7; 58:6–10). Indeed, Isaiah 1:10–18 opens with a harsh accusation to the people of Judah and its leaders: they are like Sodom and Gomorrah, cities that both the Hebrew Bible and the NT associate with wickedness and destruction (e.g., Gen. 18–19; Isa. 13:19; Amos 4:11; Zeph. 2:9; Matt. 10:15; 2 Pet. 2:6). Ezekiel 16:49, however, offers another interpretation of Sodom and Gomorrah that better fits the context of Isaiah 1:10–17. Ezekiel identifies the wrongs of Sodom as "pride, excess of food, and prosperous ease," ignoring the needs of the poor. The inhabitants of these cities were living a life of self-complacency in which social justice did not play a part.

The reference to Sodom and Gomorrah connects Isaiah 1:10–18 with the immediately preceding verses. Isaiah 1:9, for example, expresses the relief of having escaped the fate of these nations. However, if the people believed that their fate was far away from that of Sodom and

Gomorrah, the next verse, Isaiah 1:10, attests to the contrary: destruction has not come, but Judah's violence and lack of commitment to social justice upset God. Indeed, Isaiah 1:11–14 describes God's reaction to their wickedness using strong language. God hates their behavior, their offerings are an abomination, and the people are a burden impossible to carry. Their rituals no longer delight the Lord. In other words, God is sick of them.

For the Isaianic author, justice is not detached from the cult. The same people who offer the blood of bulls, lambs, or goats (v. 11) are the ones who spill the blood of the innocent. Isaiah condemns the practice of rituals that do not translate into actions of social justice. Despite their sacrifices and offerings, the people cannot be made clean by just going through the motions (Isa. 1:4; 5:19, 24; 10:20). Rather, their purification will come, Isaiah states, when they learn to take care of the most disadvantaged from society. This is true worship according to Isaiah (1:16–17)—a message that Isaiah 58 reaffirms.

Another prophetic voice from the eighth century BCE, Micah, also confronts the people of Judah for hollow cultic observances (Mic. 6:6–8), that is, their willingness to fulfill their rituals with no commitment to justice. Micah clearly declares what the Lord really expects and desires instead: to do justice, to enact social solidarity (NRSV "kindness"), and to walk humbly with God. If the people and their leaders are willing to make social justice their way of life, they will receive forgiveness and be cleaned. As Isaiah makes clear, true redemption comes only from justice (Isa. 1:27). The preacher, following Isaiah and Habakkuk, does well to highlight the importance of social justice for the believer.

Like the Hebrew prophets, Jesus also preaches about the importance of justice. The story of Zacchaeus in Luke 19:1–10 offers an example of how an encounter with Jesus moves a person to amend their wrongs and do right to those who he has harmed. Even in the eschatological time, justice has a primary role. Jesus' message emphasizes that tending to the needs of the most disadvantaged from society is the same as doing this to him who gives access to the kingdom of heaven (Matt. 25:31–40). Only through such actions can society and church become a community abounding in love, in whom "the name of our Lord Jesus may be glorified" (2 Thess. 1:1–4, 11–12).

LYDIA HERNÁNDEZ-MARCIAL

Commentary 2: Connecting the Reading with the World

"How long, O Lord?" is a familiar cry, in the Scriptures and in the world. The psalmist asks repeatedly "How long, O LORD, will you look on" my suffering while doing nothing? (Ps. 35:17). "How long shall my enemy be exalted over me?" (Ps. 13:2). It is not just the Scriptures. We too say to friends, "How long will this mess continue?" Here it is Habakkuk who takes up the same anguished query: "LORD, how long shall I cry for help, and you will not listen? Or cry to you 'Violence!' and you will not save?" (Hab. 1:2). There is a decided aurality to this passage. We can hear the sound of Habakkuk crying for help. The Lord is depicted as one who might, or might not, listen.

Underneath this emphasis on sound, there is an insistence on *seeing*. After all, before you can cry out to the Lord about violence, you must first *see* the violence. For readers today, the passage contains an invitation to notice and to allow our gazes to linger on the violence in our midst. What violence in our homes, neighborhoods, communities, and nations might we see, if we stop to look? What practices can we adopt to help train ourselves in seeing what we are habituated to blink away? What practices can help us notice what we are habituated to race past? Perhaps, among other practices, *lectio divina* can school us in slowing down and looking again and again at the same text, expecting to somehow be blessed by our repeated looking.

"How long?" questions are sometimes rhetorical. Indeed, this is often the case when such questions aim to point out injustice. Speaking about poverty in the United States, Michael Harrington, asks for example: "How long shall we ignore this undeveloped nation in our midst? How long shall we look the other way while our fellow human beings suffer? How long?"[1] This is the kind of rhetorical question Habakkuk asks: How long shall I cry "Violence!" and you refuse to save? Neither Habakkuk nor Harrington is expecting an answer.

Habakkuk's assumption is proven incorrect, however. In this case, the Lord does answer (2:2). The answer God gives continues to press the act of *seeing*. Invoking the figure of "a runner" (2:2), God instructs the prophet to write the Lord's response to Habakkuk "plain on tablets, so that [even] a runner may read it" (2:2). The image of the runner is evocative and identifiable. The runner is not an exercise nut but is, rather, someone racing through their week, someone stressed out from too many obligations, someone who is always racing, racing, racing. We are the runner. Everyone in our parish is the runner. Our colleagues and friends are the runner. Haggai tells us that the Lord wants this message to reach even us, in our busyness, in our dash through life.

What God proceeds to say is unsettling, especially for those of us who believe we can fix things, that the world can be made right through our constant action, our busyness. In this passage, God is not interested in human beings' efforts against violence, or in what those efforts can accomplish. Rather, it is God's action that this passage stresses. In the "appointed time," at "the end," God—*not we*—will set things right. Though this healing seems to be rather slow in coming, nevertheless we are encouraged to wait. Redemption is absolutely, unequivocally coming.

God wants Habakkuk and his community of runners to look—just look. To look at the proud, and see the proud clearly. If we see what the proud are, the text suggests, we will be able to see what the contrast to pride is: living not by running frantically from one (good) deed to the next, but instead living by faith, faith that God really will heal the world of all its violence at the end. In the Christian tradition, this contrastive seeing is nurtured by the practice of Ignatian examen, a mode of praying that forms us to notice contrasts—the contrast between the moments we turned toward God and the moments we turned away from God, the contrast between the moments we loved my neighbor and the moments when we scorned her.

Habakkuk responds to God's oration with a prayer, worshipfully affirming that the God who had acted before will act again (Hab. 3). Habakkuk's response is, to be sure, the correct response, yet questions still linger. Why, exactly, are we supposed to look? Why are we supposed to gaze on the proud, and size them up? Nothing ever changes; the whole of everything is just hopelessly mired in violence. Why look at that? To these queries, God's answer is jarring: You look so that you can see the violence, and so that you can know by faith that it can be fixed, but not by you. You look so that you can be a witness, both to the injustice and also to the assured salvation of God.

The prophet Isaiah also takes up the theme of the unexpectedness—the jarringness—of God's answer. Isaiah announces to his Israelite listeners, whom he calls "rulers of Sodom" (Isa. 1:10), that the Lord has had enough of their sacrifices, offerings, Sabbaths, and religious festivals. To put it into a modern context, it is akin to hearing the Lord say that what you are doing with your valuable Sunday morning hours is "futile" (Isa. 1:13); that God "hates" your worship; that God finds it "burdensome"; that God will not listen to your prayers (Isa. 1:14–15). You have just offered a half-hour of worship, and here is God, telling you worship is not what God desires. What does God want then?

It would be a misinterpretation to hear in this just a plain rejection of these religious practices. Rather, God is saying something more ethically and religiously challenging: God *has* asked us for worship. God *does* want prayers and hymns. However, because we are not giving God some *other* things that God has also asked for, the prayers and the hymns are not useful; they are not true. In fact, the absence of some of the gifts God has requested (service to the widow and orphan, pursuit of justice) constitutes a performative contradiction of the other gifts God has requested (prayers and hymns).

1. Michael Harrington, *The Other America*, quoted in Michael Robert Rank, *One Nation, Underprivileged: Why American Poverty Affects Us All* (New York: Oxford University Press, 2004), 14.

To fail to give one contradicts the giving of the other. The failure to give God one kind of gift can invalidate the gifts we do give.

What about those of us who attend a justice-minded church—a church where feeding the poor, caring for the orphan, and seeking justice are encouraged? Congregations who are living into God's call for justice should rejoice. Nevertheless, even those congregations might ask themselves what they have neglected to give God. Giving God some of the gifts God seeks is never the same as giving God all the gifts God seeks, and each of our communities excels at some gifts, and is less devoted to others. One of the preacher's tasks, when reading Isaiah 1, is to consider the specific ways the preacher's congregation could better "do good; seek justice, rescue the oppressed, defend the orphan, plead for the widow" (Isa. 1:17). How can the congregation do what Jesus does for Zacchaeus, the tax collector, in Luke 19—that is, to seek out and save the lost, the rejected, and the sinful (Luke 19:10)?

LAUREN F. WINNER

Psalm 119:137–144

[137]You are righteous, O LORD,
and your judgments are right.
[138]You have appointed your decrees in righteousness
and in all faithfulness.
[139]My zeal consumes me
because my foes forget your words.
[140]Your promise is well tried,
and your servant loves it.
[141]I am small and despised,
yet I do not forget your precepts.
[142]Your righteousness is an everlasting righteousness,
and your law is the truth.
[143]Trouble and anguish have come upon me,
but your commandments are my delight.
[144]Your decrees are righteous forever;
give me understanding that I may live.

Psalm 32:1–7

[1]Happy are those whose transgression is forgiven,
whose sin is covered.
[2]Happy are those to whom the LORD imputes no iniquity,
and in whose spirit there is no deceit.

[3]While I kept silence, my body wasted away
through my groaning all day long.
[4]For day and night your hand was heavy upon me;
my strength was dried up as by the heat of summer.

[5]Then I acknowledged my sin to you,
and I did not hide my iniquity;
I said, "I will confess my transgressions to the LORD,"
and you forgave the guilt of my sin.

[6]Therefore let all who are faithful
offer prayer to you;
at a time of distress, the rush of mighty waters
shall not reach them.
[7]You are a hiding place for me;
you preserve me from trouble;
you surround me with glad cries of deliverance.

Connecting the Psalm with Scripture and Worship

Psalm 119:137–144. The first reading is part of an extended conversation between God and the prophet Habakkuk, in which the prophet raises the age-old question of why God remains silent in the face of injustice. Weary of waiting, Habakkuk cries out to God, then stations himself to wait for an answer. The answer comes, and God wants Habakkuk to make no mistake: justice is coming. It may seem like a long wait, but the reign of God is on the way.

The architects of the lectionary chose a portion of Psalm 119 as a response to this first reading. This is the song of the perpetual student of Scripture who has dwelt in God's Word, internalized God's vision, and trusts completely and unquestioningly in God's promise. The psalmist has suffered hardship but does not waver. "Judgment," "promise," "precept," and "decree" represent the vocabulary of faith; the terms reflect God's instruction for a righteous and fruitful life that are found in God's Word. In this Word the psalmist discovers the wonders God has done, comfort for times of trouble, and hope for the days of distress.[1] Because the psalmist dwells in God's Word, trusting in God's future is an expression of faithfulness, even as the psalmist asks that God continually increase her or his understanding. The justice God promises is indeed on the way.

Psalm 119 functions in at least two ways on this day. It reminds the church that part of the life of faith is to trust in promises that have not yet come to fruition. It also admonishes the church to continue to delve into the Word of God to attain deeper understanding of God's ways as well as to cultivate hope.

In the Gospel reading, the church sees a glimpse of that justice that is a long time coming. In the story of Zacchaeus, a crooked tax collector is converted by Jesus' teaching and repents in a big way, giving away half of all he owns and promising to make things right with those he has cheated by paying them back fourfold. Here is a sighting of the justice to come, a peek at the great reversal of which Mary sang in her Advent song, the Magnificat (Luke 1:46–55). Here at the end of the season after Pentecost, we move toward the culmination of the Christian year that comes on Reign of Christ/Christ the King. On that day the church will proclaim unequivocally that God's reign of justice and peace has already been established and will one day be complete. For now, we wait.

The psalm is instructive for those preaching and planning worship, as it urges us to wait in hope—and to hope while waiting. The prayers of intercession might be combined with the Taizé refrain "Wait for the Lord." The refrain could be sung several times before and after the prayers, with musical accompaniment continuing softly beneath spoken prayers, or sung after each of a series of brief intercessions. Hymns that focus on faith in the face of difficulty—such as "We Walk by Faith and Not by Sight" and "Trust and Obey"—may also give voice to hope.

Psalm 32:1–7. In the complementary or alternate readings, Isaiah 1:10–18 is chosen to reflect the content of the Gospel reading. The prophet exhorts the people to act justly and righteously—to do good works, to lift up the oppressed, to attend to the needs of the poor, the orphaned, and the widowed. This is what God desires, not empty rituals of contrition. God is interested in forgiveness, but only when the prayers of confession are authentic and true repentance results in doing justice. The psalm is a perfect response to the first reading, as the psalmist has confessed his or her own sin and experienced the blessing of divine forgiveness. The psalm begins with two beatitudes describing how happy are those whom God has forgiven. Verses 1 and 2 include three words for sin—*pesha'* (rebellion), *hatta'* (missing the mark), and *'avon* (perversity)—implying that God's mercy covers all forms of sin.[2] The psalmist describes suffering under the weight of sin (vv. 3–4) and the blessing that comes from being forgiven (v. 5). The psalmist's experience of mercy is so strong that she or he encourages all of the faithful to pray to God in their distress, that they might receive forgiveness

1. James L. Mays, *Psalms,* Interpretation (Louisville, KY: Westminster John Knox, 1994), 383–85.
2. Irene Nowell, OSB, *Sing a New Song: The Psalms in the Sunday Lectionary* (Collegeville, MN: Liturgical Press, 1993), 81.

The Harmony of Love

You see, brothers, how great and amazing love is, and how its perfection is beyond description. Who is able to possess it save those to whom God has given the privilege? Let us, then, beg and implore him mercifully to grant us love without human bias and to make us irreproachable. All the generations from Adam to our day have passed away, but those who, by the grace of God, have been made perfect in love have a place among the saints, who will appear when Christ's Kingdom comes. For it is written: "Go into your closets for a very little while, until my wrath and anger pass, and I will remember a good day and I will raise you up from your graves." Happy are we, dear friends, if we keep God's commandments in the harmony of love, so that by love our sins may be forgiven us. For it is written: "Happy are those whose iniquities are forgiven and whose sins are covered. Happy is the man whose sin the Lord will not reckon, and on whose lips there is no deceit." This is the blessing which was given to those whom God chose through Jesus Christ our Lord. To him be the glory forever and ever. Amen.

Let us, then, ask pardon for our failings and for whatever we have done through the prompting of the adversary. And those who are the ringleaders of the revolt and dissension ought to reflect upon the common nature of our hope. Those, certainly, who live in fear and love would rather suffer outrages themselves than have their neighbors do so. They prefer to endure condemnation themselves rather than bring in reproach our tradition of noble and righteous harmony. It is better for a man to confess his sins than to harden his heart.

1 Clement 50–51, in *Early Christian Fathers*, ed. Cyril C. Richardson, Library of Christian Classics (Louisville, KY: Westminster John Knox, 2006), 66–67.

and the same sort of comfort that the psalmist experiences (vv. 6–7).

It is likely that Psalm 32 was written to help instruct the community in the role of penitence in worship. The psalmist's experience is offered as an example to the community and underscores the importance of not keeping silent about the burden of sin. The faithful worshiper speaks a confession to God, telling the truth about one's need for grace.

The preacher may also use the first reading and psalm to teach the gathered assembly about the role of confession in the life of faith. Confession is not for the purpose of self-flagellation but rather to allow "streams of mercy never ceasing" to flow through the believer's life. Confession is always followed by forgiveness; telling the truth about our lives as individuals, as a community, and as a society allows the possibility of true repentance and makes room for the Holy Spirit to use us in the renewal of creation.

These readings also provide an occasion to highlight the connection between the church's worship and its work for justice. We bring the concerns of the world with us to worship; it is there that we lament before God and confess our part in the world's evil. We are sent from worship as agents of mercy; forgiven ourselves, we go to work for the reconciliation of the world.

If the sermon focuses on confession, a prayer or ritual of confession might follow as a response to the proclamation of the Word. Even if a corporate prayer of confession is spoken at the beginning of the service, a sung prayer may provide a bridge between the sermon and the sacrament. Since this day falls on what would be a Communion Sunday for many churches, the assembly might sing "Before I Take the Body of My Lord" by John L. Bell and Graham Maule, which begins:

> Before I take the body of my Lord,
> before I share his life in bread and wine,
> I recognize the sorry things within: these I
> lay down.[3]

3. John L. Bell and Graham Maule, "Before I Take the Body of My Lord," in *Glory to God* (Louisville, KY: Westminster John Knox, 2013), no. 428.

Although the first reading and Psalm 32:1–7 focus on penitence, the tone of the service does not need to be sober from beginning to end. The text from Isaiah builds to God's desire to wash us clean, and the psalm begins and ends with blessing. Praise is due the God of mercy, and today's congregation might express its gratitude by singing "Come, Thou Fount of Every Blessing."

KIMBERLY BRACKEN LONG

2 Thessalonians 1:1–4, 11–12

[1]Paul, Silvanus, and Timothy,

To the church of the Thessalonians in God our Father and the Lord Jesus Christ:

[2]Grace to you and peace from God our Father and the Lord Jesus Christ.

[3]We must always give thanks to God for you, brothers and sisters, as is right, because your faith is growing abundantly, and the love of every one of you for one another is increasing. [4]Therefore we ourselves boast of you among the churches of God for your steadfastness and faith during all your persecutions and the afflictions that you are enduring. . . .

[11]To this end we always pray for you, asking that our God will make you worthy of his call and will fulfill by his power every good resolve and work of faith, [12]so that the name of our Lord Jesus may be glorified in you, and you in him, according to the grace of our God and the Lord Jesus Christ.

Commentary 1: Connecting the Reading with Scripture

For the reader moving sequentially through the NT, the beginning of 2 Thessalonians will sound eerily familiar; indeed, the opening of this letter parallels the opening of the first letter to that same church. With only a few minor alterations, both texts begin with authorial invocation ("Paul, Silvanus, and Timothy"), address the church ("in God our Father and the Lord Jesus Christ"), offer a traditional Pauline greeting ("Grace to you and peace . . ."), and move to a statement of thanksgivings ("We must always give thanks . . ."). However, despite this parallelism, the letters quickly move in strikingly different directions. In 2 Thessalonians, gone is the extended warmth of 1 Thessalonians 1; in its place the second letter moves abruptly to language of persecution, suffering, destruction, and apocalypse.

This similar-but-different pairing has long attracted scholarly curiosity. If 2 Thessalonians is indeed written by Paul, why the relatively sudden change of disposition regarding the Thessalonian church? What has Paul heard about the life and ministry of that congregation that would prompt such a dramatic change of tone and disposition? Alternatively, if the letter was not written by Paul, how are we to understand the deliberate invocation of Paul's name and, indeed, the explicit declaration in 3:17 that "I write this greeting with my own hand"? While the Sunday preacher need not wrestle with sticky details of authorship in the space of worship, at the very least they suggest an interpretive approach that foregrounds the striking change in tone and emphasis that greets readers moving from the first letter to the second.

The most evident of these differences is the dramatic shift in focus from the internal moral stewardship of the congregation to the rallying of the congregation against its external threats. The thanksgiving of 1:3 quickly moves in 1:4 to concern about the church's fate at the hands of its political and religious enemies: "Therefore we ourselves boast of you among the churches of God for your steadfastness and faith during all your persecutions and the afflictions that you are enduring." The letter provides few historical clues as to the specific nature of these threats; however, if indeed the letter is not an original Pauline composition, the reference to persecutions may suggest a late-first-century composition date that would align with the rise in threats against early Christian believers. Regardless, the distinction is clear: whereas the first letter is regularly interested in the internal building up of the faith community for its worshipful and missional work, this second letter quickly sets itself to the task of naming, circumscribing, and guarding against the church's external foes.

Nowhere is this clearer than in the verses excised from this lectionary reading. In verses 5–10, the steadfastness of the Thessalonians is "evidence of the righteous judgment of God" that will be carried out with vicious wrath against those who have persecuted God's church ("those who afflict you"). At the eschaton, God will "inflict vengeance on those who do not know God," and they "will suffer the punishment of eternal destruction." While this kind of judgmental rhetoric may feel like uncomfortable territory for many Sunday preachers, it nonetheless undergirds the emphasis of the letter, strikingly contrasting with the pastoral tone that Paul sets in 1 Thessalonians 4:16–17. In those verses, he counsels a congregation's internal anxieties about the fate of those within its midst who have already died; here in 2 Thessalonians 1, the text is much more concerned with naming the church's external threats than with pastoring its internal concerns.

For the twenty-first-century Western preacher, the utility of this passage therefore hinges largely on the way in which we speak about the church in relation to its external threats. In an age of secularization and diminished religious affiliation, it is occasionally tempting to identify the contemporary church as a persecuted class; at the same time, of course, the history of the Western church abounds with a degree of political power unimaginable to the first-century audience of this letter, and any honest exegesis has to wrestle with the church's role not just as persecuted class but also as an agent of persecution itself. It is worth remembering that one of the underlying proclamations in this text is eschatological inversion: the vulnerable and politically weak will be lifted up; institutions of empire and oppression will be made low. While of course there are times when it is pastorally appropriate to speak to a congregation "during all your persecutions and the afflictions," the church as historical institution rarely fits the profile of victimhood necessary for this text to feel comfortable and heartwarming.

The enterprising lectionary preacher will note some thematic parallels with the other texts appointed for this day. The selected verses from the first two chapters of Habakkuk anticipate a similar eschatological inversion—"a vision for the appointed time" (Hab. 2:3)—as the prophet is invited, "Look at the proud! Their spirit is not right within them, but the righteous live by their faith" (2:4). While the cultural contexts of Habakkuk and 2 Thessalonians vary greatly, both ask their readers to search for signs of God's faithfulness among those normally devalued by their communities. Of course, the texts vary greatly in perspective: whereas 2 Thessalonians identifies its audience as this devalued class, Habakkuk self-identifies as a prophetic voice to religious and political authorities—much like the perspective in the lectionary reading from Isaiah, whose direct address to "the rulers of Sodom" and the "people of Gomorrah" speaks less of eschatological inversion than of a present calling to account for the powers that be.

Themes of inversion and persecution also prominently reappear in the lectionary Gospel, the story of Zacchaeus from Luke 19. Zacchaeus is of course both persecuted and persecutor, the rich tax collector who is also despised and ostracized. Luke's account presents a more nuanced portrait of social power dynamics than we find in the language of persecution in 2 Thessalonians—and therefore potentially a more fruitful point of identification for a contemporary church wrestling with the complexities of its cultural position. Whereas the eschatological promise of 2 Thessalonians hangs on God's judgment and wrath, the operating force of Luke 19 is the initiative of Zacchaeus combined with the welcoming grace of Jesus. It is this grace—the initiative of God—that finally surfaces in the closing verses of the 2 Thessalonians section, wherein the author prays that God make the church "worthy of God's call" (2 Thess. 1:11).

Such is the paradox of identifying as a persecuted church within the arc of God's faithfulness. On the one hand, Scripture asks the Thessalonians to ready themselves, gird themselves for the trials at hand—not to be the rocky ground from the familiar parable of the Sower in Matthew 13:21 or Mark 4:17, in which the rootless seeds fall away "when affliction or persecution arises." Such is the exhortation to endurance—"steadfastness" to the Thessalonians and, famously, "perseverance" to the Hebrews (Heb. 12:1). On the other hand, the church is also invited to remember God's own steadfastness, the initiative of grace summoned by the prayers of verses 11–12, the grace that calls the church into faithfulness regardless of its complicated history. Sometimes, that calling feels like the welcome offered to Zacchaeus; sometimes, it feels like the repentance Isaiah asks of the rulers of Sodom. Either way, it is a steadfastness that outlasts all troubles, as in the cadence of Romans 8:35, wherein "persecution" and "affliction" join in the familiar list of universal woes finally and eschatologically ill equipped to outlast God's grace and the love of Jesus Christ.

MATT GAVENTA

Commentary 2: Connecting the Reading with the World

This reading is an excerpt from a controversial passage, from a controversial book, concerning a cluster of controversial topics. The evidence for this tension is that the Revised Common Lectionary excises verses 5–10, even though the sense of verses 11 and 12 requires them. With this lectionary selection, then, we are thrust into the area of cultural, social, and ethical matters. What is it about our twenty-first century that would pass over these six verses—that challenge a typical contemporary congregation or individual Christian?

We come face to face with what Albert Schweitzer called the alien character of this ancient text, which spoke clearly enough in its first contexts that it was included within the canon. Reading the passage in full, we may find ourselves bewildered by its apocalyptic imagery, which reveals not just mercy but also the "judgment of God" (1:5), his "just" repayment of the violent (v. 6), the anticipated revelation of Jesus "in flaming fire" (v. 7), the "vengeance" and condemnation of disobedience (v. 8), and the threat of "punishment" and exclusion (v. 9). Verse 10, which is entirely positive, is so inextricably linked to the prior five verses that it has been, unfortunately, jettisoned with them. Thus, unhappily, we miss a gem of teaching: if we keep the apostolic testimony, we will become holy ones displaying Christ's glory. Both the bad news of 1:5–9 and the good news of verse 10 exceed the unsanctified human imagination. The careful preacher must find a point of contact, addressing the hopes as well as the fears of a contemporary congregation, and encouraging them to go further.

Without 1:5–10, this first chapter moves innocuously from its initial greeting, through its commendation of the Thessalonians' endurance, to the prayer that God will perfect their faith. Unfortunately, we miss the supplication that the Thessalonians may be part of that saintly glory shared with the Lord Jesus—a future scene that will evoke astonishment among all who have believed in the apostolic testimony (v. 10). That prayer is instead full-orbed, joining the past acts of God with present circumstances and the anticipated coming of Christ.

One cannot speak about the Parousia without also recognizing the double-edged sword of God's justice. Righteousness cannot prevail unless unrighteousness is cured or thwarted. Without the difficult verses, the reading may well, to those who are truly suffering, sound like so much wishful thinking. With them, however, we risk alienating the very people who need most to hear the message: those who are not attuned to warnings of judgment, considering them either laughable or barbaric, or both. Awareness of possible responses is called for in the preacher, whose role is at least partially to resensitize others to both God's goodness and God's justice.

It may be helpful for us to set these less palatable ideas within the context of the full gospel. If this letter (along with 1 Thessalonians) is indeed from Paul and his associates Silvanus and Timothy, it is remarkable that he does not appeal explicitly to their offices as pastors and elders. Instead of claiming apostolic privilege, he immediately moves to the recipients' strengths—faith, love, and endurance. Uppermost is not a need to chastise these loved ones, but to build them up in the strength of God. So chapter 1 is book-ended by reference to this loving God, expressed in what we could describe as "binitarian" terms—the Father and the Lord Jesus Christ (1:1, 12). At the same time, both verses 1 and 12 highlight the *koinōnia* that we have with each other and with the Lord, "glorified in you, and you in him." Those expounding this section may follow suit and give thanks for the shared life of their congregation.

Along with this overshadowing of a graceful God goes the "good news" (NRSV "gospel," v. 8), as expressed by the increasing faith and love of the community: already the glory of Jesus may be glimpsed in his saints, for they have suffered for "the name." Judgment, then, is thoroughly outshone by the righteousness, love, faithfulness, and gracious giving seen first in Christ, but also in his people. God is *not* pictured as "a strict martinet,"[1] but as "the God of peace" (3:16), who encourages us never to be weary in well-doing. Even the reference to God's future vengeance should remind us of other guidance: human retribution is not permitted, but we are to overcome evil with good (Rom. 12:9, 11). Contemporary Christians no doubt have approved feel-good films such as *Pay It Forward.* Here is an even more astonishing action: the Holy Spirit working in Christians to conquer evil not by brute power but in the mode of Christ. Not everyone is called to be a Mother Teresa, but every Christian can witness to God's character by disarming responses to personal harm.

The writer of this letter and its recipients celebrated the clement character of God and the grace-filled gospel. Our generation has absolutized inclusion, grown allergic to the idea of "obedience," and mistaken grace for tolerance. In addressing the affliction of the Thessalonians, the letter reminds them that God is just: if there are those who refuse to accept the mercy of the gospel, God will not give them free run forever. Though a douse of cold water to our sensibilities, this entire passage functions as a corrective to a day that is hearing a different "gospel" proclaimed. Consider the book and movie *The Shack*, which insist love has nothing to do with obedience or submission. Faithful Christians may be challenged to refuse such easy answers and to show the costly nature of living out the gospel, where dignity or status may be threatened.

The passage provides ample hope that many may be moved by the endurance and love of those who show forth the character of Christ. Not only "on that day" (v. 10) can the glory of Jesus be seen in the saints. Also in the present time we can see the faith and love of our brothers and sisters. This revelation of Jesus' glory is dramatic in those lands where being a Christian is a dangerous prospect; it is more subtle in our own context, where harassment for unpopular ethical positions or ridicule for one's beliefs also requires courage.

Today's churches would do well to recover the robust sense of God's justice displayed in this chapter: recognition that God is like a "flaming fire" who aims to purify us will allow us to reclaim the drama and truth of the gospel. This might mean owning unpopular positions on social issues; it might mean opening our home to those whom the world ignores or rejects; it might mean speaking in regretful truth to a family member whose lifestyle is both self-destructive and contrary to the gospel. The same God who spoke to Moses in the burning bush intends to make us, by the Holy Spirit, "worthy." The process starts now, as God strengthens our best resolutions (v. 11), both personally and as a church. At the same time, we can marvel that even in this careless age, seekers frequently glimpse the Lord's beauty in the life of those who love him. Thus, we can appropriate the epistle's prayer that God would make us worthy of this call, and that we might give thanks for those who reveal him luminously, until he comes again.

EDITH M. HUMPHREY

1. Cf. I. Howard Marshall's disclaimer in *1 and 2 Thessalonians*, New Century Bible (Grand Rapids: Eerdmans, 1983), 174.

Luke 19:1–10

[1]He entered Jericho and was passing through it. [2]A man was there named Zacchaeus; he was a chief tax collector and was rich. [3]He was trying to see who Jesus was, but on account of the crowd he could not, because he was short in stature. [4]So he ran ahead and climbed a sycamore tree to see him, because he was going to pass that way. [5]When Jesus came to the place, he looked up and said to him, "Zacchaeus, hurry and come down; for I must stay at your house today." [6]So he hurried down and was happy to welcome him. [7]All who saw it began to grumble and said, "He has gone to be the guest of one who is a sinner." [8]Zacchaeus stood there and said to the Lord, "Look, half of my possessions, Lord, I will give to the poor; and if I have defrauded anyone of anything, I will pay back four times as much." [9]Then Jesus said to him, "Today salvation has come to this house, because he too is a son of Abraham. [10]For the Son of Man came to seek out and to save the lost."

Commentary 1: Connecting the Reading with Scripture

When Zacchaeus climbs his sycamore tree in the Gospel reading, it is almost always the first week of November, when Halloween is done, and we see red and green decorations and hear the music of Christmas in our stores and malls. Attentive listeners may also hear the music of Christmas wafting through this story. Zacchaeus welcomes Jesus with overwhelming joy, vastly more than the NRSV's bland "was happy." Luke's Christmas story begins with the angel Gabriel whispering a promise of "joy and gladness" to Zechariah (Luke 1:14), and Christmas night an angel brings "good news of great joy for all the people" (2:10). In the womb John the Baptist "leaped for joy" (1:44) as Jesus approaches in utero, and now Zacchaeus fairly leaps for joy to welcome Jesus. Joy is the only adequate response to what God is doing in Jesus. The crowds in Jericho may grumble, but Zacchaeus gets it right. He rejoices!

In the Gospel of Luke salvation is surprisingly visible. When Mary and Joseph take the infant Jesus to the temple, they encounter Simeon, who cradles the baby in his arms and praises God because, he says, "my eyes have seen your salvation" (2:30). For Luke, seeing Jesus *is* seeing God's salvation. This is what Zacchaeus wants to see. Jesus is salvation walking, and as Jesus enters Jericho, Zacchaeus climbs his sycamore in order to see. This is no idle curiosity or celebrity stargazing. Zacchaeus does not seek an autograph. Zacchaeus longs to see something that is not easily spoken. The word "salvation" points to it, but the longing is deep and aching. The language of "trying to see" is phrased in terms of seeking, searching, and yearning. We may wonder at times what Jesus looked like, but Zacchaeus wants to see more than a face. He wants to see more than he can say, but he knows at least this much: it has to do with this Jesus entering Jericho.

Oddly, Luke never tells us if Zacchaeus succeeded in seeing what he was looking for. Instead Luke tells us Jesus "looked up" and saw Zacchaeus. Luke introduces the story saying that Jesus was "passing through" Jericho; now Jesus announces, "Zacchaeus, hurry and come down; for I *must* stay at your house today." Jesus is expressing more than a need for a night's lodging. The "must" of "I *must* stay" is the divine imperative that Luke uses again and again to carry heavy theological weight; it *must* be done because God wills it; it *must* be done because this is nothing less than God's plan.

"I must stay at your house *today*." The specification of today is not a casual reference to time but, rather, announces the arrival of glad tidings, just as it did in on Christmas Eve: "to you is born *today* . . . a Savior who is the Messiah, the Lord" (2:11). Jesus began his ministry in the synagogue of Nazareth reading the prophet Isaiah and announcing, "*Today* this scripture has been fulfilled" (4:21). Today is when God is doing something astonishing; *today* is the time of God's salvation.

Unlike the citizens of Jerusalem, Zacchaeus of Jericho recognizes "the time of your visitation from God" (19:44), and like Paul he understands "salvation is nearer to us . . . the day is near" (Rom. 13:11–12). Zacchaeus hears the grumbling out in the streets. He is familiar with it. By virtue of his occupation he has lived like an outcast with the envy, enmity, and resentment of his neighbors. He wants to explain himself before Jesus, but what is it that he says? "Look, half of my possessions, Lord, I will give to the poor; and if I have defrauded anyone of anything, I will pay back four times as much." This statement, in present tense in Greek, can also be translated as the claim of an observant Jew about his regular practices. Earlier, when John the Baptist was preaching "a baptism of repentance for the forgiveness of sins" (3:3), tax collectors came asking, "What should we do?" John said simply, "Collect no more that the amount prescribed for you" (3:12–13). Is that what Zacchaeus in fact does?

It is difficult to know whether Zacchaeus is repenting and resolving improvements for the future or declaring himself a righteous man who deals generously and fairly at his work. Could Habakkuk have described this situation, "Look at the proud! Their spirit is not right . . . but the righteous live by their faith" (Hab. 2:4)? The Hebrew name Zacchaeus is rooted in words connoting "clean, pure, innocent." Psalm 32:1–2 declares as "happy" those whose transgressions are forgiven, whose sins are covered, to whom "the Lord imputes no iniquity" and whose "spirit has no deceit." Which of these "happy" persons might Zacchaeus be? Indeed, we should ask: What does happiness mean in the biblical text? What should it mean in our lives? In what ways are happiness, forgiveness, and repentance linked?

The way Luke tells the story does not resemble a repentance narrative. Zacchaeus does not ask for mercy like the tax collector in the preceding chapter (18:13). Jesus does not acknowledge his faith, as he did when he told a woman who was a sinner, "Your faith has saved you; go in peace" (7:50). Jesus does not announce Zacchaeus has been forgiven, as he has done elsewhere (5:20). Luke is not a careless writer. Why is this not clearer?

Earlier Luke told a story about a centurion whose servant was ill and who wished for Jesus to heal him. The elders of the synagogue come to Jesus on behalf of the centurion, saying, "He is worthy of having you do this for him, for he loves our people, and it is he who built our synagogue for us" (7:4–5). Other friends of the centurion appear with his message, "Lord, do not trouble yourself, for I am not worthy to have you come under my roof" (7:6). Well, which is he? Worthy or not worthy? We wonder. Jesus does not wonder but declares that the centurion's faith—"speak the word, and let my servant be healed" (7:7)—is not only sufficient but exceeding all others.

As the centurion's story only appeared to be about whether he was worthy, Zacchaeus's story is not about what he does or does not do, but about what God is doing through Jesus. Jesus announces, "Today salvation has come to this house," because Jesus has invited himself into Zacchaeus's home. The plan is nothing less than God's design.

Like the shepherd searching for the lost sheep and the woman searching for the lost coin (15:3–10), Jesus has come "to seek out and save the lost." Years earlier the prophet Ezekiel had heard God's indictment of the sorry shepherds who had been kings and God's fierce determination to do better: "thus says the Lord God: I myself will search for my sheep, and will seek them out" (Ezek. 34:11). Zacchaeus is lost in the resentment of his neighbors. Even his small stature resulted in his marginalization, as short people were understood also as short on courage, character, and spirit. Zacchaeus can indeed pray the prayer of Psalm 119: "I am small and despised, yet I do not forget your precepts" (Ps. 119:141).

Though the crowds of Jericho may not know who Zacchaeus truly is, and though Zacchaeus himself may have wondered himself, Jesus sees distinctly the face of the family: "He too is a son of Abraham" (19:10). Earlier Luke had named Jesus a "son of Abraham" (3:34) and Jesus had healed a crippled woman, naming her "a daughter of Abraham" (13:16). God's salvation strides through Jericho as Jesus seeks and saves the lost.

PATRICK J. WILLSON

Commentary 2: Connecting the Reading with the World

What does hospitality look like when Jesus is on the scene? It is not difficult to be blinded by our own theological assumptions about God, how God works, and whom we deem qualified or disqualified to receive from God's bounty when blessings are bestowed and forgiveness is meted out. Luke's accounting of the chief tax agent Zacchaeus's conversion represents one among several episodic acts of Jesus in which he intensifies hostilities with various community gatekeepers. Jesus' extension of mercy to the "wealthy despised," which takes the form of table fellowship, sets off alarms in the case of Zacchaeus. Not only does Jesus earn the religious community's contempt for what he does for the tax collector; it unsettles everyone onsite, even perhaps Jesus' own disciples.

How might we situate ourselves if somehow we found ourselves among the onlookers in Jericho that day? The story line is uncomplicated. As a crowd gathers around Jesus, Zacchaeus, simply identified as a short and rich chief tax collector, climbs up a tree so that he can survey the commotion down below undetected. Jesus beckons him down and invites Zacchaeus to host him as his houseguest. To this Zacchaeus happily assents, which leads to grumbling from the crowd. Ostensibly feeling the crowd's condemnation, Zacchaeus's mood of elation turns to seriousness. Voluntarily, Zacchaeus solemnly vows to pay restitution, four times the original amount if he has defrauded anyone. In reply, Jesus lavishly bestows on him and his household the gift of salvation.

This is what Jesus does and was purposed to do—to seek and save the undesirables and lost ones. Could this passage have a message for religiously disaffected teenagers and millennials? Such passages must be pressed into the service of God to speak not only to an individual's need for salvation, but also to address the importance of spiritual growth and active involvement in the life of the Christian disciple and what it means to develop a mature faith. The passage moreover beckons preachers to see more when attempting to comprehend the societal implications attached to the character of God's inbreaking reign-dom and what our response as Christians should be in light of it.

Wealthy landholders, not tax collectors, stood to profit most in the corrupt Roman tax system. Taxation and confiscation of property led to the consolidation of landholdings program that enriched a small segment of society, who after their acquisition of property leased land and hired slaves to cultivate what they possessed. As Rome gave contracts to wealthy landholders, foreigners and Jewish aristocrats collected the residuals earned by local tax officials.[1] Zacchaeus, who according to Luke was Jericho's most influential tax man, can therefore be viewed as a metaphor for corporate greed. Homiletically, one could wage moral and ethical critique and analogously associate Zacchaeus as a private owner of a for-profit prison authorized by the federal government.

Zacchaeus imposed tariffs (indirect taxation) on goods going to market on the border along the trade route in the Jordan Valley between Perea and Judea. Auctioned to the highest bidder "chief toll collectors" set up toll stations and collected tariffs, characteristically collecting more than was authorized. Without question the taxation system of which Zacchaeus is a part by virtue of profession and association was inherently corrupt and socially abusive.

1. Anthony J. Saldarini, "Publicans," in *Harper's Bible Dictionary*, ed. Paul Achtemeier (San Francisco: HarperSanFrancisco, 1985), 841.

Although Zacchaeus experiences conversion, he does not become a social reformer, nor is there any indication that he intends to abandon a profession so culturally despised. Though he pledges compensation and donation of half his wealth, Zacchaeus still participates in an evil system that he is likely not going to challenge or work to change.

There are many privileged people who offer parallel examples. Take for example celebrity athletes. Many of them are both beneficiaries of a market-driven culture and commodities in it because of their talent. Stadiums and arenas are built on their backs as well as those of less-celebrated athletes who receive a fraction of the revenue owners and sponsors command. Even if charitable and most well intentioned in their regard for the poor, such socially and economically privileged persons in hypercapitalistic economies require others to accept fixed status to maintain the systemic evil. This in turn stymies the social progress and upward mobility of the vulnerable masses. As long as the most economically impoverished find themselves caught in the crosswinds of unscrupulous payday lending practices, high rents, and unjust social policies that protect the interests of the state and "the one percenters" who control 80 percent of the country's wealth, no person of means escapes such a system with clean hands.

Before we who preach the gospel innocently celebrate Zacchaeus's spiritual transformation, preachers must come to this text with tears in their eyes, lamenting the social reality into which the saving power of Jesus arrives. Life in Jericho is less than perfect, and certain religious strictures against ritual defilement were widely accepted as community safeguards. Tax gatherers that collected funds at the borders, as did Zacchaeus, were in frequent contact with Gentiles. For this reason, tax collectors were often deemed unclean, which further ostracized them.

Where would we find ourselves in the crowd thronging Jesus? Upholding perceived community safeguards that buttress the status quo? Disgruntled by the fact that a revolutionary charismatic figure is uprooting protected norms of established generations of recognized leaders? Standing on the fringes unaware of what is going on? Jesus' agenda is discipleship oriented. The Zacchaeus story is a useful picture for understanding what having wealth implies in the realm of faith. Zacchaeus, for example, is a saint when his story is juxtaposed with the parable of Lazarus the Rich Man (16:19–31) and the story of the rich ruler (18:18–25). For they, at the expense of the poor and for fear of poverty, reveal that neither was predisposed or persuaded enough to abandon their possessions to follow Jesus.

In the end, the Zacchaeus story is about personal gratitude and discipleship in the context of hospitality and hostility. Social psychologists claim that gratitude not only can be deliberately cultivated, but it also carries with it the positive benefits of increased energy, optimism, and empathy. This is especially important in a market-driven and consumer-driven culture. Zacchaeus happily accepts Jesus as guest in his home and takes seriously Jesus' bestowal of restored dignity. At Jesus' word human life is honored and fellowship is made possible.

Zacchaeus is found rightly disposed of heart. Rightness of heart means remaining open to the prophet's voice, which calls us from our hiding places, meets us in our curiosity, and restores our human dignity in the face of social rejection. Salvation has come to Zacchaeus's household, and for the onlookers Jesus provides one explanation: he too is a son of Abraham (v. 9). The hospitality of God meets sinners—even the most culturally despised—at the intersection of their obedience, discipleship, and trust.

KENYATTA R. GILBERT

Proper 27 (Sunday between November 6 and November 12 Inclusive)

Haggai 1:15b–2:9 and Job 19:23–27a
Psalm 145:1–5, 17–21 or Psalm 98,
Psalm 17:1–9
2 Thessalonians 2:1–5, 13–17
Luke 20:27–38

Haggai 1:15b–2:9

[15]In the second year of King Darius, [2:1]in the seventh month, on the twenty-first day of the month, the word of the LORD came by the prophet Haggai, saying: [2]Speak now to Zerubbabel son of Shealtiel, governor of Judah, and to Joshua son of Jehozadak, the high priest, and to the remnant of the people, and say, [3]Who is left among you that saw this house in its former glory? How does it look to you now? Is it not in your sight as nothing? [4]Yet now take courage, O Zerubbabel, says the LORD; take courage, O Joshua, son of Jehozadak, the high priest; take courage, all you people of the land, says the LORD; work, for I am with you, says the LORD of hosts, [5]according to the promise that I made you when you came out of Egypt. My spirit abides among you; do not fear. [6]For thus says the LORD of hosts: Once again, in a little while, I will shake the heavens and the earth and the sea and the dry land; [7]and I will shake all the nations, so that the treasure of all nations shall come, and I will fill this house with splendor, says the LORD of hosts. [8]The silver is mine, and the gold is mine, says the LORD of hosts. [9]The latter splendor of this house shall be greater than the former, says the LORD of hosts; and in this place I will give prosperity, says the LORD of hosts.

Job 19:23–27a

[23]"O that my words were written down!
O that they were inscribed in a book!
[24]O that with an iron pen and with lead
they were engraved on a rock forever!
[25]For I know that my Redeemer lives,
and that at the last he will stand upon the earth;
[26]and after my skin has been thus destroyed,
then in my flesh I shall see God,
[27]whom I shall see on my side,
and my eyes shall behold, and not another."

Commentary 1: Connecting the Reading with Scripture

Hope, which helps people and communities stand firm in times of crisis and contention, is a running theme that connects all the biblical passages of this lection. Haggai encourages the people to rebuild the temple after the exile. Job deals with accusations of his innocence while persisting in his search for vindication. Moreover, the Christian interpretation of these OT lessons finds eschatological hope fulfilled in Jesus. This eschatological hope is also present in the texts from the NT for this Sunday. The Thessalonians are assured of their hope for the second coming of Jesus, while Luke affirms the hope of the resurrection.

The four oracles of the book of Haggai, received during the second year of King Darius I of Persia (520 BCE), revolve around the hope for the rebuilding of God's house and the restoration of the Davidic kingship (Hag. 2:20–23). Judah was suffering drought, famine, and economic difficulties (1:6–11). With the little they had, the people dedicated themselves to the reconstruction of their houses.

Despite the rebuilding of the domiciles, the temple remained in ruins. Isaiah's promise of a joyful return and a successful reconstruction of the city (e.g., Isa. 49:14–26; 51:11) had not yet come to fruition. Haggai tries to make sense of what has happened: the problem is that the returning exiles have neglected the rebuilding of God's house, the temple. The temple in Jerusalem was God's dwelling place. Now that the exiles have returned to Judah, the reconstruction of the temple is imperative if the people of Judah want the presence of the Lord among them. Haggai's words appear to have moved the people to restart the construction of the temple.

There is hope in the assurance of God's presence. Haggai 1:15b–2:9 addresses Judah's disappointment after the first month of reconstruction. The temple looked like nothing compared to the former one (2:3). Ezra 3:10–13 states that the people had mixed feelings about the temple, a combination of joy and weeping. Haggai's second oracle serves as encouragement for Zerubbabel and Joshua, the political and religious leaders of the land, as well as the rest of the people. First, the prophet pronounces a phrase of assurance reminiscent of Joshua 1:8–9: "Take courage . . . do not fear" (2:4–5). Second, God repeats the promise of God's presence, which was originally made after the exodus from Egypt (2:5; cf. Exod. 29:43–45). This affirmation is crucial to the people, who probably do not see the need for a temple if God is not in their midst.

Hope is also present in the promise of provision. Haggai's words affirm to a disappointed people with limited resources that God will provide necessary resources for the restoration of the temple to its former glory. Indeed, this construction will even surpass the original (2:9). The text uses eschatological language—that is, language referring to future times, to describe how God will indeed provide. After a cosmic event shaking all creation and the nations, their treasures ("the desired things of all the nations") will be at Judah's disposal because the silver and the gold belong to God (2:6–8). The Christian church read the expression "the desired of all nations" in Haggai 2:7 as a prophecy referring to Jesus, the one who can bring *shalom* to the nations. Rendering *shalom* as "prosperity" limits the polysemic nature of the word. More than prosperity, this word commonly translated "peace" conveys the idea of well-being.

Only after the completion of construction will well-being return to Jerusalem. Even though these are words affirming the hope of restoration to the people, the expression "the treasure/the desired things of all nations" can be problematic from the perspective of the rest of the nations. Powerful nations have justified the conquest and plunder of other countries by using texts such as this one. The preacher should take care, therefore, to avoid using language justifying the oppression of one nation over the others.

The second text for this Sunday, Job 19:23–27a, focuses on Job's hope, however small, of proving his innocence. None of his three friends believes that Job is innocent. Their assumption of Job's guilt is based on the concept of retribution, in which good deeds and right behavior guarantee well-being and blessings, and bad behavior and wickedness lead to punishment and suffering (Deut. 28; Prov. 10:3; 11:18; 12:21). According to the concept of retribution, Job must have done something to deserve such afflictions. So, desirous of proving his innocence, in this second cycle of discourses between Job and his three friends (Job 12:1–20:29), Job wishes aloud for a witness of his integrity and affirms his belief in the existence of a vindicator who will restore his honor.

Alienated from family and friends (19:9–19), Job states that he is persecuted and oppressed by

God and his friends alike (19:22; cf. 30:11). He is like a cornered animal falling into the trap of its hunter (19:6, 22). Job, moreover, states that God acted perversely with him (19:6). Later in the book, he even says that God has taken away his right of defending his innocence (27:2). Job is no longer the man portrayed in the first chapters of the book, willing to accept from God both the good and the bad. To whom, then, can Job go to vindicate his name?

Job 19:23–27a describes Job's hope. He states that the concept of retribution is untenable. Not every suffering person has done something bad to deserve suffering. He desires to leave a permanent witness of his innocence (19:23–24); thus, he mentions the possibility of a record inscribed in stone with an iron stylus. Lead would make the inscription resistant to the weather conditions.

Job's hope rests in the certainty that he has a vindicator (Heb. *go'el*, NRSV "redeemer"). The concept comes from the legal context and refers to family situations in which a relative can buy back property, deliver a relative sold into slavery, or avenge a murdered relative (Lev. 25; Ruth 4). Who is this *go'el* in verse 25? There are several alternatives: Job's outcry, a member from the heavenly host serving as Job's attorney, and God. Even when elsewhere God is known as a redeemer (e.g., Isa. 41:14; 43:14; Jer. 50:34), the way in which Job has described God as his adversary makes this hardly a possibility. He wanted someone who could help him to defend his innocence and restore his honor. C. L. Seow claims that this text is a call to God to action (see Ps. 44:23–26).[1] Thus, Job reminds God that vindication is a divine function, and urges God to rise and do God's duty. Because of the emphasis in verse 25 on Job's faith in a redeemer, coupled with Job's assertion that he will see God even after his "skin has been thus destroyed," Christians have read Job 19:25 as a prophecy referring to Jesus and his resurrection.

The book of Job, especially the dialogues between Job and his friends, invites the preacher to explore the complexities of the relationship between Job and God. As Job shows, questioning God does not make someone a sinner or an evil person. On the contrary, the book of Job invites people to challenge theological positions in conflict with the character of God, just as Habakkuk does (Hab. 1:13). Through Haggai and Job and the NT readings for this Sunday, Christians reaffirm their hope of redemption, vindication, well-being, and resurrection in Jesus for tough times.

LYDIA HERNÁNDEZ-MARCIAL

Commentary 2: Connecting the Reading with the World

The passage in Haggai 1 begins with a description, simply, of how things are and of how most people, when they are not nurturing their denial, already know things to be: "Is it not in your sight as nothing?" the Lord asks (Hag. 2:3). Everything is as nothing. The temple is destroyed, and the people are exiled and under the rule of a foreign king. The body politic, the whole of society, both religious authority as represented by Joshua and secular authority as represented by Zerubbabel, are as nothing. Indeed, none of these religious or secular leaders was around when things were good, vibrant, or made sense. Maybe they nurse nostalgia for a past they have heard about but cannot themselves remember. At any rate, all they have ever known as society is decayed, rotten, horrible.

Nevertheless, God does not intend to leave Zerubbabel and Joshua in despair. Rather, Haggai affirms that God is with the community: "I am with you, says the LORD of hosts"; therefore, "work" (2:4). In so doing, the text emphasizes the difference between hopelessness and hope. Situations become hopeless when it feels as if the God who created us and is redeeming us has vanished. When God is present, we have hope. Despair diminishes our capacity to act. Hope makes action possible. In preaching this

1. C. L. Seow, *Job 1–19: Interpretation and Commentary* (Grand Rapids: Eerdmans, 2013), 807.

text, then, the preacher might ask what kind of work is being commended. What tasks would we undertake if we were to work with hope?

Those two moves—an acknowledgment of how hollowed out the body politic has become, and the insistence that we should work with hope because God accompanies us—would be plenty. Verse 6 begins a third move, a strange and lovely move, a declaration of God's power and God's ownership: "The silver is mine, and the gold is mine" (2:8). All of the wealth in the universe belongs to God, and all the power belongs to God. God promises that God will "shake" and dispose of the silver and gold so that it will return to the rightful place (2:6–7). That is, God will restore to the chosen people the wealth, health, and security that has long been missing.

Haggai's statement has theological implications. We do not own anything, at least not in the typical sense of ownership. Sometimes, we get our hands on silver and gold, but we did not create the wealth and, per this passage, we do not dispose of it. Though it seems that we "have" silver or gold, we are only its caretakers. Is Haggai 2 the basis for a rousing stewardship sermon then? Haggai invites us to give an account of what it means for us to "own" silver and gold, especially when, as Haggai states, everything ultimately belongs to the Lord (2:8). Like language, money has been given to us and shapes us. Our duty is to be a responsible, grateful conduit of this divine gift.

Other theological and political implications are also present in this pericope. Theologically, it offers strong support for the idea that redeemed creation will be better than the first creation: "The latter splendor of this house shall be greater than the former" (v. 9). At the same time, the passage seems to pertain specifically to "the house" (v. 3); God is promising to give "prosperity" "in this place" (v. 9). The promise has a location, a placed-ness—a location specific to the Jewish people. Though we Christians analogically receive and participate in the promise, we do not quite participate in its placed-ness as Haggai's first audience did. The place of Christians rather is mainly theological; it is wherever the body of Christ is, and that is a movable feast.

For Christians, then, this might be an apt passage to explore in a Communion service. How is God giving us prosperity through and in the place of the Eucharist? What does it mean to proclaim that, however bad things look for the church, the church will never become as nothing? Attendance may be down in your congregation or in your denomination; some of the reports on the state of religious affiliation may look grim, but the Lord still disposes and the Lord still builds up, and we hear God's insisting that we resist despair and get to work.

Like Haggai, Job 19 also reminds us to hold on, to have hope in the midst of despair. For Job too, everything is as nothing. Having lost his health, his wealth, and his family, all Job has are loquacious, fair-weather friends. In the midst of these losses, Job's own future is disclosed to him: he can see his own corpse, decaying (Job 19:26). Yet surprisingly, this vision of his death gives Job hope. At the end, he will see God (v. 26). We readers see too; bodies molder, yet these bodies will also be resurrected.

Considering the topic matter, it is unsurprising that this passage, especially Job 19:25, plays a central role in many Christian burial practices. The phrase "I know my Redeemer lives" or "I know my Redeemer liveth" features in many funeral liturgies, and in some communities "I know my Redeemer lives" is commonly inscribed on tombstones. Indeed, Job 19:23–27 is the *locus classicus* of the Christian word to mourners, a twinned word that simultaneously acknowledges the reality of death, and looks forward to the resurrection of the dead, which will wash away all grief.

Unsurprisingly, the depth of Job 19 makes it a frequent topic of novels, oratorios, visual art, and poetry. Perhaps most famously, in Handel's *Messiah* the "Redeemer" is envisioned as the one who lives to Christ. Vittore Carpaccio also connect Job's words to Christ in his painting *The Meditation on the Passion*, which features a wounded Christ, Jerome, who wrote a commentary on Job, and Job himself, perched on a stone with the Hebrew of 19:25.

The 1842 funeral of African American abolitionist James Forten also offers a telling example of the use of Job 19. On this deathbed, Forten gathered his nearest and dearest around him and confidently proclaimed Job 19:25–26 ("For I know that my redeemer lives") before quietly sinking "into the arms of death."[2] The tension between expecting and pursuing liberation from suffering and bondage in the here and now, and expecting ultimate liberation from suffering in the hereafter is evident in Forten's last words. We have to take care, however, not to misread the eschatological liberation in Job 19 as a way to distract people from seeking to challenge the human, political causes of suffering.

The reality of death is not the only bodily reality Job 19 discloses. It also refutes the notion that God must be encountered separate from our bodies. For those of us who live in cultures that largely evade the reality of death, Job's corpse shows us something important: not just Job's future, but ours. As Charity, a character in Edith Wharton's *Summer*, realizes when she hears Job 19, *people can see God through and in their bodies*. In this, Wharton acknowledges the idea of embodiment in Job 19, a text that invites affirmation of our flesh as it is and as it will be.[3]

LAUREN F. WINNER

2. For Forten, see Mark S. Schantz, *Awaiting the Heavenly Country: The Civil War and America's Culture of Death* (Ithaca, NY: Cornell University Press, 2008), 24–26.

3. Laura E. Rutland, "The Law of Sex and Death: Religious Language and Practice in Edith Wharton's *Summer*," *Christianity and Literature* 58, no. 3 (2009): 429–49.

Proper 27 (Sunday between November 6 and November 12 Inclusive)

Psalm 145:1–5, 17–21

[1]I will extol you, my God and King,
and bless your name forever and ever.
[2]Every day I will bless you,
and praise your name forever and ever.
[3]Great is the LORD, and greatly to be praised;
his greatness is unsearchable.

[4]One generation shall laud your works to another,
and shall declare your mighty acts.
[5]On the glorious splendor of your majesty,
and on your wondrous works, I will meditate.

. . . .

[17]The LORD is just in all his ways,
and kind in all his doings.
[18]The LORD is near to all who call on him,
to all who call on him in truth.
[19]He fulfills the desire of all who fear him;
he also hears their cry, and saves them.
[20]The LORD watches over all who love him,
but all the wicked he will destroy.

[21]My mouth will speak the praise of the LORD,
and all flesh will bless his holy name forever and ever.

Psalm 98

[1]O sing to the LORD a new song,
for he has done marvelous things.
His right hand and his holy arm
have gotten him victory.
[2]The LORD has made known his victory;
he has revealed his vindication in the sight of the nations.
[3]He has remembered his steadfast love and faithfulness
to the house of Israel.
All the ends of the earth have seen
the victory of our God.
[4]Make a joyful noise to the LORD, all the earth;
break forth into joyous song and sing praises.
[5]Sing praises to the LORD with the lyre,
with the lyre and the sound of melody.
[6]With trumpets and the sound of the horn
make a joyful noise before the King, the LORD.

[7]Let the sea roar, and all that fills it;
the world and those who live in it.
[8]Let the floods clap their hands;
let the hills sing together for joy
[9]at the presence of the LORD, for he is coming
to judge the earth.
He will judge the world with righteousness,
and the peoples with equity.

Psalm 17:1–9

[1]Hear a just cause, O LORD; attend to my cry;
give ear to my prayer from lips free of deceit.
[2]From you let my vindication come;
let your eyes see the right.

[3]If you try my heart, if you visit me by night,
if you test me, you will find no wickedness in me;
my mouth does not transgress.
[4]As for what others do, by the word of your lips
I have avoided the ways of the violent.
[5]My steps have held fast to your paths;
my feet have not slipped.

[6]I call upon you, for you will answer me, O God;
incline your ear to me, hear my words.
[7]Wondrously show your steadfast love,
O savior of those who seek refuge
from their adversaries at your right hand.

[8]Guard me as the apple of the eye;
hide me in the shadow of your wings,
[9]from the wicked who despoil me,
my deadly enemies who surround me.

Connecting the Psalm with Scripture and Worship

As the church moves closer to the climactic end of the Christian year on Reign of Christ/ Christ the King (Proper 29), the anticipation of the coming realm of God continues to build. Psalms 145 and 98 are both hymns of praise for the great works of God—what God has done for God's people in the past as well as the promise of a future reign of justice and righteousness. Both psalms are a fitting response to Haggai's prophecy, which declares that God will bring peace and prosperity to the people after their time in exile.

Haggai was instrumental in encouraging the political and religious leaders of Judah to rebuild the temple when the people returned from exile, so God's promises of restoration are tangible. The splendor of God will be visible once again, the community will gather for worship, and the land will be distributed fairly so that all may enjoy the fruits of their labors. While Haggai is talking about renewal and revival in the present age, his prophecy also anticipates the messianic age. God's *shalom* will be complete one day, but in the meantime, God's glory will be revealed in God's own time as the people once again live in peace and prosperity.

Psalm 145 is an exuberant response to the announcement of this good news. Through the psalmist's words, the community sings praise for all of God's mighty acts: abundant goodness, righteousness, mercy, compassion, and faithfulness. Expressions of praise tumble forth, one after the other, as if the psalmist cannot find enough ways to declare the goodness and graciousness of God. God has thought of everything and has provided for all people. The whole world will know about this astonishing God, and God's idyllic realm will be eternal.

In the meantime, however, God will attend to the needs of the people in the present, picking up those who fall, lifting the eyes of those who are bowed down, feeding the hungry and fulfilling the needs of everything that lives. God hears the cries of those in distress and watches over all who love God. In what seems almost like an afterthought, the psalmist says that God will destroy all the wicked; it is as if they are hardly worth the breath it takes to mention them. The justice and compassion of God is too great to allow evil to have a hold. As with Haggai's prophecy, the psalm gives voice to the people's praise to God for restoring Judah, while also extolling the Divine for the eternal realm of peace that is on its way.

Psalm 98 sounds similar themes: all the works of God are caught up in praise, and the whole creation sings in joy. The people bring whatever they have to praise; voices, strings, and brass all join the song. Even the sea shouts its praise and the hills sing in joy, because God is on the way to judge the earth. For those who love God, there is no fear, for God has already upheld God's people with faithfulness.

This vision of the world as God intends it is cause for the church to praise as well, for Christians profess that the restoration of all creation has already been secured in Jesus Christ. Even though we continue to live in times of distress, we can look back and see how God has brought us this long way. Even while we continue to pray for wars to end to and for justice to prevail, we can see where we are headed. Let the church praise God with the enthusiasm of the psalms; let joy prevail, even in the face of hardship, for God's realm is on the way.

The readings prescribed for the complementary stream also anticipate the coming reign of God, but here the tone is different. Both Job and the psalmist beseech God from the midst of suffering. The psalmist calls on God to hear his case: he does not sin, he is not wicked, and he has been faithful to God, yet he is surrounded by enemies who accuse him unjustly. He cries out for protection and counts on God to vindicate him, for he knows that God's love is steadfast and is confident that God will see him as righteous and blameless.

This makes Psalm 17 a fitting response to the first reading, in which Job asserts his confidence in his redeemer, or vindicator, the one who will right all wrongs and judge the powers that persecute him. It is important to honor the biblical use of the term "redeemer." Although Christians have come to interpret this as a reference to Jesus Christ, Job uses the term to refer to a defender who is a kinsman, one who—according to Jewish family law—restores what is lost and seeks vindication for any wrongdoing. Here in chapter 19, Job anticipates his own death and expresses his deep desire for his defender to set things right.

The reading from Job and the accompanying psalm may well be used to express the despair and anxiety of contemporary Christians. In this age of the twenty-four-hour news cycle, we are more aware than ever of the troubles of the world. These readings call us to lament—for our own sorrows, our own failings, and our complicity in the world's evil. They also exhort us to hope in the God who has promised to deliver the world from its trials, restore justice, and establish a commonwealth of *shalom*.

In recent years, scholars and practitioners have been urging the church to engage in lament in addition to proclaiming hope. We lament oppression and the abuse of power; we lament violence in nations, cities, and homes; we lament the despoiling of the earth. Our prayers and our songs must express our helplessness, despair, and anger, even as we declare our faith in God's coming reign.

Worship planners might include hymns and songs that do not move too quickly to an expression of hope but stay in a posture of lament, such as Ruth Duck's "When We Must Bear Persistent Pain" or the African American spiritual "I Want Jesus to Walk with Me." John L. Bell and Graham Maule's song collection *When Grief Is Raw* includes laments that may be sung by soloists, choirs, or congregations. Other songs acknowledge the healing power of God in the present, such as Marty Haugen's "Healer of Our Every Ill." Hymns that exhort the assembly to action in the present, even while hoping in the future, might be used at the sending; examples include "Live into Hope" by Jane Parker Huber and "Heaven Shall Not Wait" by John L. Bell and Graham Maule.

Psalm 17 might be spoken or sung. A simple, chant-like setting might best express the plaintiveness of the psalm. Jeffery Honore's setting of "Lord, Bend Your Ear" (in *Psalms for All Seasons*) is simply textured, creating a soundscape of vulnerability and honest pleading. An optional descant adds to the sense of earnest supplication. The refrain of this responsive psalm might also be used to punctuate a series of intercessions during prayers of the people.

Job 19:23–27a and Psalm 17:1–9 do sound a tone of lament, but they also express deep confidence in God who redeems and restores. Even when worshipers voice their despair, they also profess their assurance in the coming reign of God. Even when we weep, we hope.

KIMBERLY BRACKEN LONG

Proper 27 (Sunday between November 6 and November 12 Inclusive)

2 Thessalonians 2:1–5, 13–17

[1]As to the coming of our Lord Jesus Christ and our being gathered together to him, we beg you, brothers and sisters, [2]not to be quickly shaken in mind or alarmed, either by spirit or by word or by letter, as though from us, to the effect that the day of the Lord is already here. [3]Let no one deceive you in any way; for that day will not come unless the rebellion comes first and the lawless one is revealed, the one destined for destruction. [4]He opposes and exalts himself above every so-called god or object of worship, so that he takes his seat in the temple of God, declaring himself to be God. [5]Do you not remember that I told you these things when I was still with you? . . .

[13]But we must always give thanks to God for you, brothers and sisters beloved by the Lord, because God chose you as the first fruits for salvation through sanctification by the Spirit and through belief in the truth. [14]For this purpose he called you through our proclamation of the good news, so that you may obtain the glory of our Lord Jesus Christ. [15]So then, brothers and sisters, stand firm and hold fast to the traditions that you were taught by us, either by word of mouth or by our letter.

[16]Now may our Lord Jesus Christ himself and God our Father, who loved us and through grace gave us eternal comfort and good hope, [17]comfort your hearts and strengthen them in every good work and word.

Commentary 1: Connecting the Reading with Scripture

After opening with concern for the various threats faced by the Thessalonian congregation, 2 Thessalonians turns its focus in the second chapter to the church's internal spiritual wellness. Specifically, the congregation has come to believe that the eschatological Day of the Lord has already arrived. The letter withholds a detailed description of the day itself, but rather presumes that the Thessalonians church already understands something of what to expect, as evidenced by the question in verse 5: "Do you not remember that I told you these things when I was still with you?" However, by way of contrast to the joyful reunion of the deceased predicted in 1 Thessalonians 4, the prospect of the Day of the Lord here in 2 Thessalonians is treated not with eager anticipation but with fear and trembling. The author seeks to correct misinformation that may have "shaken" or "alarmed" the Thessalonian church: *despite whatever you may have heard, the Day of the Lord is not yet at hand.*

The author's evidence for this comforting claim comes in surprising form: a cosmic minidrama. Briefly put, the Day of the Lord cannot be at hand because it must first be preceded by the revealing of "the lawless one," the one who "takes his seat in the temple of God" (2:4). The lectionary then excises an elaboration of this scene in verses 6–12, including reference to the contemporary working of Satan, "who uses all power, signs, lying wonders, and every kind of wicked deception." The temptation in surveying this passage is to conjure a degree of historical particularity out of characterizations that may seem otherwise confusing: interpreters have long speculated that the author is making oblique reference to specific figures of Roman political power during the time of the early church. However, because the letter presents this drama as not yet having unfolded, and because said drama will unfold in an explicitly theological arena (the lawless one "declares himself to be God," 2:4), the best modern readings will resist the lingering temptations of excessive political allegory.

The central concern of the letter, however, is not the content of this cosmic minidrama, nor even the timetable for its approach; rather, these issues simply reveal the real problem, which is the congregation's inability to distinguish between a variety of true and false gospels. As something of a prescription for this indeterminacy, the author puts substantial weight on the durable work of words themselves. After the cosmic minidrama resolves, the author exhorts the congregation to remember his own prior instructions to that congregation, "either by word of mouth or by our letter," as a counterpoint to this new false teaching. Two verses later, the author encourages the congregation to "comfort your hearts . . . in every good work and word," and, in the pericope that immediately follows, the author seeks prayers so that "the word of the Lord may spread rapidly." Words, in the logic of this letter, have the capacity to transcend the whims of mood and fashion; words offer something permanent and immutable, as they do for Job in one of the lectionary parallels for the morning, "O that my words were written down! O that they were inscribed in a book! O that with an iron pen and with lead they were engraved on a rock forever!"

Unfortunately—and, it should be said, somewhat ironically, given that many modern scholars doubt the Pauline authorship of this letter—words here can also be used for the purpose of deception. The cadence of 2:15—"either by word of mouth or by letter"—is already undone by its parallel in 2:2, wherein the false information about the Parousia has arrived in Thessalonica "either by spirit or by word or by letter, as though from us." What therefore emerges is a passage in which the very possibility of truth itself is explicitly on the line. "Let no one deceive you," the author cautions, before introducing the cosmic minidrama in which the works of Satan explicitly include "lying wonders" and "wicked deception." For the twenty-first-century preacher, the language of this cosmic minidrama offers some predictable challenges—which largely explains why the lectionary editors have removed so much of it. For a modern congregation saturated with subjectivities and adrift in a fragmented, truth-weary culture, this passage's insistence on truth's singular importance may be just as challenging.

However, 2 Thessalonians does not see truth simply as an objective characteristic or moral virtue. In 2:13, the author describes the work of salvation in this congregation "through sanctification by the Spirit and through *belief in the truth*" (emphasis mine). NT occurrences of these Greek roots for "belief" (sometimes "trust" or "obey") and "truth" often arrive paired in sequence, as in 1 Timothy 2:7 ("a teacher of the Gentiles in faith and truth") or Revelation 22:6 ("these words are trustworthy and true"). It is somewhat less frequent, though somewhat more Pauline, to speak of belief *in* truth itself: Romans 2:8 speaks of those "who [believe] not the truth but wickedness"; Galatians 5:7 asks, "Who prevented you from [believing] the truth?" These moments seem to consider truth not simply as an ontological quality but rather as a subject unto itself, with echoes of the christological claim in John 14:6 ("I am the way, and the truth, and the life"). In such a scenario, the Thessalonian goal of "belief in the truth" is not only a strategy for discerning the accuracy of eschatological claims; it may also be a theological affirmation about the lordship of Jesus Christ.

The implications of this claim extend into the Lukan lectionary pairing for the day, which pits Sadducees in an argument with Jesus about a matter of eschatology and legal orthodoxy. However, the dramatic irony in Luke's Gospel is thick on the ground, as the Sadduceean denial of resurrection stands face to face with the one who will himself be resurrected only a few chapters later. In both texts, arguments about the objective truth of eschatological claims face off against a personified, incarnate, capital-T Truth—a christological truth—even in 2 Thessalonians 2:16, where the author wishes for the church that "the Lord Jesus Christ himself" continue to work in and through the congregation with love and grace. For the preacher addressing congregations so often seeking the tools to distinguish between true and false gospels, in a cultural context in which the notion of truth itself seems regularly so antiquated, it may be helpful to recognize in these passages the way in which truth becomes personified in the living Christ, acting on the church for its "eternal comfort and good hope."

In the meantime, the charge offered to the Thessalonian church strongly resembles the charge offered to the Jewish remnant in the morning's reading from Haggai: to remember God's former promises. "I am with you, says the Lord of hosts, according to the promise that I made you when you came out of Egypt," God speaks to Haggai (2:4–5); or, in the words of this letter, "Stand firm and hold fast to the traditions" (2 Thess. 2:15). Both texts sit in historical moments of deep uncertainty, but the joint refrain is clear, and the words still matter. Both speakers invite these anxious congregations to remember the old stories, to practice the well-worn liturgies, and to seek out the deep truths about who God's people are and who they are called to be. As personified by the words of the Lord on Haggai's lips, and as promised by the incarnate Truth proclaimed to this Thessalonian church, even when God's people forget the old stories, God's truth has a way of speaking for itself.

MATT GAVENTA

Adored Forever Be the God Unseen

Arise, my soul, on wings enraptur'd, rise
To praise the monarch of the earth and skies,
Whose goodness and benificence appear
As round its centre moves the rolling year,
Or when the morning glows with rosy charms,
Or the sun slumbers in the ocean's arms:
Of light divine be a rich portion lent
To guide my soul, and favour my intent.
Celestial muse, my arduous flight sustain
And raise my mind to a seraphic strain!
Ador'd for ever be the God unseen,
Which round the sun revolves this vast machine,
Though to his eye its mass a point appears:
Ador'd the God that whirls surrounding spheres,
Which first ordain'd that mighty Sol should reign
The peerless monarch of th' ethereal train:
Of miles twice forty millions is his height,
And yet his radiance dazzles mortal sight
So far beneath—from him th' extended earth
Vigour derives, and ev'ry flow'ry birth:
Vast through her orb she moves with easy grace
Around her Phoebus in unbounded space;
True to her course th' impetuous storm derides,
Triumphant o'er the winds, and surging tides.
Almighty, in these wond'rous works of thine,
What Pow'r, what Wisdom, and what Goodness shine!

Phillis Wheatley, "Thoughts on the Works of Providence," in *Poems on Various Subjects, Religious and Moral* (London: A. Bell, 1773), 43–44.

Commentary 2: Connecting the Reading with the World

While 2 Thessalonians 1 puts before us the mercy and the judgment of God, encouraging Christians to persist, the next chapter goes on to teachings the Thessalonians have received concerning the complexity of this age: Christ is victorious, but his enemies retain a certain power. The lectionary excises 2:6–12, perhaps due to uncertainty concerning the "man of lawlessness," and who was "restraining him." The apostle asks the Thessalonians, "Do you not remember" what I told you? Readers in our day wish *they* had heard such words to remember! Yet the mystery of this rebellion should not fixate us on the occult: the letter intends not to fascinate, but to prevent spiritual deception.

Paul's teaching is not idiosyncratic; Jesus spoke in Mark 13:5 (and parallel passages in Luke and Matthew) concerning "the abomination of desolation" (cf. Dan. 11:31). Daniel's mysterious phrase indicated the blasphemy of Antiochus IV Epiphanes, who offered swine's flesh to Zeus in the Lord's temple. In the Gospels, it may imply the desecration of Jesus' body, the fall of the temple in AD 70, or future blasphemies that may threaten God's people, the new "temple" (1 Thess. 2:4; 1 Cor. 3:17). It is not so important to decode the mystery as to grasp our fragility. We depend on the Lord in extremity, whether personal (unforeseen illness), social (marginalization for our faith), or caused by natural or humanly engineered disasters.

After the initial warning, we hear that God is sovereign. Some in Paul's day speculated that the Parousia (the second coming) had already taken place in secret; but a Parousia in the ancient world was *public*—the ceremonial entrance of a conqueror into a city, greeted by its residents. (This is the picture of 1 Thess. 4:17, now problematically interpreted as "rapture" eschatology: those who are alive when Jesus returns will rush to greet the Savior, coming to bring the judgment, give the final resurrection, and dwell among us in a union of new heaven and earth.) Jesus' arrival cannot happen in a corner: "as the lightning comes from the east and flashes as far as the west, so will be the coming of the Son of Man" (Matt. 24:27). This is not something discerned by those with special knowledge. Novels like Morris West's *Clowns of God* make for excitement, but the premise of a hidden Messiah among us is mistaken. Instead, the assurance of his public return directs us to daily preparation and constant worship.

For those who are seduced by end-time scenarios, 2 Thessalonians 2 is salutary. We are not to be deceived—and should speak against misguided teachings for the sake of others. Paul warns against all sources of distorted teaching: ecstasies "by spirit" that claim revelation, "words" that purport to be especially informed, or writings that offer secret information. Moreover, we should meditate on those things that are certain, just as the apostle does. He gives thanks for God's sovereignty, God's call to believers, and their sanctification (2:13): beginnings and endings, so to speak. Encompassed round about by God, we begin and end our faith journey, hoping to attain the "glory of our Lord Jesus Christ." Preachers may encourage the faithful to carefully and confidently "practice the presence" of Christ, seeking his enormous plans for us.

Paul has seemingly harsh words concerning unbelievers (2:11–12). It is helpful to remember that God's election is matched by human response, and that those who are struck with spiritual blindness have "*refused* to love the truth and so be saved" (2:10). Elsewhere, we see a clement God, who died for us while we were still sinners and who wills that all should be saved, coming to a knowledge of the truth (Rom. 5:8; 1 Tim. 2:4). God's "sending of a delusion" (2 Thess. 2:11) is troublesome if we see it as *preventing* faith, but the apostle is writing in a long tradition that ascribes to the sovereign God *all* that happens in our lives. Further, the delusion comes *after* human refusal; it does not cause it. Divine hardening is mysterious, but does not qualify God's universal love.

In contrast, the Thessalonians are pictured as "first fruits" (2:13)—martyred harbingers of a huge harvest of the saved. We are to remember such forebears in Christ and all that they have given us. This may be counterintuitive in our forward-looking age. Christians are both to live for future hope and to conserve the treasures given to them. We rightly extend our own thanksgiving, embracing Paul and others who transmitted and interpreted the gospel to us. Not simply forgiveness, but the means to sanctification, and the hope of glory have been given to us (vv. 13–14). These insights are helpful in inculcating attitudes of astonished thanksgiving and enlarged hopes among some who may be weary or even bored by the faith.

Looking back to the early fathers and mothers honors the command of Paul, who enjoins this congregation to "stand firm and hold fast to the traditions" they had received "either by word of mouth or by our letter." Paul uses the technical word for tradition (*paradosis*) that means "a gift given over." Alas, some translations will not use the word "tradition" in a positive sense (e.g., the KJV, which was in reaction to the medieval fixation on unhealthy traditions). We also see this tendency in the original NIV, the NIB, and the NLT, which retain the word "tradition" for *paradosis* only while referring to pagans and Pharisees, but substitute words like "teaching" wherever Paul approves of tradition (2 Thess. 2:15 is only *one* of the places where such translations avoid a positive connotation of tradition). As a result, generations of Christians have been predisposed to assess "tradition" as something foreign to biblical faith. Those who proclaim the Word might use this chapter as an antidote to this misapprehension that tradition is a dead thing that will bind rather than free Christians.

We who honor the Bible do well to take Paul at his word. Here and elsewhere (e.g., 1 Cor. 11), he values apostolic tradition, written and oral, as from the Lord. Not all traditions are brittle or dead. Of course, it is important to distinguish between local, impermanent traditions, and that which has been passed on to us for all time. The latter would include ecumenical creeds, or prayers to the Holy Spirit (not mentioned in the Bible) as life-giving, nonnegotiable traditions. This passage leads those who honor the Bible to question whether they can sustain a rigid *sola Scriptura* position. Intriguingly, Paul connects these traditions with life, comfort, and hope, for they strengthen us "in every good work and word" (2:17). We see a link of holy tradition with the Holy Spirit, since the Spirit works in the personal transmission of such matters in the *living* church.

Mention of the Holy Spirit leads us to notice all the triune God in this passage. "God the Father," "the Lord Jesus Christ" (whose name "Lord" recalls the YHWH/Kyrios of the OT), and the Holy Spirit work together, sanctifying (v. 13), teaching (v. 14), and comforting us in the "heart" (v. 17), so that we can speak and work for God. The triune God is as concerned with our outer life ("work and word") as our inner life; body, lips, hands, and feet matter. Worship in the body, using movement, sight, smell, sound, and touch, is pleasing to God, and has been practiced in the Christian East and the West for centuries; liturgical recovery of these dimensions is significant in an age that has grown tired of mere words. We stand amazed at the sweep of Paul's vision, which illumines the beginning and the end, inside and outside.

EDITH M. HUMPHREY

Proper 27 (Sunday between November 6 and November 12 Inclusive)

Luke 20:27–38

[27]Some Sadducees, those who say there is no resurrection, came to him [28]and asked him a question, "Teacher, Moses wrote for us that if a man's brother dies, leaving a wife but no children, the man shall marry the widow and raise up children for his brother. [29]Now there were seven brothers; the first married, and died childless; [30]then the second [31]and the third married her, and so in the same way all seven died childless. [32]Finally the woman also died. [33]In the resurrection, therefore, whose wife will the woman be? For the seven had married her."

[34]Jesus said to them, "Those who belong to this age marry and are given in marriage; [35]but those who are considered worthy of a place in that age and in the resurrection from the dead neither marry nor are given in marriage. [36]Indeed they cannot die anymore, because they are like angels and are children of God, being children of the resurrection. [37]And the fact that the dead are raised Moses himself showed, in the story about the bush, where he speaks of the Lord as the God of Abraham, the God of Isaac, and the God of Jacob. [38]Now he is God not of the dead, but of the living; for to him all of them are alive."

Commentary 1: Connecting the Reading with Scripture

After Jesus enters Jerusalem "he was teaching in the temple" (Luke 19:47), and Luke tells us, "All the people were spellbound by what they heard" (v. 48). Well, perhaps not all the people. Some were "looking for a way to kill him" (v. 47). Others came asking questions "to trap him by what he said" (20:20). Among the interrogators were some Sadducees, a group Luke introduces with the explanation: they "say there is no resurrection." This was not a simple matter of incredulity. The Sadducees recognized only the Torah, the books of Moses, the first five books of the Bible, as Scripture, and they found no hint of resurrection there. Later, in his second volume, the Acts of the Apostles, Luke clarifies further, "The Sadducees say that there is no resurrection, or angel, or spirit; but the Pharisees acknowledge all three" (Acts 23:8). Resurrection, angels, and spirit figure dramatically in Luke's narrative.

That the Sadducees have a question about the resurrection will come as no surprise to pastors. Worshipers have no end of questions about what resurrection means for them, those they love, and the loving relationships that make our lives rich and truly human. This text provides opportunity briefly to proclaim and illumine the hope that Christian faith dares to entertain.

The question the aristocratic, urban Sadducees propose risks no interest in resurrection but only means to impale this rustic rabbi on his own theology. Their question concerns Moses' teaching in Deuteronomy that if a man dies "and has no son," that man's brother should marry his widow and produce children "to the name of the deceased brother" (Deut. 25:6). This practice, known as Levirate marriage, had an important ethical function. In an ancient patriarchal society without social security, insurance, or occupational opportunities for women, those who did not have husband, father, or sons to care for them were left destitute, unprotected, and marginalized. The biblical command to protect the widows, the poor, and the orphans springs from this stark reality. The practice may sound strange to us and probably was strange to the Sadducees as well. Their question is largely hypothetical. They reason, "Moses wrote for us; let's see how this teacher handles the dilemma."

Calling Jesus "teacher," the Sadducees ask a question that is a rough mixture of hostility and absurdity. Jesus graciously treats their story with more seriousness than it deserves. Luke likely inherited the story of the encounter with the Sadducees from Mark and here has softened Jesus' answer. In Mark Jesus brusquely retorts to the Sadducees, "Is not this the reason you are wrong, that you know neither the scriptures nor the power of God?" (Mark 12:24). Here in Luke, however, Jesus does not catalog their errors but as a wise, gentle teacher sets about correcting them. "In the resurrection . . . whose wife will the woman be?" is the wrong question to ask because the resurrection is not merely an extension of our current way of life but a completely new existence transformed by a gracious God. Marriage, family, and the begetting of children belong to our age, a preresurrection time. Of the age that follows resurrection Jesus employs three images to describe the human situation: "they are like angels," "children of God," and "children of the resurrection" (Luke 20:35–36).

The language is evocative, reminding us that imagination is necessary to entertain the possibilities of a totally transformed life. The NT employs a variety of metaphors to describe this present and coming existence. Paul writes that "we will all be changed, in a moment, in the twinkling of an eye, at the last trumpet," when "the dead will be raised and we will be changed" (1 Cor. 15:51–52). John the Elder stretches language to explain that "when he is revealed, we will be like him, for we will see him as he is" (1 John 3:2). When 2 Thessalonians declares that we are called to "obtain the glory of our Lord Jesus Christ" (2 Thess. 2:14), that glory is resurrection language. The multiplied images remind us that we inevitably speak of things vastly beyond imagination's capacity. Jesus the spellbinding teacher teaches us how to teach others about the resurrection, entertaining evocative images ("like angels," "children of God," "children of the resurrection"), relying on the Scriptures, and finally, trusting God.

Jesus knows the Scriptures and reminds the Sadducees what they remember well. "The story about the bush," Jesus calls it, is nothing less than God's initial encounter with Moses. God calls, "Moses, Moses" (Exod. 3:4), initiating a conversation that concludes only with Moses' death (Deut. 34) and that, from the evidence of this text and our continued preaching of it, has not ended yet. While we expect Moses in the book of Exodus, Moses also appears in Luke's Gospel, where he and Elijah join Jesus at the transfiguration. Matthew, Mark, and Luke all report that Moses and Elijah "were talking with Jesus" (Mark 9:4; Matt. 17:3), but only Luke describes the content of the conversation: "They appeared in glory and were speaking of his departure, which he was about to accomplish at Jerusalem" (Luke 9:31). The word "departure" translates the Greek *exodos*, a departure often connected with connotations of death, as in our English reference to "the departed." Moses and Elijah are conferring with Jesus about his departure to Jerusalem but also about events that will take place there: his suffering, crucifixion, and death, but also his resurrection and ascension. That Moses in some sense becomes a prophet of resurrection in the Gospel of Luke supplies the interpretative model for Jesus' final teaching to the Sadducees.

Since the Sadducees are interested in what Moses said, Jesus calls their attention to "where he [Moses] speaks of the Lord as the God of Abraham, the God of Isaac, and the God of Jacob." Actually it was the Lord, YHWH, who voiced that identification as "God of Abraham, the God of Isaac, and the God of Jacob" (Exod. 3:6; also 3:15). The Lord speaks in present tense about these patriarchs (counted as ancestors of Jesus earlier in Luke's narrative, 3:34). That present tense rules out the possibility that the Lord was once upon a time "the God of Abraham, the God of Isaac, and the God of Jacob," but is no longer, now that they are dead and gone.

No, Jesus teaches, when Moses "speaks of the Lord as the God of Abraham, the God of Isaac, and the God of Jacob," Moses means that the Lord is and continues to be and everlastingly will be "the God of Abraham, the God of Isaac, and the God of Jacob." Whatever relationship the Lord has to Abraham, Isaac, and Jacob is in present, not simply past tense, and can be counted on in every future we imagine.

Abraham, Isaac, and Jacob are not merely denizens of a richly remembered heritage but citizens of a new age characterized by God's triumph over death and an unimagined and unexplored resurrection life. In the Acts of the Apostles Luke portrays Paul on Mars Hill quoting a Greek poet to say that in God "we live and move and have our being" (Acts 17:28), thereby echoing Jesus' affirmation that for God "all of them are alive." We long to know more about what it means that to God "all of them are alive," and we have our own questions about what life as "children of the resurrection" might mean. It is not necessary for the preacher to answer every question about the resurrection. It would be enough to enrich our wonderings and point to their consummation in God.

PATRICK J. WILLSON

Commentary 2: Connecting the Reading with the World

Do dead things come back to life? Better and more specific to the question this pericope raises for us, "Can life rise from death?" Resurrection is not to be confused with resuscitation or reanimation of the physical self; rather, it signals the active work of a divine sovereign to bring about a complete psychosomatic transformation of the human body. Resurrection is an absurd notion to accept unless one's faith claim is premised on the assumption that the historical process is not theologically closed. To believe in the resurrection of the dead insists on the understanding that only a free God can work wonders in history, has the power to liberate, to heal, and yes, to raise the dead. What resurrection symbolizes, if it communicates nothing else, is that only a God unharnessed can keep the historical horizon open. In short, a God who raises life from death stands outside the expectation, prediction, and horizon of human control.

When lectionary preachers have turned the ears of their congregations to Matthew 28:1–8; Mark 16:1–8; or Luke 24:1–12, preaching about what the resurrection is, what it means, and how it was understood in the context of Jesus' earthly ministry can open up creative possibilities for Easter Sunday preaching. In the liturgical context, what if the preacher placed this Lukan passage, which highlights Jesus' interpretation of resurrection, side by side with the Lazarus account in John 11 in which Jesus performs resurrection? What if both these passages were utilized as an interpretive lens through which to understand Jesus' own resurrection recorded in John 20:1–4? Each account speaks to what it means to be raised from death under divine authority.

Indeed, this passage in Luke presents one of several vignettes that raises the question about the nature and origin of Jesus' authority. The dispute pits the Sadducees, the strict keepers of the Torah, whose philosophical riddles sought to make the belief in the afterlife sound completely absurd, against Jesus, the wise rabbi who scrambles and puzzles their logic. What is revealed is a strictness of the theological imagination on the Sadducees' part and radical truth-telling grounded in well-timed perception on Jesus' part. What is at stake in the dialogue is the manner in which one sees and understands the reign of God.

Unlike the Pharisees, their religious rivals, the Sadducees (*tsaddiqim*, "righteous ones"), denied the teachings of the resurrection and the presence of angels. Sadducees were not a religious sect per se but could be better described as a philosophical school closely linked to and influential in temple leadership. They recognized only the written Torah (the five books of Moses) as authoritative. The Torah, in their judgment, made no conspicuous reference to the resurrection.

So in the spirit that they had perfected by casting aspersions on the Pharisees for their adherence to oral-tradition scriptural interpretation, the Sadducees, as textual legalists, approach Jesus with a question about Levirate marriage (brother-in-law marriage). This institution obligated the brother of a dead man to marry and impregnate his childless widow so that the deceased would not be left without any male heirs (Deut. 25:5–6). Referencing Levirate marriage, the Sadducees ask Jesus whose wife the widow will be in the resurrection if she is given in marriage to seven brothers, all of whom died without giving her children (Luke 20:28–33). The absurdity of the question is meant to point to the absurdity of belief in the resurrection.

Jesus, who naturally assumes they intend to trap him in his words, responds with an answer that in effect declares the question of the Sadducees as misguided: "Those who belong to this age marry and are given in marriage; but those who are considered worthy . . . in the resurrection from the dead neither marry nor are given in marriage" (vv. 34–35). The afterlife is different from life on earth, Jesus explains. The world of the present reality is not the only reality there is. The world to come into which humans are resurrected from death is radically discontinuous with a dying world. After Jesus deftly discredits the Sadducees' ploy, we are told that "they no longer dared to ask him another question" (v. 40).

What is the lesson for the body of Christ? One ecclesiological lesson is that the church must understand that the resurrection is the believer's gateway to hope. To believe in its power in faith gets to the very heart of why the church exists. God's revelation, as this narrative shows, is not contained and not restricted. Rather, pursuing the life of the Spirit means that life before God is unbounded and continuous. Divine revelation and disclosures have not ever stopped.[1] Rather, God continues to speak to God's people.

Another possible message that emerges is that bearing witness to the good news of the kingdom of God may engender opposition. For example, Dr. Martin Luther King Jr.'s speech on April 3, 1968, in which the kingdom of God was interpreted as freedom, justice, and equality for sanitation workers, invited his death. A possible sermon might therefore wrestle with how the people of God, despite and in the face of opposition and ridicule, can speak of the kingdom of God by addressing social woes such as the lack of justice and inequality. As preachers of God's word, it is incumbent that Scripture be used as a lens through which we concretely name God's intervening work in today's world affairs.

If eternal life is simply an extension of life in the present and nothing more, is there any reason to hope? Jesus seems to think that human relationships with the Creator matter beyond the grave. What this means sociopolitically is that bound up in life is the possibility of having a truly personal relationship with a God who transcends death itself. Empirical datum will never sufficiently verify what the heart of faith knows: that the God of Abraham, Isaac, Jacob, and Jesus honors our faith and promotes human flourishing, for the one with whom we have to do "is not God of the dead but of the living" (v. 38).

An illuminating current example comes from neurosurgeon Eben Alexander, who was rendered comatose for seven days from a bacterial meningitis infection. His experiences during his coma affirmed for him that there is "consciousness beyond the body."[2] What makes Alexander's story so compelling, though, is that here is a scientifically trained expert in the field of neurosurgery framing his experience with convincing intellectual prowess—what one respects in the earth realm. To the Sadducees of the medical community of which Alexander is apart, he writes: "The universe that I experienced in my coma . . . is the same one Einstein and Jesus were speaking of in (very) different ways."[3]

In ways personal and beyond the bounds of logic, the preacher who proclaims the gospel must be able to say to hearers that hope is not hope without the evidences of faith. In the end, and in view of Jesus' assertion that in heaven no one dies anymore but one becomes a heavenly being, like the angels (v. 36), the message of the resurrection that Christians must persistently announce is, "Seeing is not believing; rather, believing is seeing."

KENYATTA R. GILBERT

1. Luke Timothy Johnson, *The Gospel of Luke*, Sacra Pagina 3 (Collegeville, MN: Liturgical Press, 1991), 318.
2. Dr. Eben Alexander, "Proof of Heaven: A Doctor's Experience of the Afterlife," *Newsweek*, October 8, 2012. http://www.newsweek.com/proof-heaven-doctors-experience-afterlife-65327.
3. Alexander, "Proof of Heaven."

Proper 28 (Sunday between November 13 and November 19 Inclusive)

Isaiah 65:17–25 and Malachi 4:1–2a
Isaiah 12 and Psalm 98
2 Thessalonians 3:6–13
Luke 21:5–19

Isaiah 65:17–25

[17]For I am about to create new heavens
    and a new earth;
the former things shall not be remembered
    or come to mind.
[18]But be glad and rejoice forever
    in what I am creating;
for I am about to create Jerusalem as a joy,
    and its people as a delight.
[19]I will rejoice in Jerusalem,
    and delight in my people;
no more shall the sound of weeping be heard in it,
    or the cry of distress.
[20]No more shall there be in it
    an infant that lives but a few days,
    or an old person who does not live out a lifetime;
for one who dies at a hundred years will be considered a youth,
    and one who falls sort of a hundred will be considered accursed.
[21]They shall build houses and inhabit them;
    they shall plant vineyards and eat their fruit.
[22]They shall not build and another inhabit;
    they shall not plant and another eat;
for like the days of a tree shall the days of my people be,
    and my chosen shall long enjoy the work of their hands.
[23]They shall not labor in vain,
    or bear children for calamity;
for they shall be offspring blessed by the LORD—
    and their descendants as well.
[24]Before they call I will answer,
    while they are yet speaking I will hear.
[25]The wolf and the lamb shall feed together,
    the lion shall eat straw like the ox;
    but the serpent—its food shall be dust!
They shall not hurt or destroy
    on all my holy mountain,
        says the LORD.

Malachi 4:1–2a

[1]See, the day is coming, burning like an oven, when all the arrogant and all evildoers will be stubble; the day that comes shall burn them up, says the LORD of hosts, so that it will leave them neither root nor branch. [2]But for you who revere my name the sun of righteousness shall rise, with healing in its wings.

Commentary 1: Connecting the Reading with Scripture

This week's lectionary reading brings together two prophetic texts that both can be said to offer a "vision over visibility" (to cite the lyric of one of U2's songs).[1] Both these texts emerge out of a context of destruction and despair as the prophets in the books of Isaiah and Malachi respectively envision a world in which there will be healing and salvation for their constituencies, who for a very long time have been living in a world marred by the effects of the violence and injustice enforced by one empire after another.

Isaiah 65:17–25, part of Third Isaiah (Isa. 56–66), emerges from a time after the return from exile, when the people continued to experience political strife and economic hardship. Tellingly, Isaiah 65 dreams of a restored and healed world—a world where there will be food security, where people will be able to enjoy the fruits of the crops and vineyards they have planted (v. 21); where people will have access to adequate housing, building houses and actually getting to live in them (v. 21); where there will be no more infant mortality; and people will not be cut off in the prime of their lives by the violence of war but instead will grow to be a hundred—in hyperbolic fashion much older than the average life expectancy of the time (v. 20).

This eschatological vision of a world restored pertains to real concerns experienced by the community, particularly in light of the upheaval of the Babylonian invasion. This was indeed a time when houses were destroyed, crops were burnt down due to the enemy's scorched-earth policy, and too many people died before their time, due to the military invasion and the famine and pestilence that followed in its wake.

After this time of hardship, probably amid the ongoing economic struggles and political discontent that marked the postexilic context, Isaiah 65 envisions a return of joy and delight that all but erases the painful memories of the past (note the reference to not remembering the former things, which echoes Isa. 43:18).

The vision of a new heaven and earth where there will be no more tears, where "the wolf and the lamb shall feed together" and "the lion shall eat straw like the ox" (v. 25), exhibits some strong connections within the larger book of Isaiah and the biblical corpus as a whole. Tellingly, Israel's enemies, as well as corrupt Israelite leaders, were often imagined as lions or wolves that savagely devoured the people (Jer. 50:17; Hab. 1:8; Ezek. 22:25; 25:27; 32:2; Zeph. 3:3).

A particularly striking allusion to Isaiah 65 is found in the messianic text in Isaiah 11. The peaceable kingdom is imagined in terms of wild animals peacefully coexisting, which serves as a metaphor of warring nations who have laid down their weapons. Though similar, there are also are some distinct differences between these texts. For instance, gone in Isaiah 65 is the phrase "little child shall lead them" of Isaiah 11:6, a figure who has come to be associated with the messianic king who will herald in this hopeful future where there will be peace and hope and joy. Rather, in Isaiah 65, focus seems to fall on Godself to bring about transformation; this alternation might speak to changing circumstances and thus a revised theology in which the hope of a specific ruler (e.g., Cyrus, Isa. 45:1–4) has dissipated.

1. U2, "Moment of Surrender," *No Line on the Horizon* (Interscope, 2009).

Indeed, this focus on God as the ultimate transforming agent is evident in the later text of Revelation, which plays on images and ideas found in Isaiah 65. For example, Revelation 5:5–6 links the Messiah both to a lion ("the Lion of the tribe of Judah") and a slaughtered lamb. This text in Isaiah 65:17–25 also very much forms the inspiration for the vision of the new heaven and earth in Revelation 21:1–4. However, the description of the new Jerusalem coming down from heaven like a bride moves beyond Isaiah 65. In Revelation, there will be no more pain and no more weeping in this new heaven and earth, as death will be no more. This vision of the end of death in Revelation 21, aside from referring to Isaiah 65:17–25, also draws on another eschatological text in Isaiah 25:6–8, which offers a vision of a great banquet held on God's holy mountain, in which it is explicitly said that there will no more tears and where death is no more (cf. God's destruction of the shrouds and swallowing up death forever in Isa. 25:7–8). Thus, in contrast to Revelation 21, Isaiah 65's vision of a healed and restored world occurs very much amid the contention and strife of this world, where mortality is still thought to be an inevitable fact of life.

Malachi 4:1–2a offers yet another image of restoration that envisions salvation and healing for the righteous. This text employs the striking metaphor of the sun of righteousness that will shine on those who revere God's name (v. 2a). The sun of righteousness speaks of the breaking of a new dawn, of light shining in darkness. This same sun whose rays benevolently shine on the righteous, offering them warmth and comfort, also has the potential to fiercely burn down on the wicked. In Malachi 4:1, God's judgment on the wicked is imagined in terms of a burning fire that will utterly destroy the trees of the orchard, consuming even the roots of these trees underground, hence ensuring that no new life would ever be able to sprout again.

Malachi 4:1–2, like Isaiah 65:17–25, thus acknowledges the presence of the wicked that have afflicted hardship on the believers. Hope for deliverance, healing, and restoration implies that the threat of the wicked will be removed in an act of judgment by the righteous God. For those who believe in God, there will be salvation and healing, evident in the beautiful image of healing in the wings of the sun of righteousness (v. 2a). In the second part of Malachi 4:2, this joyful deliverance is compellingly imaged in the metaphor of fattened calves designated for slaughter who are jubilantly skipping around as they are released from their pens.

What is interesting about these two prophetic texts being read together in this week's lectionary selection is that from very different times and places one finds this yearning for a world that looks different from the one in which believers currently find themselves. These texts suggest a strong sense of discontent with the current economic hardships and ongoing political strife that followed in the aftermath of the Babylonian invasion and under the new Persian regime. These texts, though, cling to the hope for God's delivering presence that will have transformative effects on the entire community.

This hope in God's deliverance also features in some of the other lectionary readings of this week. This firm belief in God's steadfast love and faithfulness, of which Psalm 98:3 sings, forms the basis for the charge to the believers in every time and place to persevere and not to grow tired in doing what is right (2 Thess. 3:13). This is true even—one could say especially—in the very difficult circumstances evident in Luke 21:5–19, the Gospel reading of this week. The hope for a world where God will make all things right plays a vital role in the Gospel writer's call to believers to endure, for as Luke 21:19 puts it, "by your endurance you will gain your souls."

L. JULIANA M. CLAASSENS

Commentary 2: Connecting the Reading with the World

The eschatological vision of Isaiah 65—its promise of a new heaven and a new earth, and its images of wolves, lambs, and vegetarian lions—reimagined in Malachi as a day when the sun will rise and the healed people of God will leap "like calves from the stall" (Mal. 4:1–2), powerfully resonates as a longed-for, yet still unrealized dream. This sense of longing evinced by Isaiah and Malachi is historically fitting. Both Isaiah 65 and Malachi are dated after the return from Babylonian exile, when lived realities came into conflict with the ways in which the returnees had imagined their restored community. Despite appearances, the prophets declare that the world promised by God was indeed forthcoming.

The Isaianic passage and, to a lesser degree, the truncated verses from Malachi are rife with preaching possibilities. In offering assurances of an improved heaven and earth, Isaiah challenges the church to think about ways in which it can become cocreators in the fulfillment of this divine eschatological vision. It also challenges the people of God to consider how they have been apathetic toward and at points have even hindered the manifestation of this new divine order.

Indeed, Malachi elucidates a possible hindrance: the powerful desire for revenge against "all the arrogant and all evildoers" (Mal. 4:1). This desire for recompense, especially from those who commit injustice—people who, as Malachi clarifies in 3:5, perjure and lie and oppress workers, widows, orphans, and immigrants—is understandable. Yet this desire for retribution is in direct contrast to the new world envisioned by Isaiah, in which weeping and hurt are abolished (Isa. 65:19, 25). Preachers will do well to explore the tension that emerges when Malachi 4:1–2a is juxtaposed to Isaiah 65: How can the people of God hate injustice and oppression without despising those who commit wrongdoing? How do we participate in the advent of new creation prophesied by Isaiah without succumbing to the desire to settle the score?

One such way is to promote and work toward that which is promised in the new creation. For example, the declaration in Isaiah 65:20 that the premature deaths of babies and children will be eradicated speaks to current concerns for the health, care, and well-being of children and babies. Issues that involve the welfare of children, such as health care, poverty, immigration, and political and military conflicts, all emerge as possible topics for a sermon. This subject, likewise, can easily be widened to address concerns of child abuse, gun control, malnutrition, food deserts, and anything else that puts a child at risk. Surely the vision of this new heaven and earth espoused by the prophet—and which, in turn, should be exhorted by the preacher—is envisioned as one in which every child has the opportunity to live, grow up, and flourish in safety, security, and peace.

Relatedly, the promise of flourishing children speaks to a concern for the well-being of the mother. Mothers will no longer "bear children for calamity" (Isa. 65:23). Replete with sermonic potential, this passage can be used as a springboard to address current medical and socioeconomic issues affecting women, especially as it relates to pregnancies, reproductive concerns, and child care. The deaths of women from birth-giving complications still constitute a major worldwide problem in both the developing and developed worlds.[2] Especially at risk in the United States are women who are poor, African American, or live in rural areas.[3] Sermons on racial, gender, and socioeconomic inequality, especially as it affects women and children, stem directly from this prophecy in Isaiah 65, which promises a better and fairer universe—a universe in which every child and every woman who gives birth will not only survive but thrive.

Isaiah promises further that in this new world someone "who dies at a hundred years will be considered a youth"—that there will be no "old person who does not live out a lifetime" (Isa. 65:20a). The elderly and their treatment and whether they are able to live out a full and fulfilling life therefore appear to be major concerns of Isaiah. So this passage opens up space for sermons about senior citizens and issues affecting them, such as elderly abuse, scams, poverty, health care, and isolation.

The new creation envisioned by Isaiah and Malachi concerns issues of fairness and equality. Malachi condemns those "who oppress the

2. Nina Martin and Renee Montagne, "Focus on Infants during Childbirth Leaves U.S. Moms in Danger," n.p. https://www.npr.org/2017/05/12/527806002/focus-on-infants-during-childbirth-leaves-u-s-moms-in-danger.

3. Jacqueline Howard, "Birth Is Killing Black Women in the U.S., and Here's Why," n.p. https://www.cnn.com/2017/11/15/health/black-women-maternal-mortality/index.html.

hired workers in their wages" (Mal. 3:5), while Isaiah prophesies that builders will be able to dwell in the houses they have built, and those who plant will eat of their crops (Isa. 65:22). In short, both prophets promise that no one in the new kingdom will labor in vain. These promises open up preaching opportunities to address issues of socioeconomic oppression and inequity that prevent those who work from receiving a fair and living wage. Worthy of mention is the rise of the gig economy, with its dependence on short-term, contract labor, and the concerns it raises about workers' rights. It is significant that the new creation envisioned by the prophets—the one in which God's people will "enjoy the work of their hands" (v. 22)—is the very opposite of the one in which a worker struggles to earn a just wage for their labors.

Isaiah's mention of inhabiting houses (v. 21) suggests another possible sermon topic: the issue of fair, stable, and affordable housing. Isaiah prophesies that displacement will cease in the new creation. This concern over housing and displacement is directly connected to poverty, which in turn stems from socioeconomic and racial oppression and injustice.[4] Housing is used to keep economically disadvantaged people, many of whom are minorities, continually impoverished. Isaiah's assurance that the people of God in the new creation will inhabit houses (vv. 21–22), when reimagined for our present context, constitutes a promise of stability and safety that result from fair access to affordable habitation for all.

Cultural connections are also evident. The vision of the wolf, lamb, and straw-eating lion in Isaiah 65, an image also in Isaiah 11:6–8, has been utilized by artists to convey theological sentiments. A series of paintings called *Peaceable Kingdom* by the Quaker artist Edward Hicks uses the Isaianic visions of animals and children as a way to symbolize his hope for intrafaith unity and as a means by which to reflect upon the tension between the promised new creation and the yet untransformed world. Hicks's interpretation opens up the possibility of sermons on denominational unity and the continued hope for spiritual transformation.

This tension emphasized by Hicks fits the lectionary context. In terms of the lectionary placement of Isaiah 65 and Malachi 4, the sentiments of both radical, outward-looking hope and impatience at its fulfillment are fitting. These passages constitute the lection for the Sunday immediately preceding the Reign of Christ, when the church expectantly looks forward to the eschatological fulfillment of the new heaven and earth. During this period of waiting, this passage offers a moment of reflection on how the people of God can mirror and encourage, in some small measure, this renewed creation promised by God's messengers.

SONG-MI SUZIE PARK

4. Matthew Desmond, *Evicted: Poverty and Profit in the American City* (New York: Penguin, 2016).

Proper 28 (Sunday between November 13 and November 19 Inclusive)

Isaiah 12

[1]You will say in that day:
I will give thanks to you, O LORD,
for though you were angry with me,
your anger turned away,
and you comforted me.

[2]Surely God is my salvation;
I will trust, and will not be afraid,
for the LORD GOD is my strength and my might;
he has become my salvation.

[3]With joy you will draw water from the wells of salvation. [4]And you will say in that day:

Give thanks to the LORD,
call on his name;
make known his deeds among the nations;
proclaim that his name is exalted.

[5]Sing praises to the LORD, for he has done gloriously;
let this be known in all the earth.
[6]Shout aloud and sing for joy, O royal Zion,
for great in your midst is the Holy One of Israel.

Psalm 98

[1]O sing to the LORD a new song,
for he has done marvelous things.
His right hand and his holy arm
have gotten him victory.
[2]The LORD has made known his victory;
he has revealed his vindication in the sight of the nations.
[3]He has remembered his steadfast love and faithfulness
to the house of Israel.
All the ends of the earth have seen
the victory of our God.

[4]Make a joyful noise to the LORD, all the earth;
break forth into joyous song and sing praises.
[5]Sing praises to the LORD with the lyre,
with the lyre and the sound of melody.
[6]With trumpets and the sound of the horn
make a joyful noise before the King, the LORD.

[7]Let the sea roar, and all that fills it;
the world and those who live in it.
[8]Let the floods clap their hands;
let the hills sing together for joy
[9]at the presence of the LORD, for he is coming
to judge the earth.
He will judge the world with righteousness,
and the peoples with equity.

Connecting the Psalm with Scripture and Worship

The world as we know it is coming to an end, and we thank God for it. We can even anticipate that day with rejoicing, because God is "about to create new heavens and a new earth" (Isa. 65:17). The prophet Isaiah announces the divine plan; if the people feel anxious or fearful, God assures them that what is coming is very, very good. They will be caught up in joy and delight, and grief will be expunged forever. No longer will they work for someone else's benefit; they will live peacefully and prosperously, and their children will be born for blessing. There will be no predators and no prey, for there will be no evil force left in the world.

After hearing this incredible promise of a new creation, worshipers are invited to sing one of the prophet's own songs of thanksgiving (Isa. 12:1–6). In the context of Isaiah, this song marks the end of the first section of the book, in which Isaiah has prophesied that Judah and Jerusalem will be saved. These expressions of thanksgiving are both individual (v. 1) and communal (v. 4); the community is exhorted to trust in God's promises, to call on God for help, and to broadcast to all the nations that their God is exalted. They sing their thanks and their praise because God is not far off but in their very midst (v. 6).

These texts stand in contrast to the Gospel reading for the day, which is full of warnings about the end of the world order. Where Luke accentuates the destruction of the old, Isaiah focuses on the new. As we proclaim the coming of God's reign, we need both the judgment and the re-creation, and the thoughtful worship planner will let that juxtaposition be clear.

Even while we wait for God to destroy evil and establish righteousness forever, we know that we have already been claimed for the new realm by Christ. As the church prepares for Christ's coming reign, we might take a cue from Isaiah's song and give thanks for baptism. "With joy you will draw water from the wells of salvation," sings the prophet (Isa. 12:3). Although this is not an allusion to Christian baptism, Christians regularly give thanks for the ways that God has been at work through water. As we stand ready to receive a new heaven and a new earth—and as we acknowledge the destruction of the "devil that we know"—we might well give thanks for the gift of baptism, which assures us of our eternal life with God.

Liturgies for thanksgiving for baptism are found in several denominational worship books. Ritual acts may include approaching a font or baptistery to touch the water as a physical reminder of baptism, or aspersion (the sprinkling of water on the people), perhaps during the singing of a baptismal hymn or song. The Taizé chorus "In the Lord I'll Be Ever Thankful" might be sung during similar ritual acts; in ten short bars, this refrain enables worshipers to give thanks, to encourage one another to not be afraid, and to announce the coming of the Lord, who is near. Language from Isaiah 12 might also be incorporated into a confession/pardon sequence led from the baptismal font.

A musical setting of Isaiah 12, "Canticle of Thanksgiving," can be found in *The Psalter—Psalms and Canticles for Singing*. This chant-like setting could be sung by a cantor, choir, or small vocal ensemble while people move forward to touch water. It could also be sung as part of a processional while water is brought forward to the baptismal font and poured visibly and audibly.

While the musical setting is restrained, it can be sung with joy. Another setting of Isaiah's song, "Surely, It Is God Who Saves Me," can be sung in a variety of ways: as a congregational song, or with a cantor or ensemble singing the verses and the congregation joining in on the refrain. The arrangement found in the hymnal *Glory to God* provides both piano and guitar accompaniment, and the music is well suited to a variety of worship contexts. The tone of this setting by Jack Noble White is flowing and joyful and could be sung as part of a processional or ritual act or as part of the proclamation of the Word. Singing Isaiah 12 offers a rare opportunity to highlight the fact that there are songs (canticles) throughout Scripture in addition to the Psalter.

The readings from the complementary stream of the lectionary, Malachi 4:1–2a and Psalm 98, present a stark contrast of destruction and renewal. These verses from Malachi come near the end of the book—indeed, they are among the last verses of our OT—and serve to announce the day that is to come. The prophet warns the people that "all the arrogant and all evildoers" will be burned to nothing (Mal. 4:1a). They will be destroyed forever, for they will be left with "neither root nor branch" (v. 1b). The prophet is quick, however, to address those who are righteous; for them, "the sun of righteousness will rise, with healing in its wings" (v. 2). The prophet's words are full of light—fire and sun announce the justice that is coming.

Psalm 98 is said to be the "theological heart of the psalter: God reigns."[1] As an enthronement psalm, it declares the sovereignty of God, who is holy and victorious. The psalmist elicits songs from the people, from their instruments, from the seas and the hills and every creature that lives on land and in the water. There is no holding back praise for this God, because as J. Clinton McCann puts it, "the good news is that God rules the universe with faithfulness and love, and the ecumenical, ecological, economic, social, and political implications of this message are profound."[2] No wonder the psalmist exhorts every living being to praise.

This is the time of the liturgical year when, more than ever, the church is called to preach and pray eschatologically. In a time when oppressors grow stronger and genocide is part of the daily news, we must proclaim that a new day is coming. In a time when the rich get richer and the poor get poorer, we must proclaim that justice is on the way. In a time when it seems that the forces of greed and destruction are stronger than the powers of generosity and generativity, we must proclaim that the sun of righteousness will indeed rise. To do so is not to resign ourselves to the evil of this day while we wait for the glory of the next. To preach and pray eschatologically—to sing of the day that is to come—is to reassure the people of God (and the world) of God's future, but it is also a call to action in the present. As John L. Bell and Graham Maule have written,

> Heaven shall not wait for triumphant
> Hallelujahs,
> when earth has passed and we reach another
> shore:
> Jesus is Lord in our present imperfection;
> his power and love are for now and then for
> evermore.[3]

On this penultimate Sunday of the Christian liturgical calendar, praise not only prepares us for future glory, but propels us to be about Christ's work until that great day comes.

KIMBERLY BRACKEN LONG

1. J. Clinton McCann, "The Book of Psalms," in *The New Interpreter's Bible*, ed. Leander E. Keck, 10 vols. (Nashville: Abingdon, 1996), 4:1073.
2. McCann, "Psalms," 4:1073.
3. John L. Bell and Graham Maule, "Heaven Shall Not Wait," in *Glory to God* (Louisville, KY: Westminster John Knox, 2013), no. 773. Text © 1987, WGRG, Iona Community (admin. GIA Publications, Inc.). All rights reserved. Used by permission.

Proper 28 (Sunday between November 13 and November 19 Inclusive)

2 Thessalonians 3:6–13

[6]Now we command you, beloved, in the name of our Lord Jesus Christ, to keep away from believers who are living in idleness and not according to the tradition that they received from us. [7]For you yourselves know how you ought to imitate us; we were not idle when we were with you, [8]and we did not eat anyone's bread without paying for it; but with toil and labor we worked night and day, so that we might not burden any of you. [9]This was not because we do not have that right, but in order to give you an example to imitate. [10]For even when we were with you, we gave you this command: Anyone unwilling to work should not eat. [11]For we hear that some of you are living in idleness, mere busybodies, not doing any work. [12]Now such persons we command and exhort in the Lord Jesus Christ to do their work quietly and to earn their own living. [13]Brothers and sisters, do not be weary in doing what is right.

Commentary 1: Connecting the Reading with Scripture

A central issue confronting an interpreter of this text concerns the various renderings of the behavior being called into question with Paul's command "to keep away from believers who are living in idleness [*ataktous*] and not according to the tradition that they received from us" (2 Thess. 3:6). English translations move in different, though not contradictory, directions. Is the behavior "idleness" (NRSV, ESV), "disorderliness" (KJV, ASV), or perhaps both "idleness and disruptiveness" (NIV)?

Given Paul's twice repeated reference (2 Thess. 3:7–8 and 1 Thess. 2:9) to his own time among the Thessalonians as including toil and labor, so as not to burden his friends in that nascent Christian community, "idleness" certainly appears close to the heart of his concern. He is adamant that he and his missionary partners were determined to earn their keep in their ministry amid the Thessalonians, lifting rather than adding to any burden their presence might involve.

Two other connections to 1 Thessalonians enlarge what "idleness" entails. In 4:9–12 there is another mention of the theme of working "with your hands," set in the context of an account of the love that binds the Christian community together. Acknowledging that the Thessalonians have demonstrated love to "all the brothers and sisters throughout Macedonia," Paul urges them "to aspire to live quietly, to mind your own affairs, and to work with your hands, as we directed you." In this way, Paul believes they will "behave properly toward outsiders and be dependent on no one." Idleness appears problematic because it undermines the mutually supportive character of Christian community.

As Paul draws the First Letter to the Thessalonians to a close, he summarizes his concerns for how the community is undergirded and sustained: "admonish the idlers, encourage the fainthearted, help the weak, be patient with all of them" (5:14). Addressing "idlers" is part and parcel of maintaining the bonds of Christian love, just as are encouraging "the fainthearted" and helping "the weak." Overcoming idleness is not merely for instilling virtue in the individual inclined to it, but also for the sake of restoring the fullness of community.

As Abraham Malherbe has observed, Paul is particularly disturbed by the manner in which their disruptive behavior has social consequences. "Conscious of the destructive effect that idleness could have within the community, and on its relationships to the larger society, he directs the community to be sharp in its admonition of those who threaten the fabric of its social relationships."[1]

Thus, the choice of the NIV translators with respect to rendering the problematic behavior that Paul has in focus seems apt. Even though using two words ("idleness" and "disruptiveness") to translate one word (*ataktous*) is cumbersome, it comes closest to gathering up all that concerns Paul in the matter. Fundamentally he wants to ensure that no one takes advantage of the altruism of the Christian community, undermining generosity as a trustworthy bond of life together.

The most infamous illustration of such a problem of "freeloading" is doubtless found in the story of Ananias and Sapphira (Acts 5:1–11). However one regards the episode of early Christians sharing their material abundance with those who had need, Ananias and Sapphira represent the skeptical option. They manifest an especially disruptive impact on community by appearing to join in its generosity without being truly committed to it. It is difficult to imagine a more effective way to undermine generosity as a community norm than by pretending to honor it while simultaneously ignoring it. Such behavior amounts to idleness vis-à-vis the norm of generosity, resulting in disruption of the overall life of the community. Small wonder that it was met with such revulsion in this story.

A preacher might well ponder the ways the altruism of the Christian community is still taken advantage of or exploited. Perhaps some bask in the glow of a congregation's community outreach without supporting it with prayer or personal engagement. Maybe some broader forms of social support for human need are withdrawn in a community, leaving such aid to the church and other nonprofit organizations. Perhaps it is simply the assumption that there will always be others to provide the financial support for the church's mission and ministry, thus excusing them to employ their financial resources elsewhere.

To be sure, Jesus' own instruction for the mission of the twelve disciples in Matthew's Gospel does allow them to proceed unencumbered by worried provision of money, clothes, or food, precisely because of the anticipated generosity of those to whom they carried the gospel. "Take no gold, or silver, or copper in your belts, no bag for your journey, or two tunics, or sandals, or a staff; for laborers deserve their food" (Matt. 10:9–10). However, in the Didache there are at least two instances in which some constraints are suggested, precisely to avoid the freeloading syndrome. The first involves how Christians should relate to apostles and prophets: they are to be welcomed as the Lord, but only for a day (or at most two); and sent out with only enough food to sustain them until the next night's lodging is reached. Most emphatically, such a visitor is to be regarded as a false prophet if they either stay for three days or ask for money (Didache 11:3–6). There is no doubt of the need to safeguard the norm of generosity in the early Christian church from such intrusions—the point being that such "idle" presence in the community disrupted its common life based on reciprocal generosity.

Something similar is said in the following section of the Didache when it focuses not on prophets or apostles but on "everyone who comes in the name of the Lord." They are welcome without question for up to two days (or for three in case of necessity). However, should they want to settle within the community, they should be ready to join a body of mutual generosity, through an existing craft or readiness to learn one, rather than intending to freeload as an idle and dependent presence (Didache 12:1–5). Paul's concern to avoid a disruptive idleness that erodes communal generosity was appreciated in wider reaches of the early church.

Paul's widest concern in this passage is precisely the preservation of the new community that has come in Christ, one in which brothers and sisters do not grow "weary in doing what is right" (2 Thess. 3:13). The lectionary pairing of Isaiah 65:17–25 is salutary for maintaining such a focus. By depicting the eschatological vision of "new heavens and a new earth," Isaiah summons attention to God's desire for a community of generosity not plagued by some taking selfish advantage. "They shall not build and another inhabit; they shall not plant and another eat; for like the days of a tree shall the days of my people

1. Abraham J. Malherbe, *Paul and the Thessalonians: The Philosophic Tradition of Pastoral Care* (Philadelphia: Fortress, 1987), 92.

be, and my chosen shall long enjoy the work of their hands" (Isa. 65:22). Moreover, God's intention for generous, flourishing community includes not only the human family, but the whole realm of nature. "The wolf and the lamb shall feed together, the lion shall eat straw like the ox. They shall not hurt or destroy on all my holy mountain, says the LORD" (v. 25).

What Paul encourages in the concrete practices of the Christians in Thessalonica is foreshadowed in Isaiah's grand imagining of what God intends for the whole creation: communities of persons in which special advantage is not sought and communities of nature in which harm does not prevail.

D. CAMERON MURCHISON

Commentary 2: Connecting the Reading with the World

As a missionary, Paul had stayed in Thessalonica long enough to preach three times in the synagogue, start a Christian community hosted by Jason, and anger the Jews enough to barely escape with his life (Acts 17:1–9). Paul went to Thessalonica during his second missionary journey as a result of his vision to visit Macedonia (Acts 16:9).

Thessalonica was founded in 315 BCE and named after Thessalonike (Alexander the Great's half-sister), the wife of Macedon's King Cassander. In Paul's day, this was a key city for trade, with a famous harbor and the Egyptian Road east to Asia. This was a key city for Alexander the Great on his route to conquer Asia Minor and Persia. While Paul would certainly have been very aware of the strategic importance of this city, Paul did not want to conquer it militarily or for trade; rather, Paul went to Thessalonica to share the good news of Jesus as the Messiah.

Paul's second letter to the church in Thessalonica, like his other letters, is in response to a specific issue or concern. In this case, there are Christians who are not working, depending on others for their well-being, and meddling in others' business. As a result of this unbecoming behavior, they are impeding the growth of the gospel.

Paul addresses these concerns directly in this letter and exhorts them to "earn their own living" (2 Thess. 3:12). Paul, a tentmaker, refers to his example of working to earn his keep. He asks the congregation to continue his example so as not to be a burden to those around them.

This passage is consistent with a work ethic that dates back to the creation narrative in Genesis 1–2, in which God concludes his work with a day of rest. In the Jewish tradition, even the rabbis were expected to have a trade and work. The text even goes as far as to say that those who do not work should not eat. Paul's words to the Thessalonians are therefore not only a rebuke for those who are not pulling their own weight. They are also an encouragement to the Christian community to have a strong work ethic.

Many communal societies have ways built into the culture and family networks to provide for those less fortunate. Such programs are frequently disparaged by those who frown on people who are unable to help themselves. A possible sermon might examine and reflect on the questions that arise when thinking about labor: Should a society be responsible for the well-being of those who are unable to care for themselves? What about the churches? What roles do they have in helping those who are unable to work?

It is important to recall that this letter is written from the perspective of a guest, a visitor to Thessalonica, who does not want to be a burden to his hosts. Paul has shared the gospel with the community and wants his witness to invite and not detract from his message. If we are witnesses to those around us, then we should set an example that would draw our friends, families, and neighbors closer to Christ. Being a burden or being lazy was not an attractive witness to others.

Equally deterimental, however, is to set ourselves up on a pedestal and portray ourselves as perfect. Indeed, Henry Nouwen in his book *The Wounded Healer* writes that someone who is vulnerable and open is actually a more effective minister than someone who is closed and unrelatable. A possible sermon might explore and contemplate how we, the people of God, can responsibly reflect the God we serve.

Indeed, this message of Paul to the Thessalonians reminds us that the church has a mirroring effect on society that is intertwined with its missionary purpose. As the quote often attributed to Francis states: "Preach the gospel at all times. Use words if necessary." The message is that Christians should teach by example and behavior. The passage in 2 Thessalonians 3:6–13 therefore raises some important questions about how Christians reflect Christ: How are we as individual Christians perceived by our surrounding communities? Are the churches making a positive impact on the neighborhoods, towns, and cities in which they are located? Are they viewed as a community that others would like to join?

Paul's exhortation to not be a busybody (v. 11), moreover, raises the perilous question about boundaries. Boundaries become more and more important as we increasingly hear about the rampant cases of sexual harrassment and abuses of power. Many churches have installed windows in the pastor's office to increase accountability. Employers are sending their employees to required sexual harrassment training. This text offers a message about boundaries toward those who we are attempting to serve. It invites us to be willing to assist, but never to be overly entangled, dependent on, or taking advantage of those whom we serve.

The danger of taking this position to an extreme is to fall into the trap of doing the work of God from a distance. Churches have often been criticized for being paternalistic and starting outreach programs that serve the poor "from an arm's length." How many times have we heard of a clothing closet or food pantry where the "poor" go to receive a handout, but there is little human interaction. This is a Band-Aid type of service that attends to the symptoms, rather than the root causes of poverty. So how do we heed the epistle's warning against being busybodies and at the same time avoid this temptation of being paternalistic and distant from those whom we serve?

Recently books such as *When Helping Hurts* by Brian Fikkert and Steve Corbett and *Toxic Charity* by Robert Lupton have shed light on this issue. A theme in both of these books is human dignity. Too often we are not cognizant of the power differentials between those who serve and those being served. This is where Paul's exhortation to the community to work and earn one's own living is helpful. This interpretation is consistent with the longer Jewish and Christian tradition that work is associated with blessing (cf. Prov. 12:11; Ps. 128:2).

The message in this pericope is consistent with this teaching. The philosophies behind Habitat for Humanity and many microloan programs take these biblical teachings into account, while also avoiding paternalistic temptations. Habitat for Humanity requires future homeowners to assist in building their own home by investing sweat equity; that is, each future homeowner must work a certain number of hours as a way of demonstrating commitment. Similarly many microloan programs have the recipient sign a contract where they agree to pay back the loan and offer some type of collateral to guarantee the loan. In a more communitarian society, collateral can often be one's friends, neighbors, and family members who can vouch for the signee. The payback rate is very high. Both of these programs allow the participant to work, have human dignity, and feel as though they are "subjects" working to earn their own living rather than the "objects" of someone's mission. In so doing, these programs offer us "an example to imitate" (v. 9) and push us to consider how we too can better reflect the Christ we serve.

PHILIP WINGEIER-RAYO

Proper 28 (Sunday between November 13 and November 19 Inclusive)

Luke 21:5–19

[5]When some were speaking about the temple, how it was adorned with beautiful stones and gifts dedicated to God, he said, [6]"As for these things that you see, the days will come when not one stone will be left upon another; all will be thrown down."

[7]They asked him, "Teacher, when will this be, and what will be the sign that this is about to take place?" [8]And he said, "Beware that you are not led astray; for many will come in my name and say, 'I am he!' and, 'The time is near!' Do not go after them.

[9]"When you hear of wars and insurrections, do not be terrified; for these things must take place first, but the end will not follow immediately." [10]Then he said to them, "Nation will rise against nation, and kingdom against kingdom; [11]there will be great earthquakes, and in various places famines and plagues; and there will be dreadful portents and great signs from heaven.

[12]"But before all this occurs, they will arrest you and persecute you; they will hand you over to synagogues and prisons, and you will be brought before kings and governors because of my name. [13]This will give you an opportunity to testify. [14]So make up your minds not to prepare your defense in advance; [15]for I will give you words and a wisdom that none of your opponents will be able to withstand or contradict. [16]You will be betrayed even by parents and brothers, by relatives and friends; and they will put some of you to death. [17]You will be hated by all because of my name. [18]But not a hair of your head will perish. [19]By your endurance you will gain your souls."

Commentary 1: Connecting the Reading with Scripture

The writer of Luke highlights the counterintuitive idea that lies at the heart of Jesus' mission. At the center of Jesus' ministry, he suggests, is a radically different concept of hope—not the kind of hope that is obvious and visible, but the opposite: one that is invisible, beyond our senses (Rom. 8:24) and still to be fulfilled, the kind that requires trust and commitment to see it through. This theme of trust in the midst of difficulty resonates throughout the lectionary texts for this day.

This idea of faith and hope is not unique to Luke but is found throughout Scripture. "If you do not have faith," Isaiah states, "you will not stand" (Isa. 7:9). So also in the immediately preceding pericope, Jesus highlights the poor widow whose meager offerings are worth more than the gifts of the rich, precisely because it expresses more faith to give a higher percentage of limited means (Luke 21:1–4).

Honoring the "least" goes hand in hand with a deemphasis on grand and obvious expressions of power (21:5–19). The great temple, built by Herod, was a majestic structure that expressed Herod's wealth and civic generosity. The grandeur inspired thoughts of its beauty and devotion by those who contributed to it. Jesus uses the visible richness of the temple as a teaching device, cautioning listeners against putting their trust in false hopes and limited powers. Do not trust in the beauty or the apparent devotion. Do not trust in the signs of success in this world. Even the great temple will not last, Jesus says (v. 6).

Also to be distrusted, according to Jesus, are false prophets and untrustworthy leaders (v. 8)—a sentiment repeated in Colossians 2:16–23. They should not be followed simply because they talk with authority. Rather, if they are authentic, they should reflect the values and methods that Jesus displayed in his own ministry. Luke's audience would have been well acquainted with such false prophets, such as Theudas (Acts 5:36) and Simon the magician (Acts 8), who takes on almost mythic stature as the archheretic in early church writers such as Irenaeus and Justin Martyr. The Didache, chapter 11, likewise gives clear guidance on how to tell false prophets and teachers from real ones.

Instead of listening to these deceivers, Jesus states that signs, wars, social upheaval, and natural events will hint that the destruction is near (vv. 10–11). Such events were already quite familiar to Luke's audience, who would have experienced earthquakes as well as the occasional volcano eruptions, such as that of Vesuvius in 79 CE. Mention, moreover, is made of famines (Acts 7:11) and a prediction and fulfilment of famine (Acts 11:28).

By telling Jesus' prophecy of the destruction and razing of the temple in 70 CE, Luke offers a radical reinterpretation of this event. The destruction was not evidence of God's rejection and disfavor. Rather, it was the fulfillment of God's plan. Hence, rather than anxiety, Luke argues, this disaster should instill expectation and hope. What might bring terror should result instead in trust: Jesus said these things would happen. Therefore, though it appears as if God's plan and work has been undermined, it is not so. Despite the seeming signs of disaster, God is still in charge. God is faithful. The people, thus, should remain faithful to God.

In a similar vein, Jesus' prophecy that his followers will experience persecution (v. 12) is also meant to instill hope and faith. Examples of persecution abound throughout Acts in the martyrdoms of James and Stephen and in the work of Saul of Tarsus, who sought out Christians to persecute. The early church endured focused persecution under Roman emperors and governors, all seeking to undermine Christian testimony about the supremacy of Christ, up until the time of Constantine nearly three hundred years later. The seeming humiliation is not a cue for discouragement but an opportunity for confession of God's kingdom. God is not only still involved but actively using the situations to bring about renewal—a sentiment echoed in Hebrews 10:32–39.

While not directly mentioned, the work of the Holy Spirit is implied as the source of "words and wisdom" that God's people will receive in such situations (Luke 12:11–12). Alongside the help of the Holy Spirit, what is necessary is obedience to God, holding on to the calling in the midst of the counternarratives (vv. 32–40). There are examples of faithful, transforming witness throughout Acts, such as Stephen's testimony in Acts 7, often accompanying persecution and difficult experiences. To this we can add the stirring testimony of Polycarp before the Romans and other early martyr testimonies that led to a curious growth of the early church. "The blood of martyrs is the seed of the church," Tertullian wrote, as the early church grew despite the opposition. The world will fight and struggle to its utmost, and Luke does not spiritualize or relativize this, emphasizing again in verses 16–17 that there will be social and physical suffering.

The passage ends with a promise that no ultimate harm will come to those who persist—a curious promise in light of verse 16, which states that some will die because of the persecution, as Stephen later did. Thus the implication is not one of absolute physical shielding, but something deeper and greater. These systems will bluster with all their might but will not have an ultimate say. As in the cross itself, death is an experience but not a finality. As Paul states in 1 Corinthians 15:54: "Death has been swallowed up in victory." There is, in other words, much more to the story than what the world knows and much more activity by God than what the world can see.

The lectionary texts for this day likewise emphasize God's faithfulness that invites human faithfulness. In Isaiah 65:17–25, God speaks of renewal after destruction, emphasizing that God's victory will come in full. Trust in this end, not in the current experiences. God's anger and judgment will not last forever, we read in Isaiah 12. God is full of mercy and love, and when God

We Are All in God's Power

A few days later there was a rumor that we were going to be given a hearing. My father also arrived from the city, worn with worry, and he came to see me with the idea of persuading me.

"Daughter," he said, "have pity on my gray head—have pity on me your father, if I deserve to be called your father, if I have favored you above all your brothers, if I have raised you to reach this prime of your life. Do not abandon me to be the reproach of men. Think of your brothers, think of your mother and your aunt, think of your child, who will not be able to live once you are gone. Give up your pride! You will destroy all of us! None of us will ever be able to speak freely again if anything happens to you."

This was the way my father spoke out of love for me, kissing my hands and throwing himself down before me. With tears in his eyes he no longer addressed me as his daughter but as a woman. I was sorry for my father's sake, because he alone of all my kin would be unhappy to see me suffer.

I tried to comfort him saying, "It will all happen in the prisoner's dock as God wills; for you may be sure that we are not left to ourselves but are all in his power."

"The Martyrdom of Perpetua and Felicitas," in *Acts of the Christian Martyrs: Introduction, Texts, and Translations*, trans. Herbert Musurillo (Oxford: Clarendon Press, 1972), 113.

comes to save, we will celebrate. Have hope in this day! God will in fact punish the evildoers, as Malachi reminds us, so God's faithfulness to us invites our faithfulness in perseverance. Revering God's name will lead into healing. God will not forget his people, and indeed the psalmist notes how a new salvation will take place where God is revealed in the whole earth, and creation itself will rejoice in this victory. Wait for this celebration!

This narrative of God's faithfulness in the midst of "distress and persecution" likewise leads Paul to admonish those in Thessalonica to stand firm, praying and yearning for God's salvation. They show trust by being faithful to the calling they have been given. Rather than panic, rather than competition, the people are to experience a love that increases and overflows, a counterintuitive expression of hope that resonates throughout their community and beyond, a love filled with courage.

This faithfulness is a message for us even still, as we wade through discouraging news and constant negativity. The world seems to be getting worse and that is overwhelming. But our calling in God is to hope, and to trust that what we might see, what might very well be real, is not definitive for our hearts or our actions. We are to trust, and in trusting we are to live out with faithfulness the calling we have been given. We are to be careful, not be weighed down, as Jesus says in Luke 21:34. Redemption is indeed drawing near, but it takes eyes of faith to see and hearts of hope to trust.

PATRICK ODEN

Commentary 2: Connecting the Reading with the World

Luke's account of Jesus teaching in the temple takes place on the journey to Jerusalem that will reach its completion with his death on a cross. On the Twenty-eighth Sunday after Pentecost, the church hears this reading as a pilgrim people who find themselves in the middle of the story. Luke 21 evokes memory and hope, both a "looking back" and a "looking forward" by which the Spirit conforms the church to the way of Jesus Christ that finds its end in the fullness of love for God and neighbor. The whole of Luke's Gospel has pointed in this direction in presenting Jesus as the Son of God, Israel's Messiah, and Savior of the world. This presentation, however, cannot be separated from the particular contours of Luke's narrative that render the identity of Jesus as the one who announces and establishes God's reign in the world by the empowerment of the Spirit who is prominent at every stage of his life and ministry.

That there is an eschatological mood, tone, and orientation in Luke 21 is undeniable. In preparing for a sermon from this passage, the preacher would do well to follow closely the manner in which the words of Jesus "show" rather than "explain" the eschatological reality of God's reign, to encourage the endurance of faith during the "time of the world."[1] Luke's narrative, then, invites the preacher to see more clearly the reality of God's reign that is made present in all that Jesus says, does, and suffers. This is particularly important in preaching from Jesus' eschatological discourse in the temple, a message that is often extracted from the narrative of Luke's Gospel and treated as a formula that provides knowledge for calculating the time of the world's end.

A sermon from Luke 21 could be informed by the location of Jesus' teaching concerning the approaching end of God's time. He has entered the temple, the visible manifestation of God's presence in the midst of Israel as a blessing to the nations. This location is not incidental for the third Gospel, since Luke's narrative of Jesus Christ begins and ends with scenes in the temple, a liturgical space in which the whole of life is referred to Israel's God as Creator and Redeemer of all that is. Preaching from Luke 21 could be seen as a liturgical act—oriented to the praise of God—that calls the church to connect its life and work in the world to its worship, as an offering of thankful surrender to God in following after the way of Jesus Christ.

The preacher might also be helped by considering Luke's introduction to Jesus' eschatological discourse in the temple, the remarkable story of a poor widow whose complete self-offering points to God's self gift in the passion and death of Jesus (vv. 1–4). Luke tells us Jesus looked up and saw many wealthy people placing their gifts in the temple treasury, offerings of money for the maintenance of the sanctuary and its daily sacrifices. There are people from Jerusalem and the surrounding regions, as well as pilgrims from across the Diaspora. Jesus, however, directs attention to a poor widow who put in two copper coins, the smallest unit of money there was. His response to the widow's action must have surely been startling to those around him. "Truly I tell you, this poor widow has put in more than all of them; for all of them have contributed out of their abundance, but she out of her poverty has put in all she had to live on."

If we read this scene as an introduction to the eschatological discourse of Luke 21, the widow's offering provides a way of seeing the reign of God proclaimed by Jesus, "that God turns to human beings completely and without any reservation in order to bring divine abundance to the world."[2] God's self-giving is a decisive historical event; it is happening now in Israel and in the new community raised up with Jesus by the Spirit. The story of the widow's offering then opens a window on the world as the space in and through which God is at work completing all things under Christ as Lord. The world is the space in which the church experiences and bears witness to the glory of the overflowing self-giving of Jesus, offering wholehearted devotion to God as exemplified by the act of the poor widow.

The story of the poor widow's total self-offering directs attention away from the architectural magnificence and splendor of the temple, a sign of Israel's enduring religious strength and stability, to the glory of God displayed by Jesus in his manner of living, suffering, and dying. This is the significance of the temple for the world: "You shall love the Lord your God with all your heart, soul, mind, and strength." In light of the poor widow's offering, the eschatological words of Jesus also open up a window onto the "time of the world" as one of yearning, weakness, uncertainty, vulnerability, and incompleteness. The social conditions described by Jesus point to the constant temptation to satisfy the longing for completion, finality, and satisfaction through historical commitments, arrangements, and achievements. A sermon that follows the words of Jesus might point to the witness of the church during the "time of the world" as displaying a particular

1. On "the time of the world," see Charles Mathewes, *A Theology of Public Life* (Cambridge: Cambridge University Press, 2007), 145.
2. Gerhard Lohfink, *Jesus of Nazareth: What He Wanted, Who He Was* (Collegeville, MN: Liturgical Press, 2012), 220.

ethic of disciplined love—for God and neighbor. This ascetic way of life nourishes and sustains the hope of a community whose vision is kept open by adoring praise of God.

There is a great temptation to read the "signs of the times" as possessing a kind of eschatological finality, certainty, and completion that demand the church's wholehearted commitment in the name of doing God's will. Many preachers have been fond of citing a popular assertion that has been attributed to theologian Karl Barth, that sermons should be preached with the Bible in one hand and the newspaper in the other. The words of Jesus, however, relativize the "news" reported by sources such as, say, the *New York Times* in light of the gospel of God's reign he proclaimed and embodied completely. Political conflict and partisanship; uprisings, insurrections, and terrorist attacks; military action and threats of war; natural disasters and devastating loss; religious persecution and betrayal; cultural isolation and marginalization, are acknowledged but relativized by Jesus. Such events, including their crises and consequences, should not be seen as signs of "ends" that command the total reverence, loyalty, and devotion owed to God.

The reign of God revealed in the self-giving of Jesus is the end that is the church's one and only hope. Luke 21 opens up any number of windows onto the joys and struggles of the church as a people "on the way" into the fullness of God's reign during the "time of the world." Preaching from this text provides an opportunity to call the church to renewed trust in God. As a pilgrim people called to a life of wholehearted surrender to God in all things, its endurance in the way of Jesus Christ summons the world to recognize that it is neither the source nor the end of its own life, but is rather a gift and expression of God's self-giving love.

MICHAEL PASQUARELLO III

Proper 29 (Reign of Christ)

Jeremiah 23:1–6
Luke 1:68–79 and Psalm 46
Colossians 1:11–20
Luke 23:33–43

Jeremiah 23:1–6

> [1]Woe to the shepherds who destroy and scatter the sheep of my pasture! says the LORD. [2]Therefore thus says the LORD, the God of Israel, concerning the shepherds who shepherd my people: It is you who have scattered my flock, and have driven them away, and you have not attended to them. So I will attend to you for your evil doings, says the LORD. [3]Then I myself will gather the remnant of my flock out of all the lands where I have driven them, and I will bring them back to their fold, and they shall be fruitful and multiply. [4]I will raise up shepherds over them who will shepherd them, and they shall not fear any longer, or be dismayed, nor shall any be missing, says the LORD.
>
> [5]The days are surely coming, says the LORD, when I will raise up for David a righteous Branch, and he shall reign as king and deal wisely, and shall execute justice and righteousness in the land. [6]In his days Judah will be saved and Israel will live in safety. And this is the name by which he will be called: "The LORD is our righteousness."

Commentary 1: Connecting the Reading with Scripture

Jeremiah 23:1–6 begins with a dramatic divine denunciation, when God through the prophet Jeremiah quite dramatically voices God's disdain for the bad shepherds or leaders who were supposed to have guarded and protected God's people, but scattered, destroyed, and drove their sheep away instead (vv. 1–2). In response, an angry God, in an ironic fashion, vows to do to the shepherds exactly what they had done to their sheep: scatter and drive *them* away instead (v. 2). This threat likely is a veiled reference to the impending Babylonian invasion during which the Solomonic temple in Jerusalem was destroyed, Davidic rule put to an end, and the privileged elite of Judean society, that is, the shepherds of the people, were taken into exile (597–587 BCE).

As response, *God* personally will take over the role of the good shepherd and "will gather the remnant of my flock out of all the lands where I [God] have driven them." God proclaims to "bring them back to their fold, and they shall be fruitful and multiply" (v. 3). In this time, God will raise up good leaders (shepherds) over God's people. These good shepherds are exemplified in the reference to the righteous king, a descendant, that is, a branch of the house of David who "shall reign as king and deal wisely, and shall execute justice and righteousness in the land" (v. 5). This vision of a Davidic branch or a shoot reverberates throughout the prophets (Jer. 33:15; Isa. 4:2; 11:1; Zech. 3:8; 6:12). This hope for a future time in which the people of Judah will be free from their enemies is transposed to a distant time when a just king will reign who will be called by the name: "The LORD is our righteousness" (v. 6). As the name shows, this long-awaited king will epitomize, embody, and enact God's justice and righteousness.

Jeremiah 23:1–6 forms part of a larger literary unit, Jeremiah 21–24, in which the focus falls on the failure of the leaders of Judah, the kings, the priests, and the prophets, to live up to this ideal of justice as expressed in the covenant. Immediately following the promise of restoration focused on the hope for a just king, Jeremiah 23:11–14 offers a sharp critique of the false prophets and the priests whose wickedness extends even into the temple. These prophets and priests are, according to God, "ungodly," and hence God will send disaster as their deserved punishment.

The condemnation of the priests in Jeremiah 23 finds a prelude in Jeremiah 22, a diatribe against the kings for their failure to "act with justice and righteousness." The list of their transgressions includes acts such as unfair labor practices (see the reference to the king building his house in unrighteousness and injustice, 22:13–17), mistreatment of the vulnerable (doing "wrong or violence to the alien, the orphan, and the widow"), and unnecessary violence ("shed[ding] innocent blood in this place," 22:3). The devastating events of the Babylonian invasion and exile, as Deuteronomistic theology made clear, serve as just punishment for Judah's apostasy. The kings were particularly guilty. Not only did they turn away from God and worship other gods (22:9), but, as is evident in the metaphor of the shepherd who has scattered their sheep, they led the people astray. Deservedly they too, God promises, will be scattered.

The language of scattering throughout the book of Jeremiah is used as a metaphor for God's judgment. In Jeremiah 13:24, God vows to "scatter you like chaff driven by the wind from the desert." In Jeremiah 18:17, God likens Godself to "the wind from the east" who "will scatter them before the enemy." The scattering recalls the literal dispersion and displacement—scattering—that will occur to the people and leaders of Judah during the exile. Indeed, Jeremiah 9:16 spells out the analogy as God promises to scatter the people "among nations that neither they nor their ancestors have known."

Not all will be lost forever, however. The scattered, God promises, will eventually be gathered (Jer. 31:10). Jeremiah 23:1–6 ends with a rare word of hope that reaffirms the people's belief in the deliverer God who brought the people of Israel up out of the land of Egypt. This cherished belief of their ancestors, however, is applied to a new time when God will lead an exodus out of Babylon, the land of the north, and out of all the lands where God had scattered the people. According to this hopeful vision, the people shall one day once more live in their own land (23:7–8). This word of hope aligns with what has been called the Little Book of Comfort (Jer. 29–33), which centers on God's promise to restore the fortunes of the people and gather them from all the places where they have been sent into exile (29:14). As Jeremiah 31:10 maintains: "He who scattered Israel will gather him, and will keep him as a shepherd a flock" (cf. also Jer. 31:8).

There are a number of important connections that extend beyond the book of Jeremiah. The metaphor of the good shepherd featured in Jeremiah 23:1–6 resonates throughout the biblical corpus. In one of the best known biblical passages, the Lord is professed to be "my shepherd," who is responsible for the believer's declaration of trust, "I shall not want" (Ps. 23:1). In this iconic psalm, the actions of leading, feeding, and protecting associated with a good shepherd are used in order to describe God's delivering and sustaining presence in the life of the believer.

The image of the bad versus the good shepherds in Jeremiah 23:1–6 is further extended in the exposition of this image in Ezekiel 34:1–10, where the shepherds are indicted for feeding themselves instead of the sheep, not helping the injured, and not searching for the lost sheep. Instead, the sheep find themselves scattered, vulnerable to predators. Aligned with Jeremiah 23's image of the good shepherd, God in Ezekiel 34:11–16 will serve as the shepherd who seeks out the lost sheep, who will bring back those who have strayed, who will bind up the injured and strengthen the weak, and who "will feed them with justice" (v. 16). This section in Ezekiel 34 concludes with the reference to this "one [good] shepherd" that God will raise up, that is, God's servant David, who shall "feed them: he shall feed them and be their shepherd" (v. 23).

This tradition is picked up in the NT, when Jesus in John 10:1–18 proclaims himself to be the Good Shepherd, hence drawing on the notion of the ideal king who will reign in justice, which counters the many examples of bad kings in Jeremiah's time, who harm the most vulnerable of individuals. In terms of the Gospel reading this week, Luke too reiterates the promise of a Messiah who is to come when it states that God will raise up a mighty savior from the house of David (Luke 1:69). This Savior will liberate those who find themselves in life-denying circumstances, giving them peace from their enemies (v. 74) and "light to those who sit in darkness and in the shadow of death" (v. 79). In this way, the lectionary texts of this week work together in order to offer a word of healing to those who are hurting, proclaiming words of hope and deliverance to people who still find themselves in the grip of oppression, violence, and despair.

L. JULIANA M. CLAASSENS

Commentary 2: Connecting the Reading with the World

Jeremiah addresses the timeless issue of leadership. Leaders and their decisions affect our lives. They can lead us to safety and well-being, or they can lead us into alienation and despair. Indeed, the history of the world, including that of Israel, consisted of the terrible suffering and injustice that stemmed from bad leadership. Jeremiah had firsthand knowledge of the consequences of bad governance. He witnessed three times the pain and disillusionment caused by incompetent and self-serving leaders. Jeremiah, like the prophets before him, calls out those destructive leaders and reminds them that God is watching (Jer. 23:2).

"Woe," is how Jeremiah begins his prophecy (v. 1). In today's vernacular, "woe" is equal to "look out," and it immediately signals to the reader and listener that they should pay attention. This term signals alarm and warning for something that has gone wrong and astray from the intentions of God. The prophet Jeremiah sends the alarm that God is not pleased with what is going on.

Jeremiah utilizes a powerful metaphor to which most of his audience would relate: shepherding sheep. God, Jeremiah prophesies, is disturbed with the "shepherds who destroy and scatter the sheep" (v. 1). Like a classroom teacher responsible for the well-being and growth of the students, Jeremiah uses "shepherd" as a code word for a "leader"—someone responsible for the well-being of the flock. Indeed, ancient Near Eastern kings were often pictured with a shepherd's staff. Unsurprisingly, many of Israel's great leaders, such as Moses and David, were said to have been shepherds. Through the use of the metaphor shepherd, Jeremiah creatively translates a complex political issue into understandable language and imagery.

Jeremiah is speaking at a politically chaotic time for God's people in ancient Judah. The Babylonian Empire was gaining strength and asserting power throughout the region, and Judah was not exempt from the Babylonian expansionist agenda. At the time that Jeremiah spoke his prophecy about shepherds, Judah had been led in failed succession by three kings, Jehoiakim, Jehoiachin, and Zedekiah. They are likely the shepherds Jeremiah was referring to when he said they had "destroyed and scattered the sheep" (v. 1).

All three kings failed to lead with sound decisions. Jehoiakim showed arrogance and pride and in turn drew the ire of the Babylonians. The Babylonian invasion came shortly after his untimely death, during the reign of his successor king Jehoiachin, who had no preparation or plan for Judah against the Babylonians. His leadership ultimately resulted in great destruction and scattering of the people at the hands of the Babylonians. Finally, Zedekiah, who followed, became defiant and arrogant, even at the warning of Jeremiah to do otherwise. This quality of leadership was met by the most destructive dispersal of the people during the Babylonian exile.

Jeremiah's lived account of the suffering caused by these failures in leadership offers several questions that are worthy of consideration on the pulpit. As the people of God, how can we aid in the creation and promotion of good leaders who accept and utilize power with humility, dedication, and wisdom? Conversely, what role should the church have in speaking out against bad leaders and bad policies? To what degree is it the duty of the people of God to be like Jeremiah and call out and deter the rise and influence of narcissistic and power-hungry autocrats who cause great suffering and harm?

This passage from Jeremiah also reminds the church to engage in critical self-reflection. As representatives of God, how have we failed at shepherding? How have we used the power given to us to thwart and hinder the unfolding vision of God? Conversely, what can we now do to better reveal and participate in God's salvific plan for the world? How can we, the church, become better shepherds, better protectors of our flock?

At first it appears that Jeremiah is addressing the leaders themselves, but as his forceful words unfold, we realize that these are words spoken to the victims, the scattered people. This is evident when the prophet states that God will not pass leadership on to another king. Rather, God will be the one to gather them and comfort the people so that they shall again be "fruitful and multiply" (v. 3). God, Jeremiah states, is always on the side of those who suffer because of bad leadership—those who are scattered, fleeing, and displaced. If so, how can we, the people of God, also side with these sufferers? What can we, the church, do to alleviate the difficulties faced by those who are oppressed by bad leaders? How can we help, for example, the refugees and migrants, many of whom are fleeing countries because of the misery and hardship caused by unethical and wicked shepherds?

Fortunately, God is always moving us forward and beyond that which has broken our hearts and our lives, to a new reality. The paradox of God's work is that while it may restore the condition of well-being and harmony, it places this restored condition at a new future time, a time coming. The recurring pronouncement "I will" underscores the promise of moving forward, a new future coming.

Jeremiah outlines the essential aspects of this new future. The people shall "not fear any longer, or be dismayed, nor shall any be missing, says the LORD" (v. 4). God's promises offer much for the preacher and the church to reflect on. Imagine a world without fear. What would our community look like? Perhaps more hedges and fewer walls, more walks and fewer locked-in rides, more greetings and less avoidance, more friendships and less

The Glorious Hour

God speed the year of jubilee,
The wide world o'er!
When from their galling chains set free,
Th' oppressed shall vilely bend the knee,
And wear the yoke of tyranny,
Like brutes, no more: —
That year will come, and Freedom's reign
To man his plundered rights again
Restore.

God speed the day when human blood
Shall cease to flow!
In every clime be understood
The claims of human brotherhood,
And each return for evil, good—
Not blow for blow: —
That day will come, all feuds to end,
And change into a faithful friend
Each foe.

God speed the hour, the glorious hour,
When none on earth
Shall exercise a lordly power,
Nor in a tyrant's presence cower,
But all to Manhood's stature tower,
By equal birth!—
That hour will come, to each, to all,
And from his prison-house the thrall
Go forth.

Until that year, day, hour arrive,—
If life be given, —
With head and heart and hand I'll strive
To break the rod, and rend the gyve, —
The spoiler of his prey deprive, —
So witness Heaven!
And never from my chosen post,
Whate'er the peril or the cost,
Be driven.

William Lloyd Garrison, "The Triumph of Freedom," in *Selections from the Writings and Speeches of William Lloyd Garrison* (Boston: R. F. Wallcut, 1852), 316.

loneliness, more garden tools and fewer guns. Imagine a world without dismay. What would our lives be like? Perhaps more desire to vote and less indifference, more enthusiasm to get involved and less apathy, more passion to give and less desire to steal. Imagine a world without the missing. What would our hearts be like? Perhaps more courage to speak and less silence, more laughter and fewer tears, more love and less betrayal.

Unless the conditions that create the realities of fear, dismay, and the missing are eradicated, we will continue to suffer their ill effects. What Jeremiah promises is that God has a plan to set the conditions right for a new future for God's people. The plan for a new future is in God's hands always, but we must understand that it will never be God's accomplishment alone. In the unfolding story of God's work throughout history we see a pattern. God creates and restores on our behalf, but always, and without exception, gives the work back to us to carry forward. This is what Jeremiah is saying when he concludes with the words of God, "I will raise up for David a righteous Branch" (v. 5). This is pointing to us, calling us out of droopiness to prepare for the handover to continue and sustain the work that God has begun. We are the righteous branch. We are the participants in God's unfolding restoration.

God does not give up and has not given up on our capacity to help shepherd a better world that is in right relationship with God. The ultimate vision of God is to see our humanity step up and take leadership. Leadership of our own personal lives and destiny. Leadership in our families and communities. Leadership for our people and even our nation, with the clear mandate to be responsible for the conditions that include life without fear and dismay, because we choose to lead our lives wisely and execute justice and righteousness in the way of the Lord (v. 5).

CARLTON J. "COBBIE" PALM

Luke 1:68–79

[68]"Blessed be the Lord God of Israel,
for he has looked favorably on his people and redeemed them.
[69]He has raised up a mighty savior for us
in the house of his servant David,
[70]as he spoke through the mouth of his holy prophets from of old,
[71]that we would be saved from our enemies and from the hand of all who hate us.
[72]Thus he has shown the mercy promised to our ancestors,
and has remembered his holy covenant,
[73]the oath that he swore to our ancestor Abraham,
to grant us [74]that we, being rescued from the hands of our enemies,
might serve him without fear, [75]in holiness and righteousness
before him all our days.
[76]And you, child, will be called the prophet of the Most High;
for you will go before the Lord to prepare his ways,
[77]to give knowledge of salvation to his people
by the forgiveness of their sins.
[78]By the tender mercy of our God,
the dawn from on high will break upon us,
[79]to give light to those who sit in darkness and in the shadow of death,
to guide our feet into the way of peace."

Psalm 46

[1]God is our refuge and strength,
a very present help in trouble.
[2]Therefore we will not fear, though the earth should change,
though the mountains shake in the heart of the sea;
[3]Though its waters roar and foam,
though the mountains tremble with its tumult.

[4]There is a river whose streams make glad the city of God,
the holy habitation of the Most High.
[5]God is in the midst of the city; it shall not be moved;
God will help it when the morning dawns.
[6]The nations are in an uproar, the kingdoms totter;
he utters his voice, the earth melts.
[7]The LORD of hosts is with us;
the God of Jacob is our refuge.

[8]Come, behold the works of the LORD;
see what desolations he has brought on the earth.
[9]He makes wars cease to the end of the earth;
he breaks the bow, and shatters the spear;
he burns the shields with fire.

[10]"Be still, and know that I am God!
I am exalted among the nations,
I am exalted in the earth."
[11]The LORD of hosts is with us;
the God of Jacob is our refuge.

Connecting the Psalm to Scripture and Worship

Jeremiah 23:1–6 (the first reading and the alternate first reading for this day) is both political and personal. This text employs the picturesque imagery of shepherds and sheep, but under this pastoral metaphor lies a blunt political message: Judah has been scattered into exile, an abandoned flock of sheep, because of unjust politics practiced by wicked shepherds, that is, evil kings. In particular, Jeremiah fingers the malevolent King Jehoiakim, who was, ironically, the son of Josiah, a wise and just king, an advocate for the poor, and one who ruled in communion with God (Jer. 22:16). Unlike his father, Jehoiakim exploited the needy while pampering himself. He fancied himself not as an heir to his father's reign of righteousness but as a successor to the gilded age of Solomon. While he "made his neighbors work for nothing" (22:13), he built for himself a lavish royal residence with extravagant interior decor, "paneling it with cedar and painting it with vermilion" (22:14). "You have not attended to my people," God warns Jehoiakim and all like him. "Therefore I will attend to *you* for your evil deeds" (Jer. 23:2, paraphrase, emphasis added).

This passage, with its political message, is also personal—personal to God. Judah, suffering in exile because its kings were shepherds guilty of malfeasance, is not some anonymous tribe. To God, Judah is *my* flock, *my* people, and *my* pasture, and Jeremiah announces that God intends to save God's own, gathering these scattered people and bringing them home. God will raise up real shepherds to lead them, rulers who will protect the people and banish their fears. This assurance of just kings and restoration in the near future leans forward toward a more lasting and glorious eschatological promise: "The days are surely coming, says the LORD, when I will raise up for David a righteous Branch, and he shall reign as king and deal wisely, and shall execute justice and righteousness in the land" (23:5).

Luke 1:68–79. Luke 1:68–79 serves in lieu of the usual psalm for the day. This canticle sings of what Jeremiah spoke of so long ago: the divine promise of a lasting and just king has at last been fulfilled. Jesus is that long-expected king for all of lost and fearful humanity, the king who will "deal wisely, and shall execute justice and righteousness in the land" (Jer. 23:5).

The canticle appears in the first chapter of Luke, which is a maternity ward for the promises of God. Two women are pregnant here, Elizabeth and her relative Mary, and the birth of their children will mark the turning of the ages. Elizabeth's child will become John the Baptist, "a prophet of the Most High" (1:76). Mary's child will, of course, be Jesus, the long-expected "Son of the Most High" (1:32), "a mighty savior for us" (1:69).

The canticle is sung by John's father, Zechariah. At first, he could not believe that God was coming, at long last, to save the people, fulfilling the divine promises through the births of these sons. There were too many reasons not to believe. So many centuries had passed since the promise had been made; Zechariah and Elizabeth were far too old to have children; the oppressive and unrelenting grip of the Roman Empire made exile in Babylon seem mild; the people had begun to lose zeal. So, when the angel Gabriel came to Zechariah to tell him that God was about to act powerfully and that, as a part of this divine redemption, he and Elizabeth would have a son who would "make ready a people prepared for the Lord" (1:17), Zechariah responded with doubt. Gabriel answered

Zechariah's doubt by silencing him "until the day these things occur" (1:20). At the circumcision service eight days after John's birth, Zechariah, filled with the Holy Spirit and tongue loosed, startled all of his neighbors by singing God's praises and chanting that the promises made by "holy prophets from of old" (1:70) had now come to joyful fruition.

Putting this canticle together with the passage from Jeremiah, we see two things. First, we see the "job description" of this promised king, whom the Christian faith identifies as Jesus. This king will gather the sheep, seeking out the lost (Jer. 23:3); he will protect them, saving them from their enemies (Luke 1:71) and will reign over them with wisdom, justice, and righteousness (Jer. 23:5). Second, both passages point to the overall goal of this king: to allow the people to serve and worship God free from fear. Jeremiah promises that the people will be "saved and . . . will live in safety," calling out that "the Lord is our righteousness" (Jer. 23:6), and Zechariah sings that the people will be rescued from their enemies and will serve God "without fear, in holiness and righteousness before [God] all our days" (Luke 1:74–75). What we see here is the theological affirmation that God saves the people not merely to give them momentary relief from their enemies, but to bring them back into God's protective embrace. All true peace, all real prosperity, all political justice, all lasting freedom from fear radiate from a community in right relationship to God.

Psalm 46. Psalm 46 is the alternate psalm reading for this day, and the theme, already named in Jeremiah and Luke—God gathering and protecting the people—continues here. "God is our refuge and strength" (v. 1), says the psalmist. Notice that the place of refuge and strength is not the temple, not the city of Jerusalem, not any humanly constructed fortress, but God. Only when God has decided to make the city "the holy habitation of the Most High" (v. 4) do the rivers of the city flow with gladness, and the city becomes secure and immovable only when "God is in the midst of the city" (v. 5).

In Jeremiah, what threatens the people is bad kings like Jehoiakim and the humiliation and oppression of Babylonian exile. In the psalm, the dangers are also twofold. First, there is nature with its storms, earthquakes, floods, and volcanoes (vv. 2–3). James L. Mays has pointed out that these menaces of nature carried supernatural overtones, because "in the worldview of Canaan, sea and river were hostile gods whose threat to earth was constant."[1] The second danger to the people is the political instability of the world, especially the tendency of human hostility to erupt into war. "The nations," says the psalmist, "are in an uproar" (v. 6). In short, the world is shaking with violence, and the people are quaking with fear.

To these fears the psalmist says, "Do not be afraid; God's light is breaking over us" (see v. 5). As for convulsions in the earth, God speaks and the earth melts (see v. 6). As for warring nations, God "breaks the bow and shatters the spear" (v. 9). "Be still, and know that I am God" (v. 10) is best understood not as an invitation to quiet piety but as a command to leave the battlefield: "Stop fighting . . . and know that I am God" (TEV). To borrow the imagery of Jeremiah, God is acting as shepherd, providing refuge for the flock, and "they shall not fear any longer, or be dismayed" (Jer. 23:4).

These texts suggest a tone of confidence in the promises of God, which can be reflected in anthems and congregational song. A suitable hymn, for example, is Luther's "A Mighty Fortress." Preaching might focus on the eschatological promise of God's coming justice as well as the call to work in faith toward that coming reign of peace.

THOMAS G. LONG

1. James L. Mays, *Psalms*, Interpretation (Louisville, KY: Westminster John Knox, 1994), 184.

Colossians 1:11–20

[11]May you be made strong with all the strength that comes from his glorious power, and may you be prepared to endure everything with patience, while joyfully [12]giving thanks to the Father, who has enabled you to share in the inheritance of the saints in the light. [13]He has rescued us from the power of darkness and transferred us into the kingdom of his beloved Son, [14]in whom we have redemption, the forgiveness of sins.

[15]He is the image of the invisible God, the firstborn of all creation; [16]for in him all things in heaven and on earth were created, things visible and invisible, whether thrones or dominions or rulers or powers—all things have been created through him and for him. [17]He himself is before all things, and in him all things hold together. [18]He is the head of the body, the church; he is the beginning, the firstborn from the dead, so that he might come to have first place in everything. [19]For in him all the fullness of God was pleased to dwell, [20]and through him God was pleased to reconcile to himself all things, whether on earth or in heaven, by making peace through the blood of his cross.

Commentary 1: Connecting the Reading with Scripture

Colossians is well known for extending Pauline thought in new directions, not least because of the unique philosophical and religious milieu in which that early Christian community had taken shape. The lectionary's association of this text with the Sunday demarcating the reign of Christ is intuitively appropriate because of the receptivity of that milieu to the theme of divine sovereignty. One of the intriguing features of Colossians' expression of the reign of Christ is the blend of the cosmic and the specific in its testimony to what God has done in Jesus Christ.

The passage begins with a rehearsal of God's bringing the saints at Colossae into "the inheritance of the saints in the light," a rescue from the reign of darkness and a transfer to the reign of God's "beloved Son" (Col. 1:12–13). Cosmic darkness is displaced by cosmic light that is intensely specific; that is, it is light that shines and reigns from the forgiveness of sins accomplished in Christ. Thereby, Paul assures the Colossians at the outset that the cosmic power of their redemption is rooted in the particularity of the One who embodies God's own forgiveness to them. The power reigning over heaven and earth is the power of this specific love.

As the passage continues with the employment of an ancient Christian hymn (vv. 15–20), nuanced as it may be with Paul's editing, the emphasis moves back from the specific to the cosmic. This particular One who embodied God's forgiveness is the cosmic One prior to all creation, through whom and for whom all things have been created and in whom they find their unity and coherence, thus their "holding together" (vv. 15–17). More than an echo may be acknowledged here of John's Gospel: "In the beginning was the Word, and the Word was with God, and the Word was God. . . . All things came into being through him, and without him not one thing came into being" (John 1:1–3). God's work of redemption in the specific loving action of the beloved Son has cosmic significance, embracing "all things" both in creation and redemption, in holding together and reconciling.

The lectionary texts that surround the Colossians passage connect in interesting ways to its alternating focus on the cosmic and specific work of the reign of Christ. Jeremiah 23:1–6 utilizes the imagery of the faithless shepherds who failed to attend the flock, allowing it to scatter in fear and disarray, coupling the account of that failure with the promise to raise up shepherds who provide help and healing for the flock. Employing the classic Hebrew association of shepherd with king, Jeremiah modulates into a promise of a righteous Branch from David who will "deal wisely, and shall execute justice and righteousness in the land" (Jer. 23:5). Thereby the prophet serves as herald of the promise that Colossians declares kept, the advent of the One in whom "all the fullness of God was pleased to dwell" (Col. 1:19). The arc of prophecy stretches from the hope for the good shepherd and a righteous king to the actual appearance of the beloved Son in whom all things hold together.

In a different way, the lectionary presentation of Luke 23:33–43 reinforces Colossians' account of the reign of Christ by stressing the ironic humiliation of crucifixion through which it comes to pass. The inscription over Jesus on the cross is, "This is the King of the Jews" (Luke 23:38). Thereby Luke provides a resounding repetition of the way Colossians concludes its hymn of praise to the cosmic reign of Christ. Colossians does so by referring to God reconciling "to himself all things, whether on earth or in heaven, by making peace through the blood of his cross" (Col. 1:20). Both Luke and Colossians see God's reign accomplished in what humanly considered appears to be its opposite. The reign of God comes in the shape of a cross. Thus, in both anticipation and fulfillment, surrounding lections reiterate Colossians' affirmation of the reign of Christ in both its specific occurrence and cosmic implications.

There are two other connections of the Colossians passage to wider reaches of Scripture worthy of mention. One has to do with the universal scope of redemption as witnessed in Colossians, while the other has to do with the unique role of humanity in that genuinely broader scope. Though it has frequently been overlooked in the study of Scripture, the Genesis account of the covenant that God makes after the flood reinforces the breadth of redemption on which Colossians insists. Genesis 9 is often characterized as "God's Covenant with Noah" or the Noahic covenant. Such a description reduces the scope of God's redemptive purposes to one narrow species—the human one. In fact, the covenant is explicitly stated much more broadly. "As for me, I am establishing my covenant with you and your descendants after you, and with every living creature that is with you, the birds, the domestic animals, and every animal of the earth with you, as many as came out of the ark. I establish my covenant with you, that never again shall all flesh be cut off by the waters of a flood, and never again shall there be a flood to destroy the earth" (Gen. 9:9–11).

Just as the specific redemption wrought in Jesus Christ has cosmic significance in Colossians, so in Genesis the specific covenant introduced to Noah after the flood incorporates all of creation. Anthropocentric interpretations of the redemption to which Scripture testifies notwithstanding, Colossians and Genesis join forces in making sure that readers do not miss God's redemptive intention toward all that God has made. Fittingly, Psalm 148 gives testimony regarding the distinctive place of humanity—and especially the people of God—in that broad, indeed cosmic, redemption scheme. The psalm opens with a call for all the citizens of heaven, animate and inanimate (angels, sun, moon, stars), to render praise to God (vv. 1–6). Next it summons denizens of earth, again both the animate and inanimate, the ordinary and the marvelous (sea monsters, deeps, fire, hail, snow, frost, wind, mountains, trees, wild and domestic animals, reptiles, and birds), to join the chorus of praise (vv. 7–10). Then and only then it turns to humans, beginning with rulers but also including ordinary folk, old and young alike, and finally God's own people Israel, inviting them all to join the chorus (vv. 11–14).

In one sense, Psalm 148 maintains the cosmic scope of God's redemptive purpose, incorporating all of these elements of the universal whole into one grand choir of praise. In another sense, it acknowledges that the human realm in general and the people of God in particular have a special vocation. Though all elements of creation should and do render praise to God, it is the human members of creation who can be drawn self-consciously into the relationship of praise and thanksgiving to God. It is the human family, led by that part of the family awakened to the splendor of God and

God's purposes with all things, that is called to make sure that all creation endures for the sake of rendering such praise.

The reign of Christ is an important theme to ponder in relation to Colossians 1:11–20, not least because it both renders that reign cosmic in its scope and grounds it in the specific life and destiny of Jesus Christ. Both lectionary texts surrounding this passage, and several others that echo and magnify its themes, ensure that its testimony is not lost but endures.

D. CAMERON MURCHISON

Commentary 2: Connecting the Reading with the World

The Colossians passage for this Sunday divides nicely into two parts. In so doing, it offers two different interpretative paths. The first part offers encouragement, strength, and thanksgiving for deliverance from the dominion of darkness and entrance into the kingdom of God (Col. 1:11–14). The lengthier second section offers a robust Pauline Christology (vv. 15–20). Both the encouraging first section and the christological elucidations in the second section offer sermonic possibilities.

The encouragements that Paul offers are pertinent and timely. We all have doubt in the face of daily challenges and need the strength that comes when we are part of something larger than ourselves. We may not always see the spiritual forces working in the world or have the same dualistic cosmic vision as Paul, but it is still encouraging to believe that we part of the coming kingdom of God and that our efforts are worthwhile. A possible sermon might therefore remind the church, especially in present times of stress and discouragement, that the people of God are indeed part of divine transformation of this world. A wise preacher would encourage the church to think about the ways in which it can be active participants in Christ's coming reign.

Martin Luther King Jr. derived great strength from, and inspired others with, his imagery of the kingdom of God. In his last speech Dr. King boldly and prophetically states: "I just want to do God's will. And He's allowed me to go up to the mountain. And I've looked over. And I've seen the Promised Land. I may not get there with you. But I want you to know tonight, that we, as a people, will get to the Promised Land!"[1] This speech was given in the context of the civil rights struggle in the United States to encourage the Memphis sanitation workers to endure personal sacrifice in the fight for safer working conditions and better pay. Similarly, Paul's vision of being part of the kingdom of God encourages Christians that it is worthwhile to turn our backs on the forces of evil and believe in God's promise of the kingdom of God.

This is helpful imagery for an evangelistic sermon or an invitation for people to remember their baptism and be children of the light. There are occasions when we want to avoid simple, dualistic interpretations of complex issues. However, evangelistic sermons often are more effective when we are presented with a choice between the forces of good and the forces of evil. This passage presents such an opportunity to preach that we are invited to participate in the inaugurated kingdom of God. Here there is no gray area. We are either part of the "power of darkness," or we have been delivered and share in the "inheritance of the saints in the light" (v. 12). New Christians and long-term church members alike need to be reminded that we have been "transferred . . . into the kingdom of his beloved Son" (v. 13).

Indeed, Paul's christological images powerfully emphasize the divine more than the human characteristics of Jesus. For example, Christ is the firstborn from the dead, the dwelling of the fullness of God, and through him all things are reconciled. These are cosmic images of transformation through Christ. As the people of God, this passage therefore powerfully reminds us that, despite appearances, we through Christ

1. Martin Luther King Jr., "I Have Been to the Mountain Top," Memphis, TN, April 3, 1968, https://kinginstitute.stanford.edu/king-papers/documents/ive-been-mountaintop-address-delivered-bishop-charles-mason-temple.

are already transformed, already part of God's coming reign.

This second section invites us into a deeper philosophical reflection on bigger cosmic and existential questions. We live in a world that is threatened by global warming, nuclear proliferation, and even species extinction. There are rising sea levels caused by melting icebergs at the poles and changing weather patterns such as El Niño and La Niña. While nations create treaties to restrict the use of carbon fuels and limits on nuclear weapons, countries break the rules and strive for more weapons and economic development. A wise preacher might therefore pose the following questions to their congregation for reflection and contemplation: How do we reconcile Paul's message of hope with a seemingly more complex and pessimistic geopolitical reality? Where do we find peace of mind and hope in the midst of despair?

One response that people often have to these modern dangers is to isolate ourselves from the world's problems by building walls that protect us. More and more people choose to live in gated communities with security systems, isolated from the harsh realities around us. Countries threaten to build walls and equip border patrols, armies, and police forces to protect citizens. We also pass tougher immigration laws to keep out those who look different from ourselves. We often fall into the trap of emphasizing our differences rather than our similarities.

It is incumbent on the preacher to remind the people of God that these divisions are constructs—constructs that will be eradicated in Christ's coming kingdom. The founding of the modern ideal of a nation-state (sovereign state) is generally attributed to Frederick II of Prussia (ruled 1740–86). Historically borders have been much more porous, and the Hebrew Bible commands Israelites to be kind to sojourners. Race is generally considered to be a construct to emphasize difference, as genetically all human beings share 99.9 percent of a common gene pool. According to the biblical creation story, all human beings come from the same source.

Despite the loudest among us, who emphasize differences, Paul's Christology reminds us that Christ is the one who unifies us. Christ is above these created and superficial human differences and divisions. The last verse states that God chose "through [Christ] . . . to reconcile to himself all things, whether on earth or in heaven, by making peace through the blood of his cross" (v. 20). This image offers us hope for reconciliation of these earthly differences in the unity of all persons under the lordship of Christ.

Moreover, this passage reminds us that Christ is both creator and redeemer of this world. Some people may place their hope for humanity in governments, the United Nations, science, or other faith traditions. Paul, however, emphasizes that Christ "is before all things" (v. 17). All these human institutions are created, while Christ is eternal. As Christ is creator of all life, including human beings, he is also the redeemer. He is the beginning and the end, the Alpha and the Omega. In him all things will be restored and reconciled. A wise preacher might therefore reflect upon the hope that is offered by the unlimited, eternal nature of Christ.

Paul's eschatological Christology reminds me of the work of the late Jesuit theologian and geopaleontologist, Pierre Teilhard de Chardin (1881–1955), who wrote *The Phenomenon of Man*.[2] De Chardin participated in the excavation of the Neanderthal remains in China and prehistoric cave paintings in Spain, which came to form part of his evolutionary theology. He is an early pioneer in the struggle to reconcile science and faith. This was just as controversial then as it is now. In fact, his writings were banned by the Vatican until after his death. Teilhard de Chardin writes that while Jesus Christ was born in the past, he was the ideal human to which all humans and all of creation are aspiring and spiritually evolving. Creation will reach the "omega point" or divine destiny where all of heaven and the earth will be reconciled into Christ.

PHILIP WINGEIER-RAYO

2. Pierre Teilhard de Chardin, *The Phenomenon of Man* (1955, repr. New York: Harper Perennial, 1976).

Luke 23:33–43

[33]When they came to the place that is called The Skull, they crucified Jesus there with the criminals, one on his right and one on his left. [[[34]Then Jesus said, "Father, forgive them; for they do not know what they are doing."]] And they cast lots to divide his clothing. [35]And the people stood by, watching; but the leaders scoffed at him, saying, "He saved others; let him save himself if he is the Messiah of God, his chosen one!" [36]The soldiers also mocked him, coming up and offering him sour wine, [37]and saying, "If you are the King of the Jews, save yourself!" [38]There was also an inscription over him, "This is the King of the Jews."

[39]One of the criminals who were hanged there kept deriding him and saying, "Are you not the Messiah? Save yourself and us!" [40]But the other rebuked him, saying, "Do you not fear God, since you are under the same sentence of condemnation? [41]And we indeed have been condemned justly, for we are getting what we deserve for our deeds, but this man has done nothing wrong." [42]Then he said, "Jesus, remember me when you come into your kingdom." [43]He replied, "Truly I tell you, today you will be with me in Paradise."

Commentary 1: Connecting the Reading with Scripture

Throughout his account, Luke shows continued interest in the interpersonal: the interaction of Jesus with real people in real ways, challenging them to accept his status as Savior. Earlier in Luke 23, we find a near-unanimous rejection of Jesus, with the trial against Jesus and the absence of his supporters. Jesus himself never gave up hope, of course, and the cross is anything but the end of the narrative.

At issue is the identity of Jesus as Messiah, a key theme throughout Luke. The crucifixion is the moment at which Jesus is either confirmed in his mission or rejected. At the same time, it carries continued personal connection. Jesus repersonalizes those society has negated and, along the way, reorients for his listeners what it means to be a person in this world. Jesus conflicts with established powers, who, unable to seduce him into their patterns of identity, proceed to work at depersonalizing him. Rather than fight it, Jesus enters even more fully into the negation of Luke 23:33–43, bringing hope even to this place of suffering.

Luke spends no time on the crucifixion process itself. He tells us where it happened, the place of the Skull, which was named after the shape of the hill, where passersby could easily see the crosses (v. 33). We are also told Jesus was crucified between two criminals (v. 33). We are not told their names. It is a bare entry of setting and characters that leads into Luke's emphasis in this passage.

Crucifixion was familiar to any of that era, and the familiarity brought with it a clear understanding of its grotesque implications. This was death by torture. Rome was asserting its right and power. Crucifixion carried a message, and the message was radical: the crucified one is not a person. Rome was declaring the nonpersonhood of Jesus and those crucified alongside him.

After setting the scene, Luke begins with the reaction of Jesus in verse 34. Despite his overwhelmingly dismaying situation, he affirms his identity before God and others, following his own teaching in Luke 6:27–28 and Luke 21:12–19. His prayer is an intimate one to his Father. As one who continues to love, he intercedes on behalf of his accusers. This prayer anticipates the widened mission of the church in Acts to include Gentiles. All are forgiven. All are invited.

The Roman soldiers cast lots for his clothing, showing the clothes had more value than the person crucified (v. 34). This note about the clothing connects Jesus to the sufferer in Psalm 22:18. In verse 35, the emphasis on rejection continues. The people watch the humiliation, which was the purpose of the crucifixion. The religious leaders exult in their seeming victory, mocking Jesus with his own claims, echoing the messianic prophecy of Isaiah 42:1. Jesus is clearly cursed, the circumstances make this quite clear. God is making his choice, and they see themselves on the side of God. Luke continues to allude to Psalm 22 here as a way of establishing a connection to God's work. Counterintuitive though it is, the experience of the cross is seen as a prophecy given and fulfilled.

In verse 36, the Romans join in mocking him. The offer of sour wine, commonly used by the poor and soldiers, is part of the ridiculing, along with the sign over his head, an ironic display of his claimed sovereignty. Even one of the criminals joins in (v. 39). He may be a loser in this game, but he does not dispute the rules or structures. The way for Jesus to prove himself in light of the established systems, the only way, is for him to save himself from the crucifixion. Everyone seems to agree—except Jesus and, we find out, the other criminal also dying beside him. The nature of blaspheming places the issue back into one of divine validation. Whom does God support in this confrontation? Whom do the people trust? Whom does Jesus trust?

In a curious scene of cross-talk, the other criminal defends Jesus (v. 40). While some have assumed the criminals were punished for political unrest, the criminal's statement here suggests otherwise. He begins by admitting the justice of their own situation. He then counters the blasphemy itself, which suggests a firm belief that while the cross is horrific, there is still more to fear if God turns against them. He defends the innocence of Jesus, going even further and acknowledging Jesus as a bearer of God's mission. This death is not the end of the story, but it takes faith to see beyond the moment.

While others were willing to confess the lordship of Jesus in the midst of his ministry, only the criminal offers such a confession at the point at which Jesus and the systems of this world collide. This matches a pattern throughout Scripture of using the marginalized to offer proactive confessions, which serves to confirm the work of God while also shaming those who may lose heart in the face of their own loss (e.g., the slave girl and the servant in 2 Kgs. 5 and Rahab in Josh. 2:8–13).

Jesus, in a supreme act of his own identity, receives this confession with a message of hope. He offers grace and forgiveness from a position of authority and love (v. 43). He is in a dehumanizing position but is not dehumanized. Just the opposite. Jesus humanizes and personalizes the situation, establishing his continuing confidence in God's mission. "You," he says to this other man, "will be with me" (v. 43). These personal pronouns bring relationality and affirmation into an otherwise social-shattering moment.

As in the story of the bronze snake in Numbers 21:8–9, Jesus, instead of being cursed by being hung on a pole (cf. Gal. 3), removes the curse of death for those who gaze on him, as a person, on the pole. By identifying Jesus for who he is, the criminal confesses the kingdom of God, and in this finds immediate salvation. The language of paradise brings to mind the garden of Eden, a restoration of all that had gone wrong in contrast to the burning judgment of Hades and the present experience of the cross. The criminal, who acknowledges his guilt, is comforted with the clemency of the king.

The lectionary texts for this day share this theme of God's salvation in the midst of crisis, calling for firm faith even when—especially when—life is overwhelming. In Jeremiah 23, it is the people of Israel who are facing destruction, one brought on by the failure of the establishment. God does not need, it seems, the systems of the world to provide salvation to those he cares about—a good reminder in politically charged eras. God is indeed our refuge and strength, as the psalmist reminds us. He is the God who works in the face of utter trauma, who brings salvation during times of despair. We can trust God even when things seem the worst. This power of God, the power affirmed in Jeremiah and the Psalms, is the confidence Jesus has in the midst of his obedience. The writer of Colossians nicely connects this vision of who Christ is —the one in whom we should trust, not despite the cross, but because of it. This is good theology. Even more important, it is a vital reminder in times when we lose sight of Christ and our calling in the difficulties of life. It is in these moments, when the apparent contrasts with the calling, that we need reminders about God's faithfulness, even unto and beyond death, in making real and thorough peace.

PATRICK ODEN

Commentary 2: Connecting the Reading with the World

Reign of Christ Sunday marks the end of the Christian year. It also points to the final destiny of creation: the consummation of God's reign by the Holy Spirit under the lordship of Christ. That Jesus is revealed in all four canonical Gospels as God's anointed ruler, Israel's Messiah, and Savior of the nations, is unmistakable. However, all four lessons for this Sunday point to the particular character of Christ's way of ruling in accomplishing God's will for the world. A sermon on Reign of Christ will need to make clear that the lordly rule of Christ is not merely the power exercised by human rulers, only increased exponentially to embrace the whole world. This is where the lessons may bring clarity to distorted, confused, and compromised visions of God's way with the world that are little more than projections of humankind's "will to power."

The OT lesson (Jer. 23:1–6) attests to a king who will be raised up by YHWH and will "deal wisely, and shall execute justice and righteousness in the land." The psalm, or act of praise, is taken from the prophecy of Zechariah in Luke 1:68–79 in response to the birth of John the Baptist, the one who will prepare the way for God's anointed ruler, "to give knowledge of salvation to his people by the forgiveness of their sins." The epistle lesson (Col. 1:11–20) provides helpful commentary on the Gospel by means of what was probably a recognized hymn sung by first-century Christians. The doxological nature of this hymn in praise of Christ summons the church to confess him as Lord in acknowledging that the effects of his life, death, and resurrection extend to the whole of reality. "For in him all the fullness of God was pleased to dwell, and through him God was pleased to reconcile to himself all things, whether on earth or in heaven, by making peace through the blood of his cross" (vv. 19–20).

A sermon from the Gospel on this important day might consider pointing to the astonishing reach of God's saving work; the reconciliation of "all things" to God through the self-giving of Jesus. This is not a time to dwell on the mechanics of atonement theory, nor is it an occasion to present the death of Jesus as a therapeutic transaction with individuals. The details of the Gospel narrative summon the preacher to courageous proclamation that directs listeners to perceive the world of "all things" God was pleased to reconcile by making peace through Christ's self-offering on the cross. The work of Christ thus implicates the church in a way of life made possible in, with, and through Christ. "He has rescued us from the power of darkness and transferred us into the kingdom of his beloved Son, in whom we have redemption, the forgiveness of sins" (vv. 13–14).

Jesus was executed on a Roman cross, surrounded by common criminals. One hung at his right hand, another at his left hand. He exercised his divine authority with these words: "Father, forgive them; for they do not know what they are doing." This is the way God rules the world in the person and work of Jesus Christ. His throne is a wooden cross; his constituents are convicted sinners. God's reign in Jesus, however, was not recognized by most who witnessed his death. He was ridiculed and mocked, called upon by onlookers to use his presumptive authority for securing his own survival and success: "If you are the King of the Jews, save yourself."

Here the preacher might listen to the voices in the Gospel narrative, since they reveal that both the church and the world are recipients of God's judgment and reconciling love. One of the criminals who was hanged with Jesus joined with Roman soldiers and the crowd in taunting him, "Are you not the Messiah? Save yourself and us!" The church is often tempted in a similar manner; to imagine itself as possessing God-given power sufficient for solving the world's problems, fixing its brokenness, and asserting itself as a significant moral, political, and cultural force. Here a sermon could name the temptation to accommodate the rule of God revealed in the self-giving of Jesus to the powers of the world that constitute competing or opposing visions of "life."

The second criminal who was hung with Jesus also gives voice to the gospel. He acknowledges his sin and guilt, that he cannot save himself from condemnation and death. In Jesus, the righteous one who suffers condemnation with convicted sinners, he perceives the power of forgiveness and reconciliation that identifies God's reign. "Jesus, remember me when you come into your kingdom." What Jesus says to the man in response to his request is astonishing: "Truly, I tell you, today you will be with me in Paradise." Paradise is the "today" of God's salvation realized in the company of Jesus. Paradise is beholding the self-giving of Jesus as the way God rules and works in the world.

Arthur McGill provides a helpful way of connecting the vision of God beheld in worship with God's way of acting in the world as revealed in the person and work of Christ.[1] Following the wisdom of Scripture and the creeds, McGill affirms that service, defined as the power of God, is a "shockingly impractical creed." He describes the character of the church in light of the rule of Christ: "Self-expenditure is self-fulfillment. He who loses his life is thereby finding it. Loving is itself life, and not just a means to life. He who expends himself for his neighbor, even to death, truly lives. But he who lives for himself and avoids death truly dies: 'He who does not love remains in death'" (57).

In Jesus, divine power is vindicated in that it does not dominate, manipulate, or impose itself by force or violence, but serves by sharing itself. The distinctive mark of God's power that works in the weakness of human beings is service, "the self-giving love which dwells with the poor and not the rich, with the sinful and not the righteous, with the weak and not the strong, with the dying and not those full of life" (62).

McGill's work illumines the church's calling to discern and make visible God's way with the world in Christ. If force is no attribute of God, then God's divinity, as revealed in the humanity of Christ, does not consist in his ability to push things around, to impose the divine will and purpose from the security of detached, self-enclosed remoteness, or to sit in grandeur while the world carries out his demands. Far from being a neutral, impersonal force, distant and external to the world, God sends his glory into the world in the form of slavery, humiliation, suffering, and death on a cross. Luke 23 invites the preacher to contemplate a significant but often neglected theological and moral truth: "we are as the power that rules us" (90). A sermon on Christ the King Sunday might well consider beginning with the following question: *What kind of power do we worship, and what kind of power informs the way we perceive and participate in God's way with the world?*

MICHAEL PASQUARELLO III

1. Arthur C. McGill, *Suffering: A Test of Theological Method* (Philadelphia: Westminster, 1982). Hereafter page references will be included in the body of the text.

Contributors

JARED E. ALCÁNTARA, Assistant Professor of Homiletics; Director of the MA in Ministry Program, Trinity Evangelical Divinity School, Deerfield, IL

O. WESLEY ALLEN JR., Lois Craddock Perkins Professor of Homiletics, Perkins School of Theology at Southern Methodist University, Dallas, TX

RONALD J. ALLEN, Professor of Preaching and Gospels and Letters, Christian Theological Seminary, Indianapolis, IN

WM. LOYD ALLEN, Professor of Church History and Spiritual Formation, McAfee School of Theology, Mercer University, Atlanta, GA

DAVID L. BARTLETT†, Professor of New Testament Emeritus, Columbia Theological Seminary, Decatur, GA

SUZANNE WOOLSTON BOSSERT, Chaplain Volunteer for "Healing Paws" (canine therapy), Boston Medical Center; Boston Healthcare for the Homeless, Needham, MA

STEPHEN BOYD, John Allen Easley Professor of the Study of Religions, Wake Forest University, Department of the Study of Religions, Winston-Salem, NC

BRAD R. BRAXTON, Director, The Center for the Study of African American Religious Life, Smithsonian National Museum of African American History and Culture, Washington, DC

LINDA MCKINNISH BRIDGES, Former President, Baptist Theological Seminary at Richmond, Richmond, VA

E. CARSON BRISSON, Associate Professor of Bible and Biblical Languages, Union Presbyterian Seminary, Charlotte, NC

JOHN M. BUCHANAN, Pastor Emeritus, Fourth Presbyterian Church; Former Editor/Publisher, *The Christian Century*, Chicago, IL

ELIZABETH F. CALDWELL, Professor Emerita, McCormick Theological Seminary; Adjunct Faculty, Vanderbilt Divinity School, Nashville, TN

L. JULIANA M. CLAASSENS, Professor of Old Testament, Stellenbosch University, Stellenbosch, South Africa

JOSEPH J. CLIFFORD, Pastor, Myers Park Presbyterian Church, Charlotte, NC

GREGORY L. CUÉLLAR, Associate Professor of Old Testament, Austin Presbyterian Theological Seminary, Austin, TX

R. ALAN CULPEPPER, Dean Emeritus, McAfee School of Theology, Mercer University, Hartwell, GA

CAROL J. DEMPSEY, OP, Professor of Theology: Biblical Studies, Department of Theology, University of Portland, Portland, OR

MAGREY R. DEVEGA, Senior Pastor, Hyde Park United Methodist Church, Tampa, FL

DAN R. DICK, Assistant to the Bishop, Wisconsin Conference, United Methodist Church, Sun Prairie, WI

LEWIS R. DONELSON, Professor of New Testament, Austin Presbyterian Theological Seminary, Austin, TX

JILL DUFFIELD, Editor/Publisher, *The Presbyterian Outlook*, Richmond, VA

KEN EVERS-HOOD, Pastor, Tualatin Presbyterian Church, Tualatin, OR

FAIRFAX F. FAIR, Pastor, Presbyterian Church (U.S.A.), Houston, TX

STEPHEN FARRIS, Professor of Preaching Emeritus, Vancouver School of Theology; Dean Emeritus, St. Andrew's Hall, Vancouver School of Theology, Etobicoke, Ontario

RENATA FURST, Associate Professor of Scripture and Spirituality, Oblate School of Theology, San Antonio, TX

DAVID GAMBRELL, Associate for Worship, Presbyterian Church (U.S.A.), Louisville, KY

MATT GAVENTA, Pastor/Head of Staff, University Presbyterian Church, Austin, TX

KENYATTA R. GILBERT, Professor of Homiletics, Howard University School of Divinity, Washington, DC

DONNA GIVER-JOHNSTON, Pastor, Community Presbyterian Church of Ben Avon, Pittsburgh, PA

BRIDGETT A. GREEN, Assistant Professor of New Testament, Austin Presbyterian Theological Seminary, Austin, TX

ANGELA DIENHART HANCOCK, Associate Professor of Homiletics and Worship, Pittsburgh Theological Seminary, Pittsburgh, PA

LYDIA HERNÁNDEZ-MARCIAL, PhD Candidate, Lutheran School of Theology at Chicago, Chicago, IL

SALLY SMITH HOLT, Professor of Religion, Belmont University College of Theology and Christian Ministry, Nashville, TN

PAUL K. HOOKER, Associate Dean for Ministerial Formation and Advanced Studies, Austin Presbyterian Theological Seminary, Austin, TX

CAMERON B. R. HOWARD, Associate Professor of Old Testament, Luther Seminary, St. Paul, MN

EDITH M. HUMPHREY, William F. Orr Professor of New Testament, Pittsburgh Theological Seminary, Pittsburgh, PA

GEORGE R. HUNSBERGER, Professor Emeritus of Missiology, Western Theological Seminary, Holland, MI

DAVID SCHNASA JACOBSEN, Professor of the Practice of Homiletics; Director of the Homiletical Theology Project, Boston University School of Theology, Boston, MA

LYNN JAPINGA, Professor of Religion, Hope College, Holland, MI

JOSHUA W. JIPP, Associate Professor of New Testament, Trinity Evangelical Divinity School, Deerfield, IL

DAVID W. JOHNSON, Associate Professor of Church History and Christian Spirituality, Austin Presbyterian Theological Seminary, Austin, TX

EUNJOO MARY KIM, Professor of Homiletics and Liturgics, Iliff School of Theology, Denver, CO

ELIZABETH C. LAROCCA-PITTS, Senior Pastor, Saint Mark United Methodist Church, Atlanta, GA

CLEOPHUS J. LARUE, Francis Landey Patton Professor of Homiletics, Princeton Theological Seminary, Princeton, NJ

GERALD C. LIU, Assistant Professor of Worship and Preaching, Princeton Theological Seminary, Princeton, NJ

KIMBERLY BRACKEN LONG, Editor, *Call to Worship*, Presbyterian Church (U.S.A.), Louisville, KY

THOMAS G. LONG, Bandy Professor Emeritus of Preaching, Candler School of Theology, Emory University, Atlanta, GA

DONYELLE MCCRAY, Assistant Professor of Homiletics, Yale Divinity School, New Haven, CT

DONALD K. MCKIM, Honorably Retired, Presbyterian Church (U.S.A.), Germantown, TN

SCOT MCKNIGHT, Julius R. Mantey Professor of New Testament, Northern Seminary, Lisle, IL

TIM MEADOWCROFT, Senior Lecturer in Biblical Studies, Laidlaw College, Auckland, New Zealand

D. CAMERON MURCHISON, Professor Emeritus, Columbia Theological Seminary, Decatur, GA

VANTHANH NGUYEN, SVD, Professor of New Testament Studies, Catholic Theological Union, Chicago, IL

PATRICK ODEN, Visiting Assistant Professor of Theology and Church History, Fuller Theological Seminary, Pasadena, CA

HIERALD E. OSORTO, Candidate in the Evangelical Lutheran Church in America; Researcher, Austin Presbyterian Theological Seminary, Austin, TX

CARLTON J. "COBBIE" PALM, Mission Facilitator and Spiritual Formation Director, Silliman University Divinity School, United Church of Christ in the Philippines, Dumaguete City, Philippines

SONG-MI SUZIE PARK, Associate Professor of Old Testament, Austin Presbyterian Theological Seminary, Austin, TX

MICHAEL PASQUARELLO III, Methodist Chair of Divinity, Director of the Robert Smith Jr. Preaching Institute, Beeson Divinity School, Samford University, Birmingham, AL

ROBERT A. RATCLIFF, Executive Editor, Westminster John Knox Press, Louisville, KY

STANLEY P. SAUNDERS, Associate Professor of New Testament, Columbia Theological Seminary, Decatur, GA

MATTHEW RICHARD SCHLIMM, Professor of Old Testament, University of Dubuque, Dubuque, IA

C. MELISSA SNARR, Associate Dean for Academic Affairs; Associate Professor of Ethics and Society, Vanderbilt Divinity School, Nashville, TN

BENJAMIN M. STEWART, Gordon A. Braatz Associate Professor of Worship; Director of Advanced Studies, Lutheran School of Theology at Chicago, Chicago, IL

LEONORA TUBBS TISDALE, Clement-Muehl Professor of Homiletics, Yale Divinity School, New Haven, CT

EMRYS TYLER, Teaching Elder and Co-Director, Sonlight Christian Camp, Pagosa Springs, CO

ALLIE UTLEY, Fellow, Theology and Practice, Vanderbilt Divinity School, Nashville, TN

LEANNE VAN DYK, President and Professor of Theology, Columbia Theological Seminary, Decatur, GA

RICHARD W. VOELZ, Assistant Professor of Preaching and Worship, Union Presbyterian Seminary, Richmond, VA

ROBERT W. WALL, Paul T. Walls Professor of Scripture and Wesleyan Studies, Seattle Pacific University and Seminary, School of Theology, Seattle, WA

NANCY LYNNE WESTFIELD, Professor of Religious Education, Drew University Theological School, Madison, NJ

DAVID F. WHITE, C. Ellis and Nancy Gribble Nelson Professor of Christian Education, Professor in Methodist Studies, Austin Presbyterian Theological Seminary, Austin, TX

PATRICK J. WILLSON, Retired Pastor, Presbyterian Church (U.S.A.), Santa Fe, NM

PHILIP WINGEIER-RAYO, Academic Dean and Professor of Missiology and Methodist Studies, Wesley Theological Seminary, Washington, DC

LAUREN F. WINNER, Associate Professor of Christian Spirituality, Duke Divinity School, Durham, NC

JOHN W. WRIGHT, Professor of Theology and Christian Scriptures, Point Loma Nazarene University, San Diego, CA

STEPHEN I. WRIGHT, Vice Principal (Academic Director), Spurgeon's College, London, UK

Author Index

Abbreviations

C1	Commentary 1	G	Gospel
C2	Commentary 2	OT	Old Testament
E	Epistle	PS	Psalm

Contributors and entries

Scripture Index

Scripture citations that appear in boldface represent the assigned readings from the Revised Common Lectionary.

OLD TESTAMENT

NEW TESTAMENT

Matthew

Mark

Luke

Comprehensive Scripture Index for Year C

Scripture citations that appear in boldface represent the assigned readings from the Revised Common Lectionary.

ABBREVIATIONS

C1 Year C, Volume 1
C2 Year C, Volume 2
C3 Year C, Volume 3

OLD TESTAMENT

NEW TESTAMENT

Acts *(continued)*

Romans 367 (C3)

1 Corinthians

2 Corinthians

2 Corinthians (*continued*)

Galatians 57 (C1); 417 (C3)

APOCRYPHA

Wisdom

Tobit

Sirach

1 Maccabees

2 Maccabees

3 Maccabees